The European Union

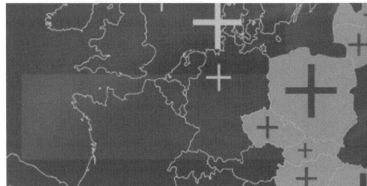

Economics, Policies and History

Susan Senior Nello

The **McGraw·Hill** *Companies*

London	Boston	Burr Ridge, IL	Dubuque, IA	Madison, WI	New York
San Francisco	St. Louis	Bangkok	Bogotá	Caracas	Kuala Lumpur
Lisbon	Madrid	Mexico City	Milan	Montreal	New Delhi
Santiago	Seoul	Singapore	Sydney	Taipei	Toronto

The European Union: Economics, Policies and History
Susan Senior Nello
ISBN-10: 007-710781-0
ISBN-13: 9780077107819

 **Education**

Published by McGraw-Hill Education
Shoppenhangers Road
Maidenhead
Berkshire
SL6 2QL
Telephone: 44 (0) 1628 502 500
Fax: 44 (0) 1628 770 224
Website: www.mcgraw-hill.co.uk

British Library Cataloguing in Publication Data
A catalogue record for this book is available from the British Library

Library of Congress Cataloguing in Publication Data
The Library of Congress data for this book has been applied for from the Library of Congress

Acquisitions Editor: Kirsty Reade
Marketing Director: Petra Skytte
Senior Production Editor: Eleanor Hayes
Editorial Assistant: Laura Dent

Text design by Smith Cowan & Wilson
Cover design by Ego Creative
Printed and bound in the UK by Bell & Bain, Glasgow

Brief Table of Contents

Detailed Table of Contents

Guided Tour

Learning Objectives

Each chapter opens with a set of learning objectives, helping readers to quickly grasp the essentials to be learned in the chapter.

2
A Brief History of European Integration

LEARNING OBJECTIVES

By the end of this chapter you should be able to understand:

▶ the decision to create a supranational organisation in Europe after the Second World War;
▶ the purpose of setting up the European Coal and Steel Community;
▶ the failure of early attempts to promote European co-operation on defence;
▶ the reasons for setting up a common policy on agriculture, and its initial failure;
▶ why the integration process gained a new impetus in the mid-1950s;
▶ the principal objectives and policies set out in the Treaty of Rome;
▶ the main elements of the EEC in the fields of trade and agriculture;
▶ the 1969 Hague Summit: deepening, widening and completion of the integration process;
▶ the years of eurosclerosis in the 1970s;
▶ the main events in the development of the EU (the Single Market project, the Maastricht Treaty, the EU's enlargement, the Amsterdam and Nice treaties, the Mediterranean Programme, the Lisbon Process, enlargement and the Constitutional Treaty).

Important Terms

These are highlighted in the relevant chapters providing ease of reference.

Figures and Tables

Each chapter provides a number of figures and tables to help illustrate and summarize important concepts.

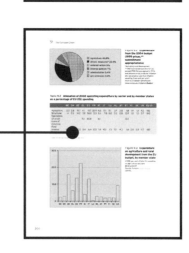

Summary of Key Concepts

This briefly reviews and reinforces the main topics you will have covered in each chapter to ensure you have acquired a solid understanding of the key topics.

Questions for Study and Review

These questions encourage you to review and apply the knowledge you have acquired from each chapter and can be undertaken to test your understanding.

Appendices

Relevant chapters end with an Appendix which aims to expand on themes explored in the chapter.

TECHNOLOGY TO ENHANCE LEARNING AND TEACHING

Visit www.mcgraw-hill.co.uk/textbooks/senior today
Online Learning Centre (OLC)

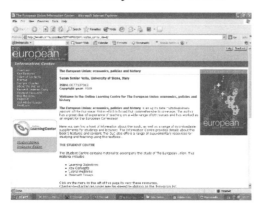

After completing each chapter, log on to the supporting Online Learning Centre website. Take advantage of the study tools offered to reinforce the material you have read in the text, and to develop your knowledge of European economics in a fun and effective way.

Resources for students include:
- Learning Objectives
- Key Concepts
- Relevant Essays
- Useful Weblinks

Also available for lecturers:
- Lecture Outlines
- Guide Answers to Study Questions

FOR LECTURERS: PRIMIS CONTENT CENTRE

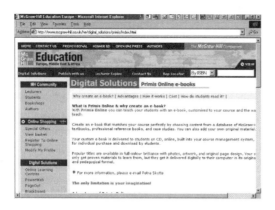

If you need to supplement your course with additional cases or content, create a personalized e-Book for your students. Visit

www.primiscontentcenter.com
or email
primis_euro@mcgraw-hill.com for more information.

Study Skills

Open University Press publishes guides to study, research and exam skills to help undergraduate and postgraduate students through their university studies.
Visit **www.openup.co.uk/ss/** to see the full selection.

Computing Skills

If you'd like to brush up on your computing skills, we have a range of titles covering MS Office applications such as Word, Excel, PowerPoint, Access and more.

Get a £2 discount off these titles by entering the promotional code **app** when ordering online at **www.mcgraw-hill.co.uk/app**

Preface

Many years ago when I was studying European integration at the College of Europe in Bruges, one of my professors organized a trip to the First World War battlefields of Flanders. The day seemed a little like a school outing, but with the relentless rain falling in the former trenches, the lesson was well taken. One of the main aims of integration was to render war in Europe not only inconceivable but 'materially impossible'. Today, despite tensions in areas such as the divided Cyprus or Northern Ireland, in the EU we tend to take this success almost for granted. One of the aims now is to extend this achievement to other less stable areas of Europe such as the former Yugoslavia.

Of the many experts working on East–West studies, few predicted the collapse of communism in 1989. Right from the start of transition, the Central and Eastern European countries wanted to join the integration process. At first the European Community seemed rather unprepared and overwhelmed at the prospect, but after a long and difficult process of preparation, in 2004 much of Europe was again 'reunified'.

European integration has therefore a strong political impetus, but the method of implementation has been primarily economic. The first successful initiative was the European Coal and Steel Community created in 1951, while in the early years of the European Economic Community (EEC) the main progress was in trade and agriculture (though the policy mechanisms chosen for the latter can be criticized). Numerous studies suggest that the Single Market Programme introduced from 1985, and bolstered in many member states by the euro, has fostered trade and other closer economic ties between countries.

This book is aimed mainly at students of economics, European studies, business, political science and international relations. Though the approach is grounded in economics, the aim is to provide a multidisciplinary account of EU integration. The debate about whether the EU is primarily an economic or political entity is of long standing, but the view here is that in order to understand the process of integration a combination of economics, politics and history is necessary. The textbook is intended to have a strong policy orientation.

The objective has also been to organize the material in a flexible way so it can be directed at different audiences. For this reason the theory has been concentrated in Chapters 4 and 5 and in separate sections in other chapters. Omitting Chapters 4 and 5, and the theoretical sections, the book can and has been used in various courses where the students have little or no economics background. The aim has also been to write chapters that stand individually and can be used independently from the rest of the book. A basic introduction to the EU could cover Chapters 1–3, Chapters 6–9 and Chapter 20. Depending on where the reader comes from, this could, for example, be supplemented with Chapters 17 and 18 or, in the case of US students, Chapters 18 and 19. Those interested in individual policies can select from Chapters 10 to 16. A course on the external relations of the European Union could use Chapters 17–20. The intention has been to permit the use of different combinations of chapters depending on the needs or interests of the reader.

Because each chapter has been written so that it can stand independently, the aim is also to provide a text that can be consulted by researchers or policy-makers. For this purpose each chapter sets out references for further reading and relevant websites.

The EU is evolving constantly, and though every effort has been made to ensure that the text is up to date, more recent developments are necessarily covered by the OLC website for this book.

Acknowledgements

Our thanks go to the following reviewers for their comments at various stages in the text's development:

Niels Blomgren Hansen, University of Copenhagen
Jim Campbell, Glasgow Caledonian University
Jan Colijn, Erasmus University
Tom Craven, University of Ulster
Charlotte Lythe, University of Dundee
Roxana Radulescu, University of Newcastle
Ivonia Rebelo, London Metropolitan University
Malcolm Sawyer, University of Leeds
Jette Steen Knudsen, Copenhagen Business School
Barbara Timms, Napier University
Thomas Verbeke, University of Ghent
Pam Whisker, University of Plymouth

Few would be foolhardy enough to sit down and begin writing a textbook on the European Union these days. This book was never actually planned but emerged as a result of teaching various aspects of EU integration over the years. As many of the courses were repeated, it seemed a good idea to keep a written record, and gradually the book emerged. My first thanks therefore go to the many students on whom (often inadvertently) the material was tried out. These include the students of the Faculty of Economics and the Faculty of Political Science of the University of Siena, the California State University Florence Program and Cornell College, Iowa.

University work is invariably a combination of teaching and research, and this book has grown out of many years of research into European integration. I would therefore like to thank the many colleagues (who are too numerous to mention individually), in particular those at Siena University, the European University Institute, and the European Commission, who offered opportunities for discussion of topics related to the book, including seminars, summer schools and conferences.

Recognizing that it would be difficult to pull together a final version of this text, I hesitated for some time before presenting the manuscript. The various members of the publishing team were invaluable in helping me to complete this final step. I am very grateful to them for their encouragement and assistance, in particular for organizing numerous reviews by referees. These reviews have radically shaped the final version of the book, but any eventual mistakes that remain are, of course, my responsibility.

I would like to thank the following organizations and publishers for permission to reproduce material in this book.

CABI Publishing
Carocci editore, Roma
ECRE
European Commission
Financial Times

Acknowledgements

OECD
Oxford University Press
International Institute for Management Development (IMD)
Taylor & Francis, incorporating Routledge
UNCTAD
UNHCR
John Wiley & Sons Inc.
WTO

Every effort has been made to trace and acknowledge copyright and to obtain permissions to reproduce material in the text. The publishers would be pleased to make arrangements to clear permission with any copyright holders it has not been possible to contact.

Dedication

This book is inevitably dedicated to Paolo, Matteo and Caterina, and to the many friends I made throughout Europe and elsewhere while studying and teaching EU integration.

An Introduction to European Integration: Definitions and Terminology

LEARNING OBJECTIVES

By the end of this chapter you should be able to understand:

► The difference between the terms 'European Economic Community', 'European Community' and 'European Union';
► How the membership of the European Union has changed over the years;
► What we mean by integration, and its various stages;
► The different approaches to integration;
► What is the *acquis communautaire*;
► What we mean by the term 'subsidiarity';
► The importance of the EU in the world economy.

QUESTIONS OF TERMINOLOGY

The term 'European Economic Community' dates from the Treaty of Rome (which came into force 1 January 1958). It was one of the then three European Communities, the others being the

European Coal and Steel Community (1951) and Euratom (1958). The institutions of the three Communities were fused from 1967.[1] The widespread use of the term 'European Community' dates from a resolution of the European Parliament of 1975 when it was decided to drop the term 'economic' because the Community was considered to have extended its activities beyond the purely economic sphere.

In the Treaty of Rome the founders of the original EEC laid the foundations for working towards 'an ever closer union'. According to the opening words of the Maastricht Treaty this objective has been reached: 'By this Treaty, the High Contracting Parties establish among themselves a European Union, hereinafter called "the Union".' With the Maastricht Treaty the European Community was reinforced and flanked by two other 'pillars': the Common Foreign and Security Policy (CFSP) and Justice and Home Affairs (JHA).[2] The three together form the European Union (see Fig. 1.1). The reason for creating two additional pillars was that, at least initially on such sensitive issues, the member states were reluctant to give up responsibility to a supranational authority (the European Community), and preferred to take decisions in these spheres on the basis of inter-governmental co-operation.[3] This policy implies that initiatives on the second and third pillars are reached by direct negotiation between governments and require a unanimous agreement. The Community, or first pillar, includes areas such as the Common Agricultural Policy, the Common Commercial Policy, the Single Market, Competition Policy and Economic and Monetary Union.

The proposed Constitutional Treaty (see Chapter 3) would merge the three pillars, though special procedures would be maintained in the fields of foreign policy, security and defence.

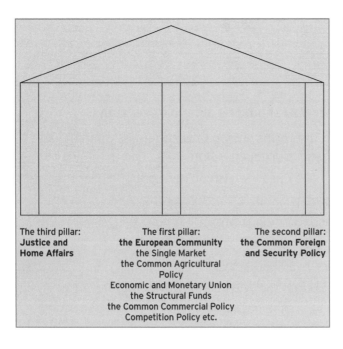

FIGURE 1.1 **The European Union**

The third pillar:
Justice and Home Affairs

The first pillar:
the European Community
the Single Market
the Common Agricultural Policy
Economic and Monetary Union
the Structural Funds
the Common Commercial Policy
Competition Policy etc.

The second pillar:
the Common Foreign and Security Policy

---

[1] When the 1965 Merger Treaty came into force. In July 2002 the ECSC was formally wound up, and its assets and liabilities were transferred to the EU.
[2] According to the Amsterdam Treaty, many aspects of JHA were to be brought under the Community pillar by 2004, and the name of the third pillar was to be changed to Police and Justice Co-operation in Criminal Matters (PJCCM).
[3] The meaning of a 'supranational authority' is discussed below.

THE CHANGING MEMBERSHIP OF THE EU

There were six original members of the European Economic Community, the European Coal and Steel Community, and Euratom: Belgium, France, Germany, Italy, Luxembourg and the Netherlands. Allowing for a time span of five years in the case of the Mediterranean countries, enlargement has generally taken place in groups of three countries: Denmark, Ireland and the UK in 1973, Greece in 1981 and Spain and Portugal in 1986, and Austria, Finland and Sweden in 1995.

Ten new member states joined the EU in May 2004: Cyprus, the Czech Republic, Estonia, Hungary, Latvia, Lithuania, Malta, Poland, Slovakia, and Slovenia, while Bulgaria and Romania could join in 2007. In December 2004 a decision will be taken on whether Turkey is ready to become a member; if so, negotiations would be opened without delay. In 2004 the European Commission published an Opinion favourable to starting accession negotiations with Croatia.

THE DEFINITION OF INTEGRATION

Economic integration can be defined as the elimination of barriers to the movement of products and factors of production between a group of countries and the introduction of common policies. Tinbergen (1954) made the distinction between negative integration (the removal of barriers) and positive integration – the introduction of common policies, and building of common institutions. However, this distinction only remains clear when a state's intervention is limited to measures taken at the border, such as tariffs, import quotas and so on. If a state's more active role in the economy is considered, many measures with 'domestic' objectives will have repercussions for trade. For example, subsidies to domestic production in a particular country (e.g. by the Italian government to Fiat) could constitute a barrier for foreign firms. As a result, in a modern, mixed economy with wide-scale state intervention, the effective elimination of barriers may require common policies.

THE STAGES OF INTEGRATION

Following the pioneering work of Balassa (1961), the traditional literature on integration refers to different 'stages' in the process. However, if the more active role of the state in the economy is taken into account, these should not be regarded as steps in an ascending scale since even complete realization of one of the 'lower stages' may require full economic, monetary and political union. None the less, the classification remains useful to indicate different forms of integration.

Free trade areas
The member states remove all barriers on trade between themselves but retain the freedom to implement different commercial policies towards third countries. In order to get around the problem of importing for re-exporting, free trade areas require rules of origin. In other words, when a good is traded it has to be accompanied by documentation stating where it was made. Rules of origin may be complex to administer, and the regulatory uncertainty to which they give rise means that market access is conditional.

An example of a free trade area is the EFTA (the European Free Trade Association), which was set up in 1960 by seven European countries as an alternative to joining the EEC (see Chapter 2).[4]

---

[4] The UK, Norway, Sweden, Denmark, Austria, Switzerland and Portugal.

A further example is NAFTA (the North American Free Trade Agreement), which came into operation between the USA, Canada and Mexico in 1994.

Customs unions

The member states remove all barriers on trade between themselves and introduce a common external commercial policy (for instance a common external tariff) towards the rest of the world. An example of a customs union is that between the EU and Turkey which came into operation from 1995 but which largely excluded agricultural products.

Common markets

These are customs unions, which also allow for free factor mobility. In other words, a common market entails the so-called four freedoms: freedom of movement of goods, services, labour and capital. During the early years the Community was sometimes called the 'common market', although this description was not very accurate as the then EEC was more like a customs union with certain sectoral policies (notably the Common Agricultural Policy) financed largely through a Community budget.

Economic and monetary union

An economic and monetary union should include the following elements: a common market; co-ordination or central control of monetary and fiscal policies; a common money or complete convertibility among national currencies with no possibility of exchange-rate adjustments; and a common authority which acts as a central bank. As will be seen in Chapter 8, in the case of the EU it was decided to introduce a single monetary unit (the euro), a common monetary policy, co-ordination of fiscal policy and a European Central Bank in Frankfurt.

Political union

The definition of this term in the literature is often imprecise and ambiguous, reflecting different conceptions of what it entails. In very general terms, political union involves a central authority that has supranational powers similar to those of a nation's government over various policy areas including, for example, foreign policy and security matters, and is responsible to a directly elected central parliament. As will be discussed in Chapter 2, the different conceptions of political union, and the reluctance of member states to give up sovereignty on certain issues, mean that in practice political union has not been realized by the EU.

APPROACHES TO INTEGRATION

There are differing views about how political and economic integration should be achieved: [5]
1. According to the **pluralist approach,** the member states should retain their sovereignty, but should co-operate to achieve certain economic or political objectives, such as trade liberalization. This is the idea of a *Europe des patries*, based on intergovernmental co-operation rather than transfer of power to a supranational authority.

A supranational authority can be defined as an international organization which either has direct authority for certain matters over its member states (in the sense that its legislation is directly binding and does not have to be transposed into national laws), or takes decisions on the basis of majority voting by its members, i.e. the member states give up their right of veto in deciding on certain issues.

---

[5] For a more detailed discussion of these approaches see Hitiris (2003).

2. The **functionalist approach** maintains that in the modern world, technical, economic and social forces lead to interdependencies and shared problems for nation states. Individual countries acting in isolation cannot decide on issues such as the environment, the control of multinational enterprises, telecommunications and information technology. International co-operation is needed to deal with such matters, and it is believed that this will ultimately lead to economic and political unity. In other words, political integration inevitably follows economic integration.

3. The **neo-functionalist approach** is essentially a strategy that entails using functionalist techniques to realize federalist objectives. Again the starting point is a network of international economic linkages, but unlike the functionalist approach importance is attached to sub-state actors, such as interest groups, which try to exploit these linkages. To deal with these groups, individual countries have to delegate to international organizations, which gradually evolve into supranational authorities. The interest groups and supranational organizations become the drivers of integration. Also at the core of neo-functionalism is the idea that integration in one sector will generate impetus for integration in other sectors.[6] Thus, for example, integration of the defence effort will require democratic control, thus creating a spill-over leading to integration in the political sphere.

4. The **federalist** approach calls for the transfer of many of the sovereign rights and obligations of the member states to a supranational federal authority. In contrast to the functionalist and neo-functionalist approaches, which envisage a federal authority as the final stage in an ongoing process, the federalist approach favours introducing that stage directly. It is therefore in direct contradiction with the pluralist approach, which views creation of a supranational federal authority as anathema.

Early US history offers many examples of the federalist approach. For instance, the Constitutional Convention of 1787 was concerned with wresting powers from the individual states in a way that was palatable to them. The various states had distinct histories, often dating back nearly two centuries, and were reluctant to relinquish their autonomy to an untried central authority.

THE *ACQUIS COMMUNAUTAIRE*

The *acquis communautaire* is literally 'what the Community has achieved'. It consists of the body (sometimes called 'patrimony') of EU legislation, practices, principles and objectives accepted by the member states. It is composed of:

■ The treaties, especially the Treaties of Rome (1958), the Single European Act (1987), the Maastricht Treaty (1993), the Amsterdam Treaty (1999) and the Treaty of Nice (2003);[7]

■ Legislation enacted at the EU level and judgments of the European Court of Justice;

■ Foreign and Security Policy;

■ Justice and Home Affairs; and

■ Treaties of the EU with third countries.

The *acquis* has been accumulating over the years and now amounts to about 12 000 legislative acts (consisting of some 80 000 pages). Progress in EU accession negotiations depends to a large extent on the speed with which the candidate countries can take on and implement the *acquis communautaire*.

---

[6] See, for example, Haas (1958) who is generally acknowledged to be one of the founders of this approach.
[7] Unless otherwise stated, these dates refer to when the treaties entered into force.

SUBSIDIARITY

In practice difficulties may arise in deciding which is the appropriate level of government to take decisions on various policy areas. In other words, is a particular issue best decided at the EU, national, state, regional or local level? Subsidiarity is the principle that decisions should be taken at the lowest level that permits effective action. The idea of subsidiarity is linked to that of taking decisions 'as closely as possible to the citizens'. It is also maintained that by limiting action at the Community level to where it is really necessary, the quality of EC legislation could be improved. As Jacques Santer, a former president of the Commission, stated:[8] 'I have a different notion of subsidiarity: it means not harmonizing every last nut and bolt, but stepping up our co-operation wherever this is really worth it. We should take as our motto "Less action, but better action".'

In the EU context the word 'subsidiarity' first appeared in the EC Commission's submission to the 1975 Tindemans Report on European Union and the steps to be taken to create a more united Europe, closer to the citizens.[9] However, the principle was not taken up in the final version of the report, partly because the proposals were less far reaching than the Commission had suggested, so there was less need to reassure those member states fearing a loss of their sovereignty.[10]

Since the late 1980s the term has frequently been used by the EC member states and regions wanting to limit the powers of the Community, in particular Britain, Denmark and the German Länder. It was largely to assuage the fears of these countries that a subsidiarity clause was introduced in Article 3b of the Treaty of Maastricht:

> In areas which do not fall within its exclusive competence, the Community shall take action, in accordance with the principle of subsidiarity, if and only in so far as the objectives of the proposed action cannot be sufficiently achieved by the member states and can therefore, by reason of the scale or the efforts of proposed action, be better achieved by the Community. Any action of the Community shall not go beyond what is necessary to achieve the objectives of this Treaty.

A protocol to the Amsterdam Treaty confirms that Community actions should not exceed what is necessary to realize the objectives of the Treaty, and this has become known as the 'principle of proportionality'.

Article 8 of the proposed new Constitutional Treaty (see Chapter 3) establishes that any competence not conferred on the Union by the constitution rests with the member states. In the EU context the term 'competencies' refers to the allocation of tasks. Article 10 indicates those areas of exclusive Union competence, which include the internal market (though some member states had reservations about including the four freedoms in this category), the organization of agricultural markets, economic and social cohesion, and the Union's financing. In other areas the EU either shares competence with the member states (Article 11), or does not have competence to legislate and simply supports or co-ordinates action by the member states (Article 12). In practice it is difficult to establish which measures should be centralized, and to what extent.[11] The treaties allow for an extension of EU tasks if this is necessary to realize the objectives of the EC Treaty.[12]

---

[8] In a speech to the European Parliament, Strasbourg, 17 January 1995.

[9] The first reference to the principle was in the Papal Encyclical, *Rerum Novarum* of 1891, and it was again taken up in the 1931 Encyclical, *Quadragesimo Anno*. In this context the principle warned against the ever-increasing powers of the state (Bainbridge, 1998).

[10] The principle reappeared in the 1984 European Parliament's Draft Treaty establishing the European Union. Although the 1987 Single European Act contained no general reference to it, it specified that subsidiarity was to be used for environment policy. 'The Community shall take action relating to the environment to the extent to which (objectives) can be attained better at the Community level than at the level of the member states.' Article 130r, since repealed.

[11] So much so that in a speech to the European Parliament Jacques Delors, then president of the European Commission, offered a job and ECU 200 000 to anyone who could define subsidiarity in one page!

[12] According to Article 308 (ex Article 235) of the EC Treaty: 'If action by the Community should prove necessary to attain, in the course of the operation of the common market, one of the objectives of the Community and this Treaty has not provided the necessary powers, the Council shall, acting unanimously on a proposal from the Commission and after consulting the European Parliament, take the appropriate measures.'

Over the years there has been a tendency towards 'competence creep', or an increase in the sphere of activities of the EU.

In April 1996 Eurobarometer[13] carried out a survey to assess which decisions EU citizens felt were best carried out at the national level and which at the EU level. Not surprisingly, according to the survey EU decisions were preferred in areas such as the fight against drugs, assistance to developing countries, research and development. The policy areas where national decisions were favoured included health and social protection, education, cultural policy, workers' rights and questions relating to the media (radio, TV and press).

THE EU IN THE WORLD

The success of the EU as an integrated bloc has meant that it has emerged as one of the main partners in world trade and investment, as shown in Figures 1.2–1.5. In 2003, foreign direct investment (FDI) outflows of the EU(25) to the rest of the world grew by over 80 per cent, to

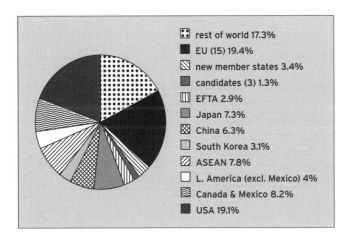

rest of world 17.3%
EU (15) 19.4%
new member states 3.4%
candidates (3) 1.3%
EFTA 2.9%
Japan 7.3%
China 6.3%
South Korea 3.1%
ASEAN 7.8%
L. America (excl. Mexico) 4%
Canada & Mexico 8.2%
USA 19.1%

FIGURE 1.2 Share in world trade of goods (2002)

Source:
www.europa.eu.int.comm/trade

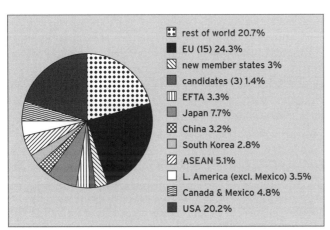

rest of world 20.7%
EU (15) 24.3%
new member states 3%
candidates (3) 1.4%
EFTA 3.3%
Japan 7.7%
China 3.2%
South Korea 2.8%
ASEAN 5.1%
L. America (excl. Mexico) 3.5%
Canada & Mexico 4.8%
USA 20.2%

FIGURE 1.3 Share in world trade in services (2001)

Source:
www.europa.eu.int.comm/trade

[13] 'Eurobarometer top decision-makers survey of September 1996': www.europa.eu.int/comm/public_opinion. Eurobarometer is the public opinion analysis section of the European Commission.

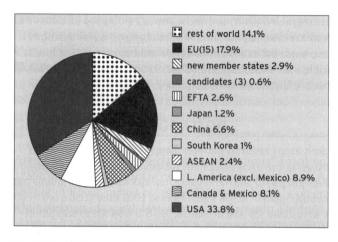

FIGURE 1.4 **Share in world FDI inflows 1998–2001**

Source: www.europa.eu.int.comm/trade

- rest of world 14.1%
- EU(15) 17.9%
- new member states 2.9%
- candidates (3) 0.6%
- EFTA 2.6%
- Japan 1.2%
- China 6.6%
- South Korea 1%
- ASEAN 2.4%
- L. America (excl. Mexico) 8.9%
- Canada & Mexico 8.1%
- USA 33.8%

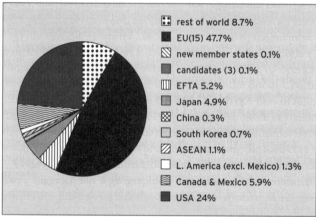

FIGURE 1.5 **Share in world FDI outflows 1998–2001**

Source: www.europa.eu.int.comm/trade

- rest of world 8.7%
- EU(15) 47.7%
- new member states 0.1%
- candidates (3) 0.1%
- EFTA 5.2%
- Japan 4.9%
- China 0.3%
- South Korea 0.7%
- ASEAN 1.1%
- L. America (excl. Mexico) 1.3%
- Canada & Mexico 5.9%
- USA 24%

reach 118 billion euros, compared to 65 billion in 2002, while FDI inflows to the EU(25) from extra-EU(25) countries decreased by 15 per cent, from 91 billion in 2002 to 77 billion in 2003.[14]

Table 1.1 presents comparative statistics for EU economic weight and performance *vis-à-vis* the USA and Japan. Its weight in the world economy and the repercussions of EU policies for other countries imply a growing need for the EU to adopt a more active and responsible role for the international economy, a topic that is taken up in more detail in Chapters 17 to 19.

The functions of the GATT (General Agreement on Tariffs and Trade) and its replacement, the WTO (the World Trade Organization), are discussed in some detail in Chapter 17, but it is useful at this point to give a brief indication of their roles.[15] The GATT came into operation in 1948 in order to provide a framework for international trade negotiations in an attempt to regulate world trade. The GATT aimed at setting out regulations governing the conduct of international trade by making provisions for the settlements of disputes and retaliatory actions, and providing the framework for multilateral negotiations to liberalize world trade. In 1995 the WTO replaced the GATT, and differs from its predecessor in having full institutional status, a legal personality and reinforced powers to settle trade disputes. In 2004, 148 countries were members of the WTO.

---

[14] Eurostat data.
[15] For a discussion of the links between the EU and international organizations such as the GATT/WTO, the IMF and the World Bank, see the website for this book. Some of the other international organizations with which the EU has close relations, such as the OECD, are discussed in Chapter 2.

TABLE 1.1 Key EU indicators (2003)

	Population 1 January 2003 (millions)	Area (thousand sq km)	GDP US$ using current PPPs	Inflation rate	Unemployment rate	Growth
EU(15)	380.4	3240	10130	2.0	8.1	2.3
EU(25)	454.6	4342	11100	2.0	9.1	2.4
Japan	126.8*	378	3582	-0.9	5.3	2.3
US	278.1*	9372	10871	2.3	6.0	3.2

*2001 data
Source: World Bank, OECD, European Commission, www.europa.eu.int/comm.

Summary of Key Concepts

● The term 'European Economic Community' dates from the Treaty of Rome of 1958. The widespread use of 'European Community' dates from a resolution of the European Parliament of 1975 when it was decided to drop the word 'economic'. With the Maastricht Treaty the European Community was reinforced and flanked by two other 'pillars': Justice and Home Affairs, and the Common Foreign and Security policy. The three together form the 'European Union'.

● There were six original members of the European Economic Community: Belgium, France, Germany, Italy, Luxembourg, and the Netherlands. Denmark, Ireland and the UK joined in 1973, Greece in 1981, Spain and Portugal in 1986 and Austria, Finland and Sweden in 1995. Ten countries joined the EU in 2004: Cyprus, Malta, the Czech Republic, Estonia, Hungary, Latvia, Lithuania, Poland, Slovakia and Slovenia. Bulgaria and Romania are expected to join in 2007. A decision will be taken on Turkey in December 2004, and in 2004 the Commission published an Opinion in favour of opening accession negotiations with Croatia.

● Economic integration can be defined as the elimination of barriers to the movement of products and factors of production between a group of countries (negative integration) and the introduction of common policies (positive integration).

● The stages of integration are: free trade areas, customs unions, common markets, economic and monetary union, and political union.

● The approaches to integration are: the pluralist approach, the functionalist approach, the neo-functionalist approach and the federalist approach.

● The *acquis communautaire* is the body of EU legislation, practices, principles and objectives accepted by the member states.

● Subsidiarity is the principle that decisions should be taken at the lowest level that permits effective action.

● The EU has become one of the major global actors in terms of trade and foreign direct investment (FDI).

Questions for Study and Review

■ Define integration and indicate the different stages of integration. What are the different approaches to integration?

■ What do we mean by the term '*acquis communautaire*'?

■ What do we mean by the term 'subsidiarity'? What policies do you think should be the responsibility of the EU?

■ Describe the economic weight of the EU in the world.

References

Bainbridge, T. (1998) *The Penguin Companion to European Union,* 2nd edn, Penguin Books, London.

Balassa, B. (1961) *The Theory of Economic Integration,* Irwin, Homewood, IL.

Haas, E.B. (1958) *The Uniting of Europe*, Stanford University Press, Stanford, CA.

Harrop, J. (2000) *The Political Economy of Integration in the European Union*, 3rd edn, Edward Elgar, Cheltenham, UK.

Hitiris, T. (2003) *European Community Economics,* 5th edn, Pearson Education Limited, Harlow, UK.

OECD (various years) *Main Economic Indicators.*

Swann, D. (1995) *The Economics of the Common Market*, 8th edn, Penguin Books, London.

Tinbergen, J. (1954) *International Economic Integration,* Elsevier, Amsterdam.

Useful websites

The website of the European Union:

www.europa.eu.int

For the treaties and EU legislation see:

www.europa.eu.int/eur.lex

The OECD and the WTO provide statistics and analysis of the world economy:

www.oecd.org

www.wto.org

The IMF (see the OLC website for this book) provides reports and international financial statistics:

www.imf.org

The World Bank is mainly concerned with development issues (see the OLC website for this book) but publishes numerous studies on the world economy:

www.worldbank.org

List of Abbreviations

ASEAN	Association of South-East Asian countries
CFSP	Common Foreign and Security Policy
EC	European Communities
ECSC	European Coal and Steel Community
EEC	European Economic Community
EFTA	European Free Trade Association
EU	European Union
FDI	foreign direct investment
GATT	General Agreement on Tariffs and Trade
JHA	Justice and Home Affairs
NAFTA	North American Free Trade Agreement
OECD	Organization for Economic Co-operation and Development
PJCCM	Police and Justice Co-operation on Criminal Matters
WTO	World Trade Organization

2

A Brief History of European Integration

LEARNING OBJECTIVES

By the end of this chapter you should be able to understand:

▶ The initial failure to create a supranational organization in Europe after the Second World War;

▶ The purpose of setting up the European Coal and Steel Community;

▶ The failure of early attempts to promote European co-operation on defence;

▶ The reasons for setting up a common policy on agriculture, and its initial failure;

▶ Why the integration process gained a new impetus in the mid-1950s;

▶ The principal objectives and policies set out in the Treaty of Rome;

▶ The main elements of the EEC in the 1960s: trade and agriculture;

▶ The 1969 Hague Summit: deepening, widening and completion of the integration process;

▶ The years of eurosclerosis in the 1970s;

▶ The main events in the development of the EU (the Single Market Project, the Maastricht Treaty, the EFTA enlargement, the Amsterdam and Nice Treaties, the Mediterranean Programme, the Lisbon Process, enlargement and the Constitutional Treaty).

The main aim of this chapter is to provide a brief overview of the chief events leading to the creation of the EEC in 1958, and the most important developments in its subsequent history. Discussion of almost all of these later developments is taken up in more detail in later chapters.

THE ORIGINS OF EUROPEAN INTEGRATION

The idea of a united Europe dates back several centuries, but in the years following the Second World War it acquired a greater urgency.[1] The aim was to make another war in Europe materially impossible, and to co-operate in the post-war reconstruction process. At the same time, the creation of the Eastern bloc and the perceived Soviet threat left Western Europe feeling divided and vulnerable. After the war the USA and the USSR emerged as the two superpowers (an international scenario to last until the 1990s), and it became increasingly evident that only a united Europe would carry weight at an international level.

During the early years, most of the initiatives to carry forward the integration process came from France, usually backed by Germany and the Benelux countries. Despite widespread popular belief in the European ideal, the position of the other 'large' founder-member of the Community, Italy, often appeared confused and contradictory, possibly reflecting the overriding concern with the internal political situation.

British ambivalence towards the integration process soon became apparent. Britain had emerged victorious from the war, participating in meetings such as Yalta to create a new world order. Great importance was attached to the 'special relationship' with the United States. In addition, much trade was still carried out with former members of the Empire rather than with continental Europe.

BACKGROUND TO THE INTEGRATION PROCESS: THE 1940S

The first European organization to be created after the war was the **UNECE** (United Nations Economic Commission for Europe) which was set up as a regional organization of the UN in Geneva in 1947. Its initial aim was to carry out economic reconstruction and encourage co-operation among all the states of Europe: East, West and Central. Soon after creation of this organization, the East–West division of Europe became a reality and the USSR feared Western influence on its satellites. The UNECE was to prove the last pan-European organization for many years. It remained in operation as a useful research centre for East–West studies, and subsequently for analysis of the transition of countries in Central and East Europe and the former Soviet Republics into market economies and functioning democracies.

The European integration process gained a new impetus in 1947 with the introduction of the **Marshall Plan.** A bad harvest in 1946 increased food prices, and the severe winter of 1947/8 led to a fuel crisis. The continental European countries faced an acute shortage of foreign reserves as the result of a combination of huge import requirements and limited exports. US General George Marshall proposed a programme to aid Europe. It was initially suggested that the programme would be administered through the UNECE, but this was opposed by the USSR, which feared an increase of Western influence on its satellites. The Marshall Plan involved US and Canadian aid to 16 European countries. The aid was to be conditional on the European countries dismantling barriers to trade among themselves, and co-operating in the creation of a European organization to administer the aid programme.

---

[1] See Swann (1995) and Milward (1984 and 1992) for more detailed accounts of the historical background.

In 1948 this led to the creation of the OEEC (Organization for European Economic Co-operation). There was a difference of opinion between Britain and France as to whether this organization should be based on inter-governmental co-operation, or whether a supranational element should be injected, as favoured by the French (with US support). The French pushed for an international secretariat that could take initiatives on major issues, but in the end the British view prevailed. The OEEC led to the setting up of the European Payments Union in 1950, and was the forum in which the six founding members of the EEC began the discussions that led to the Treaty of Rome. After the winding up of Marshall aid, in 1961 this organization was transformed and became the **OECD** (Organization for Economic Co-operation and Development) (see Box 2.1).[2]

Box 2.1 The OECD (Organization for Economic Co-operation and Development)

Based in Paris, the OECD unites 30 major industrial countries and plays an important role in international economic co-operation. Its main functions include the co-ordination of development aid, the promotion of trade liberalization and economic growth, and the analysis of economic performance, including international trade questions. It is well known for its statistics, and for its publications that include country surveys and reviews.

The economic division of Europe was formalized in 1949 with the creation of the **Comecon or CMEA** (Council for Mutual Economic Assistance).[3] In addition to the USSR and smaller Central–East European countries, Cuba, Mongolia and Vietnam were also CMEA members. The founding of the CMEA was largely a political response to the Marshall Plan, but the organization really only became active after the signing of the Treaty of Rome in 1957. Though the CMEA never became a supranational body like the Community, Soviet hegemony implied a certain degree of political integration. The CMEA was formally dissolved in September 1991.

In 1948 pro-European statesmen (including Churchill) rallied at a Congress of Europe in The Hague and called for progress towards economic and political union in Europe, if necessary by sacrificing some national sovereignty. It was decided to create the **Council of Europe**, but again attempts to create a supranational European organization failed, largely due to opposition from Britain and the Scandinavian countries, who were among the founder-members. The French and Belgians were in favour of a European parliamentary assembly which could use majority voting, but the powers finally agreed for the first Consultative Assembly were so limited that its first president, the Belgian, Paul-Henri Spaak, resigned.

Set up in Strasbourg in 1949, the Council of Europe is *not* an institution of the European Community. Though the Council of Europe disappointed the federalists, it provided the seat for various debates and initiatives in the European integration process, and continues to play an important role in the field of human rights, rule of law and democracy (see Box 2.2).

Box 2.2 The Council of Europe

The Council of Europe deals with areas such as culture, education, the environment, control of the international drugs trade and medical ethics. Since 1989 it has been active in promoting constitutional and institutional reforms to assist democratic consolidation in Central and Eastern Europe and certain former Soviet Republics.

---

[2] Following the EEC/EFTA division, see below.
[3] For many years the term 'Comecon' was generally avoided in Central–East Europe as it was considered reminiscent of the cold war.

In 1950 a European Convention on Human Rights was also drawn up, and recently a Framework Convention for the Protection of National Minorities was also adopted. The organs of the Council of Europe include a parliamentary assembly, a committee of foreign ministers and, probably the best known and most effective of its institutions, the Court of Human Rights. Previously separate, two of the organs of the Council of Europe, the European Commission of Human Rights and the Court of Human Rights, were merged in 1998.

Membership of the Council of Europe has been growing rapidly, reaching 45 countries in 2003. In theory membership of the Council of Europe is only for those countries able and willing to sign and implement its treaties, but in practice tensions may arise. It is frequently argued that the Council is in a stronger position to influence countries if they are members. At the time of their accession there was much controversy about countries such as Russia and Croatia, which were considered to have shortcomings with regard to freedom of expression and the rule of law. When Georgia joined in 1999 it was given a list of needed reforms and deadlines for introducing them. Other countries, such as Belarus, have been excluded on the grounds that they are undemocratic and fail to respect human rights.

The Council of Europe can play an important role for countries outside the EU as membership may provide evidence that they belong to Europe, as well as giving such countries some say in a pan-European organization. In 2003 Liechtenstein (population 34 000), a member of the Council of Europe, risked monitoring by the Council for its democratic deficit, sharing the fate of countries such as Turkey, Azerbaijan and Armenia. The principality of Liechtenstein, ruled by Prince Hans-Adam II, introduced revisions of its 1921 constitution. It was claimed that the revisions gave the prince virtually feudal powers, including *de facto* veto on legislation and on key appointments (*Financial Times*, 22–23 November 2003).

Box 2.3: The OSCE (Organization for Security and Co-operation in Europe)

There is a certain overlap of functions between the Council of Europe and the Organization for Security and Co-operation in Europe (OSCE). Created in 1975 during the era of *détente*, the aim of what was then known as the CSCE (Conference on Security and Co-operation in Europe) was to promote East–West dialogue. The 'final act' of the CSCE was signed in Helsinki and was primarily of interest to Western countries as a means of improving human rights in the Eastern bloc, while the Eastern partners were mainly concerned with economic and technological co-operation. The final act set out four Helsinki 'baskets': security and disarmament; economic and technological co-operation and protection of the environment; co-operation in humanitarian and other fields; and the commitments of the signatory states. Following the collapse of communism, this organization was transformed into the OSCE, and became focused on an ongoing process of ensuring that commitments were being implemented. The main function of the OSCE is to provide a forum for its members to discuss and co-operate on security issues, and to ensure the operation of democratic practices (in particular, free and fair elections). It is active in early warning, conflict prevention, crisis management and post-conflict rehabilitation. The OSCE had 55 members in 2003, including most European countries, the USA, Canada and various former Soviet Republics. At least in theory, the Council of Europe is responsible for codifying and upholding legal rules, while the obligations of the OSCE are only politically binding; its main function is to encourage improved practices in areas of tension.

INTEGRATION BY SECTOR

The failure of federalist attempts to create a supranational European architecture in both the OEEC and Council of Europe brought about a change in tactics, with subsequent proposed initiatives in European integration adopting a more neo-functionalist approach. It was felt that less ambitious plans to co-operate in specific economic sectors might provide experience in working together, and could also induce spill-over into increased political co-operation.

THE ECSC (EUROPEAN COAL AND STEEL COMMUNITY)

The combination of US aid and the determination of the German people soon led to post-war recovery of the German economy. The question became how to allow Germany to regain her powerful position in what were then the strategic industries of iron, steel and coal production without endangering peace in Europe. Moreover, it was realized that Allied control of coal and steel production in the Ruhr could not continue indefinitely.

The proposed solution was the Schuman Plan which was elaborated by Jean Monnet (then in charge of the French *Commissariat du Plan*; see Box 2.4), and put forward by the French foreign

Box 2.4 Jean Monnet (1888-1979)

Jean Monnet* was a French economist and diplomat, at times called the 'Father of Europe'. As director of the post-war planning commission in France, he was the initiator of the Monnet Plan (1947–53) for the modernization and re-equipment of French industry. Monnet was instigator of the Schuman Plan in 1950, and first president of the European Coal and Steel Community. In 1950 he also fostered the eventually unsuccessful plan to create a European Defence Community.

During the war Monnet turned down an invitation to join de Gaulle's government-in-exile in London. In the summer of 1940 he persuaded Churchill to make an offer of Franco-British Union. He was convinced of the importance of US support for the war effort, and for several years was technically a senior British civil servant in Washington with his French passport personally endorsed by Churchill. In some French circles Monnet's vision, which led him to work so closely with the USA and Britain, was criticized. An interesting account of his life is provided in his memoirs (Monnet, 1978).

*Not to be confused with the French painter Claude Monet!

minister, Robert Schuman (Box 2.5). The Schuman Plan aimed at making war in Europe not only 'unthinkable, but materially impossible' through the creation of a common market for iron, steel and coal in Europe. For Germany this offered a passport to international respectability, and an end to Allied occupation and checks on economic recovery (Swann, 1995). For France the plan provided a means of concluding French occupation of the Saarland, since handing the Saarland back to Germany would be more acceptable if Germany formed part of a common market in coal

> ## Box 2.5 Robert Schuman (1886-1963)
>
> Although born in Luxembourg, Schuman's family came from Lorraine and he grew up in Metz while it was under German rule. A prominent statesman in post-war years, Schuman always emphasized the importance of Franco-German *rapprochement*.
>
> Schuman entered politics when Lorraine was returned to France, becoming prime minister (1947-48) and foreign minister (1948-53) in the Fourth Republic. He was a member of the Mouvement Républicain Populaire (MRP), a centrist, Christian Democrat party.
>
> The 9th May, which is the day on which Schuman announced the plan for setting up the ECSC, is still celebrated as a holiday in EU institutions.

and steel. The plan was also attractive to the federalists, who were disappointed by the failure to transform the OEEC into a supranational organization.

According to the Schuman Plan, production of steel and coal should be 'pooled' (the famous 'black pool') and placed under a supranational High Authority. The aim was to eliminate trade barriers and increase competition, but since in such highly regulated sectors many exceptions had to be allowed, the approach was essentially that of 'regulated competition'. The High Authority could levy taxes, influence investment and fix minimum prices and production quotas in times of 'imminent' and 'manifest' crisis.

Abhorring the transfer of sovereignty to an authority that was 'utterly undemocratic and responsible to nobody' (Attlee, speaking in the House of Commons[4]) the UK remained out of the initiative. France, Germany, Italy and the Benelux countries (who were to become the founder members of the EEC) went ahead and signed the Treaty of Paris, establishing the ECSC in 1951. The new Community was to lay the foundations for Franco-German post-war reconciliation, which was to prove the cornerstone and driving force in the integration process.

ATTEMPTS AT CO-OPERATION IN DEFENCE

Given the aim of rendering war in Europe impossible, and the fear of the perceived Soviet threat, it was to be expected that a common defence policy would be one of the main aims of the European integration process. As a first response to creation of the Eastern Bloc, in 1948 France, the UK and the Benelux signed the Treaty of Brussels which provided for a system of mutual assistance in the event of attack. Western defence efforts acquired an Atlantic flavour from 1949 when these countries joined with the USA, Canada, Denmark, Italy, Norway, Portugal and Iceland to form **NATO (North Atlantic Treaty Organization).**

With the outbreak of the Korean War in 1950, the USA and the UK were in favour of German rearmament. France was against this idea and also opposed Germany becoming a member of NATO, instead proposing the creation of a European army with West German participation (the Pleven Plan). The UK was not opposed to such an initiative but was against being directly involved, partly because of the 'special relation' with the USA and partly because the French proposal contained supranational elements.

Negotiations among the six future founding members of the EC went ahead with a view to creating a **European Defence Community (EDC)**. The institutional structure of the Community was to be similar to that of the ECSC, with a Joint Defence Commission, a Council of Ministers,

---

[4] Quoted in Swann (1995).

a Parliamentary Assembly and a Court of Justice. There was to be a combined army with a single uniform and flag, and its own budget. In order to ensure control of the European army, political integration was also to be strengthened, and in 1953 a draft proposal for the creation of a European Political Community was also presented. It was envisaged that after a transitional period, the institutions of the ECSC, the EDC and the European Political Community would be fused.

In 1952 the Treaty on the European Defence Community was signed, but required ratification by the six participating states. In 1954 the French parliament refused to ratify the Treaty (though the other five countries involved had done so). There was reaction to the supranational element of the proposal, with the French Right objecting to the creation of an army under European control,[5] especially as the UK was not involved. At the same time the French Left feared German rearmament.

The solution to this impasse was the creation of the **Western European Union** (WEU) in 1955. This is a traditional inter-governmental organization whose founding members were the original EC (6) plus the UK. Its aim was to provide a European framework in which Germany could be rearmed and enter NATO, and in which the last vestiges of Allied occupation of Germany could be removed. The WEU remained relatively ineffective for almost 30 years before the question of an EU security initiative was revived (as described in Chapter 19).

AGRICULTURE: TOWARDS THE CREATION OF THE COMMON AGRICULTURAL POLICY

For many years the Common Agricultural Policy was considered the cornerstone of the integration process.[6] In the immediate post-war period there were strong reasons for creating a common market for agricultural products:

- The initial deal is frequently regarded as an exchange of interests between France who was seeking markets for her agricultural exports, and Germany who was anxious to reduce tariffs in order to ensure outlets for her industrial exports. Germany had a tradition of heavy protection and substantial income support for the agricultural sector, and was also keen to transfer part of the burden of such policies to the Community level. Italy and the Netherlands also considered that a common agricultural market would provide opportunities for developing their typical forms of production (Mediterranean, and dairy products and vegetables respectively), though in the event the latter was more successful in realizing this objective.
- At the time agriculture was extremely important economically, socially and politically. In 1958 agriculture accounted for 20 per cent of the labour force in the original EC (6) countries and generally incomes were lower than in non-agricultural sectors. In some countries and areas the farm vote was a strong force to be reckoned with.
- The farm policies in the original EC (6) countries were very different and had to be harmonized; otherwise, differences in agricultural price levels and support measures would cause distortions in intra-EC trade.
- The introduction of a common market for agriculture would encourage competition and specialization according to the principle of comparative advantage (see Chapter 4), thereby increasing the productivity of the sector. Insofar as this resulted in lower food prices, there might be less pressure for wage increases.

[5] News that the Treaty had failed ratification led to a rendering of the 'Marseillaise' in the French parliament.
[6] See Tracy (1989) for a more detailed account of the foundation of the CAP.

■ The harmonization of agricultural prices was envisaged as the first step towards harmonization of wage levels which was considered necessary for the creation of a common market in industrial products and services.

THE PROPOSED 'GREEN POOL'

In 1950 in response to a French initiative, the Special Committee of the Council of Europe agreed to consider the prospects for agricultural integration in Europe. The French presented a proposal, known as the Charpentier Plan, to create a 'green pool' in Europe similar to the 'black pool' of the ECSC. This would entail:

■ Common agricultural prices;
■ The elimination of trade barriers between the member states;
■ Preference for the producers of the member states, i.e. they could sell at lower prices on the domestic market than producers from third countries; and
■ A High Authority with supranational powers.

Although the UK and Denmark were strongly opposed to the supranational element of the Charpentier Plan, the Special Committee of the Council of Europe accepted the proposals, and it was agreed to prepare a draft treaty along the lines of the plan.

In 1951 the main elements of the proposal were presented formally in the Pfimlin Plan (taking the name of the French agricultural minister), and they were discussed at the Paris Conferences of 1952 and 1954, which enabled the positions of the various countries to become more precisely defined. However, during these years little progress towards an agreement on agricultural integration was made as France was distracted by the turbulent internal politics of the last days of the Fourth Republic.

TOWARDS THE TREATIES OF ROME

By 1955 the rift between the European countries who wanted to limit integration to inter-governmental co-operation and those who preferred the creation of a supranational authority could no longer be breached. The UK and the Scandinavian countries were in favour of the creation of a free trade area and co-operation on agricultural questions within the OEEC framework. In this context any supranational initiative could be blocked as each of the member states had the power of veto.

The 'Six' founding members of the EEC were not satisfied with this arrangement and in 1955 the Benelux countries presented a Memorandum. This called for the creation of a common market, and specific action in the areas of energy and transport. Though political union was recognized as an ultimate aim, the practical difficulties encountered in its implementation suggested that it was preferable to concentrate on more specific, concrete aims of economic integration.[7] It was considered that the experience gained in working together would then pave the way for political integration. The aim was to: 'work for the establishment of a United Europe by the development of common institutions, the progressive fusion of national economies, the creation of a common market and the progressive harmonization of social policies' (1955 Memorandum).

The foreign ministers of the Six at the Messina Conference considered the ideas of the

---

[7] See Swann (1995).

Memorandum, and it was agreed to set up an intergovernmental committee under the Belgian foreign minister, Paul-Henri Spaak, which would study the problems and prepare the treaties necessary for establishing a common market and energy pool. Initially the UK (as a member of the WEU and associate of the ECSC) participated in the activities of the Spaak Committee, but withdrew in 1955 because the UK remained in favour of simply strengthening the OEEC framework, and preferred a free trade arrangement to the creation of a customs union.

In Venice in 1956 the foreign ministers of the Six accepted the results of the Spaak Committee, and work began on the drafting of the two treaties establishing the European Economic Committee and Euratom. These were signed in Rome in March 1957, and entered into force from January 1958.

Two external events help to explain the speed with which the Six worked towards agreeing the Rome treaties: Suez and the Soviet invasion of Hungary. In 1956 as a reaction to Egyptian raids across the border, Israel invaded Egypt and was subsequently supported by an Anglo-French force. France and Britain opposed Nasser's nationalization of the Suez Canal in which they held shares. Fearing Soviet intervention, the USA exerted diplomatic and economic pressures, which led to the withdrawal of the Anglo-French troops. British and French relations with the USA became very strained, and it was again demonstrated that a weak and divided Europe would have no hope of standing up to the superpowers.

The same lesson emerged from the example of Hungary. In 1953 the Nagy government was permitted to introduce certain reforms such as the freeing of political prisoners, the relaxing of political and economic controls and the ending of collectivization. In less than two years Rakosi replaced Nagy, but in the face of wide-scale demonstrations, he was allowed to return to power in 1956. Nagy then declared Hungarian neutrality and the withdrawal from the Warsaw Pact, and released Cardinal Mindszenty, the Primate of Hungary, from prison. In 1956 despite fierce resistance, Soviet troops occupied Hungary and Nagy was executed, and the West European countries were left feeling weak and vulnerable.

Faced with the decision of the Six to proceed with more ambitious forms of integration, in 1960 the European countries that then preferred intergovernmental co-operation decided to create EFTA (European Free Trade Association). The founder members of EFTA were the UK, Norway, Sweden, Denmark, Austria, Switzerland and Portugal. Subsequently Iceland (in 1970), Finland (in 1986) and Liechtenstein (in 1991) joined. As its name suggests, EFTA involved the creation of a free trade association for industrial products. Agricultural products were largely excluded from this arrangement.

THE TREATIES OF ROME

The Treaties of Rome provide the legal basis for establishment of the European Economic Community and the Euratom. The former is of greater concern here, with Euratom being created mainly in response to a French request, and subsequently shelved, again largely thanks to France. The Treaties are among the most fundamental elements of the *acquis communautaire*.

The Treaty of Rome establishing the EEC consists of 248 Articles. Article 2 sets out the main objectives:

- ◼ 'Harmonious development;
- ◼ Continuous and balanced expansion;
- ◼ Increased stability;
- ◼ Ever more rapid growth in living standards;
- ◼ Closer links between the member states.'

This short list has been the subject of considerable debate and controversy. The Treaty left open the fixing of priorities and the question of how possible conflicts between objectives were to be resolved. In particular, the list raises the fundamental economic question of how to reconcile equity ('harmonious development' and 'balanced expansion') with efficiency ('ever more rapid growth in living standards'). Subsequent treaties added new priorities so that in the Nice Treaty Article 2 reads:[8]

> to promote throughout the Community a harmonious, balanced and sustainable development of economic activities, a high level of employment and of social protection, equality between men and women, sustainable and non-inflationary growth, a high degree of competitiveness and convergence of economic performance, a high level of protection and improvement of the quality of the environment, the raising of the standard of living and quality of life, and economic and social cohesion and solidarity among Member States.

Article 3 lists the mechanisms by which these objectives were to be realized. A 12-year transition period from 1958 until 1969[9] was envisaged for their implementation. These measures include:

- The abolition of tariffs, and of quantitative and qualitative restrictions in intra-EC trade;
- The creation of a common external policy and, in particular, a common external tariff;
- The elimination of obstacles to the free movement of people, capital goods and services;
- A common agricultural policy;
- A common transport policy;
- The introduction of means to ensure fair competition;
- The co-ordination of the economic policies of the member states to avoid balance-of-payments disequilibria;
- The creation of a European Social Fund (ESF) to improve employment opportunities and raise living standards for workers;
- The creation of a European Investment Bank (EIB) to help reduce regional disparities;
- Special trade and development arrangements for colonies and former colonies.

Progress in implementing these measures has been very uneven. The elimination of tariffs on intra-EC trade and the introduction of the common external tariff were largely completed by mid-1968, 18 months ahead of schedule.

However, despite many proposals, only limited steps were taken to remove non-tariff barriers and to free factor movements within the Community. As a result, these objectives had to be relaunched many years later in the programme to complete the Single Market from 1993. Linguistic and cultural differences partially account for the relatively limited increases in the movement of people, and similarly for the slow progress in the recognition of qualifications and in obtaining social security benefits in other member states. The Treaty called for liberalization of capital movements only insofar as this was necessary for the creation of a common market. The main instruments of the Common Agricultural Policy (CAP) were in operation from 1967. Already during the 1960s and 1970s some steps were taken in applying competition policy to limit the abuse of dominant position by private firms and against restrictive business practices.

Progress on transport was slow, partly because the Treaty was remarkably unencumbered with details concerning the implementation of a common policy. As late as 1985 there was a judgment of the European Court of Justice against the Council for failing to introduce a common transport policy, and calling for the situation to be remedied as soon as possible.[10]

---

[8] See also Chapter 3 for the changes in EU objectives proposed in the Constitutional Treaty.
[9] Divided into three four-year periods.
[10] See Chapter 16 for a more detailed discussion of EC transport policy.

Despite the mention of co-ordination of economic policies, the Treaty contains no specific commitment to macroeconomic co-ordination or to economic and monetary union. Various considerations (Tsoukalis, 1997) help to account for the reticence of the Treaty on this point:

■ The importance of the dollar in the international monetary system at the time meant that there was little need or purpose to establish a regional monetary arrangement in Europe;

■ Reasons of political feasibility (quite enough was already being taken on with the creation of the common market);

■ Differences among the member states;

■ In the golden age of Keynesian demand management (which entailed active intervention in an attempt to regulate economic activity) member states were reluctant to sacrifice autonomy of fiscal and monetary policies.

The European Social Fund and European Investment Bank envisaged by the Treaty were operational at an early stage. With the exception of the Italian Mezzogiorno, regional disparities among the original Six were relatively limited and the European Investment Bank was conceived essentially as an instrument to assist the Mezzogiorno.

At the time of the Treaty, the prevailing view appears to have been that the transfers to and from the Community budget by the member states should roughly balance. Despite the references to 'harmonious' development and 'balanced expansion' in Article 2, extensive redistributional policies were not foreseen by the Treaty. Though various Community structural (social and regional) measures were introduced over the years, the spending involved was fairly limited, at least until 1988 when the Structural Funds were doubled (see Chapter 13).

The provision for special trade and aid arrangements with colonies and former colonies was a concession to France who wanted to maintain her links, but with the other EC members (and Germany in particular) helping to foot the bill. Trade preferences to these countries were extended throughout the Community, and aid was granted through the European Development Fund (EDF). From the 1960s many of these countries gained independence, and in 1963 (renewed in 1969) the Yaoundé agreements covering trade and aid arrangements were signed between the EC and former French colonies in Africa.

The entry of the UK into the Community in 1973 led to a reappraisal of development policy, resulting in the first Lomé Convention of 1975. Subsequent agreements followed in 1980, 1985 and 1990 (which was extended to cover a ten-year period) and the Cotonou Agreement of 2000. Seventy-seven ACP (African, Caribbean and Pacific) countries are now covered by the Cotonou Agreement (see Chapter 18).

THE EUROPEAN COMMUNITY IN THE 1960S

The 12-year transitional period in which the provisions of the Treaty of Rome were to be implemented coincided with a particularly favourable international economic climate. Growth was rapid and employment in the EEC countries reached unprecedented levels, while inflation was rising but had not reached dangerous levels (see Tables 2.1–2.3 and Figures 2.1 and 2.2). The economic performance of the Six outshone that of the USA and the UK.

It was in this climate that the tariffs and quantitative restrictions on intra-EC were dismantled and the common external tariff was introduced (by mid-1968). Internal developments in EC commercial policy were linked to external events as the Six prepared common positions to negotiate as a single actor in the GATT (General Agreement on Tariffs and Trade) Kennedy Round over the

TABLE 2.1 The economic growth of OECD countries (average percentage change in real GDP at constant prices)

	1960-69	1970-1980	1980-1990	1991-2000	2001	2002
Belgium	4.8	3.3	2.3	2.2	0.8	0.7
France	5.5	3.3	2.2	1.9	1.8	1.2
Germany	4.5	2.7	2.1	1.5	0.6	0.2
Italy	5.7	3.6	2.5	1.6	1.8	0.4
Lux.	3.6	2.6	3.3	5.5	4.0	1.1
NL	4.4	2.9	1.9	2.9	1.3	0.2
Denmark	4.8	2.2	1.8	2.4	1.4	1.6
Ireland	4.3	4.7	3.0	7.3	6.0	6.0
UK	2.9	1.9	4.4	2.4	2.1	1.8
Greece	7.6	4.7	1.6	2.4	4.1	4.0
Portugal	6.1	4.7	3.1	2.8	1.6	0.5
Spain	7.7	3.5	3.0	2.7	2.7	2.0
USA	4.3	3.1	2.7	3.1	0.3	2.4
Japan	10.4	4.4	4.2	1.5	-0.7	-1.0
OECD	5.1	3.6	2.8	2.7	1.6	0.9

Source: OECD and own calculations on the basis of OECD.

TABLE 2.2 Unemployment in OECD countries (average of annual rates, percentage of labour force)

	1960-67*	1974-1979*	1980-1990	1991-2000	2001	2002
Belgium	2.1	5.7	10.9	8.5	6.7	7.3
France	1.5	4.5	9.1	10.9	8.5	8.8
FRG	0.8	3.5	6.8	7.8	7.8	8.6
Italy	4.9	6.6	10.1	10.6	9.4	9.0
Lux.	0.0	0.6	2.5	2.5	2.1	2.8
NL	0.7	4.9	9.6	5.1	2.4	2.8
Denmark	1.6	-	7.8	6.6	4.3	4.5
Ireland	4.9	7.6	14.4	11.1	3.9	4.4
UK	1.5	4.2	9.2	7.9	5.0	5.1
Greece	5.2	1.9	6.8	9.9**	10.4	10.0
Portugal	2.4	6.0	7.1	5.6	4.1	5.1
Spain	2.3	5.3	17.5	16.0	10.6	11.3
USA	5.0	6.7	6.9	5.6	4.7	5.8
Japan	1.3	1.9	2.5	3.3	5.0	5.4
OECD	3.1	5.1	7.3	7.1	6.5	7.0

* This column is taken from Table 2.2 from *The New Economy Revisited* 2/e by Tsoukalis, Loucas. By permission of Oxford University Press.
**Commonly used definitions of unemployment rather than standardized rates.
Source: OECD and own calculations based on OECD data.

1964–7 period.[11] A precondition for agreeing tariff reductions for third countries was that the common external tariff should be in place. During the 1960s trade and, in particular, intra-EC trade grew faster than output, and a 'virtuous circle' of trade liberalization and rapid growth seemed to be in operation. Growth eased the adjustment process rendering the reduction or elimination of trade barriers less painful.

The emergence of the EEC Six as a single actor and their successful economic performance encouraged the UK to apply for membership in 1961 and 1967, but on both occasions De Gaulle

---

[11] The GATT is described in Chapter 17.

TABLE 2.3 Inflation in OECD countries: consumer price index (average annual percentage change)

	1961-70	1974-1979*	1980-1990	1991-2000	2002
Belgium	2.8	8.5	4.5	1.9	1.8
France	4.0	10.7	6.7	1.8	2.3
FRG	2.5	4.7	2.8	2.3	1.2
Italy	4.0	16.1	10.4	3.8	2.8
Lux.	2.3	7.4	4.4	2.2	2.2
NL	4.2	7.2	2.7	2.1	3.0
Denmark	5.2	10.8	6.3	2.1	2.5
Ireland	4.8	15.0	8.3	2.6	5.0
UK	3.7	15.6	7.3	3.3	2.9
Greece	2.2	16.1	19.4	9.2	3.4
Portugal	3.7	23.7	16.7	4.7	4.0
Spain	5.8	18.3	9.7	3.9	4.0
USA	2.5	8.5	5.4	2.8	2.3
Japan	5.7	9.9	2.5	0.8	-0.3
OECD	3.3	10.5	6.6	4.2	2.7

* This column is taken from Table 2.3 from *The New Economy Revisited* 2/e by Tsoukalis, Loucas. By permission of Oxford University Press.
Source: OECD and own calculations based on OECD data.

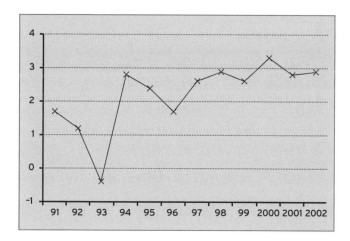

FIGURE 2.1 Growth in the EU (15) 1991-2002

Source: Own elaborations based on Eurostat data.

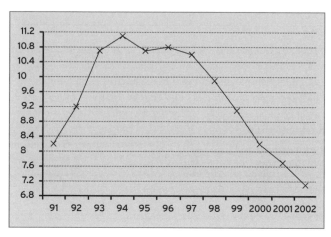

FIGURE 2.2 Unemployment in the EU (15) 1991-2002

Source: Own elaborations based on Eurostat data.

vetoed the application. The opposition of de Gaulle to any transfer of French sovereignty to the Community also meant that agreement on financing of the EC budget had to wait until 1970,[12] and an initiative to strengthen European political integration was blocked.

The 1960s also marked the birth of the Common Agricultural Policy, which was then regarded by many as the greatest achievement in integration. In 1962 agreement was reached on the mechanisms for agricultural support, with the decision on the level of the common prices for agricultural products following in 1964 and being applied from 1967. The Mansholt Plan was presented in 1968 with radical proposals for restructuring EC agriculture in order to raise incomes and efficiency.

THE 1969 HAGUE SUMMIT

With the end of the transition period due in 1970, the search was on for new ways of relaunching the integration process. This gained new impetus in 1969 when Pompidou replaced de Gaulle. At the Hague Summit of 1969 a package was presented, which was described by Pompidou as containing three main elements: completion, deepening and enlargement.

The completion of the integration process referred essentially to placing the financing of the CAP on sounder footing. This entailed agreement on the own resources for the EC budget, and a slight increase in the budgetary powers of the European Parliament. The deepening process was to consist of gradual progress towards the creation of an Economic and Monetary Union (EMU) by 1980, and the introduction of European political co-operation. The first EMU programme met with little success, though in 1979 the EMS (European Monetary System) was introduced.

At the Hague Summit, it was agreed to study the best way of implementing European Political Co-operation (EPC), and a report was presented in 1970.[13] The basis for EPC was to be intergovernmental co-operation, and member states would attempt to work out common positions and agree on common actions. However, progress in developing common positions on foreign policy issues was slow before the 1990s. With de Gaulle no longer on the political scene, the path to further enlargement of the Community was now open. This occurred in 1973 when the UK, Ireland and Denmark became members, while Norway (not for the last time) voted against membership in a referendum.

THE COMMUNITY IN THE 1970S: THE YEARS OF EUROSCLEROSIS

After the successes of the first 12 years, the Community entered a long period of stagnation when little progress was made in integration. Particularly after the 1973 oil crisis, the EC economy entered a phase of slower growth, higher unemployment, more rapid inflation and falling competitiveness (see Tables 2.1–2.3 and Figures 2.1 and 2.2). The process of trade liberalization wavered, and non-tariff barriers were applied on trade both within the EC and with third countries in what became known as the 'new protectionism'.

Divergence in the economic policies and performance of the EC member states, and the more unstable international monetary situation meant that the first programme to introduce monetary union had to be shelved. The main energies of the EC member states seemed concentrated on the

---

[12] As described in Chapter 9.
[13] Though the membership was to be the same, the EPC was to be separate from EC institutions. There was to be no majority voting (qualified or otherwise), and member states were not obliged to agree.

seemingly endless squabbles about the level of agricultural price support and the EC budgetary mechanisms. As Tsoukalis (1997) notes, the energy expended on these debates would seem excessive given that the sums involved accounted for such a tiny fraction (then less than 1 per cent) of the Community's GDP.

These are often called 'the years of Eurosclerosis or Europessimism', but none the less a few successes must be noted: the 1973 enlargement; the creation (albeit on a small scale) of the European Regional Development Fund in 1975; the establishment of the European Monetary System; the introduction of direct elections to the Parliament in 1979, and the entry of Greece in 1981. The path was also prepared for Spanish and Portuguese accession in 1986.

THE RELAUNCHING OF INTEGRATION: THE INTERNAL MARKET PROGRAMME

By the mid-1980s there was growing discontent in the Community about poor economic performance and loss of competitiveness, particularly when compared with rivals such as Japan and the USA. Some governments of the EC member states, such as those of Thatcher, Kohl and even Mitterand, were committed to deregulation as a means of stimulating output and trade.

Against a background of increasing frustration with the slow pace of integration, Jacques Delors became president of the Commission in 1985. The strategy chosen to revive the integration process was the completion of the internal market. The objective was to eliminate barriers at the frontiers between member states and promote the freedom of movement of labour, capital, goods and services. In 1985 France, Germany and the Benelux countries signed the Schengen Agreement, which aimed at the removal of checks on people at borders. Schengen was incorporated into the Amsterdam Treaty of 1999, and its membership was gradually extended to all member states except the UK and Ireland.

Freedom of movement of goods and services entailed eliminating the remaining non-tariff barriers on trade between the member states, one of the most important of which was differences in standards. A key element of the Community's strategy in tackling differences in standards was to rely as far as possible on the principle of mutual recognition. This was defined in the much-cited *Cassis de Dijon* case of 1979 when the European Court of Justice established the general principle that all goods lawfully manufactured and marketed in one member state should also be accepted in other member countries. Certain exceptions were allowed if they were necessary to protect public health, the fairness of commercial transactions and the defence of the consumer.

The introduction of the Single or Internal Market Programme had the effect of launching a new phase in the integration process, spilling over into renewed efforts in institutional reform, reinforced EC social, regional and competition policies, and economic and monetary union. Reform of the Community decision-making process was necessary to ensure that all the legislation could be introduced in time to meet the January 1993 deadline for introduction of the Single Market. The programme was initially presented as an exercise in deregulation and received wholehearted support from the EC member states and business community. However, the weaker countries and regions of the Community feared that they might not be able to meet the increased competitive pressure implied by the Single Market, and that as a result regional disparities might worsen. To assuage these fears, in 1988 it was agreed to double the Community Structural Funds and to reform the way in which they operated. The Single Market Programme spurred a spate of mergers in the Community and led to a tightening of competition policy. Introduction of a single currency could be regarded as a further step in completing the Single Market.

THE MAASTRICHT TREATY

In addition to creating the European Union, the Maastricht Treaty envisaged a strengthening of the Community. This would consist of EMU, greater economic and social cohesion, some institutional reform (including increased powers for the European Parliament), the creation of European citizenship (see Chapter 7) and the extension of EU competence to new areas.

The Treaty of Maastricht set out the three stages in the process of implementing EMU, fixing dates and describing the objectives to be reached in each stage. In addition, it presented criteria to be satisfied before member states could participate in EMU and allowed for certain countries to opt out. The third stage of economic and monetary union began on 1 January 1999 with 11 countries as full participants; Greece also subsequently joined, Denmark and the UK chose to opt out, and Sweden decided not to participate and remained out on technical grounds.

The objective of greater economic and social cohesion in the Treaty was translated into an increase in transfers through the Structural Funds to the poorer regions of the Community. The Treaty was also accompanied by a separate protocol known as 'the Social Chapter' which aimed at improving living and working conditions. Initially the Social Chapter was accepted by only 11 of the then member states and had to wait for the advent of the Blair government to be adopted by the UK. The new areas of competence introduced by the Treaty of Maastricht refer to an increased role for the Community in education, culture, public health and the environment. In addition, there were to be the development of trans-European networks in transport and energy.

EU ENLARGEMENT

In part because they feared that with the Single Market Programme their industries would lose relative competitiveness, the EFTA countries began to negotiate the creation of a European Economic Area (EEA). This would enable the EFTA countries to participate in a unified market but imposed strong limits on their ability to participate in decision-making. In the event, three of the EFTA countries (Austria, Sweden and Finland) opted for EU accession, joining in 1995. In a referendum Norway again decided against EU membership, while the Swiss voted even against participation in the EEA. When the EEA came into operation from January 1994, the EFTA members were limited to Norway, Iceland and Liechtenstein.

TABLE 2.4 Economic indicators for Austria, Sweden and Finland (per cent)

	Growth 1991–2000	2001	2002	Unemployment 1991–2000	2001	2002	Inflation 1991–2000	2001	2002
Austria	2.4	0.8	1.4	5.2*	3.6	4.3	1.9	2.3	1.7
Finland	2.0	1.2	2.2	12.5	9.1	9.1	2.1	2.7	2.0
Sweden	2.0	1.1	1.9	7.6	4.9	4.9	2.6	2.6	2.4

*Commonly used definitions of unemployment rather than standardized rates.
Source: Own elaborations based on OECD data.

Following the fall of communism in 1989, the smaller Central and East European countries wanted tighter links and eventual membership of the EC.[14] The Community responded first by offering trade and co-operation agreements to these countries, but was slow to offer them an accession strategy. The 1993 Copenhagen European Council set out the conditions that the

---

[14] Economic indicators for the countries that joined the EU in 2004 and for the candidate countries are presented in Chapter 20.

application countries have to fulfil in order to join the EU. Between 1994 and 1996 ten CEECs applied for EU membership. All these countries signed association agreements with the EU and all were participants in the EU pre-accession strategy to help prepare them for membership.

In July 1997 the EC Commission published the document Agenda 2000, which analysed the steps needed to prepare both the EU and accession countries for enlargement, and included 'Opinions' on the readiness of each of the applicant countries to join the EU. At the Luxembourg Summit[15] of December 1997 it was decided to open accession negotiations with Cyprus and five CEECs: the Czech Republic, Estonia, Hungary, Poland, Romania and Slovenia. These negotiations began in March 1998.

At the Helsinki Summit it was also decided to begin negotiations for accession with six further candidates: Bulgaria, Latvia, Lithuania, Malta, Romania and Slovakia, and to declare Turkey a candidate. Malta's application had lapsed in 1993 but was subsequently resumed in 1998. Negotiations with these six countries began in February 2000.

The Gothenburg Summit of June 2001 set the objective of trying to complete negotiations with the first applicant countries by the end of 2002 so they could participate in the European Parliament elections of 2004. The Copenhagen European Council of December 2002 confirmed this timetable and, as described in Chapters 1 and 20, ten new member states joined the EU in May 2004, while Bulgaria and Romania could join in 2007. In December 2004 a decision will be taken on whether Turkey is ready to join; if so negotiations would be opened without delay. In 2004 the Commission published an Opinion favourable to starting accession negotiations with Croatia.

The prospect of enlargement gave a new urgency to the question of institutional reform of the EU as it was necessary to ensure that the decision-making process was operable with a growing number of members.

The Treaty of Amsterdam that came into operation in 1999 was intended to resolve these questions but fell well short of expectations. For that reason there were further attempts to tackle the question of institutional reform with the Nice Treaty and Constitutional Treaty. In June 2004 the European Council reached agreement on the Constitutional Treaty, but this has to be ratified (either by a vote in the national parliament or a referendum) by all the member states before it can come into operation, a process that is likely to prove lengthy and hazardous.

THE MEDITERRANEAN POLICY

There was an attempt to counterbalance the eastward developments of the European Union with a strengthening of the EU Mediterranean Policy. This is strongly favoured by the present southern members of the Union, partly as a means of stemming the growing flow of immigration across the Mediterranean but also to increase security in the area. At the Barcelona Summit of 1995 it was agreed to set up the Euromed Programme to increase aid and create a free trade area in the Mediterranean area by 2010.

EMPLOYMENT, PRODUCTIVITY AND THE LISBON STRATEGY

In 1997 the Luxembourg Process, or European Employment Strategy (EES), was launched. This aimed at improving 'employability' and encouraging the adaptability of businesses and their employees. Concerns with relatively low EU productivity led in March 2000 to the decision of the

---

[15] These summits, or European Councils, are attended by heads of state and of the government of the EU member states (see Chapter 3).

Lisbon European Council to launch a 'new strategic goal' for the following ten years aimed at creating a knowledge-based economy focusing on better use of information science and research and development, and more flexible labour markets.

The Lisbon Strategy was confirmed at the March 2002 Barcelona European Council, which called for measures to guarantee EU competitiveness, promote sustainable development and improve employment across skills and geographical areas (also by increasing labour mobility). To date, however, it is difficult not to conclude that the process has produced a great deal of rhetoric and rather less concrete change.

Summary of Key Concepts

- After the unsuccessful efforts to set up a supranational organization in Europe, there was a change in tactics. In line with the neo-functionalist approach, there were various attempts at integration by sector.
- The European Coal and Steel Community (or 'black pool') was set up in 1951 with the aim of making war in Europe 'materially impossible'.
- Attempts to set up a European Defence Community and a 'green pool' for agriculture failed, largely because of France.
- Article 2 of the Treaty of Rome sets out the main objectives of the EEC, while Article 3 sets out the mechanisms by which these were to be realized. Progress in implementing the measures was very uneven, but a common commercial policy and the Common Agricultural Policy were soon operating.
- The 1969 Hague Summit called for widening (enlargement), deepening (economic and monetary union) and completion (a settlement to the budgetary question) of the Community.
- The 1970s and early 1980s were the years of Eurosclerosis or Europessimism, when much of the energy of the Community was spent on quarrels over the budget and agricultural spending.
- When Jacques Delors became president of the Commission in 1985, his strategy to relaunch the integration process was the completion of the Single Market.
- In addition to creating the European Union, the Maastricht Treaty set out the steps for establishing economic and monetary union.
- The EFTA countries began to negotiate the creation of a European Economic Area (EEA) which would enable them to participate in the Single Market but which limited their ability to participate in decision-making. In the event, three of the EFTA countries (Austria, Sweden and Finland) opted for EU accession in 1995. In a referendum Norway again decided against EU membership, while the Swiss even voted against participation in the EEA.
- In 2004 ten new countries joined the EU, with Bulgaria and Romania possibly joining in 2007, and a decision being taken on Turkey in December 2004. In 2004 the Commission published an Opinion in favour of opening accession negotiations with Croatia.
- The Treaties of Amsterdam and of Nice, and the Constitutional Treaty, were intended to introduce the necessary institutional changes for an enlarged EU.
- At the Barcelona Summit of 1995 it was agreed to set up the Euromed Programme to increase aid and create a free trade area in the Mediterranean area by 2010.
- In 1997 the Luxembourg Process, or European Employment Strategy (EES), was launched.
- In March 2000 the Lisbon Strategy was introduced to create a knowledge-based economy in ten years.

Questions for Study and Review

■ **How far do the federalist and neo-functionalist approaches to integration help to explain the initiatives of the 1940s and 1950s?**

■ **Compare the trade and aid measures from 1989 for post-communist countries with the Marshall Plan (see also Chapter 20).**
■ **Describe the main functions of the OECD.**
■ **What are the main differences between the Council of Europe and the OSCE?**
■ **Describe the main objectives of the Treaty of Rome, and the mechanisms by which these objectives were to be realized. How far has the Community been successful in implementing these mechanisms?**
■ **What strategy was used to overcome the years of Europessimism or Eurosclerosis?**
■ **What were the main European integration initiatives in the 1990s?**

Appendix
Key dates in the history of European integration

1950
In a speech inspired by Jean Monnet, Robert Schuman proposed the pooling of coal and steel resources between France and Germany, and any other European country that wished to join them.

1951
The Six (France, Germany, Italy and the Benelux countries) signed the Paris Treaty establishing the European Coal and Steel Community.

1952
Treaty establishing the European Defence Community (EDC) was signed in Paris.

1954
French parliament rejected the EDC Treaty.

1955
The Western European Union (WEU) was created.
At Messina the foreign ministers of the Six decided to launch a new integration initiative aimed at the creation of a common market, and common policies for agriculture, transport and the civilian use of nuclear energy.

1958
The Treaties of Rome entered into force, and the EEC and Euratom were created.

1960
The European Free Trade Association (EFTA) was set up.

1962
Key decisions on the Common Agricultural Policy were taken. The decision on common prices was not reached until 1964 and came into operation from 1967.

1963
De Gaulle vetoed UK application to join the EC. A second veto followed in 1967.

1966

The Luxembourg compromise entered into force, with France resuming its seat in the Council in return for use of the unanimity rule when any country deems an issue to be of 'vital national interest'.

1967

The Treaty merging the EEC, the European Coal and Steel Community (ECSC) and Euratom entered into force.

1968

Remaining customs duties in intra-EC trade in manufactured goods were removed 18 months ahead of schedule, and the Common External Tariff was introduced.

1969

The Hague Summit agreed on proposals to deepen (EMU by 1980), widen (allow Denmark, Ireland and the UK to join) and complete (by introducing own resources) the Community.

1973

Denmark, Ireland and the UK joined the Community.

1975

The European Fund for Regional Development was established.
The Treaty giving the European Parliament wider budgetary powers and establishing the Court of Auditors was signed and entered into force in 1997.
The first Lomé Convention was signed between the Community and developing ACP (African, Caribbean and Pacific) countries. Later Lomé Conventions entered into force in 1980, 1985 and 1990.

1979

EMS started to operate.
First direct elections to the European Parliament.

1981

Greece joined the EC.

1985

Jacques Delors was appointed president of the Commission and announced the Single Market Programme.
France, Germany and the Benelux countries signed the Schengen Agreement, committing themselves to the gradual removal of checks on people at borders. The Amsterdam Treaty that came into force in 1999 incorporated the Schengen Agreement, which was extended to all EU countries except the UK and Ireland.

1986

Spain and Portugal became members of the Community.

1987

The Single European Act entered into force.
Turkey applied to join the EU.

1988

Financial perspective for 1988–92 was agreed and included a reform of the Structural Funds.

1991

Agreement was reached on setting up a European Economic Area.

1992

The MacSharry Reform of the Common Agricultural Policy was agreed.
The Edinburgh European Council decided the financial perspective for 1993–99 ('Delors 2' or the bill for Maastricht), and on further reform of the Structural Funds with the introduction of the Cohesion Fund.

1993

1 January: introduction of the Single Market.
November: the Maastricht Treaty entered into force.

1994

April: the GATT Uruguay Round was signed at Marrakech.

1995

Austria, Finland and Sweden joined the EU.
Barcelona European Summit: decision to create Euromed, a free trade area involving Mediterranean countries, by 2010.

1997

July: Agenda 2000
The Amsterdam Treaty was signed.
The Luxembourg Process, or European Employment Strategy (EES), was launched.
The Luxembourg European Council decided to open enlargement negotiations with the Czech Republic, Estonia, Hungary, Poland, Slovenia and Cyprus.

1998

March: accession negotiations started with five countries of Central and Eastern Europe and Cyprus.
Brussels Summit of May: the decisions to set up the European Central Bank and on member states ready to enter the third stage of EMU were taken.

1999

Beginning of third stage of EMU (1 January).
Berlin Agreement (March) on Agenda 2000 (including financial perspective for the period 2000–06).
The Amsterdam Treaty entered into force.
The Helsinki European Council (December) took the decision to open enlargement negotiations with Malta and the other five CEECs that had applied for membership and to treat Turkey as a candidate.
Agreement to create an EU rapid-reaction force to assist peacekeeping.

2000

February: accession negotiations began with Bulgaria, Latvia, Lithuania, Malta, Romania and Slovakia.

The Lisbon European Council set the creation of a 'knowledge-based economy' as a priority for the EU.

December: the Nice European Council.

2001

The Gotenberg European Council reaffirmed the objective to complete negotiations with a first wave of candidate countries so they could join the EU in time for the European Parliament elections of 2004.

June: ratification of the Nice Treaty was rejected by the Irish in a first referendum, but passed in a second referendum in October.

December: the Laeken European Council decided to set up the European Convention.

2002

1 January: euro notes and coins came into circulation.

Coins and notes in national currencies were withdrawn in the euro countries.

December: Copenhagen European Council confirmed the deadline of 2004 for accession of ten applicant countries and indicated 2007 as a possible date for Bulgarian and Romanian accession. A decision on Turkey is to be taken in December 2004.

2003

June: the European Convention presented its results.

December: the Brussels European Council failed to decide on the Constitutional Treaty.

2004

May: 10 new member states joined the EU.

June: elections to the European Parliament.

June: the European Council agreed the Constitutional Treaty.

References

Milward, A.S. (1984) *The Reconstruction of Western Europe 1945-1951*, Methuen, London.

Milward, A.S. (1992) *The European Rescue of the Nation State*, Routledge, London.

Monnet, J. (1978) *Memoirs*, Collins, London.

Swann, D. (1995) *The Economics of the Common Market*, 8th edn, Penguin, London.

Tracy, M. (1989) *Government and Agriculture in Western Europe 1880-1988*, Harvester Wheatsheaf, London.

Tsoukalis, L. (1997) *The New European Economy Revisited*, 3rd edn, Oxford University Press, Oxford.

Useful websites

The OECD (Organization for Economic Co-operation and Development): www.oecd.org

The OSCE Organization for Co-operation and Security in Europe: www.osce.org

The UNECE United Nations Economic Commission for Europe: www.unece.org

The Council of Europe:
www.coe.int
The European Union:
www.europa.eu.int

List of abbreviations

ACP	African, Caribbean and Pacific countries covered by the Lomé Conventions and the Cotonou Agreement
CAP	Common Agricultural Policy
CEECs	Central and Eastern European countries
CFSP	Common Foreign and Security Policy
CMEA	Council for Mutual Economic Assistance
CSCE	Conference on Security and Co-operation in Europe
EC	European Communities
ECSC	European Coal and Steel Community
EDC	European Defence Community
EDF	European Development Fund
EEA	European Economic Area
EES	European Employment Strategy
EIB	European Investment Bank
EMS	European Monetary System
EMU	economic and monetary union
ESF	European Social Fund
EU	European Union
GATT	General Agreement on Tariffs and Trade
OEEC	Organization for European Economic Co-operation
OSCE	Organization for Security and Co-operation in Europe
NATO	North Atlantic Treaty Organization
UNECE	United Nations' Economic Commission for Europe
WEU	Western Economic Union

3

The Decision-Making Institutions of the European Union

LEARNING OBJECTIVES

By the end of this chapter you should be able to understand:

▶ What are the main decision-making institutions of the Community;

▶ What we mean by the 'democratic deficit';

▶ The main changes that would be introduced by the Constitutional Treaty;

▶ The structure and functions of the European Commission;

▶ The role of the Council of Ministers;

▶ What is the European Council;

▶ The system of voting in the Council of Ministers;

▶ The organization and role of the European Parliament;

▶ The role of the Court of Justice;

▶ The role of the Court of Auditors;

▶ The decision-making procedure of the European Community;

▶ What we mean by 'differentiated integration';

▶ The debate on the future architecture of Europe.

THE DEBATE ABOUT REFORM OF THE EU INSTITUTIONS AND THE CONSTITUTIONAL TREATY

One of the main difficulties of the European Union is that of accommodating its institutional structure to a growing membership, at the same time ensuring that decision-making respects democratic principles and is 'as close to the citizens as possible'. An increasing membership adds to the difficulty of ensuring 'efficiency', or what is usually defined in the EU context as ability to take decisions. Respect for democratic principles generally entails legitimacy of the decision-making process, but there has been growing criticism of EU institutions as not being answerable to the preferences of its citizens. The European initiative has been driven mainly by political elites, and opinion polls and referendums often reveal a disturbing lack of confidence in the EU on the part of the public. As will be shown in this chapter, in recent years there have been various attempts to correct the 'democratic deficit' of the EU, but to date these have met with limited success.

Difficulties arise in analysing EU decision-making because the EU is neither a country nor a 'traditional' international organization. The institutions of the EU appear messy and complex, and are very different from those of a country such as the USA which are based on the distinction between legislature, executive and judiciary. EU institutions have been evolving over time and reflect successive compromises to balance various (and varying) interests.[1]

In 2001 an EU summit at Laeken in Belgium agreed on the creation of a Constitutional Convention aimed at drawing up a Constitutional Treaty to render Community decision-making more democratic, transparent and efficient. Both the name and the rhetoric deliberately echoed the 1787 Philadelphia Constitutional Convention, whose role had been to mould a federation out of the 13 original states.

The EU Convention was composed of representatives of the governments of member states and of the candidate countries, the European Parliament, Commission and Council, and of national parliaments. Giscard D'Estaing was chosen as president of the Convention, with two vice-presidents, Amato and Dehaene (former prime ministers of Italy and Belgium, respectively). The results of the work of the Convention were presented in June 2003. The heads of government and of state of the EU countries failed to agree on the proposals at a summit in December 2003 in Brussels but subsequently reached agreement in June 2004 (see Box 3.1).[2]

Before coming into operation the Treaty has to be ratified by all the member states, either by a vote in the national parliament or by a referendum. The UK, France, Spain, Portugal, Denmark, Ireland and Luxembourg have announced that they will hold referendums, and Belgium, the Czech Republic and Poland might also do so. In the UK the referendum seems unlikely to obtain a positive result. There have been numerous instances of referendums on EU issues having a negative outcome. For instance the Irish voted against the Nice Treaty in a first referendum of June 2001 (though the decision was reversed in a second referendum in October 2002), and the Swedish voted against the euro in a referendum in 2003 (see Chapter 8). The ratification process therefore seems likely to be prolonged and full of pitfalls. In the meantime the Nice Treaty will continue to apply.

The draft Constitutional Treaty consists of four main parts (see Box 3.2 and the more detailed descriptions below). The first part contains the 'constitutional' elements, setting out what the Union is, its objectives, values, what it does, the method of legislation and the functioning of its institutions. Part 2 sets out a Charter of Fundamental Rights. The third part indicates the various policy areas in which the EU operates and the financial procedures to be used. Part 4 sets out

---

[1] For more detailed accounts of these institutional aspects see Bainbridge (1998), Borchardt (1999), Dinan (1994), Edwards and Spence (1995), Hix (1999), McCormick (2002), Nugent (1999), Peterson and Shackleton (2002), Schmitter (2000), Wallace and Wallace (2000) and Westlake (1994 and 2001).
[2] For the text of the draft treaty agreed in June 2004, see Conference of the Representatives of the Governments of the member states (2004) available on the Commission website www.europa.eu.int/comm. Earlier versions of the proposed Constitutional Treaty are also available on this website.

> **Box 3.1 Key dates in the evolution of the Constitutional Treaty**
>
> **1997** The Amsterdam Treaty was agreed (and came into operation in 1999) but fell well short of expectations that it would prepare EU institutions for enlargement.
>
> **December 2000** The Nice Summit agreed to reform EU decision-making, but the compromise was complex and not very transparent.
>
> **December 2001** The Laeken Summit agreed to set up the European Convention.
>
> **June 2003** The results of the European Convention were presented.
>
> **December 2003** An attempt to agree the text of the Constitutional Treaty at the Brussels Summit failed.
>
> **June 2004** Brussels: the European Council agreed on the Constitutional Treaty.

'General and Final Provisions'. These indicate how earlier treaties are to be repealed, how the new Constitutional Treaty enters into force and how it can be amended in the future.

The first part of the Treaty containing the constitutional elements begins with a Preamble, which recalls the 'cultural, religious and humanist' inheritance of Europe. There was much debate about whether some reference to Europe's Christian roots should be included, but some felt this might be divisive, and could hinder eventual accession by Turkey.

Article 2 defines the values of the EU as 'human dignity, fundamental rights, democracy, the rule of law, tolerance, respect for obligations and for international law'.

Article 3 sets out the general objectives of the EU as:

- 'Protection of the common values, interests and independence of the Union;
- Promotion of economic and social cohesion;
- Strengthening of the internal market, and of economic and monetary cohesion;
- A high level of environmental protection;
- Encouragement for technological and scientific progress;
- Creation of an area of liberty, security and justice;
- Development of a common foreign and security policy, and a common defence to defend and promote the Union's values in the wider world.'

Article 5 defines EU citizenship, and establishes that every citizen of a member state also has European citizenship. As described in Chapter 1, Articles 8–11 deal with the division of competences between the EU and member states.

A Charter of Fundamental Human Rights (see Box 3.3) was approved at Nice. At the time, British misgivings that certain provisions would add to labour market rigidities led to the charter remaining outside the Treaty. However, the charter will be incorporated into the Constitutional Treaty.

To date Intergovernmental Conferences (IGCs) have been necessary for any revision of the treaties, and have been convened with growing frequency over the past few years. These entail frequent meetings between national representatives at various levels to prepare the drafts of treaty changes, or new treaties. One of the objectives of the Constitutional Treaty was also to streamline and divide the treaties, splitting off the less fundamental components that would be subject to a less cumbersome process of change.

Important novelties would also be introduced with Articles 45 and 46 of the Constitutional Treaty. Article 45 establishes the procedure for suspension of Union membership if a member state violates the principles and values of the Union. Article 46 sets out the procedure for voluntary withdrawal from the union by a member state.[3]

---

[3] The only withdrawal to date has been that of Greenland, whose status was renegotiated in 1994. Greenland remains associated with the EU and has an agreement covering fisheries.

Box 3.2 Main changes that would be introduced by the Constitutional Treaty (as agreed by the European Council of June 2004)

- ■ A simplified, single Treaty indicating the values, objectives and role of the EU;
- ■ A European Council president holding office for up to five years;
- ■ A new EU foreign minister who will head the newly created EU diplomatic service;
- ■ Greater scope for co-operation on defence (including procurement) among member states;
- ■ A Charter of Fundamental Human Rights to be included in the Treaty;
- ■ Abolition of national vetoes in some areas such as immigration and asylum policy;
- ■ National vetoes are to be maintained over tax issues, defence and foreign policy, and over financing the EU budget;
- ■ A reduction in the size of the Commission from 2014, with Commissioners from only two-thirds of member states on a rotation basis;
- ■ Simplification of the voting rule in the Council of Ministers, with the introduction of a 'double-majority' system so that at least 55 per cent of member states comprising at least 65 per cent of the population are necessary to pass a measure;
- ■ Increased power of the Eurogroup (composed of the economic and finance ministers of countries that have adopted the euro);
- ■ The minimum number of seats for a small country in the European Parliament is raised from 4 to 6, and the maximum number for large member states is fixed at 96;
- ■ The possibility of suspension of a member state from the EU, or its voluntary withdrawal.

Box 3.3 The Charter of Fundamental Human rights

- ■ Right to respect for the integrity of the human person, including bans on eugenics and reproductive cloning of human beings;
- ■ Right to education;
- ■ Workers' right to information and consultation;
- ■ Rights of collective bargaining action;
- ■ Freedom of assembly and association, including the right to join a union;
- ■ Right to reconcile family and professional life;
- ■ Right to rest periods and annual leave, including the right to limits on working hours;
- ■ Safe and healthy working conditions;
- ■ Right to vote and to stand as a candidate for the European Parliament and in municipal elections.

THE DECISION-MAKING INSTITUTIONS OF THE EU

The main decision-making institutions of the European Union are:[4]

- ■ The European Commission;
- ■ The Council of Ministers;
- ■ The European Parliament (EP);

---

[4] This list does not include the other institutions of the European Union, and, for example, the financial institutions such as the ECB (European Central Bank), the ESCB (European System of Central Banks), the EMI (European Monetary Institute) etc. that are discussed in Chapter 8.

■ The Economic and Social Committee (ESC);
■ The Committee of Regions;
■ The European Court of Justice (EJ); and
■ The Court of Auditors.

THE EUROPEAN COMMISSION

In a strict sense the term 'European Commission', or more correctly 'the Commission of the European Communities', denotes the commissioners (described below), but more generally the term is used to refer to all the officials (*fonctionnaires*) working for the institution. Roughly the language staff takes up 15 per cent of this full-time, permanent bureaucracy (see Box 3.4).

> **Box 3.4**
> For many years the Commission was housed in the famous Berlaymont Building in Brussels. It was extremely easy to get lost in the curved corridors of a building shaped like a Maltese cross and 13 floors high. Considered the symbol of the Commission, and appearing on the news nearly every time Brussels was mentioned, the Berlaymont was riddled with asbestos, and was evacuated for 10 years while the asbestos was removed. During that time white protective sheeting shrouded the building, provoking the inevitable comment that it looked like a work by the Bulgarian-born artist Christo.

The commissioners at the head of the Commission are responsible for one or more areas of policy and required to act independently of national interests. Many come from prominent political careers in their own countries. The Commission is headed by a president, who can play an important role in influencing the image of the Commission and determining the pace of integration. For instance, the personal role of Commission President Jacques Delors (from 1985 to 1995) was fundamental for the introduction of the Single Market Project and economic and monetary union. From 2004 José Barroso from Portugal will replace Romano Prodi as president of the Commission. The commissioners generally try to take decisions by consensus on a 'collegial basis', and a small cabinet backs each. The president may be assisted by one or more vice-presidents.

Immediately following the 2004 enlargement, there were 20 commissioners for the EU(15) and one from each of the ten new member states. In the new Commission from 2004, France, Germany, Italy, Spain and the UK will have given up their second commissioner. According to the Protocol on Enlargement annexed to the Nice Treaty, when the EU reaches 27 members the number of commissioners 'shall be less than the number of member states and will be agreed by the Council acting unanimously'. A future rotation system based on 'the principle of equality' will have to be agreed. The proposed Constitutional Treaty envisages a smaller Commission from 2014, with commissioners being sent only from two-thirds of the member states on the basis of equal rotation. It is argued that a smaller Commission would be less cumbersome and more efficient and would be freer from national ties. However, the full participation of each member state in the Commission is felt to increase its public acceptability and to ensure that the interests of each member state are taken into account.

The commissioners are chosen for a five-year period. The governments of the member states nominate the president of the Commission by 'common accord', after consulting the European Parliament. The nominee president then has to be approved by the European Parliament, and in

1995 this almost resulted in the rejection of Jacques Santer. The new draft Constitutional Treaty proposes election of the new president by the European Parliament based on nominations by the heads of state and of government of the EU countries.

The Commissioners are appointed by their national governments after consultation with the European Parliament and the new president of the Commission. Once chosen, the commissioners as a body are subject to a vote of approval by the European Parliament. Until 2003 the 'collegial' nature of the Commission (which implies collective responsibility) meant that the European Parliament could only dismiss it as a whole.[5] There were calls for dismissal of the Commission 1997 over the treatment of the 'mad cow disease' scandal and again over the 1999 scandal (see Box 3.5).

According to the Nice Treaty, the president will be able to force a member of the Commission to resign after obtaining the approval of the whole Commission. A Commission anti-fraud office, OLAF, was also set up, and the president of the 1999–2004 Commission, Romano Prodi, promised a 'zero tolerance' policy on corruption.

When a new Commission comes into office, a complex and controversial process of deciding the allocation of portfolios begins. Each commissioner is responsible for one or more portfolios, or policy areas, and balancing the relative importance of the portfolio(s) given to each commissioner is a delicate process.

Each commissioner also takes charge of at least one of the Directorates-General (DGs) into which the Commission is divided. Each DG covers a main policy area such as external affairs or agriculture (the largest DG of all). The system of vertical hierarchies means that at times there is insufficient co-ordination between the various DGs. Following the 1999 scandal (see Box 3.5), various reforms in the organization of the Commission were introduced, including an attempt to substitute names for numbers of the various DGs, so that, for example, DGVI was to be called the Agriculture DG.

Box 3.5 The 1999 Scandal

The events of 1999 constitute one of the most profound institutional crises in the history of the EU, and a milestone in the shift in the balance of power between the Commission and the European Parliament. The starting point was the reluctance of the European Parliament to approve the accounts relating to the 1996 budget, accusing the Commission of mismanagement, cronyism and fraud. In January 1999 a motion of censure against the Commission was tabled, but in the event the European Parliament voted in favour of a compromise measure consisting of an independent inquiry into allegations against the Commission. The results of this inquiry were published in March 1999, and accused the Commission on a number of counts. Irregularities were found in programmes relating to humanitarian aid (with the discovery of fictitious contracts supposedly granting aid to Rwanda and former Yugoslavia), tourism and educational and training programmes. There was said to be evidence of nepotism, and of bending staff rules to appoint acquaintances, in particular in the case of Edith Cresson, the commissioner responsible for health and educational programmes. The most famous attack was against the appointment of a 70-year-old dentist from her home town as a 'scientific adviser', on a salary said to be $4,500 a month, with his son also receiving a consultancy contract (*The Economist*, 6 March 1999). The Security Office, which was directly responsible to the president, was accused of operating as a regulation-free zone granting 'small favours' to colleagues such as the

---

[5] A two-thirds majority vote of the European Parliament is necessary to dismiss the Commission.

cancellation of parking fines, practising dubious recruitment practices (so that it appeared like a private club for retired Belgian policemen) and permitting irregularities such as the disappearance of office furniture and equipment. The president of the Commission, Santer, was said to have lost control of the institution he was supposedly running, allowing a 'culture of complacency' to arise. The immediate reaction was a press release in which Santer announced that he was 'whiter than white' and protested that it was misleading and distorting to judge the output of the Commission on the basis of a few cases of fraud. A code of conduct was drawn up for those working in the Commission, but the damage was done and in March 1999 the Santer Commission resigned.

In the literature, the phrase 'The Commission proposes and disposes' is frequently used to describe its functions, but a more complete list would include the following:

1. The Commission has the **right of initiative** and is involved at each stage in the EU legislative process.[6] Commission proposals are not drawn out of thin air but are generally the result of a lengthy process of consultation involving interest groups, national civil servants, politicians and so on. The Treaty of Rome reserved the right to initiate Community legislation almost exclusively for the Commission, and in this role the Commission has often been referred to as the 'motor of European integration'. The Maastricht Treaty introduced the 'request clause' which permits the Parliament to 'request' the Commission to submit any proposal where the EP decides by absolute majority that new legislation is needed.

2. The Commission has to 'exercise the powers conferred on it by the Council [of Ministers] for the **implementation of rules** laid down by the latter'.[7] This 'management' role of the Commission is important in the day-to-day running of policies such as the CAP (Common Agricultural Policy) and CCP (Common Commercial Policy).

3. The Commission has **certain autonomous powers** in areas such as competition policy, and negotiates for the Community on some policy issues including foreign trade. It represents the EU in international organizations such as the OECD, the United Nations and the WTO.[8]

4. **The Commission prepares the annual preliminary draft Budget** for the Community and is responsible for implementing the Budget and submitting accounts at the end of each financial year.

5. The Commission acts as **Guardian (or 'Watchdog') of the Treaties.** Article 155 of the Treaty of Rome stated that the Commission must 'ensure that the provisions of this Treaty and the measures pursuit thereto are applied'. If a firm, institution or member state is found to be acting contrary to the treaties, the Commission may issue a reasoned Opinion, impose a fine or even refer the matter to the Court of Justice.

6. The Commission makes recommendations or opinions on matters related to the treaties (see Box 3.6).

7. The Commission may publish formal presentations (White and Green papers) on specific policy areas in order to make the position of the Commission known and obtain reactions

---

[6] In order to safeguard the principle of subsidiarity (see Chapter 1), the new draft Constitutional Treaty proposes the introduction of the 'yellow card procedure'. This entails the parliaments of member states receiving legislative proposals brought forward by the Commission. When a third of the parliaments of the member states express concern, the Commission would be obliged to reconsider its proposal. The draft Constitutional Treaty as agreed by the European Council in June 2004 also envisages the principle of participatory democracy by which over a million citizens, coming from a significant number of member states, could invite the Commission to submit a proposal.
[7] Article 155 of the Treaty of Rome.
[8] See Chapter 2 for a description of the OECD, and the OLC website of this book for the WTO.

> ## Box 3.6 EU legislative instruments
>
> According to the Treaty of Rome (Article 189), a **Regulation** is directly binding in all EC member states. The draft Constitutional Treaty proposes that these should be called 'European laws'.
>
> A **Directive** fixes an objective which is binding, but leaves the choice of method to achieve that aim to the member states. Unlike a Regulation, a Directive therefore has to be transposed into national legislation before entering into force. According to the draft Constitutional Treaty, these would be called 'European framework laws'.
>
> **Decisions** deal with specific problems and are binding on those to whom they are addressed, which may include member states, companies or individuals.
>
> In contrast, **Recommendations** and **Opinions** have no binding force.

before the start of the legislative procedure. Green papers present broader, initial ideas of the Commission, while White papers set out more detailed guidelines for policy proposals.

In the shifting balance of power between EU institutions, the Commission appears to have been losing power. Successive reforms of EU institutions have strengthened the European Parliament, while the European Council (see below) has increasingly gained responsibility for setting priorities and establishing the policy agenda. This tendency has been reinforced by the fact that the Commission is not elected (but rather is composed of technocrats) and is not directly accountable to the public.[9]

The Commission also plays a less active role with respect to the second (CFSP) and third pillars (JHA), where much decision-making is intergovernmental. Although the Commission is associated with these policy areas, it does not have exclusive right of initiative. The lack of accountability and transparency of the Commission is one aspect of the problem of the 'democratic deficit'.

THE COUNCIL OF MINISTERS

The Council of Ministers is the principal decision-making institution of the European Union, although since the Maastricht Treaty it can be overridden in certain cases by a veto of the European Parliament. It is also the only EU institution that directly represents the member states, and is sometimes referred to as the 'brake on European integration', reflecting the (rather simplistic) view that Commission proposals presenting the EU position hve been checked by national interests in the Council.

The Council is composed of representatives of each of the member states at the ministerial level, plus a representative of the Commission. The composition of the Council varies according to the question considered, so there is a Council of Economic and Finance Ministers (referred to as 'Ecofin'); a Council of Foreign Ministers (known as the General Affairs Council); a Council of Agricultural Ministers; a Council of Transport Ministers and so on. In 1998 there were 23 councils of this type, but by 2002 the number had fallen to 16.

With so many specialized councils, consistency and unity of operation may be difficult to achieve. At times joint Councils may be held, when an issue affects different policy areas. The General Affairs Council is responsible for co-ordinating the activities of the various Councils

---

[9] This type of complaint was raised as early as the 1960s with, for instance, de Gaulle describing the Commission in his inimitable words as 'an embryo technocracy, for the most part foreign' (Bainbridge, 1998, p. 337).

(a role to be confirmed by the draft Constitutional Treaty), but this often proves difficult in practice. The Council generally meets in Brussels where there is a Council Secretariat served by a staff.

The Council of heads of state and of government is known as the **European Council**.[10] Though the summits of heads of state date from 1961, the European Council only received formal recognition as a Community institution in the Single European Act of 1987. The summits of the European Council should take place 'at least twice a year' (SEA, Article 2), though in practice they are more frequent. The European Council plays an important role in providing overall political direction to the Union, defining goals and strategies, and in resolving problems that have proved intractable at the Council of Ministers level.[11] At the Seville European Council of June 2002, it was decided that European Councils should agree on action programmes for the following three years. The European Council takes decisions on an intergovernmental basis, and implementation of the measures is left to the other EU institutions. The Constitutional Treaty proposed introducing use of a qualified majority vote (see below) but only after using the *passerelle*, which entails consulting the European Parliament and informing national parliaments.

The **Presidency** of the Council of Ministers and the European Council rotates among the EU member states in six-month terms.[12] Up until 1998 the sequence followed the alphabetical order of the names of member states in their own languages, but subsequently this was changed to ensure a better balance between large and small countries (see Box 3.7).

Box 3.7 The order of the Presidency

	January–June	July–December
	January–June	July–December
1999	Germany	Finland
2000	Portugal	France
2001	Sweden	Belgium
2002	Spain	Denmark
2003	Greece	Italy
2004	Ireland	The Netherlands
2005	Luxembourg	UK
2006	Austria	Finland

The Presidency may allow a particular member state to press for policy decisions and initiatives in which it is particularly interested. To date European Council meetings have generally been held in the country holding the Presidency, though it has been proposed that more summits should be held in Brussels to reduce expense and (at times) inconvenience.

The country holding the Presidency has the power to set the agenda, draft compromises and ensure the continuity and consistency of policy-making. For instance, a priority of the German Presidency was to reach a budgetary agreement at the March 1999 Berlin European Council on the financial perspective for the 2000–06 period (see Chapter 8). The subsequent Finnish Presidency took key decisions on enlargement at the December 1999 Helsinki European Council, while the Portuguese Presidency in early 2000 placed emphasis on turning the EU into a 'new economy'. The French Presidency focused on institutional questions at the Nice European Council of December 2000, while Sweden in 2001 wanted progress on the three 'e's: the environment,

---

[10] The term 'heads of state and of government' is used because France reserves the right to send both.
[11] The Nice Treaty establishes that the European Council should 'provide the Union with the necessary impetus for its development and shall define the general political guidelines thereof' (Article 4, EU Treaty), discuss the conclusions of 'broad guidelines of the economic policies of the member states and of the Community' (Article 99, EC Treaty) and should 'define the principles and the general guidelines for the Common Foreign and Security Policy' (Article 13, EU Treaty).
[12] The terms last from January to June, and July to December.

employment and enlargement. During the Danish Presidency key decisions on enlargement were taken at the Copenhagen Summit. In 2003 Italy unsuccessfully attempted to reach agreement on the Constitutional Treaty, but subsequently the member states agreed that it would be signed in Italy in order to create a new Treaty of Rome. The Irish Presidency was heralded as a success for reaching agreement on the Constitutional Treaty. During the Dutch Presidency a decision must be taken on whether to accept Turkey as an EU member.

In order to provide a certain continuity, and assist smaller countries holding the Presidency, the **Troika** entails that countries immediately preceding and following flank the current holder of the Presidency. However, difficulties remain and will increase with enlargement as a result both of the large number of applicant countries and the small size of many of them.

The Constitutional Treaty proposes introducing a President of the European Council who would hold office for two and a half years, renewable for a following term. The president would have functions similar to those of the present Presidency, driving forward the proceedings of the European Council. The Constitutional Treaty also envisages creating a Union Minister for Foreign Affairs to replace the External Relations Commissioner (Chris Patten for the period 1999–2004) and the High Representative for the Common Foreign and Security Policy ('Mr CFSP' or Javier Solana, see Chapter 19). The minister would chair the Council for Foreign Affairs and would act according to the strategic guidelines defined by the European Council. The minister for foreign affairs would also be a member of the Commission, and would hold office for five years. According to the proposals of the Constitutional Treaty, the Presidency of other specialised Councils would continue to rotate on a six-month basis, though within a team Presidency of three countries holding office for 18 months.

The Council is assisted in its work by the **Coreper** (Committee of Permanent Representatives), which is composed of ambassadors of the member states in Brussels. The Coreper helps to prepare Council meetings, and may take decisions on issues that are not controversial. On agricultural questions the Special Committee for Agriculture carries out this role. It is estimated that some 90 per cent of all Council decisions are taken by Coreper and the Special Committee on Agriculture, or in working groups of national officials before the Council of Ministers even meets, though the 10 per cent that remains almost invariably concerns the more controversial questions. The Council may adopt common positions or joint actions under the Common Foreign and Security Policy, and Justice and Home Affairs. It is also responsible for authorizing, monitoring and concluding agreements with third countries.

THE WEIGHTING OF VOTES AND THE THRESHOLD FOR QUALIFIED MAJORITY VOTING

The Council of Ministers may take decisions by **unanimity, simple majority or qualified majority voting (QMV)**. According to the treaties, unless otherwise specified, simple majority will be the rule. However, almost invariably the treaties specify that QMV or unanimity voting should be used.

QMV is the most widely used system of voting in the Council (covering about 80 per cent of Council decisions), although in practice attempts are generally made to reach consensus. Each of the ministers in the Council is allocated a certain number of votes (very roughly) reflecting the population of the country of origin. With each enlargement of the European Union adjustments have been necessary in the allocation of votes and the number of votes necessary to block a proposal. Tables 3.1 and 3.2, and Figure 3.1 illustrate the weights of each of the EU(25).

Prior to the May 2004 enlargement the qualified majority rule required that 62 of a total of 87

Member states	Population millions	Pre-Nice vote in the Council	Post-Nice vote in the Council
Germany	82.0	10	29
UK	59.2	10	29
France	59.0	10	29
Italy	57.6	10	29
Spain	39.3	8	27
NL	15.8	5	13
Greece	10.5	5	12
Belgium	10.2	5	12
Portugal	10.0	5	12
Sweden	8.9	4	10
Austria	8.1	4	10
Denmark	5.3	3	7
Finland	5.2	3	7
Ireland	3.7	3	7
Lux.	0.4	2	4

TABLE 3.1 The changes in weights in the Council of Ministers agreed at the Nice Summit

Source: Protocol on the enlargement of the European Union, annexed to the Nice Treaty.

New member states and candidate countries	Population 2003 (millions)	Vote in the Council on basis of previous system	Vote in the Council agreed at Nice	European Parliament allocation of seats
Poland	38.2	8	27	50
Romania	21.8	6	14	33
Czech Rep.	10.2	5	12	20
Hungary	10.1	5	12	20
Bulgaria	7.8	4	10	17
Slovakia	5.4	3	7	13
Lithuania	3.5	3	7	12
Latvia	2.3	3	4	8
Slovenia	2.0	3	4	7
Estonia	1.4	3	4	6
Cyprus	0.7	2	4	6
Malta	0.4	2	3	5

TABLE 3.2 The weights agreed for the new member states and candidate countries at the Nice Summit

Source: Protocol on the enlargement of the European Union, annexed to the Nice Treaty, and Eurostat data for population.

votes had to be in favour of a measure for it to be adopted, i.e. 71.3 per cent of the vote. With the Accession Treaty (which implements some of the changes agreed at Nice) the rule for passing a measure became:[13]

■ 232 out of a total of 321 votes, or 72.3 per cent of the votes;
■ a majority of member states (a two-thirds majority in some cases); and
■ a member of the Council may request verification that the qualified majority represents at least 62 per cent of the EU population, and if that condition is not met the decision will not be adopted.

The increase in number of votes for each country was intended to allow more discretion in allocating weights to different countries. The requirement that a majority of states should back a

---

[13] The Protocol on Enlargement of the EU annexed to the Nice Treaty indicates a threshold of 258 votes out of 345 in an EU of 27 members, which represents 74.8 per cent of the vote.

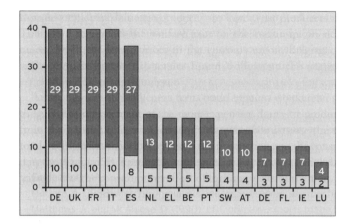

measure was introduced to favour the interests of smaller member states, while the population requirement reflected the interests of larger countries.[14]

Although the introduction of these two additional voting rules renders decision-making more complex and less transparent, its aim was to increase legitimacy in an attempt to reconcile two views of the EU. The EU can be regarded either as a union of states or as a union of people. In the case of a union of states equality of power (or the ability to influence decisions) would require each state to have equal voting power. For a union of people each citizen should have the same voting power. The hybrid nature of the EU requires some compromise between the two. Prior to enlargement this was achieved through over-weighting the votes of the smaller member states in QMV. As can be seen from Figure 3.1,[15] the Treaty of Nice increased the weight of larger countries in QMV, implying a shift of the compromise away from of the union-of-states concept. This is to some extent corrected by the requirement that at least 50 per cent of member states support a measure. The introduction of the two additional rules renders this dual nature of the EU more explicit.

One of the aims of the Nice Treaty was to increase the efficiency of EU decision-making, or the ability to pass legislation. This can be defined as 'passage probability', or the chances of reaching a majority on an issue given a particular voting rule. Baldwin and Wyplosz (2004) found that compared with applying the status quo in either an EU of 15 or 27, the Nice Treaty actually reduced the passage possibility of QMV in the Council.[16]

The Nice Treaty also changed the relative weights of the member states in the Council. The parity of votes in the Council between France and Germany was maintained, despite the increase in German population after unification. However, the relative weight of Germany in the European Parliament was increased (see below). The traditional parity of votes in the Council between the Netherlands and Belgium was broken, and Spain increased its relative weight.

These debates about the relative weights of countries were heated and acrimonious both in the context of the Nice Treaty and the Constitutional Treaty. This is because weights in the Council are generally assumed to reflect the power of a member state to influence the outcome of the decision-making process. Various empirical studies have been carried out to test this hypothesis. Baldwin et al. (2001) find a close correlation between the number of votes of the poorer member

---

[14] On previous QMV rules, a decision could be voted by countries representing as little as 58 per cent of the EU population, and without reform this percentage would fall to less than 50 per cent in an EU of 27 countries. In addition, countries representing only 13.8 per cent of the EU population could block a measure, and this percentage was destined to fall to 10 per cent with enlargement if procedures remained unchanged.

[15] See Laruelle and Widgren (1998), and Baldwin and Wyplosz (2004) for more detailed analyses of this issue.

[16] 'Passage possibility' is defined as the number of all possible winning coalitions divided by the number of all possible coalitions.

states and spending on the Structural Funds.[17] Kandogan (2000) finds a similar result both for structural actions and for the link between the number of member states with a strong interest in agriculture and agricultural spending. On the basis of the experience of successive enlargements Kandogan concludes that the allocation of voting power in the Council is more important than the initial budgetary deal for the new member state, as voting power will determine successive budgetary outcomes.

Given the complexity of the solution agreed at Nice, the Constitutional Treaty proposed a simpler system based on a dual majority, so that 55 per cent of member states representing at least 65 per cent of the EU population would be required to pass a measure. In order to avoid a situation where only three large member states could block legislation, a blocking minority would require at least four member states.[18] A change in the system was initially opposed by Spain and Poland, who argued that their weight would be less than in the voting procedure agreed at Nice.

THE VOTING RULES USED IN THE COUNCIL OF MINISTERS

During the early years of the Community (1958–65) unanimity voting was generally used. In 1965 the Commission (under the aegis of its then president, Hallstein) put forward proposals for the financing of the Common Agricultural Policy, the introduction of own resources for the Community Budget and increased powers for the European Parliament, which were also aimed at ensuring democratic control of Community spending. At the same time, the third phase of the transitional period for introducing the Community was due to begin in 1966, and the Commission called for implementation of the Treaty of Rome with respect to the use of the qualified majority vote.

The French President, de Gaulle,[19] fiercely contested these proposals, and instructed his ministers to boycott meetings of the Council of Ministers. The non-participation of France in Council meetings became known as the 'Empty Chair' crisis, and had the effect of paralysing EC decision-making for six months. The crisis coincided with presidential elections in France, and following the failure of de Gaulle to win outright in the first ballot of December 1965, he let it be known that a more conciliatory tone would be adopted towards the Community. As an important agricultural producer, France was also concerned to ensure adequate financing for the Common Agricultural Policy, which then absorbed about 90 per cent of EC spending.

Following de Gaulle's success in the second ballot, negotiations with the Community were resumed, leading to the Luxembourg compromise in early 1966. This entailed that whenever any member state declared that a measure affected a 'vital national interest', the Council would endeavour to reach solutions within a reasonable time that could be adopted by unanimity. Though in practice during the following years the Luxembourg compromise was seldom invoked, unanimity became the rule, and majority voting was rarely used, except occasionally on details of agricultural policy or budgetary matters.

It was only with the Single European Act (SEA) that this situation changed, with the number of areas subject to the QMV rule being substantially extended. The SEA specified that all measures relating to completion of the Single Market were to be decided on the basis of QMV, which was probably the only way of ensuring that the 1993 deadline could be reached. The Maastricht and

---

[17] See Chapter 13 for a discussion of the Structural Funds.
[18] In addition a number of member states comprising three-quarters of a blocking minority (either in terms of population or number of states) can require a vote to be postponed.
[19] According to de Gaulle, the provisions for QMV in the Treaty of Rome had been negotiated during the IV Republic when France was politically weak, and he was in favour of 'taking our destiny back into our own hands' as it was unacceptable that 'a foreign majority can constrain recalcitrant nations' (quoted in Bainbridge, 1998, pp.337–338).

Amsterdam Treaties brought limited extensions of the areas where QMV was to be used, but unanimity continued to be used in many areas.

The fact that so many areas remained under the unanimity-voting rule (with any member state able to threaten use of a veto) raised a spectre of even greater risk of deadlock and the breakdown of decision-making in an enlarged EU. To meet this problem the Nice Summit aimed at increasing the use of qualified majority voting in the Council, and in the event it was agreed that QMV would be extended to 29 of the 70 Treaty articles, that were still subject to unanimity. The most important changes were in immigration and asylum, trade in services, decisions on senior appointments (including appointment of the president of the Commission) and measures to streamline the Court of Justice. However, national sensibilities meant that the right of veto in the Council was maintained in many crucial areas. For instance, the UK managed to ensure that unanimity remained for tax questions and social security. Spain insisted on keeping unanimity for decisions relating to the Cohesion Fund,[20] while Germany demanded it for movement of professionals. France was able to block an extension of qualified majority voting for trade in audiovisual services, culture, education, health and social services. Denmark and Greece obtained exceptions from the QMV for maritime transport.

The Constitutional Treaty proposes that unanimity be limited to a dozen or so policy areas, some of which relate to constitutional issues and the EU Budget, while others raise sensitive questions for certain member states (such as taxation, the Common Foreign and Security Policy, and some aspects of social policy).

THE EUROPEAN PARLIAMENT

The European Parliament (EP) is primarily a consultative body, and its legislative powers are relatively limited. It is elected every five years, and since 1979 a system of direct election has been used.[21] The EP is the only directly elected EU institution, but the elections tend to be fought mainly on national issues. The elections often seem to be a vote of confidence about the incumbent national government. As Figures 3.2–3.4 indicate, the low turnout in some member states illustrates how the European Parliament has failed to secure a hold over public opinion.

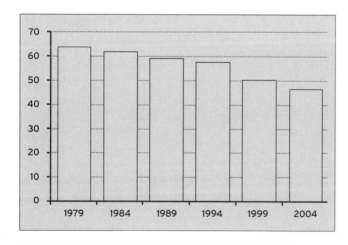

FIGURE 3.2 Percentage turnout in successive European Parliament elections

Source: www.elections2004.eu.int

---

[20] See Chapter 13.
[21] See Westlake (1994) for a detailed description of the European Parliament.

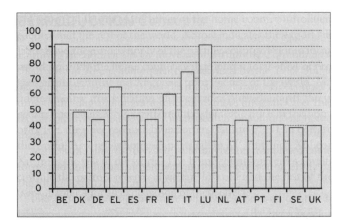

FIGURE 3.3 Percentage turnout in the June 2004* European Parliament elections EU(15)

*The data for Italy, Luxembourg and the UK are provisional. The division of countries between Figures 3.2 and 3.3 was simply for reasons of space. Source: www.elections2004.eu.int

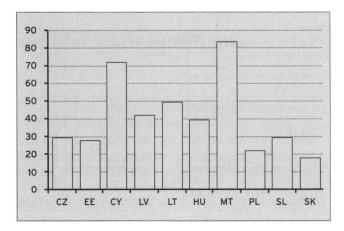

FIGURE 3.4 Percentage turnout in the June 2004 European Parliament elections: new member states

Source: www.elections2004.eu.int

The Amsterdam Treaty set a ceiling of 700 on the future size of the European Parliament, but this was happily exceeded. Following enlargement the number of members of the Parliament was increased from 626 to the 732 elected in June 2004 (see also Tables 3.2 and 3.3, and Figure 3.5). The seats are apportioned roughly according to the populations of the member states (though again there is a bias to ensure adequate representation of the smaller states). The Constitutional Treaty proposes a maximum of 750 MEPs, and a digressively proportional rule for representation, with a minimum of six seats and a maximum of 96 seats per member state.

The MEPs are organized into large groupings that reflect political leaning rather than nationality. Following the 2004 elections, the largest of these are the European People's Party (Christian Democrats) and European Democrats (268 MEPs), the Party of European Socialists (200 MEPs), the European Liberal, Democrat and Reform Party (88 MEPs), the Greens/European Free Alliance (42 MEPs), the Confederal Group of the European United Left/Nordic Green Left (41 MEPs), the Independents/Democrats (33 MEPs), the Union for a Europe of the Nations (27 MEPs), and the non-attached (33).[22] Many MEPs were initially national politicians, or in the media and sport.[23]

The party relationships of members of these broad groups tend to be loose, but advantages such

---

[22] These data are taken from www.elections2004.eu.int.
[23] On one famous occasion the Italian MEPs included a famous porno-star, 'Cicciolina'.

as increased possibility of obtaining places on committees or other official positions can be derived from membership. The Parliament has 23 committees dealing with different policy areas, and most of the detailed work takes place there.

The European Parliament of the EU(15) made use of 11 official languages,[24] and with enlargement to 27 members the number of additional languages could increase by 10 (see also Box 3.8). A consequence of using so many languages is that debates tend to be dull, with little scope for repartee.

TABLE 3.3 Representation in the European Parliament

Current members	Population (millions) 2003	European Parliament seats 1999–2004	Inhabitants per MEP (1000) in the EP before June 2004	European Parliament allocation of seats from 2004	Inhabitants per MEP (1000) in the EP after June 2004
Germany	82.5	99	833	99	833
France	59.6	87	685	72	827
UK	59.3	87	682	72	823
Italy	57.3	87	658	72	796
Spain	41.6	64	650	50	832
NL	16.2	31	523	25	648
Greece	11.0	25	440	22	500
Belgium	10.4	25	416	22	473
Portugal	10.4	22	472	22	473
Sweden	8.9	21	423	18	494
Austria	8.1	16	506	17	476
Denmark	5.4	16	338	13	415
Finland	5.2	15	347	13	400
Ireland	4.0	15	267	12	333
Lux.	0.4	6	67	6	67

Source: Protocol on the enlargement of the European Union, annexed to the Nice Treaty; and own elaborations based on Eurostat data.

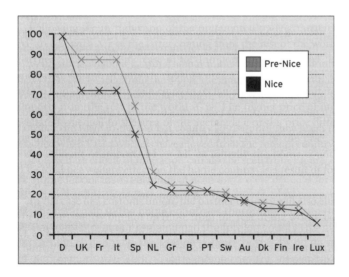

FIGURE 3.5 Pre-Nice votes in the European Parliament and votes according to the Nice Treaty (by country)

---

[24] Spanish, Danish, German, Greek, English, French, Italian, Dutch, Portuguese, Finnish and Swedish.

Box 3.8 The problem of languages in the EU

With 15 member states the EU employed 550 translators, and the Council alone had an interpreting budget of €50 million per year. For many years French was the dominant language of the Community, but English and German are more widely spoken in the countries that joined the EU in 1995 and in 2004. According to the *Financial Times* (28 November 2003), an analysis of candidates from the new member states for Commission posts found that 83 per cent spoke English, 34 per cent German and 24 per cent French.

One of the proposals to meet the problem of languages with enlargement was to charge member states for using their native language. The proposal would not apply to ministerial meetings where full interpreting services would be provided, but it was suggested for working groups. In 2004 the Commissioner responsible for administrative reform, Neil Kinnock, also called for Commission reports to be shorter and not exceed 15 pages.

Box 3.9 Reform of the European Parliament

During the debate on the European Convention, one of the proposed reforms of the European Parliament entailed setting up a second chamber drawn from representatives of national parliaments. Elections to the European Parliament have been contested largely on the basis of national issues in the various member states, and the Italian experience suggests a further drawback of the proposed reform. Many of the Italian members of the European Parliament are also national politicians. In March 1999 a survey carried out by the French *Journal du Dimanche* found that on average Italian MEPs had been absent from 41.6 per cent of the plenary sessions of the European Parliament, followed by the Danes (35.7 per cent) and the French (30 per cent). An article in the Italian newspaper *La Repubblica* of 8 March 1999 confirmed that party secretaries who are also MEPs rarely attended the European Parliament. For instance, the head of the Northern League, Umberto Bossi, attended only 6 per cent of the sessions, and Gianfranco Fini of the National Alliance attended 11 per cent. At the time the Italian MEPs were also the most highly paid in the EU.

In 2002 there was a failed attempt in the European Parliament to ensure that receipts backed expenses. MEPs are entitled to club class travel, but many fly economy and pocket the difference as they are only required to produce a boarding card to claim expenses. A coalition including Italians, Spanish and Germans also blocked an attempt to introduce the same salary for all MEPs. The salary of German MEPs would have increased to the average, but the German government was against such a measure at a time of fiscal austerity.

The official seat of the European Parliament is Strasbourg, but its committee meetings take place in Brussels, and its secretariat is divided between Luxembourg and Brussels; hence the famous trunks in the corridors to accommodate the various moves of personnel.

The European Parliament has powers relating to legislation, the EU Budget, the conclusion of international agreements and supervision (see also Box 3.9):

The Parliament has the right to be consulted during the legislative process (described below). It can make amendments to legislative proposals in a variety of ways, and, since the Maastricht Treaty, it also has the power of veto in certain circumstances.

The Parliament may adopt or reject the whole EU Budget. The European Parliament's committee on budgetary expenditure is responsible for monitoring expenditure. Parliament makes an annual assessment of the management of the budget before approving the accounts and granting 'discharge' to the Commission on the basis of the Annual Report of the Court of Auditors.

The EP has budgetary powers (i.e. it can propose amendments) over non-compulsory expenditure. The proposed Constitutional Treaty would increase the budgetary powers of the European Parliament.

Compulsory expenditure is defined as spending 'necessarily resulting from this Treaty or from acts adopted in accordance therewith' (Article 272 EC Treaty). Compulsory spending is said to have a priority claim as it is considered necessary for the Community to meet its internal and external obligations. Most compulsory spending relates to agricultural price support and certain forms of foreign aid to third countries. The underlying logic is that when, for example, the level of common agricultural prices was decided, this became Community law, and the necessary financing should be forthcoming (and consequently not subject to possible cuts by the EP). The EP can only propose modifications of compulsory expenditure to the Council.

In contrast **non-compulsory expenditure** does not emanate from the commitments of the treaties, or the conventions and contracts signed by the European Union. The largest component of non-compulsory expenditure is spending on the Structural Funds (the European Social Fund, FEOGA Guidance, the European Regional Development Fund and the Financial Instrument for Fisheries Guidance; see Chapter 13). A related instrument is the Cohesion Fund. Other categories of non-compulsory expenditure include internal policies (education, the internal market, research and the environment), external programmes and administrative expenditure.

If the Parliament proposes an increase in non-compulsory expenditure, this will only come into effect if backed by a vote of the Council using QMV. Ceilings set by the Commission on the growth of that expenditure may further limit the power of the European Parliament over non-compulsory expenditure. Moreover, some types of expenditure (for example, until 2006 that of the European Development Fund which gives assistance to developing countries)[25] are excluded from the budget completely.

The division between compulsory and non-compulsory expenditure is essentially political and relates to the balance of power between the EU institutions. As described above, in the 1960s the Commission and federalists envisaged a Community with its own resources subject to control by the European Parliament as an important step in the creation of a federalist Europe. In contrast, France objected to transfers of sovereignty to the Community, but wanted to ensure adequate financing for the Common Agricultural Policy. The compromise, involving the division of types expenditure and the inclusion of agricultural support under compulsory spending, ensured that the Council had the final say on most EC agricultural spending. This, together with the use of unanimity voting after the Luxembourg compromise, offered a guarantee that the interests of French farmers would not be overridden. The EP has campaigned for the distinction between compulsory and non-compulsory expenditure to be abolished.

Parliamentary assent[26] is necessary before important agreements can be concluded with third countries or international organizations, and, in particular, its assent is necessary for treaties of accession or association. Assent is also necessary on decisions regarding the objectives of the

---

[25] It is proposed to bring EDF spending under the EU budget for the 2007–13 financial perspective.
[26] See the section on Community decision-making below.

Structural and Cohesion Funds, and the functions of the European Central Bank. The EP has no power to amend decisions under this procedure, but it can comment on them.

The EP has supervisory powers over the work of the Commission. It has to be consulted when a new Commission president and Commission are being chosen, and their appointment is also subject to a vote of approval by the Parliament. It can dismiss the whole Commission, and the Treaty of Nice also envisages the power to dismiss individual Commissioners. The Constitutional Treaty proposes that the EP elect the new Commission president.

The Maastricht Treaty gave the European Parliament the power to investigate alleged contraventions of Community law and to appoint an ombudsman[27] to receive complaints from any EU citizen about suspected maladministration on the part of any EU institution.[28] The ombudsman may take the initiative in making investigations. The results of any inquiry are sent to the European Parliament and to the institution concerned, but the ombudsman has no right of sanction. The first ombudsman, elected for the 1995–2000 period, and again from 2000, was a Finn, Jacob Magnus Soderman, who had previously acted as Parliamentary ombudsman in Finland. In the Parliament elected in 2004 the new ombudsman was the Greek, P. Nikoforos Diamandouros.

The EP is an important forum for discussion. The Parliament sets its own agenda for discussions, invites important outside speakers and can send out delegations and fact-finding missions.

THE ECONOMIC AND SOCIAL COMMITTEE

The Economic and Social Committee (also known as Ecosoc or the ESC) has its origins in the French notion of including the 'social partners' (and, in particular, trade unions and employers) in social dialogue; this entails consulting them on proposed legislation. In practice, the representatives from each member state in the Ecosoc are drawn from three categories: trade unions, employers and 'other interests'. The Ecosoc represents the various economic and social components of the European Union, including 'producers, farmers, carriers, workers, dealers, craftsmen, professional occupations, consumers and the general interest' (Article 257, EC Treaty). Based in Brussels, following the 2004 enlargement the Ecosoc has 317 members.[29]

According to the Treaty of Rome, the ESC has to be consulted during the legislative process, but there is no obligation for the Council to take its Opinions into account. The ESC can also prepare Opinions on its own initiative. Though its influence on the legislative process is less than that envisaged in the Treaty of Rome, the expertise of the ESC can prove a useful source of information and is valued in many circles, including the European Parliament and Commission.

Since the Maastricht Treaty the ESC shares its secretariat with the **Committee of the Regions**. The latter consists of regional and local representatives appointed for four-year terms, whose function is to advise the Council and Commission on regional problems and policies. The Committee of the Regions has the same number of representatives per member state as Ecosoc. It must be consulted on matters affecting regional interests; it can also issue opinions on its own initiative but suffers from a low profile.[30]

---

[27] The ombudsman is an institution of Scandinavian origin, and the first ombudsman was appointed in Sweden in 1809.

[28] The term 'maladministration' is used to cover both incompetence and deliberate wrongdoing.

[29] The four largest EU member states each have 24 members; Spain and Poland have 21; Belgium, Greece, the Netherlands, Austria, Portugal, Sweden, Hungary and the Czech Republic have 12; Denmark, Ireland, Finland, Lithuania and Slovakia were to have 9; Latvia, Slovenia and Estonia were to have 7; Luxembourg and Cyprus were to have 6, with 5 for Malta. Romania will have 15, and Bulgaria will have 12.

[30] In 2003 the Committee of the Regions was involved in a financial scandal when the European Court of Justice forced its most senior civil servant to resign over severe irregularities. The decision awaits the outcome of an investigation by OLAF, the Commission's anti-fraud office. The Committee of the Regions was accused of travel expense fraud, and falsification of records to claim expenses by, for example, arranging 'fake' meetings on the eve of official meetings (*Financial Times*, 14 April 2003 and 19 September 2003).

THE EUROPEAN COURT OF JUSTICE

The European Court of Justice (EJ) is composed of one judge from each member state, assisted by eight advocates-general.[31] All appointments are for six-year renewable terms, and the judges choose a president every three years. In 1989, in order to speed up procedures, a Court of First Instance was created, which is also composed of one judge from each member state. According to the Nice Treaty, the Court of First Instance has powers to hear direct actions and deliver preliminary rulings in certain areas. The Nice Treaty also envisaged a third tier of courts known as 'judicial panels' to relieve the higher tiers of certain cases.

The European Court of Justice is responsible for interpreting Community law and adjudicating on disputes arising from the interpretation of the treaties and the legislation based upon them. If national law and EU law conflict, the latter takes precedence: in other words the EJ may overrule both national courts and governments. The Court of Justice is the highest court to which disputes on EC law can be taken, and national courts must abide by its judgments. The Maastricht Treaty permits the Court to impose fines on recalcitrant countries.[32] The Court cannot initiate cases, but makes judgments on cases referred to it by EU institutions, national governments and courts, corporate bodies and individuals. The Court can only act within the powers given by the treaties.

Despite being handicapped by a relatively small staff, the Court has played a 'discrete but substantial role in furthering the objectives laid down in the Treaties' (Bainbridge, 1998). Some of its rulings have established important principles, in particular in fields such as competition policy and equal pay. The ruling in the famous 1979 *Cassis de Dijon* case formed the basis for mutual recognition of each other's standards by EU member states. This role of the Court in carrying forward the integration process has frequently been criticized, and certain member states have accused the Court of being the unguarded back door through which national sovereignty is being carried away.[33]

The Court has, however, been criticized for not being sufficiently transparent and being too slow in its procedures. On average in 2000 it took 30 months for cases to come to judgement (Jones, 2001), but this is still less than in certain member states. The delays are largely due to the overload of work of the Court, and the Nice Treaty aimed at reducing the burden on the Court by delegating more work to lower levels.

THE COURT OF AUDITORS

The expenditure of all the EU institutions is subject to internal control by the Commission (DG XX), and since 1977 to external control by the Court of Auditors. The Court's authority also extends to all institutions (including those in third countries) receiving or handling EU funds.

The Court is responsible for ensuring that all expenditure corresponds to the legal provisions, that correct accounting practices have been used and financial objectives have been met. In practice to date, it has mainly been concerned with checking on fraud and the proper use of funds. The findings of the Court are published in an annual report, and other reports on specific topics may also be produced. Initially the Court could simply bring irregularities to the notice of the authorities responsible for the institution concerned (and its findings were frequently ignored), but since the Treaty of Maastricht it can refer cases to the Court of Justice.

---

[31] A system of rotation is used for the smaller countries.
[32] Fines have been imposed on Italy, for example, for non-application of the milk quotas.
[33] The *Economist*, 17 May 1997.

THE DECISION-MAKING PROCEDURES OF THE EUROPEAN COMMUNITY

Until the Single European Act, the EC legislative procedure was based on what is known as the **consultation procedure,** which, unlike the present combination of procedures, was relatively straightforward. As shown in Figure 3.6, this consisted essentially of a Commission proposal being passed to the European Parliament and Economic and Social Committee, and, since the Maastricht Treaty, to the Committee of the Regions for 'consultation'. The significant feature of this procedure was that there was only one reading by the European Parliament. The Council would take the final decision, using the appropriate voting rule. It is important to note that neither the Commission nor the Council were bound to accept eventual amendments proposed by the European Parliament.

The 1987 Single European Act introduced the **co-operation procedure** as a means of strengthening the role of the European Parliament in the legislative process. The procedure allowed the European Parliament to amend legislation. This required two readings by the European Parliament (see Figure 3.6). This procedure is now hardly ever used, and the Treaty of Amsterdam transferred most of the areas formerly dealt with under this procedure to the co-decision procedure.

The Maastricht Treaty introduced **the co-decision procedure**, and both the Amsterdam and Nice Treaties entailed an extension of its use so that it now covers about 80 per cent of Community legislation. The Constitutional Treaty proposes near generalization of the co-decision procedure. The aim of wider use of the co-decision procedure was to reinforce the power of the European Parliament in the legislative process and shift the balance of power away from the Commission. The main innovations of this procedure were to allow the EP to veto legislation in certain cases, to add the possibility of a third reading of legislative proposals for the European Parliament and the creation of a Conciliation Committee to help the Parliament and Council to reach agreement.

As mentioned above, the **assent procedure** applies to important international agreements, decisions concerning the objectives of the Structural and Cohesion Funds, and the functions of the European Central Bank. According to this procedure, the European Parliament can give or withhold its assent to a legislative proposal, but it does not have the power to amend it.

'FLEXIBILITY' OR 'ENHANCED CO-OPERATION'

The number of policy areas dealt with by the EU is growing, and so too is its membership. There is increasing concern about the efficiency of EU decision-making and the need to ensure that progress in integration is not limited to the pace of the slowest. The widening membership of the EU is bringing growing diversity,[34] and with it the idea that more 'flexibility' or 'differentiated integration' will be necessary. Flexibility or differentiated integration allows those countries that are willing and/or able to proceed faster in some areas of integration. This is also referred to as 'enhanced co-operation'. Various concepts have been advanced in this context:[35]

- A **multi-speed EU** that assumes that all member states will arrive at the same destination but require different speeds to do so. In other words, all the member states will be allowed transitional periods before they fully apply certain policies.

---

[34] On differentiated integration, see Ehlermann (1995); Hughes (1996), pp. 8–10; and Wallace and Wallace (2000).
[35] See Jones (2001).

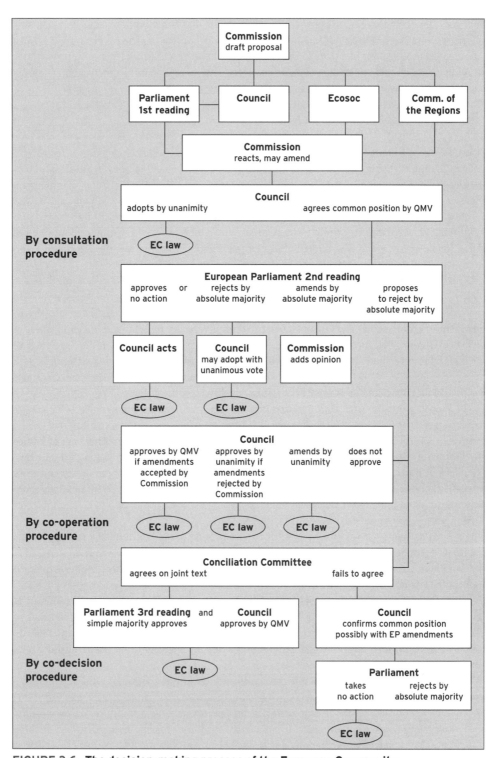

FIGURE 3.6 The decision-making process of the European Community.

Source: *European*, Special Supplement, 1992

- A **variable geometry EU**, or Europe *à la carte*, in which all the member states can pick and choose whether to participate in different policies. In contrast to the first option, it is not assumed that all member states will arrive at the same destination.
- A **Europe of concentric circles** by which countries are placed in different circles according to the degree of integration which they are able and willing to pursue.
- A **core or pioneer group of countries,** which are most committed to and able to carry forward vanguard integration projects.

A 'multi-speed' EU would entail allowing member states time before they sign up for certain policies. It implies that the goal for all member states would be that of membership in all aspects of the Union, but that member states may need time to prepare for such membership.[36] For instance, there was a delay until 2001 before Greece began to participate in full membership of the EMU.

In the case of the new CEEC member states, the concept of a multi-speed EU translated into long transitional periods in certain areas such as labour movement, the Common Agricultural Policy, land ownership and environmental regulations. Derogations were also used in the past, and were granted, for example, to Spain and Portugal when they joined the Community.

With 'variable geometry', or a Europe *à la carte*, the member states could sign up to different policies on the basis of preference rather than ability. In other words, the member states could choose voluntarily to remain outside certain policies or co-operation frameworks. There are various precedents for this such as the UK opt-out of the Social Charter in 1989 and Social Chapter in 1993 (see Chapter 14), and the UK and Danish opt-outs of full participation in the third stage of the EMU. However, here there is a risk that a 'hard core' of member states, having all signed up for the same policies, would decide to proceed with even deeper integration, and other member states would find that their options of eventually joining the hard core are excluded.

The French prime minister, Balladur, first proposed the idea of 'concentric circles', which, as its name suggests, has a geographical dimension. Other countries also strongly committed to the integration process, such as the other original member states, would flank an inner core of France and Germany. These would be surrounded by a second circle of member states, and finally by a periphery of other partner countries. The flaw in this conception is that some of the countries consigned outside the central circle (such as Finland or Ireland) are among those generally more enthusiastic about integration, while candidate countries have usually objected to being fobbed off with anything short of full membership.

Proposals to create a 'core group' of EU countries generally rotate around the concept of the Franco-German relationship as being the driving force of integration. For example, in a speech at the Humbolt University of Berlin in May 2000 German Foreign Minister Fischer expressed support for a federalist vision of Europe based on a European superstate. A core group of states (headed by Germany and France) would represent the centre of gravity in furthering this initiative, though membership of the group would be open to all countries. Nation states would continue to play a role in order to ensure a 'union of citizens and states that wins public legitimacy. The EU would become a lean federation capable of action and fully sovereign, but based on fully self-confident nation states.'

The French president, Chirac, then presented his rather different vision of a future EU to the Bundestag in June 2000. Again this was to be centred on a core group or *avante-guarde* (vanguard) of pioneers committed to closer co-ordination on matters such as economics, defence, crime and immigration. This vanguard could forge ahead with joint projects, and might have its own secretariat. The vanguard was seen as having possibly half-a-dozen member countries. However,

---

[36] See Ehlermann (1995), pp. 5–7.

Chirac differed from Fischer in calling not for a 'United States of Europe', but a 'United Europe of States'.

Although the Franco-German alliance had long provided the momentum for many of the initiatives in European integration, there was a growing feeling that it might prove inadequate to propel the EU after enlargement. The misgivings were reinforced because at times co-operation between the two countries seemed increasingly geared to furthering national rather than EU interests, as in the October 2003 agreement on the CAP (see Chapter 10), or the 2004 controversy over the Growth and Stability Pact (see Chapter 8).

Partly as a reaction, in 2004 Prime Minister Tony Blair proposed that the UK join France and Germany in a summit of the 'big three' countries. The aim was to extend their newfound co-operation in defence matters and foreign policy (see Chapter 19) to other issues such as employment, the economy, finance and social policy. Countries such as Italy, Spain and Poland immediately expressed their concern at such an initiative.

If the EU fails to permit sufficient possibilities for enhanced co-operation within its structures, there is a risk of flexibility by default with initiatives taking place outside the EU. The problem becomes one of finding a middle road, with some variable geometry to allow flexibility within EU structures, while at the same time avoiding excessive variable geometry that might undermine the cohesion and common core of the EU.

A flexibility clause was included in the Amsterdam Treaty of 1999, according to which flexibility must:

■ respect the treaties and objectives of the EU;
■ involve a majority of member states;
■ not affect the rights and obligations of states not participating;
■ allow any other member state to join at a later stage;
■ be introduced as a last resort;
■ not impede the operation of the *acquis*; and
■ be allowed to be vetoed by any single country that feels that vital interests are being threatened.

It was soon realized that these conditions were too restrictive to realize in practice. The Nice Treaty aimed at rendering flexibility easier, in particular by removing the simple right of any member state to veto the process. According to the Amsterdam Treaty, enhanced co-operation required a majority of states, but this was modified to participation by eight member states in the Nice Treaty (at the time the 'critical mass' of eight corresponded to a majority of member states).

EVALUATION

In recent years the 'democratic deficit' of the EU has proved far from simply a concept for academic debate. On various occasions when EU decision-makers have appealed to their citizens for approval, the outcome has not been what they expected. As a result, decisions have increasingly been taken in the European Council and various Councils, with national representatives 'looking over their shoulders' at the likely reaction of their national electorate. While this has added to accountability, debates have become more confrontational, and compromises are more difficult to reach. After enlargement this tendency can only become more accentuated.

The Constitutional Treaty attempts to address the questions of legitimacy and transparency and would make a notable contribution to simplifying and rationalising existing treaties. However, the process of ratification is lengthy and hazardous, and even if the Treaty succeeds in becoming more than an academic exercise and opportunity for debate, some time will elapse before it comes into operation. In the meantime, the discussion about the future architecture of the EU seems set to continue for many years.

Summary of Key Concepts

- The main decision-making institutions of the European Union are: the European Commission; the Council of Ministers; the European Parliament; the Economic and Social Committee; the Committee of Regions; the European Court of Justice and the Court of Auditors.
- It is frequently claimed that EU legislative process suffers from a 'democratic deficit'. The Constitutional Treaty aims at rendering EU decision-making more efficient and legitimate, and at simplifying the treaties, but its ratification process could prove difficult.
- The functions of the Commission are: to present legislative proposals; to implement decisions; to exercise certain autonomous powers in areas such as competition policy and trade negotiations; to prepare the annual preliminary draft budget for the Community; to act as Guardian (or 'Watchdog') of the treaties; to make recommendations or opinions on matters related to the treaties, and to present White and Green papers on specific policy areas.
- The Council of Ministers is the principal decision-making institution of the European Union, though since the Maastricht Treaty it can be overridden in certain cases by a veto of the European Parliament.
- The composition of the Council varies according to the question considered.
- The Council of heads of state and of government is known as the European Council. The European Council plays an important role in providing overall political direction to the Union and in resolving problems that have proved intractable at a lower level.
- The Presidency of the Council of Ministers and the European Council rotates among the EU member states in six-month terms. The country holding the Presidency has the power to set the agenda and further policy objectives in which it has a particular interest.
- The Council of Ministers may take decisions by unanimity, simple majority or qualified majority voting. Successive treaties have increased the number of policy areas subject to QMV.
- The European Parliament is primarily a consultative body, and its legislative powers are relatively limited. Since 1979 a system of direct election every five years has been used.
- The functions of the Parliament are: to be consulted during the legislative process and to use the power of veto in certain circumstances; to adopt or reject the whole EU Budget; to exercise budgetary powers over non-compulsory expenditure; to grant assent to important agreements with third countries or international organizations; to exercise supervisory powers over the work of the Commission; to investigate alleged contraventions of Community law and to appoint an ombudsman, and to act as a forum for discussion.
- The Economic and Social Committee and the Committee of the Regions are consulted during the legislative process.
- The European Court of Justice is responsible for interpreting Community law and adjudicating on disputes arising from the interpretation of the treaties and the legislation based upon them.
- The expenditure of all the EU institutions is subject to control by the Commission and European Parliament, and since 1977 to external control by the Court of Auditors.
- The decision-making procedure of the European Community may operate through the consultation procedure, the co-operation procedure or the co-decision procedure.
- The question of allowing flexibility or differentiated integration is rendered more urgent as the increasing membership of the EU is bringing growing diversity. Flexibility may take various forms: multi-speed Europe; a variable geometry EU, or Europe *à la carte*; a Europe of concentric circles, or an EU with a core or 'pioneer' group of countries.

Questions for Study and Review

■ Describe the organization and functioning of the European Commission. What are the main criticisms levelled against the Commission?

■ Why was it necessary to reform the system of voting in the Council of Ministers? What system of voting do you consider appropriate for the EU?

■ Why does the system of Presidency of the Council of Ministers need to change, and what reforms would you consider most effective?

■ Describe the European Parliament and indicate its main functions. What reforms are necessary to increase the democratic accountability of the European Parliament?

■ How would you resolve the problem of languages in the European Union?

■ Describe and criticize the reforms agreed at the Nice Summit and the proposals of the Constitutional Treaty.

■ What are the dilemmas posed by flexibility or differentiated integration?

■ How do you envisage the future architecture of Europe?

References

Bainbridge, T. (1998) *The Penguin Companion to European Union,* 2nd edn, Penguin Books, London.

Baldwin, R., Berglof, E., Giavazzi, F. and Widgren, M. (2001) *EU Reforms for Tomorrow's Europe*, CEPR, London.

Baldwin, R. and Wyplosz, C. (2004) *The Economics of European Integration*, McGraw-Hill Education, Maidenhead, UK.

Best, E. (2001) 'The Treaty of Nice: Not beautiful but it will do', *Eipascope*, No. 1.

Borchardt, K.-D. (1999) *The ABC of Community Law*, www.europa.eu.int/euro-lex

Conference of the Representatives of the Governments of the Member States, IGC (2004) Provisional consolidated version of the 'Draft Treaty establishing a Constitution for Europe, CIG 86/04', 25 June 2004, available on the website of the European Commission, www.europa.eu.int/comm

De Witte (2002) 'Anticipating the institutional consequences of expanded membership of the European Union', *International Political Science Review*, Vol. 23, No. 3, pp. 235–48.

Dinan, D. (1994) *Ever Closer Union. An Introduction to European Integration,* 2nd edn, Palgrave, Basingstoke, UK and New York.

Edwards, G. and Spence, D. (eds) (1995) *The European Commission*, Longman, Harlow.

Ehlermann, C-D. (1995) 'Increased differentiation or stronger uniformity', Robert Schuman Centre Working Paper no. 95/21, European University Institute, Florence.

Hix, S. (1999) *The Political System of the European Union,* Palgrave, London.

Hughes, K. (1996) 'Eastward enlargement of the EU: EU strategy and future challenges', RIIA European Programme Working Paper no. 2. Royal Institute for International Affairs, London.

Jones, R.A. (2001), *The Politics and Economics of the European Union. An Introductory Text,* 2nd edn, Edward Elgar, Cheltenham, UK.

Kandogan, Y. (2000) 'Political economy of eastern enlargement of the European Union: Budgetary costs and reforms in voting rules', *European Journal of Political Economy*, Vol. 16.

Laruelle, A. and Widgren, M. (1998) 'Is the allocation of voting power among the EU member states fair?', *Public Choice*, Vol. 94.

McCormick, J. (2002) *Understanding the European Union*, 2nd edn, Palgrave, Basingstoke, UK and New York.

Nugent, N. (1999) *The Government and Politics of the European Union*, 4th edn, Palgrave, Basingstoke, UK and New York.

Peterson, J. and Shackleton, M. (2002) *The Institutions of the European Union*, Oxford University Press, Oxford.

Schmitter, Philippe C. (2000) *How to Democratize the European Union – and Why Bother?* Rowman & Littlefield, Lanham, MD.

Senior Nello, S.M. and Smith, K.E. (1998) *The Consequences of Eastern Enlargement of the European Union in Stages,* Ashgate Publishers, Aldershot, UK.

Wallace, H. and Wallace, W. (2000) *Policy-Making in the European Union*, Oxford University Press, Oxford and New York.

Westlake, M. (1994) *The Commission and the Parliament: Rivals in the European Policy-Making Process,* Butterworths, London.

Westlake, M. (2001) *The Council of the European Union,* John Harper Publishers, London.

Useful websites

See the European Union website for a description of the various institutions:
www.europa.eu.int
The Centre for Economic Policy Research has carried out extensive research on EU institutions and voting rules:
www.cepr.org
Committee of the Regions:
www.cor.eu.int
Economic and Social Committee:
www.esc.eu.int
The European Commission:
www.europa.eu.int/comm
The European Council:
http://ue.eu.int/council
European Court of Auditors:
www.eca.eu.int
European Court of Justice:
http://curia.eu.int
The European Parliament and, in particular its factsheets provide information on institutions and decision-making procedures:
www.europarl.eu.int
Information is also available from the Swedish Parliament at:
www.riksdagen.se/english/eu/eufacts/index.asp

List of abbreviations

CAP	Common Agricultural Policy
CCP	Common Commercial Policy
CFSP	Common Foreign and Security Policy
Coreper	Committee of Permanent Representatives
ECB	European Central Bank
Ecofin	Council of Economic and Finance Ministers
Ecosoc	Economic and Social Committee
EDF	European Development Fund
EJ	European Court of Justice

EMI	European Monetary Institute
EMU	economic and monetary union
EP	European Parliament
ESC	Economic and Social Committee
ESCB	European System of Central Banks
FEOGA	European Agricultural Guidance and Guarantee Fund
IGC	Intergovernmental Conference
JHA	Justice and Home Affairs
OLAF	European Anti-Fraud Office
MEP	Member of the European Parliament
QMV	Qualified majority vote
SEA	Single European Act
WTO	World Trade Organization

4

Basic Instruments: The Theory of Trade and the EU

LEARNING OBJECTIVES

By the end of this chapter you should be able to understand:

▶ The main arguments in favour of free trade;

▶ The effect of introducing a tariff in a small nation;

▶ The effect of introducing a tariff in a large nation;

▶ The impact of introduction of a tariff on the partner country;

▶ What are the most frequently used barriers to trade, and how they are applied in the EU;

▶ The main arguments given in favour of protection;

▶ What we mean by the political economy of protectionism.

INTRODUCTION

The aim of this chapter is to introduce the different concepts used in the theory of trade, which will be used in the following chapter to explain integration. Integration is generally advocated for motives that are a mixture of politics and economics, and can perhaps be summarized as the desire to spread 'peace and prosperity' though other aims have also always played a role. The idea of using integration to avoid further wars in Europe ('peace') emerged clearly in the process of constructing the European Community in the years after the Second World War (see Chapter 2). Prosperity is generally associated with the benefits to be obtained by removing barriers to trade, and by permitting freedom of movement of goods, services, labour and capital.

In order to explain how integration is expected to lead to prosperity, it is first necessary to indicate the main arguments in favour of free trade. Then follows a description of the most commonly used obstacles to trade and an explanation of the reasons for their introduction. Those who are already familiar with international economics can skip this chapter and move straight to the analysis of integration in Chapter 5.

THE MAIN ARGUMENTS IN FAVOUR OF FREE TRADE

Many of our arguments in favour of free trade still owe much to the work of the classical economists Adam Smith and David Ricardo.[1] These writers illustrated that trade between two countries could be mutually beneficial (a 'win-win' game, to use more recent terminology) thanks to the specialization of production. The possible conflict between free trade and other policy objectives such as the environment or labour standards is discussed in Chapter 17.

ABSOLUTE ADVANTAGE

Adam Smith illustrated the principle of absolute advantage, arguing that 'what is prudent in the conduct of every private family can scarce be folly in that of a great kingdom. A family will not make at home what it costs less to buy from outside. A taylor [sic] will not make his own shoes, but will buy them from a shoemaker.'

With two nations, if one country is more efficient in the production of one good, and less efficient in the production of the other, then each country should specialize in the production of the good where it has an absolute advantage. Part of the output of that country can be exchanged for the good for which it has an absolute disadvantage. In this way resources will be used in the most efficient way possible. For instance, according to this principle, in trade between the two countries Ecuador should specialize in the export of bananas and Argentina in that of beef.

COMPARATIVE ADVANTAGE

In practice Smith's concept of absolute advantage explains only a small share of international trade. From this point of view, the concept of comparative advantage developed by David Ricardo is much more useful. According to the principle of comparative advantage, even when one country is less efficient in the production of both goods there is a basis for mutually beneficial trade. An example frequently given in the textbooks is that of Justice Holmes of the US Supreme Court. Justice Holmes was, apparently, a very speedy typist, and could type twice as fast as his secretary. She could earn $10 an hour with the amount she typed, but he could earn $20. However, he would receive $100 an hour from his legal activity, so it was in his interest to concentrate on that. With every hour he spent typing he would earn $20 but would forgo $100, so the net loss would be $80.

According to the principle of comparative advantage, even if one country has an absolute disadvantage in the production of both goods, it should specialize in the production and export of

---

[1] Smith's *Wealth of Nations* was published in 1776, while Ricardo's *Principles of Political Economy and Taxation* was published in 1817.

the good where its absolute disadvantage is smaller and import the product where its absolute disadvantage is greater. The country with an absolute advantage in the production in both goods should specialize in the production and export of the product where its absolute advantage is greater, and import the good for which its absolute advantage is smaller. Thus, for example, if the USA has an absolute advantage in the production of grain and clothing compared with the EU, but its absolute advantage is greater for grain, it should specialize in grain production, and export grain in exchange for clothing.

Comparative advantage still remains an important element of the toolkit in explaining the advantages of free trade, so it useful to provide an example of how this principle works in practice. Ricardo based his approach on the labour theory of value, by which the price of a product is said to depend exclusively on the amount of labour used in its production. This theory requires:

■ either that labour is the only factor used in making products, or that the ratio between labour and other factors such as land or capital is constant; and

■ that labour is homogeneous and there are no differences in skills between people.

Clearly, these are extremely restrictive assumptions, and have been eliminated in most later evolutions of the theory.[2]

To illustrate the principle of comparative advantage it is useful to take a simple example with only two partners involved in trade, the EU and the USA, and two products, wheat and wine. It is assumed that with one hour of work the USA can produce 6 units (tonnes) of wheat, or 4 units (litres) of wine. With one hour of work an EU labourer can produce 1 unit of wheat or 2 units of wine (quality differences are ignored in this highly simplified model). The USA has an absolute advantage in the production of both goods, but its advantage is greater in the production of wheat. Similarly, the EU has a disadvantage in the production of both goods, but the disadvantage is less in the production of wine (see Table 4.1).

	USA	EU
Wheat (tonnes produced in a man-hour)	6	1
Wine (litres produced in a man-hour)	4	2

Table 4.1 Comparative advantage

In the USA, 6 units of wheat can be exchanged for 4 units of wine. If in international trade more than 4 units of wine can be obtained for 6 units of wheat, it is to the advantage of the USA. In the EU 2 units of wine can be exchanged for 1 unit of wheat. If more wheat could be obtained, it would be to the advantage of the EU.

Assume that with the opening of trade between the EU and USA it is possible to exchange 6 units of wine for 6 units of wheat. The EU will gain, because before the opening of trade 12 units of wine had to be given for 6 units of wheat and now only 6, so there is a saving of three man-hours. The USA will also gain, as before 6 units of wheat could only be exchanged for 4 units of wine, and now it can obtain 6 units of wine, so there is a saving of 2 units of wine (30 minutes of labour).[3] If the EU is less efficient than the USA in the production of both goods, how can it export to the USA? The answer is that wages are lower in the EU, so that when the prices of the two products are expressed in the same currency, wine will be cheaper in the EU, and grain will cost less in the USA.

If the wage in the USA is $6 an hour, 1 unit of grain will cost $1 and 1 unit of wine will cost

[2] See, for example, Salvatore (2001) for a discussion of this point.
[3] The only exception is the unlikely case in which the absolute disadvantage that one country has with respect to the other is the same for the two products. This would occur in the above example if the EU could produce 3 units of grain with one man-hour.

$1.50. If the wage in the EU is €2 per hour, then the price of a litre of wine is €1, and that of a tonne of grain is €2. With an exchange rate of $1 = 1 euro, then the prices in the EU will be $1 for a unit of wine, and $2 for a unit of grain. Traders will have an incentive to buy wine in the EU and trade it for grain in the USA. With an exchange rate of $0.5 per euro, then the EU price would be $1 for grain and $0.5 for wine. There would be very strong pressure to sell EU wine in the USA, but no incentive to sell US grain in the EU. The value of the dollar against the euro would have to fall.

With an exchange rate of $2 = €1, then the EU price would be $4 for grain, and $2 for wine. There would be very strong pressure to buy grain in the USA, but it would be impossible to sell EU wine to the USA, and so the euro rate against the dollar would have to fall.

THE HECKSCHER-OHLIN THEOREM

Classical economists such as Ricardo explain the advantages of international trade on the basis of specialization according to comparative advantage, but fail to analyse in any detail what determines the comparative advantage of a country. Later developments in trade theory, and in particular, the Heckscher–Ohlin theorem, try to explain the pattern of comparative advantage between countries. In other words, why does a country have a comparative advantage in the production of a particular good? According to this approach, trade can be explained by the pattern of endowment of countries with different factors of production.

For purposes of simplification, in textbooks the Heckscher–Ohlin theorem is usually presented using a highly simplified case of two countries, two products (x and y) and two factors (labour and capital). A country is said to have an abundance of a certain factor if the ratio of the total amount of one factor, say labour to capital, is higher than in the other country, and if the cost of labour relative to capital is less than in the other country.[4] If the production of one of the goods, say x, requires more labour relative to capital than the other good, then product x is said to be labour-intensive. According to the Heckscher–Ohlin theorem, a country will export the commodity whose production is intensive of the factor in which the country is relatively abundant.

For example, if China has an abundance of cheap labour, and the production of clothing is labour-intensive, China will tend to export clothing. In contrast, if the USA has a factor abundance of capital (or skilled labour), and computers are intensive of capital (or skilled labour), China will specialize in textiles and import computers, while the USA will specialize in computers and import textiles.

This explanation works rather well in accounting for trade between countries with different endowments of factors of production such as land, labour or capital. For example, it may explain certain trade flows between developing and industrialized countries. However, it works less well for trade between similar countries, such as most of those of Western Europe.

Figure 4.1 can be used to illustrate the Heckscher–Ohlin theorem. The highly simplified model is based on two countries, 1 and 2, and two products, X and Y, and two factors of production, labour (L) and capital (C). Country 1 is assumed abundant in labour, while country 2 has an abundance of capital. Product X is assumed intensive of labour, while product Y is intensive of capital. In Figure 4.1 quantities of product X are indicated on the horizontal axis, and quantities of product Y are indicated on the vertical axis.

The model is based on various simplifying assumptions.[5] The two countries are assumed to have the same technology and to be operating under conditions of perfect competition. They are also

---

[4] In case of conflict between the two criteria, the second is decisive.
[5] See Salvatore (2001) for a discussion of these assumptions and what happens when they are relaxed.

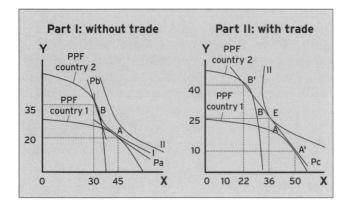

Figure 4.1 The Heckscher-Ohlin Theorem

Source: From *International Economics* by Dominick Salvatore, Copyright © 2001, John Wiley & Sons, Inc. This material is used by permission of John Wiley & Sons, Inc.

assumed to produce some of both goods X and Y, and production of both goods takes place with constant returns to scale. This implies that if the amount of inputs is increased in the production of a good, the amount of the good produced will increase by a proportional amount. The preferences of consumers are assumed to be identical in the two countries. All resources are used in each country (i.e. there is no unemployment in the factors of production). It is assumed that there is perfect mobility of factors of production within a country, but no mobility between countries. There are no transport costs or barriers to trade, such as tariffs. The exports and imports between the two countries are assumed to balance.

The production possibility frontier (PPF) shows the alternative combinations of the two products that a country can produce by fully utilizing its resources and making use of the best technology available. Each country must be on the production possibility curve to be in equilibrium, since points below the curve are inefficient, while points above cannot be reached. The slope of the production possibility curve in absolute terms indicates the opportunity cost of X, or the amount of Y which has to be given up to release enough resources to produce one additional unit of X. Under conditions of perfect competition each country will produce a combination of the two goods such that opportunity cost is equal to the ratio between prices of X and Y (Px/Py).

As shown in the diagram, the production possibility frontier for country 1 is flatter and wider than that of country 2. This is because country 1 has an abundance of labour, and product X is intensive of labour, so country 1 can produce a greater quantity of X than country 2.

The curves I and II are community indifference curves which show the various combinations of the two products that yield the same level of satisfaction or utility to a country.[6] Higher indifference curves indicate higher levels of satisfaction. For simplicity, in the example here, preferences of consumers in the two countries are assumed identical so the same collective indifference curves can be used for each.

The marginal rate of substitution (MRS) is the amount of good Y that the country has to give up in order to consume an additional unit of X while remaining on the same indifference curve. The MRS is given by the slope of an indifference curve in absolute terms at the point of consumption of the two goods. Moving down along the indifference curves shown in Figure 4.1, the MRS will decrease because of diminishing marginal utility. This implies that after a certain point increasing quantities of a good consumed yield smaller and smaller increases in utility.

In the absence of trade the equilibrium of each country is at the point where its production possibility curve is tangent to the highest collective indifference curve possible. This occurs at A

---

[6] A discussion of the well-known problems with collective indifference curves is beyond the scope of the analysis here.

for country 1 and B for country 2. Country 1 will produce and consume 45 X and 20 Y, while country 2 will produce and consume 30 X and 35 Y. The tangent of the PPF and highest indifference curve at point A indicate the relative price −Px/Py of the two goods, or Pa, in country 1. Similarly the relative price of the two goods in country 2 is Pb. In country 1 the relative price of X is lower (Pa is less than Pb in absolute terms) than in country 2 and Country 1 has a comparative advantage in the production of X, while country 2 has a comparative advantage in the production of Y.

With trade (see Part II of Figure 4.1) it will be to the benefit of country 1 to export good X to country 2 in exchange for good Y. Country 1 will therefore specialize in the production of X, moving along down its production possibility curve to the right. As it does so, the increasing slope of the production possibility curve implies that the opportunity cost of X will rise, and the price of X relative to Y will increase.

Without trade the price of Y relative to X in country 2 is lower than in country 1. With trade country 2 has an advantage in specializing in the production of Y moving up along its production curve and selling Y to country 1 in exchange for X. In this case the price of X relative to Y will fall (or, in other words, the price of Y relative to X will rise) in country 2.

This process of specialization will continue until the relative price Px/Py is the same in both countries. This occurs when production of the two goods reaches A′ in country 1 and B′ in country 2. At this point country 1 produces 50 X and 10 Y. Country 2 produces 22 X and 40Y. At the relative price Pc country 1 will export 14 X in exchange for 15 Y from country 2. In this way both countries reach equilibrium at E in Part II of the diagram, where they consume 36 X and 25Y. Both countries benefit from trade since they can reach the higher indifference curve II.

INTRA-INDUSTRY TRADE AND PRODUCT DIFFERENTIATION

A large percentage (70–80 per cent in many cases) of trade between EU countries consists of exports and imports of the same product or group of products. For instance Italy exports Fiat, and imports BMW from Germany and Renault from France. This is known as **intra-industry trade** and arises when products are substitutes for each other but are slightly different (see Box 4.1). This kind of **product differentiation** means that a firm or plant can specialize in a few varieties of the product, making use of longer production runs, more specialized machinery and labour, and so on. Other varieties of the product can be imported. As a result consumers may have a wider range of products available at lower prices. The products are differentiated but similar and therefore substitutes.[7]

> ### Box 4.1 The Grubel-Lloyd index
> One of the most widely used measures of intra-industry trade is the Grubel-Lloyd index:
>
> $$T = 1 - \frac{[Xi - Mi]}{(Xi + Mi)}$$
>
> where X and M represent respectively the exports and imports of a particular commodity group i. The straight-line parenthesis indicates value in absolute terms. T may take values between 0 and 1. If T is zero there is no intra-industry trade, and the countries are

---

[7] Models of monopolistic competition are frequently used to analyse this type of market.

specialized in different product categories indicating inter-industry trade. If T is 1 all trade is intra-industry, and the countries are specialized in the same product categories.

The index is frequently calculated using the SITC or Standard International Trade Classification. This breaks trade down by product category, and the number of digits indicates the level of disaggregation (OO, OO1, OO15 etc.). One of the difficulties in using the Grubel-Lloyd index is that the results may reflect the level of disaggregation of the statistics used.

A further shortcoming of the index is that products within the same classification group may be very different in terms of quality. Distinction is therefore sometimes made between vertical intra-industry trade (reflecting quality differences) and horizontal intra-industry trade in products of similar quality.

STATIC ECONOMIES OF SCALE

Product differentiation and intra-industry trade allow a firm to exploit static and dynamic economies of scale. Static economies of scale occur when an increase in the use of inputs results in a more than proportional increase in output. In other words, the unit costs of production fall as the scale of production rises. This may arise, for example, from the use of more specialized machinery, or from the division of labour with workers specializing in the tasks they perform. A classic example is the assembly-line production introduced by Henry Ford.

Static economies of scale occur when an increase in the use of inputs results in a more than proportional increase in output. In other words, the unit costs of production fall as the scale of production rises. Figure 4.2 can be used to illustrate how mutually beneficial trade between countries can arise from economies of scale.[8] The same highly simplified model is based on two countries, 1 and 2, and two products, X and Y, and two factors of production are used. In Figure 4.2 quantities of product X are indicated on the horizontal axis, and quantities of product Y are indicated on the vertical axis. The two countries are assumed to be identical in all respects so the same production possibility frontier B'B in Figure 4.2 can be used for both of them. In the case of

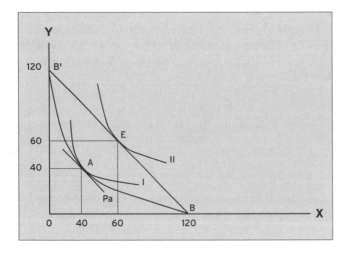

Figure 4.2 Static economies of scale

Source: From *International Economics* by Dominick Salvatore, Copyright © 2001, John Wiley & Sons, Inc. This material is used by permission of John Wiley & Sons, Inc.

---

[8] The analysis here is based on Salvatore (2001).

economies of scale, the production possibility curve is convex to the origin. The two countries are assumed identical, so the same indifference curves can be used for both.

The equilibrium position before trade, A, will therefore be identical for both countries. At A each country is at the point where the production possibility curve is tangent to the highest collective indifference curve possible. At A both countries can produce and consume 40 units of X and 40 units of Y. The equilibrium point before trade A is not stable since if for any reason one of the countries, say country 1, increased its production of X, the price of X relative to Y would fall, and the country would move along its production curve until it became fully specialized in the production of X (i.e. producing only X and no Y) at point B. In the same way, if for some reason country 2 increased its production of Y, it would continue moving up and left along its production possibility frontier until it became fully specialized in the production of Y at B'. As the two countries are assumed identical, it is purely a matter of accident which country specializes in the production of which good.

At the equilibrium point B, country 1 produces 120 units of X, while at B' country 2 produces 120 units of Y. With trade country 1 could exchange 60 units of X for 60 units of Y and move to the new equilibrium point E that is on the higher collective indifference curve II. Similarly country 2 could sell 60 Y for 60 X and also move to E. As a result of specialization based on economies of scale and trade, both countries gain 20 X and 20 Y compared to the equilibrium point A. This is a highly simplified model, and in practice the two countries do not have to be identical to draw mutual benefit from trade based on economies of scale.

DYNAMIC ECONOMIES OF SCALE

Dynamic economies of scale are associated with the learning process. This process entails that a firm will have a unit cost advantage because of the experience it acquires through cumulative production of goods and services. The fall in cost may be due to technological improvements, better organizational structures and/or performance of workers. For example, the experience gained by McDonald's in producing hamburgers (how many billion sold?) enables it to compete against new firms attempting to enter the market and facing much higher initial costs. Economic policy could therefore aim at ensuring that markets are on an adequate scale to allow such learning effects to be exploited.

The learning process refers to the unit cost advantage that accrues to a firm because of the experience it acquires through cumulative production of goods and services. The fall in cost may be due to technological improvements, better organizational structures and/or performance of workers. The firm that first moves down the 'learning' curve of a strategic industry will gain a cost advantage over its competitors. Economic policy should therefore ensure that markets are on an adequate scale to allow such learning effects to be exploited. The existence of these experience economies may render it difficult for new entrants to enter the market. According to strategic trade theory (see below), there may be a case for subsidizing or protecting strategic industries to help domestic firms move down the learning curve first.

Figure 4.3 illustrates a learning or experience curve, which can be expressed by the formula:[9]

$$Cn = an^{-b}$$

where Cn is the cost of the nth unit produced, a is the cost of the first unit, and b is the learning rate.

---

[9] This example is taken from Healey (1995).

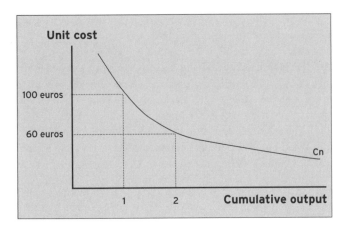

Figure 4.3 Dynamic economies of scale

Source: Figure 1.7 (p. 37) from *The Economics of the New Europe* (1995) by Healey, N.M. By permission of Taylor & Francis incorporating Routledge.

TARIFFS

In most economic textbooks the discussion of the theory of trade policies begins with an analysis of tariffs.[10] This is because at least up until the First World War it was widely accepted that if trade barriers were introduced for protectionist purposes they should be confined to tariffs. In the GATT/WTO context tariffs are considered the 'lesser evil' compared with other trade barriers because they are more transparent.[11] The GATT/WTO favours the conversion of other non-tariff barriers into tariffs.

An import tariff is a tax or duty levied on a product when it is imported into a country. Tariffs can be *ad valorem*, specific or compound. An *ad valorem* tariff entails a percentage increase in the price of the imported product. If, for example, p is the price of the good before the tariff, when a tariff rate t is applied the price will become (1 + t)p. A 10 per cent tariff on a bicycle worth 100 euros would increase the price of the bicycle in the importing country to €110. *Ad valorem* tariffs are the type most frequently used by the EU. A specific tariff is a fixed lump sum levied on an import. For instance, a specific tariff of €5 would increase the price of the bicycle to €105. The USA uses both *ad valorem* and specific tariffs. A compound tariff combines an *ad valorem* and a specific tariff.

> ### Box 4.2 Tariff levels
>
> As explained in Chapter 2, the Treaty of Rome envisaged the elimination of tariffs on trade between member states, and the EU met this objective six months ahead of schedule in 1968. The EU continues to apply tariffs (the common external tariff) on trade with third countries, but over time the level of these tariffs has shrunk as a consequence of the various GATT rounds.
>
> Though difficult to measure in practice, the average level of world tariffs fell from roughly 40 per cent in 1948 to about 3 per cent by the early 2000s. Problems arise in calculating average tariff rates for a number of reasons: actual tariffs are often lower than the rates 'bound' by GATT agreements; in order to calculate averages, account has to be taken of weights of the good in trade; in practice there are likely to be exceptions to non-discrimination (i.e. to most favoured nation treatment; see Chapter 17); if tariffs are too high they are prohibitive and no trade will take place, and tariffs change over time.

---

[10] See Chapter 10 for an analysis of the economic effects of other policies such as production subsidies, quotas on production and export subsidies.
[11] See Chapter 17 for a discussion of the GATT/WTO.

With a 10 per cent *ad valorem* tariff, and a specific tariff of €5, the price of the imported bicycle would rise to 115 euros.

THE ECONOMIC EFFECTS OF INTRODUCING A TARIFF IN A 'SMALL NATION'

In order to analyse the economic effects of a tariff on imports, it is useful to make certain simplifying assumptions. The analysis here is partial equilibrium in that it only considers the market of the good on which the tariff is levied, ignoring the implications for other economic sectors or for factor markets. It is assumed that there are no stocks of the product, and transport costs or possible externalities are not taken into account.

For simplicity, the discussion here relates to an *ad valorem* tariff so, if p is the price of the good before the tariff, when a tariff rate t is applied, the price will become (1 + t)p. Initially it is assumed that the country is a 'small nation', so that any changes in its supply or demand for that product will have no impact on the international terms of trade or world price level for that product.

The demand and supply curves (assumed linear for simplicity) of a country for the traded good in question are shown in Figure 4.4. Prior to the introduction of the tariff, the domestic price of the product in the country is assumed equal to the world price Pw. At this price the country will produce Qs and demand Qd of the product. The country will therefore import Qd – Qs (equivalent to the excess demand) of the product.

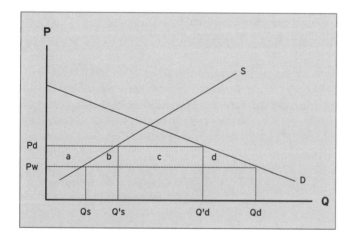

Figure 4.4 A tariff in a small nation

With the introduction of the tariff t the domestic price for the product will rise to (1 + t)Pw, or Pd in the diagram. Assuming a small nation, the world price will remain unchanged at Pw. The new higher internal price will be Pd. The introduction of the tariff will entail the following effects on demand, supply and foreign trade:

- The quantity demanded will decline from Qd to Q'd.
- The quantity supplied will increase from Qs to Q's.
- The quantity imported will fall from (Qd - Qs) to (Q'd - Q's).

The tariff will also have the following 'financial' effects:

- Consumer expenditure on the product will change from QdPw before introduction of the tariff to Q'dPd with the tariff.

■ Producer revenue will increase from QsPw before the tariff to Q'sPd after the tariff is introduced.

■ The trade balance (or, in this case, the amount spent on imports) will improve from (Qs – Qd)Pw to (Q's – Q'd)Pw.

Introduction of the tariff will redistribute welfare between the three main groups in society: taxpayers, consumers and producers. In order to assess these effects, it is first necessary to introduce two concepts: consumer and producer surplus.

Consumer rent or **surplus** is defined as the difference between the price a consumer is prepared to pay for a certain quantity of a product and the price that is effectively paid for that quantity. This concept may be applied to an individual consumer or to the overall demand curve in a particular market. As shown in Figure 4.5, with a demand curve D and price OA, consumer surplus is indicated by the triangle ABC.

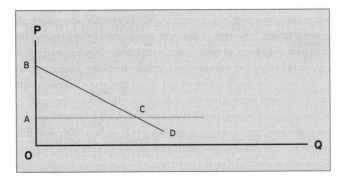

Figure 4.5 Consumer surplus

Producer rent is the difference between the total revenue and total cost of the producer and can be considered as the profits of the producer. Ignoring fixed costs, the total cost of producing a certain quantity is given by the area under the marginal cost curve (which coincides with the supply curve). As mentioned above, producer revenue is given by the price received by the producer multiplied by the quantity produced. In Figure 4.6, with a supply curve S, and price OF, producer revenue is equal to OFGQ and total cost is OHGQ, so that producer rent is indicated by the triangle HFG.

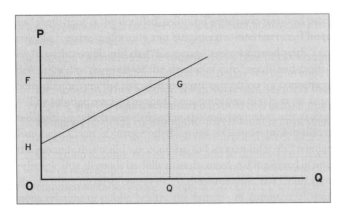

Figure 4.6 Producer surplus

The introduction of the tariff will alter consumer and producer surplus and the income of taxpayers. The tariff entails an increase in the price received by producers so, as Figure 4.4 above shows, there is an increase in producer surplus equivalent to area a. The consumers also have to pay a higher price for the product, so there will be a reduction in consumer surplus equivalent to area a + b + c + d. There is an increase in government revenue of area c.

The tariff is a source of revenue for the government budget.[12] The total revenue for the budget will be equal to the unit value of the tariff (Pd – Pw) multiplied by the quantity imported after introduction of the tariff (Q′d – Q′s). In the diagram this corresponds to the area of the rectangle c, or (Pd – Pw) × (Q′d – Q′s). If this revenue is used in a socially useful way, it represents a welfare benefit to the country. This benefit could be considered an increase in the income of taxpayers in that, *ceteris paribus*, in the absence of the tariff the government would have to impose higher taxes to obtain the same amount of revenue. It is, however, possible that the revenue from the tariff is not used in a socially useful way. For instance, a share of the revenue may be used to cover the administrative costs of levying the duty, and government funds spent in this way represent a net welfare loss to the community.

In order to calculate the overall net welfare effect of the tariff, it is necessary to assume that value of each euro lost by any individual is the same as that of any euro gained, regardless of who undergoes the loss or gain. With this assumption it can be seen that only part of the loss in consumer surplus is compensated by the gain in producer rent and the increase in government revenue. The net welfare cost of the tariff is indicated by the two triangles b and d.

Triangle b represents the net economic cost on the production side. It reflects the worsening in the allocation of resources as a result of introduction of the tariff. Triangle d represents the net welfare cost on the consumption side, because the tariff raises the price of the good relative to other products, causing a distortion in consumption. A numerical example of the effects of introducing a tariff in a small nation is included in Appendix 1.

THE EFFECT OF INTRODUCING A TARIFF IN A 'LARGE NATION'

In Figure 4.4 it was assumed that introducing a tariff would leave the world price for the product unchanged. However, it is possible that the introduction of a tariff will lower the world price for a product. The tariff raises the domestic price for that product, increasing production and reducing consumption. The country will therefore import less after the tariff is introduced, reducing the demand for that product on world markets. The *ceteris paribus* clause implies that supply on world markets remains unchanged. If that country accounts for a large share of world trade, the reduction in net imports for the product, with supply on world markets unchanged, will reduce the price on world markets. The assumption that the country is a 'large nation' implies that the introduction (or removal) of a policy such as a tariff will affect the price for that product on world markets or, in other words, that country's terms of trade.

If, as in the case being considered here, the country is a net importer, the reduction in world price will constitute a net welfare gain for that country. In other words there will be a transfer from exporters in the rest of the world to that country. This situation is shown in Figure 4.7. In the diagram, the introduction of a tariff leads to a reduction in the world price level to P′w. As a result, the internal price after introduction of the tariff will be P′d, or (1 + t)P′w, which is less than (1 + t)Pw.

In this case the reduction in consumer surplus is indicated by area f + g + h + k; the increase in producer rent is area f. The increase in government revenue is area h, which represents a transfer from internal consumers (because of the higher domestic price now paid) and area m, which

[12] See the discussion on the sources of revenue of the EU Budget in Chapter 9.

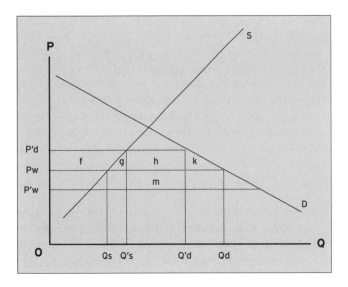

Figure 4.7 The introduction of a tariff in a large nation

consists of a transfer from producers in the rest of the world (because of the lower world price which they now receive).

The net welfare effect for the country introducing the tariff now consists of: the net welfare cost on the consumption side, triangle k; the net welfare cost on the production side, triangle g, and a net welfare gain, rectangle m, which represents transfers from the rest of the world.

It is possible that the net welfare gain represented by rectangle m outweighs the net welfare loss represented by the two triangles g and k. In this case the introduction of a tariff entails an increase in net welfare for the country. This has encouraged countries to seek the so-called optimal tariff, which leads to the maximum increase in net welfare possible for the country imposing a tariff (see below). A numerical example of the effects of introducing a tariff in a large nation is included in Appendix 1.

THE EFFECTS OF INTRODUCING A TARIFF ON THE EXPORTING COUNTRY

It is useful to show the effects of introducing a tariff by the home country on an exporting country.[13] For simplicity it is assumed that there is only one foreign country (called 'foreign'). The two countries are assumed to be small nations and have increasing production costs.[14] Figure 4.8a illustrates the demand and supply curves in the home country, and Figure 4.8b illustrates MDh, or the home income demand for X. At price P' home supply equals home demand and there is no import demand for X. At price P'' home demand exceeds home supply of X by HJ, and this is equal to import demand OM.

Figure 4.9a illustrates the supply and demand curves for X of the foreign country that are used to derive the export supply of X by the foreign country XSf in part (b) of the figure. At price P' demand and supply are in equilibrium on the foreign market, and foreign export supply is zero. At price P'' foreign supply exceeds foreign demand by amount FG of product X, and foreign export supply OH is equal to FG. In the simple two-country model, foreign export supply XSf is equal to home import supply, so can be labelled MSh.

---

[13] The discussion here follows Baldwin and Wyplosz (2004).
[14] The analysis is extended to the case of a large nation in Chapter 5.

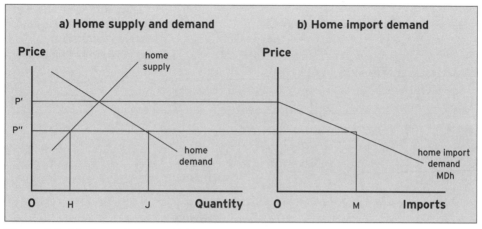

Figure 4.8 The import demand of the home country

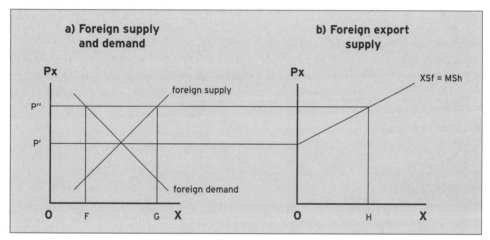

Figure 4.9 The import supply of the home country, or the export supply of the foreign country

The left part of Figure 4.10 shows the export supply of X by the foreign country, while the right part of Figure 4.10 combines the import demand and import supply for X in the home country and shows the effect of the tariff T on home imports and foreign exports. The tariff raises the price faced by home consumers and producers from Pft to P′. The border price or the price received by foreigners falls to P′ – T. The volume of imports falls from Mft (or Xft exports) to M' (which is equal to X').

The welfare loss from the tariff to the foreign country is rectangle b (because of the lower price received) and triangle c (because of loss of sales). The home country receives a welfare gain from tariff revenue equal to the unit value of the tariff (t) times the volume of imports M', indicated by rectangles m and n. The loss in private surplus (i.e. the sum of changes in consumer and producer surplus) is equal to areas f and m. The overall impact on welfare for the home country is therefore area n minus area f. In terms of the analysis in Figure 4.4 above, triangle f is equal to the sum of triangles b and d.

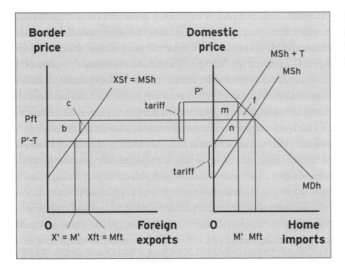

Figure 4.10 The effect of a tariff on the home and foreign countries
Source: Baldwin and Wyplosz (2004).

NON-TARIFF BARRIERS AND THE 'NEW PROTECTIONISM'

Despite the success of the GATT in reducing tariffs, from the 1970s international trade became increasingly subject to non-tariff barriers (NTBs), in what is referred to as the 'new protectionism'. In particular, the Uruguay Round attempted to extend the jurisdiction of GATT regulations to cover these NTBs. The following list includes some of the main non-tariff barriers, but does not pretend to be exhaustive:[15]

- quotas on imports;
- voluntary export restraint agreements (VERs);
- cartels;
- anti-dumping duties;
- export subsidies;
- differences in standards and technical specifications, and administrative measures;
- discrimination in public procurement.

A **quota on imports** is a quantitative restriction imposed by the state on imports of a particular product. The quota may entail a limit on all imports of a particular product (or group of products)

Box 4.3 EU Quotas

The EU applies seasonal quotas to the imports of some agricultural products and quotas on the imports of certain textiles and clothing under the Multifibre Agreement, though the latter have to be phased out by January 2005 in line with the Uruguay Round Agreement (see Chapter 17). Another exception permitted by GATT/WTO is on imports from non-market economies, so the Community applied quotas on the imports of certain goods (such as footwear, glass products, some agricultural goods and so on) from the former centrally planned countries of Central and Eastern Europe. These were eliminated as part of the trade concessions granted from 1989 on.[16]

---

[15] For reasons of space a formal analysis of these various measures based on the use of diagrams is not included here. For a study of this type see, for example, Salvatore (2001) or Krugman and Obstfeld (1997).
[16] See Senior Nello (1991) for a description of how these quotas operated, and their elimination.

or it may relate to imports of a product from a particular country or group of countries. In general, a system of import quotas is implemented through the granting of import licences. In principle the GATT forbids quotas on imports, but in practice various exceptions have been allowed (see Box 4.3).

Voluntary export restraint agreements (VERs) entail an export restriction which in formal terms was imposed unilaterally by the exporting country, but in practice was usually introduced in response to pressure from the government or industry in the importing country (see Box 4.4).[17] VERs were essentially bilaterally negotiated agreements. The export restraint involved could operate through quotas and/or minimum export prices. Although these arrangements appear to be an improvement on the autonomous setting of policy, it must be questioned how far they were in fact 'voluntary'. Often the exporter had to accept the demands made by the importing country, or risk the unilateral imposition of a tariff, quota or anti-dumping measures against its products. According to the GATT Uruguay Round Agreement, VERs were to be phased out by 1999.

VERs were probably less effective than quotas in limiting the quantity of imports, as exporters were generally reluctant to cut their market share. VERs also tended to lead to a continual upgrading of products since the limit on quantity encouraged exporters to supply products of higher quality and price. As the VER usually applies to the main supplier, at times there was a tendency to switch to other exporters, or even for the main supplier to redirect exports through other countries.

Box 4.4 VERs

VERs have been used by the EU and US to limit exports of steel, electronic products, automobiles and other products, in particular from Japan, Central and Eastern Europe and Korea. Following the 1973 oil crisis there was a sharp drop in the demand for steel, and the Community threatened its major suppliers with anti-dumping measures unless they signed VERs. The Community applied VERs on steel, textiles and some agricultural products from most of the smaller Central and Eastern European countries during the 1970s and 1980s.[18]

An international **cartel** is an agreement between suppliers in different countries to restrict production and exports in order to increase their prices and profits. The most famous example of a cartel is that of OPEC (Organization of Petroleum Exporting Countries) (see Box 4.5). The USA

Box 4.5 The OPEC

In February 2004 the OPEC (Organization of Petroleum Exporting Countries), probably the most famous example of an international cartel, decided to cut production by 10 per cent in order to keep prices up in the summer, when demand in its main markets falls steeply. The OPEC countries resolved to stop cheating on the overall production quota of 24.5 million barrels a day. The new quota in terms of millions of barrels was allocated among members as follows:

Saudi Arabia 7.9, Iran 3.6, Venezuela 2.82, UAE 2.14, Nigeria 2.02, Kuwait 1.97, Libya 1.31, Indonesia 1.27, Algeria 0.78, and Qatar 0.64.

Source: *Financial Times*, 11 February 2004.

---

[17] Orderly marketing arrangements (OMAs) are a sub-category of VERs involving government-to-government arrangements. VERS may also include agreements with the direct participation of industry.
[18] Senior Nello (1991).

prohibits cartels between national producers but, as explained in Chapter 15, in the EU they are simply heavily regulated.[19]

Dumping consists essentially in the practice of international price discrimination, when the price charged by an exporter to a foreign market is lower than the domestic price for that product. Distinction is frequently made between sporadic, predatory and persistent dumping.

As the name suggests, sporadic dumping occurs occasionally when, because of a change in the pattern of demand or an error in production plans, a firm finds itself with an unsold surplus. Rather than risking disruption of the domestic market, the firm will sell this surplus at a low price abroad. In this case below-cost sales may occur. Predatory dumping is aimed at eliminating competing firms from international markets. The firm will charge low prices in order to drive its competitor(s) out of the market. Even though this may entail setting prices below costs for a time, the firm will be able to raise prices again once the competitor has been eliminated. Persistent dumping is practised by a producer with monopoly power who attempts to use price discrimination between different markets in order to maximize profits. This price discrimination is only possible if the markets are separate, for instance as a result of incomplete information, transport costs, trade barriers and so on. In other words retrading between the individual markets is impossible.

If dumping is found to cause injury or threat of injury to domestic producers, the WTO regulations permit a country to impose an **anti-dumping duty** (see Box 4.6). A frequent complaint is that countries may use anti-dumping duties as an instrument of protectionism.

Box 4.6 EU Anti-dumping

EU anti-dumping legislation is a sphere where authority is very much in the hands of the Community rather than its member states. The legislation draws heavily on the GATT/WTO Articles relating to dumping. According to EC legislation, dumping is said to occur when the price of an export to the EC is lower than its 'normal value'. The Commission acting on its own initiative never opens EC anti-dumping procedures; it is always at the request of one or more producer who represents the 'Community industry'. If dumping is found to cause injury or threat of injury, and the 'interest of the Community' so requires, the EC Commission may impose an anti-dumping duty, though in most cases it simply insists on a price undertaking from the exporting country involved.

The total number of EU anti-dumping investigations opened was 25 in 1996, 47 in 1997, 29 in 1998 but rose to 86 in 1999, reflecting world-wide difficulties in the steel industry in the wake of the Russian and Asian crises. In 1999 25 investigations were in the iron and steel sector, a further 28 were in chemicals and allied products, and 12 were in electronics products. In 2000 only two new cases were opened, one against China and the other against Russia.

Export subsidies may involve giving direct payments, tax breaks or low interest loans to exporters, subsidised loans to foreign purchasers, and assistance in export promotion (through advertising, trade fairs, meetings and so on). Though export subsidies are subject to a general ban by the WTO, in practice there are many exceptions to this rule. These include the agricultural export subsidies for which the EU is highly criticized by its trading partners (see Chapter 10). The WTO permits the granting of credits to clients by exporting firms and government-backed guarantees for certain risks to foreign direct investment, though the OECD tries to ensure that

---

[19] Chapter 15 also contains a formal analysis of the effects of a cartel.

these are not used to promote domestic firms in an unfair way.[20] Countries sometimes use tax breaks to promote exports, but the WTO ruled against the system of Foreign Sales Corporations used by the USA (see the OLC website of this book).

Technical restrictions and standards and other administrative regulations may act as barriers to trade. These include safety regulations (for instance for electrical equipment), health regulations (in particular for food products) and labelling requirements. **Differences in standards and technical barriers** probably represent the main barrier in trade between developed countries. Firms also frequently complain about **customs formalities**, which may cause delays, additional costs, and even block trade. Differences in tax systems may also have to be offset at the border. The Single Market Project aimed at removing these barriers between EC member states (see Chapter 6), and there have been attempts to reduce their impact on trade with third countries (see Box 4.7).

Box 4.7 Standards, technical restrictions and other administrative regulations in EU-USA trade

A major objective of the Single Market Programme is to prevent differences in standards, technical restrictions and other administrative regulations from acting as barriers to intra-EU trade, but the problem also arises in trade between the EU and other countries such as the USA. Annual publications such as the *US Trade Review* or the European Commission's *Report on United States Barriers to Trade and Investment* describe many of these barriers.

For example, the 1999 EU Report[21] complains of excessive invoicing requirements on exports to the USA, with information requirements that far exceeded normal customs requirements and tariff procedures. User fees on harbour services etc. were also said to constitute a barrier to trade. A further complaint was against the US 'gas-guzzler' tax that was an excise duty of $1000–7700 on any car not meeting the fuel economy standards of the USA Environmental Protection Agency. EU cars with a total market share of 4 per cent in the US accounted for 85 per cent of payments of the gas-guzzler tax. The report also criticized the complexity of the US regulatory system, and the 'lack of a clear distinction between essential safety regulations and optional requirements for quality'. As described in Chapter 18, the US and EU authorities are discussing methods such as mutual recognition of standards to overcome these barriers.

Lack of transparency in **government procurement** may also act as a barrier to trade since local, regional and national authorities tend to buy from firms of their own country (see Chapter 6).

THE MAIN ARGUMENTS PRESENTED IN FAVOUR OF PROTECTION

Protectionism may be advocated for **non-economic reasons,** such as for defence, national pride or to further foreign policy objectives. For instance, the need to ensure sufficiency of supply in times of war has frequently been advanced to justify protection in sectors such as agriculture, ship-building, energy, steel production and so on. However, such explanations seem incomplete as an

---

[20] Export credit subsidies and foreign investment guarantees are generally granted by special government-backed agencies. In France for example there is the Banque Française pour le Commerce Extérieur, and in Britain, the Export Credit Guarantee Department. In certain other countries the loan is granted by commercial banks, but interest rate payments are subsidised by a transfer from the government to the bank.
[21] European Commission (1999).

account of the behaviour of Western industrialized countries and are difficult to apply to some of the sectors most affected by protectionism.

The **infant industry** case is probably the oldest and best-known argument advanced in favour of protection. When an industry is first set up it may need time to acquire experience or competence (in terms of managerial resources, networks of suppliers, financial capabilities etc.), or to reach a sufficient size to benefit from economies of scale. A new industry will therefore not be able to compete with a foreign industry that is already well established. According to this argument, the new industry should therefore be protected, for instance by a tariff, until it is large enough to compete with foreign firms.

However, for this argument to be valid the industry must eventually succeed in becoming competitive with foreign industry at the free trade world price; moreover the eventual benefit from the industry must exceed the cost of protection. Protection initially increases the price consumers have to pay, and for this to be justified it must be offset by the lower costs and prices that consumers will pay when the industry is established. Even if these two conditions are satisfied, it would be preferable to use a production subsidy rather than a tariff since subsidies are more transparent, less distorting and also tend to be easier to remove.

The practical implementation of protection of infant industries also encounters difficulties. For instance, how is the decision concerning which industries to be protected taken? And is there a risk of this selection process becoming politicized? When is the industry to be weaned, and is there likely to be pressure to prevent the protection ending? Even where protection helps an industry to become established, could this have occurred even without the protection? Clearly a general answer cannot be given to such questions and the outcome will depend on the particular case in question.

Another argument in favour of protectionism that has a long history is that of the **optimal tariff**. John Stuart Mill noted that if Britain introduced a tariff on a good widely used, consumption would decline causing the world price to fall. As a result, foreign producers would bear part of the cost of the tariff. This argument only applies in the case of a large nation that is able to influence the level of world prices.[22] The risk of introducing a tariff for this reason is that of retaliation on the part of other countries.

The **senescent industry** argument is frequently used, and maintains that protectionist measures may be necessary to avoid unemployment. However, the probable impact of such measures is simply to delay adjustment, and it is likely that the jobs saved in the declining sectors will be less numerous and will have less favourable prospects than those lost or foregone in non-subsidized sectors.

SECOND BEST

The traditional theory advocating free trade according to the principle of comparative advantage is based on some extremely restrictive assumptions, and in particular that there is perfect competition in factor and product markets both at national and international levels. This assumption is violated at a national level by cases of monopoly, oligopoly and imperfect competition, while at an international level the assumption appears even more heroic.

If the conditions of perfect competition are not verified, then we are in a situation of **second best**. Second best implies that if the conditions of perfect competition are violated in some part of

---

[22] For the country to benefit from introduction of the optimal tariff, it is also necessary that the transfer from the rest of the world following introduction of a tariff exceeds the net welfare loss to domestic producers and consumers.

the economy, it need not be optimal for the rest of the economy to attain a perfectly competitive equilibrium. In other words, it is not possible to know whether the introduction of an additional distortion will increase (while still remaining in a suboptimal situation) or reduce total welfare. The situation may actually be improved by violating further conditions of perfect competition. In the context of the debate on protectionism this implies that it is impossible to say a priori whether a move towards free trade will improve the situation, or that the introduction of a protectionist measure will worsen it. Under such conditions it is necessary to examine the specific case in question to decide on the most appropriate policy.

Meade (1962) provided a useful analogy for understanding the concept of second best. Let us consider a person trying to reach the highest possible peak in a group of mountains. Going towards the highest peak, the mountaineer will at times have to climb smaller mountains and descend the other side: the path to the highest peak is not always upwards. Assume, for example, in Figure 4.11 the mountaineer has reached B, but discovers that there is a deep gorge at D over which it is impossible to cross. If the climber wants to reach the highest peak possible under the circumstances, he should not remain at B, nor move to D in order to try and reach V, but should return to A.

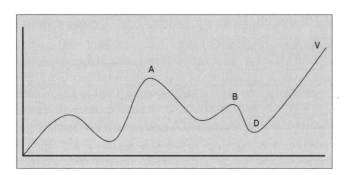

Figure 4.11 An illustration of second best

Source: elaborated on the basis of Meade (1962).

MORE RECENT ARGUMENTS IN FAVOUR OF PROTECTION: STRATEGIC TRADE THEORY

Given the shortcomings of the traditional theory, there have been numerous attempts to develop new approaches to the study of international trade, which no longer rely on the assumption of perfect competition. The differences among authors are such that it is difficult to present a synthesis of this type of approach. What emerges from the literature, however, is an emphasis on dynamic phenomena that may influence the productive conditions of a firm. In this world, technology, and both static and dynamic economies of scale, may play a crucial role. These phenomena may enable a firm to gain a competitive advantage regardless of the initial endowments of factors of production in that country. This implies that comparative advantage may in some sense be created and may be of a temporary nature.

This view underlies **strategic trade theory**, which advocates an active government trade policy and protectionism. According to this approach, a government may create a competitive advantage for its firms in high-technology industries through temporary protection, subsidies and tax breaks. Strategies to promote investment in infrastructure, people and research and development may also play an important role. Unfortunately, this approach shares many of the shortcomings of the infant industry argument: choosing which sectors will be future winners is as difficult as betting on horses, and too much government intervention may invite similar measures by major competitors.

THE POLITICAL ECONOMY OF PROTECTIONISM

The effect of trade protection for a particular product, say steel, is to raise domestic steel prices. Steel producers in that country will benefit, while consumers will have to pay higher prices. However, the benefits to the producers can be very high, while the cost to consumers is spread. The expected benefits to producers from protection may be sufficient to induce them to take on the costs of lobbying governments to introduce protectionist measures. The costs of lobbying may include the time, effort and expense needed to obtain information, organize a pressure group, signal preferences and carry out lobbying activities (see Box 4.8). The cost to consumers of the higher steel prices may be insufficiently high to induce them to organize any kind of protest. The government may have an incentive to give in to the requests of the steel lobby, knowing that consumers will be unlikely to organize any kind of effective resistance.

Box 4.8 The political economy of protectionism

The work by Olson (1965) provides a key in identifying the elements of success in pressure group activities. Olson explains the decision to join and participate in the activities of a pressure group in terms of expected benefits and costs. In the case of lobbying, the benefits relate to the probability of obtaining a favourable policy outcome, and the size of the per capita transfer to the beneficiary group.

The costs of pressure group activities include the costs of signalling preferences, organization and administration of the group and lobbying. According to Olson, the costs of organization and co-ordination may be higher, and the group may be rendered less effective with numerous members, each of whom feels that, whether they participate in the activities of the group or not, will not be noticed.[23] In other words there is a tendency for the members to 'free ride'. Olson argues that one way of overcoming free riding is by offering selective incentives to ensure membership or participation in the activities of a group. Alternatively, Olson maintains that the problem of free riding can be avoided in the case of what he calls a 'privileged group'. This involves one or more members of the group whose size or interest in having the goal of collective action is sufficient to induce them to take on the task of obtaining the common goal.

Downs (1957) provides an explanation of how, in a 'democratic system', a policy can serve the interests of a special group rather than those of the public as a whole. According to Downs, politicians are assumed to maximize their chances of re-election by competing for votes. They will adopt or reject a proposal on the basis of how many votes are expected to support or oppose it. However, voters will only reveal their preference if there is some advantage in doing so, such as action by the politician in favour of the voter. Information and signalling costs are involved in forming and expressing a preference. The rational voter will only undertake these costs if there is some incentive to do so. The fundamental theoretical insight of Downs is to illustrate why taxpayers and consumers may be 'rationally ignorant'.

This type of political economy argument is very powerful in explaining the pervasiveness of protectionist measures. In the EU and USA, aside from steel, protection tends to be high in agriculture, textiles and clothing, and the automobile industry.

---

[23]Olson refers to this type of group as a 'latent' group.

Summary of Key Concepts

- Many of our arguments in favour of free trade still owe much to the pioneering work of the classical economists Adam Smith and David Ricardo who illustrated that trade between two countries could be mutually beneficial thanks to the specialization of their production.
- Much trade between EU countries consists of intra-industry trade. This arises from product differentiation and means each country (or producer) can specialize in a few varieties of the product and exploit economies of scale.
- Static economies of scale occur when the unit costs of production fall as the scale of production rises. Dynamic economies of scale are associated with the learning process.
- An import tariff is a tax or duty levied on a product when it is imported into a country. Tariffs can be *ad valorem*, specific or compound.
- Among the main non-tariff barriers are: quotas; voluntary export restraints (VERs); cartels; anti-dumping measures; trade facilitation measures (including customs procedures, measures to promote exports and so on); differences in standards and technical specifications; and lack of transparency in government procurement.
- The effect of trade protection for a particular product is to raise domestic prices. Producers in that country will benefit, while consumers will have to pay higher prices. However, the benefits to the producers can be very high, while the cost to consumers is diffused. Producers may have an incentive to lobby government to introduce protection in their favour, while it may not be worth their while for the consumers to object.

Questions for Study and Review

- What are the main arguments in favour of free trade?
- What are the main obstacles to trade and how are they used in the EU?
- Why are protectionist measures so diffuse?
- Illustrate how political economy reasons may help to explain the high levels of protection in sectors such as agriculture, steel or textiles.
- Exercise on the effects of a tariff in a small nation (see Appendix 1 for an example of how to carry out the exercise). The quantity of a commodity supplied in a country is 24 tonnes, the quantity demanded (Qd) is 60 tonnes, and the world price (Pw) is €6/tonne. A tariff is introduced which raises the domestic price (Pd) to €7/tonne. The elasticity of demand is -0.3 and the elasticity of supply is 0.5. Calculate the effects of the tariff on: producer revenue, consumer expenditure, the trade balance and total welfare.[24]
- Exercise on the effects of introducing a tariff in a large nation (see Appendix 1 for an example of how to carry out the exercise). It is assumed initially that in conditions of free trade the quantity supplied (Qs) by a country is 200 tonnes, the quantity demanded (Qd) is 400 tonnes, and the world price (Pw) is €4/tonne. A tariff is introduced which raises the domestic price (Pd) to €5/tonne and as a result the world price P'w falls to €3.5/tonne. The elasticity of demand is -0.5 and the elasticity of supply is 0.4. Calculate the effects of the tariff on: producer revenue, consumer expenditure, the trade balance and total welfare.

---

[24] As a tip, calculate the total welfare effects using both approaches to ensure that they coincide. The country is a small nation, and for simplicity the demand and supply functions are assumed to be linear. It is also assumed that there are no stocks of the product or externalities. The approach used is partial equilibrium.

Appendix 1
A numerical example of the introduction of a tariff in a small nation[25]

A simple numerical example can be used to calculate the effects of introducing a tariff. It is assumed initially that the quantity supplied (Qs) by the country is 8 tonnes, the quantity demanded (Qd) is 30 tonnes, and the world price (Pw) is €2/tonne. A tariff is introduced which raises the domestic price (Pd) to €3/tonne (see Figure A4.1).

The elasticity of supply with respect to price can be defined as the ratio of the proportional change in the quantity supplied to the proportional change in price that brought it about. In symbols we have:

$$Es = \frac{\frac{\Delta Qs}{Qs}}{\frac{\Delta P}{P}}$$

Which can be rewritten as:

$$\frac{\Delta Qs}{Qs} = Es \frac{\Delta P}{P}$$

Assuming an elasticity of supply of 0.5 we can now calculate the new quantity supplied (Qs) after introduction of the tariff.

$$\Delta Qs = Qs\ Es \left(\frac{\Delta P}{P}\right) = 8\left(\frac{0.5 \times 1}{2}\right) = 2$$

$$Q's = 10$$

In the same way the new quantity demanded (Q'd) can be calculated. The elasticity of demand with respect to price can be defined as the ratio of the proportional change in the quantity demanded to the proportional change in price that brought it about. In symbols we have:

$$Ed = \frac{\frac{\Delta Qd}{Qd}}{\frac{\Delta P}{P}}$$

Which can be rewritten as:

$$\frac{\Delta Qd}{Qd} = Ed \frac{\Delta P}{P}$$

---

[25] The exercises presented here are a slightly different version of those developed by Prof. Secondo Tarditi in 1992 in an unpublished manuscript 'Esercitazioni' at the Faculty of Economics 'Richard Goodwin' of the University of Siena.

Assuming a price elasticity of demand of −0.4 (in general the price elasticity of demand is negative since in most cases an increase in price provokes a reduction in the quantity demanded).

$$\Delta Q = Q_d \left(E_d \frac{\Delta P}{P} \right) \qquad \Delta Q = 30 \left(\frac{-0.4 \times 1}{2} \right) = -6$$

$$Q'_d = 30 - 6 = 24$$

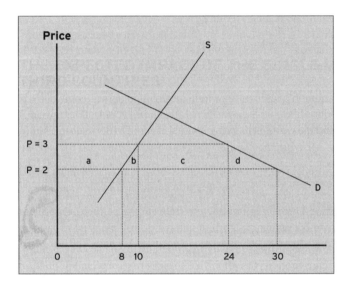

Figure A4.1 A tariff in a small nation: a numerical example

Before introduction of the tariff, producer revenue is:

$$Q'_s(P_w) = 8 \times 2 = 16$$

With the tariff it becomes:

$$Q'_s(P_d) = 10 \times 3 = 30$$

Before the introduction of the tariff, consumer expenditure is:

$$Q_d(P_w) = 30 \times 2 = 60$$

After the introduction of the tariff it becomes:

$$Q'_d (P_d) = 24 \times 3 = 72$$

Before the introduction of the tariff, the trade balance is:

$$(Q_s - Q_d)P_w = (8 - 30)\,2 = -44$$

With the tariff it becomes:

$$(Q'_s - Q'_d)\,P_w = (10 - 24)2 = -28$$

n.b. The world price is used to calculate the trade balance, but the domestic price is used to calculate producer revenue and consumer expenditure.

The loss in consumer surplus is given by:

$$-0.5 \ (Pd - Pw) \ (Qd + Q'd) = -27$$

The increase in producer surplus is given by:

$$0.5 \ (Pd - Pw) \ (Qs + Q's) = 9$$

The impact on the government budget (or the income of taxpayers) is:

$$(Pd - Pw)(Q'd - Q's) = 14$$

The total effect of introducing the tariff on welfare is given by:
loss in consumer surplus, plus the increase in producer surplus and the increase in government revenue:

$$-27 + 9 + 14 = -4$$

Alternatively, the effect of introducing the tariff on total welfare can be calculated using the net welfare effects:
triangle d is the net loss of welfare on the consumer side:

$$= -0.5 \ (Pd - Pw) \ (Qd - Q'd)$$
$$= -0.5 \ (3 - 2) \ (30 - 24)$$
$$= -3$$

Triangle b is the net loss of welfare on the production side (reflecting the worsening in the allocation of resources):

$$= -0.5 \ (Pd - Pw) \ (Q's - Qs)$$
$$= -0.5 \ (3 - 2) \ (10 - 8)$$
$$= -1$$

The total effect on welfare is the sum of the two net effects -4
Clearly the result must be the same as the total welfare effect calculated using the alternative method above.

Appendix 2
A simple numerical example of the effects of introducing a tariff in a large nation (see Figure A4.2)

Before the tariff is introduced it is assumed that:

$$Pw = 40 \text{ euro/t}$$
$$Qd = 1400t$$
$$Qs = 800t$$
$$Ed = -0.5$$
$$Es = 0.6$$

Assume that a tariff of €20/t is then introduced causing the world price to fall to 37. The new domestic price will be 57.

Recalling the formula for the elasticity of supply with respect to price, it is possible to calculate the new quantity supplied $(Q's)$ after introduction of the tariff:

$$Es = \dfrac{\dfrac{\Delta Qs}{Qs}}{\dfrac{\Delta P}{P}}$$

Which can be rewritten as:

$$\dfrac{\Delta Qs}{Qs} = Es \dfrac{\Delta P}{P}$$

$$\Delta Qs = \dfrac{Qs \; Es \; (\Delta P)}{P} = \dfrac{800 \; (0.6 \; 17)}{40} = 204$$

$$Q's = 800 + 204 = 1004$$

Similarly, the formula for elasticity of demand can be used to calculate the new quantity demanded (Q'd):

$$Ed = \dfrac{\dfrac{\Delta Qd}{Qd}}{\dfrac{\Delta P}{P}}$$

Which can be rewritten as:

$$\dfrac{\Delta Qd}{Qd} = Ed \dfrac{\Delta P}{P}$$

$$\Delta Q = \dfrac{Qd \; (Ed \; \Delta P)}{P} \qquad \Delta Q = \dfrac{1400 \; (-0.5 \; 17)}{40} = -297.5$$

$$Q'd = 1400 - 297.5 = 1102.5$$

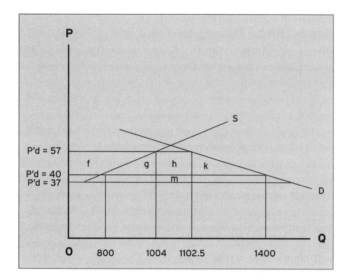

Figure A4.2 The introduction of a tariff in a large nation: a numerical example

Foreign trade without the tariff (i.e. net imports) is given by:

$$Q_s - Q_d = 800 - 1400 = -600 \, t$$

With the tariff it becomes:

$$Q's - Q'd = 1004 - 1102.5 = -98.5$$

Before introduction of the tariff producer revenue is:

$$Q_s(Pw) = 800 \times 40 = 32\,000$$

With the tariff it becomes:

$$Q's(Pd) = 1004 \times 57 = 57\,228$$

Before the introduction of the tariff consumer expenditure is:

$$Q_d(Pw) = 1400 \times 40 = 56\,000$$

After the introduction of the tariff it becomes:

$$Q'd \,(Pd) = 62\,842.5$$

Before the introduction of the tariff the trade balance is:

$$(Q_s - Q_d)Pw = -24\,000$$

With the tariff it becomes:

$$(Q's - Q'd) \, P'w = -36\,445$$

n.b. The world price is used to calculate the trade balance, but the domestic price is used to calculate producer revenue and consumer expenditure.

The loss in consumer surplus is given by:

$$-0.5 \, (Pd - Pw) \, (Qd + Q'd) = -21\,271.25$$

The increase in producer surplus is given by:

$$0.5 \, (Pd - Pw) \, (Qs + Q's) = 15\,334$$

The impact on the government budget (or the income of taxpayers) is:

$$(Pd - P'w)(Q'd - Q's) = 1970$$

The total effect of introducing the tariff on welfare is given by:
loss in consumer surplus, plus the increase in producer surplus and the increase in government revenue:

$$-21\,271.25 + 15\,334 + 1970 = -3967.25$$

Alternatively, the effect of introducing the tariff on total welfare can be calculated using the net welfare effects:
triangle k is the net loss of welfare on the consumer side:

$$
\begin{aligned}
&= -0.5\,(Pd - Pw)\,(Qd - Q'd) \\
&= -0.5\,(57 - 40)\,(1400 - 1102.5) \\
&= -2528.75
\end{aligned}
$$

Triangle g is the net loss of welfare on the production side (reflecting the worsening in the allocation of resources):

$$
\begin{aligned}
&= -0.5\,(Pd - Pw)\,(Q's - Qs) \\
&= -0.5\,(57 - 40)\,(1004 - 800) \\
&= -1734
\end{aligned}
$$

Rectangle m represents the transfers from producers in the rest of the world to consumers in that country (a reduction in world prices is a welfare gain for an importing country).

$$(Pw - P'w)\,(Q'd - Q's) = 295.5$$

The total effect on welfare is the sum of the three net effects:

$$-2528.75 - 1734 + 295.5 = -3967.25$$

Clearly the result must be the same as the total welfare effect calculated using the alternative method above.

References

Baldwin, R. and Wyplosz, C. (2004) *The Economics of European Integration*, McGraw-Hill Education, Maidenhead, UK.

Downs, A. (1957) *An Economic Theory of Democracy*, Harper & Row, New York.

European Commission (1999) 'Report on United States barriers to trade and investment'.

Falcone, F. (1990) *Commercio internazionale e integrazione europea. Aspetti teorici ed esperienza italiana*, Il Mulino, Bologna.

Healey, N. M. (1995) 'From the Treaty of Rome to Maastricht: The theory and practice of European integration', in Healey, N. M. (ed.), *The Economics of the New Europe*, Routledge, London and New York.

Krugman, P. and Obstfeld, M. (1997) *International Economics. Theory and Policy*, Addison Wesley Longman Inc., Reading, MA.

Meade, J. E. (1962) *The Theory of International Economic Policy, Vol. 2: Trade and Welfare*, Oxford University Press, Oxford.

Olson, M. jr. (1965) *The Logic of Collective Action: Public Goods and the Theory of Groups*, Harvard University Press, Cambridge, MA.

Salvatore, D. (2001) *International Economics*, 7th edn, John Wiley & Sons, New York.

Senior Nello, S. M. (1991) *The New Europe: Changing Economic Relations between East and West*, Harvester Wheatsheaf, Hemel Hempstead, UK.

Tarditi, S. (1992) 'Esercitazioni', Unpublished manuscript, Facoltà di Economia 'Richard Goodwin', University of Siena.

Useful websites

Statements of the EU position and studies of various trade issues are provided by the European Commission:

www.europa.eu.int/comm.

International trade statistics are available from Eurostat, www.eurostat.org, the Organization for Economic Co-operation and Development www.oecd.org and the United Nations www.un.org.

Studies of US positions on trade and international monetary issues include: the US Department of Commerce, International Trade Administration www.ita.doc.gov; the US Trade Representative www.ustr.gov and the US International Trade Commission www.usitc.gov. The Institute for International Economics in the USA also produces numerous studies of international economic issues www.iie.com

Oxfam generally presents a critical position on trade issues, taking the side of developing countries:

www.oxfam.org.uk

The World Bank generally concentrates on development issues but also publishes reports on the state of the world economy and trade:

www.worldbank.org

The World Trade Organization provides statistics, analysis of trade issues and information about the state of negotiations:

www.wto.org.

List of abbreviations

GATT	General Agreement on Tariffs and Trade
NTB	non-tariff barrier
OECD	Organization for Economic Co-operation and Development
OMA	Orderly Marketing Arrangement
OPEC	Organization of the Petroleum Exporting Countries
SITC	Standard International Trade Classification
VER	voluntary export restraint
WTO	World Trade Organization

5

The Economics of Integration

LEARNING OBJECTIVES

By the end of this chapter you should be able to understand:

▶ The concepts of trade creation and trade diversion;

▶ The effects of forming a customs union on the home and partner countries;

▶ The different effects of non-discriminatory liberalization of trade, preferential trade arrangements and customs unions;

▶ The conditions under which a customs union is likely to increase welfare;

▶ The reasons that countries may prefer preferential trade arrangements to non-discriminatory trade liberalization;

▶ What we mean by the dynamic effects of integration;

▶ The link between growth and integration;

▶ Why there may be a tension between regional trade blocs and multilateral trade liberalization.

INTRODUCTION

The early economic analysis of integration relies heavily on what is known as 'customs union theory'. One of the questions to arise was why preferential arrangements should be preferred to unilateral trade liberalization. Traditionally, 'customs union theory' attempted to address this question and assess the effects of customs unions using instruments based on the concepts of welfare economics. More recent analysis has taken into account the dynamic effects of integration and phenomena such as economies of scale, increased competition and better opportunities for more rapid technology transfer. According to empirical studies, these dynamic effects of integration seem far more important than the static welfare effects.

THE COSTS AND BENEFITS OF INTEGRATION

The early literature on integration used customs union theory to analyse the so-called **static effects** of integration on welfare, making use of the distinction made by Viner (1953) between trade creation and trade diversion.[1] **Trade creation** arises when domestic production is replaced by cheaper imports from a partner country. **Trade diversion** involves low-cost imports from suppliers in third countries being replaced by more expensive imports from a partner country. It was generally assumed that integration would lead to a welfare gain because the positive effect of trade creation would exceed the possible negative effects of trade diversion.[2]

Viner considered the costs and benefits of forming a customs union only from the point of view of production, and assumed that products were always consumed in the same proportion. Lipsey (1957) pointed out that the customs union is also likely to have an effect on the consumption side. It is also ambiguous as to whether the terms 'trade creation' and 'trade diversion' refer to trade flows or welfare effects, but Pelkmans and Gremmen (1983) have illustrated that changes in trade flows can be a misleading indicator of welfare changes.

TRADE CREATION

The 'static' effect of a customs union can be illustrated with the help of a diagram similar to that of Figure 4.4 in Chapter 4. Figure 5.1 shows the domestic demand and supply curves for product X of a country that imports that product, say Belgium. Assume that the free trade price of a commodity is $Px = €1$ in country 1 (say Germany), and $Pw = €2$ in country 2 (or the rest of the world). For simplicity Belgium is assumed to be a 'small nation' in the sense that its economy is too small to affect the prices in Germany or the rest of the world. Assume initially that Belgium imposes a non-discriminatory *ad valorem* tariff of 100 per cent on imports from all sources. S1 represents the perfectly elastic supply curve of Germany with free trade, and S1 + T is the tariff-inclusive German supply curve. Belgium will import commodity X from Germany at a price of $Pd = €2$, reflecting the effect of the tariff. It will not import from the rest of the world, since after the tariff the price in Belgium would be €4.

If Belgium now forms a customs union with country 1 (Germany), the tariffs will be removed on German imports but not on those from the rest of the world. Belgium can now import at $Px = €1$ from Germany, and at this price Belgium will produce 10 million units of X, consume 65 million units, and import 55 million units.

The increase in consumer surplus as a result of creation of the customs union is area a + b + c + d. The loss in producer surplus is indicated by area a. Belgium loses its tariff revenue on imports from Germany (rectangle c). The net positive impact on welfare as a result of the customs union is therefore comprised of triangles b and d. Triangle b represents the welfare gain on the production side as a result of improved allocation of resources with the shift in the production of 10 million X

---

[1] In the subsequent literature there was further refinement of the different effects of integration. For example, external trade creation was said to arise when the faster growth of the integration unit led to higher imports from the rest of the world. Trade suppression may arise when creation of the customs union leads to production in one of the partners stopping and production shifting to the other partner, which had previously imported from the rest of the world.
[2] The rules of the GATT/WTO were aimed at ensuring that this is the case (see Chapter 17).

from less efficient domestic producers to lower cost producers in the partner country Germany. Triangle d represents the welfare gain on the consumption side from creation of the customs union. With the lower prices in the customs union, Belgian consumption will increase by 15 million units. Together, triangles b and d illustrate the net increase in welfare as a result of establishing the customs union.

A strict application of Viner's term 'trade creation' would refer simply to the production side and the effect of replacement of the more expensive domestic production of 10 million X by imports from the partner country, Germany. Many economists use the term 'trade creation' to cover the total net increases in welfare on both the production and the consumption sides, i.e. triangles b and d in the diagram. It is probably more precise to refer to triangle b as the trade-creation effect, and triangle d as the consumption effect of forming a customs union.

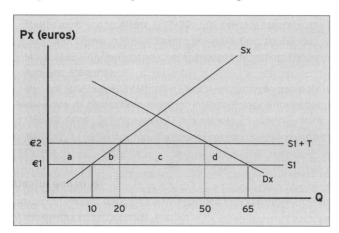

Figure 5.1 **Trade creation (million units of product X)**

TRADE DIVERSION

Figure 5.2 illustrates the case of trade diversion.[3] Again Dx and Sx are domestic demand and supply of commodity X in the country in question (Belgium). S2 and S3 are the free trade, perfectly elastic supply curves of commodity X in country 2 (say the USA) and country 3 (say Luxembourg) respectively. With a 100 per cent non-discriminatory tariff, the home country (Belgium) will import from country 2 (the USA) at a price of €2. At this price Belgium will produce 35 million units and consume 60 million, so 25 million units are imported from country 2 (the USA). There will be no imports from Luxembourg as the price inclusive of tariff is €3.

Assume that Belgium now forms a customs union with country 3 (Luxembourg) but not with country 2 (the USA). As a result tariffs are removed on imports from Luxembourg, but the 100 per cent tariff remains on imports from the USA. After formation of the customs union Belgium will import from Luxembourg at price €1.50. At this new price Belgium will produce 30 million units, and consume 70 million, importing 40 million units from country 3 (Luxembourg).

With the customs union the imports of Belgium have been diverted from more efficient producers in country 2 (the USA) to less efficient producers in country 3 (Luxembourg), so there is a worsening in the allocation of resources. Five million units of X (35 − 30 million) are now imported from the partner country, Luxembourg, rather than being produced at home in Belgium, while 25 million units (60 − 35 million) that were previously imported from the USA are now imported from Luxembourg.

Belgium will no longer receive tariff revenue. The welfare loss from trade diversion is indicated

---

[3] This type of analysis was first used by Kindleberger (1973).

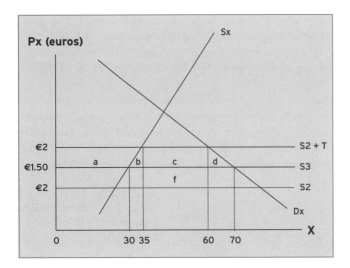

Figure 5.2 Trade diversion (million units of product X)

by the area of rectangle f. The 25 million units that were previously imported from more efficient country 2 (the USA) whose free trade price is €1 per unit are now imported from country 3 (Luxembourg) with a free trade price of €1.50. In this case the welfare loss will be €12.5 million.

Triangles b and d reflect the welfare gain from the customs union as more expensive production in Belgium is now replaced with cheaper imports from Luxembourg. The welfare gain on the production side due to trade creation (triangle b) is equal to €1.25 million, while that on the consumption side (triangle d) is €2.5 million.

The total impact on welfare as a result of formation of the customs union is given by the sum of the areas of the two triangles (b and d), representing a welfare gain due to the trade creation and consumption effects, minus the area of the rectangle (f) representing welfare loss due to trade diversion. In this case the total effect on welfare is equal to −8.75 million euros (2.5 million +1.25 million −12.5 million), so creation of the customs union causes a net welfare loss.

If the sum of the areas of the two triangles representing welfare gain is greater than the area of the rectangle representing the welfare loss due to trade diversion, formation of the customs union will cause a net welfare gain for the home country. The idea that a customs union is either 'trade creating or 'trade distorting' is misleading; Figure 5.2 illustrates that a customs union may give rise to both effects.

THE EFFECT OF A CUSTOMS UNION ON THE PARTNER COUNTRY

The analysis can be extended to consider the effect of forming a customs union on the partner country. Figure 5.3a illustrates the demand and supply curves for product X in the partner country, while Figure 5.3b illustrates the demand and supply curves for the home country. The two countries are assumed to be small and have increasing production costs. The costs of production are assumed to be higher in the home country, and for simplicity it is assumed that at the initial level of protection the partner country is just self-sufficient at the perfectly elastic world price Pw.[4] The partner country therefore does not need to protect its industry from world competition. Before creation of the customs union, the home country applies a tariff that raises its domestic price to Ph. With the creation of the customs union trade is liberalized between the home and partner country,

---

[4] The simplifying assumption of initial self-sufficiency of the partner country is taken from Robson (1984).

and they introduce a common external tariff in trade with the rest of the world. The price including the common external tariff is indicated by Pcu in Figure 5.3.

In the home country the reduction in the apparent price of imports will lead to a welfare gain of a on the production side due to trade creation, a welfare gain on the consumption side of c, and a welfare loss of m due to the diversion of imports from the rest of the world.

In the partner country prices will rise because of increased protection. Equilibrium occurs in the customs union when the combined supply of the two countries equals their combined demand (and Q1Q3 = Q4Q7). The increase in price from Pw to Pcu in the partner country causes an increase in producer surplus of e + f + g and a reduction in consumer surplus of e + f. The partner country is able to increase its exports to the home country to Q1Q3 and obtain a net welfare gain of area g.

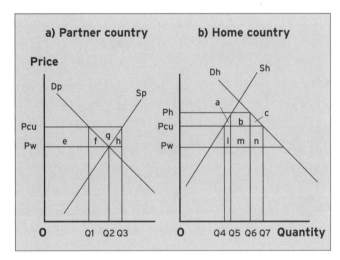

Figure 5.3 The effects of a customs union on home and partner countries

In the example the net welfare benefit of the partner country rises. This is sometimes called 'trade creation'. However, more accurately this is an income transfer from the home country to the partner country. The home could have imported quantity Q4Q7 from the rest of the world, rather than from the partner country at Pcu. In this way the home country would have received revenue of l + m + n from the common external tariff. Instead, this passed to the partner country with areas f + g representing profit, while area h is the additional cost of production compared with the lower world price Pw.

In this example there is a net welfare loss for the home country (rectangle m is greater than the sum of triangles a and c) and a net welfare gain for the partner country of triangle g. There will be a net welfare loss for the rest of the world whose exports are replaced by exports from the partner country.

THE DIFFERENCE BETWEEN NON-DISCRIMINATORY TARIFFS AND PREFERENTIAL ARRANGEMENTS

The analysis based on import demand and supply curves shown in Chapter 4 is also useful to illustrate the difference between non-discriminatory tariffs and preferential arrangements.[5] As explained in Chapter 17, non-discriminatory tariffs could be, for example, those extended to all WTO members on the basis of the most-favoured-nation clause (MFN).

---

[5] The analysis in this section follows Baldwin and Wyplosz (2004).

Figure 5.4 illustrates the effect of the home country introducing an MFN tariff on the partner country and the rest of the world. XSrow indicates the export supply of the rest of the world, and ESp shows the export supply of the partner country. Prior to introducing the tariff, at the free trade world price Pft the home country will import a total of M of product X of which Xp comes from the partner country and Xr comes from the rest of the world. MS shows the import supply of the home country in a situation of free trade. With the tariff the import supply curve in the home country becomes MS + tariff, and the domestic price in the home country rises to P'. The border price (i.e. the price received by exporters) falls to P' − T in both the partner country and the rest of the world. As a result home imports fall to M', of which Xp' come from the partner country and Xr' from the rest of the world. The home country receives a welfare gain of b and a welfare loss of c, while the partner receives a welfare loss of f and the rest of the world suffers a welfare loss of e (see Chapter 4 for an explanation of these effects).

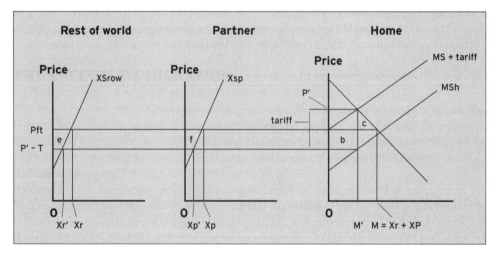

Figure 5.4 The effect of a non-discriminatory tariff on the partner country and the rest of the world
Source: Baldwin and Wyplosz (2004).

A customs union involves all members eliminating trade barriers with their partners and introducing a common external tariff towards the rest of the world. In the interests of simplification, before analysing the effect of a customs union on the partner country, it is useful to consider the effect of just one country introducing a unilateral preferential trade arrangement.

In Figure 5.5 MSmfn shows the supply of imports of product X in the home country with a non-discriminatory (or MFN) tariff, and MSh shows the import supply in a situation of free trade. MSpta shows the import supply in the home country with a preferential trade arrangement. As the trade liberalization is preferential, MSpta is assumed to be lower than MSmfn. In this simple model with two exporters, a partner and the rest of the world, preferential trade liberalization applies only to the partner, and MSpta can be assumed to lie halfway between MSh and MSmfn. However, the rest of the world cannot supply the home market at a price less than Pa, which represents their zero export supply price (P*) plus the tariff T. Up to Pa only firms from the partner country will supply imports. The import supply curve MSpta with a preferential trade arrangement therefore takes the form shown in Figure 5.5.

With a non-discriminatory tariff, the import supply curve MSmfn and the import demand curve in the home country intersect at price P'. The border price received by exporters in both the rest of the world and the future partner country is P' − T.

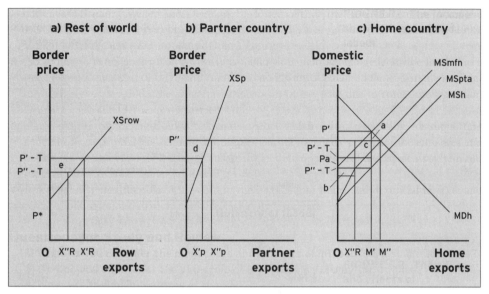

Figure 5.5 The impact of introducing a preferential trade arrangement on the home country, the partner and the rest of the world
Source: Baldwin and Wyplosz (2004).

With the preferential trade arrangement the new domestic price becomes P″, and this is also the border price in the partner country joining the preferential arrangement. The border price in the partner country therefore rises from P′ − T to P″ as a result of creating the preferential trade arrangement. In contrast, following the introduction of the preferential trade arrangement, the border price in the rest of the world falls from P′ − T to P″ − T. The exports from the partner country rise from X′p to X″p, while those of the rest of the world fall from X′R to X″R.

The welfare effects of introducing the preferential trade arrangement can also be shown in the diagram. The partner country gains area d because it can sell a larger quantity at a higher price. The rest of the world has a welfare loss of e since it sells a smaller quantity at a lower price.

Following the introduction of the preferential trade arrangement home imports increase from M′ to M″, with X″r of the latter coming from the rest of the world and M″ − X″r coming from the partner country. The increase in total imports from M′ to M″ leads to a welfare gain due to the increased volume of imports equal to area a and the lower price of imports from the rest of the world leads to a welfare gain equal to rectangle b (the price difference (P′ − T) − (P″ − T) times the imports from the rest of the world X″r). The higher price of imports from the partner implies a welfare loss equal to the area of the rectangle c or the price difference (P″) − (P′ − T) multiplied by the quantity of imports (M′ − X″r). The effect of the price difference does not apply on the extra amount of imports M″ − M′ as initially the home country did not import this quantity. The total net welfare effect on the home country as a result of formation of the customs union is: a + b − c.

In the case of a customs union, the partner country will also eliminate tariffs on its imports from the home country but not on those from the rest of the world. For simplicity, to illustrate the case of a customs union it can be assumed that the home country imports good X from the partner country and exports good Y to the partner country. The rest of the world exports product X to the home country, and product Y to the partner country. The home, the partner and the rest of the world are also assumed symmetric in all aspects, including the tariffs initially applied on imports.

Figure 5.5 can also be used to analyse the effect of the partner eliminating the barrier on imports of Y from the home country. This simply requires inverting the partner and home countries as parts (b) and (c) of Figure 5.5 (which is possible due to the symmetry assumption). The partner country then becomes the importing country (of Y), and the home country is an exporter (of Y).

The total welfare effects of forming a customs union for the home country are shown in Figure 5.6. To explain the welfare effects more precisely, area c of Figure 5.5 is divided into areas g and h, and area d is broken down into f and j. On the import market for product X the home country gains areas a and b and loses areas g and h (g + h are equal to area c in Figure 5.5), while on its export market for product Y it gains areas f and j (area d in Figure 5.5). The welfare loss of areas h and g to the home country is the result of paying the higher price after the tariff cut on imports from the partner. Part of this loss, area h simply represents a transfer to the partner country who receives higher prices for its exports. Area h is equal to area f. The home country's loss of area h on its imports of product X will be offset by a gain of area f for the partner country's exports of X. Similarly for product Y (because of the assumption of symmetry) the loss of area h on the partner country's imports of Y will be equal to the home country's gain of f on its exports of Y.

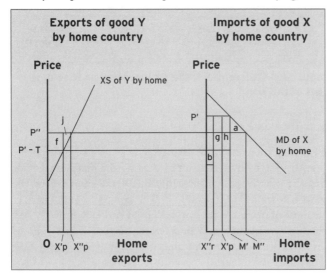

Figure 5.6 The welfare effects of forming a customs union on the home country
Source: Baldwin and Wyplosz (2004).

In contrast, area g represents trade diversion because of switching from cheaper exports from the rest of the world to exports from the higher-cost partner country. The size of this welfare loss is given by the quantity of supply switching $X'p - X''r$ multiplied by the price difference $P'' - (P' - T)$. Given that h = f, the total net welfare effect on the home country from formation of the customs union is a + b+ j − g.

THE CONDITIONS UNDER WHICH A CUSTOMS UNION IS LIKELY TO INCREASE WELFARE

From the analysis here it emerges that the net effect of forming a customs union on the welfare of the home country may be positive, negative or zero. This is known as 'Viner's ambiguity'. *Ex ante* general predictions of the welfare effects of introducing customs unions cannot be given as they will depend on the case in question. The analysis of the introduction of a customs union is a case of second best in which a shift from one sub-optimal situation to another does not permit generalizations about the overall effect on welfare.

However, even from this simplified analysis, certain principles about the effect of introducing a customs union on welfare can be deduced and, in general, the benefits are likely to be higher:

- The higher the original level of the tariff before forming the customs union;[6]
- The lower the common external tariff towards the rest of the world;[7]
- The higher the number of countries joining a customs union, and the greater their size. Under these circumstances there is more likelihood of low cost producers within the customs union;
- The smaller the differences in costs of production between the members of the customs union and third countries;[8]
- The closer the countries are geographically, as transport costs will be lower;
- The more competitive (producing the same goods) rather than complementary (producing a different range of goods) the economies of the member states are. In this way there will be more opportunities for specialization;
- The greater the trade flows and economic relations between the countries before forming the customs union.

PREFERENTIAL TRADE LIBERALIZATION VERSUS NON-DISCRIMINATORY MEASURES

The traditional static analysis assesses the overall impact of a customs union by comparing the situation before and after creation of the customs union. However, Cooper and Massell (1965) challenged this approach, arguing that the comparison should be made between discriminatory reduction of tariffs, as in the case of a customs union, and a non-discriminatory elimination of tariffs.[9] They argue that a non-discriminatory removal of tariffs would not involve trade diversion and would be superior. The question then becomes: why do countries create customs unions (or preferential trade liberalization) rather than use non-discriminatory trade arrangements?

One reason given is the possible terms-of-trade loss from unilateral trade liberalization, and the possible terms-of-trade gain that may arise for the customs union as a whole as result of discrimination against the rest of the world.[10] The individual member states may be too small to affect their external terms of trade individually, but together they are able to affect the terms of trade with third countries. Given the weight of the EU in world trade, this argument could be quite important. However, some countries in the rest of the world are also large nations (such as the USA or Japan) so, as indicated in Chapter 4 in the context of the optimal tariff argument, the customs union could risk retaliatory measures from other countries.

It has also been argued that a customs union may be preferred to non-discriminatory liberalization since the former can create opportunities for exploiting economies of scale, but these presumably could also be exploited at the level of a wider world market.

Johnson (1965) introduces political economy arguments to maintain that countries with a strong preference for industrial production that are (or feel themselves to be) at a comparative disadvantage *vis-à-vis* the rest of the world may favour the creation of a customs union.[11] According to this view, governments use tariffs to achieve certain non-economic objectives. Countries are assumed to have a preference for industrial production, so consumers are prepared to expand industrial production beyond what would occur in a free trade scenario. Governments are assumed to respond rationally to the demands of the electorate and will use protection to expand industrial

---

[6] This can be seen by using Figure 5.2 or 5.5 to consider the effect of a higher initial tariff.
[7] To verify, consider the effect of applying a lower common external tariff in Figure 5.3 or 5.5.
[8] Again Figures 5.2 or 5.3 can be used to see this effect.
[9] The approach used in Figures 5.5 and 5.6 provides a toolkit for carrying out this type of comparison.
[10] See the discussion of Figure 4.7 or Figure 5.6 for an explanation of the terms of trade effect.
[11] The argument is easily extended to countries having a preference for agricultural production.

production. Tariffs are the usual instrument used, since most types of export subsidy are ruled out by the WTO, and domestic political considerations lead to a preference for tariffs rather than production subsidies because of the burden posed by the latter on domestic taxpayers.

El-Agraa (2004) modifies Johnson's model by considering industrial production not as a single aggregate but as a variety of products for which countries have varying degrees of comparative advantage. In this way countries can be both exporters and importers of industrial products.

Considering a simplified case with only two countries, one will be a net exporter and the other a net importer of any industrial product. For each country the prospective gain from tariff reduction lies in the expansion of industrial production. With non-discriminatory trade liberalization the reduction of the home country's tariff is considered a source of loss that must be compensated by tariff reductions on the part of the other country.

With a customs union, trade creation is not considered as a means of replacing higher cost production with cheaper imports but is regarded as the price to be paid for expanding export markets. Trade diversion offers a chance for increasing production within the customs union by replacing imports from the rest of the world with imports from the partner. As a result trade diversion is preferable to trade creation for the home country since no sacrifice of domestic production is necessary. Stress is also placed on the gains to domestic industry from economies of scale, increased competition and the growth potential of a larger market area as a result of establishing the customs union. Preferential trade liberalization gives rise to chances for expanding industrial production to an extent not possible through non-discriminatory liberalization.

The choice for a country then becomes whether to form or join a customs union. According to Johnson's model as refined by the El-Agraa assumption, a country will join a customs union only if it considers that its comparative advantage in some forms of industrial production is strong enough for its industrial production to increase (or for any loss in industrial production to be compensated by greater efficiency). Other member states will only allow the country to join if they think that there is no threat of the new member increasing its industrial production at the expense of their own. As a result, customs unions are likely to be negotiated between countries with a similar preference for industrial production and a similar degree of comparative advantage in industrial production (or, in other words, a similar level of economic development).

As Johnson argues, this approach helps to explain why the Treaty of Rome attempted to ensure that each of the member states maintained a 'fair share of production', even if this required additional mechanisms such as the measures to promote growth in Southern Italy.

EMPIRICAL RESEARCH ON THE EFFECTS OF INTEGRATION

Many of the early empirical studies of the formation and successive enlargements of the EC were based on customs union theory. This type of approach generally involves an attempt to measure the effects of passing from free trade to a customs union. Over time customs union theory became somewhat anachronistic, as in later enlargements most countries joining the EU already had a free trade area or customs union with the Community. For instance, thanks to the Europe Agreements (see Chapter 20) the new CEEC member states had a free trade area for manufactures and passed to a single market (with some derogations) with enlargement. Turkey already has a customs union with the EU.

Early empirical research based on the customs union approach found the effects of integration surprisingly small. Though there are considerable variations in the results, in general the gains from creation of the Community were found to be in the order of 1–2 per cent of GDP (Harrop,

2000, p. 65). This seemed a remarkably small reward for all the effort of creating the Community, so led to questioning of the approach, and the emergence of the view that integration might also involve dynamic effects (see next section).

The aim here is not to present a comprehensive survey of the research on integration effects, but some clarification of the different approaches used by these studies is useful. Surveys of the early studies are available, for instance in Mayes (1978), El-Agraa and Jones (1981), and (in Italian) Falcone (1990).

A first distinction can be made between *ex-ante* and *ex-post* **analyses** of the effects of integration. An *ex-ante* analysis attempts to estimate the future effects of setting up an integration bloc, or enlargement to new members. In this case information is available concerning the present, pre-integration situation, but predictions have to be made about the likely impact of beginning or extending the integration process.

Ex-post analyses of the effects of integration take place after the process has been in operation for some time. In this case data are available on what has occurred with integration, but the difficulty lies in attempting to assess what would have happened in its absence. In other words it is necessary to assess likely developments in economic variables such as trade, production and consumption if there had been no integration. This entails constructing an ***anti-monde*** or fictitious world in which the integration bloc is absent or the country in question remains outside it. The *anti-monde* is then compared with actual developments in order to assess the integration effect by 'residual imputation'. As the approach is based on an unknowable *anti-monde* that cannot be tested against experience, ultimately the evaluation of estimates based on this type of approach is largely a matter of judgement about the plausibility of the simplifying assumptions made about the *anti-monde*.

A further distinction between studies of integration is based on whether they took into account effects on trade or income, and each will be considered in turn.

Estimates of the trade effects of integration

Most of the early studies concentrated on the trade effects of integration. As Grimwade (2004) describes, attempts to estimate these effects generally fell into three broad categories:

- Residual models;
- Econometric models; and
- Computable general equilibrium models.

Residual models impute hypothetical trade flows from existing trade flows, using various methods:

- Extrapolating developments existing prior to the creation or extension of the integration process;
- Comparing developments in the integration bloc with developments in third-party countries.

An early survey of empirical estimates of the trade effects of the EC using extrapolation is provided in Mayes (1978). The survey suggests that there was evidence for trade creation in the 1970s and 1980s, and though trade diversion was estimated to be much lower scale, it appeared to be substantial in the agricultural sector. Among the best-known studies of this type for the EEC are those by Truman (1969), Sellekaerts (1973) and Balassa (1967, 1974 and 1975).

Balassa (1967, 1974) proposed a method that uses the *ex-post* income elasticity for imports, and assumes that this would have remained constant in the absence of integration. The *ex-post* income elasticity of demand is defined as the ratio of the average annual rate of change in imports to that of GDP, both expressed in constant prices. The method consists of comparing the elasticities for intra-EC trade and extra-EC trade for periods before and after integration. Under *ceteris paribus* conditions, a decline in the income elasticity of demand for extra-EC imports indicates trade diversion. Alternatively, according to Balassa, a rise in this elasticity for intra-EC imports indicates gross trade creation, while an increase in these elasticities from all sources indicates overall trade creation. Balassa compared the pre-integration period (1953–59) with two post-integration periods (1959–65 and 1965–70) and found evidence for overall trade creation, though there appeared to have been trade diversion for foodstuffs.

There are, however, certain drawbacks to the approach and, in particular, that of defining the *anti-monde* and assuming that all, and only, integration effects are picked up in changes in the income elasticity of demand for imports. Moreover the results of the approach depend on the choice of base period, and supply-side effects are ignored.

A comparison of EEC performance with that of third countries such as the USA, the UK and other industrial countries outside Europe was carried out by Kreinen (1972). Clearly, the results depend heavily on the country chosen as a control group to 'normalize' trade shares. Kreinen's results suggested that trade creation was far more substantial than trade diversion.

One way of avoiding the shortcomings of constructing an *anti-monde* is by using an **econometric model**. This involves identifying the various factors (including integration) having an impact on trade and trying to assess their explanatory power. Two main types of model have been used to assess the effect of integration: gravity models and analytic models.

The **gravity model** approach involves attempting to predict the level of bilateral trade flows on the basis of variables such as GNP, population, geographical distance, and preferential trading arrangements. Gravity models are often relatively successful in predicting trade flows between countries but have been criticized for lacking theoretical underpinnings. Gravity models were developed by Tinbergen (1952), and have been applied to the EC by Verdoorn and Schwartz (1972), Aitken (1973) and, more recently, Frankel (1997). Recent studies (Frankel and Rose, 2000; Rose 2000 and 2002) have used gravity models to show how introducing a common currency appears to have encouraged trade growth (see Chapter 8).

Following the collapse of communism in Central and Eastern Europe in 1989, various authors used gravity models to assess the 'normal' level of trade with the EC, i.e. what trade would have been had communism never been introduced in those countries. Among the most well-known studies of this type are those of Wang and Winters (1992), Hamilton and Winters (1992), Baldwin (1994), Faini and Portes (1995) and various studies of the European Bank for Reconstruction and Development.[12]

Analytic models attempt to take into account all the main variables influencing trade, including integration. When all the coefficients have been estimated, the model can be used to estimate what trade would have been without integration. These models generally take into account variables reflecting the level of economic activity (measured by GDP, GNP or apparent consumption) and the ratio(s) between domestic and import prices. Applications of models of this type to European integration include the studies by Resnick and Truman (1975), Winters (1984 and 1985) and CEPR/European Commission (1997).

A **computable general equilibrium model (CGE)** attempts to overcome the limitations of partial equilibrium models by taking into account the repercussions of trade liberalization on the whole of the domestic economy and on trading partners. The aim of a CGE model is to specify the conditions for equilibrium in all markets and countries. As described in Chapter 6, models of this type were used to assess the impact of the Single Market programme and, as shown in Chapter 13, the evolution of regional disparities in the EU.

---

[12] See European Bank for Reconstruction and Development, Transition Report, various years. For a discussion of the application of gravity models to the CEECs see Senior Nello (2002).

Estimates of the income effects of integration

Analysis of income effects often took the form of attempts to assess the welfare effects of integration. Many of these used a partial equilibrium approach of the type illustrated in Figure 5.2 above, despite the limitations of this approach in not taking into account the repercussions on the markets of factors of production or of other products.

Early studies of the impact of integration on income generally attempted to assess the impact of trade liberalization as a share of GDP. Studies of this type include those by Johnson (1958) and Balassa (1975). In general the impact of integration was found to be very limited, partly because trade was generally a rather small share of GDP. Most of the studies concentrated on tariff reductions, but tariffs were already relatively low. These models tended to be highly simplified because of data problems, and agriculture was often left out.

As mentioned in Chapter 4, much trade between developed countries is intra-industry trade in differentiated products, and this poses an additional complication for empirical estimates of integration effects. If imports and importables are not perfect substitutes, with liberalization a fall in price of imports may not lead to a corresponding fall in the price of importables. Against this, liberalization of trade in differentiated products may stimulate higher intra-industry trade. This will result in consumers having a wider range of choice of product, though estimation of the size of this gain to consumers may prove difficult. Moreover intra-industry trade is often associated with the dynamic effects of integration such as increased competition and opportunities for exploiting economies of scale. Balassa (1974) attempted to take into account the effect of the larger scale of production, while Owen (1983) considered the effect of integration on competition and the scale of production.

THE DYNAMIC EFFECTS OF INTEGRATION

Partly because of the relatively small size of empirical estimates of the static effects of integration, over time the emphasis shifted towards dynamic effects. Among the most comprehensive studies of these dynamic effects were those carried out in the context of the Single Market Programme (see Chapter 6). Studies such as the Cecchini Report and Emerson (1989) suggested that the benefits from these dynamic effects could be as much as five or six times as large as the static effects of integration.

The dynamic effects of integration include:

- **specialization**
  Integration leads to improved location of industry.
- **increased competition**
  By bringing down the barriers integration should lead to reductions in costs and prices and encourage the restructuring of industry (see Figure 6.1 in Chapter 6).
- **economies of scale**
  With integration, firms operate in a larger market and have more opportunities for exploiting economies of scale (see Chapter 4). The issue then becomes whether there is more scope for exploiting economies of scale at the EU rather than the international level (see Chapter 6).
- **technological progress**
  It is frequently argued that economic integration also contributes to technological progress. This is increasingly a global rather than a regional phenomenon though; as explained in Chapter 13, location counts.

■ **increased bargaining power at an international level**

By presenting a more united front, a regional bloc such as the EU would be able to carry more weight *vis-à-vis* its main trading partners.

■ **more rapid growth**

The link between growth and integration is taken up in more detail in the next section.

GROWTH AND INTEGRATION

According to orthodox neo-classical growth theory (based on the pioneering work of Solow, 1956), the key determinant of growth is capital accumulation. As more capital is added to a fixed amount of labour, output per worker increases, but by a progressively smaller amount for each additional unit of capital due to diminishing returns. The basic assumption of the Solow model is that since people save and invest a certain percentage of their income each year, the inflow of investment is a fixed fraction of output per worker. If y is output per worker, the curve sy in Figure 5.7 shows investment per worker (which is equal to savings per worker). The shape of the sy curve reflects diminishing returns.

The ratio of capital to labour in an economy will depend on investment, but also on depreciation, since old capital has to be replaced and repaired. A constant fraction of stock capital n is assumed to depreciate each year. The straight line n(k/l) shows the depreciation per worker that increases in proportion with the amount of capital per worker. At E investment is sufficient to keep capital per person constant. At E the inflow of investment just equals depreciation. At this point the capital/ labour ratio reaches its equilibrium k/l*, or steady state. Below E investment exceeds depreciation and capital per worker will rise. Above E depreciation exceeds investment so capital per worker will fall. Accumulation of capital cannot be an ongoing source of long-run growth.

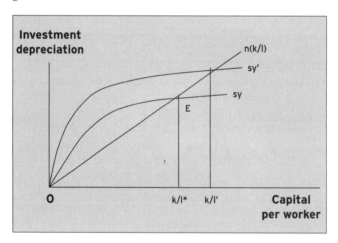

Figure 5.7 The Solow growth model

In order to explain ongoing rates of growth other elements have to be introduced into the Solow model. If, for instance, technological progress is introduced, this will lead to increased output per worker, thus raising investment and the capital/labour ratio. Technological progress causes the sy curve to rotate upwards each year. Figure 5.7 shows the effect of one such rotation in which the sy curve is translated to sy′, and the new capital/labour ratio becomes k/l′.

Endogenous growth theory as developed by Romer (1986) provides other explanations of long-term growth. Continual growth of output per person in the long run requires ceaseless accumulation of factors of production. In order to endogenize growth, it is necessary to endogenize investment. The decision to accumulate factors of production will depend on the costs and benefits of investment. Continual accumulation therefore requires that the return on investment does not fall as capital stock rises.

Various accounts of how this may occur have been advanced. Much of the literature relies on the concept of productivity-boosting knowledge capital. For example, a firm may invest in knowledge to increase its advantage *vis-à-vis* other firms. The additional profits from exploiting this knowledge represent the return on investment in knowledge capital for the firm. However, the investment will have a spill-over effect in increasing the stock of knowledge in the economy. It is assumed that this spill-over will increase the productivity of resources used in innovating.

The model developed by Lucas (1988) focuses on the role played by human capital in contributing to growth.[13] Individuals will invest in skills because they expect that there will be adequate capital for their higher skills to be reflected in higher salaries. Firms invest in capital as they anticipate that there will be sufficient skilled workers for the firm to earn a profit. There is a positive spill-over as those investing in human capital do not consider the output-boosting effect that their investment will have.

The elimination of barriers implied by integration may facilitate international flows of knowledge. This could reduce the cost of innovation, thereby increasing the private return on R&D and encouraging more resources to be drawn into innovation. At the same time, the creation of a larger market could increase the profitability of innovation.

According to this approach, integration could also have a positive effect on financial markets, thereby leading to higher levels of investment and long-term growth. In particular, greater competition might encourage more efficiency in financial markets, enabling a reduction in the spread between the return earned by savers and the costs of funds to investors (Baldwin, 1994).

A lesson from approaches based on the new growth theory is that public intervention can contribute to growth by encouraging R&D and rendering the appropriation of new technology easier. The message for the EU is therefore that in order to foster growth, measures to promote R&D, improvements in human capital and more efficient financial markets are necessary.

As Deardorff and Stern (2002) maintain, empirical estimates of the impact of European integration on growth run into difficulties since it is difficult to isolate integration from other variables influencing growth. Baldwin (1989) and Italianer (1994) have analysed the possible growth effects of the Single Market Programme (see Chapter 6). Marques-Mendes (1986) made use of a foreign trade multiplier to assess the impact of integration on growth over the 1961–72 and 1974–81 periods. During the first period, despite a negative effect in France and, to a lesser extent, Germany, according to the analysis the EC contributed to faster growth in the Benelux countries and Italy. During the second period, Marques-Mendes found that the EC contributed to growth in all member states except Denmark, so that by 1981 the GDP of the EC was 5.9 per cent higher than it would have been without integration.

REGIONALISM *VERSUS* MULTILATERALISM

The most recent addition to the theoretical toolkit is the emerging literature on regional co-operation which dates from the 1990s. This approach places the issue of regional integration in the wider context of multilateral trade liberalization. The literature attempts to address the question of

---

[13] This could be regarded as a special case of the knowledge capital argument.

whether regional co-operation acts as a stumbling block to or a building block for multilateral trade liberalization (Bhagwati et al., 1998) and to identify the conditions for successful regional initiatives.

The domino effect described by Baldwin (1993) may be used in favour of the argument that regional integration promotes world-wide trade liberalization. According to this model, outsiders want to become insiders, increasing the incentives to add members to the integration bloc. This enlarges the market, causing other countries to be pulled in as well. At the limit this could lead to a situation where trade barriers are freed world-wide. Alternatively, according to Ethier (1998), regionalism is the means by which new countries enter the multilateral system and attempt to attract FDI.

However, not all the literature is so confident of regionalism promoting multilateral trade liberalization. Bhagwati et al. (1998) refer to the 'spaghetti bowl' phenomenon caused by the overlapping of complex systems of trade concessions. This may help to explain why the EU has generally preferred free trade associations to customs unions with the applicant countries (with the notable exceptions of Turkey, and the proposed customs unions with Malta and Cyprus, where the motives were political as much as economic).

The new regionalism approach may also help to identify the characteristics that are likely to lead to success (or failure) of a regional bloc. A study by the World Bank (2000) argues that a strong liberalizing arrangement with the right partner (preferably rich, large and open) may lead to a virtuous circle of increased credibility, investment, growth and political stability. This may help to explain the interest of Mexico in NAFTA and of the successive waves of applicant countries in joining the EU.

Summary of Key Concepts

- Viner introduced the concepts of trade creation and trade diversion on which customs union theory is based. Trade creation arises when domestic production is replaced by cheaper imports from a partner country. Trade diversion results from low-cost imports from suppliers in third countries being replaced by more expensive imports from a partner country. Usually these concepts are taken to refer to welfare effects rather than trade flows. The welfare effects of forming a customs union on the consumption side also have to be taken into account
- The net effect of forming a customs union on the welfare of the home country may be positive, negative or zero. This is known as Viner's ambiguity.
- The benefits of forming a customs union are likely to be higher: (1) the higher the original level of the tariff before forming the customs union; (2) the lower the common external tariff towards the rest of the world; (3) the higher the number of countries joining a customs union and the greater their size; (4) the smaller the differences in costs of production between the members of the customs union and third countries; (5) the closer the countries are geographically; and (6) the more competitive (producing the same goods) rather than complementary (producing a different range of goods) the economies of the member states are.
- In order to explain why a country should prefer a customs union to non-discriminatory trade liberalization the early literature advanced arguments such as terms-of-trade effects and economies of scale. Johnson argued that the political economy argument – that governments may have a preference for industrial production – can be used to explain why they favour preferential trade arrangements.
- Early empirical research based on the customs union approach found the effects of integration surprisingly small.

- The dynamic effects of integration are: economies of scale, increased competition, specialization, increased bargaining power at an international level and technological progress. These effects are generally considered to be greater than the traditional static integration effects.
- Integration may contribute to long-term growth by encouraging R&D, technology diffusion, improved human capital and more efficient financial markets. In practice empirical studies may encounter difficulties in isolating integration from the other variables having an impact on growth.
- There has been much recent debate as to whether regional co-operation helps or hinders multilateral trade liberalization.

Questions for Study and Review

■ Describe the static and dynamic effects of integration.

■ Compare the effects of non-discriminatory trade liberalization with a preferential trade arrangement or customs union.

■ What explanations have been given of why countries may prefer preferential trade agreements to non-discrimination?

■ Under what conditions is a customs union likely to lead to an increase in welfare?

■ What are the main approaches used in empirical studies to assess the effect of integration?

■ Does regional integration promote multilateral trade liberalization?

■ Exercise on trade creation. Use the example of trade creation in the text to calculate the effects of formation of a customs union on: producer revenue, consumer expenditure, the trade balance and total welfare in Belgium (see also Annex 4 for examples of how to calculate these effects).

■ Exercise on trade diversion. Assume that the free trade price of commodity X is equivalent to €2 in the USA, and €3 in Luxembourg. Initially Belgium applies a 100 per cent tariff on all imports, and produces 60 million units of X and consumes 80 million units. Belgium then forms a customs union with Luxembourg, but maintains the 100 per cent tariff with the USA. After formation of the customs union Belgium produces 50 million units of X, consumes 100 million X and imports 50 million X. Calculate the net impact on welfare as a result of formation of the customs union.

References

Aitken, N.D. (1973) 'The effects of the EEC and EFTA on European trade: A temporal cross-section analysis', *American Economic Review,* Vol. 68.

Balassa, B. (1967) 'Trade creation and trade diversion in the European common market', *Economic Journal,* Vol. 77.

Balassa, B. (1974) 'Trade creation and trade diversion in the European Common Market: An appraisal of the evidence', *Manchester School,* Vol. 42.

Balassa, B. ed. (1975) *European Economic Integration,* North-Holland, Amsterdam.

Baldwin, R. (1989) 'The growth effects of 1992', *Economic Policy,* Vol. 2, pp. 247-81.

Baldwin, R. (1993) A domino theory of regionalism, CEPR Working Paper No. 857, London.

Baldwin, R. (1994) *Towards an Integrated Europe,* Centre for Economic Policy Research, London.

Baldwin, R. and Wyplosz, C. (2004) *The Economics of European Integration,* McGraw-Hill Education, Maidenhead, UK.

Bhagwati, J., Greenaway, D. and Panagariya, A. (1998) 'Trading preferentially: Theory and policy', *The Economic Journal,* Vol. 108, pp. 1128-48.

CEPR/European Commission (1997) 'Impact on trade and investment', Vol. 3, *The Single Market Review*, Office of Official Publications of the European Communities, Luxembourg.

Cooper, C.A. and Massell, B.F. (1965) 'A new look at customs union theory', *Economic Journal*, Vol. 75, pp. 742-75.

Deardorff, A. and Stern, R. (2002) *EU Expansion and EU Growth,* Ford School of Public Policy Working Paper No. 487, University of Michigan, Ann Arbor.

El-Agraa, A.M. (2004) 'The theory of economic integration' in El-Agraa, A.M. ed. *The European Union: Economics and Policies,* 7th edn, Prentice Hall, Harlow, UK.

El-Agraa, A.M. and Jones, A.J. (1981) *Theory of Customs Unions*, Philip Allan, Oxford.

Emerson, M. et al. (1989) *The Economics of 1992: The EC Commission's Assessment of the Economic Effects of Completing the Single Market*, Oxford University Press, Oxford.

Ethier, W.J. (1998) 'The new regionalism', *The Economic Journal*, Vol. 108, pp. 1149-61.

European Bank for Reconstruction and Development (various years) *Transition Report*.

Faini, R. and Portes, R. eds (1995) *European Union Trade with Eastern Europe: Adjustment and Opportunities*, Centre for Economic Policy Research, London.

Falcone, F. (1990) *Commercio internazionale e integrazione europea. Aspetti teorici ed esperienza italiana*, Il Mulino, Bologna.

Frankel, J.A. (1997) *Regional Trading Blocs in the World Trading System*, Institute for International Economics, Washington DC.

Frankel, J.A. and Rose, A. (2000) *Estimating the Effect of Currency Unions on Trade and Output*, National Bureau of Economic Research Working Paper 7857, Cambridge, MA.

Gandolfo, G. (1989) *Corso di economia internazionale*, UTET, Torino.

Grimwade, N. (2004) 'Measuring the impact of economic integration' in EL-Agraa, A.M. ed. *The European Union: Economics and Policies,* 7th edn, Prentice Hall, Harlow, UK.

Hamilton, C.B. and Winters, L.A. (1992) 'Opening up international trade with Eastern Europe,' *Economic Policy*, No. 14.

Harrop, J. (2000) *The Political Economy of Integration in the European Union*, 3rd edn, Edward Elgar, Cheltenham, UK.

Hitiris, T. (2003) *European Community Economics,* 5th edn, Prentice Hall, Harlow, UK.

Italianer, A. (1994) 'Whither the gains from European integration?' *Revue Economique*, Vol. xx, pp. 689-702.

Johnson, H.G. (1958) 'The gains from freer trade in Europe, an estimate', *Manchester School,* Vol. 26, No. 3, pp. 247-55.

Johnson, H.G. (1965) 'An economic theory of protectionism, tariff bargaining and the formation of customs unions', *Journal of Political Economy,* Vol. 73, pp. 256-83.

Kindleberger, C.P. (1973) *International Economics*, 5th edn, Irwin-Dorsey, Homewood, IL.

Kreinen, M.E. (1972) 'Effects of the EEC on imports of manufactures', *Economic Journal*, Vol. 82.

Lipsey, R.G. (1957) 'The theory of customs unions: Trade diversion and welfare', *Economica*, Vol. 24.

Lucas, R.E. (1988) 'On the mechanics of economic development', *Journal of Economic Literature*, Vol. 22.

Marques-Mendes, A.J. (1986) 'The contribution of the European Community to economic growth', *Journal of Common Market Studies*, Vol. 24, No. 4.

Mayes, D. (1978) 'The effects of economic integration on trade', *Journal of Common Market Studies*, Vol. 17, No. 1, pp. 1-25.

Nielsen, J. Ulff-Moller, Heinrich, H. and Hansen, J.D. (1991) *An Economic Analysis of the EC*, McGraw-Hill Education, Maidenhead, UK.

Owen, N. (1983) *Economies of Scale, Competitiveness and Trade Patterns within the European Community*, Oxford University Press, Oxford.

Pelkmans, J. and Gemmen, H. (1983) 'The empirical measurement of static customs union effects', *Rivista Internazionale di Scienze Economiche e Commerciali*, Vol. 30, 7 July.

Resnick, S.A. and Truman, E.M. (1975) 'An empirical examination of bilateral trade in Europe', *Journal of International Economics*, Vol. 3.

Robson, P. (1984) *The Economics of International Integration*, 2nd edn, Allen & Unwin, London.

Romer, P. (1986) 'Increasing returns and long run growth', *Journal of Political Economy*, Vol. 94.

Rose, A. (2000) 'One money, one market: The effect of common currencies on trade', *Economic Policy*, Vol. 30, pp. 7-33.

Rose, A. (2002) 'The effect of common currencies on international trade: Where do we stand?', unpublished manuscript available at http://faculty.hass.berkeley.edu/arose/RecRes.htm

Salvatore, D. (2001) *International Economics*, 7th edn, John Wiley & Sons, New York.

Sellekaerts, W. (1973) 'How meaningful are empirical studies on trade creation and trade diversion?', *Weltwirtschaftliches Archiv*, Vol. 109, pp. 519-51.

Senior Nello, S.M. (2002) 'Progress in preparing for EU enlargement: The tensions between economic and political integration', *International Political Science Review*, Vol. 23, No. 3, July.

Solow, R. (1956) 'A contribution to the theory of growth', *Quarterly Journal of Economics*, February.

Tinbergen, J. (1952) *On the Theory of Economic Policy*, North-Holland, Amsterdam.

Truman, E.M. (1969) 'The European Economic Community: Trade creation and trade diversion', *Yale Economic Essays*, Spring.

Verdoorn, P.J. and Schwartz, A.N.R. (1972) 'Two alternative estimates of the effects of the EEC and EFTA on the pattern of trade', *European Economic Review*, Vol. 3.

Viner, J. (1953) *The Customs Union Issue,* The Carnegie Endowment for International Peace, New York.

Wang, Z.H. and Winters, L.A. (1991) *The Trading Potential of Eastern Europe*. CEPR Discussion Paper No. 610. Centre for Economic Policy Research, London.

Winters, L.A. (1984) 'Separability and the specification of foreign trade functions', *European Economic Review*, Vol. 27.

Winters, L.A. (1985) 'EU's preferential trade agreements: Objectives and outcomes' in van Dijk, P. and Faber, G. eds, *The External Economic Dimension of the European Union*, Kluwer Law International, Dordrecht and London.

World Bank (2000) 'The road to stability and prosperity in South Eastern Europe: A regional strategy paper', World Bank, Washington DC.

Useful websites

Studies of various trade and integration issues are provided by the European Commission: www.europa.eu.int/comm

List of abbreviations

CGE   computable general equilibrium
CEEC   Central and Eastern European country

FDI	foreign direct investment
GDP	gross domestic product
GNP	gross national product
MFN	most favoured nation
NAFTA	North American Free Trade Agreement
WTO	World Trade Organization

6

From the Single Market to the 'New Europe'

LEARNING OBJECTIVES

By the end of this chapter you should be able to understand:

▶ That specialization of industry appears to be greater in the USA than the EU;

▶ The main forms of non-tariff barrier still applied in the EU;

▶ What advantages were expected from the Single European Market (SEM) Programme;

▶ What were the main steps in introducing the SEM;

▶ How important the Single European Act was in the integration process;

▶ What were the estimated effects of the Single Market on the European economy;

▶ How the Lisbon Summit of 2000 advocated completion of the Single Market but aimed to improve EU economic performance through the creation of a 'knowledge-based economy', and an EU education and training system of 'world quality reference' by 2010;

▶ How the 2002 Barcelona European summit reiterated the Lisbon objectives but also placed emphasis on encouraging labour mobility and strengthening the social agenda.

BACKGROUND TO THE SINGLE MARKET PROGRAMME

Following the 1979 increase in oil prices, the European economy experienced a prolonged recession with stagnating output, rising unemployment and declining world export shares. During these years the terms 'Eurosclerosis' and 'Europessimism' were coined to describe the flagging process of integration. The main energies of the Community appeared absorbed by budgetary squabbles and the annual marathons to fix 'common' agricultural prices.[1]

The EC member states were becoming increasingly concerned about the growing lag between their economic performance and that of countries such as Japan and the USA, especially in high-technology sectors.[2] The Community was not only losing its world market share in industries such as automobiles and industrial machinery but also in rapidly growing sectors such as information technology and electronics. Moreover EC markets were increasingly being penetrated in these sectors by foreign firms.

In searching for the explanation for this lack of competitiveness, European industrialists and policy makers laid the blame on the fragmentation of the EC market. The EC business lobby soon began to press for EC initiatives to overcome this disadvantage, and the initial response of the Community was to introduce a series of measures to promote co-operation in research and development among European firms.

Theoretical studies, such as that of Krugman (1991), also provided evidence of the fragmentation of the EC market. Krugman argued that the four large countries of the EC were comparable in size and population to the four great regions of the USA: the North-East (New England and the mid-Atlantic), the Midwest (the north-central and western north-central states), the West and the South. Examining industrial specialization as measured by share of manufacturing employment, Krugman found that the level of specialization in the USA was higher than in the EC, even though the distances were greater. The Midwest could be compared to Germany in that both were centres of heavy, traditional industry, while the South was similar to Italy with light, labour-intensive industry. However, while there was almost no textile production in the Midwest, Germany still accounted for a substantial share. As shown in Table 6.1, Italy had a far higher share of machinery and auto production than the South. Krugman attributed the lower level of specialization in the EU to the continued existence of non-tariff barriers.[3]

	Germany	Italy	Midwest	South
Textiles	3.7	9.1	0.3	11.7
Apparel	2.6	5.6	2.4	10.6
Machinery	15.8	12.9	15.0	7.1
Transport equipment	13.2	10.4	12.8	5.9
Automobiles	38.4	17.6	66.3	25.4

Table 6.1 **Industrial specialization (share of manufacturing employment) in Germany, Italy and the USA (%)**

Source: Krugman (1991)

In 1985, when Jacques Delors became president of the Commission, the Single or Internal Market Programme was announced as a strategy to raise EC competitiveness.[4] The idea was to return to and complete the original objectives set out in the Treaty of Rome. The removal of tariffs on intra-EC

---

[1] See Chapter 10 for an explanation of why these prices were not 'common' for many years.
[2] Where possible, in this chapter the terms 'EC' or 'Community' have been used when reference is prior to implementation of the Maastricht Treaty, and the term 'EU' is used subsequently.
[3] In the literature various indices to measure specialization have been developed. For an overview of these indices see Coombes and Overman (2004).
[4] The term 'Internal Market' is generally used by the Commission.

trade was considered a major factor contributing to the quadrupling of that trade in the first decade of the Community, with intra-EC trade growing twice as fast as world trade over that period. If the Community could now eliminate non-tariff barriers between its members, the earlier success of the Community could perhaps be repeated.

The main non-tariff barriers identified were:

- Frontier controls;
- Differences in technical specifications and standards;
- Restrictions on competition for public purchases;
- Restrictions on providing certain services (in particular financial and transport services) in other EC countries;
- Differences in national tax systems.

The Commission divided these barriers into three somewhat arbitrary categories: physical barriers, fiscal barriers and technical barriers (all the rest). The third category lumps together measures such as differences in technical specifications and public procurement procedures with institutional restrictions on the free movement of people and capital, etc.

The choice of completion of the Single Market to relaunch the integration effort represented a major strategic decision on the part of Delors and the Commission. Following the Hague Summit of 1969, economic and monetary union was the main integration objective of the 1970s. The difficulties encountered and limited success realized help to explain the search for an alternative.

EXPECTED ADVANTAGES OF THE SINGLE MARKET

The EC Commission sponsored what was probably the most extensive single assessment of the likely effects of an economic policy ever carried out. The results were published in 16 volumes and are known as the Cecchini Report, or 'Costs of non-Europe'.[5] As will be shown below, many of the results of the study have been subject to heavy criticism, but the description of the various approaches used in the analysis is interesting both as a guide to many of the prevailing theories on integration at the time and as an insight into the views of the Commission.

Traditionally, in order to assess the impact of economic integration, customs union theory made use of the 'static' concepts of trade creation and trade diversion (see Chapter 5). However, empirical studies of integration effects increasingly pointed to the gap between the traditional theory and real issues and stressed the need to take dynamic effects such as increased competition and the scope for exploiting economies of scale into account.[6] As will be shown below, dynamic effects figure strongly in the analysis of expected benefits of the Single Market.

Studies such as the Cecchini Report emphasize the impact that the Single Market was likely to have in reducing prices and costs. Prior to the 1993 Programme large price differences existed between EC states,[7] and these were taken as an indication of the degree of market fragmentation.

Figure 6.1 provides a useful shorthand illustration of the expected effect of the Single Market on costs and prices. The elimination of barriers would enable firms from other EC member states to sell at lower prices in a particular EC country, say Italy. The increased competition from other EC firms selling at lower prices on the Italian market would first induce Italian firms to reduce excess

---

[5] Cecchini (1988).
[6] See Chapter 4 for a formal treatment of economies of scale.
[7] According to Emerson et al. (1989), the average variation from EC mean price without indirect taxes in 1985 across countries was 15 per cent for consumer goods and 12 per cent for capital products (taking the EC-9 members prior to 1981 as 100). In the service sectors these variations were even greater, amounting to 28 per cent for road and rail transport, 29 per cent for financial services, 50 per cent for telephone and telegram services and 42 per cent for electrical repairs.

Figure 6.1 The effects of eliminating cost-increasing trade barriers

*Economic rents consist of the margin of excess profit or wage rates that result from market protection.

** X-inefficiency consists of, for example, the costs of over-manning, excess overhead costs and excess inventories (i.e. inefficiencies not related to the production technology of the firm's investments). Because the firm is not operating in a competitive environment, there is inadequate pressure to cut these costs.

***Economies from restructuring include, for example, greater economies of scale, or the benefits obtained when inefficient production capacity is eliminated and new investments are made.

Direct costs include delays at the frontier and the cost of differing technical regulations, which would immediately fall if market barriers were eliminated.

Indirect costs are those that would fall as foreign suppliers adjust to the more competitive situation with more efficient production and marketing.

Source: Figure 2.2 (p. 26) from *The Economics of 1992* (1989) by Emerson, Michael et al. By permission of Oxford University Press.

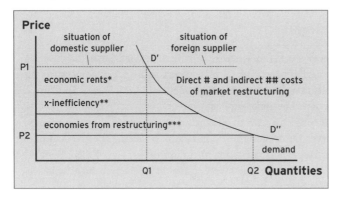

profits and wages and eliminate inefficiencies within the firms. Subsequently, the increased demand resulting from lower prices would encourage restructuring and attempts to exploit economies of scale, both through mergers and new investment.

It was argued that these processes would free resources for alternative productive uses, so raising the levels of investment and consumption sustainable in the Community. The rationalization of production and distribution would increase productivity, thereby reducing prices and costs.

In the case of public procurement, the cost savings would release resources enabling governments either to cut taxes or carry out other growth-inducing activities. The liberalization of financial services was of particular importance to the programme since the reduced cost of credit would stimulate increased consumer demand and investment. It was estimated that these benefits would be apparent after a period of 5–6 years.

THE TIMETABLE FOR THE INTRODUCTION OF THE SINGLE MARKET

In March 1985 the new president of the Commission, Jacques Delors, presented his programme for the Single Market to the European Parliament. Later that year the Cockfield White Paper, 'Completing the Internal Market', was presented at the European Council in Milan. This called for the elimination of barriers between EC countries by the end of 1992 and set out 282 measures necessary to achieve this aim.

Many of these measures had been around as draft proposals for many years, and although the completion of the Single Market was not a new idea, it now acquired a new impetus. The way in which the Programme was presented represents a major marketing success: the timetable set out deadlines that represented precise targets, and focused the attention of politicians and business. The Commission, and in particular Delors, were largely responsible for introducing what was to become a self-fulfilling prophecy. The personal style of Lord Cockfield, commissioner for the

Internal Market, who emphasized the technical and low-key nature of the programme, also contributed to its success (Tsoukalis, 1997).

The emphasis on deregulation meant that the programme coincided with the economic doctrine being advocated at the time by politicians such as Thatcher and Reagan. Initially the programme seemed to be concerned with rules, not money, so did not appear a threat to national governments. However, it was soon to emerge that the programme would have to be flanked by redistributive measures to compensate the weakest regions and sections of the population.

The Milan Summit also had to decide on the intergovernmental conferences to prepare the necessary revision to the existing treaties. Initially the UK, Denmark and Greece were opposed to the proposed institutional reforms that would increase the use of majority voting in the Council, strengthen the European Parliament and extend the use of European Political Co-operation. The decision of the Italian Presidency to go ahead on a majority vote was 'unexpected and without precedent' (Tsoukalis, 1997).

The three governments that had initially opposed institutional reform soon overcame their misgivings. In part this reflected a fear of being excluded and not being able to influence the decision-making process. However, in the case of the UK in particular, institutional reform was seen as the necessary price to pay for the Single Market, which was an objective strongly favoured by national politicians and businessmen.

THE SINGLE EUROPEAN ACT

The Single European Act sets out the formal procedure necessary to implement the 1993 programme. It also modified the EC decision-making process and called for a revived integration effort in other fields such as technology and in monetary, social, regional and external policies. The Single European Act (SEA) defined the Single Market as 'an area without internal frontiers in which the free movement of goods, persons, services and capital is ensured'.

The SEA represented the first major revision to the treaties, but at the time its importance was underestimated. With the benefit of hindsight it can be argued that the SEA launched a new phase in the integration process, spilling over into renewed efforts in political union, institutional reform, economic and monetary union, and reinforced EC social, regional and competition policies. The way in which the Single Market Programme pushed the integration process forward in other areas lends itself well to interpretation according to the neo-functionalist approach.

In order to implement the harmonization of national rules and regulations, qualified majority voting was to be used in the Council. This voting rule was also extended to the liberalization of capital movements and of sea and air transport.[8] The rule of unanimity voting was still to be used in the Council for questions relating to fiscal policy, the free movement of persons, and the rights and interests of employees. This was because these were sensitive issues on which the EC member states held divergent views.

Though the SEA contains formal recognition of the European Monetary System (EMS) and the role of the ECU, Article 102 stipulates that any institutional change in economic and monetary policy would require a new intergovernmental conference to revise the treaties, a prospect that seemed unlikely at the time. EMU is linked to completion of the internal market in that exchange rate uncertainty between currencies can be regarded as another obstacle to trade. The introduction of a single monetary unit would confirm the reality of the Single Market, but this in turn would

---

[8] The *quid pro quo* for wider use of majority voting was a safeguard clause that would allow member states to continue to apply national provisions after the introduction of new EC rules in certain circumstances. This was to ensure that standards for the protection of the environment or working conditions would not deteriorate.

push the integration process further. Democratic control of the new European Central Bank would require further steps in the direction of political union.

Title V of the Single European Act deals with 'economic and social cohesion' to ensure harmonious development and the reduction of regional disparities. The weaker regions, and in particular the periphery of the Community, feared that they would not be able to withstand the increased competition implied by the Single Market. In response to their requests, Article 130d of the SEA calls for effective co-ordination and rationalization of the Structural Funds.

Certain derogations and special provisions were permitted in order to take account of the heterogeneity and different levels of development of EC member states, but the outcome was far from permitting a multi-speed Europe.

The Treaty also called for increased Community responsibility for social policy, in particular on questions relating to the health and safety of workers. In 1988 the idea of a 'Social Europe' was launched, which entailed identifying the regions and industries most likely to be negatively affected by the 1993 programme and offering some measures of compensation. It was also argued that social policy measures were necessary in order to ensure a 'level playing field' and prevent the Internal Market being undermined by the phenomenon of 'social dumping'.

Social dumping refers to fear that employment will be lost in member states where better social standards are reflected in higher labour costs. There may be downward pressure on wages, social security conditions and minimum health and safety regulations in those countries in order to prevent loss of market share. This phenomenon is attributed to 'unfair competition' from countries in which labour laws are less restrictive. A major aim of both the 1989 Social Charter and the Social Chapter of the Maastricht Treaty was to prevent this type of 'social dumping'.

One of the immediate effects of announcement of the Single Market Programme was to induce a rapid increase in the number of cross-border mergers of EC firms, which rose from 200 in 1985 to some 2000 in 1989 (Tsoukalis, 1997). This led to a tightening of EC competition policy and, in particular, the introduction of *ex ante* Community authority over mergers from 1989 (see Chapter 15).

IMPLEMENTATION OF THE SINGLE MARKET PROGRAMME

At the EC level rapid progress was made in passing the necessary measures for the Internal Market Programme and, according to the Commission, by 31 December 1992 95 per cent of the legislative programme set out in 1985 was complete.[9] The transposition of EC measures into national legislation was to prove a slightly more lengthy process, but the real difficulties arose in implementation of the measures and the granting of temporary derogations.

Progress still appears to be slow with regard to public procurement, the recognition of higher education diplomas, and (at least in certain EU states) the liberalization of financial services, telecommunications, transport, intellectual property and the environment. According to the European Commission, substantial differences in the prices between new cars in different member states was evidence that the Internal Market was still not operating fully in this sector in 2004 (see Box 6.1).

Subsequently, the European Commission attempted to tighten up on enforcement and implementation procedures.[10] The 1997 Amsterdam European Council endorsed an Action Plan that entails the Commission drawing up a 'Single Market Scoreboard' every six months. This indicates the shortcomings of the various member states in implementing Single Market measures.

---

[9] The main exceptions related to company legislation, fiscal harmonization and intellectual property rights.
[10] See European Commission (2003c) for a description of the various measures taken.

> ## Box 6.1 Car prices in the EU
>
> Each year the Commission carries out a survey of price differences of new cars net of taxes between the member states. There appeared to be some price convergence for the 90 best-selling models in the eurozone considered in 2004.* In the eurozone the cheapest cars were in Finland, and the most expensive were in Germany and to a lesser extent Austria. For 18 models sold in Germany the prices were between 20 per cent and 31 per cent higher than in the cheapest eurozone country. In the new member states the cheapest cars were in Poland, which were 9 per cent below Finnish prices on average, although luxury cars were more expensive in Poland.
>
> *European Commission Memo/04/202 of 29 July 2004, www.europa.eu.int/comm

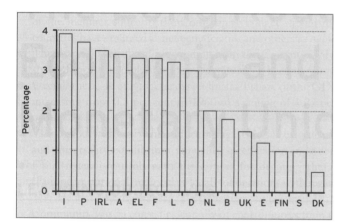

Figure 6.2 The share of Single Market Directives not yet transposed into national legislation*

*The situation as at 15 April 2003
Source: Internal Market Scoreboard of May 2003.

According to the May 2003 Single Market Scoreboard,[11] the transposition deficit in 2002 was 2.4 per cent, well above the objective of 1.5 per cent set by the Stockholm European Council. The worst offenders with regard to implementing legislation were Italy, Portugal, Ireland, Austria, Spain and France (see Figure 6.2). The best performers were Denmark, Sweden and Finland. The 2002 Barcelona European Council also called for a 'zero tolerance' target for transposition of directives two or more years overdue. In April 2003 only Denmark, Finland, Portugal and the UK met that target (see Figure 6.3).

The November 2002 Scoreboard suggested that 80 per cent of EU citizens felt that the Single Market had led to a wider choice of products and 67 per cent believed it had improved quality, but only 45 per cent felt well informed. Of the businesses interviewed 46 per cent believed that the Single Market had a positive effect. The European Commission has proposed increasing EU and national initiatives to ensure that citizens and firms are more aware of their Internal Market rights.[12]

The countries with most cases of infringement of Single Market legislation at the end of February 2003 were France, Italy and Spain, while the countries with least infringement cases were Sweden, Luxembourg and Denmark (see Figure 6.4).

Since 1987 there have been 'package meetings' of experts from the member states and the Commission to discuss a 'package' of cases under examination by the Commission for violation of

---

[11] European Commission (2003c).
[12] European Commission (2002a).

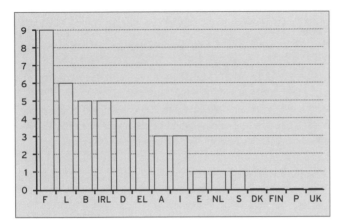

Figure 6.3 The number of Single Market Directives still not transposed into national legislation after two years*

*The situation as at 15 April 2003
Source: Internal Market Scoreboard of May 2003.

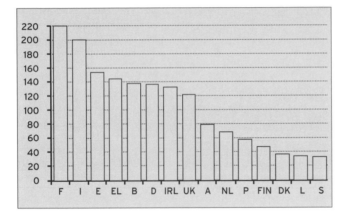

Figure 6.4 Number of cases of infringement of Single Market legislation*

*The situation as at 15 April 2003
Source: Internal Market Scoreboard of May 2003.

Community law. The aim is to solve cases without the need for further legal action, and in recent years the use of these meetings has increased.

In 2002 the SOLVIT redress system was introduced in order to improve implementation of Internal Market rules (see Box 6.2). Previously victims of failure to apply rules (such as non-recognition of a valid diploma or denied market access for a product) had to appeal to national courts or to the Commission. Under the new system the victim can refer the case by Internet or

Box 6.2 SOLVIT Cases

A Portuguese breakdown vehicle was transporting a damaged Portuguese car from Belgium to Portugal and was fined €600 by the Spanish police because the breakdown vehicle was not fitted with tachograph equipment. The Portuguese SOLVIT office pointed out that breakdown vehicles were not required to have this equipment by EU regulations, and the fine was refunded.

A Danish citizen was registered as an EU job seeker in the Netherlands, but the Dutch authorities only granted her Mexican husband the same status after intervention by the Dutch SOLVIT office.

Source: Internal Market Scoreboard No. 12 of May 2003, www.europa.eu.int/comm/internal_market/en/update/score/index.htm

telephone to the SOLVIT office it their own member state, and the office will raise the case with the country in which the misapplication has occurred. In 2002 most use of SOLVIT was made by Germany, Portugal and the Netherlands, while the time taken to resolve a case through SOLVIT varied from an average of 101 days in Italy to 40 days in Belgium and 38 days in Iceland (see Figure 6.5).[13]

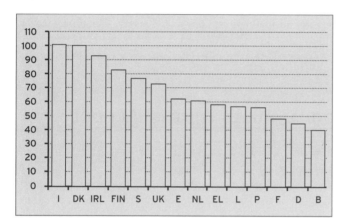

Figure 6.5 Average length of time to resolve SOLVIT cases (number of days)*

*The situation as at 15 April 2003
Source: Internal Market Scoreboard of May 2003.

THE MAIN ELEMENTS OF THE SINGLE MARKET PROGRAMME: THE REMOVAL OF FRONTIER CONTROLS

A key aim of the removal of frontier controls is to facilitate free movement of people within the Community. Key to this strategy is the Schengen Agreement which, according to the Amsterdam Treaty, was to be incorporated into the Community pillar (see Chapter 7). Other aspects of the elimination of border controls include the abolition of customs formalities, veterinary and road safety checks at frontiers. In addition, quantitative restrictions could no longer be applied at the national level by EC member states and had to be replaced by EC measures.[14] The Cecchini Report estimated that industry would save €8 billion a year, and government would save €1 billion per year if frontier controls were removed.

> **Box 6.3 Football integration**
>
> One of the effects of the Single Market was to encourage integration of soccer. Football integration has paralleled the overall integration process. In 1956 the first European Cup was played and, as in the case of the EEC, initially the UK failed to participate.* With the Single Market objective of free movement of labour it was no longer legal for EU teams to limit the number of citizens they had from other EU states. At about the same time the European Court decided that footballers were free to move anywhere after the end of their contract without their club demanding a transfer fee. Wages and transfers increased, and the Champions League emerged.
>
> *_Economist_, 31 May 2003.

---

[13] European Commission (2003c). The Internal Market also applies in three EFTA countries, Iceland, Liechtenstein and Norway, as a result of the EEA agreement.
[14] This had important implications for the quotas on textile products permitted by the MFA Multifibre Agreement (MFA), and entailed abolition of the monetary compensatory amounts of the Common Agricultural Policy (a system of taxes and subsidies levied at the border to cushion the impact of exchange rate changes on the system of price support). The Single Market Programme and the transition of Central and Eastern Europe from 1989 also account for the elimination of the different quotas applied by the member states on imports from the former CEEC 'non-market economies'.

A series of measures was introduced to facilitate the right to work in other member states and to develop exchange programmes, including the Socrates and ERASMUS (university exchanges), Leonardo da Vinci (traineeships) and LINGUA (language) programmes of the EU. By 2003 it was estimated that 1 million students had participated in ERASMUS programmes (European Commission, 2003a). There was also a renewed effort to encourage recognition of university diplomas and other professional qualifications in respective member states. The EURES network was established to provide information on job opportunities in EU states. Though legislation permitting the residence of EU workers and their families in other member states had existed for some time, measures to promote easier residence for other categories, such as pensioners and students, were also passed.

DIFFERENCES IN NATIONAL RULES AND REGULATIONS

According to Mattera (1988), differences in standards and technical barriers accounted for some 80 per cent of the remaining barriers to intra-EC trade. Though the words are sometimes used interchangeably, technical regulations refer to legally binding rules relating to the health and safety of consumers, while 'standards' are voluntary and aim to provide adequate information and ensure the quality of a product.

Barriers, supposedly on 'health' grounds, were levied, for example, on chocolate and French mineral water by the FRG, and by Italy on imports of pasta not using durum wheat. In some cases differences in technical regulations prevented cross-border trade, while in others it added to the costs of firms that had to modify their products to meet the requirements of other EC countries. It is estimated that some 75 per cent of intra-EU trade is covered by these technical norms (Molle, 2001).

Article 30 of the Treaty of Rome prohibits quantitative restrictions on intra-EC trade and 'all measures having an equivalent effect'. In the 1974 Dassonville ruling of the European Court of Justice, it was argued that 'measures having an equivalent effect' included 'all trading rules enacted by member states which are capable of hindering directly or indirectly, actually or potentially intra-EC trade'.

One way of eliminating these barriers to trade between EC member states is by harmonizing the national standards and technical regulations of member states. This 'old approach' has proved slow and inefficient as the detailed, technical legislation involved is complex and costly. It also runs the risk of excessive uniformity and bureaucratic interference. The topic is one on which feelings run high, with complaints that 'Eurocrats' are concerned with 'measuring the size of sausages', or determined to bring about the demise of rare breeds and crops. Against this, however, excessive deregulation runs the risk of inadequate protection for consumers.

The solution reached by the Community was to rely as far as possible on the principle of mutual recognition, which was defined in the much-cited *Cassis de Dijon* case of 1979. In this case the European Court of Justice ruled against a German prohibition of imports of a French liqueur on the grounds that it did not conform to German rules and regulations, and established the general principle that all goods lawfully manufactured and marketed in one member state should be accepted also in other member countries. At the same time, the Court recognized the need for some exceptions relating to public health, the fairness of commercial transactions and the defence of the consumer. By 2003 the mutual recognition principle covered about half intra-EU trade in goods[15] and had also been extended to some dealings with third countries, including the USA.

---

[15] European Commission (2002a and 2003d).

According to surveys carried out by the Commission,[16] mutual recognition works well for relatively simple products but less so for more complex goods. When a product is denied access to a country there is no clear procedure for a company to challenge a negative decision so the company is forced to modify the product or abandon that market. In 2003 the Commission called for new legislation to enhance the transparency of mutual recognition and set out the key principles on which it is based.[17] These could include mandatory notification when mutual recognition is refused.

To speed up the process of harmonization, in 1985 a 'new approach' was developed. Wherever harmonization of rules at the EC level was deemed necessary, it was decided that this should be limited to essential objectives and requirements. Directives cover large groups of products and/or hazards, and specify the essential safety or other requirements the product must meet. The manufacturers are free to choose between applying either the appropriate EU standard (see below), or any other technical specifications that meet these essential requirements. Any product conforming to the requirements can circulate freely in all the member states.

The task of defining technical specifications was left to private standardization bodies. At EC level standardization bodies included the CEN (Centre Européen de Normalisation), the CENELEC (Centre Européen de Normalisation Electrotechnique) and the ETSI (European Telecommunications Standards Institute). The membership of these organizations consists of national standardization bodies. Between 1990 and 2002 some 2000 of these standards were introduced.[18]

According to the European Commission,[19] the new approach has proved relatively successful but needs improved conformity assessment procedures, increased administrative co-operation and better market surveillance to ensure that effective action is taken when products fail to meet essential requirements. A product manufactured according to EU standards can carry the mark 'CE' if it conforms to the basic safety requirements laid out in the relevant directive. Compliance is voluntary and manufacturers may choose not to observe Community standards, but the onus is on them to prove that their product is safe.

In 2003 the European Commission began to discuss plans of introducing a 'made in the EU' label, but many national governments and firms felt this would add to costs and render it difficult to promote products on the basis of national origin. It was argued that while a mark of origin for certain member states could act as a mark of distinction in the production of some goods, this was not necessarily the case for the EU. One option raised by the Commission was that national markings could accompany the EU label.

The average time needed to adopt an EU standard increased from 4.5 years in 1995 to 8 years in 2001, and the European Commission called for measures to speed up this process and ensure uniform quality in the production and application of standards.[20]

The Community and, in particular, the DG for Consumer Affairs of the Commission are also active in the field of protecting consumer rights, and its initiatives can be divided into four main categories:

- ■ Actions for the protection of consumer health and safety. These include rules on the testing and registration of pharmaceutical, medical and cosmetic products, measures to ensure the safety of toys, health controls, labelling for food and agricultural products and so on.

---

[16] European Commission (2002b).
[17] European Commission (2003b).
[18] European Commission (2003a).
[19] European Commission (2003b).
[20] European Commission (2003b).

- Protection of the economic interests of consumers by, for instance, measures against unfair contracts and misleading advertising.
- Actions to ensure that consumers have comparative information, through rules on packaging and labelling, and support for consumer organizations.
- Measures to ensure the right of consumers to redress, with simple clear procedures.

The Commission set out a Consumer Policy Strategy for the 2000–06 period which is focused on three main objectives: a high common level of consumer protection, effective enforcement of consumer protection rules and the involvement of consumer organizations in EU policies.[21]

FISCAL HARMONIZATION

Differences in national tax systems represented a barrier to completion of the internal market in two ways. In the first place, tax differences may cause price distortions and so undermine the competitive process. Secondly, differences in national taxation have to be adjusted at the border, thereby necessitating controls at the frontier. Moreover, operating with different tax systems adds to the cost and complexity of doing business in other EU countries. In a survey of EU companies in 2002, 77 per cent called for national tax systems to be more closely aligned.[22]

The Community has made slow progress in introducing fiscal harmonization, partly because this is one of the areas where unanimity voting is required in the Council of Ministers since taxation raises sensitive issues. The power to tax is central to the sovereignty of a country, and differences in tax systems frequently reflect underlying differences in culture and tradition.

Article 99 of the Treaty of Rome called for harmonization of indirect taxes, but the Treaty is rather vague on what is meant by harmonization (Ardy and El-Agraa, 2004). Article 100, for example, states only that 'laws should be approximated'.[23]

Although the Single European Act (Article 17) called for 'harmonization of legislation concerning turnover taxes, excise duties and other forms of indirect tax', to date the approach adopted has been that of approximation rather than harmonization of taxes. The emphasis on indirect taxation reflects the assumption that goods and capital are more mobile than labour, and so more sensitive to differences in national tax systems (Tsoukalis, 1997).

At the time of the Treaty of Rome the system of indirect taxation adopted by the member states varied considerably.[24] One of the main achievements of the Community was to introduce a common system of turnover tax from 1967, based on the French VAT (value added tax).[25] This was considered necessary as a percentage of VAT returns constituted one of the own resources of the Community Budget (see Chapter 9).

VAT accounts for some 10–20 per cent of the total tax revenue of the member states (Molle, 2001). Although the EC members agreed on a uniform method for calculating VAT in 1979, its application differs greatly from country to country. Differences relate to tax coverage (i.e. which products are liable to tax), the number of VAT rates and their levels. As shown in Table 6.2, Denmark applied only one VAT rate in 1991/2, while Ireland applied six. The standard rate applied varied from 15 per cent in Spain, the FRG and Luxembourg to 25 per cent in Denmark. Differences

---

[21] European Commission (2002c).
[22] European Commission (2002a).
[23] Harmonization entails introducing common legislation, while approximation involves bringing national laws more in line with each other.
[24] With the exception of France, the other original EC members applied a cascade system. This was a multi-stage tax levied on the gross value of output at each stage of the production process. At each stage the tax was levied on selling price, and this price might reflect tax paid at an early stage. The system was therefore cumulative and provided an incentive to vertical integration. In contrast, VAT is neutral towards vertical integration and has the advantage that it is self-policing since the purchasing firm has an interest in obtaining an invoice from suppliers showing that taxes on inputs have been paid.
[25] VAT is paid at each stage in the productive process (including marketing) on the value added at that stage.

also arose as to which products were subject to reduced rates either to compensate for the regressive nature of VAT, or for merit goods, such as books and cultural services. For example the UK applied zero rating for foodstuffs, gas and electricity.

Table 6.2 VAT rates in the Community in 1991/2 and 2003 (per cent)

Country	Standard 1991/2	Reduced 1991/2	Increased 1991/2	Standard 2003	Reduced 2003
Belgium	19.5	1, 6 and 12	–	21	6
Denmark	25	–	–	25	–
FRG	15	7	–	16	7
Spain	15	6	28	16	4/7
France	18.6	2.1 and 5.5	–	19.6	2.1/5.5
Greece	18	4 and 8	–	18	4/8
Italy	19	4, 9 and 12	38	20	4/10
Ireland	21	0, 2.7, 10.0, 12,5 16	–	21	4.3/13.5
Lux.	15	3 and 6	–	15	3/6
NL	18.5	6	–	19	6
Portugal	16	5	–	19	5/12
UK	17.5	0	–	17.5	5

Source: Hitiris, T. (1994) *European Union Economics*, 3rd edition. Prentice Hall: Harlow, UK.

The 1985 White Paper called for the reduction or elimination of fiscal barriers, and in 1987 the Commission produced detailed proposals of how to reach this objective in the case of VAT. The negotiations were heated and prolonged. Higher rate countries such as Ireland, France and Denmark feared the loss of VAT revenue. Low rate countries such as Germany feared that increased VAT could add to inflationary pressures. The UK and Ireland wanted to maintain zero rating on 'social necessities' such as foodstuffs to offset the regressive nature of VAT.

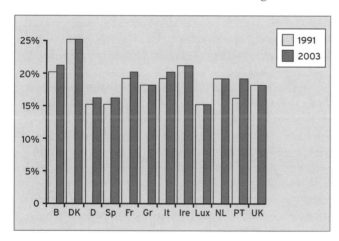

Figure 6. 6 The difference in standard VAT rates in 1991 and 2003

Source: Hitiris, T. (1994) *European Union Economics*, 3rd edition. Prentice Hall: Harlow, UK.

A compromise was eventually reached, which entailed a standard minimum rate of VAT of 15 per cent and a list of products (food, pharmaceuticals, energy, water, hotels, passenger transport etc.) on which a reduced rate of 5 per cent could be applied. Subsequently a band of 15–25 per cent was introduced for the standard rate. Existing zero rates could be continued but not extended.

As can be seen from Table 6.2 and Figure 6.6, over time convergence has been minimal. In November 2000 a European Commission survey indicated that 26 per cent of businessmen still considered that differences in VAT rates and procedures were an obstacle to doing business in the Internal Market.[26] In 2003 the Commission proposed measures to simplify the VAT regime, which included abolishing the zero VAT rating on children's clothes in Britain and Ireland. The UK and Irish governments fiercely opposed the proposal, but, according to the Commission, the exemption was not necessarily passed on as lower prices.

Traditionally VAT in the Community was applied according to the principle of destination, in other words it was paid in the country of consumption. If a product were traded between two EU countries, the tax would be paid in the importing country, and VAT paid in the exporting country would be refunded. This may be complex and costly for firms as businessmen may not be acquainted with the legislation and language of the country to which they are exporting. The Commission proposed that with the introduction of the Single Market, the destination system should be replaced by a system based on the principle of origin (also known as the 'common market' principle). In practice little progress has been made in this direction, and reform of the system remains a long-term goal.

Excise duty accounts for about 6–12 per cent of the total tax revenue of the member states (Molle, 2001). There are also considerable differences in the level and coverage of excise duties (on petrol, alcohol, cigarettes, wine, beer etc.) in the various EC countries (see Box 6.4). These reflect differences in social customs, public health considerations and the revenue requirements of governments of the member states. In some cases decisions are also influenced by the existence of state monopolies (for example tobacco for many years in Italy).

Box 6.4 Excise duties in the Single Market

According to Commons (2002), the duty on a pint of beer was 30p in the UK, 5p in France, 3p in Germany and 7p in the Netherlands. Duty on a 70cl bottle of spirits was £5.48 in the UK, £2.51 in France and £1.19 in Spain. Duty on a 75cl bottle of wine was £1.16 in the UK, 2p in France and zero in Spain. Total excise duty on a packet of cigarettes was £2.80 in the UK, £1.22 in France, £1.00 in the Netherlands and 99p in Belgium.*

Under the Single Market, the quantity of products subject to excise duty that could be taken from one country to another for 'personal consumption' initially amounted to 800 cigarettes, 10 litres of alcohol, 90 litres of wine, 110 litres of beer etc. For private individuals going to another member state this was subsequently increased to an 'unlimited quantity' of goods for personal use on which excise had been paid. Differences in excise duties between the member states were sufficient to stimulate a lively trade exploiting these personal allowances, creating significant losses of revenue for some of the member states (notably the UK).

Sweden and Finland were allowed to maintain state monopolies on retailing alcohol and, together with Denmark, tighter limits on how much alcohol travellers can bring back from other EU states. The European Commission has, however, been pushing for liberalization by the Nordic member states. In December 2003 the Danish government lowered duties on alcohol, because so much was being bought in Germany. From 2004 the Swedish government applied EU-wide limits on the importation of alcoholic beverages, and travel to Denmark and Germany was frequent.

*See also European Commission (2004c).

---

[26] European Commission (2003c).

Little progress has been made in reducing differences in national systems of excise duties in the Community. The member states have adopted common lists of products on which excise duties apply, and these are divided into alcoholic, tobacco and petroleum products. The 1993 programme simply entailed minimum rates of duty for alcohol,[27] tobacco, cigarettes and mineral oil, and an imprecise commitment to harmonization in the medium term. In the meantime goods could circulate an interconnected circuit of customs deposits and were subject to duty only when and where they left that circuit.

The quantity and value of products subject to excise duty that could be taken from one country to another for 'personal consumption' was increased. It is likely that the increased mobility of products in the Single Market will force governments into further measures of market-induced harmonization (see Box 6.4).

Duty-free sales have no place in an internal market, but their abolition entailed a serious loss of revenue for airports and ferry companies. It was eventually decided to allow sales of duty-free on intra-EU trips to continue until 1999 when, despite protests by certain member states (the UK, France and Germany), they were abolished.

Though the Commission has presented various proposals, little progress has been made in harmonizing direct taxes, which account for 40 per cent of total tax revenues,[28] also because a unanimity vote is required. The principle of mutual recognition has been applied to corporation taxes.

The fear of 'tax competition' again came to the fore from the late 1990s. It was argued that removal of the barriers, with capital and labour becoming more mobile, would lead workers and investment to move to low-tax destinations. Ireland, for example, was accused of setting its taxes on profits low, helping to contribute to high levels of inward foreign direct investment. New member states were warned that if they attempted to emulate the successful Irish model (see also Chapter 13), they would not be permitted to introduce what were considered as unfair tax concessions. However, in many new member states tax rates are lower than in the EU(15). 'Tax competition' does not appear to have occurred to any great extent for taxes on incomes, also because labour mobility within the EU seems to be relatively low (see Chapter 7).

In 1999 a heated dispute arose over a Commission proposal to introduce a 20 per cent withholding tax on incomes from cross-border, non-resident savings. Germany and the Scandinavian countries were in favour of such a measure, claiming that they forgo a large share of tax revenue because their wealthier citizens transfer savings to non-resident accounts. The UK and Luxembourg were thought to be the prime beneficiaries of such flows. The UK was strongly opposed to such a measure since it would hit the London-based eurobond market and encourage investors to place their holdings in Switzerland and Liechtenstein. Instead the UK argued in favour of improved information exchange and a delay before introducing the withholding tax.

In June 2003 agreement was reached among 12 of the member states to start exchanging information from 2005 on non-residents' savings so that each country could tax its citizens on such savings.[29] Austria, Belgium and Luxembourg will be exempt from exchanging information and will levy a withholding tax instead. Three-quarters of the proceeds from this tax will go to the saver's own country with the rest remaining with the three countries. The tax rate will rise from 15 per cent in 2005 to 35 per cent in 2010. The aim is to ensure that non-EU tax havens such as Switzerland and the Channel Islands also apply the withdrawing tax.

---

[27] The minimum rate on wine is zero, because of its importance for the Mediterranean countries.
[28] Molle (2001).
[29] Italy threatened to veto the agreement until the question of the fines on Italian milk farmers not respecting their quotas was resolved (see Chapter 10).

THE LIBERALIZATION OF PUBLIC PROCUREMENT

Public orders account for about 16 per cent of EU GNP, but, according to the Cecchini Report, only one public procurement contract out of 50 was granted to a firm from another country. As a result, the Cecchini Report maintained that governments were overspending by the equivalent of 22 billion euro, often paying 25 per cent more than their private counterparts.[30] Only part of public purchases (public procurement) is subject to tender or formal contract (7–10 per cent of GDP). The aim was to introduce common rules and greater transparency in tenders.

A series of new Directives was introduced relating to public procurement in the sectors of telecommunications, water, energy and transport. Measures have been taken to assist small and medium enterprises in competing for public procurement and to provide legal remedies to firms that feel they have been unfairly excluded from contracts. However, in practice public procurement has proved one of the most difficult markets to open. According to the Commission, the estimated value of cross-border procurement as a share of all public procurement only rose from 6 per cent in 1987 to 10 per cent in 1998.[31]

In 2003 the Commission called for simplification of national rules, standardization of procedures and modernization of public procurement systems to make it easier for foreign companies to participate in calls for tender.[32] In view of initiatives to develop the European Security and Defence Policy (see Chapter 19), the Commission also maintained that high priority should be given to increasing co-operation end efficiency in EU defence procurement. In 2003 a Public Procurement Network was established to resolve cross-border difficulties, share 'best practices' and improve the access of small and medium enterprises to public procurement in other member states.

LIBERALIZATION OF THE SERVICE INDUSTRIES

The advantages of liberalizing services is said to be similar to those of the international goods market, and are based on the improved allocation of resources with international specialization and the opportunities for exploiting economies of scale.

However, traditionally countries tend to apply restrictions on trade in services. These are said to be necessary, for example, to protect consumers, to ensure safety (air travel) and minimum standards (medical services), and financial solidarity (the banking system). Alternatively, restrictions are said to be justified to protect national industries, for instance for strategic or prestige reasons (air transport), to control key technologies (information science or telecommunications), for regional, social or environmental reasons (rail transport) or for cultural reasons (audiovisual services).

Restrictions on free trade in services may take various forms:[33]

- Authorization procedures;
- Quantitative restrictions;
- Reserving a certain share of the market for home producers;
- Government procurement;
- Requirements with regard to labour qualifications;
- Technical requirements and standards;
- Exchange controls;
- Subsidies.

---

[30] European Commission (2003a).
[31] European Commission (2003a).
[32] European Commission (2003c).
[33] This list is a modified version of that in Molle (2001).

The Treaty of Rome (Article 50) defined services as 'all those activities normally provided for remuneration insofar as they are not governed by the provisions relating to the freedom of movement of goods, capital and persons'. The Treaty called for two types of freedom in this context:

- ■ To provide services: any company of a member state can provide services in other member states without having to set up an office there (Article 49); and
- ■ To set up an establishment (Article 43): companies (or persons) from one member state may set up an establishment in another member state on the same conditions as nationals of the other member state (the principle of national treatment).

Progress in liberalizing the EU service sector in the Community has been slow. By 2003 services accounted for 70 per cent of the EU economy, but only 20 per cent of intra EU cross-border trade.[34] The task is rendered more complex by the different ways that services can be provided in the EC member states: across the border (for example Internet services), by the customer moving to the producer (such as in tourism) or by the producer moving to the customer (for instance in the construction trade).

A further factor rendering liberalization of services complicated is that the various service industries have very different characteristics. For this reason most of the discussion here is limited to a few key service sectors: financial services and two of the so-called network services (which in fact were not included in the 1985 White Paper) – telecommunications and energy. Transport is discussed in Chapter 16. Water is not dealt with here but was singled out by the European Commission in 2003 as an area where EU initiatives could prove beneficial.[35]

Common to all the network industries is a need to improve infrastructure and, given the financial constraints on governments, it seems likely that private financing will play a growing role in this area. However, care must be taken to ensure that all measures to improve infrastructure conform to EU competition policy and, in particular, to the rules on state aid.

In January 2004 the Commission proposed a Directive to create an effective Single Market for services. According to the Internal Market commissioner, Frits Bolkenstein, the Directive was 'potentially the biggest boost to the Internal Market since its launch in 1993'.[36] The proposed Directive would establish a general legal framework for a wide variety of services, while attempting to take into account the distinctive features of each. The services covered account for about 50 per cent of EU GDP, and include activities such as the distributive trades, construction, leisure services (notably travel agencies and tour operators), information technology-related services, advertising, car rental, employment agencies, security services, audiovisual services and healthcare. It does not include services already covered by EU legislation (such as financial services, telecommunications and transport), or services provided directly by public authorities in fulfilment of their social, cultural, education or legal obligations.

The Directive would remove a large number of barriers that prevent or discourage cross-border trade in services. Member states would no longer be able to make access to their market conditional on discriminatory requirements based on nationality. The country-of-origin principle would mean that if a service operator were operating legally in one member state, it could offer its services freely in others.

The aim of the Directive is also to make it easier for companies to open offices in other EU countries by:

- ■ No longer requiring companies to have their principal place of 'establishment' on their territory;

---

[34] European Commission (2003a).
[35] European Commission (2003b).
[36] European Commission (2004a).

■ Mutual recognition of the documents necessary for companies to provide services;
■ Introduction of a 'one-stop shop' for permits to do business in each member state by December 2008;
■ No longer obliging companies to follow the legislation of their host country rather than their country of origin.

The Directive also proposes aligning legislation on transporting cash, gambling and debt recovery.

Financial services

According to the Cecchini Report, roughly one-third of the gains from completion of the Internal Market were to come from liberalization of financial services. The 1985 White Paper identified the main barriers in this sector as controls on capital movements and different regulatory frameworks for banks and other financial institutions. Liberalization was to be based on mutual recognition, with harmonization being limited to essential legislation such as the taxation of savings and incomes from investment.

Freedom of movement of capital is generally advocated because it improves efficiency by increasing the supply of capital (additional savings will be mobilized if the prospects for investing them are better) and by enabling entrepreneurs in need of capital to raise greater amounts more tailored to their needs.

The Treaty of Rome was very cautious with regard to liberalization of capital movements, requiring liberty of movement only 'to the extent necessary to ensure proper functioning of the Common Market'. In part this reflected a fear of potential instability in capital markets, but capital controls were also considered a means of maintaining autonomy of monetary policy and of securing some exchange rate stability.[37] The treaty allowed restrictions on capital movements, which were permitted in certain circumstances such as if movements of capital would cause disturbances in the capital market or for balance-of-payments reasons.

Essentially the Treaty of Rome was a framework agreement to be padded out by later legislation. Directives were introduced for this purpose in 1960 and 1962, and distinguished various types of transaction according to the degree of liberalization of capital movements.[38]

Until the mid-1980s, despite various proposals, there were few Community initiatives to liberalize capital movements. Some of the member states, such as Germany, the UK, the Netherlands and Belgium also proceeded with liberalization in transactions with countries outside the Community (Molle, 2001). However, France, Italy and the three new Mediterranean member states continued to make use of capital restrictions.

By the 1980s there was growing world-wide support for deregulation and liberalization of capital movements. Increasingly capital controls were felt to be ineffective on a number of grounds, in particular because:

■ Technological innovations, such as the use of computers and telecommunications, increased the ease and speed of capital movements, rendering it simpler to evade controls.
■ Unregulated offshore financial centres provided a means of avoiding restrictions.

---

[37] A theoretical justification for this kind of position is given by the Mundell–Fleming model (see Annex 6).
[38] Three categories were introduced for capital movements:

■ *Fully free.* This included foreign direct investment, the purchase of real estate, short-term export credits, personal transactions such as the repatriation of earnings and former investments, and the purchase of quoted stocks in another member state.
■ *Partly free.* These were: the issue of shares on the stock market of another member state, the purchase of non-quoted shares or shares in an investment fund by non-residents of that country and long-term trade credits.
■ *No obligation to liberalize.* This category included short-term treasury bonds and other capital stocks, and the opening of bank accounts by non-residents of that country.

- Innovations in financial instruments, and the emergence of new and larger actors (such as financial conglomerates), rendered the task of regulation more complex.

Following a first modest step in 1986, in 1988 a Directive called for complete elimination of controls on capital movements both between EC member states and with third countries. This was achieved from July 1990, with the later deadlines of 1992 for Ireland and Spain, and 1994 for Greece and Portugal.[39]

With regard to the **banking system,** the main obstacles to establishing banks in other EC member states included authorization procedures, capital endowment requirements and restrictions on foreign acquisitions. In 1988 the average market share of foreign banks in member states was only 1 per cent.[40] According to the White Book, liberalization was to proceed through mutual recognition and harmonization of essential legislation but also on the basis of control by the home country.

In 1989 three Directives were passed which formed the basis for liberalization of the banking sector and a model for liberalization of other financial services. Of particular importance was the Second Banking Directive[41] which established a single banking licence. Any bank that has received authorization by the appropriate authority in any EC state can provide services over the border and can open branches in any other EC state without the need for further authorization. The home country has main responsibility for control of the bank's activities, while the host country shares responsibility for supervision of the liquidity of branches in their own territory, as well as for measures related to the implementation of national monetary policy. Similar systems of single licences were subsequently introduced for insurance and investment services.

The division of responsibility for supervision between the home and host countries was blurred from the outset and reflects a reluctance on the part of the EC member states to give up their authority. The immediate response of the banking system to the liberalization process was to embark on a spate of mergers and co-operation agreements.

In 1999 **a Financial Services Action Plan (FSAP)** was launched. The Commission argued that EU financial markets had difficulty competing on an international scale and that an integrated EU capital market was important to ensure sustainable investment-driven growth and employment. According to Commission estimates, integrated EU financial markets would increase EU GDP by at least 1.1 per cent, or €130 billion, in 2002 prices over about a decade. Total employment would increase by 0.5 per cent, while the cost of equity capital would decrease by 0.5 per cent and that of bond finance by 0.4 per cent.[42]

The FSAP was to be delivered by 2005, but the target to create an integrated market for securities and risk capital was 2003. The FSAP included measures to:

- create a single wholesale financial market to allow firms to raise capital on an EU-wide basis;
- complete a single EU retail market;
- ensure state-of-the-art prudential rules and supervision.

---

[39] A safeguard clause permitted the reintroduction of certain controls when the monetary or exchange rate policy of a member state was threatened. However, such controls could only be applied on capital movements liberalized under the 1988 Directive, were limited to a maximum of six months and required approval of the EC Commission.

[40] European Commission (2003a).

[41] The other Directives established principles and definitions regarding bank capital and the establishment of a minimum solvency ratio of 8 per cent.

[42] European Commission (2003d), www.europa.eu.int/comm/internal_market/en/finances/actionplan. The Commission estimates were based on a background study by the CEPR (Centre for Economic Policy Research).

According to the European Commission's 9th Progress Report on the Financial Services Action Plan, published in November 2003, 36 of the 42 original measures had been finalized.[43] Measures introduced include the Directives on: taxation of savings income (see above in the section on fiscal harmonization), insider dealing and market manipulation, pension funds and market abuse (see Chapter 15). High priority has also been given to improved arrangements for the effective supervision of financial institutions and the management of financial crises with a cross-border dimension.

When the FSAP was introduced there was concern about ability to meet the deadlines to implement measures. A further issue was whether regulation of the EU securities market should be carried out on the basis of co-operation and mutual recognition among the national authorities of the member states (as favoured by many in the City of London), or whether there should be a single central regulator of trading in EU securities. A single supervisor would require cross-border enforcement, and it is difficult to see how this could operate in practice in the EU where there are substantial differences in criminal and civil law among member states.

A Committee of Wise Men chaired by Alexandre Lamfalussy (a former Belgian banker) was set up to examine these questions and in February 2001 presented its report. In what has become known as the 'Lamfalussy procedure' the EU is responsible for passing broad framework laws, while committees of experts work out the technical details. In 2002 it was agreed to set up a Securities Committee composed of national officials. The aim was to permit flexibility and effective regulation of a fast-changing sector and ensure adequate consultation of market professionals. The European Parliament was granted a three-month period to scrutinize and give its opinion on all draft implementing measures. The Commission agreed to accept 'sunset' clauses in financial legislation that will enable the European Parliament to review the Lamfalussy procedure after four years.[44] There have been proposals to extend the procedure to the banking and insurance sectors.

One of the difficulties with the procedure is that the framework Directives leave the member states to fill in the details of what is a very complex field of legislation, and this process could prove difficult to amend as market conditions change.[45] The procedure was agreed too late to influence much of the Financial Services Action Plan. A further shortcoming is that at times consultation can lead to uneven results, and outcomes may reflect undue pressure by certain parties. Defenders of the system argue that it is still too early to judge its effectiveness.

In 2003 the Lamfalussy procedure was used to introduce new legislation on market abuse and investment services. The investment services Directive sets rules for investment business carried out by banks and stock exchanges. There was substantial consultation of Commission and European Parliament officials, but in the Council the positions of the UK and four other member states (Sweden, Ireland, Finland and Luxembourg) were overridden. The proposed Directive allows banks to compete with stock markets throughout the EU but requires them to keep to pre-published prices. Under a process known as 'internalization' a bank would match buyers and sellers and send the aggregated order to a stock exchange. France and Italy, in particular, were anxious to ensure 'pre-trade' transparency by requiring prices to be published in advance. The UK is the only EU country where investment banks already match 'buy' and 'sell' orders internally on a substantial scale, and the British government argued that the Directive would increase the risk for bankers and so was likely to be passed on as higher prices to consumers.[46]

[43] European Commission (2003d); www.europa.eu.int/comm/internal_market/en/finances/actionplan.
[44] *Financial Times*, 6 February 2002.
[45] *Financial Times*, 1 December 2003.
[46] *Financial Times*, 8 October 2003.

Telecommunications

The telecommunication and information sectors were traditionally characterized by national monopolies in the provision of equipment and services. It was considered that with more than one supplier costly networks would be duplicated, leading to an overall loss in welfare. The Cecchini Report found price differences in telephone and telegraph services of as much as 50 per cent among EC member states prior to the introduction of the Single Market.

With the rapid technological progress in the information and telecommunications industry, the argument in favour of natural monopolies was undermined. There was strong pressure to liberalize both from corporate users of telecommunication services, and at the international level, despite the rather limited results obtained in the Uruguay Round agreement on GATS (General Agreement on Trade in Services, see Chapter 17).

A 1988 Directive was aimed at the ending of national monopolies on equipment, and a further Directive of 1990 called for liberalization of the provision of services (except basic telephone services). New Regulatory Agencies (NRAs), which were to be independent from both government and operators, were set up in all the member states to implement EU regulations. The EU has also launched programmes such as RACE (Research in Advanced Communications in Europe) and ESPRIT (European Strategic Programme for Research and Development in Information Technologies) to help Community firms develop new technologies.

According to the European Commission (2003d), developments in technology combined with the Single Market Programme caused a fall in telephone charges by 50 per cent for national calls, and 40 per cent for international calls. In line with world telecommunications, the EU industry has been undergoing a process of radical structural change, characterized by large-scale mergers and acquisitions such as that of Vodafone and Mannesmann. This process of restructuring and mergers to capture market shares seems far from over.

Energy

Since 1996 successive Directives have set out the steps necessary to open gas and electricity markets both for business consumers and households. The aim has been to open gas and electricity for non-householders by 2004 and for household consumers by 2007. Where users are free to choose their supplier, the evidence suggests that prices fall.[47] Only 8 per cent of electricity consumed is supplied across borders, and the 2002 Barcelona European Council set the objective of cross-border supply of 10 per cent of capacity by 2005 (see also Chapter 12).

THE INTERNAL MARKET STRATEGY FOR THE 2003-06 PERIOD

In May 2003 the European Commission published a 10-point plan to improve the working of the Internal Market. The plan was intended to help the EU meet the three challenges of:

- enlargement;
- increasing growth capacity through structural reforms; and
- becoming the world's most competitive economy by 2010.

The priorities of the plan for the Internal Market were to improve the implementation and enforcement of Internal Market legislation, encourage the free movement of services, remove the remaining barriers to trade in goods and create a free market for public procurement.[48]

---

[47] The data in this section are taken from European Commission (2003a).
[48] European Commission (2003b).

Box 6.5 sets out the 10 points of the Strategy. Many of the proposed initiatives have been discussed above in the context of the various barriers to be removed by the Internal Market Project (services, taxes etc.) and the difficulties of implementation. In order to improve the conditions for business, the Commission aims at fostering innovation and entrepreneurship, building in particular on the European Charter for Small Enterprises endorsed by the Feira Council of 2000. Measures would be introduced to improve accounting and auditing techniques, and to combat piracy and counterfeiting with, for example, the introduction of a Community patent. In order to help meet the demographic challenge, there would be initiatives to encourage cross-border co-operation on pensions and health services. Among the efforts to improve the regulatory framework, the Commission proposed introducing a 'compatibility test' to ensure that the Internal Market implications are taken into account in deciding national legislation in the member states.

Box 6.5 The 10-point plan to improve the working of the Internal Market

- enforcing the rules
- integrating service markets
- improving the free movement of goods
- meeting the demographic challenge
- improving essential services
- improving conditions for business
- simplifying the regulatory environment
- reducing tax obstacles
- introducing more open public procurement markets
- providing better information

ESTIMATES OF THE EFFECTS OF THE SINGLE MARKET PROGRAMME

The Cecchini Report was based on the following methods of evaluation:

- **Opinion surveys of business.** These were based on questionnaires about the costs of given barriers and likely responses to their removal.
- **Industry case studies** of the cost structure of enterprises and the likely market barriers they face, including attempts to estimate the possible impact of restructuring the industry branch in response to increased competitive pressures.
- Micro- and macroeconomic analyses of the expected effects.[49]

---

[49] Various approaches were used, including:

A static, partial equilibrium approach which uses information obtained from the industry studies and other surveys to assess the net welfare effects on producers, consumers and government spending. The analysis is 'partial' in the sense that each barrier and each economic sector is considered one at a time and then the results are aggregated. The approach ignores the extent to which barriers overlap and markets are interconnected. In other words, no account is taken of the consequences of changes in factor prices or in the relative prices of products as a result of reducing the barriers.

A general equilibrium microeconomics approach which attempts to take into account the interactions between different sectors.

The use of macroeconomic models in attempt to show the evolution of costs, prices, income and other macroeconomic variables (including policy) as a result of introduction of the Single Market. The emphasis here is on what happens during the adjustment period, considering questions such as how quickly workers made redundant by the restructuring process can find work elsewhere.

Estimates of dynamic effects were carried out, attempting to estimate how market conditions affect the rate of technological progress, innovations and the strategic reactions of business (through the learning process and so on). Such effects are extremely difficult to explain with economic rigour or to quantify.

The most discussed and controversial estimates were those based on a macroeconomic approach, which suggested that in the case of passive macroeconomic policies, the overall impact (after an estimated 5–6 years) of the Single Market Programme could be a 4.5 per cent increase in GDP, a 6 per cent reduction in the price level and the creation of about 2 million jobs. With a more active macroeconomic policy (reflecting the improved economic performance), there would be a 7 per cent increase in GDP, a 4.5 per cent reduction in inflation and the creation of 5 million jobs.[50]

According to a study carried out by the EC Commission 10 years after the 1 January 1993 deadline, the Internal Market added 1.8 per cent (or €164.5 billion) to the EU GDP in 2002. The cumulative extra prosperity due to the Single Market was estimated at €877 billion and, according to the Commission, 2.5 million jobs had been created since 1992.[51]

THE EXPECTED IMPACT OF THE SINGLE MARKET PROJECT ON THIRD COUNTRIES

Emerson et al. (1989) estimated that the completion of the Internal Market would increase the competitiveness of EC industry, leading to a decline in imports from the rest of the world by as much as 10 per cent.[52] Fear of loss of relative competitiveness was a major factor in causing the EFTA countries to negotiate the European Economic Area, and this in turn led to EU accession by Austria, Sweden and Finland.

Countries such as Japan and the USA feared the prospect of a 'Fortress Europe' and attempted to ensure a foothold within the fortress through increased foreign direct investment. The rapid increase in Japanese firms operating in the Community led to a tightening of 'screwdriver' legislation in 1987 aimed at ensuring a minimum EC share of components in goods produced in the Community.

At the time the Commission argued that this possible negative effect of increased EC competitiveness in reducing imports from the rest of the world would be offset insofar as higher GDP would lead to increased demand for imports.[53] Ultimately, the impact on third countries would depend very much on the level of EU trade restrictions after the completion of the Single Market. Dealing with EU or mutually recognized standards, and EU rather than national quotas, also simplifies procedures for producers in third countries. Indirect effects (of inducing changes in policy) could play a crucial role. A more buoyant economy would be reflected in greater confidence at a world level, rendering the Community more willing to improve access to its markets. In the last resort prospects for the liberalization of trade depend on the overall macroeconomic climate of the EU and world economy.

THE GROWTH EFFECTS OF THE SINGLE MARKET

One of the criticisms of the Cecchini study to attract most attention at the time was that of Baldwin (1989), who argued that the expected gains from the Single Market Programme might be far larger than those estimated in the Cecchini Report. The Cecchini study attempted to estimate

---

[50] The results of the general equilibrium microeconomic approach suggest possible gains of 2.5 per cent of GDP (or 70 billion ECU) for a narrow conception of the gains from removing barriers to a range of 4.5–6.5 per cent (125–90 billion ECU) for a more competitive, integrated market.
[51] The estimates here are taken from European Commission (2003a).
[52] Emerson et al. (1989, p. 182) also estimate the possible percentage changes in extra-EC imports for various sectors. These range from 0 for agriculture, −5.8 for textiles and clothing to −30.9 for communications, and −61.3 for credit and insurance.
[53] It has also been argued that the Single Market Programme could lead to changes in trade distribution, or the substitution of one third-country supplier for another. This may occur, for instance, because the removal of national restrictions involving preferences for a particular third country, or group of countries, or because some countries are better able to adjust to the new situation than others (Matthews and McAleese, 1990).

how the Single Market Programme would increase the level of output rather than the rate of growth. In other words, according to Baldwin, the Cecchini Report was considering a one-off rather than a continuing effect. This one-off effect is shown by line 1 in Figure 6.7. Baldwin presented two distinct arguments as to why this approach underestimated the gains.

In the first place, even with a one-off increase in output, if savings and investment stay as constant percentages of output, they will rise in absolute terms. As a result, the stock of capital will increase leading to higher output, which in turn implies higher saving and investment. According to this first argument, a growing share of investment will simply replace capital stock owing to depreciation. Eventually (possibly after 10 years) investment will match depreciation, so the economy will return to its earlier growth rate but with a higher level of output and capital stock. Baldwin estimated that this 'medium-term bonus' could add some 3.5 per cent to 9 per cent of the GDP of the Community. The medium-term bonus is indicated by line 2 in Figure 6.7.

In addition to this medium-term bonus, drawing on endogenous growth theory (see Chapter 5), Baldwin argued that there may also be a permanent increase in the rate of growth. As a result there could be a total medium- and long-term bonus of some 9 per cent to 29 per cent of GDP. If this is added to the increase in GDP estimated by Cecchini, the total benefit would amount to about 11 per cent to 35 per cent of GDP. This effect is shown by line 3 in Figure 6.7.

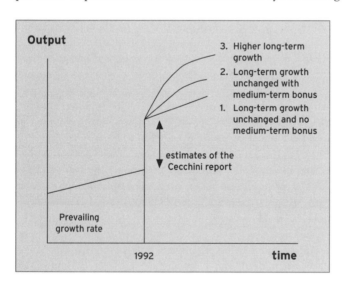

Figure 6.7 The growth effects of the Single Market

Source: Adapted from Baldwin (1989).

CRITICISMS OF THE CECCHINI REPORT

With the benefit of hindsight, various other criticisms of the Cecchini predictions of the Internal Market effects can be made. In the Report the estimates of direct benefits from reduced controls at the border were relatively small, while the estimates of secondary dynamic effects (economies of scale, restructuring, increased competition) were large. It is difficult to produce more than 'guestimates' or 'speculative ranges' concerning the size of such dynamic effects. In fact, the more important the effects are said to be, the more vague and less precise the Commission's analysis appeared.

Too much emphasis was put on economies of scale in the Cecchini analysis. It has to be shown they are only possible in a European rather than a national market and that they promote efficiency. Too little account is taken of the costs of adjustment or of the impact on regional disparities. The approach tends to emphasize the supply rather than the demand side, and the results are very sensitive to changes in the economic environment.

The analysis of the economic consequences of the Internal Market Programme shares the difficulty of all empirical analysis of integration in that it is almost impossible to separate the integration effect from overall economic developments. None the less the picture that emerges is that the outcome was rather different from what was expected, or at least was different from the stated objectives of the Commission.

As described above, the implementation of the Internal Market was subject to substantial delays, and part of the reaction of the EC economy to the programme seems to have occurred *before* 1993. As mentioned above, the late 1980s was associated with a boom in mergers between European (and not simply EC) firms, and Italianer (1994) argues that the expectations concerning the 1993 programme appear to have contributed to rapid EC growth in 1988 and 1989. Italianer compared actual growth rates for Japan, the USA and the Community with average growth rates for the 1981–90 decade. The latter is assumed to be the trend growth rate or *anti-monde*.[54] Italianer found a higher cumulative difference in the growth rate of the EC in 1988–89 than for Japan or the USA. Italianer attributes the EC boom in 1988–89 to business confidence. Subsequently the economic climate changed, with the increase in German interest rates following unification, speculation against the weaker EMS currencies and the growing uncertainty about EMU in the early 1990s (see Chapter 8).

A later study by Geroski and Gugler (2001) found that the overall effect of the Single Market Programme on specialization in the EU and the distribution of companies by size was relatively limited. The two authors studied 65 000 firms employing more than 100 people in the EU. The study suggests that there may still be barriers to trade that prevent the full benefits of increased competition, restructuring and efficiency from being realized. Evidence is cited to indicate incomplete liberalization in sectors such as automobile sales and telecommunications. However, the authors conclude that it may still be too early to assess the impact of the Internal Market Programme, and that the impact of the single currency on industrial structuring may be greater.

FROM THE SINGLE MARKET PROGRAMME TO THE LISBON STRATEGY

More than 10 years after the 1993 Internal Market deadline the EU continued to lag behind the USA in terms of competitiveness and productivity, with the gap actually widening. Though it can be argued that the Single Market Project is still not complete, the assumption that all the shortcomings of the European economy could be attributed to market fragmentation became increasingly questionable.

Subsequently, low EU productivity has been more frequently explained in terms of factors such as labour market rigidities, shortcomings in education and training and a technology gap, in particular with regard to information science. These were the basis of the decision of the March 2000 Lisbon European Council to launch a 'new strategic goal' aimed at economic, social and environmental renewal in the following 10 years. The goals were:[55]

■ To prepare 'the transition to a knowledge-based economy and society by better policies for the information society and R&D'. This includes measures to create closer links between research institutes and industry, to develop conditions favourable to R&D, to improve access to finance and know-how and to encourage new business ventures.

---

[54] The trend growth rate for the EC is assumed to be 2.3 per cent.
[55] Lisbon European Council Presidency Conclusions. See also OLC website for this book.

- To step up 'the process of structural reform for competitiveness and innovation by completing the internal market'.
- To ensure full employment, by emphasizing the need to open employment opportunities, to increase productivity at work and to promote life-long learning.
- To ensure an inclusive labour market in which unemployment is reduced and social and regional disparities are narrowed by 'modernizing the European social model, investing in people and combating social exclusion'.
- To connect Europe, in particular through closer integration, and by improving transport, telecommunications and energy networks.
- To protect the environment.[56]
- To sustain 'the healthy economic outlook and favourable growth prospects by applying an appropriate macro-policy mix'.

A Work Programme was to be introduced to make EU training and education systems a 'world quality reference' by 2010.

The Lisbon Strategy was confirmed at the March 2002 Barcelona European Council which called for measures to guarantee EU competitiveness, promote sustainable development and improve employment across skills and geographical areas (also by increasing labour mobility).[57] Priorities included developing the information society, encouraging entrepreneurship and a well-functioning internal market, and reinforcement of the social agenda.

In 2002 a Competitiveness Council was created with the aim of relaunching the competitive drive of the EU. The role of the Competitive Council was to give an opinion on all matters affecting competitiveness, and in this way it was hoped to exploit the synergies between different policies such as the Internal Market, industrial policy, competition policy and research and development. At the end of 2003 there were criticisms that the Competitiveness Council was still not being given a high enough profile.[58]

The Lisbon Strategy is linked to the European Employment Strategy (EES) launched in 1997 (see Chapter 14). The aims of the European Employment Strategy for the 2003–06 period include full employment, improved quality and productivity of work and increased social cohesion (European Commission, 2004b).

Each spring the Commission publishes a report on progress in implementing the Lisbon Strategy.[59] The 2003 report regarded the Internal Market and introduction of the euro (see Chapter 8) as evidence of the EU capacity to 'deliver ambitious reforms' but pointed to the vulnerability of the European economy to political uncertainty and economic downturn. The 2004 report was pessimistic about progress and predicted that many of the midterm targets would be missed. It called for three new priorities:

- Improving investment in networks and knowledge;
- Strengthening competitiveness in industry and services; and
- Promoting active aging.

Employment is discussed in Chapter 14, but the Union seems likely to miss the midterm Lisbon target of ensuring participation of 67 per cent of the labour force by 2005, though the midterm target of employing 57 per cent of women seems likely to be met.

There were also mixed results in providing the labour force with the skills necessary to create a

---

[56] The Gothenburg European Council added environment as the third strand to the Lisbon Strategy for economic and social development.
[57] Presidency Conclusions, Barcelona European Council of March 2002.
[58] The criticisms were expressed in a report by the UNICE, or organization of EU industries, as reported in the *Financial Times* of 14 November 2003.
[59] European Commission (2003e).

'knowledge-based society'. The economic downturn and complex and incomplete regulatory environment meant that business was not investing enough in knowledge and innovation, while the Commission repeatedly called on the member states to spend more on education, research and the knowledge economy. More effort in combating poverty and social exclusion (see Chapter 14) and in implementing environmental legislation (see Chapter 12) were also considered necessary.

The Brussels European Council of December 2003 announced a series of measures to further the Lisbon Strategy through the creation of a European Action for Growth.[60] The Action covers investments in the trans-European network infrastructure, including transport (see also Chapter 16), telecommunications and energy, R&D and also environmental technology. The Action was to take the form of a 'quick start programme' and was to be based on private as well as public financing.

EVALUATION

The Single Market Programme was an important stimulus to restructuring of the EU economy, and in its absence there might have been slower growth and less job creation in Europe. One of its most visible effects has been on frontier controls within the EU, an issue taken up in the context of labour movement in the next chapter. The Internal Market Programme has also been important for its spill-over into other areas of integration, including EMU, institutional reform, the 1995 enlargement, regional and social measures and competition policy.

The Lisbon Strategy of 'economic, social and environmental renewal' set out an ambitious programme for transforming the EU into a 'knowledge-based economy' of world quality reference by 2010. The slow-down in the world economy and international political uncertainty did not render the task any easier, but it is difficult not to conclude that the EU and its member states engaged more in rhetoric than practical steps to render the strategy a reality. In many member states additional funds for education, training and R&D were rarely forthcoming, and job-creation projects were on a relatively limited scale. The Internal Market Programme was considered a central element of the Lisbon Strategy, and important steps have been taken towards its 'completion', in particular with regard to services and the financial sector. It is still too early to assess how effective these measures will prove in practice.

Summary of Key Concepts

- During the 1970s and early 1980s the EC member states were becoming increasingly concerned about the growing lag between their economic performance and that of countries such as Japan and the USA, especially in high-technology sectors. The explanation given was the fragmentation of the EC market.
- Krugman (1991) found that the level of specialization in the USA was higher than in the EC, even though the distances were greater.
- In 1985 Jacques Delors launched the Single Market Programme as a strategy to raise EC competitiveness.
- The main non-tariff barriers that the SEM Programme aimed at removing were: frontier controls; differences in technical specifications and standards; differences in national tax systems; restrictions on competition for public purchases and restrictions on providing certain services (in particular financial and transport services) in other EC countries.

---

[60] European Council (2003).

- The Cockfield White Paper, 'Completing the Internal Market', of 1985 called for the elimination of barriers between EC countries by the end of 1992 and set out 282 measures necessary to achieve this aim.
- The Single European Act of 1987 set out the formal steps necessary to introduce the Single Market.
- In practice incomplete implementation of the measures and the granting of temporary derogations have undermined the effectiveness of the SEM.
- One of the main aims of removing frontier controls is to permit the free movement of people, as described in Chapter 7.
- Standards and technical restrictions may act as barriers to trade but may be needed to protect consumer interests.
- The Community has made slow progress in bringing the national tax systems of the member states in line with each other.
- Little progress has been made in opening up public procurement to foreign firms.
- In 2004 the Commission presented a proposal for a Directive to create an effective Single Market for services.
- With the SEM programme the movement of capital between member states was liberalized. With regard to financial services, any bank that has received authorization by the appropriate authority in any EC state can provide services over the border and can open branches in any other EC state without the need for further authorization.
- The FSAP (Financial Services Action Programme) proposed 42 measures to liberalize financial markets by 2005.
- The SEM programme ended national monopolies of telecommunications and information services.
- The Cecchini Report suggested that if macroeconomic policies remained unchanged, the overall impact (after an estimated 5–6 years) of the Single Market Programme could be a 4.5 per cent increase in GDP, and a 6 per cent reduction in the price levels.
- Later Commission studies estimated the increase in GDP at about 1.8 per cent in 2002, and the creation of jobs at 2.5 million compared with the situation without the 1993 Programme. The cumulative extra prosperity due to the Single Market was estimated at 877 billion euros.
- The Lisbon European Council of 2000 attributed poor EU economic performance to lack of completion of the Single Market, labour market rigidities and a technology gap between the EU and USA, in particular with regard to information science.
- Possibly the most lasting effects of the Single Market Programme are the kick-start it gave to the deregulation process and the spill-over effect into other areas of integration such as institutional reform, EMU and social and regional measures.

Questions for Study and Review

■ Describe the main barriers causing fragmentation of the European market.

■ What were the expected advantages of the Single Market Programme?

■ Indicate the main steps in introducing the SEM Programme.

■ What was the significance of the Single European Act in the integration process?

■ Describe, with examples, the areas where implementation of the SEM Programme has been particularly slow.

■ In practice the effects of the Single Market Programme were different from those initially predicted. Explain why you think that this was the case.

■ What are the main objectives of the Lisbon Strategy, and why do you consider it has met with limited success?

Appendix
The Mundell-Fleming model

The Mundell–Fleming model can be used to show how it is impossible to carry out an independent monetary policy with fixed exchange rates and perfect capital mobility.

Figure A6.1 presents the usual textbook version of IS and LM curves. The IS curve illustrates the various combinations of interest rates (i) and national income (y) that yield equilibrium in the goods market. It is negatively sloped, since lower interest rates are associated with higher levels of investment and income (and higher saving and imports) for the quantities of goods and services demanded and supplied to remain equal. The LM curve illustrates all the points at which the money market is in equilibrium. As can be seen from Figure A6.1, the curve is positively sloped. The derivation of the LM curve is based on the assumption that the money supply is fixed. Higher incomes imply higher transaction demand for money. Higher incomes will therefore have to be associated with higher interest rates to ensure lower demand for money for speculative purposes (the opportunity cost of holding speculative money balances is greater with high interest rates), and thereby ensure that the total amount of money demanded remains equal to the fixed amount of money supplied.

An expansionary monetary policy will shift the LM curve to the right (from LM to LM′ in Figure A6.1) since at each level of interest rate the level of national income must be higher to absorb the increase in money supply. Tighter monetary policy will shift the LM curve to the left.

With perfect capital mobility, assume that the interest rate prevailing on international markets is i*. Along the BP curve the balance of payments is in equilibrium, but this will only occur when the domestic interest rate i is equal to that prevailing on international markets. If, for example, the government attempts monetary expansion moving the LM curve to LM′, at the new equilibrium E′ the domestic interest rate is below i*. Perfect capital movement means that this will cause an outflow of capital. The balance of payments will be in deficit, and there will be pressure on the exchange rate; so the central bank must sell foreign currency and buy national currency until the LM curve has moved back to its original position, LM. If, in contrast, the government attempts a tight monetary policy, shifting the LM curve to the left so that the domestic interest rate is above i*, the result will be an inflow of capital and the LM curve will have to shift back to its original position where i = i*. According to the model, autonomous monetary policy is incompatible with fixed exchange rates and free capital movements.

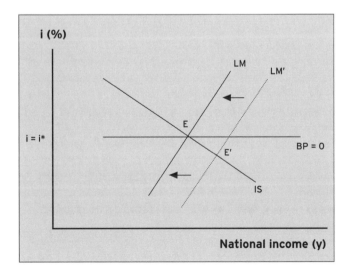

Figure A6.1 The Mundell-Fleming Model

References

Ardy, B. and El-Agraa, A. (2004) 'The general budget' in El-Agraa, A. *The European Union: Economics and Policies,* Prentice Hall, Harlow, UK.

Baldwin, R. (1989) 'The growth effects of 1992', *Economic Policy,* Vol. 2, pp. 247–81.

Baldwin, R. (1994) *Towards an Integrated Europe,* Centre for Economic Policy Research, London.

Cecchini, P. (1988) *The European Challenge: The Benefits of a Single Market,* Wildwood House, Aldershot.

Commons (2002) 'Crossborder shopping and smuggling', *House of Commons Library*, Research paper 02/40, London.

Coombes, P. and Overman, H. (2004) 'The special distribution of economic activity in the EU' in Henderson, V. and Thisse, J.F. eds, *Handbook of Regional and Urban Economics,* Vol. 4, Elsevier, Amsterdam.

El-Agraa, A. (2001) *European Union: Economics and Policies*, 6th edn, Prentice Hall, Harlow, UK.

Emerson, M. et al. (1989) *The Economics of 1992: The EC Commission's Assessment of the Economic Effects of Completing the Single Market*, Oxford University Press, Oxford.

European Commission (1985) 'Completing the Single Market', COM(85)310.

European Commission (1996) 'Impact and effectiveness of the Single Market', COM(96)920.

European Commission (2002a) 'Internal Market Scoreboard No. 11', November, www.europa.eu.int/comm

European Commission (2002b) 'Second Biennial Report on the application of the principle of mutual recognition in the Single Market', COM(2002) 419 final.

European Commission (2002c) 'Consumer policy strategy', COM(2002) 208 final, www.europa.eu.int/comm

European Commission (2002d) 'Functioning of EU product and capital markets, the "Cardiff Report"', December, www.europa.eu.int/comm/internal_market

European Commission (2003a) 'The Internal Market: Ten years without frontiers', www.europa.eu.int/comm/internal_market

European Commission (2003b) 'Internal Market strategy. Priorities 2003–2006', COM (2003) 238 final, www.europa.eu.int/comm/internal_market

European Commission (2003c) 'Internal Market Scoreboard No. 12', May. www.europa.eu.int/comm/internal_market

European Commission (2003d) 'Financial services. Ninth report, November', www.europa.eu.int/comm/internal_market/en/finances/actionplan

European Commission (2003e) 'Choosing to grow. Knowledge, innovation and jobs in a cohesive society'. Report to the Spring European Council, March 2003 on the Lisbon Strategy of economic, social and environmental renewal, *www.europa.eu.int/comm/internal_market*

European Commission (2003f) 'Services: Commission proposes Directive to cut red tape that stifles Europe's competitiveness', *www.europa.eu.int/comm/internal_market*

European Commission (2003g) 'VAT rates applied in the member states and accession states of the European Community', DOC 2402/2003.

European Commission (2004a) 'Implementation Report on the Internal Market Strategy', January, www.europa.eu.int/comm/internal_market

European Commission (2004b) 'Joint employment report', www.europa.eu.int/comm/internal_ market

European Commission (2004c) 'Excise duty tables', www.europa.eu.int/comm/taxation

European Council (2003) 'Presidency conclusions of the Brussels European Council', 12 December, 2003.

Fleming, M.J. (1962) 'Domestic financial policies under fixed and floating exchange rates', *International Monetary Fund Staff Papers,* November, pp. 369-79.

Geroski, P. and Gugler, K.P. (2001) 'Corporate growth and convergence in Europe', Centre for Economic Performance Discussion Paper 2838, June, CEPR, London.

Hitiris, T. (1994) *European Community Economics,* 3rd edn, Prentice Hall, Harlow, UK.

Italianer, A. (1994) 'Whither the gains from European integration?', *Revue Economique,* Vol. xx, pp. 689-702.

Jones, R.A. (2001) *The Politics and Economics of the European Union. An Introductory Text,* 2nd edn, Edward Elgar, Cheltenham, UK.

Krugman, P. (1991) *Geography and Trade,* Leuven University Press, Leuven and The MIT Press, Cambridge, MA.

Mattera, A. (1988) *Marché unique européen: Ses règles, son fonctionnement,* Jupiter, Paris.

Matthews, A. and McAleese, D. (1990) 'LDC primary exports to the EC: prospects post-1992', *Journal of Common Market Studies,* Vol. XXIX, Dec., pp. 157-80.

Molle, W. (2001*) The Economics of European Integration. Theory, Practice, Policy,* 4th edn, Ashgate, Aldershot.

Mundell, R. (1963) 'Capital mobility and stabilisation policy under fixed and flexible exchange rates', *Canadian Journal of Economics and Political Science,* November, pp. 475-85.

Mundell, R. (1968) *International Economics,* Macmillan, New York.

Tsoukalis, L. (1997*) The New European Economy Revisited,* 3rd edn, Oxford University Press, Oxford.

Useful websites

Studies of various trade issues are provided by the European Commission:
www.europa.eu.int/internal_market
Other international organizations that deal with standards are:
The United Nations Economic Commission for Europe (UNECE) www.unece.org
World Intellectual Property Organization www.wipo.org
World Trade Organization www.wto.org

List of abbreviations

CEN	Centre Européen de Normalisation
CENELEC	Centre Européen de Normalisation Electrotechnique
ECU	European Currency Unit
EFTA	European Free Trade Association
EMS	European Monetary System
EMU	economic and monetary union
ERASMUS	European Community Action Scheme for the Mobility of University Students
ESPRIT	European Strategic Programme for Research and Development in Information Technologies
ESTI	European Telecommunications Standards Institute
EURES	European Employment Services
FSAP	Financial Services Action Plan
GATS	General Agreement on Trade in Services
GDP	gross domestic product
Leonardo da Vinci	action programme for the EU's vocational training policy

LINGUA	programme for the learning and teaching of European languages
NRAs	New Regulatory Agencies
RACE	Research in Advanced Communications in Europe
SEA	Single European Act
SEM	Single European Market
Socrates	European programme for education
SOLVIT	the redress system for implementation of Internal Market rules
VAT	value added tax

7

Movement of Labour, Immigration and Asylum

LEARNING OBJECTIVES

By the end of this chapter you should be able to understand:

▶ The main advantages said to arise from freedom of labour movement;

▶ The most frequent justifications given for introducing restrictions on immigration;

▶ The main factors influencing the decision to migrate;

▶ How migration may influence wage levels and unemployment;

▶ The most common forms of immigration;

▶ How the pattern of immigration has changed in the EU over time;

▶ What we mean by Justice and Home Affairs;

▶ What the Schengen Agreement is;

▶ What Europol is;

▶ What is implied by the aim of the EU to create an area of 'freedom, security and justice';

▶ What are the main criticisms levied by human rights organizations against the EU.

INTRODUCTION

Ensuring freedom of labour movement within the Community was one of the main objectives of the Treaty of Rome, subsequently reinforced by the 1993 Single Market Programme. However, allowing free movement of people involves a trade-off – control of international crime, terrorism, drug trafficking and migration becomes more difficult. Over the years the emphasis of EU policy has gradually shifted towards increased co-operation on home affairs, and police and judicial matters.

At the same time the pressure of immigration from third countries to the EU has acquired new forms and dimensions, urgently requiring co-ordination of the positions of EU member states and the introduction of common policies.

The aim of this chapter is first to provide a brief account of some of the theoretical aspects of labour movement. Then follows a description of the main developments in migratory flows within the EU and from third countries, before outlining the evolution of EU policies.

THE EFFECTS OF MIGRATION

Freedom of movement of labour on an international scale is generally advocated because the removal of restrictions is said to increase efficiency and improve the allocation of resources. Workers will have higher chances of using their qualifications in the best possible way. Employers will be able to overcome possible labour shortages and increase their possibilities of finding labour with the skills required.

More specific arguments are also advanced in favour of immigration. For example, in the country of destination it is sometimes claimed that the inflow of young workers can be used to offset possible negative effects of aging of the population, or immigrants can be used to cover a skill shortage.[1] Labour-exporting countries may favour emigration so that the balance of payments can benefit from workers' remittances, though these often tend to be invested in housing and consumption and may have little lasting positive effect on the home economy.

The effects of migration can be analysed using a simple model. It is assumed that there are two factors of production, capital C and labour L; two countries, home and foreign; that both countries produce one good and that there is perfect competition. The marginal product of labour shows how the output of a product increases when one additional unit of labour is used. Diminishing returns means that as additional units of labour are added to a given amount of capital, output will increase but by ever smaller amounts for each additional unit of labour.

Figure 7.1 shows the marginal product of labour in the home country MPLh. With the stock of home labour Lh, the equilibrium wage in the home country is Wh. Total earnings by home labour are given by the wage Wh multiplied by the amount of labour Lh. Under perfect competition the payments to the two factors of production will just equal the value of total production. The area under the curve indicates the total output of the home country. The payment to capital is therefore given by the area under the MPLh curve minus the payment to labour.

In order to show the effects of migration the marginal product of labour curves for both the home and foreign countries can be shown in a single graph. Assume initially that immigration is not allowed. Figure 7.2 reproduces the MPLh curve for home labour from Figure 7.1 but adds a second vertical axis and shows the marginal product of labour curve for the foreign country

---

[1] In 2000 the Irish government announced a plan to recruit up to 200 000 skilled specialists, while the German government introduced a programme to attract 20 000 information technology experts from abroad. It was estimated that to offset the effects of aging of the population, Germany would have to allow some 500 000 working-age immigrants a year (Boeri et al., 2000).

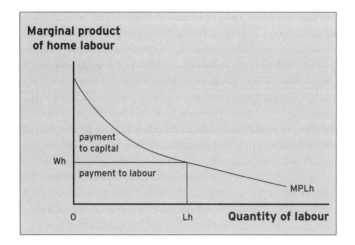

FIGURE 7.1 The income shares of capital and labour

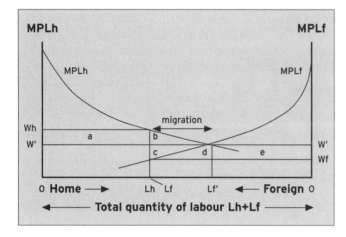

FIGURE 7.2 The causes and effects of immigration

Source: Adapted from Baldwin and Wyplosz (2004).

running right to left. The total horizontal distance between the two axes indicates the total amount of labour in the two countries (Lh + Lf).

With stock of labour Lf (total labour minus Lh), the equilibrium wage in the foreign country will be Wf. As can be seen from the graph, the equilibrium wage Wh in the home country is higher than Wf, so if migration is now allowed, there will be an incentive for workers to move from the foreign country to the home country to earn higher wages. The immigration will cause the wage at home to fall, and the wage in the foreign country to rise until they reach the same level W'. Equilibrium is reached when Lf'Lf workers have moved from the foreign country to the home country.

The welfare effects of migration can also be seen from Figure 7.2:

- Home labour loses earnings of area a.
- Home capital gains earnings of a + b.
- The total gain to the home country is therefore b.
- Payments to labour remaining in the foreign county rise by e.
- Earning by capital in the foreign country fall by d + e.
- If foreigners now working in the home country are also taken into account, the earnings to foreign workers rise by c + d + e, the earnings of foreign capital fall by d + e, so there is a net gain of c.

Various effects of migration are therefore shown by this simple model:

■ There is convergence of wages in the two countries with wages falling at home and rising in the foreign country.
■ Total world output, which is given by the area under the two curves MPLh and MPLf, rises. This is because migration has the effect of increasing efficiency.
■ There are winners and losers from the migration.

Annex 7 presents a slightly more elaborate model which also takes into account the impact of migration on the demand and supply of labour in the two countries and the costs of migration.

THE CAUSES OF MIGRATION

The simple model above attributes migration to wage differences, but in practice various factors influence the decision to migrate, so the list becomes:

■ The wage gap between the home and host country;
■ Political and ethnic disturbances (which emerge as the main cause of major large-scale migration flows in Europe);
■ The employment possibilities in both countries; [2]
■ Economic expectations;
■ The geographical proximity of the two countries;
■ Emigration traditions;
■ Ethnic and family networks;
■ Cultural and linguistic factors.

Migration involves economic and psychological costs to the person involved. Individuals have a preference for living in their own country for social, cultural and linguistic reasons. Migration entails costs of travel, finding a house, job and so on. An individual will only undertake migration when the expected benefit is large enough to offset the costs of migration. [3]

RESTRICTIONS ON MIGRATION

In practice most countries use restrictions on immigration. These generally consist of border controls, and work or residence permits, but may also take other forms such as limited access to certain jobs and professions, or financial disincentives such as limits on access to social security benefits, or unfavourable tax treatment. Other factors such as inability to find housing may also inhibit migration.

In the case of countries receiving immigrants the most frequently cited negative effects are: [4]

■ Increased government expenditure in order to provide the necessary social provisions for foreigners; [5]
■ Societal disruption due to cultural differences and so on;

---

[2] Faini (1995) also argues that, *ceteris paribus*, countries with a large informal sector tend to be attractive to immigrants because lower skills are generally required for employment.
[3] As Faini and Venturini (1994) argue, migration is an 'inferior' good, and staying at home is the 'normal' good.
[4] This list is taken from Molle (2001).
[5] As Molle (2001) points out, empirical studies do not produce a consistent picture as to whether immigrants add to the public expenditure of the host country.

- Increased regional disparities as the foreign workers tend to be attracted to urban agglomerations where jobs are more readily available;
- A worsening of the balance of payments as foreign workers send their earnings home;
- The downward pressure on wages (see next section);
- Increased unemployment (see next section).

In practice the importance of the political effects of immigration often outweigh the economic impact, because populist and nationalist political parties may exploit societal tensions, as has been the case in various EU countries.

In countries of emigration the most frequent justification for restrictions is that they are said to be necessary to avoid the possible negative effects of migration. These include the loss of human capital necessary for the development of the country as in general the younger, most dynamic and better skilled workers tend to leave (the so-called 'brain drain').

THE IMPACT OF MIGRATION ON WAGES AND EMPLOYMENT

One of the main debates about migratory flows relates to their impact on wages. Neo-classical economic theory argues that freedom of labour movement will lead to convergence of wages, as suggested by the model above. If costs of migration are also taken into account, the migratory flow will continue until the difference in wages between the two countries just matches the costs of migration.

According to the neo-classical view a similar mechanism is in operation for unemployment, and in the long run unemployment rates are likely to be independent of the size of the labour force. In the short run an increase in migration may lead to an increase in unemployment in the receiving country. As unemployment rises in the country of destination, this puts downward pressure on wages, inducing firms to take on more labour, and eventually unemployment will revert to its original level. The difficulty lies in assessing how long this process of adjustment will take.

However, the view that migration will lead to wage convergence and will not influence the long-run level of employment is based on some rather restrictive assumptions. Institutional barriers, such as restrictions on labour movement, may prevent adjustment from taking place. For example, trade unions or employee associations may prevent access to certain jobs, or employers may discriminate against certain types of workers on grounds of race or gender. Moreover, in practice the adjustment process may take some time, and in the meantime immigration may lead to lower wages and higher unemployment.

The impact of migration on wages and unemployment therefore becomes a question for empirical research. Early analyses of European integration find some evidence for wage convergence between member states.[6] The study by Boeri and Brücker et al. (2000) on the impact of immigration from the 10 Central and East European candidate states suggests that a 1 per cent increase in the share of foreign workers from these countries would lead to a fall in wages by 0.25 per cent in Austria and by 0.6 per cent in Germany, and to an increase in the risk of dismissal by 0.8 per cent in Austria and 1.6 per cent in Germany.

According to the study by Boeri and Brücker et al. (2000) the negative employment and wage effects from CEEC immigrants would be concentrated on less qualified, blue-collar workers. Initially immigrants from Central and East Europe were considered to be relatively well qualified,

---

[6] This is generally attributed to Italy's process of catching up. See Molle (2001) for a discussion of these studies.

but a closer analysis revealed that, in particular, the skills obtained in vocational schools under the old regime were often not suited to operating in a market economy.

The issue of whether immigrants are high skilled or low skilled labour is crucial to the analysis of the impact of immigration on the economy of the recipient country. As Baldwin and Wyplosz (2004) point out, the issue is one of complementarity versus substitutability. In many West European countries there is a shortage of unskilled workers. In Italy, for instance, unskilled immigrant labour is essential during the harvest and in helping in restaurants and bars during the tourist season. The unskilled work of immigrants therefore complements the skilled work of the Italian owners and managers of hotels, farms and so on. High-skilled labour can be regarded as a form of human capital, and so could be included as part of capital in Figure 7.2. Immigration of high skilled labour to a country can therefore be seen as an increase in human capital, which tends to increase the marginal product (and hence wages) of low-skilled labour.

ASYLUM AND IMMIGRATION

The policies of the member states on asylum and immigration from third countries have generally evolved separately, and reaching common EU positions has not proved easy. As a result national policies continue to play a predominant role in this policy area.

Various categories of immigrants are generally distinguished:

- ■ economic immigrants seeking permanent residence to improve their living standards;
- ■ asylum seekers looking for refuge from war or oppression;
- ■ illegal immigrants;
- ■ seasonal or temporary workers.

As it is becoming ever more difficult to enter the EU as a long-term economic immigrant, there has been a growing tendency to seek other forms of access. The 1951 Geneva Convention provided a definition of refugees as those who are fleeing persecution for 'reasons of race, religion, nationality, membership of a social group or political opinion'. However, in practice it is very difficult to distinguish whether refugees are fleeing poverty rather than persecution. The number of those seeking asylum remained fairly stable in the 1980s but increased dramatically following the collapse of communism and the Balkan wars (see Figure 7.3).

The treatment of requests for asylum varies considerably among the EU member states both

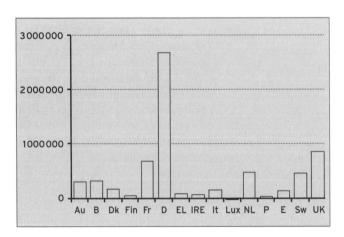

Figure 7.3 Total asylum applications in EU countries, 1982-2002

Source: European Council on Refugees and Exiles and United Nations High Commissioner on Refugees.

with regard to percentage of asylum cases accepted and the treatment of applicants while procedures are being carried out (see Table 7.1). From 1993 Germany became more restrictive in accepting requests for asylum, but few refugees were sent home. In 1997 the UN High Commissioner on Refugees (UNHCR) estimated that Germany was harbouring about 1.3 million people who had requested asylum, creating a form of covert immigration.[7] When Germany became more restrictive about asylum, the number of requests in the UK and Ireland rose, as these were considered countries with a higher record of accepting claims (see Table 7.2).

Country of asylum	Main countries of origin
UK	Iraq/Zimbabwe/Afghanistan/Somalia/China
USA	China/Mexico/Colombia/Haiti/India
Germany	Iraq/Turkey/Serbia-Montenegro/Russia/Afghanistan
France	Turkey/D.R.Congo/Mauritania/Algeria/China
Austria	Serbia-Montenegro/Iraq/Afghanistan/Turkey/India
Sweden	Serbia-Montenegro/Iraq/Bosnia-Herz./Russia/Somalia
Belgium	D.R.Congo/Serbia-Montenegro/Russia/Turkey/Algeria
NL	Angola/Sierra Leone/Afghanistan/Iraq/Iran
Ireland	Nigeria/Romania/Moldova/Zimbabwe/Ukraine

Table 7.1 Main countries of origin of asylum applications in selected countries, 2002

Source: United Nations High Commissioner on Refugees.

Table 7.2 Asylum claims

	Asylum claims (000) 2001	Asylum claims (000) 2002	Average processing time	Permission to work	Access to welfare benefits
Australia	12.4	6.0	88 days	After 6 months if not in detention	If not in detention
Britain	90.2	109.5	13 months	After 6 months	Withdrawn on rejection of appeal
Canada	44.1	30.4	11 months	Yes	Yes
Denmark	12.4	5.9	180-258 days	No	In reception centre
France	47.3	46.3	n.a.	No, unless stringent criteria are fulfilled	Yes, withdrawn on completion of procedure
Germany	88.3	71.1	2 weeks to 6 months	After 12 months	Only in kind
Italy	14.8	n.a.	180-240 days	No	Limited to 45 days
Netherlands	32.6	18.7	31 weeks	After 6 months and limited to 12 weeks a year	Not if undocumented and stopped after negative decision
Switzerland	20.6	26.1	90 days	After 3 months	In reception centre
USA	67.1	63.0	60 days	After 6 months	No

n.a. - not available
Source: *Economist*, 15 March 2003 and Inter-governmental Consultations on Asylum, Refugee and Migration Policies.

---

[7] As reported in Vachudova (2000).

In recent years there has been a rapid rise in asylum applications in the Central and East European new member states. According to the UNHCR, during the first 11 months of 2003 the number of asylum seekers rose by 92 per cent in Slovenia and 52 per cent in Poland (see also Figure 7.4).

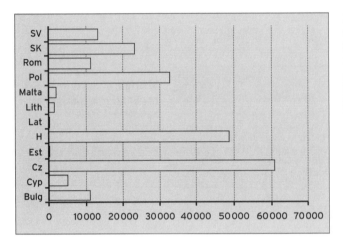

Figure 7.4 Total asylum applications in new member states, 1982–2002

Source: European Council on Refugees and Exiles and United Nations High Commissioner on Refugees.

To prevent asylum-seekers 'shopping around' the 1990 Dublin Convention requires asylum-seekers to apply for asylum in the first EU country they enter.[8] As will be discussed below in the context of policies, the EU is committed to evolving a common asylum system.

Temporary immigration generally involves a fixed-term contract, usually of less than one year. As permanent immigration to the EU has become more difficult, there has been a considerable increase in temporary immigration, which may take various forms:[9]

- Guest-workers,
- Seasonal workers,
- Project-tied workers,
- Border-commuters,
- Exchanges of trainees.

With the economic boom in Germany, from 1961 *Gastarbeiter* or temporary guest workers were recruited from Turkey and the former Yugoslavia. Many of these Turkish workers, in particular, failed to return home and were joined by their families, so that by the late 1990s it was estimated that there were still some 2 million people of Turkish origin in Germany (Vachudova, 2000).

Seasonal workers are mainly employed in agriculture and tourism. They are generally taken on at times of the year when extra labour in necessary, for example during the harvest, so the employment of these workers tends to have complementary effects on the incomes of workers in the host country (Boeri and Brücker et al. 2000).[10]

Tied-project programmes permit firms in the host country to subcontract parts of a project to foreign firms that employ workers with the wages and social security conditions of their own country. According to Boeri and Brücker et al. (2000), in 1998 32 000 project-tied workers were employed

---

[8] The Dublin Convention was extended and replaced by Regulation No. 343/2003 of February 2003.
[9] Boeri and Brücker et al. (2000).
[10] For instance, in 2003 seasonal workers in Tuscany were being paid a little over 4 euros an hour to harvest grapes, a wage few indigenous workers would be prepared to accept for such backbreaking work.

in Germany, mainly in the construction sector, and at times the wages and employment of German workers were negatively affected by this subcontracting. Border commuting is frequent in countries such as Poland, the Czech Republic and Hungary, and the main countries of destination tend to be Germany and Austria (Boeri and Brücker et al., 2000).

THE CHANGING PATTERN OF IMMIGRATION OVER THE YEARS

The 1958–73 Period

As described below, a major aim of the Treaty of Rome was to remove obstacles to the mobility of labour by 1970 when the transitional period would come to an end. During the first years of the Community, growth was rapid and, with the exception of Italy, the labour markets of the member states tended to be tight. During the 1958–73 period the only substantial migration flow within the Community was from Italy to Northern Europe.

In contrast there were large-scale migrations from third countries to the Community, and in particular:[11]

- Guest workers to Germany from Turkey and the former Yugoslavia.
- From the Mediterranean countries then outside the EC to Northern Europe. These included flows from Spain (mainly to France, Germany and Switzerland), Greece (to Germany and to a lesser extent the UK) and Portugal (mainly to France).[12] It was estimated that by the mid-1970s about 1 million people had left Franco's Spain (Chafos, 2002).
- From colonies of EC countries which gained independence.[13]

The 1973–89 Period

Over time with the growth of the Italian economy, and the process of catching up with the other member states, the number of Italians migrating to Northern Europe dwindled. Italian emigration shrank still further after the 1973 oil crisis when employment opportunities in Northern Europe became scarce. The subsequent revival of the EC economy failed to bring about a corresponding return to earlier levels of migration and, indeed, many Italians, Spanish and Portuguese returned home. This suggests that when income and employment conditions at home reach a certain minimum threshold, most workers are unwilling to undertake the costs of migration.

During this period other main categories of intra-EC migration included those working in multinational and international organizations, and Irish working in the UK. In 1973 these two categories, together with Italian emigrants in other EC states, amounted to some 3 million persons (Molle, 2001), so the degree of labour movement within the Community was relatively limited.

Between 1973 and 1989 the main trends in migration from third countries included:

- Migration from Spain, Greece and Portugal, though this dropped drastically with EC membership, and many immigrants returned home;
- Immigration from North Africa, Turkey and, to a lesser extent, Yugoslavia;
- Continuing immigration from other former colonies.

---

[11] The account here is based on Vachudova (2000) and Chafos (2002), who uses data from http://www.cnn.com.
[12] Molle, 2001.
[13] For example, there were immigration flows to Belgium following independence of the Belgian Congo in 1960; an estimated 1 million people went to France following Algerian independence in 1962 and there were flows to the UK (though in legal terms in many cases this did not involve 'foreigners') including those after the creation of Bangladesh (the former East Pakistan) in 1971, and in 1972 when Idi Amin expelled 50 000 Uganda Asians, 29 000 of whom came to Britain.

Since 1989

After 1989 immigration within the EU continued be on a limited scale. According to the European Commission, there were 5 million citizens living in another member state in 2002, and 35–45 000 qualified professionals were obtaining recognition of their right to practise in another member state each year (European Commission, 2003). From 1989 immigration from third countries increased, in particular from:

- the Mediterranean basin;
- the Middle East, Asia, sub-Saharan Africa and Latin America, where immigrants were at times subject to unscrupulous human trafficking, as for example in the case of June 2000 when 58 Chinese were found dead in a lorry at the UK port of Dover;
- Central and Eastern Europe, and the former Soviet Republics.

After 1989 some experts predicted large migration flows from the 10 Central and East Europe applicant countries (CEECs) to Western Europe as a result of lower levels of income in those countries, and the newfound freedom of citizens of those countries to travel abroad. In practice the number of people leaving the CEEC (10) was manageable and, according to Boeri and Brücker et al. (2000), in 1998 there were only about 850 000 CEEC residents in the EU, most of whom were concentrated in Germany and Austria. An updated version of the research (Alvarez-Plata et al., 2003) found an estimated 977 307 immigrants from the CEEC (10) in the EU in 2001/2002, concentrated in Germany, Italy and Austria.

The Boeri and Brücker et al. study of 2000 predicted that by 2030, the total number of CEEC residents in the EU could rise to 3.9 million, or roughly 1 per cent of the EU population, and 4 per cent of that of the CEECs.[14] In the updated version of the research (Alvarez-Plata et al., 2003), this estimate was revised down slightly to 3.8 million by 2030.

Despite the relatively low levels of migration of CEEC(10) citizens, after 1989 the EC experienced a sizeable increase in immigrants from the East, which can be divided into four main categories (Vachudova, 2000):

1. Ethnic Germans or Aussiedlers who benefited from the provisions of the German constitution to move to Germany. Between 1989 and 1994 some 2 million ethnic Germans, mainly from Russia, Poland and Romania moved to Germany. In 1993 Germany introduced quotas of some 222 000 of such persons per year, but it is estimated that some 3-4 million Germans remain in the East.
2. Roma who left Bulgaria and Romania after 1989, and the Czech Republic and Slovakia subsequently. Racial discrimination, poverty and nomadic traditions all contributed to the exodus from the East.
3. Refugees from the Yugoslav wars. Following the wars in Croatia and Bosnia, by 1995 it was estimated that there were some 2 million refugees outside the Yugoslav border in 1995, and only 40 per cent of these had returned home by 1998 (Vachudova, 2000). Following the Kosovo conflict in 1998/9 it was estimated that about 900 000 people were displaced, but many of these were ethnic Albanians who had moved to Albania and Macedonia and subsequently returned home (Chafos, 2002). According to Human Rights Watch (2003), at the end of 2002 more than 1.5 million refugees and internally displaced persons in the former Yugoslavia remained unwilling or unable to return to their pre-war homes.
4. Transit immigrants (i.e. immigrants whose ultimate aim is elsewhere)[15] from the Middle East, Asia and Africa passing through Central and East Europe to the EU. The EU declared

---

[14] The conclusion that immigration from the CEECs would be on a limited scale was confirmed by, for example, Layard et al. (1992).
[15] With increasing prosperity, some of the CEECs were also becoming the final destination.

the Central East European states bordering the Community 'safe countries' and forced them to accept readmission agreements to take back unwanted migrants even if the migrant came from elsewhere. Since these countries were candidates for EU membership they had little choice but to comply and were transformed into the EU's 'reluctant gatekeepers' (Vachudova, 2000). In their turn the Central and East European countries declared neighbouring countries to be 'safe' and triggered a chain of readmission agreements for illegal immigrants and asylum-seekers ever further to the east and south. This successive deportation of migrants at times placed human rights at risk and was criticized in 2003 by both the European Council on Refugees and Exiles (ECRE) and by the UNHCR.

Although after enlargement emigration from the CEEC(10) was expected to be limited, the Commission proposed a transition period of five years, renewable for a further two before freedom of labour movement would be applied in the new CEEC member states. During this time the EC member states would continue to apply their differing policies with regard to immigration from the CEECs (see Table 7.3).

Table 7.3 The differing policies of the EU(15) on immigration from the new member states after enlargement

Austria
Will restrict labour inflows from the CEECs for up to seven years.

Belgium
Will keep restrictions on migrants for two years and open access gradually in 2006.

Denmark
Will allow workers in, but with restrictions to prevent social security shopping, and reserves the right to refuse work permits for certain regions and jobs.

Finland
Two-year freeze with an option of extension until 2006. Workers from new member states will only be able to register for jobs when there are no suitable Finnish applicants.

France
No formal quotas on migrant workers, but existing bilateral agreements will be kept with new member states.

Germany
Will apply the option allowing it to ban labour immigration for up to seven years, and will maintain existing bilateral agreements with new member states.

Sweden
Initially announced that there would be no restrictions, but policy is being changed, in particular to prevent 'welfare shopping'.

Greece
Will suspend free flow of workers for two years.

Italy
Will apply the option allowing it to ban labour immigration for up to seven years.

Britain
No restrictions, but limits on claims for welfare benefits.

Portugal
Needs 20 000 immigrants in 2004 to meet labour needs, but will issue only 6500 work permits as 13 000 unemployed immigrants are already registered.

Spain
Work permits only if immigrants have a job offer, and they must apply for visas in their own country.

Luxembourg
Applying current rules for at least a further two years.

Netherlands
Tightened immigration and asylum laws, and is restricting immigrant access to 22 000 until May 2006.

Ireland
No restrictions on immigration from new member states.

Source: *Financial Times*, 4 February 2004.

THE EVOLUTION OF COMMUNITY POLICIES WITH REGARD TO LABOUR MOVEMENT WITHIN THE EU: FROM THE TREATY OF ROME TO THE SINGLE EUROPEAN ACT

The free movement of workers within the Community was one of the main objectives set out in the Treaty of Rome. The Treaty makes the distinction between workers and self-employed or independent persons:

- Articles 48-51 of the Treaty of Rome refer to the free movement of workers that should entail the abolition of any discrimination based on nationality between workers from member states with regard to employment, remuneration and other conditions of work.
- Articles 52-58 deal with the freedom of establishment, or the right of self-employed or independent citizens of Community member states to set up businesses (including agencies, branches and subsidiaries) in other member states.

Both the free movement of labour and the freedom of establishment were to be based on the principle of national treatment, which entails the same conditions for citizens of other EC member states and the nationals of that country. The only exception permitted by the Treaty was public employment, a rather substantial exception given the size of the public sector in the EC member states.

The Treaty of Rome (Articles 117–28) also included references to social policy, including the improvement of working conditions, equal pay for men and women, and paid holidays.[16] The European Social Fund was to be set up with the aim of 'rendering the employment of workers easier and increasing their geographical and occupational mobility' (Article 123). During the 1958–70 transitional period of the Community, great emphasis was placed on promoting free movement of labour, but progress was slow. By the end of the 1960s, such freedom of labour movement as had been achieved applied more to young, unskilled workers than older professionals (Tsoukalis, 1997). The EC member states continued to apply differing policies with regard to movement of labour from third countries.

The 1993 Single Market Project (see Chapter 6) gave a new impetus to the task of eliminating frontier controls and permitting the free movement of people. The programme was also aimed at harmonizing rules on matters such as social security, recognition of qualifications, residence permits, working conditions and so on. In addition a European clearance system was set up and consisted of a network of consultants providing information about job opportunities and working conditions in the various member states.

Subsequently the EU took further measures to encourage free movement of labour between the EU(15), but progress has been relatively slow. CEDEFOP, an EU agency, has been attempting to identify the requirements for mutual recognition of qualifications, and professional associations of doctors, lawyers etc. have also been working to encourage mutual recognition of diplomas. Directives have been passed to permit aggregation of social security rights accumulated in different member states. However, social security systems still vary considerably among member states, and this is an area where unanimous voting is required in the Council of Ministers.

As Pelkmans (2001) points out, a major factor discouraging labour movement within the EU is differences in labour market regulations among the member states. These regulations include laws on minimum wages, collective contracting, hiring and firing, the duration of the working week, flexible labour contracts and so on. Given the diversity and complexity of these laws, few workers have adequate information to assess the various opportunities and risks in other member states. In

---

[16] See Chapter 14 for a discussion of EU Social Policy.

general immigrant workers are bound by the regulations of their host country, and there have been few EU attempts to approximate legislation. Notable exceptions are the Community Directives to ensure minimum standards of health and safety in the workplace, and equal treatment for men and women (see Chapter 14).

THE LINK BETWEEN FREEDOM OF LABOUR MOVEMENT AND JUSTICE AND HOME AFFAIRS

With the introduction of the Internal Market Programme, the member states realized that the abolition of border controls would have to be compensated by greater co-operation in combating transnational phenomena such as terrorism, organized crime and migration. Freedom of movement of people within the Community could not be allowed to take place to the detriment of the security of the population, public order and civil liberties. Over time national solutions to resolve such questions appeared increasingly inadequate. The collapse of communism, the dubious ability of Russia to control sales of the former Soviet military arsenal, the increase in immigration pressures and the events of 11 September 2001 added a new urgency to the question.

However, governments are reluctant to sacrifice sovereignty on such sensitive issues, so common EU policies were slow to develop, and at least initially were decided on the basis of intergovernmental co-operation. Since the compromises necessary to reach common positions in the EU were often messy, co-operation covers a heterogeneous collection of policies, and decision-making procedures are complex and in flux.[17]

FROM JUSTICE AND HOME AFFAIRS TO 'FREEDOM, SECURITY AND JUSTICE'

Prior to the Treaty of Maastricht, at the Community level co-operation on judicial and police issues was largely on an *ad hoc* basis and outside any formal institutional framework. In 1975 the TREVI Group was set up, named after the fountain in Rome where the group first met, and after the French acronym for Terrorism, Radicalism, Extremism and International Violence.[18] The group (of ministers of the interior, and subsequently also ministers of justice) met every six months to exchange information and co-operate on issues such as terrorism, organized crime, football hooliganism, national disasters and nuclear safety. After the 1993 Treaty of Maastricht the group was incorporated into Justice and Home Affairs.

The Maastricht Treaty established Justice and Home Affairs as the third pillar of the Union. Being outside the Community made for slow progress in evolving common JHA policies as decisions generally had to be unanimous.[19] Justice and Home Affairs (JHA) involves co-operation between the police, judicial immigration and customs authorities of the member states in order to jointly prevent and combat crime (Articles 29 and 30, TEU). The areas of co-operation cover both civil and criminal law, and include:

- Combating terrorism;
- Fighting drugs and the illicit arms trade;
- Combating racism and xenophobia;

---

[17] See Jones (2001) for a description of these complex changes in decision-making procedures.
[18] The first director-general of the group was also a Mr Fonteijn.
[19] There was also a certain overlap between JHA and some Single Market provisions (which fell under the Community pillar) relating to freedom of movement of people.

■ Fighting organized crime;
■ Preventing criminal acts against children and trafficking in human beings;
■ Immigration, asylum and visas;
■ Preventing corruption and fraud (and taking common measures against money-laundering); and
■ Customs administration.

The Maastricht Treaty also aimed at promotion of a European citizenship that was to be assured in three main ways:

■ Any EU citizen living in another member state has to be treated as a national of that country, and has the right to vote or stand in local and European elections;
■ Any EU citizen can use the diplomatic and consular activities of another EU country in any part of the world where their own country is not represented;
■ A Community ombudsman was to be attached to the European Parliament in order to address alleged cases of maladministration by EU institutions.

The Treaty of Amsterdam called for the development of the EU as an area of 'freedom, security and justice'. This entailed a number of issues, including visas, asylum, immigration and other policies relating to the free movement of people being 'communitised' or brought under the first (or Community) pillar. The deadline fixed was 2004, i.e. five years after the Treaty of Amsterdam came into force.[20] Coming under the Community pillar meant an increased role for the Commission, European Parliament and Court of Justice in deciding on such questions. The remaining third pillar is to become known as 'Police and Judicial Co-operation on Criminal Matters'. The name reflects its competences, which were also extended to include fighting racism and xenophobia.

The Tampere European Council of October 1999 took key decisions on rendering the area of 'freedom, security and justice' operational, calling for:

■ A common immigration and asylum policy;
■ Minimum rights for the victims of crime; and
■ Re-enforced efforts to combat cross-border crime.

With regard to asylum policy, the deadline for implementing a common EU system was set at 2004. A scoreboard was drawn up to spell out the respective responsibilities of the member states, the Commission and the Council in achieving that task.

In February 2002 the EU Council of Ministers agreed on a plan to combat illegal immigration and trafficking of human beings. The plan identified a number of areas where common action was necessary, including visa policy, the exchange of information, readmission and repatriation policies, and border management.

The European Council at Seville of 2002 discussed proposals such as sanctions on countries of emigration that failed to co-operate in managing migratory fluxes, and a common EU effort with joint financing to patrol external borders. However, the Seville Summit failed to agree on many concrete steps in the asylum field apart from a timetable for certain asylum directives currently under discussion and a call for member states to co-operate in the management of external borders.

In January 2003 the EU, Iceland and Norway launched Eurodac, a system to fingerprint all asylum-seekers and exchange information. This will enable member states to determine whether

---

[20] This included communitizing the Schengen Agreement, as discussed below.

an individual has already applied for asylum in another EU country or whether that person was apprehended for attempting to enter the EU illegally.

The 2003 Brussels European Council called on the Commission to present a proposal to create a Border Management Agency, though the main responsibility for management of the external borders of the EU is to rest with the EU member states. The Commission was also requested to present a proposal to incorporate biometric identifiers into passports and visa and resident permit systems.

The EU also attempted to work towards minimum standards for processing the granting and withdrawing of refugee status for people arriving in the EU. A proposed Directive of 2004 would include a list of 'safe countries' outside the EU where refugees could be returned and where their cases could be processed. The United Nations High Commissioner for Refugees again expressed concern over the 'safe country principle', arguing that it could lead to erosion of standards.

THE SCHENGEN AGREEMENT

Progress in adopting JHA policies in the EU has relied heavily on a pilot project, which is generally referred to as 'Schengen'. In 1985 Benelux, Germany and France formed the Schengen Group with the aim of eliminating border controls between each other as rapidly as possible, and co-operating on visa, asylum and immigration questions.[21] This would entail the removal of all controls on people (whether they are citizens of the EU or of third countries) when they cross frontiers between Schengen countries. Subsequently other countries joined the group, and by 1999 when the Schengen Agreement was incorporated into a protocol Annex to the Amsterdam Treaty, only the UK and Ireland had opted out, while Denmark had a partial opt-out, reserving its position on all questions except visas.[22] Two non-EU countries, Iceland and Norway, signed association agreements in 1996.

In order to control immigration, international terrorism and criminal activities when police checks at frontiers were eliminated, in 1990 the Schengen countries agreed a Convention on Application of the Agreement, which entered into force from 1995.[23] In addition to a mechanism for settling disputes, this set out a series of provisions on issues such as extradition, drugs, firearms, asylum and transmission of personal data. The provisions included:

- Establishing the institutional framework for the abolition of border controls between Schengen countries.
- Setting up the Schengen Information System (SIS), a computer network for the exchange of information between national police forces. This was to act as a joint automated search system and involved setting up and maintaining data files on persons and certain objects (firearms, stolen or lost vehicles, bank notes, official documents and so on).
- Common rules and procedures for checks at the external borders.
- More co-operation on extradition.
- Harmonization of legislation governing firearms.
- Measures to facilitate cross-border transport of goods, including increased co-operation between customs authorities.
- Common lists of countries requiring visas and a common model of visa.

---

[21] The name 'Schengen' derives from the town near the Luxembourg, French and German borders.
[22] Spain and Portugal signed in 1995, and Italy, Austria and Greece signed in 1997. The UK and Ireland take part in aspects of the Schengen *acquis* dealing with police co-operation.
[23] 1997 for Italy, Austria and Greece.

■ Increased co-operation between national police forces, including the establishment of Europol (see below).[24]

Some aspects of Schengen have been challenged on grounds of privacy and accountability. For instance, it has been claimed that the SIS may run counter to national legislation on data protection and could therefore infringe civil liberties.

EUROPOL AND POLICE CO-OPERATION

The aim of Europol is to facilitate cross-border co-ordination between EU police forces and customs officials. The Maastricht Treaty lists its aims as 'preventing and combating terrorism, unlawful drug trafficking, and other serious forms of international crime, including, if necessary, customs co-operation'. Based in The Hague, Europol became fully operational in 1999 and supports the member states through:[25]

■ Exchange of data between Europol officials;
■ Analyses of crime and general strategic reports;
■ Expertise and technical support for investigations and ongoing operations.

Following 11 September 2001, stronger transatlantic ties were developed between Europol and US law-enforcement authorities. The aim was to increase strategic and technical co-operation in preventing, detecting and suppressing international terrorism.

There has been much speculation as to whether Europol would evolve into a European FBI, but Europol is a police office rather than a police force. None the less, civil rights groups fear it might develop into an operational police force, and criticize its inadequate accountability.[26] Europol officers have the power to open files on victims and witnesses, are not required to testify in court and are immune for acts they perform in the course of duty. Though they are not allowed to make arrests or search houses, in 2000 they gained the right to start criminal investigations (Jones, 2001).

A European Police Chiefs' Task Force permitting top-level communication came into operation from 2000. A Crime-Prevention Forum and a European Crime-Prevention Network (EUCPN) were set up in 2001 to share crime-prevention information and promote best practices. In 2001 a European Police College (CEPOL) to train personnel also came into operation. EU Police officers would also be involved in peacekeeping tasks (see also Chapter 19).

JUDICIAL CO-OPERATION

Judicial co-operation is aimed at facilitating and accelerating collaboration with regard to procedures and the enforcement of decisions, easier extradition between member states and establishing minimum rules in relation to the constituent elements of criminal acts and penalties in the fields of organized crime, terrorism and drug trafficking (Articles 31 and 32, TEU). The aim is also to link judicial co-operation to the work of international organizations such as the UN and the Council of Europe, and to include it in the transatlantic dialogue with the USA and Canada.

---

[24] The agreement also envisages cross-border surveillance and cross-border pursuit of suspects by police officers.
[25] The Europol Drugs Unit (EDU) was set up in 1994.
[26] The FBI, for example, is accountable to Congress.

The EU member states decided to introduce a common arrest warrant to come into operation from 2004 and faster and simpler procedures for the surrender of suspects. It was proposed that the common arrest warrant would cover 32 crimes including terrorism and financial fraud.

> ## Box 7.1 Judicial co-operation
> Initially Italy wanted to restrict the common arrest warrant to a list of six crimes, raising speculation about the personal interests of the prime minister, Berlusconi, who was under investigation for fraud charges by a Spanish judge, Baltazar Garzon. In the event compromise was reached, and Italy was given time to introduce the necessary constitutional changes before applying the measure.

Eurojust is a European Judicial Co-operation Unit set up in Brussels in 2001 and composed of magistrates, prosecutors, judges and legal experts drawn from the member states. Its aim is to facilitate co-ordination between national prosecuting authorities and support criminal investigations into organized crime (Article 31 TEU). It can also help OLAF, the EU anti-fraud organization. In 1998 a European Judicial Network (EJN) was set up to facilitate exchanges of information between EU judges and lawyers working on criminal cases.

EVALUATION

Despite the various attempts to facilitate labour movement, while at the same time co-operating on internal affairs and judicial and police matters, the EU member states continue to have difficulties in reaching common positions on such issues. What is even more worrying is that EU policies have frequently been criticized on human rights grounds. In 2000 Human Rights Watch began a project on the human rights of migrants in Western Europe.[27] The project revealed a range of abuses of rights of migrants from non-EU countries in several European Union member states including:

- Arbitrary detention;
- Gravely substandard conditions of detention;
- Procedural violations in criminal and administrative law proceedings, and in the asylum system;
- Racial and ethnic discrimination;
- Police abuse;
- Arbitrary and collective expulsions;
- Violations of children's and women's rights;
- Horrendous abuses of migrants and asylum seekers at the hands of human traffickers, often in complicity with law enforcement officials in EU member or accession states.

Unfortunately, the picture that emerges for the EU from the Human Rights Watch World Report for 2003 is not much more favourable:

> Throughout the region, the deportation of migrants was characterized by persistent rights violations, including inadequate information and translation services, insufficient access to legal representation during detention, and lack of judicial oversight or opportunities for migrants to

---

[27] As reported in Chafos (2002).

appeal their expulsions. Following the Seville summit, the EU undertook an explicit policy of linking its aid to countries to their willingness to enter into readmission agreements committing them to accept the return of migrants who had entered the union through their territory. The web of readmission agreements effectively shifted the burden of immigration control and refugee protection from EU member and applicant states to their eastern and southern neighbours, which had markedly fewer resources to devote to it ... While member states pursued migration policies and practices that violated international standards, EU joint action to combat immigration failed to specify any concomitant joint obligations to respect migrants' rights.

In developing common policies with regard to 'freedom, security and justice' the EU member states should take care that protection standards are not eroded.

Summary of Key Concepts

- Freedom of movement of labour on an international scale is generally advocated because it is said to lead to increased efficiency. More specific arguments are also advanced such as to offset possible negative effects of aging of the population or skill shortages.
- Restrictions on immigration include border controls, and work or residence permits, limited access to certain jobs and professions, inability to find housing, financial disincentives, limits on access to social security benefits, or unfavourable tax treatment.
- Various factors influence the decision to migrate: the income gap between the home and host country; employment possibilities in both countries; the geographical proximity of the two countries; emigration traditions; ethnic and family networks; political and ethnic disturbances; cultural and linguistic factors and economic expectations.
- The different kinds of immigrant are: economic immigrants, asylum seekers, illegal immigrants and seasonal or temporary workers.
- As it is becoming ever more difficult to enter the EU as a long-term economic immigrant, there has been a growing tendency to seek other forms of access, such as asylum. In practice it is very difficult to distinguish whether refugees are fleeing poverty rather than persecution.
- To prevent asylum-seekers 'shopping around', the Dublin Convention requires them to apply for asylum in the first EU country they enter.
- Temporary immigration may take various forms: guest workers, seasonal workers, project-tied workers, border-commuters and exchanges of trainees.
- During the 1958–73 period the only substantial migration flow within the Community was from Italy to Northern Europe, but there were large-scale migrations from third countries to the Community.
- Between 1973 and 1989 the degree of labour movement within the Community was relatively limited. There was immigration from Spain, Greece and Portugal, though this dropped drastically with EC membership; from North Africa, Turkey and Yugoslavia, and continuing immigration from other former colonies.
- After 1989 immigration within the EU continued to be on a limited scale, but immigration from third countries increased.
- Despite the relatively low levels of migration of CEEC(10) citizens, after 1989 the EC experienced a sizeable increase in four main types of immigrants from the East: ethnic Germans or Aussiedlers, Roma, refugees from the Yugoslav Wars and transit immigrants.
- After enlargement the EU will apply a transition period of five years, renewable for a further two, before freedom of labour movement would be applied in the new CEEC member states. During this time the EC member states would continue to apply their differing policies with regard to immigration from the CEECs.

- Articles 48–51 of the Treaty of Rome refer to the free movement of workers, and Articles 52–58 deal with the freedom of establishment.
- The Maastricht Treaty established Justice and Home Affairs as the third pillar of the Union. JHA involves co-operation between the police, judicial immigration and customs authorities of the member states in order to jointly prevent and combat crime.
- With the Treaty of Amsterdam a number of issues including visas, asylum, immigration and other policies relating to the free movement of people were to be 'communitized' by 2004. The remaining third pillar is to become known as 'Police and Judicial Co-operation on Criminal Matters'.
- The Tampere European Council of 1999 aimed at rendering the European area of 'freedom, security and justice' operational.
- The Schengen Group aims at eliminating border controls among member countries, but Britain, Ireland and Denmark (partially) have opt-outs.
- The aim of Europol is to facilitate co-operation among EU police forces.
- Judicial co-operation involves facilitating and accelerating collaboration with regard to procedures and the enforcement of decisions, easier extradition between member states and establishing minimum rules.

Questions for Study and Review

■ What are the main arguments in favour of freedom of labour movement?

■ What are the main arguments used by governments to justify restrictions on immigration? To what extent do you consider that these arguments are justified?

■ What is the effect of immigration on wages?

■ How does immigration affect unemployment?

■ Describe the main forms of immigration.

■ How has the pattern of immigration changed in the EU over the years?

■ What changes in the policy towards movement of labour in the EU are expected with enlargement?

■ What does the Justice and Home Affairs pillar involve?

■ Describe the Schengen Agreement.

■ What is Europol, and why has it been criticized by civil rights groups?

■ What do we mean by the European area of 'freedom, security and justice'?

■ Why do human rights organizations criticize policies in the EU with regard to immigration? Do you consider these criticisms justified?

Appendix
The effects of migration

A slightly more elaborate model can be used to show the impact of migration on the demand and supply of labour in the two countries.[28] The upper part of Figure A7.1 illustrates the situation when labour markets are separate, and there is no migration. The lower part of the graph shows the situation after integration of labour markets when migration takes place. For simplicity it is again assumed that there are only two countries, home and foreign. The situation for the home country is shown in the left of Figure A7.1 and that for the foreign country on the right. The horizontal axes indicate the number of workers in each country, while wage levels are measured along the vertical axes. The curves Sh and Sf show the supply of labour in the two countries respectively, while Dh and Df indicate the demand for labour in the home and foreign countries .

---

[28] The account here is taken from Molle (2001) who presents a model based on Lindert (1986).

As shown in the upper part of the diagram, before integration the intersection of the supply Sh and demand Dh for labour leads to relatively high wages in the home country, while the intersection of Sf and Df implies lower wages in the foreign county. This difference in wages will continue only if there is some restriction on movement of labour from the foreign country to the home country .

With integration and the removal of barriers to labour movement, workers in the foreign country will move to the home country. Migration involves economic, social and psychological costs which are assumed equal to C. As a result of these costs the movement of labour will not lead to complete equalization of wages in the two countries. The inflow of labour into home country will push wages down, so that less labour is supplied domestically (OaM) and more is demanded domestically (OaN). MN is the number of workers that have moved to the home country from the foreign country. In the foreign country the higher wages caused by workers leaving will reduce the quantity of labour demanded (ObP) and increase the quantity of labour

Figure A7.1 The effects of immigration

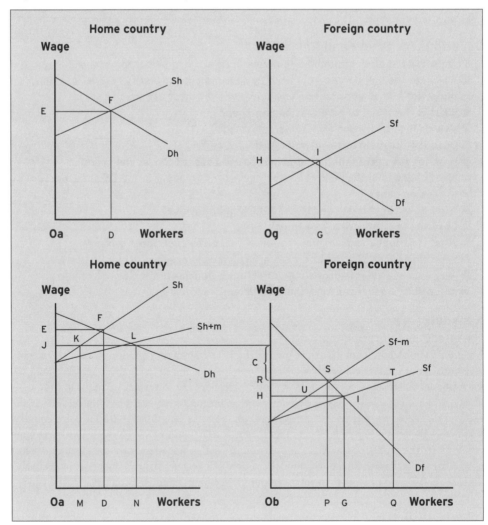

supplied (ObQ). PQ indicates the number of workers who have left the foreign country to go to the home country, and so is equal to MN. The new domestic labour supply curves are Sh + m and Sf − m respectively.

The welfare effects of migration for workers and employers can also be seen from Figure A7.1. Workers in the home country lose JEKF as wages are forced down. In the foreign country wages rise from ObH to ObR, so workers gain by HRSU (i.e. the producer surplus above the new supply curve). Migrants gain as they earn more in the home country than in the foreign country, but the costs of immigration C have to be taken into account. The gain for migrants is area USTI, or the area above the old supply curve Sf and below the new one Sf − m.

References

Alvarez-Plata, P., Brücker, H. and Siliverstovs (2003) *Potential Migration from Central and Eastern Europe into the EU-15 - An Update*, Report for the European Commission DG Employment and Social Affairs, http://europa.eu.int/comm/employment_social

Baldwin, R. and Wyplosz, C. (2004) *The Economics of European Integration*, McGraw-Hill Education, Maidenhead, UK.

Boeri, T., Brücker, H., et al. (2000) *The Impact of Eastern Enlargement on Employment and Wages in the EU Member States,* Report for the European Commission, http://europa.eu.int/comm/employment_social

Chafos, T.A. (2002) 'From immigration policy in Europe to European Union Immigration Policy: The present window of opportunity', unpublished Master's thesis, Faculty of Political Science, University of Siena.

European Commission (2003) 'Choosing to grow. Knowledge, innovation and jobs in a cohesive society. Report to the Spring European Council, March 2003 on the Lisbon Strategy of economic, social and environmental renewal', www.europa.eu.int/comm/internal_market

Faini, R. (1995), 'Migration in the integrated EU', in *Expanding Membership of the European Community*, Baldwin, R., Haaparanta, P. and Klander, J. (eds), Cambridge University Press, Cambridge.

Faini, R. and Venturini, A. (1994) 'Migration and growth: The experience of Southern Europe', CEPR Discussion Paper no. 964, Centre for Economic Policy Research, London.

Human Rights Watch (2003) *World Report 2003,* www.hrw.org

Jones, R.A. (2001) *The Politics and Economics of the European Union. An Introductory Text,* 2nd edn, Edward Elgar, Cheltenham, UK.

Krugman, P. and Obstfeld, M. (1997) *International Economics. Theory and Policy*, Addison Wesley Longman Inc., Reading, MA.

Layard, R., Blanchard, O., Dornbusch, R. and Krugman, P. (1992) *East-West Migration: The Alternatives*, MIT Press, Cambridge, MA.

Lindert, P. (1986) *International Economics,* 8th edn, Irwin, Homewood, IL.

Molle, W. (2001) *The Economics of European Integration. Theory, Practice, Policy,* 4th edn, Ashgate, Aldershot, UK.

OECD (2003) *Trends in International Migration, 2002 Edition,* OECD, Paris.

Pelkmans, J. (2001) *European Integration. Methods and Economic Analysis,* Prentice Hall, Harlow, UK.

Salvatore, D. (2001) *International Economics,* 7th edn, John Wiley & Sons, New York.

Tsoukalis, L. (1997) *The New European Economy Revisited,* 3rd edn, Oxford University Press, Oxford.

Vachudova, M. A. (2000) 'Eastern Europe as gatekeeper: The immigration and asylum policies of an enlarging European Union' in *The Wall around the West: State Borders and Immigration Control in North America and Europe*, Andreas, P. and Snyder, T. (eds), Rowman & Littlefield, Lanham, MD.

Useful websites

Information on EU policies on labour movement and immigration are available from:
The European Commission
http://europa.eu.int/comm/justice_home.
The European Parliament
www.europarl.eu.int
The EU Council of Ministers
www.europa.eu.int/pol/justice

Statistics on immigration can be obtained from:
International Organization for Immigration
www.iom.int
Organization for Economic Co-operation and Development
www.oecd.org
United Nations Development Programme
www.undp.org.

Discussion of asylum and human rights issues is provided by:
Cable News Network (CNN)
www.cnn.com
European Council on Refugees and Exiles
www.ecre.org
Human Rights Watch
www.hrw.org
Inter-governmental Consultations
www.igc.ch
The Organization for Security and Co-operation in Europe
www.osce.org
United Nations High Commission on Refugees
www.unhcr.ch

List of abbreviations

CEDEFOP	European Centre for Development of Vocational Training
CEEC	Central and East European country
CEPOL	European Police College
ECRE	European Council on Refugees and Exiles
EDU	European Drugs Unit
EUCPN	European Crime-Prevention Network
Europol	European Police Office
FBI	Federal Bureau of Investigation
JHA	Justice and Home Affairs
OECD	Organization for Economic Co-operation and Development
OLAF	European Anti-Fraud Office
SIS	Schengen Information System
TEU	Treaty on European Union
TREVI	Group on Terrorism, Radicalism, Extremism and International Violence
UNHCR	United Nations High Commissioner on Refugees

8

The Long Road to Economic and Monetary Union

LEARNING OBJECTIVES

By the end of this chapter you should be able to understand:

▶ What we mean by an optimum currency area;

▶ The main expected costs and benefits of introducing the euro;

▶ Why the aim of the 1969 Hague Summit to introduce economic and monetary union (EMU) failed;

▶ What we mean by the 'snake in the tunnel';

▶ What the main features of the European Monetary System were;

▶ What we mean by the 'contradictory quartet';

▶ Why the objective of EMU was revived in the 1990s;

▶ The way in which the Maastricht Treaty set out the conditions for joining the single currency, the timing of its introduction and its main institutional features;

▶ What the main functions of the European Central Bank are;

▶ What is the likely role of the euro in the international financial system.

INTRODUCTION

From 1 January 2002 12 EU countries replaced their national currencies with euro notes and coins. Only three EU countries remained out of what became known as 'euroland', the 'eurozone' or 'euro area': the UK, Denmark and Sweden. In May 1998 the decision concerning which countries could join the euro was taken (later for Greece which became a member from 1 January 2001), and from June 1998 the European Central Bank came into operation in Frankfurt. The countries of the eurozone adopted a common interest rate and close co-ordination of their fiscal policies.

What were the expected advantages of adopting a single currency, and what were the possible costs of giving up exchange rate changes? These are the questions addressed in the first part of this chapter.

Although there was no precise commitment to economic and monetary union (EMU) in the Treaty of Rome, subsequently various initiatives were taken in this direction. For many years these initiatives met with mixed success, but they created a framework of institutions and arrangements on which EMU could eventually be built. The second part of this chapter therefore adopts a historical approach to the evolution of EMU before the main features of its operation are described in the final part.

THE THEORY OF OPTIMUM CURRENCY AREAS

Early theoretical assessments of whether countries should join together to form an economic and monetary union generally make use of the concept of an optimum currency area.[1] A currency area is defined as a group of countries that maintain their separate currencies but fix the exchange rates between themselves permanently. They also maintain full convertibility among their currencies and flexible exchange rates towards third countries. The problem then becomes determining the optimum size of the currency area and, more specifically, deciding whether it is to the advantage of a particular country to enter or remain in a currency area.

The early literature in this field concentrates on finding individual criteria that are necessary and sufficient to identify optimum currency areas. This involves indicating alternatives which could act as substitutes for exchange rate policies *vis-à-vis* other member countries, or which would render exchange rate adjustment within the area unnecessary. Possible candidates include trade integration, international factor mobility, financial integration, the diversification of production, convergence of inflation rates and integration of economic policies. As can be seen, most of these also indicate the degree of integration between the member countries.

COST/BENEFIT ANALYSES OF ECONOMIC AND MONETARY UNION

Later authors adopt the traditional optimal currency area approach as a starting point but attempt to evolve a global framework that takes the various criteria into account. This involves using cost/benefit analysis to assess whether a country or group of countries should form an economic and monetary union. In order to decide whether membership is advantageous or not, it is necessary to identify the different costs and benefits involved and attach weights to each of these. The evaluation

---

[1] This concept was introduced by Mundell in 1961.

of whether countries should form an economic and monetary union will depend on the weight attributed to the various costs and benefits, and this can be very subjective.

According to Krugman and Obstfeld (1997), the benefits of forming an economic and monetary union will increase, and the costs will decline, as the level of integration rises. The level of integration can be measured by, for example, the ratio of intra-EU trade to GDP.

THE BENEFITS OF ECONOMIC AND MONETARY UNION

1. In changing from one currency to another, not only does a customer have to pay a commission but the price paid for buying a currency is higher than that received for selling at any given time. It has been estimated that if a citizen changed a certain sum of money successively into each of the former currencies of the European Union, at the end less than half the money would remain. The 'transaction costs' of changing money reflect the fact that real resources are used up in the provision of foreign exchange services. The bank, or *bureau de change,* has to pay the overheads for maintaining an office, the salaries of staff and so on. The benefit from elimination of transaction costs rises with the level of integration, as the savings will tend to be greater as the level of trade increases. According to the EC Commission,[2] the reduction in foreign exchange transactions as a result of EMU could amount to some 0.5 per cent of the EU GDP, or $40 billion each year.[3]

2. EMU would represent a further step towards completion of the Single Market. There is much empirical evidence to suggest prices for a given product vary considerably in the different EU countries.[4] If all prices were quoted in a single currency, it seems likely that the chances of exploiting this kind of market discrimination would decline. This is a major reason that European business embarked on a new phase of restructuring and mergers from the late 1990s, in particular in the banking and insurance sectors.

    However, it seems likely that in Europe differences in tastes, habits, culture and language will prevent the eurozone from becoming a single homogeneous market (see Box 8.1).

Box 8.1

Even in the case of multinational firms, surprisingly few homogeneous products are sold from one end of Europe to another. For instance, in the USA the same brands of soap powder are sold throughout the country, but in the EU even detergents are different from country to country to suit local conditions. As a representative from Henkel maintains, stains in the Scandinavian countries are different from those in Southern Europe because of 'the special challenges of olive oil and tomatoes'.*

* As reported in the *Financial Times,* 5/6 January 2002.

---

3. Introduction of the single currency could encourage the creation of a deeper, wider, more liquid capital market. Portes and Rey (1998) describe a circular mechanism by which this might come about. As euro markets for money and securities become more

---

[2] As reported in the *Economist,* 6 April 1996.
[3] As reported in the *Economist,* 24 October 1998.
[4] The *Financial Times, FT Guide to the Euro,* 15 November 2001 compared prices for standard products in various EU cities and found substantial differences. For example, the price of a Sony Walkman varied from €45.53 in Madrid to €61.33 in Frankfurt, while the price of the same video cassette (*Gladiator*) was €13.89 in Rome and €21.34 in Paris.

integrated and liquid, transaction costs will fall, rendering euro-denominated assets more attractive. Increased holdings of euro-denominated assets, and use of the euro as a vehicle currency, make the EU financial market deeper, broader and more liquid and so on.

The shortcoming in this argument is that one of the main European financial centres, the City of London, remains outside the euro area, but even here trading in euros has been expanding rapidly (ECB, 2003).

4. Various studies (Frenkel and Rose, 2000; Rose 2000 and 2002) have shown how introducing a common currency is likely to encourage trade growth. Rose (2000) maintained that countries with the same legal tender trade as much as three times more than other economic systems,[5] and the result spawned a vast and growing literature. Rose (2002) considers 24 recent studies of the impact of currency unions on trade, and despite the differences in approach and coverage of the studies, all seem to confirm that currency unions have a positive impact on trade.

5. There may be economies of scale in holding international reserves in dealings with third countries. It seems likely that the European Central Bank will be able to hold fewer reserves than those held by the national central banks of the EU member states. Euro-area countries will no longer have to hold reserves to cover transactions with other countries participating in the monetary union.

6. The euro is likely to become an international reserve currency, and be able to reap some benefits of seignorage as some of the printed money will end up as international reserves. In so far as non-euro countries hold euros, they will also have to pay some of the costs of seignorage.

   Seignorage refers to the capacity of governments to increase their budget receipts as a result of their right to print money.[6] A government may cover a budget deficit by printing money. The question that then arises is why the public is prepared to hold a greater stock of money, or even a stock of money that is increasing in size year after year. In part this willingness of the public may be the consequence of real growth of the economy, but it is generally also the result of inflation. Assuming that there is no real growth in an economy, the public will want to hold a constant stock of money in real terms. However, with inflation the purchasing power of a given nominal stock of money will decline. In order to maintain the real value of money holdings unchanged, the public will have to hold an increasing stock of nominal money to compensate for the inflation rate.

   Inflation can therefore be regarded as a type of tax insofar as the public can only spend a smaller share of its income and has to pay the difference to the government in exchange for money. In other words, if the government sector is financing its deficit by printing money, and the public is prepared to hold this extra money to maintain the real value of its money holdings constant, the government is imposing a kind of 'inflation tax'.

7. A monetary union would entail the introduction of a common monetary policy, which according to some was a benefit, and to others a cost (see below). This would reduce the risk of manipulation of monetary policies for electoral purposes. In the EU context a common monetary policy might allow other EU countries more say than was the case in the 'German policy leadership' model of the European Monetary System up until 1992.

---

[5] The Rose (2000) analysis was based on a cross-country dataset covering bilateral trade between 186 economic systems at five-year intervals, using a linear gravity model. One of the surprising outcomes of Rose's study is that exchange rate volatility plays little significant role in the picture.
[6] The term derives from the benefits to the *seigneur* or lord of the manor in issuing coins. The gold content of such coins was generally less than their face value. In other words, if there were confidence in holding such coins, the *seigneur* could 'clip' part of their gold content.

A common monetary policy might be considered an advantage in providing external discipline and 'borrowed' credibility for inflation-prone countries.[7] Some studies presented the likely reduction of inflation and interest rates as one of the main advantages of a monetary union.[8] This argument in favour of EMU rests on the assumption that the European Central Bank is committed to low inflation (which seems even excessively the case in the first years of the euro), and that inflation-prone countries are incapable of pursuing the policies necessary to keep inflation low outside the EMU.

8. Exchange rate uncertainty is taken into account by firms in their location decisions. If this uncertainty is removed, firms will be able to locate where their unit costs are lowest, and where they can best exploit economies of scale.

9. According to the neo-functionalist approach, introducing an economic and monetary union might further the integration process through spill-over into other policy areas. For instance, the need for democratic control of a central bank could lead to institutional reform and further steps towards political union.

10. It seems likely that members of a monetary union will carry more weight at a world level in their dealings with third countries.

THE MAIN COSTS OF ECONOMIC AND MONETARY UNION

1. The introduction of a new, single currency is likely to involve psychological costs. A survey carried out by Eurobarometer suggested that in November 1997 the share of public opinion opposed to introducing a single money was highest in Finland, Denmark, Britain and Sweden. The countries with the highest share of public opinion in favour of a single money were Italy (at least initially), Ireland, Luxembourg and Spain.

    According to a survey carried out by Cetelem,[9] 59 per cent of 5000 people surveyed in 2003 said they were worried about the effects of the euro, compared with a third in 1999. Italians were the most critical with 78 per cent expressing concern, probably because of the widespread conviction that the euro has added to inflation. The negative views of the impact of the euro on prices were confirmed by Eurobarometer surveys (see also Tables 8.1 and 8.2). According to the Cetelem survey, the second most critical vote was in Germany, and the share of British surveyed expressing misgivings about the euro rose from 48 per cent in 1999 to 65 per cent in 2003. In contrast, almost two-thirds of the Belgians in the survey felt positive about the euro.

2. The transition to the new system involves 'technical' costs such as the printing of new money (see also Box 8.2), the adjustment of slot machines, changes in accountancy etc.

3. Monetary union will entail loss of seignorage for some EU member states. On 9 December 2001 the European Central Bank indicated how the estimated €13 billion seignorage was to be allocated among the central banks of the euro members. The allocation was based on each central bank's share in the capital of the European Central

---

[7] If governments take advantage of the temporary trade-off between inflation and unemployment and raise inflation to reduce unemployment, agents will come to expect them to do so and will predict a higher level of inflation. What is needed is a way of making commitment to lower inflation credible, and an independent European Central Bank committed to curbing inflation may perform this function and bring about a lower rate of inflation. In this way the inflation-prone country may 'borrow' credibility.

[8] According to some observers this aspect of EMU is to be considered a cost as the deflationary bias of a common monetary policy may prove excessive for some countries.

[9] As reported in the *Financial Times*, 8 January 2004.

Country	A lot of difficulty	Some difficulty	No difficulty
Ireland	8	16	76
Luxembourg	4	27	69
Portugal	5	26	68
Greece	12	25	63
Netherlands	9	29	62
Belgium	6	33	61
Spain	8	32	60
Finland	3	38	59
Austria	5	40	55
Germany	15	33	52
EU (12)	14	35	51
Italy	29	28	43
France	11	51	39

Table 8.1 Attitudes to the euro in 2003 (per cent)*

*Question: It is two years since we have been using the euro instead of [NATIONAL CURRENCY]. Today, would you say that the euro continues to cause you a lot of difficulty, some difficulty, or no difficulty at all?
Source: Eurobarometer (2003).

Country	In favour of consumers	To the detriment of consumers	Rises and falls balanced out for consumers
Italy	–	96	–
Netherlands	–	93	4
Germany	–	92	7
Greece	3	92	4
EU (12)	3	89	7
Austria	–	89	7
Spain**	4	87	5
France	4	83	11
Ireland	5	81	12
Portugal***	6	76	13
Finland	–	72	26
Belgium	5	71	21
Luxembourg#	14	55	26

Table 8.2 Attitudes about the impact of the euro on prices (per cent)*

*Question: Did you personally notice that, in [OUR COUNTRY] when converted into euro, prices have been: rather in favour of consumers; rather to the detriment of consumers, or one way and another the rises and falls balanced out?
** 4 per cent don't know, *** 6 per cent don't know, #5 per cent don't know. The dash indicates that the statistic is not given by Eurobarometer.
Source: Eurobarometer (2003).

Bank, with France, Greece and Finland standing to gain most from the new system, while Germany, Spain and Italy were the greatest losers.[10]

4. Last but not least, introduction of economic and monetary union entails loss of an autonomous monetary policy and of the exchange rate mechanism.

A single interest rate may be unsuited to the differing economic situation in individual member states, being too tight for some and too loose for others. In 1998, for example, the business cycles of countries joining the euro were evidently not synchronized. Countries such as Finland and Portugal were growing faster than Italy or Germany, and in Ireland and Spain there was a risk of

---

[10] *Financial Times*, 20 December 2001. France stood to gain most: although the franc accounted for only 12 per cent of issuance across the euro area, under the capital key the economic size and population of France entailed an estimated share of 20 per cent.

> **Box 8.2**
> **What happens to the notes and coins not traded in?**
> It was estimated that central banks and governments in the eurozone were likely to collect a windfall of up to €15 billion from old currency notes and coins not handed in after introduction of the euro (*Financial Times*, 20 December 2001).
>
> The 11 euro area central banks are responsible for the physical issuing of euros. The introduction of the euro required old coins to be rounded up and eventually melted down so their metal could be recycled. In order to guard against theft, a German firm, Eurocoin, introduced a machine known as the 'decoiner' which squashes and corrugates higher denomination coins, rendering them useless to thieves (*Financial Times*, 4 December 2001). Eurocoin provides coin blanks for the euro and also for other currencies like the Thai baht and Malaysian ringgit.

overheating. However, some economists have argued that the experience of participating together in EMU will bring the business cycles of the euro countries more in line with each other and so reduce this problem of 'one size fits all'. A further complication arises because a given interest rate change may have different effects in different economies.[11]

According to economic textbooks, the role of the exchange rate mechanism is to act as a shock absorber in the event of asymmetric shocks, i.e. disturbances that affect the countries involved in different ways. Appendix 8 provides a more formal treatment of this question.[12] For instance, if it is assumed that France is relatively intensive in the production of wine, and Germany is relatively intensive in the production of beer, an asymmetric shock could take the form of a health scare concerning wine that causes consumers to start drinking beer in place of wine. To meet this situation the French franc might be devalued against the German D-mark, rendering French output cheaper relative to German output. As a result people will again start drinking more wine and less beer, so it should therefore be possible to use the devaluation to return to the original situation in each country.

However, even if French domestic prices remain the same, the devaluation will increase the franc price of German beer bought by French workers. If there is a high level of integration between the French and German economies, a large share of products in France will be imported from Germany.[13] This means that a French devaluation will have a substantial effect in raising consumer prices in France.

These higher prices reduce real wages, and may lead to requests by French workers to increase nominal wages. There is even a risk that repeated devaluations lead to a wage–price–devaluation spiral. With a higher level of integration, an exchange rate change is more likely to alter consumer prices and lead to this kind of price–wage reaction. The higher the level of integration, the less is the cost of forgoing the exchange rate mechanism. This is a major reason that the cost curve of monetary union is assumed to slope down to the right.

Although this type of price–wage reaction reduces the effectiveness of the exchange rate instrument, few economists would argue that it loses all its effectiveness. The reactions may not be immediate, so that devaluation can give governments a breathing space while other policies are introduced.

---

[11] For example, Dornbusch et al. (1998) estimate that the initial impact of a rise in short-term interest rates is twice as high in Italy as in Germany.
[12] See also Artis (1994) for a more complete description of these effects.
[13] This is one of the explanations for the cost curve in Figure 8.1 above sloping down to the right.

In the more recent literature the view has emerged that rather than neutralizing asymmetric shocks, exchange rate changes might actually cause them. For instance, Buiter (2000) maintains that with very high international financial capital mobility, market-determined exchange rates are primarily a source of shocks and instability, arguing: 'The potential advantages of nominal exchange rate flexibility as an effective adjustment mechanism or shock absorber are bundled with the undoubted disadvantages of excessive noise and unwarranted movements in the exchange rate, inflicting unnecessary real adjustments on the rest of the economy' (p. 236).

A further question that arises is whether a higher level of integration makes the likelihood of asymmetric shocks greater or less. It seems likely that a higher level of integration will lead to some convergence of consumer tastes and preferences. If this were the case, on the demand side the shocks would be more likely to affect all the partners, reducing the role for a shock absorber such as adjustment of exchange rates between the member states.

The implications for the production side are less clear. If integration leads to specialization,[14] the economies of the member states will become less similar and more vulnerable to asymmetric shocks. Against this, most trade within the EU is intra-industry and is usually explained in terms of economies of scale and imperfect competition.[15] If this is the case it seems likely that shocks would be more likely to affect all the member states. If, however, integration implies centrifugal forces leading to the concentration of industry, asymmetric shocks may affect the poles of development.[16]

The cost of forgoing the exchange rate mechanism will also be less if it can be replaced by alternative mechanisms. In the case of the European Union such mechanisms could include wage–price flexibility and factor mobility, or Community mechanisms such as regional or budgetary policy to compensate regions or countries that have been adversely affected.

Wage–price flexibility implies that in the case of a permanent adverse asymmetric shock the real wages and relative prices in that country (or region, if the production is concentrated in a particular area) will fall. There will be a strong incentive for workers to move to other regions or countries where real wages are higher. Similarly, if there is sufficient capital mobility among the member states, in the example above there will be a reduced incentive to invest in the French wine industry and a tendency towards increased investment in German beer production. If factors of production were sufficiently mobile, this process would continue until differences in the remuneration of factors in different regions were eliminated. Although much progress has been made in increasing factor mobility in the European Union, as the discussion in Chapter 7 shows, this process is far from complete, particularly in the case of labour. In the case of a single country, if the demand for a good whose production is concentrated in a particular region falls, transfers from the government budget may be used to compensate producers in that region for the loss of income.

Comparison is frequently made with the USA. At times individual states may experience asymmetric shocks as, for example, was the case of Texan oil in the mid-1980s, the property collapse in New England in the 1980s or the collapse of the defence industry in California in the 1990s and the difficulties of the computer industry subsequently. There, not only do people tend to be more mobile, and willing to change state, but transfers from the federal government play an important role. Any fall in the income of a state will lead to higher benefits received from the federal authorities and lower taxes paid to them.

At least in theory EU regional or budgetary policies could be used in a similar way to offset the repercussions of asymmetric shocks among the member states.[17] However, the scale of both the

---

[14] In terms of international trade theories, this would be the case with specialization according to a Ricardian concept of comparative advantage.

[15] See Chapter 4 for a description of these effects.

[16] See Chapter 13 for a description of these agglomeration effects.

[17] The 1977 MacDougall Report advocated an increase in the Community budget to 7 per cent of GDP to enable it to perform this stabilizing role. Some more recent work such as that by Danson et al. (2000) has suggested that a dedicated budget function may be significantly less costly, however.

EU budget and Structural Funds is too limited to enable the Community to carry out this kind of stabilizing role between member states effectively.[18]

THE CORE AND PERIPHERY

The literature on optimum currency areas and the costs and benefits of EMU contains various assessments about which countries should join. Although the results of different studies vary, in general a 'core' group of countries emerged for which it was easy to recommend EMU membership, and these include Germany, Austria and the Benelux countries. In contrast there is another group of countries, the 'periphery', for which membership was less easy to recommend and these include the UK, Ireland, Greece, Sweden and Finland, with France and Italy appearing to move between core and periphery (Artis and Bladen-Hovell, 2001). This distinction between core and periphery fails to correspond to the participation or not in the euro because in many cases the latter was ultimately decided on a political basis, and political factors are not generally taken into account in the core/periphery analysis.

THE INTERNATIONAL MONETARY SYSTEM IN THE EARLY YEARS OF THE COMMUNITY

As described in Chapter 3, the Treaty of Rome contains no specific commitment to economic and monetary union, partly because of the importance of the dollar in the international monetary system at the time. During the late 1950s and 1960s international monetary arrangements were still based on the agreement reached at the 1944 Bretton Woods Conference. This entailed that members agreed to make their currencies convertible into other currencies and gold at fixed exchange rates, and agreed not to impose import controls without permission of the IMF (which was also set up as a result of Bretton Woods).

Gold continued to play an important role in the international monetary system in the 1950s and 1960s, and was used in settlement of imbalances. The price of gold remained fixed for many years at $35 per ounce, but the supply of gold was not rising fast enough to keep pace with the rapid increase in world trade.

After the Second World War the dollar became increasingly important as the main reserve currency. During the 1950s and 1960s the USA ran large and persistent payments deficits, thereby increasing dollar balances, since surplus countries were prepared to hold short-run debt in dollars. The US deficits therefore had the effect of increasing international liquidity as long as foreigners were prepared to hold dollars.

In 1970 and 1971 the US balance-of-payments deficit reached record levels partly because of large-scale investment by US firms abroad but also because of financing of the Vietnam War. At home the fiscal deficit was also growing, in part because of Lyndon B. Johnson's 'War on Poverty'. There was widespread speculation against the dollar, and pressure on the 'stronger' EC currencies, the D-mark and the Dutch guilder.

---

[18] Moreover, as explained below, the need to meet the Maastricht criteria and the constraints imposed by the Growth and Stability Pact reduced the leeway for national budgetary spending.

THE HAGUE SUMMIT: 'EMU BY 1980'

One of the most optimistic beliefs of the founding fathers of the Common Agricultural Policy was that the introduction of a common system of prices for agricultural products (see Chapter 10) would render exchange rate adjustments between the EC currencies impossible. Theoretical support for this view was drawn from the neo-functionalist approach to integration: progress in harmonizing agricultural policy would spill over into the economic and monetary sphere. The optimism was to prove short-lived: common agricultural prices began to operate from 1967, and by 1969, with the French devaluation and the German revaluation, exchange rate instability had arrived in the Community.

In order to resolve this situation and as part of the package for 'completion, deepening and enlargement' of the EC, at the 1969 Hague Summit the Community announced its intention to proceed towards economic and monetary union as a long-term objective.

Differences of opinion were soon to emerge: in particular, the 'economist' group of countries including the FRG and the Netherlands maintained that before proceeding to monetary unification it was first necessary to reach a certain level of convergence of economic performance by setting common targets and co-ordinating economic policies. In contrast, the 'monetarist' countries (France, Belgium, Italy and Luxembourg) argued that the first step should be to narrow exchange rate fluctuations, as this would itself promote a certain degree of convergence.

The debate between the monetarists and the economists can be illustrated using the Krugman and Obstfeld (1997) analysis of the costs and benefits of economic and monetary union.[19] According to the 'monetarist' view, the exchange rate is an ineffective corrective for different developments between countries, and the cost curve is close to the origin (see Figure 8.1). Monetary integration is considered the best way to commit national governments to taking the necessary steps to reduce inflation (for instance by cutting the budget deficit or curbing the wage claims of trade unions).

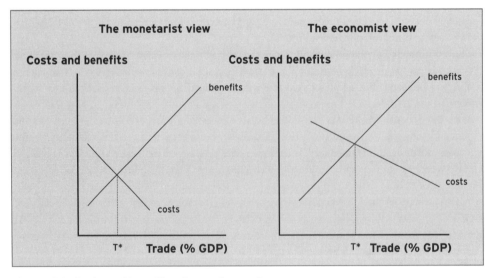

Figure 8.1   Costs and benefits of monetary union

Source: Figure 4.2 (p. 79) from *The Economics of Monetary Union* (2003) by De Grauwe, Paul. By permission of Oxford University Press.

---

[19] The account here is based on De Grauwe (2003).

According to the 'economist' view, a higher level of co-ordination of economic policies and integration is necessary before creating a monetary union. This view stresses rigidities (of wages and prices, and labour is considered immobile), arguing that the exchange rate is an effective instrument. The cost and benefit curves are considered to intersect a long way from the origin, implying that it would be in the interests of relatively few countries to join a monetary union.

A special study group was set up to examine EMU, and the results presented in 1970 are known as the Werner Report. This proposed a three-stage move to full EMU by 1980. The exchange rates of the EC member states would be irrevocably fixed and a single currency would eventually be adopted (though this was considered desirable, but not strictly necessary for the project).

THE SNAKE IN THE TUNNEL

In the event the proposals of the Werner Report were overtaken by the situation of international monetary turbulence.[20] To meet the heavy speculation against the dollar in 1971, the USA had to suspend dollar convertibility and introduce a 10 per cent surcharge on imports. A solution to the US dollar and balance-of-payments problem was reached with the 1971 Smithsonian Accords. These involved a devaluation of the dollar by 7.9 per cent against gold, an adjustment of the EC currencies against the dollar[21] and a return to fixed exchange rates with margins of fluctuation of +/−2.25 per cent around central rates. The US import surcharge was ended, and it was hoped that there would be an eventual return to dollar convertibility.

It was against this background that in 1972 the EC Six, together with the UK, Denmark, Ireland and Norway (who were expected to become the new EC members), decided to create what is known as 'the snake in the tunnel'. For the EC currencies this entailed two margins of fluctuation:

- +/−2.25 per cent against the dollar.
- The maximum divergence between the strongest and the weakest EC currency was 2.25 per cent. Italy was allowed a wider margin of fluctuation of 6 per cent, and this was also offered to Ireland, though refused as a condition of more favourable credit.

However, speculation against currencies continued, and in 1972 the UK and Ireland were forced to float their currencies. Italy began to float in 1973, and France floated between 1974 and 1975, and again from 1976. By 1977 the snake members were Benelux, Germany, Denmark, Norway and (after 1973) Sweden, so the 'snake' had lost its EC character. In 1973 the 'tunnel' collapsed, and a 'joint float' of the snake against the dollar began.

THE LAUNCHING OF EMS

Far from reaching EMU by 1980, the Community was no nearer this objective in the late 1970s than it had been in 1969. Moreover, the volatility of exchange rates was threatening to undermine such progress as had been made in integration. Exchange rate uncertainty acts as a barrier to trade and posed difficulties for the Common Agricultural Policy.[22]

Partly as a reaction to the years of 'Eurosclerosis', by the late 1970s there was growing support

---

[20] For a more detailed account of these events see Swann (1995).
[21] The D-mark and guilder were revalued, sterling and the French franc remained unchanged, and the lira was devalued by 1 per cent.
[22] As shown in Chapter 10, the operation of the agrimonetary system meant that at times during the 1970s the difference in agricultural price levels in the national currencies of EC countries was greater than it had been prior to introduction of the CAP.

for the idea of setting up a regional system of exchange rates as a first step towards EMU. The initiative would also help to bolster EC countries from the negative consequences of the US policy of benign neglect in international monetary matters (Tsoukalis 1997).

The origins of the EMS date from a speech by Roy Jenkins at the European University Institute in Florence in 1977, calling for efforts to relaunch monetary integration. With strong support from President Giscard d'Estaing and Chancellor Helmut Schmidt, the idea of creating a zone of monetary stability in Europe gained ground (Ludlow, 1982). For the French this offered the prospect of escape from US dominance and a renewed role for France in integration initiatives, while for Germany reduced speculative pressure on the D-mark should reduce inflationary pressures.

In drawing up the EMS proposals, the other EC countries implicitly accepted the traditional German priority attached to combating inflation, and both France and Italy considered participation in the EMS part of an anti-inflation strategy. The members of the former snake were pleased to see the area of exchange rate stability extended. Ireland was in favour of external discipline of monetary policy, independence from the UK and the credits offered as part of the new system. The UK was wary of the political objectives of the EMS and feared its deflationary consequences, so only became a full member 11 years later.

THE EMS MECHANISMS

The EMS was introduced in 1979 and its membership comprised all the then EC members, though the UK only participated in the provisions regarding exchange rates from 1990. The EMS built on the snake, but included new characteristics, namely:

- The exchange rate mechanism (ERM);
- The introduction of the ECU;
- A divergence indicator designed to ensure that adjustment was symmetrical;
- A system of monetary co-operation with very short-, short- and medium-term credits to defend fixed interest rates.

There are two systems that can be used to peg fixed exchange rates: a parity grid and a basket of currencies. A **parity grid** is based on bilateral exchange rates between all the participating countries.[23] A **basket of currencies** is a monetary unit made up of fixed quantities of the currencies of participating countries. For instance, the ECU[24] or European Currency Unit was composed of given quantities of each of the EU currencies, including those (such as the UK up until 1990) that did not participate in the exchange rate mechanism. The ECU consisted of so many D-marks, so many francs, so many lira etc. The quantity of each currency in the basket was decided by some agreed criterion, and in the case of the ECU it roughly reflected the share of each member state in EC GDP and intra-EC trade. The central rates of each EC currency in ECU were used to establish a parity grid of cross rates between the participating currencies. This constituted the basis of the **exchange rate mechanism**.

The EMS was a system of fixed but adjustable exchange rates. Member countries participating in the ERM were obliged to maintain their exchange rate with each other within a target band of fluctuation around their central rates. Between 1979 and 1993 the band of fluctuation for most participating currencies was +/− 2.25 per cent. A wider band of +/− 6 per cent was allowed for Italy

---

[23] If n countries participate, each country will have n − 1 exchange rates against the other currencies. The total number of exchange rates among participating countries will be n(n − 1), but it is sufficient to know n − 1 rates to calculate them all.
[24] ECU indicates both the acronym in English and a coin formerly used in France.

between 1979 and 1990, and for the countries that joined later: Spain (1989), the UK (1990) and Portugal (1992). As described below, Italy and the UK were forced to abandon the exchange rate mechanism in September 1992, and Greece remained out of the ERM because of its higher level of inflation. The bands of fluctuation for countries participating in the ERM were widened to +/– 15 per cent from August 1993, when only the exchange rate between the D-mark and Dutch guilder maintained the narrow +/– 2.25 per cent band.

The EMS was a hybrid system since the introduction of a currency basket, the ECU, is not strictly necessary for the operation of a parity grid. One of the main reasons for introduction of the ECU was its importance as a symbol, indicating commitment to the ultimate objective of EMU. Later the ECU provided the basis of what was to become the euro.

The ECU performed the following functions:

- ■ It acted as the numeraire for defining the central rates of the parity grid.
- ■ The ECU was the unit of account used for the EU budget, including all payments and credits granted by the Community.
- ■ It was used as a means of payment, initially by the EC authorities, and subsequently also by member states, international organizations and for private use.[25]
- ■ It provided the basis for a divergence indicator aimed at ensuring early and symmetrical intervention. When a country's currency was out of line, the divergence indicator was intended to act as an alarm bell and there was a 'presumption' (not obligation) that the country would take corrective action.

The aim of the **divergence indicator** was to signal the direction and extent of divergence of a currency from its central rate in ECU. It was hoped that the divergence threshold would require adjustment by both strong and weak currency countries equally. If one currency reached the trigger point against another, both countries were expected to intervene. If, however, policies to maintain an exchange rate were unsustainable, or the balance of payments indicated that a parity was out of line, then by mutual agreement exchange rates could be realigned.

Given the obligations to maintain currencies within the bands of fluctuation, if necessary through unlimited intervention on exchange markets, the EMS was accompanied by provisions to ensure **monetary co-operation** among the participating countries.[26] These operated through the European Monetary Co-operation Fund (EMCF) which was superseded by the European Monetary Institute (EMI) in 1994. The central banks of EMS participants were required to pool 20 per cent of their gold and foreign exchange reserves with the EMCF in exchange for ECU. The EMI later provided the framework for what became the European Central Bank.

THE PROBLEM OF ASYMMETRY IN THE OPERATION OF THE EMS

At the time of its inception, the EMS was envisaged as a symmetrical system, with the introduction of the divergence threshold aimed at ensuring intervention by both the authorities responsible for strong and weak currencies. However, given the dominant role of Germany, it soon became apparent that the system was operating in an asymmetrical way.

---

[25] Following the 1985 Basle Agreement.
[26] The monetary co-operation for countries in difficulty consisted of credit provisions for the very short run (45 days, but extended to 60 days with the Basle–Nyborg Agreement of 1987), the short run (up to 75 days but renewable up to three months) and the medium term (2–5 years). With the Basle–Nyborg Agreement the use of the credit facilities was extended to intra-marginal intervention, and many of the restrictions on use of the ECU were removed.

Germany provided the anchor for the system, using the money supply to control German inflation. The high inflation members of the ERM used their monetary policy to maintain their exchange rates with the D-mark with the aim of 'importing' low German inflation rates.

The strong economic performance of Germany, and the implicit acceptance of German leadership after 1983, meant that other EMS members tended to co-ordinate their monetary policies with that of Germany. Increases in German interest rates aimed at domestic stabilization were generally followed by a rise in other European interest rates (including those of countries outside the ERM). At times countries such as Italy and France introduced controls on capital movements to secure a certain degree of autonomy in monetary policy, but with the liberalization of capital movements from 1990 this was no longer possible.

All the ERM currency realignments carried out between 1979 and 1988 involved revaluation of the D-mark against other EC currencies and only the guilder–D-mark exchange rate remained unchanged over the 1984–88 period. The Bundesbank was hostile to unlimited intervention to support weak currencies. The divergence indicator never functioned particularly well in practice, and even when the divergence threshold was triggered, the Bundesbank rarely carried out intramarginal intervention. Most of the burden of intervention and adjustment was borne by the weaker currency countries.

The weight of the FRG in the system, and the importance of the D-mark as a reserve currency, meant that the Bundesbank was largely responsible for exchange rate policy with regard to third currencies (chiefly the dollar and the yen), while the other central banks were mainly concerned with intervention for adjustment within the system.

THE PHASES OF OPERATION OF THE EMS

The literature generally divides the operation of the EMS into four periods:

- 1979-83;
- 1983-87;
- 1987-92; and
- the 1992 crisis and after.

The first period from March **1979 until 1983** was characterized by an unstable international monetary environment following the second oil crisis. The frequency (seven) and size of realignments during this period was unexpected. Differentials in inflation between the EC countries were high, but from 1983 France and other EC countries adopted more determined counter-inflationary measures (Artis and Healey, 1995).

The second phase of EMS covers **the 1983–87 period** and was characterized by relatively few realignments, and when these occurred few currencies were involved and the changes in central rates tended to be small. During this period (which dates from the French decision of 1983 to attach higher priority to combating inflation) empirical evidence suggests that the EMS had a stabilizing effect on exchange rates, and that there was a convergence towards lower inflation rates. The average level of inflation in countries participating in the ERM fell from 11.6 per cent in 1983 to 2.3 per cent in 1986.

There has been considerable debate as to how far the EMS was responsible for this reduction in inflation, which was also experienced by countries not participating in the EMS. There seem to be two ways in which the EMS contributed to downward price convergence:

- Member states used the EMS as a scapegoat to justify unpopular policies to reduce inflation and to limit wage claims.

- The increased importance attached to the anti-inflationary objective implied an acceptance of the traditional German priority by other EMS members.

The third period (**1987–92**), known also as the 'hard' EMS, was characterized by great stability, if not rigidity of exchange rates. The only realignments that took place were considered 'technical', as for instance when Italy entered the narrow +/−2.25 per cent band of fluctuation in 1990.

During this period there was a gradual extension of the ERM membership, to Spain, the UK and Portugal, so that Greece was the only EC country not participating. The decision of these countries to join seems likely to have been influenced by a mixture of economic and political motives, including the desire of the Southern European countries to demonstrate their commitment to the European cause. In the case of the UK, a major factor was undoubtedly fear of remaining outside the system because of the speculative pressures against the currency.

The currency crisis of September 1992 led to the widening of most ERM margins to +/− 15 per cent in August 1993. Three events which contributed to the 1992/3 crisis are:[27]

- The liberalization of capital movements;
- The early difficulties encountered by the Maastricht Treaty and the decision to move to economic and monetary union; and
- German reunification.

Up until 1990 countries such as France and Italy were able to resort to capital controls to regain a certain degree of autonomy for monetary policy. The use of capital controls can limit the scale of a speculative attack on a weak currency and may help to isolate interest rates from fluctuations on international markets. This was especially important given the Bundesbank's objection to unlimited intervention to protect weak currencies. The liberalization of capital movements from 1990 removed this safety valve from the system.

In 1992 there was great uncertainty about the prospects for the Treaty of Maastricht and the EMU programme. In July 1992 the Danish voted against Maastricht in a referendum, though this decision was reversed in 1993. Then followed the *'petit oui'* in France in which only 51 per cent voted in favour of the Maastricht Treaty. One of the main reasons that there were no currency realignments during the 1988–92 period was to prepare the way for EMU. In 1992 EMU seemed at risk, calling into question the credibility of the EMS and encouraging currency speculation.

The operation of the EMS in the years before 1992 rested on the acceptance of German policy leadership by the other EC countries. German unification represented a shock, leading to a tightening of German monetary policy that other EMS members were unwilling to follow.

The collapse of the Berlin Wall in November 1989 was followed at breakneck speed by the monetary unification of Germany in July 1990, and political unification in October. The German government hugely underestimated the cost of reunification, which entailed transfers to East Germany of $79 billion in 1991 and $105 billion in 1992 (Nuti, 1994). As a result the public sector deficit deteriorated by more than 3 per cent of GDP. Inflation rose from 1.3 per cent in 1988 to 4.8 per cent in 1992. During the 1990 elections Kohl had promised that reunification would not lead to an increase in taxes, and the main strategy for combating inflation was through an increase in interest rates, which reached 9.75 per cent in 1992.

At the same time, fear of recession meant that in the USA the Fed reduced interest rates to 3 per cent, and the prospect of elections limited attempts to cut the deficit. The difference of 6.75 per cent between German and US interest rates led to huge capital inflows to the FRG, causing

---

[27] For a more complete discussion see Artis in Artis and Lee (1994).

upward pressure on the D-mark and leading to widespread expectation that there would be an EMS realignment. Fear of deflation (in particular in France, the UK and Italy) meant that other countries were reluctant to raise their interest rates to German levels. However, they were no longer able to use capital controls to protect their currencies from speculation. Pressure against sterling and the lira forced them to be 'temporarily' withdrawn from the ERM in September 1992, and subsequently there was speculation against the currencies of Spain, Denmark, Ireland, Portugal and France.[28] When the French franc came under attack again in August 1993, it was decided to widen the bands of fluctuation to +/− 15 per cent (with the exception of the D-mark–guilder rate). At the time many thought such wide bands were not very different from floating, but in practice EMS exchange rates did not fluctuate much more than they had previously (Artis and Bladen-Hovell, 2001). The crisis appears to have increased the commitment of policy-makers to EMU.

THE CONTRADICTORY QUARTET

Padoa Schioppa (1987) refers to the 'contradictory quartet' that no international monetary arrangement has been able to reconcile simultaneously:

- Liberalized trade;
- Free capital movements;
- Fixed exchange rates; and
- Autonomy of monetary policy.

During the first period of the EMS (1979–83) participating countries maintained controls on capital movements and there were frequent realignments of exchange rates. After 1983 Italy and France managed to acquire exchange rate stability but only through losing autonomy for monetary policy and recourse to capital controls. The UK realized free capital movements and trade during the 1980s but only at the cost of exchange rate stability.

The combination of the Single Market and EMS implied a commitment to free trade and capital movement with fixed exchange rates.[29] This system could survive only as long as the other ERM countries were prepared to sacrifice monetary autonomy and accept German policy leadership. After reunification this was no longer the case and the system broke down. EC countries regained a degree of monetary autonomy but at the price of sacrificing fixed exchange rates from August 1993.

The way forward proposed by the Treaty of Maastricht was to combine the first three elements of Padoa Schioppa's list with a common monetary policy for the euroland.

THE 1990S: BACK TO EMU

During the late 1980s, the objective of economic and monetary union was revived with a renewed vigour for a number of reasons:

- Exchange rate uncertainty between the EC currencies was another obstacle to trade that should be eliminated in order to complete the Internal Market. The increased trade

---

[28] The French franc was defended by massive intervention and by a joint statement by the French and German authorities concerning the importance of the franc/D-mark exchange rate to the EMS.
[29] As explained in Chapter 6, capital movements were only liberalized in 1992 for Ireland and Spain, and in 1994 for Greece and Portugal.

and interdependence between the EC economies would render exchange rate adjustment less effective, and a common currency would confirm the reality of the Single Market.

■ The aim was to take the relatively successful experience of co-operating in the EMS one step further.

■ The boom of the late 1980s was beginning to flag, so methods of prolonging business confidence were being sought

■ According to the neo-functionalist approach, EMU was viewed as a means of pushing the integration process further in the direction of political union, since greater Community responsibility for economic and monetary policies would require more effective democratic control.

■ The EC Commission, and Delors in particular, played an active role in relaunching the initiative, supported by the French and German governments (despite the hesitancy of the Bundesbank).

■ Following German unification, Kohl was anxious to demonstrate that an even more powerful Germany remained firmly anchored in Western Europe, and commitment to EMU provided a means of demonstrating that this was the case.

For once the role of the CAP and the need for exchange rate stability to ensure the effective functioning of the price support system played a relatively minor role. Similarly, compared with the 1960s and 1970s, the revived EMU initiative seemed less of a response to worries about the international monetary system.[30] As the process gained momentum, a further reason for its continuation was that it would have been increasingly costly to abandon the whole initiative: the result would have been speculation and currency instability, and the probable collapse of attempts at fiscal discipline, at least in some of the Southern European countries.

The EMU project was formally launched at the 1988 Hannover Summit, when it was decided to set up a committee for the study of EMU under the president of the Commission, Jacques Delors.[31] The Committee's results were presented as the Delors Report in 1989. Many of the conclusions were similar to those of the earlier Werner Report, which is not surprising as several of the members of the two committees were the same. The Delors Report differs from the Werner Report in its emphasis on the institutional changes implied by EMU, and the need for transfer of authority to the Community. In particular, the central bankers in the Delors Committee seemed concerned to draw the attention of politicians to the need for some constraints on fiscal policy.

During the debate at that time only the UK expressed doubts about the overall objective of EMU. France wanted to fix early dates for the introduction of EMU in order to ensure continuing German commitment to the project. Germany stressed the importance of stringent fiscal criteria and independent institutions mirroring so far as possible the German model. The poorer EC member states such as Ireland, Portugal and Greece called for a link between EMU and cohesion for the weaker regions and countries of the Community and wanted more flexible criteria as a condition for entering the final phase of EMU. The final compromise combines the stringency of the criteria and institutional arrangements requested by Germany with the early deadlines favoured by France.

---

[30] According to Tsoukalis (1997), this reflected a greater confidence on the part of the EC countries and, in particular, less fear that the EMS was vulnerable to fluctuations in the value of the dollar.
[31] This was composed of the governors of the central banks of the EC member states and a group of independent experts.

THE MAASTRICHT TREATY

The Maastricht Treaty followed the main indications of the Delors Report but 'put flesh on it' (Artis, 1994). The main provisions of the treaty with regard to EMU are:

- The Treaty set out convergence criteria to be met before a country could participate in EMU, though allowance was made for certain countries opting out.
- A timetable was fixed for the introduction of a single currency by 1 January 1999 'at the latest'. This was to occur in three stages, and the Treaty describes the objectives to be reached and fixes the dates for each of these stages.
- The Treaty indicates the main institutional features of EMU and, in particular, of the European Central Bank.

THE CONVERGENCE CRITERIA

Any country wanting to participate fully in the final stage of EMU had to satisfy the Maastricht convergence criteria. These were introduced in an attempt to ensure that the constraints on policy implied by the EMU were acceptable to the country concerned. The aim is to avoid destabilizing the EMU by the premature admission of countries whose underlying economic performance is not yet compatible with permanently fixed exchange rates.

The criteria entail that:

- Successful candidates must have inflation rates no more than 1.5 per cent above the average of the three countries with the lowest inflation rate in the Community.
- Long-term interest rates should be no more that 2 per cent above the average of that of the three lowest inflation countries. This is to ensure that inflation convergence is lasting, because otherwise higher than expected future inflation in a country would be reflected in higher long-term interest rates.
- The exchange rate of the country should remain within the 'normal' band of the ERM without tension and without initiating depreciation for two years. At the time of the Maastricht Treaty the 'normal' band referred to the margins of +/-2.25 per cent, but from August 1993 it was taken to refer to +/-15 per cent.[32]
- The public debt of the country must be less than 60 per cent of GDP.
- The national budget deficit must be less than 3 per cent of GDP.

The last two on the list are referred to as the 'fiscal' criteria and are subject to an escape clause. A country may be granted a waiver if the gap between the actual and reference situation is 'exceptional and temporary' or if the excess in public deficit or debt is declining 'continuously and substantially'. As will be described below, in practice there has been rather flexible interpretation of whether various countries have met the criteria.

THE THREE STAGES IN THE INTRODUCTION OF EMU

The first stage in the introduction of EMU covered the period July 1990–December 1993. The main objectives of that stage were to liberalize capital movements between EU members, to

---

[32] The new member states joining the EU in 2004 have been told that they have to respect the margin of +/−2.25 per cent.

Box 8.3 Key dates in the EMU Programme

Date	Event
1989	Delors Report on EMU.
1990	Beginning of stage 1 and abolition of capital controls in July for most member states.
1993	Maastricht Treaty.
1994	Stage 2 of EMU begins with the creation of the EMI.
1995	The Madrid European Council announced that the third stage would be launched from 1999, and adopted the name 'euro' for the single currency.
1996	Stability and Growth Pact agreed at the Dublin European Council.
1998	The European Council of May decided on the euro members, and fixed the exchange rates between the currencies of the participating countries irrevocably.
May/June 1998	The president and Executive Board of the ECB were chosen, and it came into operation from June.
1999	The ECU was converted into the euro, and the third stage of EMU began.
2001	Greece joined.
2002	Euro notes and currencies introduced, and national currencies withdrawn.

---

introduce long-run convergence programmes and to adopt multilateral monitoring of economic policies and performance through the Ecofin (Council of Economic and Finance Ministers).

The second stage in the introduction of EMU was to cover the period from 1 January 1994 until December 1996 or 1998. In the event the later date was chosen, and the 1995 Madrid European Council announced that the third stage would be launched from 1999 and adopted the name 'euro' for the single currency (see Box 8.3).

The main aims of the second phase were to encourage convergence and to prepare for the final stage in particular by putting in place the necessary institutions and deciding which countries were to participate in the final stage. Temporary derogations were to be granted for countries deemed not yet ready.[33] States subject to derogation would be reconsidered every two years. The EMI (European Monetary Institute) was set up in Frankfurt as the forerunner of the European Central Bank (ECB) which came into operation from June 1998.

The selection of the countries participating in the euro took place at the May 1998 European Council.[34] Contrary to earlier expectations, when it was expected that several member states would fail to meet the Maastricht convergence criteria, this was only the case for Greece.[35] The generous final interpretation of who was able to meet the criteria probably owes much to the then weakness of the German economy (Artis and Bladen-Hovell, 2001). Germany had insisted on introduction of the fiscal criteria and their strict interpretation but following German unification could not meet them to the letter when the time came.

It was agreed to grant the UK an 'opt-out' clause so that the decision to participate or not in the final stage would be left to future governments. Blair subsequently announced that when certain economic conditions for membership had been met (see Box 8.4), British participation would be

---

[33] The decision concerning which countries were ready was to be decided on the basis of a qualified majority vote.

[34] This summit took place in Brussels since, rather ironically, the country holding the presidency at the time was the UK, who chose not to participate fully in stage 3 of EMU.

[35] In most of the participating countries certain 'cosmetic' measures were introduced to enable the Maastricht criteria to be met. These included a payment by French Télécom, a refundable 'eurotax' in Italy and an attempt by Germany to adjust the value of its gold reserves.

> ## Box 8.4 The five tests for the UK adopting the euro
>
> ■ **Convergence**
>   Are business cycles and economic structures compatible so that the UK can live comfortably with common euroland interest rates on a permanent basis?
> ■ **Flexibility**
>   If problems emerge, is there sufficient flexibility to deal with them?
> ■ **Investment**
>   Would adopting the euro create better conditions for firms taking long-term decisions to invest in the UK?
> ■ **The City of London**
>   How would adopting the euro affect UK financial services?
> ■ **Stability, growth and employment**
>   Would adopting the euro help to promote higher growth, stability and a lasting increase in jobs?

decided in a referendum. In June 2003 the Chancellor of the Exchequer Gordon Brown announced that only one of the tests (the impact on financial markets) had been met.

Denmark secured a milder version of the 'opt out', and in 2000 the Danish people voted against participation in the euro in a referendum. In 1998 Sweden also decided to remain outside on technical grounds, and in a referendum of September 2003, 56 per cent of the Swedish people voted against adopting the euro.[36]

One of the negative consequences of remaining out of the euro is that a member state's influence over certain decisions of crucial importance to the future of the EU economy is likely to be reduced. For instance, as explained below, choices have to be made on voting rules in the ECB and the future of the Stability and Growth Pact, and it is difficult to see how non-euro area countries can carry the same weight in resolving such questions. Moreover, many important decisions are taken in the monthly informal meetings of the Eurogroup[37] which take place the evening before Ecofin meetings. After September 2003 the UK, Denmark and Sweden were no longer even able to send senior officials to help prepare Eurogroup meetings.

At the May 1998 European Council it was also decided to fix the exchange rates between the currencies of the participating countries irrevocably. Conversion rates into the euro had to wait until 31 December 1998, because the euro was to replace the ECU (with one euro being equal to one ECU) and the ECU included currencies that were not then in the euro (those of the UK, Denmark, Greece and Sweden). These decisions account for the rather awkward numbers for converting the various national currencies into the euro (see Box 8.5).

The third stage of EMU began on 1 January 1999 and entailed a three-year transition period during which the currencies of the countries participating fully in EMU continued to exist but only as subdivisions of the euro.[38] Financial markets were encouraged to use the euro increasingly. It is perhaps a reflection of how strong the political commitment to EMU was during this period that the process proceeded smoothly and without strong speculative attacks against currencies.

---

[36] In Sweden 42 per cent voted in favour of the euro. Three days before the referendum the Swedish Foreign Minister Anna Lindh was stabbed to death in a department store. She had been strongly in favour of the euro, but the expected surge in 'yes' votes as a reaction failed to take place. According to exit polls carried out at the time (and reported in the *Economist*, 20 September 2003), the Swedish people feared the loss of democracy, sovereignty, national control of interest rates and threats to their welfare state (in that order).

[37] The Eurogroup is composed only of economics and finance ministers from countries participating in the euro.

[38] From 1999 the euro began its existence as a largely virtual currency appearing in accounting systems. In theory from this date banks were to exchange euro currencies, and in particular euros, into those currencies without a commission, but in practice commissions continued to be charged.

Box 8.5 The conversion rates for the 11 currencies initially participating in the euro

€1 (one euro) =

BEF	40.3399	DEM	1.95583	ESP	166.386
FRF	6.55957	IEP	0.787564	ITL	1936.27
LUF	40.3399	NLG	2.20371	ATS	13.7603
PTE	200.482	FIM	5.94573		

From 1 January 2002 euro notes and coins were introduced, and national banknotes and coins were withdrawn in the first two months of that year.[39]

Even without participating fully in stage 3 of EMU, all EU countries are obliged to treat their economic policies as a matter of common interest and co-ordinate them in the Council (Art. 99 of the Nice Treaty). This involves participation in the procedures to monitor economic performance in the EU and its member states. It also entails the co-ordination of economic policies through national convergence programmes, broad guidelines and multilateral surveillance to assess the consistency of the policies of the EU and its member states with the broad policy guidelines.

As explained in Chapter 20, full participation of the new member states in EMU is unlikely to occur for some time. The Maastricht criterion on exchange rates entails that a country should remain within the 'normal' band of the exchange rate mechanism (ERM 2) without tension and without initiating depreciation for two years. For the new member states, this means that full participation in the third stage of EMU has to wait for two years after joining the EU.

THE EUROPEAN SYSTEM OF CENTRAL BANKS

The European System of Central Banks (ESCB) is composed of the European Central Bank (ECB) and the national central banks (NCBs) of all 15 EU member states. The 'Eurosystem' is the term used to refer to the ECB and NCBs of the countries that have adopted the euro. The NCBs of member states that do not participate in the euro area are members of the ESCB with a special status since they do not take part in decision-making with regard to the single monetary policy for the euro area.

The relationship between the ECB and the Eurosystem resembles the federal banking system of Germany,[40] though in practice it seemed likely that there would be more decentralization. This was also probable given the small initial size of the ECB, with a staff of only about 600 (though subsequently it began to expand) compared with the 60 000 working in the national central banks of the euro countries.[41]

The main tasks of the Eurosystem set out in Article 105 of the EC Treaty are:[42]

■ *'To maintain price stability'*. According to the EC Treaty, this is to be the *'primary objective'*. The ECB has adopted two policy guides to carry out this task: a reference value for monetary policy and an inflation target of 2 per cent or less over the medium term.

---

[39] Initially 1 July was indicated for the date when national notes and coins were to cease being national tender, but subsequently it was decided to shorten the time period for the changeover on practical grounds.
[40] It is also similar to the US federal system.
[41] Baldwin et al. (2001).
[42] The reference is to Article 105 of the Nice Treaty.

- ■ '*To support the general economic policies in the Community*'. This is a secondary function, only to be carried out without prejudice to price stability.
- ■ '*To define and implement the monetary policy of the Community*'. The Governing Council of the ECB was to set interest rates but not decide them unilaterally. The ECB would not normally engage in market operations, and the ESCB would be responsible for implementing monetary policy.
- ■ '*To conduct foreign exchange operations*'. Decisions with regard to the exchange rate are to be taken by Ecofin but subject to consultation with the ECB, the European Parliament and the Commission in order to ensure accountability.
- ■ '*To hold and manage the official foreign reserves of the member states*'.
- ■ '*To promote the smooth operation of payments systems*' (which included the introduction of a euro-payments mechanism called TARGET).
- ■ To contribute to '*the smooth conduct of policies pursued by the competent authorities relating to the prudential supervision of credit institutions, and the stability of the financial systems*' . However, the ECB is not to be responsible for supervision of banks and financial institutions.[43]

One of the criticisms of the interpretation of the ECB of its role in its early years was that it concentrated almost exclusively on the primary priority of price stability. As a result it virtually ignored the secondary and less well-defined objective of supporting general economic policies, covering goals such as stabilization of the business cycle and financial stability.

The Maastricht Treaty failed to define the primary goal of price stability precisely. In its early years the ECB defined this goal as a rate of inflation of at most 2 per cent over the medium term. This definition came under growing attack for encouraging the ECB to keep the inflation rate under 2 per cent, thereby adding to the risk of deflation, in particular in member states where inflation was already below 2 per cent. De Grauwe and other observers such as Fitoussi and Creel (2003) suggest moving to a more explicit inflation targeting procedure of the type that is widely adopted as best practice in central banking.[44] This would consist of a point target for inflation in the centre of a symmetric range. The Central Bank would announce its inflation forecast, and this would increase transparency and help the market to understand its policy actions.

The ECB uses three types of instrument to conduct monetary policy: open market operations, standing facilities (credit lines) and minimum reserve requirements. Open market operations involve the buying and selling of securities in order to increase or reduce liquidity on the money market. Standing facilities are used to provide or absorb overnight liquidity. By adjusting reserve requirements, the ECB can influence conditions on the money market.

In conducting monetary policy the Eurosystem uses control over short-term interest rates.[45] Short-term interest rates are close to cash, and since central banks have a monopoly in supplying cash, they can control short-term interest rates. It is the long-term interest rates that have more influence on the level of economic activity, but these are almost impossible for a central bank to control since long-term financial instruments are issued by various private and public entities. The Eurosystem focuses on the EONIA (European Overnight Index Average), a weighted average of overnight lending transactions in the interbank market of the euro area. The Eurosystem creates a floor and a ceiling for the EONIA by maintaining open lending and deposit facilities at interest

---

[43] This policy has been criticized in that the ECB is likely to obtain much information in carrying out its monetary policy operations, and this information will be wasted if it is not responsible for supervision (Artis, 1994). The narrow supervisory function of the ECB may reflect the German system in which the Bundesbank plays a limited role and supervision is carried out by a small number of large, private universal banks. However, the different institutional reality of the Community makes it likely that the system will be more open and deregulated.

[44] De Grauwe in the *Financial Times*, 3 May 2003. See also the article by Hans-Werner Sinn in the *Financial Times*, 21 May 2003.

[45] See De Grauwe (2003) or Baldwin and Wyplosz (2004) for more detailed discussions of these instruments.

rates announced in advance. The Eurosystem also conducts weekly auctions at a rate that it chooses in order to supply liquidity to the system.

THE INDEPENDENCE OF THE EUROPEAN CENTRAL BANK

One of the main debates over the constitution of the European Central Bank centred on the issue of how far that bank should be independent and insulated from political pressure, or the extent to which it should be politically accountable.

France and some members of the the UK government favoured the idea of a politically accountable bank that could act directly in the name of the EU countries and would be answerable to the governments of the member states. It was argued that certain functions of the ECB had important implications for the economic performance of the member states and, in particular, for politically sensitive issues such as unemployment. The activities of the bank should therefore be subject to adequate political control. In addition, transparency was considered essential.

Germany, in contrast, wanted an independent bank modelled so far as possible on the Bundesbank. The theoretical justification for this type of institution draws on the economic literature on credibility, which takes the technical ability of a central bank to pursue an anti-inflationary policy for granted, and concentrates on the political will of governments to do so. It was feared that a political bank would be open to political pressure to reflate, and so would be 'soft' on inflation.

The EC Treaty tries to ensure the independence of ECB by:[46]

- ■ Stipulating that the ECB should not '*seek or take instructions from Community institutions or bodies, from any Member State or from any other body*' (Article 108);
- ■ Forbidding the ECB to lend to 'national, regional, local or other public authorities or to Community institutions or bodies' (Article 101), though this implies that the ECB will not perform one of the functions usually attributed to central banks, namely, that of 'banker of the government';
- ■ Requiring that members of its Executive Board (a president, vice-president and four other members) be appointed for eight-year non-renewable terms (Article 112).[47]

THE DECISION-MAKING PROCESS OF THE EUROSYSTEM

The Governing Council is the main decision-making body of the Eurosystem taking, *inter alia*, decisions on interest rates. The Governing Council is composed of the Executive Board and the governors of the NCBs of the euro area member states (see Figure 8.2).

As the Governing Council is assumed to be independent of national interests, under the initial Maastricht Treaty there was no provision for weighting of votes by the size of country. When the countries that joined the EU in 2004 adopt the euro, the members of the Governing Council could rise from 18 to 28, increasing the difficulty of reaching common positions.

It was decided that reform of decision-making in the Governing Council would be necessary with enlargement, and the ECB's proposal was accepted by the Council but has yet to be ratified.

---

[46] Reference is to Articles in the Nice Treaty.

[47] Selection was by the participating states after consultation with the European Parliament and Governing Council of the ECB. There was a difference of opinion over the appointment of the first president between the French who favoured their own candidate, Trichet, and the Germans who wanted Duisenberg from the Netherlands. A compromise was reached whereby Duisenberg was appointed but seemed to agree that he stand down after four years on grounds of age. Subsequently, differences arose over the interpretation of this deal, but in November 2003 Trichet became president of the ECB (after having been cleared in a court case on financial irregularities in France).

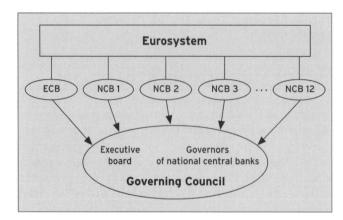

Figure 8.2 The decision-making process of the Eurosystem

Source: Figure 7.8 (p. 165) from *The Economics of Monetary Union* (2003) by De Grauwe, Paul. By permission of Oxford University Press.

Box 8.6 Voting rights in the Governing Council of the ECB
(based on a eurozone of 28 countries)
Big countries (voting 80 per cent of the time)
Germany, the UK, France, Italy and Spain
Medium-sized countries (voting 57 per cent of the time)
The Netherlands, Belgium, Sweden, Austria, Denmark, Ireland,
Poland, Portugal, Turkey, Greece, Luxembourg, Finland, Czech Republic, Hungary
Small countries (voting 30 per cent of the time)
Romania, Slovakia, Slovenia, Bulgaria, Lithuania, Latvia, Cyprus, Estonia, Malta

---

The proposal would divide the member states into three tiers on the basis of the size of their GDP (on which five-sixths of their weighting would be based) and the balance sheets of their financial institutions (determining one-sixth of their weighting). Larger EU member states (see Box 8.6) would be entitled to vote 80 per cent of the time, medium-sized countries could vote 57 per cent and small countries 30 per cent of the time. The system would lead to Luxembourg falling into the middle group of countries, while Bulgaria and Romania would class as small, and has been criticised for its failure to take population into account. It is also difficult to see how strategic behaviour with regard to voting or setting of the agenda could be avoided with such a system.

An additional complication arises because, as explained in Chapter 20, most of the new member states in Central and East Europe have relatively high levels of growth and inflation. Like Ireland they would probably favour higher interest rates than those preferred by the 'core' economies, adding to the problem of 'one size fits all'.[48] The possibility of systematic differences in priorities with regard to monetary policy renders the weighting of votes in the Governing Council an even more crucial issue.

The division of responsibility between the ECB, Ecofin, the Eurogroup and national governments is complex. The ECB is to define and implement monetary policy and hold foreign reserves. However, decisions with regard to the exchange rate are to be taken by Ecofin but subject to consultation with the ECB, the European Parliament and the Commission. National governments are to conduct fiscal policy, though subject to the constraints of the Stability and Growth Pact.

---

[48] See De Grauwe (2000) or Baldwin et al. (2001) for more detailed discussions of this issue.

THE STABILITY AND GROWTH PACT

The Stability and Growth Pact was agreed at the Dublin Council of 1996 and confirmed at Amsterdam in 1997. According to the Pact, budget deficits would be limited to 3 per cent of GDP, except if the country experienced a fall in GDP of over 2 per cent. Countries were invited to strive for a 'close to balanced budget', so that the margin between 0 and −3 per cent could be used for counter-cyclical policies in times of economic downturn. The excessive deficit procedure is designed to ensure conformity with the Stability and Growth Pact. If the Council decides that a country has an excessive deficit and insufficient action has been taken, sanctions can be imposed.[49] EU countries outside the eurozone must keep their deficits below 3 per cent, but they are not subject to disciplinary proceedings should they break the pact.

The Stability and Growth Pact was largely introduced in response to German beliefs about the need to create a system that would ensure co-ordination of budgetary policies (Verdun, 2003). It was felt that the Pact could encourage consolidation of fiscal policy, would help to avoid possible negative effects of fiscal spill-overs between increasingly interdependent countries and would prevent excessive deficits undermining the independence of the European Central Bank (even though it is expressly forbidden by the Maastricht Treaty to bail out member states).

With the slowdown of the EU economy from 2002, the Stability and Growth Pact came under attack for being excessively rigid, or 'stupid' in the words of Commission President Prodi.[50] By late 2002 the excessive deficit procedure had been initiated for Portugal, France and Germany. Portugal subsequently brought its deficit below the ceiling, but France and Germany were expected to break the Pact for the third year running in 2004. Germany announced measures to bring the deficit below 3 per cent, though these were considered inadequate by the Commission. The German finance minister, Eichel, maintained that Germany had followed the Commission's recommendations but only failed to respect the fiscal ceiling because of the sluggish economy. In November 2003 the EU finance ministers decided to suspend the sanctions mechanism of the Pact against France and Germany.

The European Central Bank warned that suspension of the Pact could lead to 'serious dangers' including higher interest rates. Smaller countries that had introduced fiscal consolidation (notably Austria, Finland, the Netherlands, Sweden and Denmark) attacked the failure of the two larger member states to respect the fiscal constraints.

In 2004 Commissioner for Monetary Affairs Pedro Solbes took the member states to the Court of Justice for failure to respect the Pact. In July 2004 the court ruled that the Council acted illegally in suspending the threat of sanctions against France and Germany. However, the Court maintained that 'responsibility for making the member states observe budgetary discipline lies essentially with the Council'. In other words, the Council can decide whether to back the Commission in its efforts to reduce budget deficits.

Though many referred to the 'demise' of the Pact, the rules and procedures remained in place, and it seems likely that it will be reformed to operate in a more flexible manner. The flexibility could take into account the need to promote sustainable growth in times of economic recession, the distinction between government expenditure on investment and current spending, and the overall public debt situation of the country.

---

[49] The country in question would have to make a non-interest-bearing deposit of 0.2 per cent of GDP plus 0.1 per cent for each point of the excess deficit, up to a maximum deposit of 0.5 per cent of GDP. The deposit would be returned when the deficit falls below 3 per cent of GDP, but if the excess deficit lasts for over two years the deposit could become a fine. If a country deviates substantially from its path, the Council can issue a recommendation to bring the country back on track. The underlying assumption appears to be that excessive public borrowing could weaken a currency, drive up interest rates or give rise to moral hazard. However, the ECB is expressly forbidden to bail governments out.
[50] In a speech on 18 October 2002.

THE EURO IN THE INTERNATIONAL FINANCIAL SYSTEM

There has been much speculation about future relations between the euro and the dollar, and whether the euro represents a challenge to the dollar and US hegemony in the international financial system (see also Chapter 18). The role of the dollar in international trade and finance is far greater than its share of world trade and output might suggest. The dollar remains the most important currency in the invoicing of trade, in the reserves of central banks and in the denomination of international private assets.

Given the economic weight of the EU, and the likely deepening and widening EU financial markets as a result of the euro, it seems probable that the euro will play a growing international role.[51] However, the extent to which the euro can challenge the dollar as an international currency will depend on how far the money and securities markets of the EU (12) become effectively integrated and on confidence in the euro as a stable currency.

In 1998 it was estimated that roughly half of total world export invoicing in the world was in dollars, while one-third was in the major EU currencies (IMF, 1998). According to ECB (2003), use of the euro as a settlement/invoicing currency in trade with non-euro member states and third countries has been rising. This increase predates the introduction of euro notes and coins, but became more prominent in 2002 when about a half of EU trade with non-euro area EU residents was priced in euros. None the less, widespread use of the dollar in invoicing seems likely to continue, in particular in oil and commodity markets.

In 1997 57 per cent of all official foreign exchange reserves were held in dollars, with a further 20 per cent being held in EU currencies and the ECU, and about 4.9 per cent in yen (IMF, 1998). Bergsten (1997b, p. 90) estimated that official reserve shifts into euro could range between $100 billion and $300 billion, but he argues that the time horizon over which such a shift might occur is extremely uncertain. Inertia is an important force, and, for example, the pound sterling continued to play an important role as a reserve currency long after the UK's decline as a hegemonic power.[52] According to ECB (2003), the share of the euro in global international foreign exchange reserves grew from 16.4 per cent in 2001 to 18.7 per cent in 2002.

Official reserves of currencies are relatively small compared with private holdings of international financial assets. Excluding intra-EU portfolios, in 1996 global holdings of international financial assets, including bank deposits and bonds, amounted to some $3.5 trillion.[53] Roughly 50 per cent of these were in dollars, and only 10 per cent in EU(12) currencies, so that, according to Bergsten (1997b, p.90), a balancing of portfolios would require a shift of $700 billion.

In its 2003 annual report of the international role of the euro,[54] the ECB found that, supported by the appreciation of the euro against the dollar, the share of euro-denominated assets in total foreign assets was increasing. Use of the euro by non-euro area residents was found to be particularly prominent in countries bordering the eurozone, including the new CEEC member states. The City of London was found to play a pivotal role regarding use of the euro outside the euro area and, depending on the market segment, the UK share ranged from one-third to two-thirds of euro-denominated financial activity outside the euro area.

The method of representing the euro countries on the international scene was decided at the Vienna European Council of December 1998. The president of the Ecofin was to participate in

---

[51] Some authors (for example, Bergsten, 1997a) warn that an integrated market might take some time to emerge, given the present decentralization of EU financial markets and the absence of a central government borrower like the US Treasury that could act as a fulcrum for the market.
[52] See Kindleberger (1984) and Eichengreen (1989).
[53] Bergsten (1997b, p. 90).
[54] ECB (2003).

meetings of the G7,[55] but if the president were from a non-euro state, representation would be by the president of the Eurogroup assisted by the Commission.

The movements of the euro in its early years defied the predictions of many observers, with an initial fall followed by a substantial rise against the dollar. Various explanations of the initial weakness of the euro were given: the faster productivity increase and more flexible markets of the USA; a few untimely statements by the first ECB president, Duisenberg; capital outflows from the EU and the untested and cumbersome nature of EMU institutions. Some observers have also argued that market nervousness about EU enlargement also contributed to the weakening of the euro.[56] Subsequently the strength of the euro was said to reflect factors such as portfolio adjustments, relatively high interest rates in the euro zone and falling confidence in the dollar (spurred also by the large US current acount and fiscal deficits).

Some concern has been expressed about the possible negative consequences of volatility of the euro against third currencies. The external trade of the euro countries accounts for only about 10 per cent of GDP.[57] The ECB is committed by the EU Treaty to price stability as its chief priority, and Ecofin seems mainly concerned with fiscal consolidation. There is therefore a risk of an inward-looking EU. At the meeting in Boca Raton, Florida, of February 2004, finance ministers and central bank chiefs of the G-7 (Group of Seven) countries called for greater exchange rate flexibility, and criticized excess volatility and disorderly exchange rate movements as being undesirable for economic growth. However, the failure to back these words with actions makes it likely that volatility will continue.

EVALUATION

Though economic and monetary union was not envisaged by the Treaty of Rome, the 1969 Hague Summit called for EMU by 1980. The unstable international monetary environment during the 1970s rendered this goal impossible, but the discussions of the time laid the basis for what was eventually to become the euro system. The launching of the EMS in 1979 provided a framework for ongoing monetary co-operation, created the ECU that evolved into the euro and set up the EMCF that became the EMI and was subsequently transformed into the ECB.

Progress in implementing the three stages of EMU set out in the Maastricht Treaty proceeded surprisingly smoothly, though the number of countries fully participating in stage 3 was larger than initially foreseen. It was only subsequently that unresolved questions began to emerge. How, for instance, was fiscal discipline to be ensured while avoiding the excessive rigidity of the Stability and Growth Pact in times of economic downturn? What balance of power between the Ecofin, Eurogroup, ECB and Commission would emerge? How effective would the decision-making process of the ECB prove, in particular after enlargement? How far would a single interest rate lead to sychronization of national economies? When would the new member states be able to take on the euro, and what difficulties would emerge?[58] How would the international role of the euro develop? The introduction of the euro was an ambitious and apparently irreversible initiative, but it is still too early too make judgements about its lasting consequences.

---

[55] The ECB as the Community body responsible for monetary policy would be granted observer status at the IMF Board. The views of the EU on other issues relating to EMU would be presented at the IMF by an official of the member state holding the Presidency, assisted by a representative of the Commission.

[56] See the statement by Bundesbank Council member, Franz-Cristoph Zeitler, as reported in the *Financial Times*, 26 September 2000. Zeitler even proposed setting additional conditions, such as that the per capita income of the CEECs should reach 70 per cent of the EU average, before they could participate fully in stage 3 of EMU

[57] Eurostat data.

[58] This issue is taken up in Chapter 20.

Summary of Key Concepts

- Most theoretical assessments of whether countries should join together to form an economic and monetary union take the traditional optimal currency area approach as a starting point but attempt to assess the various costs and benefits.

- In general it is assumed that the costs of forming an economic and monetary union will fall, and the benefits will rise as the level of integration increases.

- The main benefits of EMU are: a saving in transaction costs; increased transparency in comparing prices; encouraging the creation of deeper and wider capital markets; increased trade; possible economies of scale in holding international reserves; use of the euro as an international reserve could yield seignorage; the introduction of a common monetary policy which may permit countries to 'borrow credibility'; improved location of industry; neo-functionalist spill-over into other integration areas and increased weight of the member countries at a world level.

- The main costs of EMU are: the psychological cost of losing a national currency; the technical costs of changeover; loss of seignorage for some member states; the problem of 'one size fits all' arising with a single interest rate and loss of the possibility of exchange rate changes among the member states.

- The role of the exchange rate mechanism is to compensate asymmetric shocks, i.e. shocks that affect the countries involved in different ways.

- The cost of forgoing the exchange rate mechanism will be less if other instruments such as wage/price flexibility or budget transfers can replace it.

- The 'core' refers to those countries for which it is easy to recommend EMU membership. The 'periphery' is countries for which EMU membership seems less appropriate since their economies are less synchronized with those of euro members.

- The Treaty of Rome contained no commitment to EMU.

- The 1969 Hague Summit envisaged EMU by 1980, but the initiative failed in the face of the monetary instability of the 1970s.

- The 'snake in the tunnel' was created in 1972, but by 1973 this had become a 'joint float' of currencies linked to the D-mark against the dollar.

- The European Monetary System was launched in 1979 and entailed: the exchange rate mechanism, introduction of the ECU, a divergence indicator and monetary co-operation. The ECU was the forerunner of the euro, and the European Monetary Institute provided the institutional basis on which to build the future European Central Bank.

- The operation of EMS can be divided into four periods: 1979–83, 1983–87, 1987–92 and the 1992 crisis and after. From August 1993, the bands of fluctuation were widened to +/– 15 per cent.

- Padoa Schioppa (1987) refers to the 'contradictory quartet' which no international monetary arrangement has been able to reconcile simultaneously: liberalized trade, free capital movements, fixed exchange rates and autonomy of monetary policy

- The 1993 Maastricht Treaty set out the criteria for joining the single currency, the timetable for its introduction and the main institutional features of EMU.

- The Maastricht criteria entail that successful candidates must have: inflation rates no more than 1.5 per cent above the average of the three countries with the lowest inflation rate in the Community; long-term interest rates no more than 2 per cent above the average of the three lowest inflation countries; an exchange rate within the 'normal' band of the ERM without tension and without initiating depreciation for two years; a public debt of less than 60 per cent of GDP and a national budget deficit of less than 3 per cent of GDP.

- The decision about which countries could join the euro was made in May 1998 (though Greece joined later), and from that time no further exchange rate changes were made between their currencies. Britain, Sweden and Denmark remained outside the euro. The euro replaced the ECU from 1 January 1999. The European Central Bank began to operate from June 1998. Euro notes and coins were introduced from 1 January 2002.

- According to the Stability and Growth Pact, budget deficits should generally be limited to a maximum of 3 per cent of GDP and countries should aim at balanced budgets in the medium term. In November 2003 the sanctions mechanism of the pact due to come into operation against France and Germany was suspended.
- The main priority of the ECB is to maintain price stability. It is responsible for supporting general economic policies, defining and implementing monetary policy for the euro area and holding foreign reserves. It also has to ensure the smooth operation of the payments system and supervision by the relevant authorities.
- It seems likely that the role of the euro in the invoicing of trade, and in official reserves and private holdings of international financial assets, will increase.

Questions for Study and Review

■ What do you consider the main costs and benefits of introducing a single currency?

■ Why do you think that the objective of introducing EMU by 1980 failed?

■ What are the main features of the EMS?

■ In what ways did the EMS set the stage for introduction of the euro?

■ How does the idea of a 'contradictory quartet' explain the main developments in each of the phases of EMS?

■ What were the motives for a return to the objective of EMU in the late 1980s?

■ Describe the main features of EMU as set out in the Maastricht Treaty.

■ What was the aim of the Maastricht criteria?

■ Describe the main steps in introducing the euro.

■ How useful do you consider the Stability and Growth Pact?

■ What are the chief functions of the European Central Bank, and what difficulties is it likely to encounter in its operation?

■ How do you think the role of the euro in the world economy will change?

Appendix

An illustration of the role of the exchange rate mechanism using aggregate demand and supply curves

The role of the exchange rate as a shock absorber can be analysed using the concepts of aggregate demand and aggregate supply.[59] For simplicity, initially it is assumed that nominal wages are fixed. Figure A8.1 presents the aggregate demand and supply curves for two countries, say France and Germany prior to EMU.

The aggregate demand curve slopes down from left to right. This is because with lower prices the economy is more competitive, increasing the demand for its exports and reducing imports. At the same time, for a given money stock, lower prices will increase the value of real money balances, leading to an excess supply of money and an excess demand for bonds. This will raise the price of bonds and reduce the interest rate, leading to increased investment and a higher level of production.

The aggregate supply curve is assumed to slope upwards to the right. A possible explanation is that as prices rise, real wage costs fall and firms will take on more labour, increasing output. According to this view, the upward sloping curve is based on the assumption that there is some money illusion on the labour supply side. This implies that an increase in money wages is perceived

---

[59] The example here is taken from Artis (1994), and owes much to the work of Mundell (1961). Source: pp. 351–52 from *The Economics of the European Union* (1994) by Artis, M. and Lee, N. By permission of Oxford University Press.

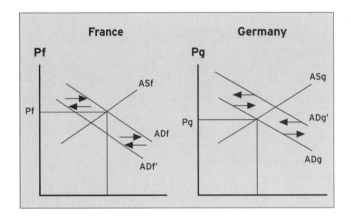

Figure A8.1 The aggregate demand and supply curves for France and Germany

as an increase in real wages so more labour is offered. If prices rise, but money wages rise less quickly, there will still be an increase in the labour supply.

Assume that the initial position of the aggregate demand curves in France and Germany are ADf and ADg respectively. An asymmetric shock then takes place because consumers' preferences change, possibly in response to a health scare. For instance, it is assumed that France is relatively intensive in the production of wine, and Germany is relatively intensive in the production of beer. As a result of a health scare concerning wine, consumers may start drinking beer in place of wine. This will shift the aggregate demand curve in France downwards to the left to ADf', and that in Germany up to the right to ADg', as shown in the diagram.

To meet this situation the French franc might be devalued against the German D-mark, rendering French output cheaper relative to German output. This will have the effect of moving the French aggregate demand curve out to the right and the German curve in to the left. According to textbook analysis, it should therefore be possible to use the devaluation to return to the original situation in each country, ADf and ADg.

However, the price levels so far considered are the domestic price levels in France and Germany (Pf and Pg respectively). Workers are not interested in the prices of domestically produced goods, but in the consumer price index, and this is also based on the price of imported goods. For instance, even if French domestic prices remain the same, the devaluation will increase the franc price of German beer bought by French workers. The French consumer price index PcF can be expressed by the following formula:

$$PcF = aPf + (1 - a)e\, Pg$$

where e is the exchange rate for converting D-marks into francs, a is the share of domestic products, and $(1 - a)$ is the share of imported goods.

Even if Pf and Pg remain unchanged, a devaluation of the franc will increase PcF. If there is a high level of integration between the French and German economies, a large share of French products will be imported from Germany. This means that $(1 - a)$ will be high, and a French devaluation will have a substantial effect in raising consumer prices in France.

These higher prices reduce real wages and may lead to requests by French workers to increase nominal wages. If these are granted, the aggregate supply curve will shift to the left offsetting part of the effect of the devaluation. Prices will be higher and French output has not returned to its original level. There is even a risk that repeated devaluations lead to a wage–price–devaluation spiral.

With a higher level of integration, an exchange rate change is more likely to alter consumer prices and lead to this kind of price–wage reaction. The cost of forgoing the exchange rate mechanism is less the higher the level of integration, and this is is a major reason that the cost curve of monetary union is assumed to slope down to the right.

References

Artis, M. (1994) 'European Monetary Union', in Artis, M. and Lee, N. eds (1994) *The Economics of the European Union: Policy and Analysis*, Oxford University Press, Oxford.

Artis M. and Bladen-Hovell, R. (2001*)* 'European Monetary Union', in Artis, M. and Nixson, F. (eds), *The Economics of the European Union. Policy and Analysis*. 3rd edn, Oxford University Press, Oxford.

Artis, M. and Healey, N.M. (1995) 'The European Monetary System' in N.M. Healey ed. *The Economics of the New Europe,* Routledge, London and New York.

Artis, M. and Lee N. eds (1994) *The Economics of the European Union: Policy and Analysis*, Oxford University Press, Oxford.

Baldwin, R., Berglöf, E., Giavazzi, G., Widgren, K. (2001) 'Preparing the ECB for enlargement', *CEPR Policy Paper*, No. 6, Centre for Economic Policy Research, London.

Baldwin, R. and Wyplosz, C. (2004) *The Economics of European Integration*, McGraw-Hill Education, Maidenhead, UK.

Bank of England (1990) 'The Exchange Rate Mechanism of the European Monetary System', *Bank of England Quarterly Bulletin*, Vol. 30, No. 4.

Bergsten, C.F. (1997a) 'The impact of the euro on exchange rates and international policy co-operation', in Masson, P.R., Krueger, T.H. and Turtelboom, B.G. (eds), *EMU and the International Monetary System*, IMF, Washington DC.

Bergsten, C.F. (1997b) 'The euro and the dollar', *Foreign Affairs*, July/August.

Buiter, W.H. (2000) 'Optimal currency areas. Scottish Economic Society/Royal Bank of Scotland Annual Lecture', *Scottish Journal of Political Economy*, Vol. 47, No. 3, August.

Danson, M., Halker, H. and Cameron, G. (2000) *Second Report on Economic and Social Cohesion*, European Commission, Brussels.

De Grauwe, P. (1988) 'Exchange rate variability and the slowdown in growth of international trade', *IMF Staff Papers*, Vol. 35.

De Grauwe, P. (2003) *Economics of Monetary Union*, 5th edn, Oxford University Press, Oxford.

Dornbusch, R., Favero, C. and Giavazzi, F. (1998) 'Immediate challenges for the European Central Bank', *Economic Policy*, Vol. 26.

Eichengreen, B.J. (1989) 'Hegemonic stability theories of the International Monetary System' in Cooper, R.N., Eichengreen, B.J. and Henning, C.R., *Can Nations Agree? Issues in International Economic Co-operation,* The Brookings Institute, Washington DC.

Eurobarometer (2003) 'The euro two years later', Flash EB No. 153, European Commission.

European Central Bank (2003) 'Review of the international role of the euro', December 2003, www.ecb.int

Fitoussi, J.-P. and Creel, J. (2003) *How to Reform the European Central Bank*, Centre for Economic Policy Reform, London.

Frankel, J.A. and Rose, A. (2000) 'Estimating the effect of currency unions on trade and output', National Bureau of Economic Research Working Paper 7857, Cambridge, MA.

Gros, D. and Thygesen, N. (1998) *European Monetary Integration,* 2nd edn, Addison-Wesley Longman, Harlow, UK.

IMF (1998) *World Economic and Social Survey*, Washington DC.

Kindleberger, C. (1984) *A Financial History of Western Europe*, Allen & Unwin, London.

Krugman, P.R. and Obstfeld, M. (1997) *International Economics: Theory and Policy*, Addison-Wesley, Reading, MA and Harlow, UK.

Ludlow, P. (1982) *The Making of the European Monetary System*, Butterworths, London.

Mundell, R. (1961) 'A theory of optimum currency areas', *American Economic Review*, Vol. 51.

Nuti, D.M. (1994) 'The impact of systematic transition on the European Community', in Martin, S. (ed.), *The Construction of Europe: Essays in Honour of Emil Noel*. Kluwer Academic Publishers, Dordrecht, the Netherlands.

Padoa Schioppa, T. (1987) *Efficiency, Equity and Stability*, Oxford University Press, Oxford.

Portes, R. and Rey, H. (1998) 'Euro vs dollar: will the euro replace the dollar as the world currency?' *Economic Policy*, April.

Rose, A. (2000) 'One money, one market: The effect of common currencies on trade', *Economic Policy*, Vol. 30, pp. 7-33.

Rose, A. (2002) 'The effect of common currencies on international trade: Where do we stand?', unpublished manuscript available at http://faculty.hass.berkeley.edu/arose/RecRes.htm

Swann, D. (1995) *The Economics of the Common Market*, 8th edn, Penguin, London.

Tsoukalis, L. (1997) *The New European Economy Revisited*, 3rd edn, Oxford University Press, Oxford.

Verdun, A. (2003) 'The past and future of the Stability and Growth Pact', Paper presented at the First EUI Alumni Conference, Governing EMU: Political, Economic, Legal and Historical Perspectives. 3-4 October 2003, European University Institute, Florence.

Useful websites

The British Treasury has carried out extensive research into the issues of exchange rates and EMU, much of which is available on:

www.hm-treasury.gov.uk

The European Central Bank for statistics, reports and analysis:

www.ecb.int

The website on Economic and Monetary Affairs of the EU:

www.europa.eu.int/pol/emu.

The EU and EC treaties available on:

www.europa.eu.int/eur.lex

The *Financial Times* publishes frequent articles on the euro, the ECB and the Growth and Stability Pact:

www.ft.com/centralbanks

The International Monetary Fund publishes statistics, theoretical research, and articles on the international financial architecture:

www.imf.org

List of abbreviations

CAP	Common Agricultural Policy
CEEC	Central and East European country
D-mark	Deutschmark
ECB	European Central Bank
ECU	European currency unit
EMCF	European Monetary Co-operation Fund
EMI	European Monetary Institute
EMU	economic and monetary union
EONIA	European Overnight Index Average
ERM	Exchange Rate Mechanism
ESCB	European System of Central Banks
Eurogroup	Group of Ministers of the Economy and Finance of the eurozone

G-7	group of seven most industrialized countries
GDP	gross domestic product
IMF	International Monetary Fund
NCB	national central bank
TARGET	euro-payments mechanism

9

The EU Budget

LEARNING OBJECTIVES

By the end of this chapter you should be able to understand:

▶ That although the Treaty of Rome envisaged the Community budget as having contributions and receipts roughly in balance, some member states have emerged as net beneficiaries and others as net losers;

▶ The main items of expenditure from the EC budget and how these have changed over the years;

▶ The basic principles of the Community budget;

▶ How the financing of the budget has changed over time;

▶ Why and when financial perspectives covering a number of years were introduced;

▶ The debate about financing enlargement.

INTRODUCTION

The changing nature of the EU with its widening and deepening processes has been reflected in the evolution of its budget. Budgetary considerations have played an important role in Community proceedings for much of the history of the EU, and the budgetary procedure is the outcome of many disputes and finely balanced compromises. There have been controversies about whether the Community should have its own resources, about the respective roles of the Community's institutions in the budgetary process and over the redistributive effects of the budget on different member states. The European Parliament, like most parliaments in history, has used its budgetary powers to increase its role and influence and to wrest concessions from the Commission and Council.[1]

---

[1] For instance, the 1999 institutional crisis described in Chapter 3 began with the European Parliament's refusal to approve the 1996 budget accounts.

THE MAIN FEATURES OF THE EU BUDGET

The underlying belief of the Treaty of Rome was that the contributions and the receipts of each of the member states to the Community budget should roughly balance. Some redistribution was expected to occur through the European Investment Bank, which was established with the main objective of encouraging development in the Italian South or Mezzogiorno. However, as can be seen from Table 9.1 and Figure 9.1, some countries have emerged as net beneficiaries, others as net losers, and the respective shares have frequently been the subject of heated disputes.

	Net receipts 2001 million euros	Receipts per capita 2001 % GDP	Net receipts 2002 million euros	Receipts per capita 2002 % GDP
Belgium	-629.5	-0.25	-256.4	-0.10
Denmark	-229.0	-0.14	165.0	0.09
Germany	-6953.3	-0.34	-5067.8	-0.24
Greece	4513.2	3.52	3387.9	2.39
Spain	7738.3	1.23	8870.8	1.29
France	-2035.4	-0.14	-2184.2	-0.14
Ireland	1203.1	1.15	1576.7	1.50
Italy	-1977.9	-0.17	-2884.5	-0.23
Luxembourg	-144.1	-0.74	-48.9	-0.25
Netherlands	-2256.8	-0.54	-2187.7	-0.51
Austria	-536.4	-0.26	-226.3	-0.11
Portugal	1794.2	1.53	2692.3	2.14
Finland	-150.4	-0.11	-5.7	0.00
Sweden	-973.3	-0.43	-746.6	-0.29
UK	707.5	0.04	-2902.8	-0.17

Table 9.1 **Operational budgetary balance (after UK rebate)**

Source: European Commission (2003).

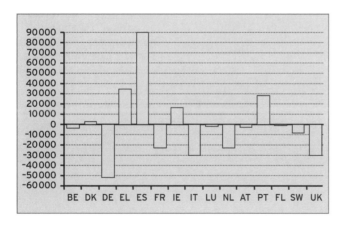

Figure 9.1 **Net contributions to the EU budget (2002, after UK rebate, 100 000 euros)**

Source: European Commission (2003).

On the expenditure side, in the early years of the Community agriculture accounted for some 90 per cent of spending from the Community budget. The share remained as high as 73 per cent in 1985, and agriculture was expected to account for 46.8 per cent of spending in 2004 (see also Figures 9.2–9.4 and Chapter 10). The share spent on structural operations has steadily been increasing, reaching 32. 4 per cent in 2004 (see Table 9.2).[2]

---

[2] The Structural Funds are: the European Social Fund; the European Regional Development Fund; FEOGA Guidance and the Fisheries Guidance Instrument. The Cohesion Fund is related but separate. See Chapter 13.

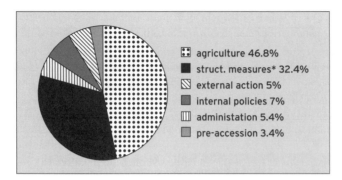

Figure 9.2 Expenditure from the 2004 budget (1999 prices, ** **commitment appropriations)**

*including rural development
**The financial perspective for the period 2002–06 was agreed in 1999, and allowance was made for inflation (the assumption was that inflation would be 2 per cent per year)
Source: European Commission
www.europa.eu.int/comm/budget

Table 9.2 Allocation of 2002 operating expenditure by sector and by member states as a percentage of EU (15) spending

	BE	DK	DE	EL	ES	FR	IE	IT	LU	NL	AT	PT	FI	SE	UK	EU 15
Agriculture	2.2	2.8	15.7	6.1	13.7	22.5	4.0	13.1	0.1	2.7	2.5	1.8	1.9	1.9	9.2	100
Structural Operations	1.1	0.3	14.7	7.9	38.0	5.5	3.3	7.8	0.0	0.2	0.8	12.9	1.0	1.0	5.7	100
Of which share of Cohesion Fund			15.1	65.8		6.1						12.9				
Internal Policies	13.4	2.4	22.0	3.4	6.4	12.0	1.4	10.1	1.5	5.1	4.3	1.6	2.0	2.8	11.7	100

Source: European Commission (2003).

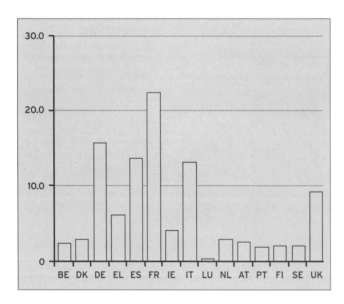

Figure 9.3 Expenditure on agriculture and rural development from the EU budget, by member state

(2002, per cent of total EU spending on agriculture and rural development)
Source: European Commission (2003).

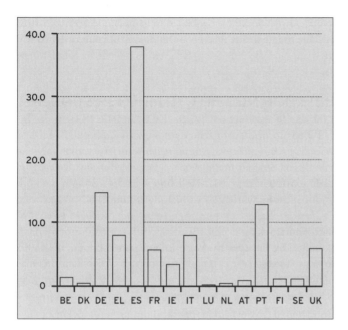

Figure 9.4 Expenditure on structural operations (including the Cohesion Fund), by member state
(2002, per cent of all EU spending on structural operations)
Source: European Commission (2003).

Overall the scale of budgetary spending as a share of the GDP of the EU has remained small, increasing from 0.3 per cent in 1960 to 0.53 per cent in 1973 and being fixed as a ceiling of 1.27 per cent of GDP for the 2000–06 period.

THE BASIC PRINCIPLES OF THE EU BUDGET

Throughout its history the budget of the EU has been guided by certain basic principles:

Unity and universality
According to Article 268 of the EC Treaty, all revenues and expenditures have to be entered into the budget. Individual revenues must not be assigned to any particular expenditure, and all revenues and expenditure must be entered in full in the budget without any adjustment against each other.

In practice there have always been certain exceptions to this rule and, for example, the activities of the European Investment Bank are outside the budget. The European Development Fund (which provides financial aid to developing countries, see Chapter 18) was outside the budget until 2006, but its inclusion in the budget was proposed from the 2007–13 financial perspective.

Equilibrium
According to Article 268 of the EC Treaty, the budget has to balance, i.e. estimated revenues for a financial year have to equal expenditure for that year.

Annuality
The budget runs for a financial year from 1 January to 31 December. In 1984 and 1985 financial difficulties led to budgets covering only the 10 months up to October in order to satisfy the principle of equilibrium, with supplementary budgets being voted for the remaining period. The European Court of Justice ruled against this expedient as being contrary to the principle of annuality.

Specification

Although revenues cannot be earmarked for particular items of expenditure, all items of expenditure must be specified in the budget.

A common unit of account

All items of revenue and expenditure have to be indicated in a common unit of account rather than in national currencies. Since 1981 the unit of account used was the ECU, and this was replaced by the euro from 1 January 1999.

Box 9.1 The budgetary procedure

Since 1977 the annual budgetary procedure of the EU has generally entailed:

■ Establishment of the preliminary draft budget by the Commission and transmission to the budgetary authority no later than 15 June.

■ First reading of the preliminary draft by the Council before 31 July and transmission of the draft to the European Parliament in the first half of September.

■ First reading by the Parliament in October.

■ Second reading by the Council in the third week of November.

■ Second reading by the Parliament and adoption of the budget.

Parallel to the debate on subsidiarity in the context of EU institutions, in the field of public finance a similar theoretical literature has emerged on what is referred to as 'fiscal federalism'. This literature deals with the criteria for deciding the appropriate level of government (European, national, regional or local) for decisions with regard to expenditure and revenue. A central concept of the literature is the idea of 'congruence', according to which each level of government has to have its own source of revenue to match its expenditure responsibilities.

Criteria for assigning functions to higher levels of government could include the presence of externalities (e.g. in fighting pollution), indivisibility or economies of scale (such as in research and development programmes) or ensuring minimum standards of services or of prosperity (as in the case of the Cohesion Fund). Criteria for assigning functions to lower levels of government could include the need for democratic control or to bring decisions closer to the citizens, flexibility, competition among units, or the aim of reflecting preferences more accurately given the greater political homogeneity that often characterizes smaller communities.

THE FINANCING OF THE COMMUNITY UP UNTIL 1970

The Treaty of Rome envisaged a transition period until 1970 during which financing of the Community was to consist essentially of contributions from the member states. The basic contribution of the three large members (France, Germany and Italy) was fixed at 28 per cent of total budget revenue, while that of the Netherlands and Belgium was 7.9 per cent, with 0.2 per cent for Luxembourg. However, the basic financing rule was adjusted according to the importance of the policy in question for each member state. For instance, Italy's contribution to the European Social Fund was reduced to 20 per cent, while those of France and Germany were raised to 32 per cent, Belgium to 8.8 per cent, with the Netherlands at 7 per cent and 0.2 per cent for Luxembourg. During the transitional period the system of financing was further complicated by the existence of separate institutions for the three Communities up until 1967.

According to Article 201 of the Treaty of Rome, a system of own resources (or self-financing) for the Community was to be introduced at the end of the transition period. Own resources consist of revenue allocated automatically to the Community without any need for further decisions by the member states.

The 1962 agreement on the basic principles of the CAP (Common Agricultural Policy) called for a decision on the rules for financing Community policies by 1965. The CAP was due to come into operation from 1967 and, backed by France and the Netherlands, the president of the Commission, Hallstein, was pushing for the new system of financing to begin operation at the same time.

The Commission's proposals for the Community Budget were presented in 1965 and, in line with the provisions of the Treaty of Rome and the logic of a customs union, the proposals entailed that the Community should be financed directly by proceeds from the common external tariff.

Federalists such as Hallstein, Monnet and Spinelli regarded the introduction of own resources as a step in the process of building a united Europe, in which the European Parliament would exercise powers of budgetary control. For example, Jean Monnet drew on his experience of international organizations and concluded that if such institutions relied on their members for financing, their powers tended to be more limited. This had been a major motive for his insistence on own resources for the European Coal and Steel Community. Altiero Spinelli used his knowledge of the history of the taxing power of the US federal government to argue that the power to tax directly was 'the essence of federal institutions'.[3]

However, the Commission's proposal to introduce own resources was opposed by France since it appeared to challenge De Gaulle's concept of national sovereignty. The budgetary issue was directly linked to the question of how Community institutions should evolve (and, in particular, the balance of power between the Commission and Council, parliamentary budgetary powers and the use of the qualified majority vote in the Council) and was at the heart of the 1965 'Empty Chair' Crisis.

It was only when de Gaulle resigned in 1969 and was replaced by Pompidou that the introduction of own resources could proceed as part of the 'completion' of the Community called for by the 1969 Hague Summit. The French government considered a solution to the budgetary question as being in its own interests as a means of ensuring adequate financing for the Common Agricultural Policy.

Treaties on Community financing came into operation in 1970 and 1975,[4] though practical difficulties meant that the full system of EC self-financing had to be delayed until 1980. In the meantime a hybrid system was adopted, based partially on contributions from the member states, and partially on own resources.

By the time agreement was reached on own resources, the system of financing envisaged by the Treaty of Rome, based on tariffs and levies on agricultural imports from third countries, was clearly inadequate to meet the growing expenditure needs of the Community and, in particular, the already high and growing cost of the Common Agricultural Policy. It was therefore decided to introduce a common system of turnover tax from 1967 based on the French tax, VAT, or value added tax. VAT is paid at each stage in the production process (including marketing) on the value added at each stage. A major reason for delaying full implementation of the system was that the VAT base varied from country to country, with differences in the products covered and the rates of VAT applied (see Chapter 6).

---

[3] The initial federal system in the USA ran into difficulty because of the refusal of states to pay their contributions.
[4] Decisions on the budgetary powers of the European Parliament and the distinction between compulsory and non-compulsory expenditure were also taken in this context.

The own resources system, which was applied fully from 1980, consisted of three elements:

■ Tariffs on manufactured imports from third countries;[5]
■ Levies on agricultural imports from the rest of the world, and on sugar and isoglucose; and
■ A percentage of VAT, fixed at 1 per cent up until 1986.

THE CONTINUING DIFFICULTIES OF THE EU BUDGET DURING THE 1980S

During the 1980s, primarily because of excess spending on the CAP but also because of its widening membership and extension into new policy areas, the Community was continually plagued by inadequate budgetary resources. In 1980 and again in 1985 the European Parliament rejected the proposed budget on the grounds of excessive growth in agricultural spending.

One of the most heated controversies over the EC budget was the so-called British budget question, which dragged on over several years. When Britain joined the Community a large share of its agricultural imports traditionally came from the rest of the world, in particular Commonwealth countries such as New Zealand. This together with its relatively small but efficient agricultural sector, meant that Britain would be a large net contributor to the EC budget. It was hoped that during the seven-year transition period following UK accession the weight of agriculture both in the Community budget and economy would decline, thereby reducing the bias against Britain. According to the terms of accession, if the situation remained unacceptable, an equitable solution would be negotiated.

An initial proposal to resolve the situation entailed establishing a European Regional Development Fund (ERDF) that would provide transfers to the economically weaker areas of the Community, including the regions of industrial decline in the UK. However, the recession after the 1973 oil crises meant that funding for the ERDF was not forthcoming on the scale initially envisaged.[6] Following a not very successful attempt by the British Labour government to renegotiate the terms of accession, from 1979 there was a determined attempt by the prime minister, Margaret Thatcher, to get Britain's 'money back'.[7]

By 1984 an increase in the VAT ceiling was urgently needed to avoid bankruptcy of the EC budget and to provide the necessary financing to permit the accession of Spain and Portugal to the Community from 1986. Any change in the VAT ceiling required ratification by all the member states, and UK acquiescence was conditional on settlement of the British budget question. The outcome was the 1984 Fontainebleau Agreement that entailed:

■ A refund of two-thirds of the UK's net contribution to the budget;
■ An increase in the VAT contribution to 1.4 per cent from 1986;
■ A limit on the growth of agricultural spending which could not grow more than the increase in own resources;[8] and
■ The introduction of quotas on the production of milk.

BUDGETARY REFORMS AND FINANCIAL PERSPECTIVES

The Fontainebleau Agreement failed to resolve the ongoing financial difficulties of the Community budget. On the expenditure side CAP spending continued to grow, and the three countries

---

[5] Member states were granted a 10 per cent reimbursement on tariffs and agricultural levies to cover the administrative costs of collecting these resources.
[6] Transfers through the EBRD amounted to only 300 million units of account in 1975 and 500 million units in 1976 and 1977.
[7] For a discussion of these issues see Pinder (1995).
[8] This could be considered a type of 'constitutional rule' to limit increases in government spending favoured by some members of the public choice school such as Buchanan and Tullock (1962).

that joined the EC in the 1980s (Greece, Spain and Portugal) were all net beneficiaries from the budget. The poorer regions of the Community feared the additional competitive pressure expected to arise from the Single Market Programme and were pressing for compensation in the form of a substantial increase in the Structural Funds.

On the revenue side all three sources of EC budgetary financing had been subject to erosion. Successive GATT rounds had reduced the average level of tariffs, thereby reducing the tariff share in budget revenue as shown in Table 9.3. The growing level of EC self-sufficiency in agricultural products meant a falling share of levies on agricultural imports in budget resources.

	1975	1980	1987	2002
Tariffs	52.5%	37.7%	25.0%	10.3%
Agricultural levies	11.0%	14.8%	8.7%	1.6%
VAT contribution	36.5%	47.5%	65.7%	28.8%
GNP/GNI**	–	–	–	59.1%

Table 9.3 The share of difference resources in EC budget revenue*

*Totals may be less than 100 per cent because of correction for budgetary imbalances
**The GNP/GNI resource was not used before 1988; see text for explanation
Source: European Commission www.europa.eu.int/comm/budget

Although, as Table 9.3 illustrates, the VAT share in budget revenue rose between 1975 and 1987, the VAT base (i.e. the goods and services on which VAT was levied) was not growing as rapidly as the overall economy. Savings and investment, and spending on services such as health and education, are not subject to VAT, and these are often higher in richer countries. The VAT contributions of different member states also depended on the level and number of VAT rates applied in each country (see Chapter 6).

By 1987 it was estimated that to balance the budget an increase in the VAT ceiling from 1.4 per cent to 1.9 per cent would be necessary. However, the regressive nature of VAT and the fact that increases in the VAT contributions of the member states failed to reflect their respective GDP performance led to the decision to introduce a new resource, or additional form of financing for the EC budget.

The creation of the fourth resource formed part of the 'First Delors Package' or 'bill for the Single Market' agreed in 1988. The package established the precedent of setting out the financial perspective of the Community for several years to come, in this case the 1988–92 period. The financial perspective fixes the maximum amount and composition of EU expenditure over the next few years. The advantage of this approach was to ensure adequate financing for projects extending over several years and to establish objectives and priorities from the outset.

Under the financial perspective the main categories of Community expenditure are divided into headings (see Tables 9.4 and 9.5). Each heading is covered by a commitment appropriation and the maximum amount of payable appropriations in each year. The margin between appropriations for payment and for commitments allows for flexibility, but the appropriations for payments must cover outstanding commitments from previous years.

With the 1988 agreement the own resources of the Community became:

■ Tariffs on imports of industrial products from third countries;
■ Variable levies on imports of agricultural products from third countries, and the levies of sugar and isoglucose minus the 10 per cent reimbursement to member states to cover the administrative costs of applying the levies;
■ 1.4 per cent of the total VAT levied by the member states from 1986; and

Table 9.4   The 2000–06 financial perspective the EU (15) agreed at the Berlin European Council March 1999
Appropriations for commitments in billions of euros, 1999 prices. The annual deflators for agriculture and structural operations were fixed at 2 per cent.

	2000	2001	2002	2003	2004	2005	2006
AGRICULTURE	**40.920**	**42.800**	**43.900**	**43.770**	**42.760**	**41.930**	**41.660**
Of which:							
Rural development and accompanying measures	4.300	4.320	4.330	4.340	4.350	4.360	4.370
STRUCTURAL OPERATIONS	**32.045**	**31.455**	**30.865**	**30.285**	**29.595**	**29.595**	**29.170**
Structural funds	29.430	28.840	28.250	27.670	27.080	27.080	26.660
Cohesion fund	2.615	2.615	2.615	2.615	2.515	2.515	2.510
INTERNAL POLICIES	**5.930**	**6.040**	**6.150**	**6.260**	**6.370**	**6.480**	**6.600**
EXTERNAL ACTION	**4.550**	**4.560**	**4.570**	**4.580**	**4.590**	**4.600**	**4.610**
ADMINISTRATION	**4.560**	**4.600**	**4.700**	**4.800**	**4.900**	**5.000**	**5.100**
RESERVES	**900**	**900**	**650**	**400**	**400**	**400**	**400**
PRE-ACCESSION AID	**3.120**	**3.120**	**3.120**	**3.120**	**3.120**	**3.120**	**3.120**
Of which:							
Agriculture	520	520	520	520	520	520	520
Pre-accession structural instrument	1.040	1.040	1.040	1.040	1.040	1.040	1.040
PHARE (applicant countries)	1.560	1.560	1.560	1.560	1.560	1.560	1.560
TOTAL APPROPRIATIONS FOR COMMITMENTS	**92.025**	**93.475**	**93.955**	**93.215**	**91.735**	**91.125**	**90.660**
Accession			4140	6710	8890	11 440	14 220
TOTAL APPROPRIATIONS FOR PAYMENTS	**89.600**	**91.110**	**94.220**	**94.880**	**91.910**	**90.160**	**89.620**
Own resources ceiling % of GNP	**1.27%**	**1.27%**	**1.27%**	**1.27%**	**1.27%**	**1.27%**	**1.27%**

Source: European Commission www.europa.eu.int/comm/budget

Table 9.5   Financial framework for EU enlargement agreed at the 2002 Copenhagen European Council: million euros, 1999 prices, commitment appropriations

	2004	2005	2006
Agriculture	1897	3747	4147
Of which:			
Rural development	1570	1715	1825
Structural actions	6070	6907	8770
Of which:			
Structural Funds	3453	4755	5948
Of which:			
Cohesion Fund	2617	2152	2822
Internal policies and additional transitional expenditure	1457	1428	1372
Of which:			
Existing policies	846	881	916
Of which:			
Transitional nuclear safety measures	125	125	125
Of which:			
Transitional institution building	200	120	60
Of which:			
Transitional Schengen measures	286	302	271
Administration	503	558	612
Total commitment appropriations	9927	12 640	14 901
Berlin 1999 scenario: total commitment appropriations	11 610	14 200	16 780

Source: EC Commission www.europa.eu.int/comm/budget

■ The 'fourth resource', which was based on the difference between VAT levies and the GNP of a member state and which can be levied up to a maximum percentage of the GNP of the Community if the budget financing from the other three resources proves inadequate. The ceiling was fixed as 1.2 per cent of GNP in 1992, or 1.31 per cent if the European Fund for Regional Development and the UK rebate from the EC Budget are also taken into account. In 1995 the concept of GNP was replaced by the concept of Gross National Income (GNI) (see Figure 9.5).

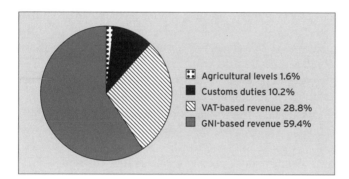

Figure 9.5 Financing of the EU budget (2002)

Source: European Commission (2003).

⊡ Agricultural levels 1.6%

■ Customs duties 10.2%

◩ VAT-based revenue 28.8%

■ GNI-based revenue 59.4%

With the 1988–92 financial perspective, the link between the Single Market and redistributive policies became explicit. The poorer regions and countries of the Community insisted on reform of the Structural Funds and a near doubling of the their financing in order to assist their adjustment to the additional competitive pressures of a less fragmented market. The strategy for rendering the necessary financing available was twin pronged: creating new resources for the Community and re-dimensioning spending on the Common Agricultural Policy.

In 1988 the 'stabilisers' were introduced to limit CAP spending. These involved fixing a 'maximum guaranteed quantity' for a product each year, and if that quantity were exceeded, the following year there would be an automatic reduction in the level of support prices. The 1988 budget package also placed a ceiling on the rate of increase in FEOGA Guarantee spending which could not exceed 74 per cent of the growth of the GNP of the Community. The European Parliament was to be responsible for ensuring that this limit was not passed.

In Edinburgh in 1992 a second 'Delors Package' also known as the 'bill for Maastricht' was agreed, setting out the financial perspective for the years 1993–99. The main innovations of the package included a further increase in spending on the Structural Funds and the creation of the Cohesion Fund to compensate the poorer areas and countries of the Community for the additional competition expected to result from introduction of the single currency. The British budget rebate was also continued. The relative importance of the VAT contributions and the fourth resource were also adjusted. With the reduction in the ceiling of the VAT contribution to 1 per cent and the gradual increase in the GNP ceiling of the budget to 1.27 per cent by 1999, it was hoped that resources paid by each of the member states to the EU budget would better reflect their overall economic performance.

THE BERLIN AGREEMENT ON AGENDA 2000

The financial perspective for the 2000–06 period was decided at the Berlin European Council of March 1999. The package is also known as 'Agenda 2000' after the document of July 1997 setting out the Commission's proposals. A main priority of the package was to prepare the way for enlargement of the EU, and the deal included agreements on reform of the Common Agricultural Policy and Structural Funds (see Chapter 20).

As shown in Table 9.4 the Berlin Agreement on Agenda 2000 entailed a total budget commitment allocation of €640 billion for the 2000–06 period. At the insistence of the main contributor countries, and Germany in particular, the ceiling on budget spending as a percentage of GNI remained at 1.27 per cent. The VAT contribution was to be decreased from 1 per cent in 2000 to 0.75 per cent in 2001 and 0.5 per cent in 2004. This would again have the effect in increasing the share of the fourth resource in total revenue, with the intention of bringing the relative contributions of the different member states closer in line with their overall economic performance. The percentage of tariffs and agricultural levies to be retained by the member states in order to cover administrative costs was raised from 10 per cent to 25 per cent.

The British budget rebate was to continue (and was worth about 4 billion euros per year), but the UK agreed to forgo certain windfall gains that it would otherwise have received, namely:

■ The benefits from reducing the VAT ceiling. This was expected to increase the relative contribution of Italy, Belgium, Denmark and France, and to decrease that of Germany and the UK.
■ The increased reimbursement to member states to cover administrative costs on traditional financing (i.e. tariffs and agricultural levies) from 10 per cent to 25 per cent.
■ The expenditure on EU enlargement was excluded from calculation of the British rebate.

The other main contributors to the EU budget (Germany, the Netherlands, Austria and Sweden) also requested a reduction in their net contribution, but in the final compromise accepted simply that their contribution to the UK rebate would be reduced. It was, however, agreed that there would be a revision of budgetary procedures before the next financial perspective.

With regard to total spending on agriculture, the initial intention was to freeze annual expenditure in real terms at the 1999 level of €40.5 billion for the 2000–06 period,[9] but in the event an additional €3 billion was agreed.

The Agenda 2000 package also entailed reform of the Structural Funds. The financial perspective earmarked some €195 billion for the Structural Funds for the 2000–06 period, with a further €18 billion for the Cohesion Fund.

The 2000–06 financial perspective allocated €3.12 billion per year in pre-accession assistance to the applicant countries. This was to consist of €1.56 billion each year in PHARE assistance.[10] Initially PHARE was aimed primarily at facilitating economic and political transition, but increasingly it became focused on preparing the applicant countries for EU accession. This entailed assistance for institution building, investment support and economic and social cohesion (see Chapter 20). The pre-accession assistance also included an allocation of €1.04 billion for ISPA (the Pre-Accession Structural Instrument) and a further €0.52 billion each year for SAPARD (the Special Accession Programme for Agriculture and Rural Development).

The Berlin Agreement on Agenda 2000 also fixed a budgetary allocation for new EU members that was to rise from €4.14 billion in 2002 to €14.21 billion in 2006. The Berlin estimates were based on the assumption of the six 'front-wave' candidates of the Luxembourg group joining in 2002,[11] even though by then accession negotiations had begun and such an early deadline was clearly unrealistic. Presumably, in confirming the hypothesis that had been set out in the initial

---

[9] Allowance was made for 2 per cent inflation each year.
[10] The PHARE programme began in 1989, and the acronym, Assistance for Economic Reconstruction in Poland and Hungary, soon became a misnomer since assistance was extended to other countries in Central and East Europe.
[11] The Czech Republic, Estonia, Hungary, Poland and Slovenia.

1997 Agenda 2000 document, the EU wished to leave a certain room for manoeuvre and avoid possible diplomatic incidents which might arise if the date were postponed.

The Copenhagen European Council of December 2002 agreed on a revised financial package for EU enlargement over the 2004–06 period (see Table 9.5). This was based on the assumption that 10 countries would join in 2004 (Bulgaria and Romania were expected to join in 2007) and that direct payments to CEEC farmers would be phased in gradually (see Chapter 10). It was agreed that no new member state should be a net contributor (which might risk happening because of delays in spending) to the Community budget from 2004.

The aim of the Copenhagen agreement was to keep within the Berlin budgetary key. As Table 9.5 illustrates, the annual budgetary allocation for enlarging to 10 countries set out at Copenhagen is below the Berlin allocation for each year for only six new members. The total allocation for commitment appropriations for accession was €42 590 million in the 1999 financial perspective and €37 468 million in the 2002 agreement.

FINANCIAL IRREGULARITIES

In recent years there has been growing concern with financial irregularities in payments from the EU budget. According to Article 274 of the EC Treaty, the Commission is responsible for implementing the budget (see Box 9.2), but in practice the Commission has to rely on the member states to implement certain policies. It is estimated that local and national authorities are responsible for administering 80 per cent of funds (in particular of the CAP and Structural Funds).

> ### Box 9.2 Control of implementation of the EU budget
> According to Community budgetary law, control of implementation is exercised by:
> - Internal control by the authorizing officers of each institution and Commission supervision of the systems to combat fraud.
> - External control by the Court of Auditors (see Chapter 3).
> - Discharge from the European Parliament. The discharge procedure 'releases' the Commission from responsibility for management of a budget by marking the end of a budget's existence.

Following the scandal that led to resignation of the Commission in 1999 (see Chapter 3), the next president of the Commission, Romano Prodi, announced a policy of 'zero tolerance' of corruption and set up an anti-fraud office, OLAF, to look into cases of financial irregularity. However, as Box 9.3 suggests, the EU continued to suffer shortcomings in financial accountability.

In 2002 after a long and acrimonious dispute, Chief Accountant Marta Andriessen was suspended on full pay for criticisms of alleged deficiencies in Community accounting methods.[12] In February 2004 Michaele Schreyer, the EU budget commissioner, proposed a 'contract of confidence' between the Commission and the member states in order to certify the systems they use for handling money.[13] Countries failing to agree to such a contract would be subject to more rigorous inspections and on-the-spot checks.

---

[12] *Financial Times*, 1 August 2002; 3–4 August 2002.
[13] *Financial Times*, 10 February 2004.

> ## Box 9.3 Financial irregularities in the EU accounts
>
> **January 2002** Marta Andriessen was appointed EU chief accountant.
>
> **March 2002** Andriessen argues with the Commission over a complete rehaul of the EU accounting system.
>
> **May 2002** Marta Andriessen is removed from her job and offered a post in the personnel department.
>
> **August 2002** Andriessen is suspended on full pay for going public to the press and European Parliament. She was also banned from Commission buildings.
>
> Following the suspension of Marta Andriessen, the commissioner responsible for the budget, Michele Schreyer, promised a vigorous programme of reform and a switch to the modern accrual system of accounting by 2005.
>
> **November 2002** The Court of Auditors strongly criticized the 2001 accounts, arguing that it could only certify that 5 per cent of spending was legal and regular.
>
> **June 2003** The chief internal auditor of the Commission, Jules Muis, attacks the Commission's 'rudimentary financial control systems', and announced that he would be leaving his job the following year. In a leaked paper, Muis accused the Directorate General for the budget as being 'a department haunted by a profound lack of qualified staff, a host of vacancies/absentees in crucial functions, a power ambience totally catered to the DG' (*Financial Times*, 10 March 2003).
>
> Eurostat was also accused of financial irregularities. Complaints had been made about Eurostat by trade unions in 1997 and by internal Commission audits in 1999 and 2000.* In 2003 the EU anti-fraud office, OLAF, maintained that Eurostat had been responsible for a 'vast enterprise of looting', with false contracts and the channelling of EU funds into unofficial bank accounts in Luxembourg. OLAF accused Eurostat officials of rewarding contracts to companies they had set up and whose boards they sat on. The value of these contracts was said to be artificially inflated, for work that was sometimes fictitious. The director general, Yves Franchet, and a director, Daniel Byk, were required to resign, and a multi-disciplinary task force comprising OLAF and Commission officials was set up to further investigate Eurostat. The commissioner nominally in charge of Eurostat, Pedro Solbes, refused to be held responsible for things he 'didn't know about'.
>
> **Financial Times, 17 July 2003.*

THE COMMISSION PROPOSALS FOR THE 2007–13 FINANCIAL PERSPECTIVE

In February 2004 the European Commission presented its proposals for the financial perspective covering the 2007–13 period.[14] The report described in some depth the main priorities of the EU for the following years before indicating the financial framework (see Table 9.6). The document also raised the issues of structure of own resources (and whether a 'European tax' should be introduced) and the British rebate (and whether a generalized 'correction mechanism' should be introduced).

For 2007–13 the Commission indicates four policy priorities:

■ **Competitiveness and cohesion for sustainable growth.** This is broken down into two sub-headings: (i) competitiveness for growth and employment, and (ii) cohesion for growth and employment. According to the Commission, in order to reinvigorate the

---

[14] European Commission (2004a).

Table 9.6 Proposed financial framework for 2007-13 (million euros at 2004 prices)

Commitment appropriations	2006*	2007	2008	2009	2010	2011	2012	2013
Sustainable growth	47528	59625	62795	65800	68235	70660	73715	76785
Of which								
Competitiveness for growth and employment	8791	12105	14390	16680	18965	21250	23540	25825
Cohesion for growth and employment	38791	47570	48405	49120	49270	49410	50175	50960
Preservation and management of natural resources	56015	57180	57900	58115	57980	57850	57825	57805
Of which: agriculture**	43735	43500	43673	43354	43034	42714	42506	42293
Citizenship, freedom, security and justice	1381	1630	2015	2330	2645	2970	3295	3620
The EU as a global partner	11232	11400	12175	12945	13720	14495	15115	15740
Administration	3436	3675	3815	3950	4090	4225	4365	4500
compensations	1041							
Total appropriations for commitments	120688	133560	138700	143140	146670	150200	154315	158450
Total appropriations for payments	114740	124600	136500	127700	126000	132400	138400	143100
Total appropriations for payments as % of GNI	1.09%	1.15%	1.23%	1.12%	1.08%	1.11%	1.14%	1.15%
Own resources as % of GNI	1.24%	1.24%	1.24%	1.24%	1.24%	1.24%	1.24%	1.24%

*2006 expenditure under the current financial perspective has been broken down according to the proposed new nomenclature for reference and to facilitate comparisons
**Agriculture includes market-related expenditure and direct payments
Source: European Commission (2004a).

Lisbon Strategy (see Chapter 6), emphasis must be placed on promoting the competitiveness of firms in the internal market, research and development, connecting Europe through networks, improving the quality of education and training and helping society to anticipate and manage social change. Cohesion policy should be more geared to increasing competitiveness so that more EU regions can contribute to growth and employment.

■ **Preservation and management of natural resources.** Environmental policy should ensure sustainable development and respect for international commitments (see Chapter 12), and a reformed fisheries policy should focus on sustainable exploitation of resources (see Chapter 11).

■ **Citizenship, freedom, security and justice.** In order to promote EU citizenship, there should be increased funding and improved instruments to encourage cultural co-operation and cross-border exchanges. There should also be a reinforced effort to follow the detailed roadmap agreed at Tampere in 1999 to create a European area of freedom, security and justice (see Chapter 7).

■ **The EU as a global partner.** The aim is to permit the EU to play a more active role at the regional and global levels. Regionally the EU should also aim to promote stability in neighbouring areas, while globally it should participate more actively in political governance and strategic security.

In order to realize these objectives, the Commission proposed an average level of appropriations for payments of 1.14 per cent of Gross National Income (see Table 9.6). The own resources ceiling would be fixed at 1.24 per cent of GNI for the whole period. The margin between own resources and payment appropriations is for unforeseen expenditure.

There would be a significant shift in EU support between headings in order to support the new priorities. This renders comparison with previous budgets difficult, even though 2006 expenditure under the current financial perspective has been broken down according to the proposed new nomenclature for reference and to facilitate comparisons.

EVALUATION AND OUTLOOK FOR THE EU BUDGET

As in the past it seems likely that the Commission proposals will mark the start of a long and probably acrimonious debate over the new financial perspective. In December 2003 the six main contributors to the EU budget (Germany, Austria, France, the Netherlands, Sweden and the UK) published a letter calling for a ceiling of 1 per cent of GNI on expenditure from the EU budget, well below the Commission proposal of a limit of 1.24 per cent. The six countries maintained that the EU budget should be subject to the same 'painful consolidation' as national budgets, but the Commission and poorer member states challenged this view.

Spending on structural measures seems set to be a further bone of contention. Michel Barnier, the commissioner then responsible for regional affairs, suggested splitting the 2007–13 expenditure on the Structural Funds so that half would go to the new member states and half remain for the poorer existing member states. Barnier proposed transitional assistance to poorer regions in existing member states which would otherwise lose their rights to assistance (see Chapter 13). The aim was to recast spending under regional policy as measures to increase 'cohesion for growth and employment'. Instead of the high-profile political projects of the past, which often did little to increase competitiveness, higher priority would be given to investing in human resources and technology.

Despite calls from many circles for a reduction in EU agricultural spending,[15] at the Brussels European Council of October 2002 the French president, Chirac (a former minister of agriculture), convinced Germany and the European Council to accept a limit of 1 per cent per year on the increase in CAP spending from 2007 until 2013. This meant that agricultural spending would continue to absorb some 36 per cent of the EU budget. Spending on rural development (about 10 per cent of Community spending on agriculture) was excluded from this limit. If this ceiling is respected, a lower level of own resources will restrict spending on the new priorities outlined by the Commission.

A further question to be resolved is the future of the British budget rebate after 2006. In July 2004 the Commission proposed a possible general rebate, extended to other net contributors (European Commission, 2004b). According to the Commission, when the UK was granted the rebate in 1984 it was one of the poorest EU countries with a GNI per capita of only 91 per cent of the EC average, but by 2003 this percentage had risen to 111 per cent, second only to Luxembourg.[16] Without correction the UK rebate would rise from €4.3 billion over the 1997–2003 period (when spending on enlargement was excluded) to €7.1 billion for the 2007–13 period, and the new member states would also have to pay part of the British rebate. Under the proposed correction mechanism Britain would contribute 0.51 per cent of GDP to the EU budget, and would become the highest contributor in terms of share of GDP. Not surprisingly this proposal was strongly contested by the UK.

---

[15] See, for example, the Sapir Report, requested by the European Commission in 2003.
[16] In terms of GDP (rather than GNI) per capita in PPP, according to Eurostat data in 2003, other member states such as Denmark, Ireland, the Netherlands and Austria were also higher than the UK. See also Table 13.5.

The aim is to reach agreement on the new financial perspective at a summit in Brussels in June 2005, in time to allow the member states to prepare programmes for when the perspective enters into force from 2007. However, before agreement is reached there seems ample scope for conflicts, which could pitch old EU members against new ones and poorer countries against richer ones.

The history of the EU budget seems essentially a process of lurching from one crisis to another. Generally compromises have been reached to resolve these crises, though often with substantial concessions and delays. Often it is difficult to justify these compromises (as, for instance, the distinction between compulsory and non-compulsory expenditure) on 'rational' grounds. The 2007–13 financial perspective seems no exception to this rule, so protracted debate ending in strange compromises can be expected.

Summary of Key Concepts

- The underlying belief of the Treaty of Rome was that the contributions and the receipts of each of the member states to the Community budget should roughly balance. Over time some countries have emerged as net beneficiaries and others as net losers.
- The share of agriculture in spending from the Community budget has been falling, while the share of the Structural Funds in expenditure has been increasing steadily.
- Overall the scale of budgetary spending as a share of the GDP of the EU has remained small, increasing from 0.3 per cent in 1960 to a ceiling of 1.27 per cent of GDP for the 2000–06 period.
- Throughout its history the budget of the EU has been guided by certain basic principles: unity and universality, equilibrium, annuality, specification and a common unit of account.
- Fiscal federalism deals with the criteria for deciding the appropriate level of government (European, national, regional or local) for decisions with regard to expenditure and revenue.
- The Treaty of Rome envisaged a transition period until 1970 during which financing of the Community was to consist essentially of contributions from the member states to be followed by the introduction of a system of own resources.
- The own resources consist of: tariffs on manufactured imports from third countries; agricultural levies; a percentage of VAT and the fourth resource based on GNP/GNI.
- During the 1980s, excess spending on the CAP, widening membership and extension into new policy areas meant that inadequate budgetary resources continually plagued the Community.
- Since 1984 Britain has had a budget refund or 'correction', but this has been increasingly contested by other member states.
- Since 1988 the financial perspective of the Community has been set out for several years to come. This was the case for the 1988–92 period (Delors 1 or the bill for the Single Market), 1993–99 (Delors 2, or the bill for Maastricht) and 2000–06 (the Berlin Agreement on Agenda 2000, which could also be termed the bill for enlargement).
- In 2004 the Commission presented its proposals for the financial perspective for the 2007–13 period.

Questions for Study and Review

■ What are the main principles underlying the Community budget, and how far have they been respected in practice?

■ Describe how the concept of fiscal federalism could be applied in the EU context.

■ Explain why the Community budget ran into difficulties on both the expenditure and revenue sides.

■ Do you see a risk of a return to the EU being dominated by budget squabbles as happened in the 1970s?

■ Indicate the main changes in the Community budget over the years.
■ What changes do you expect to see in the Community budget as a result of enlargement?
■ What innovations are likely in the 2007-13 financial perspective?

References

Buchanan, J.M. and Tullock, G. (1962) *The Calculus of Consent*, University of Michigan Press, Ann Arbor.

European Commission (2000) 'The budget of the European Union. How is your money spent?' www.europa.eu.int

European Commission (2003) 'Allocation of 2002 operating expenditure by member state', September 2003.

European Commission (2004a) 'Building our common future. Policy challenges and budgetary means of the enlarged Union 2007-13', COM(2004)101 of 10 February 2004.

European Commission (2004b) 'Proposal for a Council decision on the system of the European Communities' own resources. Proposal for a Council regulation on the implementing measures for the correction of budgetary imbalances in accordance with Articles 4 and 5 of the Council decision of (...) on the system of the European Communities' own resources', COM(2004) 501 final, 14 July 2004.

Laffan, B. (1997) *The Finances of the European Union*, Macmillan, Basingstoke.

Laffan, B. (2000) 'The budget: Who gets what, when and how', in Wallace, H. and Wallace, W. (eds), *Policy-Making in the European Union,* 4th edn, Oxford University Press, Oxford.

Pinder, J. (1995) *European Community: The Building of a Union*, 2nd edn, Oxford University Press, Oxford.

Sapir, A. et al. (2004) *An Agenda for a Growing Europe. The Sapir Report*, Oxford University Press, Oxford.

Useful websites

The European Commission:
www.europa.eu.int/comm/budget
The EU Court of Auditors:
www.eca.eu.int

List of abbreviations

CAP	Common Agricultural Policy
ECU	European currency unit
ERDF	European Regional Development Fund
Eurostat	Statistical Office of the EC/EU
FEOGA	European Fund for Agricultural Guidance and Guarantee
GATT	General Agreement on Tariffs and Trade
GDP	gross domestic product
GNI	gross national income
GNP	gross national product
ISPA	Pre-Accession Structural Instrument
OLAF	European Anti-Fraud Office
PHARE	Poland/Hungary Aid for Economic Reconstruction
SAPARD	Special Accession Programme for Agriculture and Rural Development
VAT	value added tax

10

The Common Agricultural Policy

LEARNING OBJECTIVES

By the end of this chapter you should be able to understand:

▶ The reasons for public intervention in agriculture;

▶ The objectives of the Common Agricultural Policy (CAP) set out in the Treaty of Rome;

▶ The three principles on which the CAP is based;

▶ The main mechanisms used by the CAP;

▶ Why a policy of high prices was adopted, and what were the negative consequences of that policy;

▶ Why policies to improve farm structures played such a minor role for so many years;

▶ The various attempts at CAP reform;

▶ The outlook for the CAP.

THE REASONS FOR PUBLIC INTERVENTION IN AGRICULTURE

Agriculture has always been one of the sectors most subject to state intervention, and this was also the case for the six founding members of the European Community. There are various explanations for the scale of public intervention in agriculture. The dependence of agricultural production on biological cycles, climate and natural phenomena (including epidemics) provide justification for government measures to stabilize farm prices and incomes. Empirical studies show that the elasticity of demand for food products is relatively low both with respect to price and income,[1] meaning limited outlets for sales of foodstuffs over time and rendering farmers vulnerable to shocks on the supply side.[2] Difficulties may also arise for farmers because supply may be very inelastic in the short run. This may be because some output decisions (e.g. sowing a crop) may be impossible to reverse in a changed market situation.[3] The economic and social difficulties many farmers have in leaving the sector have meant that for protracted periods farm incomes and living conditions may compare unfavourably with those in the rest of the economy.[4]

Public intervention may also be justified to deal with cases of 'market failure' as for instance may occur when information is costly or difficult to obtain. It may be extremely hard for consumers to acquire adequate information about the nature and safety of a food product even after that good has been consumed as, for instance, emerged clearly during the BSE or 'mad cow' crisis (see Box 10.1). Public intervention may be required to ensure standards are met, to carry out certification and testing, and to provide information through labelling, trademarks and so on.

Box 10.1 BSE or the 'mad cow' crisis

Identified for the first time in the UK in 1985, bovine spongiform encephalopathy (BSE) or the 'mad cow' disease causes the destruction of the animal's brain tissue, transforming it into sponge-like material. The disease is spread by simple proteins known as prions which are resistant to heat, radiation and antibiotics. In 1987 animal feed containing prions from infected animals was identified as a likely cause of the diffusion of BSE. The number of identified cases of BSE had risen to 183 716 in the EU by the end of 2002, of which 181 024 were in the UK, 958 were in Ireland, 654 were in Portugal and 601 were in France. *

At the same time as the outbreak of BSE a new variant of Creutzfeldt-Jakob disease (CJDv) appeared in humans, and the cause was soon attributed to eating infected meat. By 2001 there were 78 deaths out of 87 cases of CJDv in the UK and one death in Ireland.

Measures to contain the disease included a total EU block of imports of British beef from 1996 to 1999, a ban on eating parts of the animal at risk (the spinal cord, brain and even for a time steaks on the bone) and a prohibition on using animal waste (such as bone meal) in animal feedstuffs. EU consumption of beef fell by 20 per cent in 2001. At the height of the crisis in February 2001 beef consumption in Italy had fallen by roughly 50 per cent compared with 2000 levels, and it was only in the week of Christmas and the New Year that there was a marked recovery to earlier levels.†

*Unless otherwise stated, the statistics in this section are taken from the UK Creutzfeldt-Jakob Disease Surveillance Unit: www.cjd.ed.ac.uk

†The data on Italy are taken from Marco Buoncristiani, 'La crisi della mucca pazza', unpublished student research, University of Siena, 2001.

Public intervention may also be justified when there are externalities, i.e. when there is a difference between the costs and benefits to the individual and to the public. In other words, externalities

---

[1] According to Engel's law, as incomes rise the share of foodstuffs in household expenditure falls. Numerous empirical studies over time and across countries find support for this 'law'.

[2] The Cobweb theory suggests that when supply is more elastic than demand an explosive cycle results, and government intervention may be necessary to stabilize prices and incomes. Though the theory is based on extremely simplifying assumptions, there does appear empirical evidence for cycles in the production of certain agricultural products such as beef or pigmeat.

[3] There are various explanations of the low short-run elasticity of supply in agriculture. Fixed costs tend to be relatively high and while these have to be considered when expanding production, only variable costs are taken into account in deciding when to stop production (the shutdown point). According to Johnson and Quance (1972), the difference in the prices of certain factors of production (such as farm machinery on the new and used markets) may help to explain inelasticity of supply in the short run. If the price of second-hand factors of production is very low, they will continue to be used even when their marginal productivity in terms of value falls very low. Nerlove (1956) shows how elasticity of supply tends to increase over time.

[4] This is frequently referred to as 'the farm problem'.

are the positive or negative effects of the production or consumption by one individual on others, which are not reflected in prices. Negative externalities may arise, for example, from the impact of agriculture on the environment, with some forms of intensive production causing soil and water pollution, or the elimination of biodiversity. Positive externalities may occur when agriculture contributes to rural development, care of the landscape, protecting animal welfare or preservation of breeds in danger of extinction.

The activities of farm lobbies also help to explain the persistence and scale of state support for the farm sector.[5]

AGRICULTURE IN THE TREATY OF ROME

Given the tradition of intervention in agriculture in the founding members of the EC and the diversity of measures used, France, in particular, was adamant that the new Community policy could not simply be a collation of national policies and that some kind of common policy was necessary.

Articles 38–47 of the Treaty of Rome deal with agriculture.[6] Article 39 is probably one of the most frequently quoted articles of the treaty and sets out the objectives of the Common Agricultural Policy:

1. (a) to increase agricultural productivity by promoting technical progress and by ensuring the rational development of agricultural production and the optimum utilization of factors of production, in particular, labour;
    (b) thus to ensure a fair standard of living for the agricultural community, in particular by increasing individual earnings of persons engaged in agriculture;
    (c) to stabilize markets;
    (d) to ensure availability of supplies;
    (e) to ensure that supplies reach consumers at reasonable prices.
2. In working out the common agricultural policy and the special methods for its application, account shall be taken of:
    (a) the particular nature of agricultural activity which results from the social structure of agriculture and from structural and natural disparities between the various agricultural regions;
    (b) the need to effect the appropriate adjustments by degrees;
    (c) the fact that in the Member States agriculture constitutes a sector closely linked with the economy as a whole.

Despite the importance that has always been attached to this statement of objectives, it is vague and lacking in precision on certain crucial points and is not without contradictions. For instance, how is the increase in productivity mentioned in 39/1a to be achieved – by increases in output (which was the interpretation of the farm lobby at the time) or by reductions in the labour force? If, as turned out to be the case, support for agricultural prices is the main instrument used to achieve 'a fair standard of living' for farmers, how is this to be reconciled with 'reasonable prices' for consumers? The reference to the 'social structure of agriculture' can be interpreted as a commitment to

---

[5] See Senior Nello (1984, 1986, 1989 and 1997) for more detailed descriptions of why farmers have been so successful in organizing pressure groups and how they manage to influence policy in their favour.
[6] Article 38 defines the field of action as 'plant, livestock and fish products, including those subject to the first stage of processing'. Articles 40–47 speak in very general terms about the policies to achieve these objectives, the institutions for agricultural decision-making and the arrangements for the transitional period. See Fennel (1997) for a discussion of agriculture in the Treaty of Rome.

the family farm (which has to be read in the context of the post-war collectivization in Central and Eastern Europe). However, given the small size of many farms at that time, the question of how to ensure their efficiency arises. The stress on availability of supplies reflects the post-war concern with shortages, even though surpluses had already emerged for certain Community agricultural products (such as grains, dairy products and sugar) by the late 1950s.

What is missing from the Treaty is a precise description of what form this Common Agricultural Policy should take, and, in particular, there is little mention of the policy mechanisms to be used. These omissions from the Treaty reflect the ongoing differences among the member states about how a common policy should be constructed. After its earlier experiences of co-operation on agricultural policy matters with Luxembourg and Belgium, the Netherlands was anxious to ensure less restricted markets and effective guarantees against reintroducing restrictions on trade. In contrast, the French favoured a more interventionist approach in order to ensure adequate levels of support and protection.

THE AGREEMENT ON THE CAP MECHANISMS

As many of the key questions were still unanswered, Article 43 of the Treaty of Rome called for a conference to work out the details of the future Common Agricultural Policy. This led in 1958 to the Stresa Conference, generally recognized to be one of the milestones in the creation of the European Community. However, the conference failed to resolve many issues, and heated debate about the future form of the CAP continued. Agreement was not reached until 1962.

The second stage of the transition period was due to come into operation from January 1962, with deadlines for more dismantling of tariffs between the member states and further progress in the creation of the common external tariff. While Germany was anxious for progress on trade issues, France and the Netherlands threatened to block the move to the second stage of the transitional period (due to begin from January 1962) if sufficient progress were not made on agriculture. The issue of what mechanisms to adopt for the CAP was hammered out in the famous 23-day marathon of the Council of Ministers, and failure to meet the January deadline led to the expedient of 'stopping the clocks' until agreement was finally reached on 14 January 1962.

The package eventually agreed by the Council of Ministers included what subsequently became known as the three fundamental principles of the Common Agricultural Policy:

(1) **Unity of markets**
Trade would be progressively liberalized between the member states and common prices would be introduced for the main agricultural products throughout the Community.

(2) **Community preference**
Barriers on trade between member states were to be removed, but common levies on imports of agricultural products from the rest of the world meant that EC producers would be at an advantage *vis-à-vis* those from third countries in selling their agricultural produce on Community markets.

(3) **Financial solidarity**
A European Agricultural Guarantee and Guidance Fund (generally known as FEOGA after its French acronym) would finance agricultural policy measures. The Guarantee Section of FEOGA would be responsible for market intervention and export refunds, while the Guidance Section would cover expenditure on structural measures.

Agreement was also reached on the market organization to use for cereals and the so-called cereal-based products: poultry and pigmeat.[7] Similar mechanisms were subsequently extended to about three-quarters of all agricultural products. Figure 10.1 sets out the basic price support mechanism. Though not shown in the diagram, target prices for each year are agreed by the Council of Ministers as the basis for calculating all the other common prices. Initially target prices were calculated according to the 'objective method', which involved taking account of the evolution of costs and revenue in order to ensure that developments in farm incomes were in line with those in other sectors. This method was abandoned from the mid-1980s when a policy of price restraint for agricultural products had to be introduced.

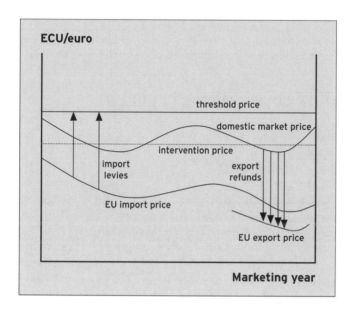

Figure 10.1 The basic price support mechanism for cereals
Source: Adapted from Tracy (1993).

Each year intervention prices, or minimum guaranteed prices, are also agreed. Intervention agencies have to stand ready to buy up the product to ensure that prices do not fall below this floor level. The intervention agencies are organized on a national basis, with, for example, the AIMA (l'Azienda Italiana per i Mercati Agricoli) and subsequently the AGEA (Agenzia per le Erogazioni in Agricoltura) in Italy, the Intervention Board in Britain and so on.[8]

The threshold price is a minimum entry price applied on imports from the rest of the world at the point of entry to the EU. In the first years of the CAP the threshold price was calculated as the target price minus the cost of transport from the main port of entry (Rotterdam) to the main consumption area (Duisberg), and was estimated at 10 per cent below the target price. In later years the ratio of threshold to other common prices also became subject to negotiation.

The level of Community preference, or advantage, that EU farmers have on Community markets over producers from the rest of the world is given by the difference between threshold and intervention price. In general the market price in the EU will oscillate between these two limits, but weakening of the intervention system in recent years (with, for example, disincentives, and time

---

[7] The introduction of the variable levy in mid-1962 on imports from the rest of the world led to the 'chicken war', or first trade dispute between the Community and the USA.
[8] Initially the intervention prices were calculated on the basis of the target price minus the cost of transport from the point of major production of grain (Ormès in France) to the point of main consumption in the Community (Duisberg in Germany), also taking into account margins of distribution, but subsequently the ratio of intervention price to the other common prices has become a matter for political compromise.

and quality restrictions before intervention can take place) means that at times market prices can descend below intervention levels.

Variable import levies were applied on imports from the rest of the world in order to bring their prices up to the threshold price. If prices on world markets fell while Community prices remained unchanged, the variable levy would simply increase, and this was regarded by the USA, in particular, as a particularly insidious form of protection. In 1995 as a result of the 1994 GATT Uruguay Round most variable import levies were replaced with tariffs on imports of agricultural products from the rest of the world (see Chapter 17).

For exports, export refunds (also called restitutions) or subsidies generally cover the gap between domestic EU prices and prices on world markets. Each week management committees in the Commission calculate the difference between EU and world prices in order to set the level of export refunds, though there is a certain leeway to take account of market conditions. On numerous occasions the EU has been criticized for its 'generous' calculation of the level of export refunds.

THE 1964 AGREEMENT ON COMMON PRICE LEVELS

The 1962 decision on the mechanisms of the CAP failed to give any indication of what the common levels of prices would be, and clearly the level of prices has crucial implications for the evolution of output and consumption in the Community.

Again the difficulties in reaching agreement reflected different national positions. At the time agricultural prices were relatively high in Germany, Luxembourg and Italy, and lower in France, Netherlands and Belgium. The solution of the EC Commission in document COM(60)105 was to propose that an average price be applied as the basis for the new common policy.

However, the national farm lobbies, and COPA (the Comité des Organizations des Producteurs Agricoles, the umbrella organization of national farm associations which had been established in September 1958) were strongly opposed to the Commission proposal. The Agricultural Committee of the European Parliament (composed mainly of farmers) also called for an increase in prices to the level of those in the main consumer country, i.e. Germany (Tracy, 1989).

In May 1964 the Kennedy Round of GATT negotiations opened formally, but France made progress on reaching a common Community position conditional on resolution of the question of grain prices.[9] In November 1964 Germany accepted a wheat price slightly below the German level, but obtained agreement that the new prices would apply only from 1967/8; that prices for barley, maize and rye (of which Germany was a major producer) would be fixed relatively close to wheat and that there would be temporary, degressive payments to compensate for the agricultural price cuts in the high-price countries: Germany, Italy and Luxembourg.

THE EFFECTS OF EU PRICE SUPPORT POLICY

The effects of the traditional Community price support system can be analysed using a partial equilibrium framework similar to that used for tariffs in Chapter 4. The world supply curve of a particular product is assumed to be perfectly elastic at Pw in Figure 10.2. The demand and supply curves (assumed linear for simplicity) of the Community for the traded product are indicated by D and S in the diagram. Without price support, the domestic price of the product in the EC is assumed equal to the initial world price Pw. At the world price Pw the Community would produce

---

[9] Tracy (1989), Fanfani (1998). See Chapter 17 for a discussion of the GATT/WTO.

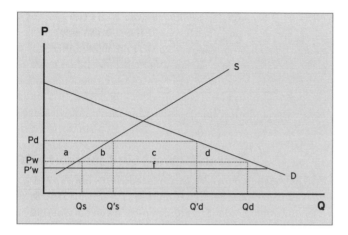

Figure 10.2 The price support system when the EC is assumed to be a large nation and net importer of a product

Qs and demand Qd of the product, so the EC would import Qs − Qd (equivalent to the excess demand) of the product.

For simplicity, the EC threshold and intervention prices are assumed to be the same and are both Pd. At Pd the Community will import $Q's - Q'd$ of the product. As can be seen from the diagram, the level of EC prices is shown to be considerably higher than the world price level, as was generally the case for many products (grain prices, for instance, were often over twice as high as world levels).

The EU is assumed to be a large nation. As can be seen from the diagram, the application of EC price support reduces net imports from Qs − Qd to $Q's - Q'd$. *Ceteris paribus* in the case of a large nation, the fall in net imports would have the effect of reducing demand on world markets, causing the world price level to fall. Conversely, the reduction or elimination of price support would increase EU net imports causing the world price to rise. The gap between the new world price P'w and the EC minimum import (or threshold) price Pd was covered by a variable import levy until 1995 and subsequently by a tariff (the difference is explained below).

The variable import levy or tariff is a source of revenue for a government budget.[10] The total revenue for the budget will be equal to the unit value of the variable import levy or tariff (Pd − P'w) multiplied by the quantity imported after introduction of the tariff $(Q'd - Q's)$. In the diagram this corresponds to the area of the rectangles c and f, or (Pd − P'w) × $(Q'd - Q's)$. If this revenue is used in a socially useful way, it represents a welfare benefit to a country. This benefit could be considered an increase in the income of taxpayers in that *ceteris paribus* in the absence of the tariff the government would have to charge higher taxes.[11]

With the introduction of price support producer surplus rises by area a, consumer surplus falls by a + b + c + d and the revenue for the budget is areas c + f. As the EC is assumed to be a net importer, the fall in world price from Pw to P'w as a result of the introduction of price support causes a transfer from producers in the rest of the world to consumers in the EU of area f (given by the quantity of imports Q'dQ's times the fall in world price PwP'w). The net welfare effect for the EC of introducing price support is therefore area f minus areas b and d.

Figure 10.3 illustrates the difference between a variable import levy and a tariff. Again the EU is assumed to be a net importer of the product, and a large nation. Introduction of price support will reduce the world price from Pw to P'w. Under the traditional price support system of the EC the threshold price Pd was fixed for the year and did not change even if world prices fell (by PwP'w).

---

[10] See the discussion on the sources of revenue of the EU budget in Chapter 9.
[11] See Chapter 4 for a description of these effects.

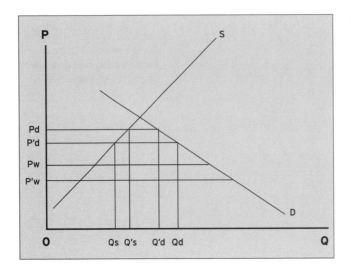

Figure 10.3 **The difference between variable import levies and tariffs**

All that happens is that the variable import levy increases to cover the gap between the new world price and the threshold price, so the unit value of the variable levy becomes Pd − P'w.

In contrast, with an *ad valorem* tariff following the fall in the world price, the internal EU price becomes P'd. With a tariff EU domestic prices are therefore more sensitive to movements in world price levels, and this was why the USA, in particular, criticized the Community's variable import levies. From 1995 EU variable import levies were converted into tariffs as a result of the 1994 GATT agreement.

The difference between the price support system and producer subsidies can be seen from Figure 10.4. In agriculture these producer subsidies are often also referred to as 'deficiency payments' after the system applied in Britain before joining the EC. The main difference between the EC price support system and producer subsidies is that the introduction of producer subsidies leaves the domestic price unchanged for consumers. As Figure 10.4 shows, with the producer subsidy the domestic price to producers rises to Pd, while the price paid by consumers remains Pw. Producer surplus rises by area a, the cost of the surplus to budget contributors is area a + b (i.e. the unit cost of the subsidy, Pd − Pw times the new quantity of output Q's). The net welfare loss is triangle b.

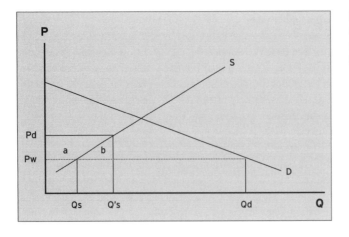

Figure 10.4 **The difference between price support and producer subsidies**

The impact of high and stable prices was to turn the EU from a net importer into a net exporter of many temperate agricultural products. As explained above, export subsidies or restitutions were used to cover the difference between the internal EU market price and the world price. Figure 10.5 shows the effect of EU export subsidies. D and S are the EU demand and supply curves for the product. With price support the internal EU price Pd is above the world price Pw, and the EU will export $Q's - Q'd$. The unit value of the export subsidy is $Pd - Pw$, and it is applied on the exports of the product $Q's - Q'd$. The export subsidy increases producer surplus by areas a, b and c, reduces consumer surplus by areas a and b and costs the budget areas b, c and d. The net welfare loss as a result of the export subsidy is equivalent to areas b and d. Appendix 10 provides a numerical example of the effects of an export subsidy as an exercise.

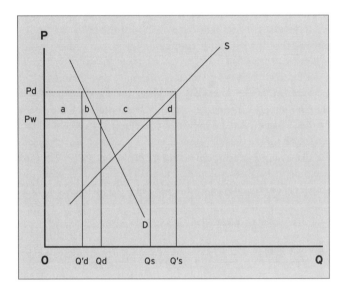

Figure 10.5 The effects of an export subsidy

THE 1968 MANSHOLT PLAN

The 1968 Mansholt Plan was probably one of the most controversial documents ever produced relating to the CAP. Published in December 1968 as Commission document COM(68)1000, the plan set out proposals to resolve the problems of surpluses and inadequate farm incomes over the following decade, so was also known as 'Agriculture 1980'.

The plan involved a dual approach, with price policy being used to achieve market balance, while structural measures (expected to account for about one-third of the agricultural budget) would be used to create large, efficient farms. A central concept of the plan was the 'modern farm enterprise' that could ensure farm incomes and working conditions (including working hours, holidays etc.) comparable with those in other sectors. A modern farm enterprise could be formed out of a single farm or by a group of farmers coming together. The plan also introduced the concept of production units, or the dimension of production required to ensure efficiency and the use of modern technology. The creation of co-operatives was to be encouraged in order to concentrate supply and render prices more stable.

The Mansholt Plan also aimed at the reduction of surpluses and the improvement of the structure of production by cutting the number of factors of production in the sector. The objective was to induce 5 million people to leave farming, 4 million of whom would be persuaded to retire, while a further 1 million would be found alternative jobs in other sectors.

It was expected that the reduction in the labour force would release 20 million hectares, most of which could be used to restructure farms. However, to cut surpluses some 5 million hectares would be withdrawn from agricultural production and used for forestry, recreational purposes etc. To meet the problem of dairy surpluses, 3 million cows would also be destroyed.

The plan also encouraged the formation of co-operatives and producer associations to improve marketing. Account was also to be taken of regional diversity (a proposal opposed by the member states) arising because farmers were operating under different natural conditions.

The reaction of the farming community to the plan was violent outrage. The proposals were thought to be too radical, and the dimension of farms proposed was considered too far removed from reality. The Commission was accused of being 'technocratic' and of attacking the family farm through back-door collectivization. Particular concern was expressed about the proposed reduction in the labour force, and about whether the means to ensure employment in other sectors would prove adequate.

In 1972 the Council finally agreed three Directives on structural measures, but these were far removed from the original Mansholt Plan.[12] The financial allocation for the Directives was extremely limited (and in general the Community contribution was only 25 per cent), and the extent to which they were taken up was far less than expected. The use of the Directives also seemed to depend more on the administrative capacity of the member state in question than structural needs. The whittling down of the Mansholt Plan is a major factor explaining the evolution of the CAP with its almost exclusive reliance on price support for many years. As late as 1983 Guarantee spending (on price support) accounted for 95 per cent of FEOGA spending, and in 1995 the share had only fallen to 92 per cent.[13]

THE AGRIMONETARY SYSTEM

What was considered to be one of the early achievements of the CAP, the introduction of common prices, was soon undermined by changes in exchange rates between the member states. Common prices were set in units of account and had to be converted into national currencies. According to the neo-functionalist approach to integration, it was hoped that the introduction of common agricultural prices would spill over into economic and monetary union in order to avoid complications to the system as a result of exchange rate changes.

This optimism was soon to prove unfounded, and beginning with French devaluation and a German revaluation in 1969, changes between EC currencies became a frequent occurrence. Special 'green' exchange rates were introduced for agriculture. Changes in these green rates lagged behind those in the central rates of EC currencies, since in that way it was possible to delay adjustment of agricultural prices in national currencies. This meant that a system of taxes and subsidies had to be set up at the border between EC countries to avoid speculative trade flows, and as a result market unity was undermined.[14] The operation of this 'agrimonetary system' led at times to price divergences between member states in national currencies larger than before the CAP had been introduced. In 1976, for example, for a time the gap between prices in the UK and Germany was

---

[12] The three structural Directives of 1972 relate to modernization of farms (72/159), early retirement (72/160) and socio-economic advice to farmers whether to continue farming or not (72/161).
[13] EC Commission, 'The Agricultural Situation in the Community'. Various years.
[14] See Senior Nello (1985) for a more complete account of the system and its effects.

over 50 per cent. It was only with the introduction of the euro that these difficulties were finally resolved (at least for euro members).

THE NEED FOR REFORM OF THE CAP

During the 1970s and 1980s, the CAP seemed increasingly to be transformed from the corner-stone to the stumbling block of the Community. The negative effects of what had begun as a high price policy were accentuated each year by substantial increases in prices for the main agricultural products (see Table 10.1). High and stable prices encouraged production leading to surpluses. Grain and butter mountains and wine lakes were the visible symbols of the malfunctioning of the CAP. It is estimated that between 1973 and 1988 EC agricultural production rose by 2 per cent per year, while consumption rose by only 0.5 per cent each year.[15]

These surpluses either had to be held in public storage, or sold on world markets with the help of

	Commission proposal (1)	Council decision (2)	Difference (2) - (1)	COPA proposal
Community of six				
1968-69		-1.3		
1969-70		0.0		
1970-71		0.5		
1971-72		4.0		
1972-73		4.7		
Community of nine				
1973-74	2.8	5.0	2.2	
1974-75	11.8	13.9	2.5	12.4
1975-76	9.2	9.6	0.4	15.0
1976-77	7.5	7.5	0.0	10.6
1977-78	3.0	3.9	0.9	7.4
1978-79	2.0	2.1	0.1	5.0
1979-80	0.0	1.3	1.3	4.0
1980-81	2.5	4.8	2.3	7.9
1981-82	7.8	9.2	1.4	15.3
Community of ten				
1982-83	8.4	10.4	2.0	16.3
1983-84	4.2	4.2	0.0	
1984-85	0.8	-0.5	-1.3	
1985-86	-0.1	0.1	0.2	
1986-87	-0.3	-0.3	0.0	
Community of twelve				
1987-88	-0.5	-0.2	0.3	
1988-89	0.0	-0.1	-0.1	
1989-90	-0.2	-0.2	0.0	
1990-91	-1.1			

Table 10.1 **Average increase in Community agricultural prices (percentage variation)**

Source: Fanfani (1998).

[15] Commission document COM(91)100.

export subsidies. Public storage was expensive, unpopular and involved the deterioration of foodstuffs over time, while the use of export subsidies antagonized other agricultural exporters, and the USA in particular. The growing EC self-sufficiency in the major foodstuffs lowered imports from the rest of the world and increased exports, thereby reducing prices of these products on world markets. Less-developed countries accused the Community of agricultural protectionism, increasing instability on world markets and lowering prices for their agricultural exports. The high and rising level of agricultural prices posed an excessive burden on the EC budget (see Chapter 9). FEOGA Guarantee spending rose from 4.5 billion ECU in 1975 to 11.3 billion in 1980 and 31.5 billion in 1991.

Linking support to prices means that those farmers who produce more benefit most from the system. It was estimated that between 1970 and 1990,[16] 80 per cent of FEOGA support went to the 20 per cent of farmers with the largest farms so the system also failed to resolve the problem of income disparities.

The CAP also tended to favour Northern European producers rather than Mediterranean farmers. For instance, in 1986 dairy products, which are mainly produced in Northern Europe, accounted for 20 per cent of the value of production, but 27 per cent of CAP spending, while grains were 13 per cent of production and 16 per cent of spending (see also Figure 10.6). In contrast the equivalent figures for typical Mediterranean products were 6 per cent for production and 3 per cent of spending for wine and 15 per cent of production and 5 per cent of spending for fruit and vegetables. The exceptions were tobacco and olive oil, which were relatively expensive regimes.[17]

The almost exclusive reliance on price support encouraged specialization and intensive methods

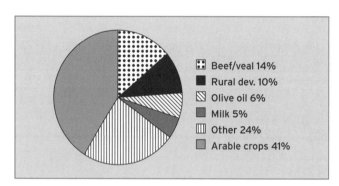

Figure 10.6 Breakdown of CAP spending by sector (2001)
Source: European Commission.

of production with negative implications for the environment and biodiversity. There has been growing public concern about water and soil pollution by fertilizers, pesticides and intensive livestock units, destruction of wildlife habitats and changes in the appearance of the countryside.

ATTEMPTS AT REFORM IN THE 1970S AND 1980S

During the early years of the 1970s reform of the CAP was still a taboo subject. It was thought that by undermining the progress achieved in the only functioning common policy, the whole fragile edifice of European integration might come tumbling down. Discussion documents of the Commission at this time refer to 'Improvement of the CAP' (1973) or 'Stocktaking of the CAP' (1975).

---

[16] European Commission document COM(91)100.
[17] Tobacco accounted for 0.6 per cent of production and 3.7 per cent of spending in 1986, while olive oil was 1.6 per cent of production and 2.9 per cent of spending. These data are taken from European Commission, 'The Agricultural Situation in the European Community' (1987).

Over time it became increasingly difficult to deny the need for change, and there were early and not very successful attempts at price restraint during the late 1970s.[18] In addition there were various reform attempts to tackle the problems of surpluses and excessive budgetary expenditure and, in particular:

■ Co-responsibility levies;
■ Milk quotas;
■ Stabilizers and the 1988 reform package.

The aim of the **co-responsibility levies** was to render farmers 'responsible' by involving them in bearing the cost of surpluses. Each year a certain level of production for an agricultural good would be fixed, and the cost of any excess production over that level would be totally or partially borne by farmers. Co-responsibility levies were introduced for milk from 1977 and cereals from 1986. In both cases the measures had a positive impact on the budget but failed to resolve the problem of surpluses largely because in practice their application became subject to negotiation.

The dairy sector was proving one of the most expensive CAP regimes, accounting for over 40 per cent of FEOGA Guarantee spending between 1976 and 1980. In 1983 Commission document COM(83)500 called for reform of the sector, arguing that a price cut of 12 per cent would be necessary to restore market balance. The member states were reluctant to accept such a large price cut and agreed on a system of **milk quotas** as a lesser evil.

The aim of the quota system was to freeze milk production at 1981 levels (1983 for Italy which imported 40 per cent of its milk and for Ireland which is a major exporter). The EC quota was then broken down by country, and the member states could decide on two methods of application. System A involved dividing the national quota by single farms. If a farm exceeded its quota, it would have to pay a fine of 75 per cent (100 per cent from 1987). According to system B quotas were granted to dairies and or other processors who paid a supplementary levy of 100 per cent if the quota was exceeded. From 1992 the two systems were fused, with quotas being allocated to farms and dairies being responsible for paying a levy of 115 per cent if quotas were exceeded. Initially quotas could only be transferred through the renting or sale of a farm, but from 1992 unused quotas could be reallocated to other producers.

Figure 10.7 uses a partial equilibrium approach to compare the welfare effects of production quotas and reductions in price support. The situation is shown for a net exporter, say the EU, even though certain member states (such as Italy) were net importers of dairy products. A reduction of support prices from Pd to P'd would have caused EU net exports of dairy products to fall from Qs − Qd to Q's − Q'd. The budgetary cost of export subsidies as a result of the reduction in price support would fall by the area b + c + f + e + d + h + g. Consumer surplus would rise by a + b, while producer surplus would fall by area a + b + c + f + e. The net improvement in welfare from reduction of price support would therefore be area b + d + h + g.

In contrast, assume that a quota of Q* for total production of milk in the EU was introduced. The EU supply curve would then become SS'S* because at Q* the EU supply curve would become perfectly inelastic. Consumers would continue to buy quantity Qd at prices well above world levels, and consumer surplus would remain unchanged. The loss in producer surplus from introduction of the quota would be area e.

Burrell (1989) has presented a more realistic version of the model with an initial loss of producer surplus of e + f + k. Area e is lost because the quota restricts output, but areas f and k are lost because of the way quotas are allocated to individual producers. If a transfer of a quota is permitted (as was

---

[18] Gundelach, the agricultural commissioner over the 1977–81 period, favoured a prudent price policy.

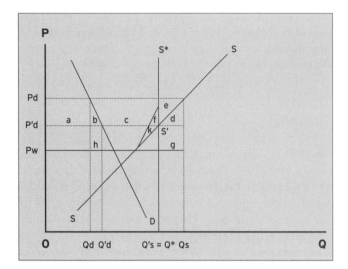

Figure 10.7 The comparison of the effects of quotas and price support reduction
Source: Burrell (1989).

the case from 1992), the purchase of quotas by low-cost producers from high-cost producers would enable k + f of producer surplus to be recovered.

Budgetary savings as a result of introduction of the quota amount to area e + d + g. The total welfare effect of introducing a quota when transferability of quotas is permitted is therefore only a welfare gain of d + g. The question then becomes: why were quotas introduced if the net welfare gain (d + g) would be less than that of a price cut (b + h + d + g)? The answer is that probably quotas were more politically acceptable to the farm lobby since they entailed less dislocation to producers (Colman, 2001).

The quota system involves freezing the structure of production, so introducing an element of economic inefficiency (though this was somewhat attenuated by introducing the transferability of quotas in 1992). It tends to be costly to administer (see Box 10.2) and may enable cuts in milk prices to be deferred. The operation of quotas may also entail windfall gains for existing producers from the sale or rent of quotas. Moreover, the operation of quotas may exert upward pressure on land prices. However, the operation of milk quotas in the EU has made a substantial contribution to reducing the problem of surpluses and slowing the rate of price increases.

Box 10.2 The Italian milk quotas

The history of the Italian milk quotas is one of long delays in applying Community legislation, huge fines, fraudulent activity and violent farm protests. One of the main complaints of Italian milk producers was that it was difficult for honest farmers to operate in such an environment.

Italy was granted a quota of 9.9 million tonnes on the basis of national statistics, and in 1984 the Italian minister for agriculture argued that there was a discrepancy between the quota and actual production of 11.4 million tonnes. Disagreements over the actual level of production and number of producers were to continue for many years.

Since Italy imports 40 per cent of its milk requirement, in order to exploit the full national quota it was decided to treat the whole country as a single national entity for two years, and not allocate individual quotas. In 1985 it applied to adopt System A, but 'administrative problems' delayed its implementation. In 1988 in order to use the quota fully, it was decided to allocate the quota to producer associations who would act as a 'single producer' and Unalat was created for this purpose. Unalat decided to apply the legislation on a voluntary basis. Unofficially Unalat and the ministry were encouraging farmers to exceed their quotas since Italy was a deficit country, and the exact level of production had not yet been established.

The non-application of the system meant that Italy was running up a fine in the order of 300 billion lira (roughly 150 million ECU) each year. In 1991 the European Court of Justice stopped 330 billion lira from payments to Italy through FEOGA, but by 1992 the fine had reached 4000 billion lira (2 billion ECU). Italy maintained that the quota was inadequate and requested a backdated increase. In 1994 a compromise was reached whereby the Italian quota was increased (not retroactively) and the fine was reduced to 3620 billion lira. In the logic of a supply-control measure, this fine should be paid by farmers, but in the face of protest by Italian farmers was passed on to taxpayers.

In 1993, nine years after the measure was introduced, a first attempt was made to collect data to establish quotas. Individual quotas were published, but their sum exceeded the national system. It was decided to rely on a system of *autocertificazione* whereby farmers provided their own data on production. Such a system was an invitation to irregular practices, with quotas representing herds of cows that only existed on paper. One famous case involved a herd of 1500 cattle based in Piazza Navona in the centre of Rome, which was said to have been rented out 12 times.

In a further moratorium in 2003, Italian dairy farmers were given 30 years to pay off the backlog of their fines.

The Green Paper of 1985 (COM(85)333), published by the EC Commission, marks the beginning of a change in priorities of the CAP. The document calls for a diversification of policy instruments in order to realize a number of objectives that cannot be reached through the almost exclusive reliance on price support. The Green Paper lists the priorities of the CAP as: reducing surpluses, promoting the quality and variety of agricultural production, improving the incomes of small family farms, supporting agriculture in areas where it is necessary for rural development, promoting awareness of farmers of environmental questions and assisting the processing industry.

The aims of the 1985 Green Paper were to some extent taken up by the package of reforms introduced in 1988. As explained in Chapter 9, these reforms were introduced in the context of the financial perspective for the 1988–92 period and involved reform of the Structural Funds, a ceiling on the growth of CAP spending and the introduction of the stabilizers and accompanying measures.

The **stabilizers** were intended to introduce an automatic check on agricultural spending. In general these entailed fixing a maximum guaranteed quantity (MGQ) for a product, and if that quantity were exceeded, the following year there would be a cut in prices or subsidies. The effectiveness of the stabilizers as a supply-control measure was undermined by the fact that the maximum guaranteed quantities tended to be set at relatively high levels.[19] In practice there was also a tendency to challenge the 'automatic' nature of the price or subsidy cut and its attempt to negotiate a compromise measure.[20]

With the benefit of hindsight, the most lasting and radical change for agriculture introduced by the 1988 package was that of the accompanying measures. These included incentives for early retirement, more extensive production methods, reforestation and set-aside.

---

[19] The maximum guaranteed quantity for cereals was fixed at 160 million tonnes in 1988 compared with a 1987 EC production of 154 million tonnes.
[20] Stabilizers had first been introduced for cereals in 1982 and should have brought about a 5 per cent cut in prices in 1985/6. A compromise was reached whereby prices were only cut by 1.8 per cent.

The set-aside scheme was voluntary and involved compensation for farms withdrawing at least 20 per cent of their arable land for at least five years. The land set aside could be left totally idle; used for forestry or non-food production (such as linen); included in a land rotation scheme or used for pasture or the production of selected crops such as chickpeas, lentils or vetches. It was hoped that set-aside would improve soil conservation and would contribute to the reduction of surpluses. However, the impact of set-aside on production is undermined by the phenomenon of 'slippage' whereby marginal land tends to be removed from production, and labour and capital tend to be used more intensively on the land that remains in production.

THE 1992 MACSHARRY REFORM

The stabilizer package failed to resolve the problem of surpluses of the main CAP products, and by 1991 reform had again acquired a new urgency. The EC became increasingly aware that CAP reform was necessary to avoid collapse of the GATT Uruguay Round negotiations (see Chapter 17). A new financial perspective was due from 1993 and spending on agriculture would have to be redimensioned. Reform of the CAP was essential to permit eastward enlargement of the CAP (see Chapter 20). The aim was to re-enforce the new priorities set out in the 1985 Green Paper, including rural development, environmental objectives and fairer distribution of support for farm incomes. A central element of the reform was cuts in administered prices for certain key products, compensated by the introduction of direct payments to farmers.

For cereals, the intervention price was to be cut by 29 per cent over three years, reaching 100 ECU/tonne in 1995/6.[21] The target price was to be reduced to 155 ECU/tonne, leaving a substantial Community preference. Farmers were to be compensated for the price cut by direct payments on a per hectare basis.[22] The compensation was calculated by multiplying a basic rate (45 ECU/tonne in 1995/6) by average yields in the past in each region. For farmers claiming compensation for an area producing less than 92 tonnes of cereals, compensation was available unconditionally in what was called the 'simplified scheme'. Farmers claiming a higher level of compensation through the 'general scheme' were required to set aside a certain percentage of their land. The percentage of land that had to be set aside varied with market conditions, and, for example, was 15 per cent in 1993/4.[23]

Oilseeds (such as soya, sunflower and colza) were at the centre of a protracted dispute between the USA and the EU. In the early years of the Community oilseed production was small, and in 1962 an EC–USA deal agreed duty-free access. Given the relatively high prices for grains in the Community, oilseeds had increasingly been replacing grains in animal foodstuffs, and production of pig-meat and poultry grew rapidly around the main ports where oilseeds were imported, such as Rotterdam, Bremen and Antwerp.

The EC introduced relatively low tariffs on oilseed imports (maximum 15 per cent) and subsidies for 'crushers' to ensure domestic producers a return compatible with that from cereals (Tracy, 1993). The USA maintained that this system ran counter to the 1962 agreement, and two successive GATT panels ruled in their favour. In 1992 the USA threatened to introduce prohibitive duties on imports worth $300 million from the EC (including pasta, white wine and so on) if the oilseed dispute were not resolved, and for a time the whole GATT Uruguay Round appeared threatened by this dispute (see Chapter 17).

---

[21] Common prices were then fixed in terms of ECU or the European currency unit, which, as explained in Chapter 8, was subsequently replaced by the euro.

[22] The use of the hectare as the basis for calculating arable compensation led to an increase in land prices.

[23] The percentages of compulsory set-aside were: 12 per cent for 1994, 10 per cent for 1995, 17.5 per cent for 1996 and 5 per cent for 1997. Initially set-aside was to be rotational, but this obligation was dropped in 1996 (also because the administrative costs involved were substantial).

As a concession to the USA the EC fixed a separate base area for oilseeds, on which a minimum set-aside area of 10 per cent was to be levied. The reform fixed the ratio of prices between cereals and oilseeds (1 to 2.1) as a basis for calculating per hectare compensatory payments for oilseeds.[24]

Since beef producers would benefit from the lower grain prices, the intervention price for beef was also to be cut by 15 per cent, and premia per head of cattle were introduced to encourage more extensive forms of production. The quota system was to remain for milk, and there was to be a cut of 5 per cent in the institutional price for butter. The tobacco regime (which was one of the most expensive common market organizations relative to the amount of production) was simplified and updated.[25]

The MacSharry Reform also included accompanying measures with a series of financial incentives for early retirement, reforestation and protection of the environment. The environmental measures were numerous, and included incentives to reduce the use of fertilizers and pesticides; to encourage extensive production methods and voluntary set-aside; to encourage the creation of natural parks, and to protect endangered species.

The MacSharry Reform represents a radical break with the past and sets a precedent for the shape of successive CAP reforms. From the point of view of economic efficiency, direct payments are preferable to price support (see Figure 10.4 above) and have the advantage of being more transparent. The reform recognizes the dual role of farmers as not only being producers of agricultural products but also playing a key role in rural development and protection of the environment. However, the funds allocated to these other objectives were limited.

The reform was instrumental in permitting a successful outcome to the GATT Uruguay Round (see Chapter 17), though at the time the Commission was adamant that the reform was not introduced in response to US pressure. The 1992 reform failed to ease the pressure of agricultural spending on the Community budget, also because there was overcompensation for the price cuts. According to Buckwell et al. (1997, p. 30), the overcompensation for cereals between 1992 and 1996 was 16 per cent. This overcompensation amounted to ECU 2.0, 4.2 and 5.0 billion for the three years 1993–96.

Although the compensation for price cuts was initially intended to be temporary, a date for its elimination was never fixed. Over time it becomes increasingly difficult to justify continued compensation for a once-and-for-all cut in prices. One of the objectives of the reform was to correct the inequity in the distribution of CAP transfers. However, compensation is highest for those who produced most and who were expected to lose most from the reform. The system of compensation payments therefore protracts the iniquity of the system.

THE 1999 BERLIN AGREEMENT ON AGENDA 2000

The lengthy document, Agenda 2000, published by the Commission in July 1997 was intended to prepare the EU for enlargement, *inter alia* by setting out the financial perspective for the 2000–06 period and proposals for the reform of the CAP and Structural Funds.[26]

The Agenda 2000 document reflects certain novelties in the agricultural policy debate, including concepts such as 'multifunctionality' and the 'European model of agriculture'. **Multifunctionality** entails that farmers should not simply be considered producers of agricultural goods but account should be taken of the role they can play in pursuing other objectives such as rural development, protecting the environment, safeguarding the countryside, guaranteeing the safety and quality of food and promoting animal welfare (see Box 10.3). **The European model of**

---

[24] See Tracy (1993) for a discussion of this reform.

[25] Intervention and export refunds were to be abolished. The number of varieties classified was reduced to eight, and each group was subject to a quota.

[26] See Chapter 20 for a discussion of agriculture and EU enlargement, and Chapter 13 for the Structural Funds.

agriculture requires social, historical and environmental considerations to be taken into account, and not just economic factors (and is sometimes seen by the USA as an excuse by the EU not to cut farm subsidies). According to Agenda 2000 (1997) the European model of agriculture should also be simplified and rendered more comprehensible as well as being brought closer in line with the expectations of society.

Box 10.3 Animal welfare

Problems for animal welfare may arise from intensive farming methods in view of the confinement and restricted movements imposed on animals, and the increased use of antibiotics. More integrated markets may subject animals to lengthy travel, with increased risk of spreading disease (as for example in the outbreak of foot and mouth disease in the UK in 2001). Many of the consequences of new developments such as genetically modified organisms and growth-producing hormones for animal health and biodiversity are still unknown.

The issue of animal welfare may have ethical, health, environmental and quality implications. EU Directive 98/58 of 20/6/98 fixes minimum animal welfare standards for all animals reared for food production. Member states are required to ensure that the conditions under which animals are kept and bred correspond to the needs of their species as well as their physiological and ethological needs.

However, implementation of the regulation may be difficult in view of:

■ The implications for trade and international trade agreements. It may be claimed that animal welfare measures are being used as a non-tariff barrier, and agreement on such issues may be difficult to reach at an international level.

■ The additional costs of production (increased expenditure on feed, energy, housing etc.), though at times this may be offset by technology and, at the level of overall welfare, may be compensated by the reduction in negative externalities.

■ Detailed labelling and traceability may be costly.

In March 1999 the European Council reached agreement on the Agenda 2000 package (overruling an earlier agreement of the Council of Agricultural Ministers). The aim was to freeze agricultural spending at the 1999 level of €40.5 billion, allowing for inflation of 2 per cent per year, but in the event a further €3 billion was agreed.

The agricultural aspects of the final agreement contained three main elements:

■ Reform of the common market organizations for products such as cereals, beef, milk and wine;

■ Increased flexibility for the member states in the use of funds through measures such as cross-compliance and modulation;

■ Rural development policy was to become the 'second pillar' of the CAP.

The main changes in common market organizations were the following:

■ Cereal prices were to be cut by 15 per cent, with farmers being compensated with direct payments for 50 per cent of the price reduction. Compulsory set-aside of land for large farmers[27] was to continue and was set at 10 per cent. Arable area payments on oilseeds and linseed were to be reduced and brought in line with those of cereals from 2002.

---

[27] Farmers claiming compensation on more than 92 tonnes of cereals.

Supplementary payments were to be made to Finland and Arctic regions of Sweden to compensate for extra drying costs.

■ The milk price was to be cut by 15 per cent with direct aids compensating farmers for 65 per cent of the price cut. Milk quotas were to continue until 2006, with a 0.9 per cent increase in the size of the quota for Ireland, Northern Ireland, Italy, Spain and Greece from 2000, and a further 1.5 per cent increase in quotas for all member states from 2005.

■ There was to be a 20 per cent reduction in beef prices, with 85 per cent compensation for farmers, and certain increases in the premia per head of cattle.

■ For wine there was to be a block on planting new vines until 2010 with limited exceptions. Quality improvement was to be encouraged, and there was to be a grubbing programme. Voluntary distillation and 'crisis' distillation in times of surplus would be permitted.

Among the more innovative aspects of the reform were those included in the so-called 'horizontal regulation' (Reg.1259/1999) relating to cross-compliance and modulation. **Cross-compliance** is a form of conditionality which entails countries indicating appropriate environmental measures which farmers have to introduce in order to receive their headage and acreage payments in full. **Modulation** allows member states, if they wish, to introduce measures to 'modulate', i.e. reduce, the acreage and headage payments a farm can receive on the basis of overall employment on the farm, overall prosperity of the holding or total amount of aid paid to the holding. The funds saved in this way can be rechannelled to other uses such as environmental measures or early retirement. The Commission had proposed a ceiling, whereby if the sum total of acreage and headage to a single holding exceeded €100 000, it would have been reduced, but this was not accepted by the Council.

Cross-compliance and modulation allowed a certain leeway for member states to increase their spending on environmental and related measures, but in the first years after the reform their use was extremely limited. By 2001 only France, the UK and Portugal had implemented modulation.

The Berlin Agreement aimed at upgrading rural development policy, even though spending on such measures continued to account for only 10 per cent of the agricultural budget. New legislation was introduced in order to:

■ Promote environmentally friendly measures through the use of 'good farming practices'; and

■ Encourage products for which there is a market, while discouraging production of those in surplus.

The definition of 'good farming practice' is flexible, but according to the Commission, compensation for the extra cost of environmentally friendly measures will be the usual good farming practice in the area to which the measure applies. Box 10.4 indicates some of the rural development measures eligible for financing.

Tighter conditions are imposed on member states in the administration of rural development schemes. Money not utilized the first year cannot be carried forward. If actual expenditure of a member state is less than 75 per cent of its forecast, in the following years the gap between 75 per cent and actual expenditure is reduced by a third.

Outside Objective 1 regions (i.e. regions whose GDP per capita is less than 75 per cent of the EU average; see Chapter 13), measures for rural development are financed by the FEOGA Guarantee section. In Objective 1 regions the accompanying measures introduced as part of the MacSharry Reform are financed by FEOGA Guarantee. As shown in Table 10.2, other rural development measures are financed by the FEOGA Guidance section, and the European Regional

> ## Box 10.4 Rural development measures
> ■ Improvement of structures of agricultural holdings (which includes encouraging early retirement) and of structures for the processing and marketing of agricultural products;
> ■ The conversion and reorientation of agricultural production potential, and the introduction of new technologies and the improvement of product quality;
> ■ The encouragement of non-food production;
> ■ Sustainable forest development;
> ■ The diversification of activities;
> ■ The raising of local breeds indigenous to an area and in danger of extinction;
> ■ The preservation of plant genetic resources adapted to a region;
> ■ The maintenance and reinforcement of a viable social fabric in rural areas;
> ■ The development of economic activities and the creation of employment;
> ■ The improvement of living and working conditions;
> ■ The maintenance and promotion of low-input farming systems;
> ■ The promotion of a sustainable agriculture safeguarding environmental requirements;
> ■ The promotion of equal opportunities for men and women.

Development Fund. This division of financing between different funds has been criticized at times for rendering the system more rigid and complex.

	FEOGA Guidance		European Fund for Regional Development	
	€ million	% total	€ million	% total
Agriculture	6786	39.1	88	6.3
Forestry	1842	10.6	27	1.9
Promoting the adoption of development of rural areas	8712	50.2	1276	91.8
Of which, outside agriculture and forestry	2588	14.9	664	47.8

Table 10.2 **Allocations for rural development through FEOGA Guidance and the European Regional Development Fund for the 2000-06 period**

Source: European Commission (2004).

THE CAP REFORM OF 2003

The Berlin Agreement envisaged a mid-term review of progress in implementing the 1999 reform. The Commission presented its initial proposals for the review in July 2002, but agreement was only reached on the proposals in June 2003. The debate was often acrimonious, and the final compromise owes much to the personal efforts of the commissioner for agriculture, Franz Fischler, and to the need to present an EU position on agriculture in the WTO negotiations (see Chapter 17). In some circles the package is already being called the Fischler reform (see, for example, De Filippis, 2004). It was also significant that reform was introduced before enlargement, as 25 countries trying to reach an agreement on such fundamental changes would have proved even more difficult.

As part of the October 2002 agreement between France and Germany over the increase in agricultural spending over the 2007–13 period, President Chirac insisted that the mid-term review should be limited to mere revision of policies and should not introduce substantial changes.

However, the Commission rightly called the agreement a 'fundamental reform' of the CAP. Although the initial Commission proposals were watered down, this was far less the case than for the 1992 or 1999 reforms (De Filippis, 2004).

The reform envisages the introduction of a single farm payment to most EU farmers that would be independent (i.e. decoupled) from production. In other words farmers would receive this payment whether they continued to produce or not. In principle this payment would be based on a reference amount of the annual average of what the farmer received during the 2000–02 period. The payment would be linked to respect of environmental, food safety and animal health and welfare standards, and to the requirement to keep all farmland in good agricultural and environmental condition (cross-compliance). Failure to respect these objectives would entail reduction of the direct payments to farmers. Member states considering it necessary to reduce the risks of abandonment of production could continue to pay limited per hectare payments for production of certain arable crops, and some premia per head of animal (partial decoupling). The single payments would be introduced from 2005, but if necessary the member states could delay their introduction until 2007.

The aim of the reform is to render the system simpler and more transparent, and to allow market forces again to play a role in influencing what (or whether) farmers decide to produce. The member states have the option of introducing a system of regionalization of the direct payments. Regions would be defined on the basis of homogeneous production conditions, and all farmers in the region would receive the same basic payment per hectare, regardless of what they received or produced during the 2000–02 period. The aim of regionalization is to reduce distortions between the single payments made to farmers, which might arise because of the different choices made in the base period.

The reform strengthens rural development policy (the second pillar of the CAP) with increased EU financing and new measures to promote the environment, quality and animal welfare, and to help farmers to meet EU production standards. EU co-financing of agri-environmental measures has been increased to 85 per cent in Objective 1 regions and 60 per cent elsewhere.

The reform also renders modulation compulsory for the member states. The 2003 reform envisages a reduction in total payments to farmers of 3 per cent in 2005, 4 per cent in 2006 and 5 per cent from 2007. The first €5000 received by a farm are exempt from this reduction. The funds released will be used to improve the environment, ensure the quality and safety of foodstuffs or to protect animal welfare. A reduction of 5 per cent a year in direct aids will release an additional €1.2 billion a year to finance these objectives.

The 2003 package introduces a wide scope for choices to be made by member states in deciding how the reform is to be applied. It is hoped that this additional flexibility will allow the CAP to be better adapted to national and local conditions. The reform also introduces national envelopes that enable the member states to cut total direct aids and use the funds saved for specific objectives. Total direct aids can be cut by up to 10 per cent to finance additional spending on environmental objectives or measures to improve the quality of agricultural products. Alternatively total aids can be cut by 3 per cent to resolve 'particular situations' and allow certain categories of farmers also to receive single payments.

A mechanism for financial discipline is to be introduced to ensure that during the period 2007–13 the agricultural budget is not overshot. Excessive spending is to induce an automatic reduction in total spending on direct payments. Measures to stabilise markets and improve common market organizations are also to be introduced. The intervention price for butter was to be reduced by 25 per cent, which is 10 per cent more than the reduction envisaged by the Berlin Agreement. There were also revisions in the cereals,[28] durum wheat, rice, nuts and dry fodder sectors. In April

---

[28] Though the current intervention for cereals was to be maintained, monthly increments were to be cut by a half.

2004 further reforms followed for cotton, olive oil, tobacco and hops. For these sectors the reforms also entailed partially decoupled direct aids.

The 2003 reform of the CAP was an important landmark in enabling WTO negotiations on the liberalization of international agricultural trade to proceed (see Chapter 17). Under the traditional CAP price system, the amount of support a farmer received was directly linked to the level of production. The price system encouraged excess production with, part of the surpluses being sold on world markets with the aid of export subsidies. Types of support that were 'coupled' or directly linked to production were considered particularly insidious to world trade, so one of the main aims of the WTO has been to encourage 'decoupled' forms of support.

THE OUTLOOK FOR FOOD AND AGRICULTURE IN THE EU[29]

Since the mid-1980s the CAP has changed fundamentally. One of the first indications of this change was the 1985 Green Paper published by the EC Commission. This document called for an end to the almost exclusive reliance on price support and listed among the priorities of the CAP: the reduction of surpluses, the promotion of the quality and variety of agricultural production, rural development and environmental objectives.

After a rather limited attempt to move the CAP in this direction with a package of reforms in 1988, radical changes followed with the 1992 MacSharry Reform, the 1999 Berlin Agreement and the mid-term review of the CAP of June 2003. By 2002 market support had shrunk to only 28 per cent of CAP spending (see also Figure 10.8), rural development had become the second pillar of the CAP and the 'multifunctionality' of farmers was recognized as a central tenet of EU policy.

Four developments influenced (and continue to influence) the pace and shape of CAP reform: the weight of agricultural spending in the Community budget, enlargement, GATT/WTO commit-

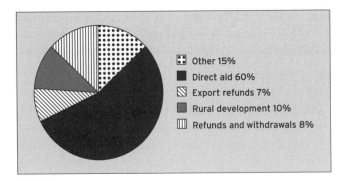

Figure 10.8 Breakdown of CAP expenditure by type (2001)

Source: European Commission.

ments and the concern of the public for safer food and more environmentally favourable agriculture.

In order to finance emerging EU policy areas (and notably the Internal Market and Single Currency Projects, which were accompanied by increased spending on structural actions), the CAP share of the EC budget had to be redimensioned, at least in relative terms. The October 2002 European Council agreed on an annual increase in CAP spending over the 2007–13 period, but the allocation now has to be shared among 25 countries. The net contributors to the Community

[29] The issue of agriculture and EU enlargement is taken up in more detail in Chapter 20.

budget (and Germany in particular) want to reduce the budget ceiling, and as explained in Chapter 9, the Commission has proposed increased spending on new priorities for the next financial perspective.

A solution to this dilemma would be to move further in the direction of co-financing of agricultural policy by the member states, as the largest net contributor to the EU budget (Germany) proposes. The aim is to place higher priority on rural development measures. An attraction of such a solution for the European Commission is that in general Community financing of such measures is only partial. In other words, by strengthening the 'second pillar' of the CAP, national co-financing of the CAP would be increased, and also in this way there would be a partial renationalization of the CAP.

A second factor influencing CAP reform is enlargement.[30] Though the results of empirical studies vary considerably, all the early estimates of how much it would cost to extend the unreformed system of CAP price support to the new member states were substantial.[31] The solution proposed by Nallet and Van Stolk (1994) was to have different levels of administrative prices in East and West Europe. Aside from the dubious political feasibility of such a proposal, it clearly contravened the principles of the Single Market. The switch to direct payments (and the delay before their full application in the new member states, see Chapter 20) was clearly influenced by enlargement.

The third factor influencing reform is the GATT/WTO framework (see Chapter 17). The 1992 MacSharry Reform has to be read against the background of fear of collapse of the Uruguay Round because of disputes on agriculture. The USA was pushing for larger cuts in domestic support and export subsidies, and easier market access than the EU was prepared to grant. When a compromise had to be reached, the EU solution was to transform price support into direct payments, thereby reducing the need for export subsidies. The 1999 Berlin Agreement and the 2003 CAP reform represent further steps in this direction, with the attempt to 'decouple' support from production, thus rendering it more compatible with GATT/WTO commitments.

The fourth factor behind reform is the growing public insistence on increased priority for rural development, environmental objectives and guaranteeing the safety and quality of food. The reform of 2003 to some extent meets these requests by rendering direct payments more conditional on furthering these objectives. After all there is little rationale for indefinite compensation for a once-and-for-all price cut. This 'greening' of the direct payments is likely to increase the chances of their being exonerated from GATT/WTO commitments to reduce domestic support (see Chapter 17).

In a Eurobarometer survey carried out in May–June 2002 on opinions towards the CAP, 90 per cent were in favour of healthier and safer food products, 89 per cent were in favour of environmental measures and 77 per cent in favour of adequate incomes for farmers. However, when asked if they thought the CAP performed those tasks well, the satisfaction levels were 37 per cent, 41 per cent and 29 per cent respectively.[32]

It is unrealistic to expect that a CAP based more on these new priorities will cost less. Health and quality controls involve high administrative costs, in particular when associated with measures such as effective labelling, animal passports and the traceability of all stages of the production and distribution processes. Budgetary constraints are likely to become even tighter in an enlarged EU. The increased emphasis on rural development and environmental measures implies a shift towards measures that already tend to be partially co-financed by national governments. A partial renationalization of the CAP seems difficult to avoid.

---

[30] See Chapter 20 for a more detailed discussion of agriculture and enlargement.
[31] See Tarditi et al. (1989) and Tarditi et al. (1995) for a review of some of these studies.
[32] For the results of the survey see www.europa.eu.int/comm/agriculture.

Summary of Key Concepts

- The scale of public intervention in agriculture can be explained by: the dependence of agricultural production on biological cycles, climate and natural phenomena (including epidemics); low elasticity of demand with respect to price and income; the inelasticity of supply in the short run; the economic and social difficulties many farmers face in leaving the agricultural sector; the need to provide consumers with adequate information and guarantees about the quality and safety of food, and the role farmers may play in protecting the environment, safeguarding the countryside, ensuring animal welfare and promoting rural development.

- The activities of farm lobbies also help to explain the persistence and scale of state support for the farm sector.

- Article 39 of the Treaty of Rome set out the initial objectives of the CAP.

- In 1962 there was agreement on the three fundamental principles of the CAP: unity of markets, Community preference and financial solidarity. There was also agreement on the price support mechanisms.

- Until 1995 variable import levies were applied on imports from the rest of the world, but as a result of the 1994 GATT Uruguay Round most variable import levies were replaced with tariffs.

- Export refunds (also called restitutions) cover the gap between domestic EU prices and prices on world markets.

- The failure of the 1968 Mansholt Plan meant that for many years structural measures played a very limited role in the EC.

- During the 1970s and 1980s, high and stable EC agricultural prices encouraged production leading to surpluses. The CAP weighed excessively on the Community budget, caused tensions with other agricultural exporters, failed to improve the relative income situation of small farmers and encouraged intensive farming methods that had a negative impact on the environment.

- Early attempts at CAP reform included co-responsibility levies, milk quotas and stabilizers. The 1988 reform package introduced accompanying measures, which included incentives for early retirement, more extensive production methods, reforestation and set-aside.

- The 1992 MacSharry Reform and the 1999 Berlin Agreement on Agenda 2000 cut prices for certain key products and compensated farmers by the introduction of direct payments. The MacSharry Reform also introduced measures for early retirement, reforestation and protection of the environment.

- With the Berlin Agreement rural development policy became the second pillar of the CAP.

- Since the late 1990s EU agricultural policy has increasingly been based on the concepts of multifunctionality and the 'European model of agriculture'.

- With the CAP reform of 2003 the EU aimed at partially 'decoupling' support from production.

Questions for Study and Review

- Why has the CAP always played such a central role in the European Community?
- What are the main defects of a price support policy?
- Why did structural policy play such a minor role in the EC for so long?
- What were the objectives of the CAP set out in the Treaty of Rome, and to what extent have they been realized? How have the objectives of the CAP changed over time?
- Why has the CAP proved so resistant to reform over the years?
- Describe the early attempts to reform the CAP.
- The 1992 MacSharry Reform, the Berlin Agreement and the 2003 CAP reform changed the mechanisms used by the CAP. Describe the fundamental aspects of these reforms.

■ What does a rural development policy involve?
■ What are the advantages and disadvantages of 'decoupling' support from production?
■ Describe the main sources of pressure for further refom of the CAP.
■ Exercise on the introduction of an export subsidy in a large nation (see Appendix for an example of how to carry out the exercise). Assume that in conditions of free trade with a world price Pw of 100 euros per tonne for a product, the quantity of that product demanded Qd by a country is 1500 t and the quantity supplied Qs is 2500 t. Assume that the price elasticity of demand for the product in that country is -0.4, and the price elasticity of supply is 0.3. The country then introduces an export subsidy of 20 euro/tonne which causes a change in world prices (i.e. the terms of trade of that country) of 3 euros/t. Calculate the effects of introducing the export subsidy on consumer expenditure, producer revenue, the trade balance and the total welfare of the country.

Appendix
A numerical example of the effects of an export subsidy

A partial equilibrium approach similar to that adopted in Chapter 4 for tariffs can be used to analyse the effects of introducing an export subsidy. For simplicity it is assumed that the country in question is a small nation, and the usual assumptions are made with regard to linear demand and supply curves, and no stocks or externalities.

In conditions of free trade it is assumed that the world price Pw is 100 euros per tonne, and the initial quantity supplied by the country Qs is 2000 tonnes, while the quantity domanded is 1000 tonnes. The price elasticity of demand Ed is −0.5 and the price elasticity of supply is Es 1.0. An export subsidy of 20 euros per tonne is then introduced, and competition between exporters will cause the price on the domestic market to rise from 100 to 120, which is the new domestic price Pd both for producers and consumers.

The formula for supply elasticity can be used to calculate the new quantity supplied, Q′s, by the country in question after introduction of the export subsidy:

$$ Es = \dfrac{\dfrac{\Delta Qs}{Qs}}{\dfrac{\Delta P}{P}} $$

$$ \dfrac{\Delta Qs}{Qs} = Es \, \dfrac{\Delta P}{P} $$

$$ \begin{aligned} \Delta P &= 20 \\ P &= 100 \\ Es &= 1.0 \\ Qs &= 2000 \end{aligned} $$

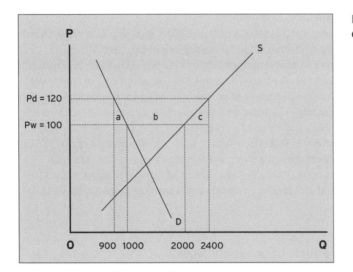

$$\Delta \text{Qs} = 2000 \ (1.0 \times 20/100)$$
$$= 400$$
$$\text{Q's} = 2000 + 400 = 2400$$

The formula for price elasticity of demand can also be used to calculate the new quantity demanded, Qd, after introduction of the export subsidy (see Figure A10.1):

$$\text{Ed} = \dfrac{\dfrac{\Delta \text{Qd}}{\text{Qd}}}{\dfrac{\Delta \text{P}}{\text{P}}}$$

$$\Delta \text{Qd} = \text{Qd} \left(\text{Ed} \dfrac{\Delta \text{P}}{\text{P}} \right) \qquad \Delta \text{Qd} = 1.000 \left(-0.5 \times \dfrac{20}{100} \right) = -10$$
$$\text{Q'd} = 1000 - 100 = 900t$$

Foreign trade without the export subsidy (i.e. net exports) is given by:

$$\text{Qs} - \text{Qd} = 2000 - 1000 = 1000 \text{ t}$$

With the export subsidy it becomes:

$$\text{Q's} - \text{Q'd} = 2400 - 900 = 500$$

Before introduction of the export subsidy producer revenue is:

$$\text{Qs(Pw)} = 2000(100) = 200\,000$$

With the export subsidy it becomes:

$$Q's(Pd) = 2400(120) = 288\,000$$

Before the introduction of the export subsidy consumer expenditure is:

$$Qd(Pw) = 1000(100) = 100\,000$$

After the introduction of the export subsidy it becomes:

$$Q'd\,(Pd) = 900(120) = 108\,000$$

Before the introduction of the export subsidy the trade balance is:

$$(Qs - Qd)Pw = 100\,000$$

With the export subsidy it becomes:

$$(Q's - Q'd)\,Pw = (2400 - 900)100 = 50\,000$$

N.B.: It is the world price that is used to calculate the trade balance, but the domestic price used to calculate producer revenue and consumer expenditure.

The loss in consumer surplus is given by:

$$-0.5\,(Pd - Pw)\,(Qd + Q'd) = -0.5(20(1000 + 900) = -19\,000$$

The increase in producer surplus is given by:

$$0.5\,(Pd - Pw)\,(Qs + Q's) = 0.5\,(20(2000 + 2400)) = +44\,000$$

The impact on the government budget (or the income of taxpayers) is the rectangle comprised of areas a, b and c:

$$-(Pd - P'w)(Q's - Q'd) = -20(2400 - 900) = -30\,000$$

The total effect of introducing the export subsidy on welfare is given by:
loss in consumer surplus, plus the increase in producer surplus and the increase in government revenue:

$$-19\,000 + 44\,000 - 30\,000 = -5000$$

Alternatively, the effect of introducing the export subsidy on total welfare can be calculated using the net welfare effects:
Triangle a is the net loss of welfare on the consumer side:

$$
\begin{aligned}
&= -0.5\,(Pd - Pw)\,(Qd - Q'd) \\
&= -0.5(120 - 100)(1000 - 900) \\
&= -1000
\end{aligned}
$$

Triangle c is the net loss of welfare on the production side (reflecting the worsening in the allocation of resources):

$$
\begin{aligned}
&= -0.5\,(Pd - Pw)\,(Q's - Qs) \\
&= -0.5(20(2400 - 2000) \\
&= -4000
\end{aligned}
$$

The total effect on welfare is:

$$-1000 - 4000 = -5000$$

In the case of a fall in world prices (because net exports from the country in question increase following introduction of the export subsidy) there will be a transfer from producers in that country to consumers in the rest of the world, causing a negative effect on total welfare of the country in question. In the case of a rise in world prices (because net exports from the country decrease after elimination of the export subsidy) there will be a transfer from consumers in the rest of the world to producers in that country, causing a positive effect on net welfare of the country in question.

References

Buckwell, A. et al. (1997) 'Towards a common agricultural and rural policy for Europe', *European Economy Reports and Studies,* No. 5.

Burrell, A. (1989) *Milk Quotas in the European Community*, CAB International, Wallingford.

Colman, D. (2001) 'The Common Agricultural policy', in Artis, M. and Nixson, F. (eds), *The Economics of the European Union. Policy and Analysis*, 3rd edn, Oxford University Press, Oxford.

De Filippis, F. (2004) *Verso la nuova PAC. La riforma del giugno 2003 e la sua applicazione in Italia,* Quaderni del Forum Internazionale dell'agricoltura e dell'Alimentazione, Edizioni Tellus, Rome.

EC Commission (1968) 'Memorandum sur la réforme de l'agriculture dans la Communauté Economique Européenne', COM(68)1000.

EC Commission (1985) 'Perspectives for the Common Agricultural Policy', COM(85)333.

EC Commission (1991) 'The development and future of the CAP: Reflections paper of the Commission', COM(91)100.

EC Commission (1997) *Agenda 2000, COM (97) 2000 final,* 15 July 1997, Supplement to the *Bulletin of the European Union*, May 1997.

EC Commission, various years, 'The agricultural situation in the European Union'.

European Commission (2004) 'Third report on economic and social cohesion'.

Fanfani, R. (1998) *Lo Sviluppo della politica agricola comunitaria,* 2nd edn, Carocci, Roma.

Fennel, R. (1997) *The Common Agricultural Policy: Continuity and Change*, Oxford University Press, Oxford.

Johnson, G.L. and Quance, C.L. (1972*) The Overproduction Trap in US Agriculture,* Johns Hopkins University Press, Baltimore.

Nallet, H. and van Stolk, A. (1994) 'Relations between the European Union and the Central and Eastern European countries in matters concerning agricultural and food production', Report to the European Commission, Brussels.

Nerlove, M. (1956) 'Estimates of the elasticities of supply of selected agricultural commodities', *Journal of Farm Economics,* No. 2.

Senior Nello, S.M. (1984) 'An application of public choice theory to the question of CAP reform', *European Review of Agricultural Economics*, Vol. 11, pp. 261–83.

Senior Nello, S.M. (1985) 'Reform of the EC agrimonetary system: A public choice approach', *Journal of European Integration*, Vol. IX, pp. 55–79.

Senior Nello, S.M. (1986) Un'analisi della riforma della politica agricola comune, in *La politica economica del settore agricolo. Atti del XXIII convegni di studi della SIDEA,* Il Mulino, Bologna, pp. 81–112.

Senior Nello, S.M. (1989). 'European interest groups and the CAP', *Food Policy,* No. 2, May, pp. 101–6.

Senior Nello, S.M. (1997) 'Applying the new political economy approach to explain agricultural policy formation in the European Union', EUI Working Paper, RSC No. 97/21, Robert Schuman Centre, European University Institute, Florence, p. 46.

Tarditi S. et al. (1989) *Agricultural Trade Liberalisation and the European Community,* Oxford University Press, Oxford.

Tarditi, S., Marsh, J. and Senior Nello, S.M. (1995) *Agricultural Strategies for the Enlargement of the European Union to Central and Eastern Europe*, Study prepared for DG-1 of the Commission, Siena.

Tracy, M. (1989) *Government and Agriculture in Western Europe 1880-1988*, Harvester Wheatsheaf, London.

Tracy, M. (1993) *Food and Agriculture in a Market Economy. An Introduction to Theory, Practice and Policy*, Agricultural Policy Studies, Genappe, Belgium.

Useful websites

The European Commission presents explanations of the functioning of the CAP, statistics, key documents on CAP reform, and news of recent developments:
www.europa.eu.int/comm/agriculture
The Food and Agriculture Organization publishes statistics and reports:
www.fao.org
The Organization for Economic Co-operation and Development provides data and analysis:
www.oecd.org
The World Trade Organization presents statistics and information on the Doha Round:
http://www.wto.org

List of abbreviations

AGEA	Agenzia per le Erogazioni in Agricoltura
AIMA	Azienda Italiana per i Mercati Agricoli
BSE	bovine spongiform encephalopathy
CAP	Common Agricultural Policy
COPA	Comité des Organizations des Producteurs Agricoles
CJDv	Creutzfeldt-Jakob variant
ECU	European currency unit
FEOGA	European Agricultural Guidance and Guarantee Fund
GATT	General Agreement on Tariffs and Trade
MGQ	maximum guaranteed quantity
WTO	World Trade Organization

11

Fisheries Policy

LEARNING OBJECTIVES

By the end of this chapter you should be able to understand:

▶ The difficulties in establishing the Common Fisheries Policy (CFP);

▶ The main instruments adopted by the CFP;

▶ The economic basis for public intervention in fisheries,

▶ The main criticisms of the CFP;

▶ The principal aspects of the 2003 reform of the CFP and the shortcomings of that reform.

INTRODUCTION: THE HISTORICAL EVOLUTION OF THE COMMON FISHERIES POLICY

The legal basis of the Common Fisheries Policy (CFP) in the treaties is the same as that of the CAP. Article 38 of the Treaty of Rome (now Article 32 of the EC Treaty) referred to a common market extending also to products of fisheries and 'of first stage processing relating to those products'. The CFP therefore also shares the objectives of the CAP, but over the years there has been increased emphasis on conservation of stock and (as in the case of the CAP) the need to take account of environmental considerations. These additional objectives were defined in Council Regulation 3760/92 which calls for 'rational and responsible exploitation of living aquatic resources and of aquaculture, while recognizing the interests of the fisheries sector in its long-term development and its economic and social conditions, and the interests of consumers taking into account the biological constraints with due respect for the marine ecosystem'.

Differences between the member states meant that the CFP was not set up until 1970, and only became fully operative from 1983. In 1970 two regulations established free and equal access to all EC fishing grounds for all EC fishermen subject to certain exceptions for sensitive coastal waters. Market support and structural measures were also introduced.

The 1973 enlargement substantially increased EC waters. The UK, Denmark and Ireland claimed that the EC principle of equal access conflicted with domestic preference and managed to obtain certain special reserved areas (6- to 12-mile zones) until 1983. In 1975 the UN Conference on the Law of the Sea failed to reach agreement on fishing rights, and subsequently various countries (including the Community) declared 200-mile zones reserved for exclusive fishing.

There were protracted negotiations over the CFP, with conflicts among EC countries over allowable catches, their allocation between the member states and access to coastal waters. The revised CFP was finally introduced in 1983 and was a 20-year agreement lasting until 2002. The instruments envisaged by the agreement were:

- **Access arrangements** that provide for national zones of up to 12 miles (19 kilometres) for member states with limited access for other EC countries, and a 200-mile exclusive Community zone. Agreements for reciprocal fishing and trade were signed with third countries including various developing countries, Norway (involving sharing of fish stocks) and Canada (reducing duties on fish imports). The EU participates in various international fisheries conventions and organizations and in international attempts to limit illegal fishing.

- **Quotas or total allowable catches (TACs)** were established for each member state for about a hundred fish species. TAC limits were (at least in theory) based on scientific evidence concerning fish stocks and then divided among member states according to the principle of 'relative stability' which takes into account the size of the fishing fleet in each country and the needs of specific fishing regions. According to the so-called Hague preferences emphasis is placed on maintaining traditional fishing methods and on assisting regions heavily dependent on fishing.[1] Technical conservation measures, including minimum size for certain types of fish, mesh sizes and so on, were used to reduce catches of young fish and ensure that stocks were renewed. Each member state was responsible for ensuring adherence to the CFP in its waters and was required to declare its catch and throw 'black landings' back into the sea. The Commission set up a small supervision unit (of 25 inspectors) to ensure enforcement of the CFP by the member states.

- **Market support measures** were introduced which entailed some support buying to maintain fish prices and stabilize incomes. However, the EU imports about 60 per cent of its fish requirements and tariffs were mainly used to maintain prices. The cost to the Community budget was therefore relatively limited compared with that of the CAP. According to the European Commission (2002), roughly €1.1 billion from the EU and national budgets was allocated to the EU(15) fisheries industry each year. This is quite high relative to the total value of EU(15) production each year of €7 billion for fish landings and €2 billion for aquaculture (fish farming). It is proposed to increase spending on the CFP from the EU budget from €0.9 billion in 2006 to €1.1 billion in 2013.

- **Structural policies** were introduced to reduce overcapacity, restructure the fishing industry and increase competitiveness. From 1983 Multi-Annual Guidance Plans (MAGPs) set the conditions for development of each country's fleet in terms of 'fishing capacity' (i.e. vessel tonnage and engine capacity). The aim was to manage the 'fishing effort', or maintain a balance between fishing capacity and the conservation of fish stocks. In 1993 the Financial Instrument for Fisheries Guidance (FIFG) was established to provide financial support for structural measures including investment in vessels, port facilities, aquaculture, and processing and marketing.

---

[1] The term 'Hague preferences' refers to the 1976 Foreign Affairs Council in The Hague which formulated the approach.

The evolution of the CFP was shaped by the withdrawal of Greenland from the EC in 1985 and by the Mediterranean enlargement. The accession of Spain and Portugal to the Community doubled the number of fishermen and added 50 per cent to the size of the Community fleet. In principle these countries were granted mutual access; however, temporary limits were introduced on allowable catches and access to the waters of certain other member states.

The Mediterranean continental shelf is narrow and this influences the form of fisheries there. Most fishing is in the coastal band and involves a large number of small vessels. In addition, highly migratory species such as tuna are found offshore. TACs for blue fin tuna were introduced from December 1997. Most of the Mediterranean has been declared 'high sea', so the 200-mile limit was not applied.

Of the new member states joining in 2004, only Poland and the Baltic states had substantial fishing sectors, but the combined fishing catch of these four countries only amounts to 7 per cent of the total EU catch.[2] As all the states bordering the Baltic except Russia are in the EU, the International Baltic Sea Fisheries Commission (IBSFC) is to be abolished and the European Commission is working with the sector on a review of the technical measures to ensure conservation and management of fisheries for the Baltic Sea.[3]

THE ECONOMIC ANALYSIS OF FISHERIES

Public intervention to control fisheries is generally justified on the grounds that the sea and the fish stock can be regarded as an example of common property. Analysis of the 'tragedy of the commons' owes much to the seminal work by Hardin (1968). The term 'common' traditionally refers to a field in an English village whose use by the villagers is free and unrestricted. If the common were privately owned, animals would be grazed on the field until their marginal product equaled their cost. However, the marginal product of each animal will decline as the number of animals grazed on the field increases. If there is free access to the common, each villager will fail to take into account the fact that grazing his animal on the common will reduce the output of other animals grazed there (i.e. the social cost is ignored), and the common will be overused.

A simple framework can be used to show the divergence between private marginal cost and marginal social cost in the case of fisheries. Figure 11.1 illustrates the conventional demand curve D and the supply curve S of the EU member states for fish. Marginal social cost (as shown by the supply curve Ss in the diagram) is above private marginal cost, reflecting negative externalities. The equilibrium taking account of externalities occurs at Es with price Ps and quantity Qs. If only private marginal costs are taken into account, the market equilibrium is E and QpQs represents the quantity of over-fishing. If one country attempts unilaterally to regulate supply and limit fishing, other EU member states will simply fish more to meet demand. A common policy is therefore needed to prevent over-fishing and reach the social equilibrium Es.

If, however, the common policy provides subsidies to fishermen, price support and financial incentives to renew and improve the fleet and fisheries infrastructure, it will reduce costs, stimulate investment and encourage a situation of over-capacity.

Figure 11.2 shows how the problem of commons can be applied to the choice of size of the fishing fleet. Assume that the number of fish caught increases with the number of fishing boats, but less than proportionately, so the number of fish caught by each boat decreases as the number of

---

[2] European Commission (2004a).
[3] European Commission (2004b). The IBSFC was composed of the EU, the three Baltic states, Poland and Russia, and set basic rules for the conservation and management of fisheries in the Baltic Sea. This included fixing total allowable catches for four species – cod, salmon, herring and sprat – and allocating them among members.

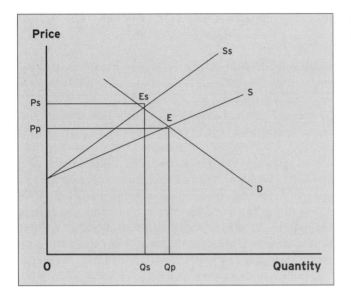

Figure 11.1 The economic analysis of fisheries

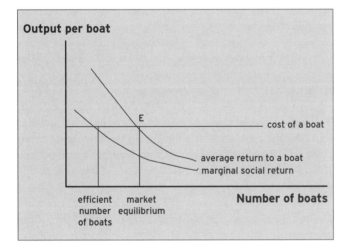

Figure 11.2 The problem of commons
Source: Stiglitz (2000)

boats increases. The marginal social benefit is therefore less than the marginal private benefit since some of the fish caught by an additional boat would have been caught by other boats. In deciding whether to buy a boat a fisherman will consider private marginal benefit, or average return, but as shown in Figure 11.2 this is greater than marginal social benefit, so market equilibrium E leads to an excess number of boats.

CRITICISMS OF THE COMMON FISHERIES POLICY

According to the 1983 agreement, some elements of the CFP were subject to review before the end of 2002. The Commission used this opportunity to launch an extensive debate on the whole of the Common Fisheries Policy. In 2002 a Green Paper was published setting out objectives for a revised policy.[4] The new EU fisheries policy came into operation from January 2003, but during

---

[4] European Commission (2001).

wide-ranging discussions leading to its adoption various criticisms of the CFP were voiced. According to the Green Paper of the Commission, these shortcomings can be expressed in conservation, economic and political terms.

With regard to **conservation**, many stocks of fish are outside safe biological levels. Some 67 per cent of stocks for which assessments are available were considered 'over-fished', while 40 per cent were 'depleted'.[5] According to the Green Paper, many stocks would collapse if trends were not changed. Over-capacity of the EU fleet and poor enforcement of decisions contributed to this situation, while the Council of Ministers systematically fixed quotas at levels higher than indicated by scientific advice.

In **economic terms**, the EU fisheries sector was characterized by falling employment, rising costs and reduced productivity. Improved technology led to increased efficiency, but the EU also worsened the problems of over-capacity and over-exploitation. Subsidies to investment and certain taxation measures (such as tax-free fuel) artificially reduced the costs and risks of investment in an over-capitalized industry.[6] Each newly subsidized vessel reduced the productivity and profitability of existing operators. It is also difficult to understand the economic rationale for maintaining price support in a situation of over-capacity. There may be a justification for maintaining incomes or employment on social or regional grounds, but price support in a declining sector is hardly the most appropriate instrument.

Politically the CFP has been criticized for shortcomings in enforcement and compliance, and insufficient involvement of stakeholders. Member states were largely responsible for ensuring application of the CFP in their waters, and the stringency of monitoring and sanctions varies considerably among countries. Even when a member state was found not to be respecting its obligations, there was a significant time lag before legal action was taken (Valatin, 2001). For instance, the Court of Justice ruled against the UK in 1999 for infringements in 1985–88 and 1990 on the grounds of failure to carry out inspections and close fisheries once the catch quota had been taken. The court simply declared that the UK had failed to respect its commitments and was required to pay court costs. Again in 2002 the court dealt with UK infringements relating to the 1985–96 period. There were too few EU inspectors and they had no legal powers to enforce legislation. Proposals to increase the authority and size of the EU supervision unit were generally rejected by the Council of Ministers.

Political discontent with the CFP also arose from criticism of the allocation of quotas among member states and, in particular, from the practice of 'quota-hopping'. Taking advantage of the EU right to freedom of establishment, many vessel operators were able to purchase or reregister vessels and thereby acquire fishing rights in another member state. It is estimated that Spanish companies managed to acquire fishing rights over 100 UK, 28 Irish and 25 French vessels, while Dutch companies accounted for 30 UK, 33 German, 11 Belgian, 1 French and 1 Danish vessel (Hoefnagel, 1998). The Multi-Annual Guidance Plans aimed at controlling the evolution of the fleet were complicated and difficult to administer. According to the Netherlands, respect for MAGP targets would have jeopardized its ability to use the Dutch TAC fully.[7]

Fishing generally accounts for less than 1 per cent of GDP in the member states, and employed about 260 000 fishermen in the EU(15) in 1995, with a further 1.5 million in associated industries.[8] However, in certain regions, such as the Atlantic coast of Spain and the east coast of Italy and of Scotland, fishing accounts for about 10 per cent of employment. The fishing industry would have declined even without the CFP in many of those regions, but in some areas, notably the

---

[5] European Commission (2000).
[6] European Commission (2001).
[7] As reported in Valatin (2001).
[8] The data in this paragraph are taken from European Commission (1998).

British ports, EU measures were blamed (in particular the policy of allowing access to fishermen from other countries, quotas, limits on days at sea, and the uneven application of rules), and there were calls for an opt-out of the CFP.

THE 2002 REFORM OF THE COMMON FISHERIES POLICY

In May 2002 proposals were presented for reform of the CFP and were subject to an intense lobbying activity. An informal grouping, 'Les Amis de la Pêche', was formed between France, Italy, Portugal, Spain, Greece and Ireland. Spain has the largest share in the EU fishing fleet, and the then president of the Council, Asnar, contacted Prodi about the proposals, while the vice-president of the Commission, Loyola de Palacio, protested to the commissioner responsible for fisheries, Fischler.

The reform of the CFP was finally agreed in December 2002 and introduced from January 2003. The reform aimed at addressing some of the shortcomings of EU measures, and its main elements included:[9]

■ **A long-term approach.** The annual fixation of TACs and related measures had prevented fishermen planning ahead and failed to ensure the conservation of stocks. With the reform two types of multi-annual plans were to be introduced: recovery plans to help rebuild stocks in danger of collapse, and management plans to help maintain other stocks at safe biological levels. Targets would be set on the basis of consultation with the interested parties, and progress assessed against these targets. The targets may be expressed in terms of the minimum weight of adult fish to be reached and maintained in a given stock. The various instruments on fishing possibilities, gear specifications and access would be co-ordinated to meet these targets. There would be tighter regulatory measures to reduce catches of younger fish, by-catches in mixed fisheries and discards. On the basis of these longer-term objectives catch limits in the form of TACs would continue to be set each year.

■ **A new policy for the fleet** places responsibility for matching capacity and fishing possibilities (or managing the 'fishing effort') with the member states, replacing the MAGPs. Public aid to renew or modernize fishing vessels was to be phased out, though assistance to improve safety and working conditions on board, and to ensure hygiene and the quality of fish products would continue. An entry-exit system would be established whereby the introduction of new fishing capacity without aid will have to be compensated by the withdrawal of at least as much capacity. Aid would be given for the decommissioning of vessels and retraining of fishermen.

■ **Better application of the rules** was to be ensured by increased co-operation between national enforcement authorities and with the Commission. There was to be greater uniformity of controls and sanctions, with an agreed list of the most serious infringements. A compliance scoreboard showing the enforcement record of the member states was to be introduced. The powers of the Commission to monitor the enforcement activities of the member states was strengthened, and the use of a satellite vessel monitoring system was extended. A European Fisheries Control Agency with powers of inspection and surveillance of fishing activities was to be set up in Spain.

■ **Stakeholders' involvement was to be increased** through greater involvement of fishermen in the management of the CFP. In order to ensure more effective conservation

---

[9] European Commission (2003).

of stocks seven Regional Advisory Councils (RACs) were to be set up to allow fishermen, scientists and other stakeholders to work together at the regional or local level. RACs were to cover areas under the responsibility of at least two member states, and to co-operate with the Commission and member states in the planning and implementation of CFP measures.

The main provider of information on marine biology to the EU, the International Council for the Exploration of the Seas (ICES), and the Scientific, Technical, Economic Committee on Fisheries (STECF) had warned the European Commission of the risk of a complete collapse in cod stocks with no eventual recovery (as occurred for cod on Canada's Grand Banks off Newfoundland) and recommended a total ban on cod fishing. The Council of Ministers agreed a multi-annual recovery plan for cod, hake and plaice, which entailed lower annual catches, new restrictions on days at sea and tighter policing. The initial Commission proposal for 2003 entailed a reduction of 80 per cent in cod fishing mortality, but the final Council agreement entailed a cut in allowable catches of only 45 per cent.

An EU strategy has been adopted to strengthen the role of aquaculture in ways that limit damage to the environment and ensure safe and good quality products. The aim is to create between 8000 and 10 000 jobs over the 2003–08 period.

The principle of equal access will continue to be applied, subject to certain exceptions, including the restrictions on 6–12-mile coastal zones of member states. The reform of the CFP aims at additional measures to ensure the sustainability of fishing in the Mediterranean area by developing a multilateral management system for Mediterranean fish resources, improving controls and tightening measures to combat illegal fishing. A new trans-Mediterranean association of fisheries organizations (Medismak) is to be created. New 'partnership agreements' are also to be signed with third countries to 'contribute to responsible fishing in the interests of all concerned'.

The 2002 reform of the CFP certainly represents a step in the right direction, but many question marks remain as to how far it will prove successful in practice. Even the substantial reduction in quotas and limitations on days at sea seem too little and too late to ensure conservation of certain fish stocks. A year after the reform, the ICES maintained that demersal fish (including cod and haddock) were at a historical low and recommended closing more fisheries. Over-capacity of the EU fleet has to be corrected, but this requires an integrated approach to the fishing-dependent regions of the EU, with active measures to reduce capacity and encourage employment in alternative occupations.

Effective monitoring and control is necessary to prevent over-fishing, but 'co-operation between national authorities', scoreboards and limited increases in EU surveillance seem rather weak instruments to resolve this question. Evidence suggests that even after the reform, quotas were not being respected and unreliable data on catches and discards were being supplied.[10]

Past experience illustrates the difficulties an enlarged EU is likely to encounter in agreeing effective measures with third countries to combat the depletion of fish stocks at a global level. Encouraging the development of aquaculture seems a promising development, but far more attention will have to be paid to the environmental implications. Even after the 2002 reform it seems likely that further efforts to improve the transparency, conservation, compliance and performance of the CFP will prove necessary.

Summary of Key Concepts

● Differences between the member states meant that the Common Fisheries Policy was not set up until 1970, and only became fully operative from 1983.

---

[10] Speech by Franz Fischler to the European Parliament's Committee on Fisheries, Brussels, 24 November 2003, www.europa.eu.comm/fisheries.

- The instruments of the CFP agreed in 1983 were: access arrangements, quotas or total allowable catches (TACs), market support measures and structural policies.
- In 1993 the Financial Instrument for Fisheries Guidance (FIFG) was established to provide financial support for structural measures, including investment in vessels, port facilities, aquaculture and processing and marketing.
- Successive enlargements of the EU have shaped the evolution of the CFP.
- Public intervention to control fisheries is generally justified on the grounds that the sea and the fish stock can be regarded as an example of common property.
- The CFP has been criticized as insufficient to guarantee conservation since many stocks of fish are outside safe biological levels. In economic terms, the EU fisheries sector is characterized by over-capacity, low productivity and falling employment. Politically the CFP has experienced shortcomings in enforcement and compliance, and insufficient involvement of stakeholders.
- The 2002 Reform of the Common Fisheries Policy involved: a long-term approach to ensure the conservation of stocks, a new policy for the fleet to reduce over-capacity, better application of the rules and increased involvement of shareholders.

Questions for Study and Review

■ **How has the Common Fisheries Policy evolved over the years?**
■ **What do we mean by the problem of 'commons', and how does it apply to fisheries?**
■ **What measures should be taken to ensure conservation of fish stocks?**
■ **What are the advantages and disadvantages of developing aquaculture?**

References

European Commission (1998) 'Factsheets: Introduction to the Common Fisheries Policy', www.europa.eu.int/comm/fisheries

European Commission (2000) 'Preparation for a mid-term review of the Multi-annual Guidance Programmes (MAGP)'. Report from the Commission to the Council, COM (2000)272 final.

European Commission (2001) 'Green Paper on the future of the Common Fisheries Policy', www.europa.eu.int/comm/fisheries

European Commission (2002) 'Communication from the Commission on the reform of the Common Fisheries Policy', www.europa.eu.int/comm/fisheries

European Commission (2003) 'The new Common Fisheries Policy', www.europa.eu.int/comm/fisheries

European Commission (2004a) 'Third Report on Economic and Social Cohesion'.

European Commission (2004b) 'European Fisheries and Enlargement', www.europa.eu.int/comm/fisheries

Hardin, G. (1968) 'The tragedy of the commons', *Science*, Vol. 162, pp. 1243-7.

Hoefnagel, E. (1998) 'Legal but controversial: Quota-hopping, the CFP and the Treaty of Rome', in Symes, D. (ed.) *Property Rights and Regulatory Systems in Fisheries*, Fishing News Books, Oxford.

Stiglitz, J.E. (2000) *Economics of the Public Sector*, 3rd edn, W.W. Norton & Co., London and New York.

Valatin, G. (2001) 'Solving the "tragedy" of the Common Fisheries Policy: What role for economic instruments?' Paper presented at the XIIIth Annual Conference of the European Association of Fisheries Economists, Salerno, Italy, 18-20 April.

Useful websites

The European Commission provides background information and documents relating to the key aspects of reform:
www.europa.eu.int/comm/fisheries

The European Parliament presents a good but rather dated description of the CFP:
www.europarl.eu.int/factsheets
The UK Department of the Environment, Food and Rural Affairs:
www.defra.gov.uk
The International Council for Exploration of the Sea:
www.ices.dk
The World Wildlife Fund:
www.wwf.org

List of abbreviations

CAP	Common Agricultural Policy
CFP	Common Fisheries Policy
FIFG	Financial Instrument for Fisheries Guidance
IBSFC	International Baltic Sea Fisheries Commission
ICES	International Council for Exploration of the Seas
MAGP	Multi-Annual Guidance Plan
Medismak	Mediterranean Association of Fisheries Organizations
RAC	Regional Advisory Council
STEFC	Scientific, Technical, Economic Committee on Fisheries
TAC	total allowable catches

12

Environmental and Energy Policies

LEARNING OBJECTIVES

By the end of this chapter you should be able to understand:

▶ The difficulties encountered in introducing a common EU environmental policy;

▶ The main instruments used in environmental policy;

▶ How EU measures have evolved over the years;

▶ The five principles of EU environmental policy;

▶ The role of the European Environmental Agency;

▶ The international dimension of EU policy, in particular with regard to the Kyoto Protocol;

▶ The main elements of EU energy policy.

INTRODUCTION

After a slow start, since the early 1970s the EU has developed a wide range of environmental policies. The evolution of such policies reflects the overall growing concern with the environment and the increased awareness that such questions need to be tackled at an international level.

The main stepping-stones in the development of EU environmental policy include the introduction of six Environmental Action Programmes, successive treaty changes increasing the EU role in environmental issues and the creation of a European Environmental Agency in Copenhagen in 1994. The EU also represents the member states on environmental issues at an international level.

However, the evolution of EU environmental measures has encountered tensions in a number of areas:

■ Differing environmental standards in the EU member states. In general the Scandinavian countries, Germany, Austria and the Netherlands tend to have higher standards than the Mediterranean countries. Disparities are likely to increase with enlargement since many standards in Central and East European countries are lower than in the EU, though these countries are attempting to take on the EU environmental *acquis*.

■ The fuzzy boundary between EU and national policies. The question is rendered even more complex in that many questions (such as the emission of chlorofluorocarbon (CFC) gases) are probably tackled better at a wider international level.

■ Environmental policy may be difficult to implement.

■ Environmental problems show no signs of abating. While in the EU there have been some improvements (such as in reducing emissions which damage the ozone layer), most projections suggest growing levels of waste and energy consumption in the future.[1]

■ It may be difficult to reconcile environmental measures with other EU policies, in particular the Single Market. Differing environmental standards may act as non-tariff barriers, and when trade is liberalized there may be a risk of a 'race to the bottom' towards environmental measures which are less restrictive and cost less to implement.

■ Member states may disagree as to how the financial burden for common environmental measures is to be shared.

INSTRUMENTS OF ENVIRONMENTAL POLICY

In general environmental measures may be divided into three broad categories, though in practice the distinction between these categories is not always absolutely clear:

1. 'Command and control' entails introducing legislation to fix norms and environmental standards that have to be complied with. These may take the form of the prohibition of certain products or substances, or emission standards combined with requirements to use certain types of technology. Strictly the term 'command and control' entails public intervention to fix both the level of pollution and the means of achieving this goal, but in practice the term is often used more widely. The Community relied heavily on 'command and control' in the early years of its environment policy, and an example of the approach was the strict standards for the quality of drinking water introduced in the 1970s and 1980s which included measures relating to the discharge of dangerous substances into rivers and seas.

2. Market-based instruments set standards (in theory on the basis of an analysis of the costs and benefits involved) and offer firms a financial incentive or penalty to encourage them to realize the objectives. These instruments give a firm a choice of how to reduce pollution. Examples of market-based instruments include charges on emissions, on products and on users, environmentally related taxes (see below), subsidies to encourage environmentally friendly production methods (which, as described in Chapter 10, are widely used in the CAP) and tradable permits. Tradable or transferable permits involve the authority issuing a number of permits to pollute on the basis of past records of pollution and allowing firms to trade these permits. Tradable permits are widely used in

---

[1] See 'Europe's environment', paper presented by the European Environment Agency at the Environment for Europe conference, Kiel, 21–23 May 2003 at http://reports.eea.eu.int.

the USA. In the past the EU tended to rely more on environmental taxes and subsidies (in the case of agriculture), but from 2005 a system of tradable emissions is to be introduced.

3. Voluntary agreements (in general between some public authority and private enterprise) may be introduced to encourage environmentally friendly measures. An example of an EU measure of this type is the Environmental Management and Audit Scheme (EMAS).[2] According to this scheme a firm voluntarily chooses to introduce an environmental programme, which is subject to external audit and publication of the results. The firm may gain from increased competitiveness and an improved image with clients, suppliers and public institutions.

Assessment of environmental policy may be carried out on the basis of cost/benefit analysis. This entails a formal comparison of the costs and benefits of a policy (or investment). The assessment may, for example, consist of a formal appraisal of the expenditure involved in adapting to the legislation, an estimate of the risks associated with the pollution addressed and an analysis of how effective the measure is likely to prove in practice. A policy should only be introduced where the expected benefits exceed the costs, and where different policies are being compared, that producing the highest net benefits should be chosen. In assessing the effectiveness of environmental measures, account has not only to be taken of their impact on the environment but also their economic and equity implications.

The Maastricht Treaty requires EU environmental measures to take into account the potential benefits and costs of action or lack of action (Article 130R). Though this has been interpreted as not necessarily requiring a fully fledged cost/benefit analysis before introducing EU measures, some form of assessment is necessary. However, it is only since the early 1990s that the Commission has begun to use cost/benefit analysis in a routine way.[3]

THE ECONOMIC BASIS OF ENVIRONMENTAL POLICY

The economic basis of environmental policy can be explained with the help of Figure 12.1.[4] In the figure there are two horizontal axes. The higher axis indicates the level of output Q of a firm that pollutes. The lower axis shows the level of pollution or waste associated with each level of output. It is assumed that as the level of output Q increases, so too does the level of pollution W. One of the main aims of environmental policy is to 'decouple' negative environmental effects from the level of economic activity.

The vertical axis indicates money units or euros. The line MNPB sloping downwards from A to Qp shows the marginal net private benefit to a firm, or the additional profit on an extra unit of output. As output increases, the marginal net private benefit is assumed to fall, finally reaching zero at Qp. The area under the MNPB line gives total profits, so at Qp the firm maximizes profits. Wp is the level of pollution associated with Qp, the profit-maximizing level of output for the firm.

The pollution causes externalities to third parties. An externality in production occurs when the activity of a firm has an unintended impact on the utility or production function of another individual or firm. The externality may be positive or negative. The diagram here illustrates the situation for negative externalities, such as the impact of the firm polluting water or the air on others. The marginal external cost line MEC shows the additional damage to third parties from

---

[2] Introduced in 1993 with Regulation 1836/93 and updated in 2001 with Regulation 761/2001.
[3] See Pearce (2001) for a discussion of cost/benefit analyses of environmental issues carried out by the European Commission.
[4] The explanation here is based on Pearce (2001).

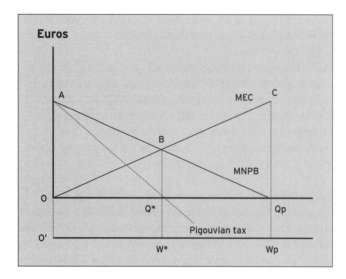

Figure 12.1 The optimum level of pollution

Source: Figure 9.1 (p. 217) from *The Economics of the European Union* 3/e (2003) by Artis, M. and Nixson, F. By permission of Oxford University Press.

each extra unit of pollution. The MEC line slopes up from O to C in the diagram because it is assumed that each extra unit of pollution will cause more damage (though in practice the line may take various shapes). The marginal external cost is also measured in money units, or euros.

The diagram can be used to show the optimum level of pollution from the point of view of society as a whole. If a firm aims at maximizing profits, and fails to take into account the effect of its pollution on others, it will produce at Qp with total profits of OAQp. However, at Qp the total external cost of the pollution on others is OCQp. The overall impact on society (i.e. taking into account the impact on the firm and on those suffering the pollution) will therefore be a net gain of OAB and a cost of BCQp.[5] This is not an optimum, because it fails to maximize the gains to society as a whole.

The optimum level of output is at output Q* with a waste level W*, where the net gain to society OAB is at a maximum. At levels of output below Q*, the net marginal private benefit to the firm is greater than the marginal external cost (the MNPB line is above the MEC line), so the net social gain could be increased by expanding output. At levels of output above Q*, the MEC line is higher then the MNPB line, so the total gain to society could be increased by cutting output. It is important to note that the optimum level of pollution is not zero since society would forgo the gain OAB.

The problem then becomes how to ensure that the firm will produce at level of output Q*, and this can be achieved in various ways:

■ Bargaining can occur between the firm and those suffering from pollution in situations where the firm is given the right to pollute.[6] As long as the marginal external cost to sufferers is greater than the net marginal benefit to the firm (i.e. the MEC line is above the MNPB line), those suffering from pollution will have an incentive to pay the firm to cut back pollution, and the firm will have an incentive to accept those payments. These payments will continue until the marginal external cost equals the marginal net private benefit (i.e. the MEC line intersects the MNPB line), which occurs at level of output Q*. In practice high transaction costs may prevent bargaining between sufferers and the firm reaching the optimal level of pollution. There may also be a tendency for individuals suffering from pollution to 'free ride' and not pay their contribution to stop the firm

[5] From the point of view of society, the benefit of OBQp to the firm and the cost OBQp of pollution on others cancel out.
[6] The classic article by Coase (1960) provides the framework for this type of analysis.

polluting, in particular if the sufferers are numerous. Individual sufferers assume that their non-payment to the firm will not be noticed and that others will bear the cost of inducing the firm to cut production and pollution.

■ In the absence of transaction costs, bargaining between the firm and those suffering from pollution will also lead to the optimum level of output Q* in situations where the firm is obliged to pay compensation for pollution. Starting from a level of output O, the firm will have an incentive to pay compensation to those suffering from pollution as long as the marginal net private benefit of the firm is higher than the marginal external cost (i.e. the MNPB line is above the MEC line), and this is the case up until level of output Q*.

■ The government may prohibit firms from emitting more than a certain level of pollution, or require them to use a particular technology, and impose sanctions (such as fines) on firms failing to comply with the legislation. This type of intervention is usually called 'command and control', though strictly the term entails the government fixing both the level of pollution and the means of achieving this goal as is usually the case in fixing technology requirements. To achieve the optimum level of pollution, the government would fix the level of pollution at W*.

■ The government may require the firm to pay a tax equal to the marginal external cost. This is called a 'Pigouvian tax' after the economist Alfred Pigou who first proposed this type of tax and is shown by the dotted line in Figure 12.1. At each level of output, the MNPB line of the firm is reduced by an amount equal to the MEC.[7] The firm will have an incentive to produce at Q*, because this is the level of output which maximizes output after tax.

In practice it is difficult to calculate the level of a Pigouvian tax, so they are not frequently used. However, other kinds of taxes and subsidies are often used to promote environmental objectives. For example, landfill taxes tax waste going to landfills to encourage more efficient means of waste disposal. These are forms of market-based instruments and offer firms financial incentives or penalties to encourage them to realize the objective.

THE EVOLUTION OF EU ENVIRONMENTAL POLICY

The number and variety of instruments now used in EU environmental policy render their description difficult. However, in recent years there has been a growing tendency to use market-based instruments rather than the strategy of 'command and control'. Such instruments generally involve lower implementation costs than command and control.

There is no mention of a role for the Community in the Treaty of Rome, reflecting the rather low priority given to such questions at the time. Though some environmental measures were implemented at a national level by the member states, it was not until the early 1970s that environmental objectives appear on the Community agenda.

According to Pearce (2001), the 1972 study by the Club of Rome, 'Limits to growth', marks a growing international awareness of environmental questions. This study drew attention to the limits of natural resources and of the Earth to absorb waste. In the same year at the Paris Summit the EC member states called for environmental issues to be included in the Community agenda.

---

[7] In other words, the vertical distance from the horizontal axis to the MEC line is subtracted from the vertical distance from the horizontal axis to the MNPB line.

In 1973 the Community embarked on the first of what are now six Environmental Action Programmes (EAPs). These are indicative programmes, even though many of their guidelines were subsequently translated into Community legislation.

The First Environmental Action Programme (EAP) covered the period 1973–76 and set out the general principles and goals of environmental policy.[8] In order to achieve these objectives the First EAP attempted to increase awareness of environmental problems, conduct impact studies, reduce pollution and improve waste management.

Box 12.1 EU policy towards waste

Each year the EU throws away roughly 1.3 billion tonnes of waste, of which about 40 million tonnes is hazardous.* Each person throws away about 1.2 kg/day in France and 1.3 kg/day in Germany, which is below the US rate of 2 kg/day (Lomborg, 2001). Most of what is thrown away is burnt in incinerators or dumped in landfill sites (67 per cent). Landfilling occupies land space and discharges chemicals such as carbon dioxide and methane into the atmosphere, and chemicals and pesticides into the soil and groundwater. Landfills are becoming so difficult to site that the term 'NIMBY' or 'not in my back yard' has been coined.

The aim of the EU is to reduce the quantity of waste disposed by 20 per cent between 2000 and 2010, and by 50 per cent by 2050. The strategy is based on three principles:

■ **Waste prevention.** This includes improving production techniques and encouraging consumers to use more environmentally friendly goods and less packaging.
■ **Recycling and reuse.** EU Directives require member states to introduce legislation on waste collection, reuse and recycling.
■ **Improving final disposal and monitoring.** Where possible waste should be incinerated, and landfills should only be used as a last resort. The EU has introduced a Directive on landfill management, which bans certain types of waste such as used tyres.

* Unless otherwise stated, the data in this box are taken from www.europa.eu.int/comm/environment/waste

---

The following three Environmental Action Programmes (1977–81, 1982–87 and 1987–92) were mainly concerned with consolidating the aims of the First EAP. Given the limited success of these programmes, the Fifth EAP (1993–2000) reflected a change in approach:

■ The emphasis of environmental policy was to be based more on prevention than correction of the damage;
■ There was to be a shift from the top-down 'command and control' approach based on regulatory legislation to a bottom-up approach based on a wider range of policies, in particular on market-based instruments, and involving a larger number of socio-economic actors.

The Sixth Environmental Action Programme, 'Environment 2010: Our future, our choice', covers the 2001–10 period and aims at using a wide range of instruments to influence decisions made by 'business, consumers, policy-planners and citizens'.[9] This is to be achieved by:

■ Improving the implementation of existing legislation;
■ Integrating environmental concerns into other policies;

---

[8] These included the first four principles subsequently included in the Maastricht Treaty, as described below.
[9] The Sixth Environmental Action Programme, 'Environment 2010: Our future, our choice', http://europa.eu.int/scadplus/leg/en/lvb/l28027.

■ Working closer with the market;
■ Empowering people as private citizens and helping them to change behaviour (see Box 12.2); and
■ Taking account of the environment in land-use planning and management decisions.

The programme identifies four priority areas:

1. Climate change;
2. Nature and biodiversity;
3. Environment and health; and
4. Management of natural resources and waste.

It is difficult to imagine a wider agenda, and the European Commission has at times been criticized for being too ambitious in setting objectives.

The first explicit statutory mandate for Community environmental policy came in 1987 with the Single European Act (SEA). The SEA included a new title, 'Environment', and Article 130R sets out its objectives:

1. Preserving, protecting and improving the quality of the environment;
2. Protecting human health;
3. Prudent and rational utilization of resources.

The Maastricht Treaty added a fourth objective to EU environmental policy: promoting measures at international level to deal with regional or worldwide environmental problems.

The Maastricht Treaty strengthened the role of the EU in environmental policy, and revised Article 2 of the Treaty of Rome which sets out the objectives of the Community. The expression 'continuous and balanced expansion' was replaced with 'sustainable and non-inflationary growth respecting the environment'. The Maastricht Treaty confirmed the four principles of Community environmental policy that had been set out in the Single European Act and added a fifth, the precautionary principle, so that the principles of EU environmental policy became:

■ **The principle of prevention**. Prevention is preferable to correction of damage.
■ **The polluter pays principle**. The polluter should bear the cost of prevention and correction of the damage.
■ **The principle of correction at source**. As a priority actions in one member state should not be allowed to affect the environment in another member state.
■ **The principle of subsidiarity**.
■ **The precautionary principle**. The precautionary principle implies that lack of scientific evidence linking cause and effect should not be considered sufficient reason to take no action when there are considered to be significant risks.[10]

In addition, the Treaty of Maastricht confirmed the practice of **environmental mainstreaming**, which requires that environmental issues are taken into account in deciding all policies. This had been mentioned in the SEA, but only as a component of good policy rather than a requirement. The Maastricht Treaty provided for qualified majority voting in the Council of Ministers on most aspects of environmental policy. The Treaty also set up the Cohesion Fund, which finances environmental and transport projects in Cohesion countries, and called for a high level of environmental protection, though taking into account 'regional diversity' (Article 174, EC Treaty).

The Treaty of Amsterdam again changed the wording of Article 2 of the European Community

---

[10] The precautionary principle is taken up again in Chapter 17.

Treaty. The rather imprecise concept of 'sustainable growth respecting the environment' was replaced by 'sustainable development', though again the concept was not defined in the Treaty. The concept of sustainable development was raised in the UN Bruntland Report of 1987 and is generally interpreted to mean economic and social development that is sustained over time. As a result future generations will have more assets per capita than the present generation. The assets in question are capital (plant and machinery), human capital (the stock of knowledge and skills), natural capital (the environment yields flows of services over time) and social capital (relations between people and between people and institutions). If the total stock of these assets per capita increases over time, development is said to be sustainable, even though environmental damage may be increasing.

The requirement that environmental issues should be taken into account in defining and implementing all EU policies (environmental mainstreaming) is also present in the Amsterdam Treaty. The European Parliament was granted powers of co-decision on most aspects of environmental policy. The Amsterdam Treaty also required the Commission to prepare assessments of the environmental impact for policy proposals with significant environmental implications.

The Treaty of Nice confirmed the objectives and principles of EU environmental policy and the obligation to carry out environmental mainstreaming. In preparing its environmental policy the Community was required to take account of:

■ Available scientific and technical data;
■ Environmental conditions in the various regions of the Community;
■ The potential benefits and costs of action or lack of action;
■ The economic and social development of the Community as a whole and the balanced development of its regions.

THE EUROPEAN ENVIRONMENT AGENCY

Situated in Copenhagen, the European Environment Agency (EEA) came into operation in 1994. The aim of the agency is to support sustainable development and to help achieve a significant and measurable improvement in Europe's environment through the provision of information to policy-making agents and to the public. The European Environment Agency is at the centre of the European Environment Information and Observation Network (Eionet). Eionet is composed of about 300 national institutes in Europe through which it collects and disseminates environment-related information and data. The European Environment Agency has 31 members: the EU (25), the three candidate countries and the members of the European Economic Area (Iceland, Norway and Liechtenstein). In 2003 Switzerland began negotiating accession.

> ### Box 12.2 Public opinion and environmental questions
> According to a survey carried out in 2003 by Eurobarometer, environmental issues remain top of their list of priorities for EU citizens.*The causes of environmental degradation most worrying EU citizens were nuclear disasters (50 per cent) and industrial disasters (45 per cent). Air pollution, natural disasters, water pollution and the elimination of tropical rainforests are also high on the list of concerns and were quoted by between 41 per cent and 44 per cent of respondents.
>
> With regard to policy, 48 per cent were in favour of tighter regulations and tougher enforcement, while 45 per cent considered increasing environmental awareness and

greater involvement as being the best way to achieve results. A preference for better enforcement of existing policy was expressed by 40 per cent.

Of the respondents 35 per cent considered the EU as the most appropriate level for tackling environmental questions, compared with 30 per cent in favour of national governments and 27 per cent preferring the local government level.

* http://europa.eu.int/comm/environment/barometer/index.htm

THE PAN-EUROPEAN DIMENSION

Since pollution is an international phenomenon, EU policy also has a wider dimension. The EU participates in the 'Environment in Europe' process launched at Dobris Castle in Czechoslovakia in 1991. The process involves regular conferences of environment ministers from countries in East, West and Central Europe, together with representatives from the UN, non-governmental organizations and the European Commission. The aim is to strengthen co-operation on environmental matters, provide comprehensive assessment of Europe's environment and evolve long-term strategies for an environmental programme for Europe.

THE INTERNATIONAL DIMENSION

The EU (the member states and European Commission acting collectively as a negotiating bloc) also takes part in global attempts to tackle transnational environmental problems such as the ozone layer, climate change and the depletion of tropical rainforests.

In 1987 the Community signed the Montreal Protocol aimed at reducing depletion of the ozone layer. Among the main causes of ozone depletion were CFCs (chlorofluorocarbons) which were used in refrigerators, spray cans and air conditioning (see Box 12.3). In 1985 a hole in the ozone layer had been noted over the Antarctic. A thinner ozone layer allows more UV-Bs to pass through,

Box 12.3 Ozone depletion

In the 1930s a new form of chemical refrigerant was developed by the Dupont Corporation, one of the oldest chemical firms in the USA. These are simple chemicals containing chlorine, fluorine and carbon, hence the name CFCs. CFCs are non-toxic stable substances which functioned significantly better than earlier substances used as refrigerants such as ammonia.

CFCs (together with halons) are referred to as 'ozone-depleting' substances. They may accidentally escape and disperse into the troposphere, and because they are stable, they may persist in the troposphere long enough to escape into the stratosphere. In the stratosphere these substances may react with ozone under the influence of intense solar radiation.

Initially the Dupont Corporation denied that there was a scientific connection between CFCs and the ozone layer. In 1983 the US Academy of Sciences released a report illustrating that CFCs had contributed to ozone depletion. Based on the Report, Dupont agreed to reduce CFC production, and in 1987 announced its commitment to developing ozone-friendly substitutes for CFCs.

increasing the risks of skin cancer and premature aging of skin. International compliance with the Montreal and subsequent CFC protocols succeeded in reducing the use of CFCs, also because relatively cheap substitutes were generally available. However, the process of halting ozone depletion is also slow because of the existing levels of ozone-depleting chemicals in the stratosphere.[11]

In 1992 at the Earth Summit at Rio de Janeiro two international agreements were signed: the Convention on Biological Diversity and the Framework Convention on Climate Change (see Box 12.4). Under the Framework Convention on Climate Change, the EU accepted a voluntary target for reducing carbon dioxide emissions to 1990 levels by 2000.

Box 12.4 Climate change

One of the main debates on the environment concerns how far current patterns of economic activity contribute to climate change. Climate change refers not just to global warming but also to more extreme weather events. Greenhouse gases such as carbon dioxide (CO_2), methane (CH_4), nitrous oxide (N_2O), hydrofluorocarbons (HFC), perfluorocarbons (PFC) and sulphur hexafluoride (SF_6) can contribute to global warming. When visible light is scattered and absorbed at the Earth's surface it changes into heat, part of which is trapped in the lower atmosphere by gases such as CO_2 and then reradiated back to the surface of the Earth. Carbon dioxide accounts for 55–60 per cent of present heat-trapping gases and is the main worry of policy-makers. The quantity of CO_2 in the atmosphere has increased as a result of the combustion of oil, gas and coal, and also because of reduced absorption arising from deforestation, in particular in tropical areas.

According to the International Panel on Climate Control (IPCC), the average temperature could rise by between 1.4 and 5.8 degrees centigrade this century, even though this wide band of prediction has been subject to much controversy. In particular, it is difficult to isolate the effect of greenhouse gases from other factors having an impact on climate change or the long-term natural variability of climate.

Most of the difficulties such as melting of the ice caps causing rising sea levels, increasingly intense storms, desertification, droughts and floods would be felt by developing countries. However, in recent years (in particular since 2001) EU Mediterranean member states have also suffered from increasing water shortages and sudden and violent weather changes, with dramatic consequences for agriculture.

One of the more controversial aspects of the climate change debate is that it might cost more for some countries (such as the USA or Japan) to cut carbon dioxide emissions than to adapt to climate change. Moreover, powerful lobbies are opposed to reduction in carbon dioxide emissions and the reduced energy consumption it implies. It is sometimes argued that certain countries such as Russia and Canada might benefit from global warning, but this view probably fails to take full account of the possibility of more extreme weather events.

Under the 1997 Kyoto Protocol to the Convention, the EU member states agreed to targets requiring a reduction in emissions by 8 per cent between 2008 and 2012. The target set for the USA was 7 per cent, but subsequently the Bush Administration refused to ratify the protocol. The USA did, however, embark on a campaign to encourage research into improved technology such as carbon sequestration (which involves slowing carbon emissions) and began to sign bilateral

---

[11] In late 2003 there were also attacks on the continuing US use of methyl bromide, a pesticide used for crops such as strawberries and tomatoes, and thought to be one of the most potent ozone-depleting compounds still in widespread use (*Financial Times*, 18 November 2003).

international deals on climate change, but many observers criticized these moves as inadequate.[12] Some individual states in the USA have started moving towards binding emission limits.[13]

The target set out under the Kyoto Protocol is for the EU as a whole (the 'EC bubble'), and the Community must ensure that the actions of the member states are consistent with the Protocol. The Commission called for the development of a strategy in all sectors that produce pollution (energy, transport, agriculture, industry etc.), the introduction of an effective monitoring system and the setting of interim targets for 2005. By the end of 2003 only Sweden and the UK seemed likely to meet their interim targets, with Spain, Austria, Belgium and Ireland, in particular, expected to exceed them (see also Tables 12.1 and 12.2).[14] In the Central and East European countries emissions declined during the 1990s, largely because of the decline in heavy industries. Energy production accounts for over half of emissions in the CEECs because of heavy reliance on fossil fuels, and though transport accounts for only 8 per cent of emissions in these countries, its share is predicted to increase. The Europe Climate Change Programme (ECCP) has been introduced with the aim of reducing emissions by some 122–78 million tonnes of CO_2 equivalent.

Table 12.1 Greenhouse gas emissions, 2000

	Index base year 1990=100	Kyoto target		Index base year 1990=100	Kyoto target
EU (15)	96.0	92.0	New member states	69.0	
BE	106.0	92.5	BG	49.4	92.0
DK	99.0	79.0	CY	140	–
DE	81.0	79.0	CZ	76.4	92.0
EL	124.0	125.0	EE	45.4	92.0
ES	135.0	115.0	HU	82.4	92.0
FR	98.0	100.0	LT	46.3	92.0
IE	124.0	113.0	LV	34.1	92.0
IT	104.0	93.5	MT	129.0	–
LU	55.0	72.0	PL	68.1	92.0
NL	103.0	94.0	RO	61.9	94.0
AT	103.0	87.0	SI	99.3	94.0
PT	130.0	127.0	SK	66.9	92.0
FI	96.0	100.0			
SE	98.0	104.0			
UK	87.0	87.5			

Source: European Commission (2004).

Table 12.2 Greenhouse gas emissions by broad sector, 2001 (percentage of total emissions)

	New member states	Cohesion countries	EU (15)
Energy and related	53.0	31.0	29.0
Industry	17.0	21.0	21.0
Transport	8.0	21.0	21.0
Agriculture	9.0	13.0	10.0
Waste	4.0	4.0	3.0
Other	9.0	10.0	16.0

Source: European Commission (2004).

[12] See, for example, Michael Grubb, director of the Carbon Trust, writing in the *Financial Times* of 13 November 2003.
[13] *Financial Times*, 23 December 2003.
[14] *Financial Times*, 3 December 2003.

To assist in meeting its Kyoto obligations the EU is to introduce a Community emissions trading system (or 'carbon trading') by 2005. Under this system member states (or companies) that expect to more than meet their target can trade the right to carbon dioxide emissions with those who cannot meet their target. The idea is that for climate, it doesn't matter who emits the carbon dioxide. If country A can cut its carbon dioxide emissions at a lower cost than country B, from the point of view of economic efficiency there is an advantage in county A cutting its emission more, and country B cutting less. Countries (or companies) motivated by the profit they can make by selling their emission allowances will be encouraged to develop and use clean technologies. In practice, however, the granting of licences seems likely to run into administrative difficulties.

About 10 000 EU firms are likely to be affected by the emissions trading system, including power generators and steel, glass and cement manufacturers. These firms cover 46 per cent of EU carbon dioxide emissions. It is estimated that the use of a Community-wide emissions trading system could reduce the cost of implementing the EU's Kyoto commitments by a fifth.[15] However, electricity prices are expected to rise since costs for power generation are likely to increase as a result of the system.[16]

Various studies have suggested that, even with full implementation, the impact of the Kyoto Protocol on climate change would be limited. By the end of 2003 120 countries had ratified the Protocol, including Japan and Canada. Emerging economies such as China and India were exempt, and Australia joined the USA in refusing to apply the Protocol. To come into operation the treaty requires ratification by countries responsible for 55 per cent of emissions, and this would be achieved with Russian ratification. The Protocol committed Russia to stabilizing emissions at 1990 levels by 2008–12, and by 2003 Russian emissions had fallen by about 30 per cent compared with 1990 levels, leaving Russia with a potential benefit from emissions trading initially estimated in the order of $8–10 billion.[17] The decision not to apply the Protocol by the USA (the largest potential customer for quotas) led to a downward revision of the potential Russian gain from carbon trading to $3–4 billion. After some prevarication, in 2004 Russia decided that it would ratify the protocol.

EVALUATION OF EU ENVIRONMENTAL POLICY

For many years environmental issues lacked the status of a fully fledged Community policy, and even now in practice the various measures do not always appear to be co-ordinated into a single approach. Successive treaties have attempted to raise the priority given to environmental issues in the EU, requiring the Community to introduce environmental mainstreaming and to take account of sustainable development, not always with complete success. Over the years there has been a shift away from the 'command and control' approach in favour of market-based instruments, which tend to have lower implementation costs.

At the EU level tensions frequently arise between environmental objectives and the Single Market Programme, and northern member states often express fears that their higher environmental standards might be undermined in a 'race to the bottom'. With enlargement an additional effort will be required to ensure effective implementation of the environmental *acquis*.

Despite frequent lip service to the Kyoto Protocol, the commitment of the EU to meeting its objectives sometimes appears questionable. It is doubtful how successful in practice the Kyoto Protocol will be in reducing emissions.

---

[15] www.europa.eu.int/scadplus/leg/en.
[16] *Financial Times*, 26 June 2003.
[17] *Financial Times*, 10 September 2003 and 2 October 2003.

EU ENERGY POLICY

Energy policy is subject to public intervention in most countries for a number of reasons:

- Ensuring security of supply is generally a priority for energy policy, in particular when a country is dependent on imports.
- In general the provision of energy requires expensive infrastructure such as gas pipelines and an electricity grid. Interconnections with other countries are also necessary.
- Energy is used by industry, transport and households and services, and is often a substantial component of costs, with no close substitutes. Ensuring energy at reasonable prices is a precondition for economic development. However, differences in energy prices (which may be caused by government subsidies) can distort competition.
- Energy policy has important implications for environmental and social policy.

During the first 15 years of the Community growth led to increased energy consumption, and the relatively low world prices for oil caused the gradual substitution of oil for coal. As a result the EC became increasingly dependent on imports of energy and of oil in particular. In 1950 coal accounted for two-thirds of energy consumption and oil for 10 per cent in what were the original six EC countries, but by 1973 oil covered 67 per cent of consumption (Kengyel and Palankai, 2003). In 1960 domestic production accounted for 60 per cent of EC energy requirements (with coal being produced mainly in Germany, France and Belgium), but by 1973 this proportion had fallen to 37 per cent.[18]

When the OPEC (Organization of Petroleum Exporting Countries) cartel increased oil prices by 475 per cent in 1973 and a further 134 per cent in 1979, the Community was therefore very vulnerable. Despite a certain lack of co-ordination, the reaction of the Community was to introduce measures to reduce dependence on oil imports, encourage the development of alternative energy sources (such as nuclear, wind, solar, water, geothermal, bioenergy etc.), hold minimum stocks against emergencies and introduce energy-saving measures. All the Western industrialized countries joined the IEA (International Energy Agency), formed under the auspices of the OECD in 1974.

The policy of developing domestic energy sources and cutting consumption met with some success. North Sea oil production began in 1976, and the UK became a net exporter of oil. However, production met less than a quarter of EC requirements and was relatively costly. The Netherlands became an important producer of natural gas, but again extraction costs were relatively high. Renewable energy sources were slow to develop, and the public in many member states increasingly opposed the use of nuclear power plants. Countries such as Austria, Denmark, Greece, Ireland, Italy and Portugal produce no nuclear energy. In contrast in 2001 nuclear energy accounted for 92.7 per cent of energy production in Belgium and 81.1 per cent in France. Spain and Germany continue to produce coal though production is heavily subsidized. See Figures 12.2 and 12.3 for a breakdown on energy consumption in the EU (25) by source.

In 2001 the EU continued to rely on imports for 50.1 per cent of its energy requirements (77.0 per cent in the case of oil but 43.3 per cent for natural gas). The main sources of supply are shown in Table 12.3. French import dependency fell from 79 per cent in 1980 to 50 per cent in 2001 (thanks also to its nuclear power programme). However, even in 2001 the import dependency of other EC member states such as Luxembourg (97.9 per cent), Portugal (87.2 per cent), Ireland (90.0 per cent) and Italy (82.1 per cent) remained high.[19]

---

[18] Kengyel and Palankai (2003).
[19] European Commission (2003), www.europa.eu.int.comm/energy_transport.

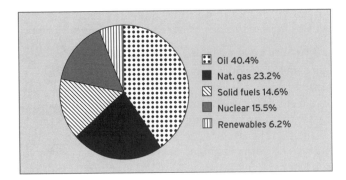

Figure 12.2 Gross inland energy consumption of the EU(15) by source of energy in 2001

Source: European Commission (2003)
www.europa.eu.int.comm/energy_transport

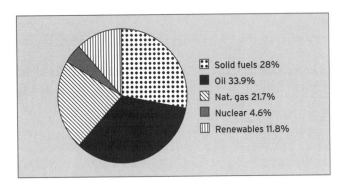

Figure 12.3 Gross inland energy consumption of the 10 new EU member states by source of energy in 2001

Source: European Commission (2003)
www.europa.eu.int.comm/energy_transport

In 2000 the dependency of the 10 new EU member states on imports of energy was 29.9 per cent. However, dependency was 95 per cent for oil, 84.3 per cent for natural gas, but −17.4 per cent for solid fuels, due, in particular, to the production of coal in the Czech Republic and Poland.

Table 12.3 The main sources of EU(15) energy imports

Main non-EU suppliers of oil to the EU in 2002 (per cent of EU imports)		Main non-EU suppliers of natural gas to the EU in 2002 (per cent of EU imports)	
Norway	23.0	Russia	38.7
Russia	22.3	Norway	26.2
Saudi Arabia	11.1	Algeria	25.4
Libya	7.9	Nigeria	4.0
Iran	5.4		
Syria	4.0		
Nigeria	4.0		

Source: European Commission (2003), www.europa.eu.int.comm/energy_transport.

THE EVOLUTION OF EU ENERGY POLICY

Two of the initial Communities were set up to deal with energy. The European Coal and Steel Community was responsible for coal, and Euratom covered nuclear energy. Oil, gas and electricity fell within the scope of the EEC, though the Treaty of Rome did not list energy policy among the specific competences of the Community. Differences in dependence on energy imports of the various member states, and in the mix of energy sources used, have acted as obstacles to the development of a common policy.

In 1964 a Protocol on Agreement on Energy represented a first attempt at co-ordination of the energy policy of the member states. This set out as common objectives: fair competition between different sources of energy, security of supply, low prices, freedom of choice for consumers and co-ordination of state aids to coal, and for coal and coke consumption by the steel industry. Introduction of a common policy was again attempted in 1968 when the three Communities were merged, but with few practical results (Hitiris, 2003).

Since 1978 the Community has tried to co-ordinate the national measures of the member states, set energy targets and fix a collective target for the rationalization of production, consumption and imports.

The Single Market Programme aimed at the liberalization of energy (which in the case of gas and electricity was generally controlled by national monopolies) and the promotion of investment in infrastructure and networks. The objective was to reduce segmentation of the market, increase competitiveness and ensure awareness of the environmental implications of energy policy.

The Maastricht Treaty confirmed the legal basis for Community measures in the sphere of energy (TEU, Article 3t) and these were reinforced in the Amsterdam and Nice Treaties. The Maastricht Treaty also called for joint efforts in the creation of trans-European networks (TENs) in energy infrastructure (EC Treaty, 129b, which subsequently became Article 154 in the Nice Treaty).

Community action for the development of TEN-Energy relates to the main transportation and transmission networks for electricity and natural gas.[20] Priority measures for the electricity sector include the connection of isolated electricity networks and the development of interconnections between member states and with third countries. TEN-Energy gas priorities include the introduction of natural gas into new regions, the interconnection of isolated networks and increased capabilities for storage and transport. With enlargement, emphasis is to be placed on integrating the new member states into priorities and projects.

The more recent guidelines for EU energy policy were set out in a Green Paper, 'Towards a European Union strategy for the security of energy supply', adopted by the Commission in 2001.[21] The Green Paper led to a heated debate which was summarized in a Commission document (COM(2002)321) in June 2002. According to the Green Paper, the EU continues to rely heavily on fossil fuels (oil, coal and natural gas) which make up four-fifths of its total energy consumption, almost two-thirds of which are imported. Without a change in policy, EU imports could rise to 70 per cent of requirements (90 per cent in the case of oil) by 2030.

The EU has relatively little room to manoeuvre with regard to energy supplies because of its low or less competitive (e.g. coal and North Sea oil) energy resources, so the strategy proposed by the Commission relies heavily on demand management. According to the Commission, energy-saving measures in buildings could cut energy consumption by 22 per cent. The Commission also proposed energy taxation and measures in the transport sector to reduce energy consumption and carbon emissions. Energy-related programmes are among the most important elements of the EU-financed framework programmes for research.

The Commission maintained that lack of harmonization of energy taxes in the member states was causing distortions in competition and called for more uniform taxes. More competitive pricing policies were also advocated. On the supply side the Commission called for measures to develop renewable energy sources, and the aim is to increase the share of energy requirements covered by such sources from 6 per cent in 2000 to 12 per cent by 2010. The Green Paper also notes that total abandonment of nuclear power in the EU would require an additional 35 per cent

---

[20] See Chapter 16 for a more detailed discussion of the TENs.
[21] Accessible at www.europa.eu.int/comm/energy_transport.

of electricity production from renewable and conventional energy sources. One of the solutions proposed by the Commission is to improve nuclear safety and the processing and transportation of nuclear waste. The Green Paper also proposed improved interconnection infrastructures to open up cross-border trade in energy. A European Energy Charter was signed with the new CEEC member states to improve infrastructure links and expand energy trade. With regard to import dependency, the Commission calls for a diversification of sources of supply. For this purpose the EU is developing an energy partnership with Russia.

EVALUATION OF EU ENERGY POLICY

The EU is frequently criticized for its slowness in developing an energy policy, but differences in the import dependency of the member states, and in the structure of energy sources used to meet consumption, render it difficult to reach common positions.

In the early years of the Community oil gradually replaced coal as the main source of energy, leading to increased import dependency. The EC member states were therefore vulnerable to the oil crises of the 1970s and reacted by attempting to reduce import dependency, develop alternative sources of domestic supply and reduce energy consumption.

Security of energy supply remains a key priority for the EU, and the present strategy relies heavily on the introduction of energy-saving measures and incentives to develop renewable energy sources. Commission proposals to harmonize taxation and liberalize energy markets in the EU have met with limited success, but in recent years there has been progress in reaching common policies to deal with the environmental implications of energy policy.

Summary of Key Concepts

- The evolution of EU environmental measures has encountered tensions because of differing environmental standards in the EU member states; the fuzzy boundary between EU and national policies; difficulties in implementing policies; the persistence of environmental problems; difficulties in reconciling environmental measures with other EU policies and disagreements about how to share the financial burden for measures.
- Environmental measures fall into three broad categories: 'command and control', market-based instruments and voluntary agreements. In recent years there has been a growing tendency in the EU to use market-based instruments rather than the strategy of 'command and control'.
- There is no mention of a role for the Community in the Treaty of Rome. In 1973 the Community embarked on the first of what are now six Environmental Action Programmes.
- The principles of EU environmental policy are: the principle of prevention; the 'polluter pays' principle; the principle of correction at source; the principle of subsidiarity and the precautionary principle.
- 'Environmental mainstreaming' requires that environmental issues should be taken into account in deciding all EU policies.
- The European Environment Agency came into operation in 1994.
- The EU takes part in global attempts to tackle transnational environmental problems such as the ozone layer (the Montreal Protocol of 1987 and subsequent agreements), climate change (the 1997 Kyoto Protocol) and the depletion of tropical rainforests.
- The Commission has proposed introducing a Community emissions trading system (or 'carbon trading') by 2005.
- Energy policy is subject to public intervention in most countries to ensure security of supply; to provide expensive infrastructure such as gas pipelines and an electricity grid; to ensure energy at reasonable prices and because energy policy has environmental and social implications.

- In the early years of the Community oil gradually replaced coal as the main source of energy, leading to increased import dependency.
- The EU is frequently criticized for its slowness in developing an energy policy, but differences in the import dependency of the member states, and in the structure of energy sources used to meet consumption, render it difficult to reach common positions.
- Security of energy supply remains a key priority for the EU, and the present strategy relies heavily on the introduction of energy-saving measures and incentives to develop renewable energy sources.

Questions for Study and Review

■ What were the obstacles to developing an EU environmental policy?

■ Describe main types of instrument used in environmental policy.

■ Describe how EU environmental policy has evolved over time.

■ What difficulties arise in applying the principles of EU environmental policy?

■ What is sustainable development? How can it be ensured in practice?

■ What role has the EU played at an international level in deciding on environmental questions?

■ What are the limitations of the Kyoto Protocol?

■ Why do most countries introduce an energy policy?

■ Describe the different sources of energy the EU uses to meet its requirements. How have these changed over time?

■ Describe the evolution of EU energy policy.

■ What strategies is the EU adopting to ensure security of energy supplies?

References

Bainbridge, T. (1998) *The Penguin Companion to European Union*, 2nd edn, Penguin Books, London.

Coase, R. (1960) 'The problem of social cost', *Journal of Law and Economics,* October, pp. 1–44.

European Commission (2001) 'Towards a European Union strategy for the security of energy supply'.

European Commission (2002) 'Final Report on the Green Paper "Towards a European Union strategy for the security of energy supply",' document (COM(2002)321) of June 2002.

European Commission (2003) 'European Union energy and transport in figures'.

European Commission (2004) 'Third report on economic and social cohesion'.

Hitiris, T. (2003) *European Community Economics*, 5th edn, Prentice Hall, Hemel Hempstead, UK.

Jones, R.A. (2001) *The Politics and Economics of the European Union. An Introductory Text*, 2nd edn, Edward Elgar, Cheltenham, UK.

Kengyel, A. and Palankai, T. (2003) 'Structural policy roles and directions' in Palankai, T. (ed.), *Economics of European Integration*, Akadémiai Kaido', Budapest.

Lomborg, B. (2001*) The Sceptical Environmentalist. Measuring the Real State of the World*, Cambridge University Press, Cambridge.

Pearce, D. (2001) 'Environmental policy', in Artis, M. and Nixson, F. (eds), *The Economics of the European Union. Policy and Analysis*, 3rd edn, Oxford University Press, Oxford.

Useful websites

Statistics, a description of environmental policies and key documents are available from the European Commission:

www.europa.eu.int/comm/environment/

www.europa.eu.int/scadplus/leg/en

The European Environment Agency provides reports and statistics on various environmental issues:

www.eea.eu.int

Various international organizations provide information on environmental questions:

Greenpeace:

www. greenpeace.org

The International Energy Agency:

www.IEA.org

The International Panel on Climate Control:

www.ipcc.ch

IUCN–World Conservation Union:

http://www.iucn.org/

Convention for Biodiversity:

http://www.biodiv.org/default.aspx

WWF International:

http://www.panda.org

For US environmental policy see:

US Environmental Protection Agency:

www.EPA.gov

The OECD provides statistics and analysis of both environmental and energy questions:

www.OECD.org

For a description of EU energy policy, statistics and key documents, see European Commission:

www.europa.eu.int/comm/energy_transport

Statistics on energy are available from *BP Statistical Review of World Energy*:

www.bpamoco.com/worldenergy/

List of abbreviations

CAP	Common Agricultural Policy
CEEC	Central and Eastern European country
CFC	chlorofluorocarbon gases
EAP	Environmental Action Programme
ECCP	Europe Climate Change Programme
EEA	European Environmental Agency
Eionet	European Environmental Information and Observation Network
EMAS	Environmental Management and Audit Scheme
IEA	International Environmental Agency
IPCC	International Panel on Climate Change
MEC	marginal external cost
MNPB	marginal net private benefit
OECD	Organization for Economic Co-operation and Development
OPEC	Organization of Petroleum Exporting Countries
SEA	Single European Act
TEN	Trans-European Network
TEU	Treaty on European Union
UV	ultra-violet rays

13

Regional Policy

LEARNING OBJECTIVES

By the end of this chapter you should be able to understand:

▶ Various views about the link between integration and regional disparities;

▶ What is the role of the Structural Funds, the Cohesion Fund and the European Investment Bank;

▶ The main stages in the evolution of EU regional policy;

▶ The extent to which there has been convergence between EU regions and countries;

▶ How effective EU regional policy has been;

▶ The ways in which regional policy might be rendered more effective.

INTRODUCTION

Regional problems are the disparities in levels of income, in rates of growth of output and employment, and generally in levels of economic inequality between different regions. Public intervention may be considered necessary to reduce these disparities through redistribution. Though the Treaty of Rome did not initially envisage a very large role for the Community in this sphere, over the years the EU has gradually evolved an active policy of redistribution between different regions and countries of the Community (the regional dimension), and different sections of the population (the social dimension, see Chapter 14).

The aims of EU regional policy figure among the objectives set out in Article 2 of the EC Treaty:

■ To promote a harmonious, balanced and sustainable development of economic activities;

■ Convergence of economic performance;

■ Economic and social cohesion and solidarity between member states.

Convergence involves a process of catching up by less favoured regions so that the disparities are narrowed. While there is no clear definition of cohesion, it can be understood as 'the degree to which disparities in social and economic welfare between different regions or groups within the Community are politically and socially acceptable' (Molle, 2001, p. 395).

Regional policies are often advocated on grounds of efficiency since they may help to remove bottlenecks and obstacles to development. For instance, public investment in infrastructure may encourage firms to move to a less favoured region, or programmes for retraining may help workers to find jobs. Regional policy may help to ease the problems of overcongestion or overheating in areas where economic activity is concentrated. The concept of social and economic cohesion also suggests a justification for redistributive policies on equity grounds: regional policies may be required to guarantee certain minimum levels of services, while social policy may ensure certain minimum incomes or living standards.[1]

Various indicators can be taken into account in assessing the degree of disparity between different regions or countries:

■ Income per capita (which is the indicator generally used by the EU);
■ Labour productivity;
■ The availability and accessibility of jobs;
■ The standard of living, which involves also taking into account the environment, the health service, cultural infrastructure, leisure activities etc.

A major, and still unresolved controversy is whether economic integration leads to greater or less convergence between different regions. The first part of this chapter will review some of the main theories advanced on either side of the argument. Then follows a survey of the instruments of EU regional policy and how they evolved over the years. The final part of the chapter addresses the question of whether there has been convergence in the EU. This is complicated by the fact that convergence may take place both within and between countries. A further difficulty arises in attributing the causes of convergence (or lack of it). To what extent was convergence due to integration, and what was the role of EU regional policy? The last part of the chapter will attempt to identify elements that make for a successful regional policy.

THE VIEW THAT INTEGRATION LEADS TO LESS INCOME DISPARITY

The view that integration will lead to greater convergence is generally based on faith in markets. Integration allows free operation of the market forces and sets in motion a process by which the return to labour and capital in different regions will tend to converge. The mechanisms by which this convergence comes about are:

■ **Free trade**, which permits regions to specialize on the basis of comparative advantage (see Chapter 4). A region with surplus labour will specialize in labour-intensive goods causing incomes to rise and unemployment to fall. The Heckscher-Ohlin-Samuelson theorem described in the next section provides an explanation of how the removal of barriers to trade may lead to the convergence of incomes in different regions. The limitation of this explanation arises from the restrictive assumptions on which the theorem is based.

---

[1] Molle (2001).

■ **Labour migration and capital mobility**. Labour will tend to leave regions with lower wage levels and move to regions where wages are higher, bringing about a process of wage equalization, as described in Chapter 7. A similar mechanism to that in Figure 7.2 can be used to explain capital movements by simply reversing the position of capital and labour.[2] Capital will be attracted to the regions where wages are lower and returns on capital are higher, setting in motion a process that leads to equalization of returns on capital in different regions.

■ **Capital accumulation**. According to orthodox neo-classical growth theory (see the description of the Solow model in Chapter 5), in regions with higher productivity and per capita incomes, growth will prove more difficult as capital accumulation runs into diminishing returns.

THE HECKSCHER-OHLIN-SAMUELSON THEOREM

According to the Heckscher–Ohlin–Samuelson theorem, the liberalization of trade will bring about the liberalization of relative and absolute returns to the factors of production between countries or regions. This theorem is a corollary of the Heckscher–Ohlin theorem explained in Chapter 4. The Heckscher–Ohlin–Samuelson theorem is based on very strict assumptions such as perfect competition, no economies of scale, free trade, full employment of resources and the same technology in both countries.

Using the same example as in Chapter 4: as China, which has an abundance of labour, specializes in the production of clothing (which is intensive of labour) the demand for labour relative to capital will increase, and as a result so will the cost of labour w (the wage rate) relative to the cost of capital r (the interest rate). According to the theorem, in the USA, which is abundant in capital, the opposite will occur. With free trade the USA will tend to specialize in products intensive of capital (say automobiles), so increasing the relative cost of capital r. With the process of specialization in the USA, labour-intensive production will decrease, releasing more labour relative to capital and pushing down the relative price of labour w. With free trade (and under the restrictive assumptions of the model), the process will continue until the relative (and absolute) prices of labour and capital are the same in the two countries.

Returning to the model used in Chapter 4 for the Heckscher–Ohlin theorem, for simplicity it is assumed that there are two countries (1 and 2), two products (X and Y) and two factors of production labour (L) and capital (K).[3] Country 1 is labour abundant, and will specialize in the production and export of product X that is labour intensive. Country 2 is abundant in capital and will specialize in the production and export of product Y which is capital intensive.

As Country 1 specializes in the production of X (which is labour intensive) and reduces the production of Y (which is capital intensive), the demand for labour relative to capital will rise. This will cause the price of labour (w, or wages) relative to that of capital (r, or the interest rate) to rise. Country 1 is labour abundant, so initially the price of labour relative to capital was lower than in Country 2, but with trade the relative price for labour will rise in Country 1. The opposite will occur in Country 2. As Country 2 specializes in the production of Y the demand for capital relative to labour will rise and so too will r relative to w. Trade will continue until the relative prices of the two factors are the same in the two countries.

Figure 13.1 can be used to illustrate this process. The vertical axis indicates the price of product X relative to product Y (Px/Py). The horizontal axis shows the price of labour relative to the price

---

[2] See Baldwin and Wyplosz (2004) for an example of how this approach is applied to capital movement.
[3] The account here is based on Salvatore (2001).

of capital (w/r). It is assumed that there is perfect competition, and that both countries use the same technology, so each value of Px/Py is associated with one and only one value of w/r.

Before trade Country 1 is at point A, with w/r = (w/r)′, and Px/Py= Pa. Country 2 is at B with Px/Py = Pb and w/r = (w/r)″. With trade Country 1 specializes in the production of X, causing Px/Py and w/r to rise. Country 2 specializes in Y, causing Px/Py (which is the inverse of Py/Px) to fall, so causing a reduction in w/r. The process will contine until both countries are at C, where Px/Py = Pc and w/r = (w/r)*.

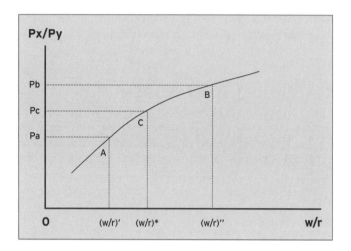

Figure 13.1 Relative factor-price equalization

Source: From *International Economics* by Dominick Salvatore, Copyright © 2001, John Wiley & Sons, Inc. This material is used by permission of John Wiley & Sons Inc.

So far what has been demonstrated is how trade leads to equalization of the relative price for the two factors in the two countries. Given the assumptions of the model (perfect competition in the product and factor markets, constant returns to scale and that both countries use the same technology), trade will also lead to the equalization of absolute factor prices. In other words, the real wage and the real rate of interest will be the same in the two countries.

Trade can therefore be said to act as a substitute for the international mobility of factors. With perfect mobility labour would move from where wages were lower to where they are higher until wages were the same in both countries. Similarly, capital would move from where interest rates were lower to where they were higher until interest rates were the same in both countries. There is, however, a difference between trade and factor mobility. Trade acts on the demand for factors of production, while factor mobility acts on their supply.

THE VIEW THAT INTEGRATION LEADS TO GREATER REGIONAL DISPARITY

Various theories are also advanced to explain why integration may lead to divergence or greater disparities between regions:

■ **Modern growth theory,** which was briefly described in Chapter 5, may explain why more prosperous areas can enjoy ongoing long-term growth. Important factors in explaining growth are market access, human capital, investment in R&D, technological change, economies of scale, institutional efficiency etc., and these may be encouraged by integration. Some countries master good combinations and grow, others fail to do so and fall behind.

■ **Technology diffusion**. According to evolutionary economic theory, knowledge and innovation tend to concentrate in certain areas.

Evolutionary economics owes much to the pioneering work of Nelson and Winter (1982) and adds new insights into the role of knowledge and innovation.[4] According to the Schumpeterian view, the evolution of the economy is constantly being 'disrupted' by technological change in a process of 'creative destruction'. Learning and evolution are seen as a disequilibrium process, and dynamic selection and mutation lead to superior responses. Structural change and growth are the result of the irruption of new technologies in the economic system which provide opportunities for investment and the opening of new sectors. Drawing on Kondratiev's concept of waves of economic activity, Schumpeter argued that radical innovations tend to be concentrated in certain periods.

Knowledge is a key concept in this framework, and evolutionary economics makes the distinction between codified and tacit knowledge. Codified knowledge is formalized and can be stored and transmitted easily, while tacit knowledge is obtained through experience, requiring a process of learning-by-doing in order to be passed on.

According to evolutionary economics a large part of knowledge needed for innovation is tacit, so contacts between people are important, and location therefore counts. There will tend to be an agglomeration of innovation in geographic clusters. In contrast codified knowledge can be transmitted easily so activities based on this knowledge can be moved to low-cost locations. According to the view that integration encourages economic concentration, by reducing barriers to the location of industry, integration will render it easier for firms to move to areas where there is an agglomeration of innovation.

■ **The New Economic Geography approach** developed by Krugman and Venables.[5] This approach involves a kind of circular causality. The possibility of exploiting scale economies is an incitement to the concentration of industry, while trade costs are reduced if firms locate close to large markets.[6] Where firms are concentrated, there will be large markets and large markets provide an incentive for firms to locate. The combination of opportunity to exploit economies of scale and reduce trade costs makes for this circular causality.

Supporters of the New Economic Geography approach argue that it explains the existence of centripetal forces in the EU. The central core area is said to lie in North-West Europe in a golden triangle running from Paris to London and including most of Belgium and the Netherlands (Harrop, 2000). In addition there is a so-called 'blue banana' in the shape of a banana that runs from the golden triangle through West German cities such as Bonn and Frankfurt, parts of Austria and Switzerland to Milan (Williams, 1996).

According to the view that integration encourages economic concentration, by freeing trade, creating a Single Market and introducing a common currency, the integration process will help remove various obstacles that could hinder the agglomeration process.

However, even when considering the various 'stages' of integration, different views emerge as to whether integration leads to more or less convergence. The customs union frees trade, creating opportunities for exploiting comparative advantage, but there may be rigidities in the process, and where adjustment takes place it may involve costs. These costs may be concentrated in certain sectors or regions. A common market introduces the four freedoms, enabling labour to move from less favoured regions, but in practice capital tends to move faster and may concentrate in

---

[4] This account is based on Navarro (2003).
[5] Krugman and Venables (1990) and Krugman (1991).
[6] Trade costs include transport costs but also the more general costs of adapting to the local market which depend on information, culture, distance etc.

faster-growing regions. Economic and monetary union removes the possibility of using exchange rate and monetary policies for adjustment between countries. However, disparities also arise within countries, and with higher levels of integration the effectiveness of the exchange rate instrument has been challenged, and it has been argued that exchange rate changes may even be a source of shocks (see Chapter 8).

THE STRUCTURAL FUNDS

EU implementation of regional and social policy operates chiefly though the Structural Funds and related instruments, though clearly other policies (such as the CAP) will have distributional implications (see Table 13.1 and Figure 13.2).

The term 'Structural Funds' refers to the European Social Fund (ESF), the European Regional Development Fund (ERDF), the Guidance Section of FEOGA (or the European Agricultural Guidance and Guarantee Fund, or EAGGF)[7] and the Financial Instrument for Fisheries Guidance (FIFG). Related instruments are the European Cohesion Fund and the European Investment Bank. Over the 1994–99 period the European Fund for Regional Development accounted for 52 per cent of the Structural Funds, followed by the FSE (30 per cent), FEOGA Guidance (16 per cent), with Fisheries Guidance accounting for only 2 per cent.

	1994-99 annual average	% of total	2000-06 Annual average	% of total	% of GDP in 2000 at 1999 prices
Austria	228	0.9	210	0.8	0.1
Belgium	293	1.2	261	1.0	0.1
Denmark	86	0.4	106	0.4	0.2
Finland	250	1.0	262	1.0	0.2
France	2070	8.6	2089	8.0	0.2
Germany	338	13.8	4022	15.3	0.2
Greece	2539	10.5	2994	11.4	2.9
Ireland	1021	4.2	441	1.7	0.6
Italy	3440	14.3	4069	15.5	0.4
Lux.	8	0.0	11	0.0	0.1
NL	369	1.5	376	1.4	0.1
Portugal	2539	10.5	2718	10.4	2.9
Spain	5671	23.5	6155	23.5	1.4
Sweden	229	0.9	273	1.0	0.1
UK	2022	8.4	2234	8.5	0.2
EU(15)	24 103	100	26 223	100	

Table 13.1 **Average annual allocations of the Structural Funds by member states (€ million, 1999 prices)**

Source: Elaboration on the basis of data taken from European Commission (2001 and 2004).

The European Social Fund

Created in 1960, according to the Treaty of Rome, the aim of the European Social Fund (ESF) was to increase employment opportunities and contribute to the improvement of living standards. The strategy for realizing this aim is dual: through creating jobs and assisting training.

During the 1960s the activities of the ESF were mainly concerned with increasing the geographical and occupational mobility of workers. During the 1970s the chief objectives became the

---

[7] The French expression, FEOGA, is usually used here since the acronym in English is a bit of a mouthful.

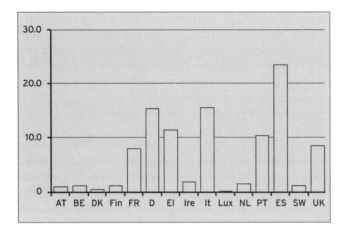

Figure 13.2 Share of the Structural Funds by member states (2000-06) (percentages)

Source: Elaboration on the basis of data taken from European Commission (2001 and 2004).

fight against long-term and youth unemployment. A reform of the Structural Funds of 1993 gave higher priority to the aims of:

- Adjustment of workers to industrial change;
- Equal opportunities for men and women;
- The creation of job opportunities for disadvantaged groups such as immigrants and disabled people.

During the 1994–99 period the European Social Fund provided support for active labour market policies, with 46 per cent of ESF spending going to training, 20 per cent for integration pathways and similar schemes, 7 per cent for employment incentives, 4 per cent for counselling and 3 per cent for job placement, though the combination of measures varied with the member state.[8]

The European Regional Development Fund

The European Regional Development Fund (ERDF) is the largest of the Structural Funds. Created in 1975, the aim of the fund is to reduce disparities between various regions in the Community. Following the 1973 enlargement and the entry of Britain with its difficulties in Northern Ireland, Scotland, Wales and the North of England (see Chapter 2), the ERDF was initially conceived as a means of assistance to regions facing industrial decline.

The ERDF provides financing for projects in disadvantaged areas, such as:

- Modernizing and restructuring production;
- Infrastructure projects (for transport, telecommunications, energy and water supply);
- Education and professional training;
- Environment;
- Health services;
- Culture;
- The reduction in disparities between regions.

The Guidance Section of the FEOGA

The Guidance Section of FEOGA was established as a result of the 1962 agreement on CAP mechanisms (see Chapter 10) and traditionally financed measures to adapt and improve farm structures and the marketing of agricultural products and to develop rural infrastructure.

---

[8] European Commission (1994).

The Financial Instrument for Fisheries Guidance

The Financial Instrument for Fisheries Guidance (FIFG) was created in 1993 in order to modernize the EU fleet, safeguard certain marine areas and improve the structures for processing and marketing of fish in the EU.

THE COHESION FUND

Though it is not strictly classified as one of the Structural Funds, the Cohesion Fund is closely related to them. Introduced as part of the Maastricht package, the Cohesion Fund provides assistance to those member states that fear that they would not be able to meet the additional competitive pressures resulting from economic and monetary union. The criterion for eligibility is that the country has a GDP per capita that is less than 90 per cent of the Community average. The countries receiving assistance through the Cohesion Fund – Greece, Ireland (though Ireland no longer meets the 90 per cent criterion, so aid is to be phased out), Portugal and Spain – are obliged to adopt economic policies conducive to convergence (see Table 13.2). In return they receive financial assistance for projects in favour of the environment and trans-European networks to improve transport infrastructure. The contribution of the fund may amount to 80–85 per cent of total financing of the project.

Table 13.2 Cohesion Fund commitments, 2000

	Environment € millions	%	Transport € millions	%	Total	% total
Greece	56.8	5.0	176.8	13.8	233.6	9.7
Spain	780.1	69.1	768.5	60.1	1548.6	64.4
Ireland	137.0	12.1	89.5	7.0	226.5	9.4
Portugal	154.9	13.7	242.6	19.0	397.5	16.5
Total	1128.8	100	1277.4	100	2406.3	100

Source: European Commission, www.europa.eu.int/comm/regional

THE EUROPEAN INVESTMENT BANK

The Treaty of Rome (Articles 129–130) envisaged the creation of the European Investment Bank (EIB). The EIB helps to finance projects in the member states and in certain third countries (such as those in the Mediterranean area, in Central and Eastern Europe and in the ACP group). The EIB raises funds on financial markets using its name as a guarantee, and provides subsidized loans to finance projects carried out by public authorities and private firms. In recent years the EIB has been involved in supporting the Lisbon Strategy with, for example, loans for investment in education, health care and high-technology sectors.

THE EVOLUTION OF EU REGIONAL POLICY

The evolution of EU regional policy can be divided into three main stages: 1959–75, 1975–88 and since 1988.

1958-75

During this period regional measures were widely implemented at a national level in the member states, but there was no real Community policy. The original six member states were a relatively homogeneous economic group, with the exception of the Mezzogiorno of Italy.[9] The European Investment Bank was set up principally with the aim of resolving the problems of Southern Italy, but in practice its activities were on a relatively limited scale. It was hoped that measures to promote labour movement in the Community would also have the effect of reducing unemployment in the Mezzogiorno. It was also considered that the CAP could play a redistributive role since farm incomes were generally below those in other sectors.

1975–88

The second phase of EC regional policy was characterized by the introduction of new measures, the wider use of existing instruments and a gradual increase in the funds available for redistributive measures (Tsoukalis, 1997).

The European Regional Development Fund was created in 1975 largely at British request. With a tradition of importing food from the rest of the world, and a small but efficient agricultural sector, the UK was expected to be a large net contributor to the EC budget (see Chapter 9). The ERDF was considered a mechanism for correcting this imbalance, though following the 1973 oil crisis its operation was on a far smaller scale than initially foreseen. The funds available for the European Regional Development Fund increased over the years, but it was criticized for poor co-ordination, insufficient flexibility in the choice of project and of being used simply to replace funding by national authorities.

In 1978 a 'Mediterranean package' was introduced as a response to criticisms that the CAP had traditionally favoured northern farmers and fear that the Mediterranean enlargement would add to competitive pressures. Requested by France and Italy, the measures were also extended to Greece from 1981, and entailed increased price and market support for certain Mediterranean products, assistance for irrigation, the infrastructure and reforestation. From 1981 similar 'integrated development programmes' were introduced for other less favoured areas such as Lozère in France, Southern Belgium and the Northwest islands of Scotland.

Building on these initiatives, and with a view to preparing for Spanish and Portuguese accession, in 1985 the Community introduced 'Integrated Mediterranean Programmes'. These mark the beginning of a new strategy aimed at overcoming some of the shortcomings of earlier redistributive measures. There was to be more co-ordination both between the then three Structural Funds (the ESF, FEOGA Guidance and the ERDF) and with the European Investment Bank. Decentralization was to increase with more involvement of local and regional authorities. The measures were directed chiefly at rural areas, but it was argued that assistance should not simply be to agriculture in these regions but should take account of the wider economic and social environment. Between 1985 and 1992, 4.1 billion ECU was allocated to these programmes, but the change in approach was probably more important than the increase in funding available.

The period since 1988

In 1985 the new president of the European Commission, Delors, announced his programme for the completion of the Internal Market. The less favoured peripheral regions and countries feared that they would not be able to meet the additional competitive pressures in the Single Market. Increased disparities in the Community following the accession of Greece, Spain and Portugal were also expected, and the limited results achieved by the separate operation of the various Structural Funds and the need to increase their effectiveness was recognized. Reform of the Structural Funds was therefore agreed in 1988.

In 1987, the Single European Act introduced the concept of economic and social cohesion and

---

[9] Tsoukalis (1997).

called for harmonious development, the reduction of regional disparities, and the co-ordination and rationalization of the Structural Funds (Articles 130A–130E).

The 1988 reform covered the 1989–93 period, and its underlying philosophy was confirmed and strengthened in the subsequent cycles of the Structural Funds covering the periods 1994–99 and 2000–06. The main aspects of the reform were:

■ A doubling of the Structural Funds from 7 billion ECU in 1989 to 14 billion in 1993;
■ The creation of so-called Community Initiatives which involve a number of member states;
■ The introduction of a series of principles of operation;
■ The concentration of the Funds on priority objectives.

The aim of Community Initiatives is to encourage co-operation between different member states on matters of common interest. Community Initiatives account for about 10 per cent of spending under the Structural Funds. During the 1989–93 and 1994–99 periods there were a number of Community Initiatives aimed at specific groups and targets, but for the 2000–06 period they were reduced to four:

■ LEADER + (rural development);
■ INTERREG II (cross-border, transnational and interregional co-operation);
■ URBAN (economic and social regeneration of cities and urban neighbourhoods);
■ EQUAL (transnational co-operation to combat all kinds of discrimination and inequalities in the labour market).

The main instrument for implementing the Structural Funds is, however, through Operating Programmes, which are drawn up and implemented on the basis of consultation and co-operation between the European Commission, national governments and local and regional authorities.

The 1988 reform introduced four principles for implementing the Structural Funds, and these have been confirmed in the funds' subsequent cycles of operation:

1. Concentration

    Measures were to be concentrated on priority objectives to ensure close co-ordination of policies (see Box 13.1). Concentration is also intended to ensure that the effectiveness of measures is not undermined by resources being spread too thinly either geographically or by policy measure, but it does not always succeed in this aim.

2. Partnership

    Partnership implies close co-operation between the European Commission and the appropriate national, regional and local authorities at all stages. This requires horizontal co-operation between organizations at the regional and local levels, and the development of vertical aspects of multi-level governance and the interplay between different tiers of government (Hardy et al., 1995). Partnership may help to disseminate information and to take a broader range of views into account in assessing needs and evaluating projects.

3. Programming

    The Structural Funds would be implemented through structured programmes lasting a number of years (1989-93,1994-99, 2000-06, and 2007-13). The cycles coincide with successive financial prospectives. Programming is intended to encourage longer-term, more strategic planning, but at times difficulties are encountered with the length of time taken to approve programming documents and with their complexity.

4. Additionality

    Additionality aims at ensuring that allocations are additional to national financing, and do not simply replace national measures. The aim is to stimulate an increase in finance (both public and private) available, and at least in Objective 1 regions this objective appears to have been realized.[10]

The main changes introduced in the Structural Funds for the 1994–99 period were:

■ The creation of the Cohesion Fund;
■ An increase in financing through the Structural Funds;
■ A change in the objectives (see Box 13.1);
■ The introduction of the Financial Instrument for Fisheries Guidance;
■ A simplification of procedures;
■ An increased role for regional and local authorities.

Box 13.1 The evolution of the objectives of the Structural Funds over time

First period 1989-93	Second period 1994-99	Third period 2000-06
Objective 1: the less well-developed areas of the Community, which are defined as those whose GDP per capita is less than 75% of the EU average in the previous three years.	Objective 1: the less well-developed areas of the Community, which are defined as those whose GDP per capita is less than 75% of the EU average in the previous three years.	Objective 1: the less well-developed areas of the Community, which are defined as those whose GDP per capita is less than 75% of the EU average.
Objective 2: regions affected by the decline of traditional industries.	Objective 2: the conversion of regions seriously affected by industrial decline.	Objective 2: the economic and social conversion of regions that were facing natural difficulties, including declining rural areas and those dependent on fishing.
Objective 3: the fight against long-term unemployment.	Objective 3: combating long-term unemployment (more than 12 months) and facilitating the integration into work of young people (under 25 years of age), women and persons exposed to exclusion from the labour market.	Objective 3: improvement of human capital by promoting employment, education and professional training.
Objective 4: integration into working life of young people.	Objective 4: facilitating the adaptation of workers to industrial change and changes in production systems.	

---

[10] European Commission (2004).

Objective 5a: assisting the structural adjustment of agriculture and fisheries. Objective 5b: aid to rural areas.	Objective 5a: assisting the structural adjustment of agriculture and fisheries. Objective 5b: aid to rural areas.	Rural development became the second pillar of the CAP.
	Objective 6: regions with a low density of population in the extreme north of Finland and Sweden.	

Note: With the 1993 reform the previous objectives 3 and 4 were integrated into a revised objective 3, and new objectives 4 and 6 were created. With the 1999 reform the old objectives 1 and 6 were incorporated into the new objective 1, the old objectives 2 and 5a were included in the new objective 2 and objective 5b was transformed into rural development, which became the second pillar of the CAP.

Despite the aims of this reform, the criticisms of complex procedures, lack of co-ordination and insufficient decentralization continued to be levelled at the Structural Funds during this period.

THE BERLIN AGREEMENT OF 1999

At the Berlin European Council of 1999 agreement was reached on reform of the Structural Funds for the 2000–06 period, also with a view to permitting EU enlargement to proceed (see Chapter 20). The reform was aimed at:

■ Simplification of the instruments;
■ Concentration of the Objectives;
■ Strengthening of subsidiarity and increased decentralization to regional and local authorities; and
■ Reinforcement of the instruments of control, monitoring and evaluation.

Simplification of the instruments refers to a reduction in the number of regulations, Objectives and sources of financing. The procedures of programming and financial management were also to be rendered less complex.

The Objectives of the Structural Funds were to be reduced to three:

■ Objective 1 regions where GDP per capita was less than 75 per cent of the EU average. These were to receive 69.7 per cent of all spending under the Structural Funds (see Tables 13.3 and 13.4), and support was available from all four funds (ESF, ERDF, FEOGA Guidance and FIFG).

	Total allocation in billion euros	% of total Structural Fund spending	% reserved for transitional support
Objective 1	135.90	69.7%	4.3%
Objective 2	22.50	11.5%	1.4%
Objective 3	24.05	12.3%	–

Table 13.3 The allocation of the Structural Funds to the various objectives (2000-06)

Source: European Commission (2004), www.europa.eu.int/comm/regional

Table 13.4 Structural Fund allocations by country and Objective, 2000-06 (million euros at 1999 prices)

	Objective 1	Phasing out Objective 1	Objective 2	Phasing out Objective 2	Objective 3	Fisheries instrument outside Objective 1	Total
Austria	261	0	578	102	528	4	1473
Belgium	0	625	368	65	737	34	1829
Denmark	0	0	156	27	365	197	745
Finland	913	0	459	30	403	31	1836
France	3254	551	5437	613	4540	225	14 620
Germany	19 229	729	2984	526	4581	107	28 156
Greece	20 961	0	0	0	0	0	20 961
Ireland	1315	1773	0	0	0	0	3088
Italy	21 935	187	2145	377	3744	96	28 484
Lux.	0	0	34	6	38	0	78
NL	0	123	676	119	1686	31	2635
Portugal	16 124	2905	0	0	0	0	19 029
Spain	37 744	352	2553	98	2140	200	43 087
Sweden	722	0	354	52	720	60	1908
UK	5085	1166	3989	706	4568	121	15 635
EU (15)	127 543	8411	19 733	2721	24 050	1106	183 564

Source: European Commission (2004), www.europa.eu.int/comm/regional

Objective 1 regions (see Figure 13.3) include Eastern Germany (except East Berlin), Greece, Portugal (except Lisbon and the Tagus Valley), ten Spanish regions, four Irish regions, the Italian Mezzogiorno (except Molise), six thinly populated regions in Sweden and Finland, the Austrian Burgenland, the French overseas departments, and four areas in the UK. There is transitional support of up to six years for regions that no longer qualify for Objective I measures.

■ A further 12.3 per cent of Structural Funds was earmarked to assist the economic and social conversion of Objective 2 regions which were facing change in industrial and service sectors or urban difficulties, declining rural areas and depressed regions dependent on fishing.

■ The remaining funds were allocated to Objective 3, which is a so-called horizontal measure in the sense it applies throughout the EU. Its aim is to improve human capital by promoting employment, education and professional training. Objective 3 schemes must promote equal opportunities between men and women.

It was hoped that by adopting these three Objectives, priorities would be fixed, and the use of funds would be rendered more effective.

The European Council in Berlin agreed €195 billion for the Structural Funds and €18 billion for the Cohesion Fund for the 2000–06 period. Each year €1.04 billion would be earmarked over the 2000–06 period for ISPA (the Pre-Accession Structural Instrument) for the CEECs, and from 2002 the financial perspective contained a budgetary heading for Structural Funds for the new member states.

During the 2000–06 period the maximum Community financial contribution was fixed at 75 per cent (85 per cent in exceptional circumstances) of the cost of a project in Objective 1 regions where normally the EU contribution is at least 50 per cent. With regard to Objective 2 and 3 measures, the maximum Community contribution was fixed at 50 per cent, and the EU

Figure 13.3 Objective 1 regions in the EU
The lighter grey areas are those qualifying for transitory support

Source: www.europa.eu.int/comm/regional_policy/objective1/map

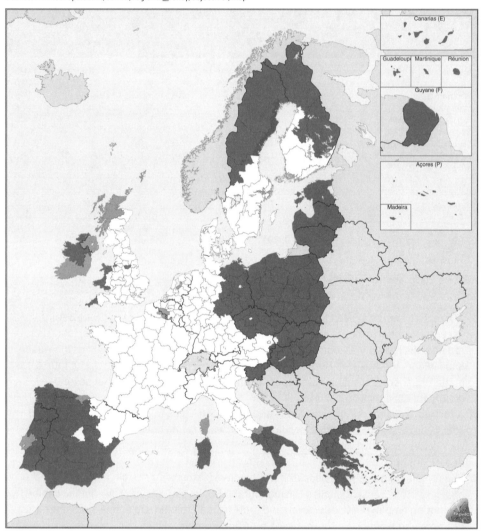

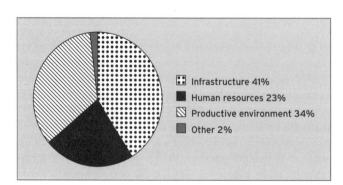

Figure 13.4 Breakdown of Structural Fund allocation in Objective 1 regions: all member states, 2000-06

Source: European Commission (2004).

contribution is usually at least 25 per cent of the total cost. However, in countries with short-comings in administrative capacity (such as Italy), the advantage of a higher percentage of Community financing in Objective 1 regions was somewhat offset by more difficult procedures in such regions.

HAS THERE BEEN CONVERGENCE IN THE EU?

The disparities in income and in employment among EU countries have narrowed over the past decade.[11] Growth in all four of the Cohesion countries was well above the average for the EU (15) between 1994 and 2001, and this translated into higher rates of GDP per capita relative to the rest of the EU (see Table 13.5).[12]

In Ireland where population grew by 1 per cent a year between 1994 and 2001, GDP per capita increased by 8 per cent a year compared with the EU average of 2 per cent a year. As a result GDP per capita in purchasing power parity terms (PPP) in Ireland increased to 22 per cent above the EU average in 2002 compared with about 25 per cent below the EU average at the beginning of the 1990s (see Box 13.2 below).

Table 13.5 Development of GDP per capita (EU15 = 100) for the EU(15)

	1950 (euros)	1990 (euros)	2000 (euros)	1990 (PPP)	2002 (PPP)	2003 (PPP) forecast
Germany	93	125	111	116	103	109
France	136	111	106	109	103	114
Italy	71	101	89	102	102	107
Netherlands	100	100	111	100	113	120
Belgium	166	104	106	105	109	117
Luxembourg	201	149	191	150	190	209
UK	140	89	113	99	103	120
Denmark	153	132	142	104	114	124
Ireland	81	71	112	74	122	132
Spain	35	69	67	77	84	96
Portugal	35	37	49	61	69	75
Greece	30	43	52	58	67	80
Austria	58	109	112	105	110	122
Sweden	170	142	122	108	102	116
Finland	114	143	110	102	102	111
EU15	100	100	100	100	100	110

Source: European Commission, www.europa.eu.int/comm/regional, and elaborations based on Eurostat data.

The increase in employment (defined as the percentage of people of working age, i.e. between 15 and 64, in jobs) in the four Cohesion countries also rose twice as quickly as the EU average increase of 4 per cent over the 1996–2002 period (see Table 13.6). As a result, the average employment rate in the four Cohesion countries was 60 per cent in 2002, compared with the EU average of 64 per cent. The rise in employment over the 1996–2002 period was particularly high in Spain (11 per cent) and Ireland (10 per cent).

---

[11] The issues of regional disparities and the application of the Structural Funds in the new member states are taken up in Chapter 20.
[12] Unless otherwise stated, the data in this section are taken from European Commission (2004).

	1996	2002
EU(15)	59.9	64.3
4 Cohesion countries	51.5	60.2
Greece	54.9	56.7
Spain	47.6	58.4
Ireland	54.9	65.3
Portugal	62.3	68.2

Table 13.6 Employment rates in the EU(15), 1996 and 2002 (per cent)

Source: European Commission (2001 and 2004).

Productivity growth over the period was also higher than the EU average in Ireland (roughly 4 per cent per year over the 1996–2002 period), Greece (2.5 per cent per year over the same period), though in Spain and Portugal it was slower (Table 13.7). However, substantial differences in GDP per head and employment rates between EU regions remain and, as explained in Chapter 20, these have been increased by enlargement.

Table 13.7 Growth in GDP and labour productivity in the EU(15) (per cent)

GDP growth				Labour productivity increase			
	1996-2000	2001	2002		1996-2000	2001	2002
Greece	3.4	4.0	3.9	Greece	2.5	4.4	3.8
Spain	4.2	4.2	2.8	Spain	0.7	0.4	0.5
Ireland	9.8	6.2	6.9	Ireland	3.9	3.1	5.5
Portugal	3.9	1.7	0.4	Portugal	1.8	0.4	0.1
Belgium	2.7	0.6	0.7	Belgium	1.4	-0.8	1.0
Germany	1.8	0.8	0.2	Germany	1.1	0.4	0.8
France	2.7	2.1	1.2	France	1.5	0.3	0.5
Italy	1.9	1.8	0.4	Italy	1.1	0.1	-0.9
Lux.	7.1	1.2	1.3	Lux.	2.8	-4.2	-1.8
NL	3.7	1.2	0.2	NL	1.2	-0.1	0.0
Austria	2.7	0.8	1.4	Austria	1.9	0.1	1.4
Finland	4.7	1.1	2.3	Finland	2.4	-0.4	1.3
Denmark	2.7	1.6	1.0	Denmark	1.6	1.2	1.6
Sweden	3.2	0.9	2.1	Sweden	2.5	-1.0	1.9
UK	3.1	2.1	1.6	UK	1.6	1.4	0.9
EU(15)	2.7	1.7	1.1	EU(15)	1.3	0.4	0.5

Source: European Commission (2004).

Econometric research carried out by the European Commission also suggests that there has been convergence of GDP per capita across the EU.[13] The analysis takes real growth for 197 regions between 1980 and 2001, dividing this into three periods (1980–88, 1988–94 and 1994–2001). There appears to be a significant tendency for growth to be inversely related to initial GDP per capita (see Table 13.8), and this tendency is generally known as 'beta convergence'. In other words beta convergence implies that the regions with the lowest GDP per capita in the base year on average experience the highest growth in GDP per capita. According to the analysis of the European Commission, beta convergence also occurred within Objective 1 regions, with the regions with the lowest GDP per capita tending to grow fastest in the 1988–94 and 1994–2001 periods.

However, a somewhat different picture emerges from other studies of whether there is convergence at the level of regions within each EU member state. Empirical studies such as those by

---

[13] European Commission (2004).

	Number of regions	GDP per head % growth rate	Beta convergence rate per year (%)*	R-squared#
1980-88				
All EU(15) regions	197	2.0	0.5	0.94
Objective 1 regions	55	1.9	0.4	0.87
Other regions	142	2.0	2.1	0.92
1988-94				
All EU(15) regions	197	1.3	0.7	0.97
Objective 1 regions	55	1.4	3.1	0.94
Other regions	142	1.2	0.8	0.95
1994-2001				
All EU(15) regions	197	2.3	0.9	0.97
Objective 1 regions	55	2.6	1.6	0.92
Other regions	142	2.1	0.0	0.96

Table 13.8 **Regional convergence**

*Beta convergence implies that the regions with the lowest GDP per capita in the base year on average experience the highest growth in GDP per capita. See explanation in the text.
R-squared is the usual statistical term.[14]
Source: European Commission (2004).

Brülhart and Traeger (2003) and Midelfart-Knarvik and Overman (2002) suggest that over time within EU countries the internal concentration of manufacturing in certain geographical areas has increased. Variations in results may arise because different time periods, regions and indicators of regional disparities are taken into account.

THE ROLE OF THE STRUCTURAL FUNDS

It is extremely difficult to assess the effectiveness of structural measures on a number of counts, and the following list does not pretend to be exhaustive:

- The impact of many projects and programmes (e.g. infrastructure) can only be assessed in the long run;
- Problems arise in isolating the effects of regional policies from other factors (including other EU policies with regional implications such as the CAP);
- It is difficult to separate the impact of national and EU regional policies;
- Recipients tend to overestimate the impact of regional measures.

Despite these difficulties, evaluation studies carried out by the Commission on structural actions for the 2000–06 period suggest that interventions in Objective 1 regions are likely to lead to the creation of about 700 000 jobs, amounting to an increase in employment of about 187 000 jobs or 4 per cent in Portugal, 100 000 jobs or 2.5 per cent in Greece and 1–2 per cent in the new German Länder, Italy and Spain (European Commission, 2004).

Simulations carried out by the European Commission using the HERMIN model suggest that structural interventions have raised growth by increasing demand and strengthening the supply

[14] R-squared is defined as the proportion of the total variation in the dependent variable y, explained by the regression of y on the independent variable. R-squared takes values between zero (when the regression model does nothing to explain the variation in y) and one (when all the sample points lie on the regression line). The values for R-squared in the table are relatively high, suggesting a good fit for the regression.

side of the EU economy (by improving infrastructure and human capital) (see Table 13.9).[15] As a result of structural actions it is estimated that GDP was 2.2 per cent higher than it would otherwise have been in Greece, 1.4 per cent higher in Spain, 2.8 per cent in Ireland and 4.7 per cent in Portugal.

Table 13.9 *Ex post* macroeconomic effects of structural policy, 1994-99: HERMIN simulation results*

	Greece	Spain	Ireland	Portugal	East Germany	Northern Ireland
GDP	2.2	1.4	2.8	4.7	3.9	1.3
Manufacturing output	3.4	3.7	4.7	10.6	3.2	0.6
Market services output	2.4	1.2	2.4	4.8	4.4	2.2
Fixed investment*	18.1	9.1	1.1	24.8	7.8	1.2
Labour productivity	2.3	2.1	2.1	6.6	1.2	0.5
Employment*	1.0	1.5	4.7	3.7	2.0	0.1

*Percentage difference from baseline without policy in 1999
Source: European Commission (2004).

THE NEED TO SELECT AN APPROPRIATE DEVELOPMENT STRATEGY

Though there is much debate about the role of structural measures (redistribution, resource allocation policy or *juste retour*; see, for example, Hardy et al., 1995), there seems widespread consensus that a low level of economic development should not be a sufficient condition for receiving transfers. Instead an effective policy should be based on a development strategy.

In evolving that strategy there are differences of opinion about whether industrial districts or clusters are preferable to more evenly spread growth. What emerges from the experience of EU member states and, in particular the Irish example, is the importance of paying adequate attention to the interaction of regional measures and the wider framework of macroeconomic policies (see Box 13.2).

The objectives of regional policy are strongly linked to the Lisbon strategy. As explained in Chapter 6, with the Lisbon strategy the EU established the goal of becoming the most competitive and dynamic economy in the world by 2010. At a national level, the Lisbon strategy requires an appropriate macroeconomic environment conducive to growth, while at a regional level various conditions are necessary (European Commission, 2004):

■ Basic infrastructure, including efficient transport, energy and telecommunications networks.
■ Environmental infrastructure (waste management, waste water treatment, drinking water supply etc.).
■ A development path that is sustainable in order to protect the environment.
■ A labour force with appropriate skills and training.
■ High priority to innovation and widespread access to information and communication technologies. This entails regions that are able to generate, diffuse and utilize technologies and a business culture that encourages entrepreneurship.
■ An efficient administrative framework providing sufficient institutional support.

---

[15] European Commission (2004). The HERMIN model was built at the beginning of the 1990s and has been used chiefly to assess the impact of EU structural actions.

EU regional policy adds certain other priority policy areas to this list:

- Modernization and restructuring of the production sector;
- Improvement of health infrastructure;
- Safeguard of cultural heritage; and
- Measures to reduce regional imbalances.

The regional policy strategies of the member states give different weights to these priorities. Ireland, for example, concentrates on human resources and training, and on infrastructure, which in the Irish context seems to have proved a happy combination (see Box 13.2). With the higher overall level of development the emphasis is now shifting to regional imbalances (Tondl, 2001). Spain places equal weight on the production sector, infrastructure and human resources, while Greece concentrates on transport infrastructure and regional development.[16]

Box 13.2 A case study of the catching-up process in the EU: the Celtic Tiger

From the early 1990s the Irish economy experienced consistently high growth both compared with the USA and average EU performances, leading to the term 'Celtic Tiger'. Irish GDP per capita increased from 71 per cent of the Community average in 1990 to 122 per cent in 2002 (see Table 13.5). Various explanations have been advanced for this exceptional performance. In general, attention is drawn to the strategy to reduce employment adopted by successive Irish governments since the 1960s, which entails attempts to attract foreign direct investment and promote export-led growth. A favourable regime of corporation tax and financial incentives was used to encourage investment by foreign companies. Active intervention by, for example, the IDA Ireland (the Industrial Development Agency Ireland) was used to select investment in what were considered sectors with a global growth potential (such as electronics and the pharmaceutical industries). The FDI strategy also encouraged upstream linkages between foreign and indigenous companies, the creation of industrial clusters and the location of industry in the less developed areas of the country such as the West. The stability offered by EU membership and the advantage of an English-speaking labour force helped to attract foreign investors. An important role was also played by a policy of improving education and human capital from the 1960s and by the introduction of appropriate macroeconomic policies and a restrained wage-setting environment in the 1980s.

Substantial financing through the EU Structural Funds (see Tables 13.1, 13.2 and 13.4) contributed to the financing of regional investments and incentives at a time when the Irish economy could not have provided these resources without undermining its corrective macroeconomic policies (Braunerhjelm et al., 2000). A relatively efficient administration also favoured the successful implementation of measures financed with the EU Structural Funds.

It is also essential to develop an appropriate system for selecting projects and programmes, for setting out clear objectives and targets and for carrying out effective evaluation and monitoring. There are also substantial differences in the ability to implement structural measures among existing EU member states. Experience suggests that the extent to which a member state can derive

---

[16] A useful approach for assessing the effectiveness of the Structural Funds would be to select examples of projects financed by the funds and assess the impact of these projects. For reasons of space this has not been attempted here, but for examples of this type of analysis see European Commission (2004).

benefits from the resources it receives depends not only on the level of financing but also on administrative capacity and the efficient use of national and Community resources (Bollen et al., 2000). The system should also be able to withstand pressure from politicians and pressure groups.

In short, it is necessary to develop a strategy for ensuring the effectiveness of regional policy, and this is likely to include the following elements:

■ Evolving an overall strategy to regional and national development to avoid the risk of piecemeal, unco-ordinated measures;
■ Ensuring stable macroeconomic policies;
■ Adopting robust selection procedures and effective monitoring of programmes; and
■ Developing an effective institutional framework for planning and implementing measures.

Summary of Key Concepts

● Regional problems are the disparities in levels of income, in rates of growth of output and employment, and in general in levels of economic inequality between different regions.
● The view that integration will lead to greater convergence assumes effective functioning of the market. Convergence is said to occur through free trade, labour migration, capital mobility and diminishing returns to capital accumulation.
● Theories explaining why integration may lead to divergence or greater disparities between regions include modern growth theories, the evolutionary economics view of knowledge diffusion and the New Economic Geography approach.
● The four 'Structural Funds' are the European Social Fund, the European Fund for Regional Development, the Guidance Section of the European Agricultural Guidance and Guarantee Fund, and the Financial Instrument for Fisheries Guidance. Related instruments are the European Cohesion Fund and the European Investment Bank.
● The evolution of EU regional policy can be divided into three main stages: 1959–75 (mainly national measures), 1975–88 (new EC initiatives were launched) and since 1988 (the development of regional policy with the reforms of 1988, 1993 and 1999).
● The four principles of operation of the Structural Funds are: concentration, partnership, programming and additionality.
● The objectives of the Structural Funds have changed over the years. Since 2000 there have been three objectives. Objective 1 covers the less well-developed areas of the Community, which are defined as those whose GDP per capita is less than 75 percent of the EU average. Objective 2 concerns the economic and social conversion of regions. Objective 3 aims at improvement of human capital.
● There appears to have been convergence between EU countries.
● It is extremely difficult to assess the effectiveness of structural measures because the impact of many projects can only be assessed in the long run; problems arise in isolating the effects of regional policies from other factors, and recipients tend to overestimate the impact of regional measures.
● To render regional policy effective, it is necessary to develop an overall strategy to regional and national development; to ensure stable macroeconomic policies, and to develop an effective institutional framework for planning and implementing measures.

Questions for Study and Review

■ Do you think that integration leads to more or less income disparity?
■ Describe the Structural Funds, the Cohesion Fund and the activities of the European Investment Bank.

■ What are the main stages in the evolution of EU regional policy?
■ How well do you consider that the principles for implementing the Structural Funds function?
■ Has there been convergence between EU countries and regions?
■ How effective were the interventions of the Structural Funds? Why is it so difficult to provide an assessment of their effectiveness?
■ What strategies can be used to render regional policy more effective?

References

Baldwin, R. and Wyplosz, C. (2004) *The Economics of European Integration*, McGraw-Hill Education, Maidenhead, UK.

Bollen, F., Hartwig, I. and Nicolaides, P. (2000) *EU Structural Funds beyond Agenda 2000: Reform and Implications for the Current and Future Member States*, European Institute of Public Administration (EIPA), Maastricht.

Braunerhjelm, P., Faini, R., Norman, V., Ruane, F., and Seabright, P. (2000) *Integration and the Regions of Europe: How the Right Policies Can Prevent Polarization*, Monitoring European Integration 10. CEPR, London.

Brülhart, M. and Traeger, R. (2003) 'An account of geographic concentration patterns in Europe', Cahiers de Recherches Economiques du Département d'Econometrie e d'Economie Politique (DEEP), Université de Lausanne, www.hec.unil.ch/deep/publications-english

European Commission (1994) White Paper: 'European Social Policy: A way forward for the Union'.

European Commission (2001) 'Second Report on Economic and Social Cohesion'.

European Commission (2004) 'Third Report on Economic and Social Cohesion'.

Hardy, S., Hart, M., Albrechts, L. and Katos, A. (1995) *An Enlarged EU: Regions in Competition?* Jessica Kingsley Publishers, London and Bristol, PA.

Harrop, J. (2000) *The Political Economy of Integration in the European Union*, 3rd edn, Edward Elgar, Cheltenham.

Krugman, P. R. (1991) *Geography and Trade*, Leuven University Press, Leuven and The MIT Press, Cambridge, MA.

Krugman, P. R. and Venables, A. (1990) 'Integration and the competitiveness of peripheral industry' in Bliss, C.J. and Braga de Macedo, J. (eds) *Unity with Diversity in the European Economy: The Communities' Southern Frontier*, Cambridge University Press, Cambridge.

Lucas, R. E. (1988) 'On the mechanics of economic development', *Journal of Economic Literature*, Vol. 22.

Martin, J.P. (1998) 'What works among active labour market policies: Evidence from OECD countries' experiences', OECD Occasional Papers, No. 35, Paris.

Midelfart-Knarvik, K-H. and Overman, H. (2002) 'Delocation and European integration: Is structural spending justified?', *Economic Policy*, Vol. 17.

Molle, W. (2001) *The Economics of European Integration. Theory, Practice, Policy*, 4th edn, Ashgate, Aldershot.

Navarro, L. (2003) 'Industrial policy in the economic literature: Recent theoretical developments and implications for EU policy', Enterprise papers No. 12, www.europa.eu.int/comm/enterprise

Nelson, R.R. and Winter, S.G. (1982) *An Evolutionary Theory of Economic Change*, Harvard University Press, Cambridge.

Salvatore, D. (2001) *International Economics*, 7th edn, John Wiley & Sons, New York.

Tondl, G. (2001) 'Regional policy', in Artis, M. and Nixson, F. (eds) *The Economics of the European Union: Policy and Analysis*, 3rd edn, Oxford University Press, Oxford.

Tsoukalis, L. (1997) *The New European Economy Revisited,* 3rd edn, Oxford University Press, Oxford.

Williams, R.H. (1996) *European Union Spacial Policy and Planning,* Paul Chapman, London.

Useful websites

European Commission Directorate-General for Regional Policy:
http://europa.int.eu/comm/regional
The Inforegio site of the European Commission which provides data and analysis of EU regional policy:
http://inforegio.cec.eu.int

List of abbreviations

ACP	African, Caribbean and Pacific countries covered by the Lomé Conventions and Cotonou Agreement
CAP	Common Agricultural Policy
CEEC	Central and Eastern European country
ECU	European currency unit
EIB	European Investment Bank
EQUAL	Community Initiative on transnational co-operation to combat all kinds of discrimination and inequalities in the labour market
ERDF	European Regional Development Fund
ESF	European Social Fund
FDI	foreign direct investment
FIFG	Financial Instrument for Fisheries Guidance
FEOGA	European Agricultural Guidance and Guarantee Fund
GDP	gross domestic product
IDA Ireland	Industrial Development Agency Ireland
INTERREG II	Community Initiative on cross-border, transnational and interregional co-operation
ISPA	Pre-Accession Structural Instrument
LEADER +	Community Initiative on rural development
PPP	purchasing power parity
R&D	research and development
URBAN	Community Initiative on economic and social regeneration of cities and urban neighbourhoods

14

Social and Employment Policies

LEARNING OBJECTIVES

By the end of this chapter you should be able to understand:

▶ What we mean by EU social policy;

▶ The main stages in the development of EU social policy;

▶ What the EU is doing to fight unemployment;

▶ What the EU is doing to combat poverty;

▶ How effective EU social and employment policy has been.

INTRODUCTION

The term 'social policy' covers a wide range of issues whose boundaries are at times indistinct. Social policies include the various measures to regulate the labour market but also measures to combat poverty and social exclusion, and to improve education, training, housing and health care.[1] One of the main ways in which social policy may reduce disparities is by improving access to employment. Social policy and the fight against unemployment are therefore intrinsically linked.

As described below, the European Employment Strategy (EES) was launched in 1997 to combat unemployment through preventive methods and active policies to promote employability. In 2003 the EES was streamlined and revised with the aim of better realizing the Lisbon Strategy in an enlarged EU (see Chapter 6).

European social policy includes the social policies of the member states and EU, and so has to be distinguished from EU social policy. EU social policy covers a relatively limited range of issues and

---

[1] European Commission (1993a) defines European social policy as the 'full range of policies in the social sphere, including labour market policies'.

amounts to just a small fraction of welfare expenditure by the member states, tending simply to complement national measures.

The aims and actions of EU social policy have evolved over the years, and since the 1990s increased priority has been given to:

- Employment policies and working conditions;
- Social exclusion, or the fight against poverty;
- Equality between men and women;
- The involvement of the so-called social partners (trade unions and employers) in the legislative process;
- The participation of workers in the decision-making of the firm.

Differences in the level of social protection between the member states may also give rise to fears of social dumping. Firms may have an incentive to locate in countries where wages and the cost of social protection is lower (usually the poorer member states). To counter this tendency countries with higher social standards may be forced to reduce social standards, giving rise to the risk of a 'race to the bottom'. One way of tackling the risk of social dumping is by setting certain minimum standards for working conditions, health and safety in all member states.

Despite the increasing role of the Community in the social sphere, there remain several obstacles to developing a fully fledged EU social policy:

- Differences in the demographic and socio-economic conditions of the member states;
- The contentious nature of social policy issues, with strong ideological differences about what the role of the state should be;
- The diversity of national social policy regimes;
- The reluctance of member states to give up control of social policy;
- The scale of budgetary transfers necessary for an extensive EU social policy; and
- The even greater diversity of social policy requirements and regimes after the 2004 enlargement.

THE EVOLUTION OF EU SOCIAL POLICY

The origins of EU social policy are to be found in all three of the original treaties founding the European Communities. Article 46 of the Treaty of Paris establishing the European Coal and Steel Community refers to the improvement of the living and working standards of workers in the coal and steel industries. The Euratom Treaty sets out provisions for the health and safety of workers in the civilian atomic energy industry. By far the most extensive treatment of social policy is to be found in the Treaty of Rome which refers to:

- Free movement of workers (Articles 48-51);
- Improvement in working conditions and in standards of living (Articles 117-128);
- Equal opportunities for men and women (see Box 14.1) (Article 119); and
- The creation of the European Social Fund (Article 123).

However, there was a dichotomy between the very ambitious objectives set out in the Treaty of Rome and the very limited means to achieve these aims. The commitments set out in the Treaty were far from being precise, and there was no fixed timetable for action. For instance, it was envisaged that improved working standards and conditions of work would be realized through operation of the common market.

Box 14.1 Gender equality in the EU

Article 119 of the Treaty of Rome (now Article 141 of the EC Treaty) guarantees equal pay for men and women. As some member states were failing to comply with Article 119, the Community introduced Directives on equal pay (1975), equal treatment (1976) and the elimination of discrimination in pension schemes (1986). The Court of Justice also reinforced EU gender policy in judgments such as Defrenne vs. Sabena on equal pay (1976), and the Marschall Judgment of 1997 which allowed priority to be given to the woman in the event of male and female candidates possessing the same qualifications.

In 1996 the Commission adopted the gender mainstreaming approach that involves 'incorporating equal opportunities for women and men into all Community policies and activities' (COM(96)67 final). The Structural Funds are also used to promote gender equality through specific actions such as the EQUAL Programme aimed at ensuring equality of opportunity for everyone.

Under the Amsterdam and Nice treaties co-decision and qualified majority voting are to be used on matters relating to equal pay for equal work or for 'work of the same value' (Article 141, EC Treaty). Article 2 includes a general objective to promote 'equality between men and women' which is reiterated in Article 3 which sets out the instruments to be used. Article 13 provides a legal basis to prevent discrimination on grounds of sex.

The European Employment Strategy aims at promoting equal pay. The Community Framework Strategy on Gender Equality covering the 2001-05 period called for tools such as gender impact assessment, training, networking and data collection to render policy more effective. The Framework Strategy identifies five fields of intervention:

- Promoting gender equality in economic life;
- Promoting equal participation and representation;
- Promoting access and full employment of social rights;
- Promoting gender equality in civil life; and
- Promoting change of gender roles and stereotypes.

However, despite these various initiatives, participation of women in the EU labour force remains lower (see below), unemployment among women is on average 3 per cent higher and the gender pay gap is still 20 per cent, also because women count for 77 per cent of low paid employees (European Commission, 2002).

In June 2003 news that the Commission was proposing legislation to prevent sexism in advertising, the media and financial services caused consternation in some of the British and German popular newspapers and Italian television.

The evolution of EU social policy can be divided into four main periods: 1958–73, 1974–85, 1985–92 and since 1993.

The 1958-73 period

The social policy of the Community maintained a low profile during this period, and its principal aim was to promote the free movement of labour.[2] This entailed co-ordinating the national social security systems of member states in order to guarantee the rights of emigrant workers. Progress in recognizing qualifications obtained in other member states was slow, so movement of labour was mainly confined to young or unskilled workers (Tsoukalis, 1997).

---

[2] See also Chapter 7.

The 1974-85 period

Following the 1973 oil crisis the economic situation in the Community degenerated rapidly, with increasing unemployment and stagnating growth. The deteriorating conditions led the Community to introduce the first Social Action Programme in 1974 aimed at:

■ The attainment of full and better employment;

■ The improvement and upward harmonization of living standards;

■ Greater involvement of employer and employee organizations in the economic and social decisions of the Community and of workers in the life of their firms.

Despite its good intentions the programme led to few concrete actions, though it served as a frame of reference for later programmes. At the time unemployment was soaring, funds were limited and the member states were reluctant to transfer responsibility for social matters to the Community. EC intervention tended to be piecemeal, but a few successes were registered (Tsoukalis, 1997). Directives were introduced to improve work standards and safety, to promote equality between men and women and to regulate the conditions for collective dismissals.

During this period EC social policy was still mainly concentrated on the co-ordination of national social security systems to permit the freedom of movement of labour and the operation of the European Social Fund. The ESF became more directed towards the fight against youth and long-term unemployment, in particular by promoting training schemes. However, EC policy was characterized by a lack of flexibility in selecting programmes and a tendency to rubber stamp decisions already taken at the national level. Moreover, in many cases it seems likely that EC measures simply replaced national financing (the so-called additionality problem; see Chapter 13).

The 1985-92 period

Given the limited success of earlier measures, many of the social policy objectives of the Treaty of Rome still had not been realized when the Single Market Programme was introduced. Although social policy was not mentioned in the White Paper of 1985, debate about a 'social dimension' to the Single Market was soon to emerge. Proponents of a more active EC role in social policy argued that this was necessary because the adjustment implied by the Single Market Project could lead to higher unemployment and that deregulation could lead to a risk of social dumping.

Though the debate about EC social policy was linked to the Single Market Project, its ideological basis was wider, reflecting different views of the role of the state in the economy. The case for an increased role for the Community was generally based on a fundamental belief that the workings of the market had to be corrected on grounds of equity and consensus. Social cohesion was necessary to correct the possible negative impact of increased competition on the weaker and more vulnerable regions and sections of the population. Minimum social standards had to be introduced to prevent the risk of social dumping. Increased participation of the workers in the decisions of firms, and of the so-called social partners (employers and trade unions) in EC decision-making, were ways of achieving consensus.

Those in favour of this type of approach included the Socialist president of the Commission, Delors, centre-left members of the European Parliament and the Socialist governments in France and some of the Southern EC countries (Tsoukalis, 1997). Most Christian Democratic parties were then in favour of legislation to protect welfare and employment. In Germany there was a long tradition of worker participation in the decisions of the firm and attempts to find consensus between the social partners.

Perhaps the main opposition in the ideological debate was to be found in the British Conservative Party, and Margaret Thatcher in particular. Increased government regulation of working conditions was considered to add to labour market rigidities, reducing competitiveness and increasing unemployment. The poor British performance when the Conservatives took office was interpreted as being largely the result of excessive trade union influence. Worse still, the attempt to strengthen the Community role in this area was considered an attack on national sovereignty and a violation of the principle of subsidiarity. The British government found support for this position among EC employers' federations and its own businessmen.[3]

Delors was among the main proponents of a more active EC social policy, or 'European Social Space', and four aspects of this position can be distinguished:[4]

- Social dialogue, or the involvement of the social partners in the EC decision-making process. In 1985 Delors arranged a meeting of associations at the Belgian château of Val Duchesse to promote social dialogue between the Commission, employers and employees. This subsequently became known as the 'Val Duchesse Process' and was institutionalized by the Single European Act (Article 118b) and the Maastricht Treaty (Article 3 of the Social Protocol).

- The Social Charter, or Community Charter of the Fundamental Social Rights of Workers. This was drawn up as a non-binding declaration of intent at the request of the Commission, European Parliament and Economic and Social Committee. It builds on the Social Charter of the Council of Europe and similar documents of the International Labour Office. An action programme accompanied the Charter with specific measures designed to assist realization of the objectives. As can be seen from Box 14.2, the objectives are couched in very general terms, but some were still the subject of heated controversy. For instance, the aim of achieving an 'equitable wage' was interpreted by some as implying the introduction of a minimum wage. Measures to protect seasonal, temporary and part-time workers were seen as an attempt to extend full social protection to such forms of atypical work, so adding to labour market rigidities. Although amended to take account of British objections, the Charter was not accepted by the UK, but it was adopted by the other 11 member states in 1989.

Box 14.2 The Social Charter

- The improvement of living and working conditions;
- The right to freedom of movement;
- The right to employment with adequate remuneration;
- The right to social protection;
- The right to freedom and collective bargaining;
- The right to vocational training;
- The right of men and women to equal treatment;
- The right to information, consultation and worker participation;
- The right to health protection and safety at the workplace;
- The protection of children and adolescents;
- The protection of elderly persons;
- Specific measures for disabled people.

- The creation of a 'Europe of the citizens', aimed at reducing the democratic deficit and bringing the Community closer to the people (see Chapter 7).

---

[3] Tsoukalis, 1997.
[4] Delors presented his vision of a European Social Space, *inter alia*, at the European Trades Union Conference (ETUC) of 1988.

■ The introduction of an EC company statute that would ensure the participation of workers in the decisions of the firm along the lines of the German and Dutch models. In December 2000 the Council agreed on the introduction of a European Company Statute which would enable a company with a European dimension to set up as a single company under EU law with a unified set of rules, management and reporting system, and provisions for safeguarding workers' rights.

Though the Single European Act contained relatively few increases in the EC role in social policy, reference was first made to the need for economic and social cohesion, social dialogue (Article 118b) and improvements in health and safety at the workplace (Article 118a).

Since 1993

The Social Charter was subsequently to form the basis of the Social Chapter of the Treaty of Maastricht, which covers issues such as minimum hours of work, social security, health and safety requirements and consultation of the social partners.

Following its earlier refusal to sign the Social Charter, the UK also opted out of the Maastricht Social Chapter during the 1993–97 period, and only under the Blair government was policy reversed. The Social Chapter was therefore added to the Maastricht Treaty as a separate Protocol, and was only incorporated into the Community pillar under the Amsterdam Treaty. However, certain other aspects of social policy (such as protection of public health) were included in the Maastricht Treaty and were applicable in all member states. As can be seen from Chapter 3, some elements of the Social Charter and Maastricht Social Chapter were similar to the Charter of Fundamental Human Rights approved at Nice in 2000.

The Amsterdam Treaty added three new objectives to EU social policy (Articles 136 and 137):

■ Proper social protection;
■ Social dialogue between management and labour; and
■ The development of human resources with a view to lasting high employment and combating forms of economic and social exclusion.

The Nice European Council of 2000 adopted a European Social Agenda that involves:

■ Measures to realize the employment potential of the EU by creating new and better jobs, managing change, exploiting the potential of the knowledge-based economy and promoting mobility;
■ The modernization and improvement of social protection and the reduction of social exclusion, gender inequality and arbitrary discrimination;
■ Preparation for enlargement and ensuring that social dialogue contributes to meeting the various challenges.

THE EUROPEAN EMPLOYMENT STRATEGY

At the time of the Treaty of Rome unemployment was relatively low in the Community, so the Treaty contained few provisions on employment. The Commission published White Papers in 1993 and 1994 aimed at promoting employment, competitiveness and growth without compromising social protection.[5] However, it was not until the Amsterdam Treaty that the legal basis of employment as a major area of EU policy was established.

---

[5] European Commission (1993b and 1994).

Title VIII of the Treaty of Amsterdam sets out the main features of EU employment policy:

- To develop a co-ordinated strategy of the member states toward unemployment;
- Employment is a matter of common concern;
- The objective of high employment must be taken into account in the formulation of EU policies and strategies;
- Multilateral surveillance;
- The Council, on a Commission proposal, may issue recommendations to member states for urgent action;
- Establishment of an employment committee to play a part in these processes and serve as a forum for debate.

The employment strategy was based on what are known as 'active labour market policies' to enable people to take up employment opportunities, increase skills and keep the unemployed in touch with the labour market. The EU adopted a dual approach to achieve these aims: setting the policy framework and guidelines and providing financing for programmes through the Structural Funds. However, the Treaty again stressed the need to 'take account of the diverse forms of national practices in particular in the field of contractual relations', and EU social and employment policy remains very much a complement to national measures.

In 1997 an Extraordinary European Council on Employment was held, and this marks the beginning of the Luxembourg Process to launch the European Employment Strategy (EES). The strategy is organized around four pillars:

- Improving 'employability' (through active labour-market policy such as training schemes for the young and long-term unemployed);
- Encouraging the adaptability of businesses and their employees (through union-negotiated work reorganization);
- Strengthening policies for equal opportunities (between men and women, and also increasing job possibilities for the disabled);
- Developing entrepreneurship (in particular through deregulation and simplification of market access for small firms).

Within each pillar, following a proposal from the Commission, the Council sets policy guidelines, some also having detailed quantitative targets with the aim of rendering monitoring easier. Member states are asked to set out annual National Action Plans indicating labour market targets and their implementation. The European Commission carries out monitoring and is also responsible for the formulation of recommendations. The Council can also make recommendations acting on a proposal from the Commission. The Commission and the Council publish annual Joint Employment Reports.

The aims of the Lisbon Strategy include achieving higher employment rates (rather than lower unemployment rates), increasing the rate of participation in the labour force to 67 per cent of the labour force by 2005 and 70 per cent by 2010 (60 per cent for women). Major challenges also included addressing skill shortages and improving the quality of work (through 'more and better jobs').

With regard to employment (see Table 14.1), the EU seems likely to miss the mid-term Lisbon target, though it has already been met by four EU countries (Denmark, Netherlands, Sweden and the UK).[6] The mid-term target of employing 57 per cent of women seems likely to be met. According to the Commission (2004), some 6 million jobs have been created since 1999. Part of

---

[6] European Commission (2004).

Employment % of labour force 2002							
	total	men	women		total	men	women
DE	65.3	71.7	58.8	BG	50.6	53.7	47.5
FR	63.0	75.2	56.7	CY	68.6	78.9	59.1
IT	55.5	62.9	42.0	CZ	65.4	73.9	57.0
NL	74.4	82.4	66.2	EE	62.0	66.5	57.9
BE	59.9	68.3	51.4	HU	56.5	63.5	50.0
LU	63.7	75.6	51.6	LT	59.9	62.7	57.2
UK	71.7	78.0	65.0	LV	60.4	64.3	56.8
DK	75.9	80.0	71.7	MT	54.5	75.3	33.6
IE	65.3	75.2	55.4	PL	51.5	56.9	46.2
ES	58.4	72.6	44.1	RO	57.6	63.9	51.8
PT	68.2	75.9	60.8	SV	63.4	68.2	58.6
FI	68.1	70.0	66.2	SK	56.8	62.4	51.4
EL	56.7	71.4	42.5	TK	45.6	65.5	25.5
AT	69.3	70.0	66.2				
S	73.6	74.9	72.3				

Table 14.1 Employment rates of men and women in the EU member states

Source: Eurostat.

proposed answer to the demographic challenge entails keeping older workers in employment longer, but this measure has encountered limited success.

In 2002 unemployment in the EU averaged 7.7 per cent of the labour force, compared with 10 per cent five years earlier, but in 2003 it increased to 8 per cent.[7] As can be seen from Figure 14.1, there are also considerable disparities in employment levels in the EU, with lower employment tending to be concentrated in certain countries of the periphery (Spain, Greece, the Mezzogiorno of Italy and Finland).

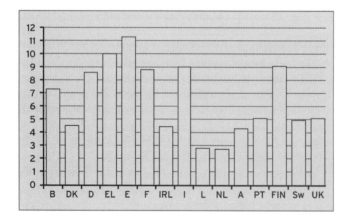

Figure 14.1 The unemployment rate in the EU member states in 2002

Source: European Commission.

The gap in labour productivity between the EU and the USA has widened and is now said to account for 40 per cent of the gap in GDP per capita between the EU and USA.[8] Since the mid-1970s EU unemployment has been consistently higher than that of the USA, while participation rates have been lower (about 60 per cent of the active population in the EU compared with 70 per

[7] The statistics in this paragraph are taken from European Commission (2004).
[8] According to European Commission (2003), at the end of 2003 EU GDP per capita was still only 72 per cent of the US level.

cent in the USA; see also Table 14.1).[9] While the USA has both relatively high productivity and participation rates, one of the difficulties in the EU is that member states either tend to have high participation rates and low productivity (such as in the UK), or relatively high productivity but low participation (Italy).[10]

One of the main ongoing debates about social and employment policies is how far the higher levels of employment and participation in the USA are the result of greater labour-market flexibility. The policy dilemma for the EU then becomes how to reconcile a relatively high level of social protection with international competitiveness.

The European Employment Strategy was evaluated in 2002 and was reinforced and streamlined in 2003 to underpin the Lisbon process in an enlarged EU. The guidelines of the EES were reduced to three:

- Achievement of the employment targets set at Lisbon;
- Quality and productivity at work as evidenced by more and better jobs;
- An inclusive labour market, in which unemployment is reduced and regional and social disparities in access to the labour market are narrowed.

With enlargement, the new member states had to take on the employment and social policy *acquis* at a time when the budgets in many of these countries were overstrained (see Chapter 20) and their welfare systems (health care, pensions, education etc.) required urgent reform. To prepare these countries for joining the European Employment Strategy, the Commission published 'Joint assessment papers' that analyse the labour market situation and trends, and identify proposals for reform.

FIGHTING POVERTY AND SOCIAL EXCLUSION IN THE EU

'Social exclusion' is the term used by the Commission for poverty and marginalization. The definition of poverty used by the EU is having an income less than 60 per cent of mean income in the country concerned (see Table 14.2 and Figure 14.2). The highest poverty rates in the EU(15) were in Ireland, Greece and Portugal.

Table 14.2 Population at risk of poverty after social transfers (2001)*

Country	%	Country	%
Belgium	13	Bulgaria	16
Denmark	11	Czech Republic	8
Germany	11	Estonia	18
Greece	20	hungary	10
Spain	19	Lithuania	17 (2002)
France	15	Poland	15
Ireland	21	Romania	17
Italy	19	Latvia	16 (2002)
Luxembourg	12	Slovakia	5 (2002)
Netherlands	11	Turkey	25 (2002)
Austria	12		
Portugal	20		
Finland	11		
Sweden	10		
UK	17		

(*Less than 60 per cent of mean income in the country concerned)
Source: European Commission (2004).

---

[9] This paragraph is based on Eurostat data.
[10] See Table 13.7 of Chapter 13 for statistics on labour productivity in the EU.

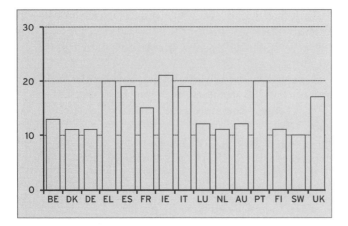

Figure 14.2 Poverty rate by member state in the EU(15) in 2001

Source: European Commission (2004).

Poverty tends to be closely linked to unemployment. In 2000 7 per cent of employed in the EU were below the poverty line in the EU(15), compared with 38 per cent of the unemployed and 25 per cent of the inactive (European Commission, 2004). The risk of poverty is also higher for single parents and old people living alone. In 2000 on average 35 per cent of single parents (mainly women) with dependent children, and almost 30 per cent of people over 65 and living alone, were below the poverty line (see Box 14.3).

Box 14.3 The aging of the EU population

In the EU(15) the share of the population over 65 is expected to rise from 25 per cent in 2000 to 36 per cent in 2025, with especially large increases projected for Italy, Sweden, Finland and Germany. In the new member states the share is expected to rise from just under 20 per cent to over 30 per cent during this period.* In the EU(15) the working age population (i.e. people from 15 to 64) is predicted to be 4 per cent lower in 2025 than in 2000, with especially large reductions for the Mediterranean countries and Italy in particular (a 14 per cent fall).

On average in the EU(15) in 2000 there were four people of working age for every person retired, but this is expected to fall to less than three to one by 2025. However, there are substantial divergencies in dependence rates between countries. In Italy in 2000 there were two people of working age for every person of 65 and over, and in Greece, Spain and Belgium there were fewer than 2.5.

Measures used to offset the effects of aging of the population in the EU include immigration policies (see Chapter 7), raising the retirement age and encouraging continued participation in the labour force by older workers.

*The data here are taken from European Commission (2004).

Though between 1975 and 1994 the Community introduced three 'poverty' programmes, EU financing of such measures has always been limited, mainly because the richer member states insist that this is primarily a policy area for national competences.

At the Lisbon European Council an 'Open Method of Co-ordination' was agreed to fight against poverty and social exclusion over the 2000–10 period. The key elements of this strategy are:

- Common objectives;
- National Action Plans against poverty and social exclusion;
- Joint reports and regular monitoring on social inclusion;
- Common indicators;
- A Community Action Programme to encourage co-operation between member states to combat social exclusion.

The Nice Summit subsequently agreed on four EU-level objectives: to promote participation and access of all to stable and quality jobs; to prevent risk of exclusion from new knowledge and technological developments; to help particularly vulnerable people and areas and to mainstream the fight against exclusion into overall policy. However, the strategy of the Community still appears to rely more on co-ordination than EU financial support.

The EU has developed policies for the disabled, though also here the primary responsibility remains with the member states. The EU supports access to jobs for the disabled through the European Social Fund and the Community Initiative, EQUAL. Support for disabled persons has also been mainstreamed into the EU's other employment policies. The National Action Plans of the member states include measures such as training, counselling and placements to encourage access of the disabled to employment. The Community also co-ordinates national measures and declared 2003 as European Year for the Disabled with a budget of €12 million.

EVALUATION OF EU SOCIAL AND EMPLOYMENT POLICIES

Until the mid-1980s EU social measures were mainly concerned with providing the legislative framework to facilitate freedom of labour movement. The announcement of the Single Market Programme in 1985 sparked a heated ideological debate about the role of the state in social policy and the role of the Community in particular. At the EC level the question was complicated by considerations of subsidiarity and the reluctance of member states to give up their sovereignty. With the 1990s priorities shifted, and the fight to promote employment gradually became a main policy concern of the EU. However, EU employment and social policy remained very much a complement to national measures, and expenditure amounted to only a small fraction of that of the member states.

Differences in national welfare systems, the socio-economic conditions of the member states, ideological conceptions concerning the role of the state in the economy and views about the appropriate balance of power make it unlikely that the EU will ever develop a fully fledged social policy.

The 'European social model' is very different from that of the USA, relying on relatively high levels of public support and a universal social protection system. An ongoing topic of debate is how to reconcile this model with EU competitiveness in particular, since the USA tends to fare better with regard to employment levels, participation rates and productivity.

Since the 1990s the EU has launched various strategies to combat unemployment and increase employment. Though at times the rhetoric and statements of intent and solidarity seem to exceed the results, there has been a slight reduction in unemployment and increase in participation in the labour force since the European Employment Strategy was launched in 1997. The EU approach relies heavily on active labour market measures (such as training and the creation of job opportunities), but financing is limited, and the effectiveness of this type of approach has sometimes been called into question.[11] At least formal EU frameworks for the formulation, development and

---

[11] See Martin (1998) for a discussion of this issue.

review of strategies to combat unemployment have been set in place, but progress remains slow in realizing the Luxembourg and Lisbon objectives.

Summary of Key Concepts

- EU social policy has evolved over the years, but includes measures for: employment and working conditions; social exclusion, or the fight against poverty; equality between men and women; the involvement of the so-called social partners (trade unions and employers) in the legislative process and the participation of workers in the decision-making of a firm.
- The EU attempts to reconcile a relatively high level of social protection with international competitiveness.
- Obstacles to developing a fully fledged EU social policy include: differences in the conditions of the member states; the contentious, ideological nature of social policy issues; the diversity of national social policy regimes; the reluctance of member states to give up control of social policy; the scale of budgetary transfers necessary for EU social policy and the even greater diversity of social policy requirements after enlargement.
- The evolution of EU social policy can be divided into four main periods: 1958–73 (a low profile for the Community), 1974–85 (piecemeal intervention), 1985–92 (the evolution of policy) and since 1993.
- The Luxembourg Process to launch the European Employment Strategy (EES) is organized around four pillars: improving 'employability'; encouraging the adaptability of businesses and their employees; strengthening policies for equal opportunities and developing entrepreneurship.
- The Lisbon European Council of 2000 aimed at higher employment rates (rather than lower unemployment rates) by increasing the rate of participation in the labour force.

Questions for study and review

■ What do we mean by the term 'social policy'?

■ How can we explain the higher unemployment rates and lower rates of participation in the labour force in the EU compared with the USA?

■ What do we mean by 'social dumping'? To what extent do you think that it poses the risk of a 'race to the bottom'?

■ What are the obstacles to developing a fully fledged EU social policy?

■ How has EU social policy evolved over the years?

■ What do we mean by the 'social dimension' of the Single Market Programme?

■ Indicate the main features of EU employment policy. What do the Luxembourg and Lisbon processes entail?

■ What policies do you think the EU should use to increase employment?

■ What policies do you think the EU should use to reduce poverty?

References

European Commission (1993a) 'Green Paper on European social policy – A way forward for the Union', COM(93)551.

European Commission (1993b) 'White Paper on Growth, competitiveness and employment: The challenges and ways forward into the 21st century'.

European Commission (1994) White Paper on 'European social policy: A way forward for the Union'.

European Commission (2002) 'EU employment and social policy 1999-2001: Jobs, cohesion productivity'.

European Commission (2003) 'Choosing to grow. Knowledge, innovation and jobs in a cohesive society'. Report to the Spring European Council, March 2003 on the Lisbon Strategy of economic, social and environmental renewal', www.europa.eu.int/comm/internal_market.

European Commission (2004) 'Third Report on economic and social cohesion'.

Martin, J.P. (1998) 'What works among active labour market policies: Evidence from OECD countries' experiences', *OECD Occasional Papers*, No. 35, Paris.

Tsoukalis, L. (1997) *The New European Economy Revisited,* 3rd edn, Oxford University Press, Oxford.

Useful websites

European Commission Directorate General for Employment and Social Affairs: http://europa.eu.int/comm/employment_social
International Labour Office provides data and analysis: www.ilo.org

List of abbreviations

EES	European Employment Strategy
EQUAL	Community Initiative on transnational co-operation to combat all kinds of discrimination and inequalities in the labour market
ETUC	European Trades Union Conference

15

Competition and Industrial Policies

LEARNING OBJECTIVES

By the end of this chapter you should be able to understand:

▶ The ways in which distortions in competition may undermine the integration process;

▶ The main features of Community antitrust policy;

▶ How merger control operates in the EU;

▶ What measures are used by the EU to prevent abuse of state aids on the part of national governments;

▶ The criticisms made of the role of the European Commission in competition policy;

▶ The reasons for industrial policy;

▶ How EU industrial policy has evolved over the years;

▶ The revived debate about supporting national and EU champions.

INTRODUCTION

Competition policy was envisaged as an essential part of the integration process both in the Treaty of Paris establishing the European Coal and Steel Community and in the Treaty of Rome. Competition policy is aimed at preventing distortions in competition caused either by private firms, or by government actions. EU competition policy is complementary to national measures, but in cases of conflict EC competition law prevails. Over time the number of cases of conflict has decreased as national measures have become more aligned with EU principles (Laudati, 1998; Martin, 1998).

Central to the analysis of the likely benefits of integration are the cost and price reductions that were expected to accrue. However, there is a risk that restrictive practices between otherwise independent firms, or the behaviour of dominant (or monopoly) firms, might prevent these price reductions from being realized. Integration is also expected to lead to increased competition, and to meet these additional pressures firms might be induced to form cartels or undertake mergers in order to reach dominant market positions. National governments may be tempted to help their firms face the additional competitive pressures by granting them state aids.

To prevent such developments undermining competition, EU policy therefore covers:

- Antitrust measures, or the fight against cartels and restrictive practices (Article 81) and against dominant position (Article 82);[1]
- Mergers (Reg. 4064/89 of 1989); and
- State aids and regulated industries (Articles 86-88).

With the prospect of EU enlargement, the EU adopted a series of new rules on competition policy to come into operation from 1 May 2004. Before discussing the various aspects of EU competition policy and its reform, it is useful to present the theoretical basis for introducing competition policy. This is followed by a description of procedural arrangements for EU competition policy, which have attracted great controversy in recent years.

THE THEORETICAL BASIS FOR COMPETITION POLICY

Though a complete analysis of different forms of behaviour by firms is beyond the present scope, the aim of this section is to compare the outcome of certain non-competitive models with a situation of perfect competition. Even these simple models can be used to show why competition policy may be necessary. Students familiar with models of monopoly and collusion can skip this section.

The simplest model of the non-competitive behaviour of a firm is that of monopoly. A monopoly entails that there is only a single seller of the product, so the firm does not have to take into account the behaviour of other suppliers. Perfect competition occurs where there are a large number of buyers and sellers, a homogeneous product, free entry of firms to the market and perfect information.

Since the monopoly is the only seller of the product, the demand curve of the firm and the demand curve of the industry are the same. The industry demand curve faced by the monopolist will slope downwards. The monopolist is a price maker. If the monopolist sets a higher price, less will be sold. For simplicity it is assumed that the aim of the monopolist is to maximize profits. In order to decide what quantity of output to produce in order to maximize profits, the monopolist will have to take into account the different revenues and costs associated with each level of output.

Marginal revenue (MR) can be defined as the change in total revenue when output is changed by one unit. When the demand curve slopes downward, marginal revenue will be less than price. This can be seen from Figure 15.1. When the price is €6 the firm can sell 2 units and total revenue is €12. To sell 3 units, the firm must reduce its price to €5 and total revenue becomes €15. When the firm increases its sales from 2 to 3 units, the first two units are sold for €5, and total revenue decreases by area a, which is equal to €2. At the same time total revenue increases by area b, which indicates the addition to revenue from selling the third unit at €5. Area b is equal to the price of the

---

[1] The references here are to Articles in the EC Treaty.

product €5. When increasing output from 2 to 3 units, total revenue rises by area b minus area a. This increase in total revenue for a one-unit change in output is marginal revenue. Marginal revenue is therefore less than price.[2]

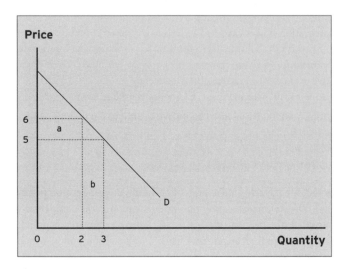

Figure 15.1 The demand curve of the monopolist

In order to maximize profits the monopolist will also have to take costs into account. Marginal cost (MC) is defined as the change in total costs of production when output is varied by one unit. The monopolist will maximize profits at the level of output where marginal cost equals marginal revenue. At lower levels of output marginal revenue exceeds marginal cost, so the monopolist can increase profits by producing more. Equilibrium occurs where marginal cost (MC) and marginal revenue (MR) intersect at point Em in Figure 15.2, where the level of output is Qm.[3] The price Pm charged for level of output Qm is given by point C on the demand curve directly above Em.

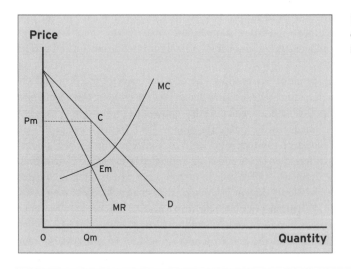

Figure 15.2 The equilibrium of the monopolist

---

[2] Another way of explaining this concept is to recall that the demand curve represents average revenue (AR). Average revenue is the total revenue divided by number of units sold. If the demand curve is negatively sloped, average revenue is falling, so marginal revenue must lie below the average.

[3] The same type of graphical analysis can be used for long- or short-term analysis, using long-term cost curves or short-term cost curves respectively. The difference between long and short run arises because in the short run a firm is not able to vary the quantities of all the inputs it uses.

The aim is now to show how the quantities produced and prices charged differ under conditions of monopoly and perfect competition. In order to render comparison simpler, a few additional assumptions are now introduced:[4]

■ An industry is initially assumed to be operating under perfect competition and then a monopoly is introduced.

■ The industry demand is assumed to be the same for the monopoly and the competitive industry.

■ The long run is considered when firms have adjusted fully to each price.

■ The industry is assumed to operate under constant costs. Average costs (AC) are defined as the total costs of producing a given number of units output divided by the number of units of output. In a constant-cost industry, the long-run marginal cost and average cost curves will coincide. The assumption of constant costs implies that input costs will be the same under perfect competition and monopoly.

■ All competitive firms are equally efficient.

The demand curve of the industry is D in Figure 15.3. With monopoly the demand curve of the industry is the demand curve of the firm. In contrast under perfect competition the two are different. Under perfect competition the firm is a price taker, and the demand curve of the individual firm is a horizontal straight line at the going price. Price will therefore equal marginal revenue for the competitive firm. In the short run the perfectly competitive firm will maximize profits when marginal costs equal price and marginal revenue.[5]

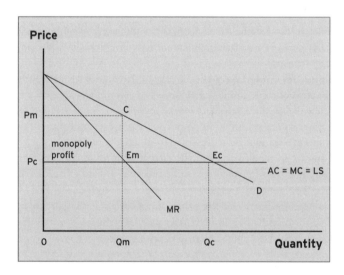

Figure 15.3 A comparison of monopoly and perfect competition

In the long run for the competitive industry to be in equilibrium, each firm must make zero profits, so there is no incentive for firms to enter or leave the industry.[6] The firm will earn zero profits if and only if the price for the product is equal to long-run marginal costs and long-run average costs.[7] The long-run competitive supply curve LS of the competitive industry will be a

[4] The analysis here follows Browning and Browning (1992).
[5] For a review of this topic see, for example, Varian (1999) or Begg et al. (2000).
[6] All competitive firms are assumed to be equally efficient.
[7] The condition for long-run equilibrium is:
Pc = MR=LMC=LAC where Pc is price, MR is marginal revenue, LMC is long-run marginal cost, and LAC is long-run average cost.

horizontal line as shown in Figure 15.3. In a constant-cost industry an increase in industry output will not raise factor prices. If industry output increases, the cost curves of firms do not change, and the expansion of industry output takes place at the same cost as new firms enter the market. Under perfect competition long-run equilibrium occurs where the industry demand curve intersects LS the long-run supply curve. In Figure 15.3 this occurs at Ec, where output is Qc and price is Pc.

Assume now that the industry becomes a monopoly. In order to maximize profits the monopolist will produce quantity Qm, at which marginal cost (MC) equals marginal revenue (MR) and the price charged will be Pm. At the level of output Qm, the difference between price Pm (or average revenue) and average costs (AC) gives the average profit per unit of output. The total profit of the monopolist is given by average profit multiplied by the quantity of output Qm, or the rectangle PcEmCPm shown in Figure 15.3.

Since it is assumed that the monopolist faces the same costs in its different plants as did competitive firms, the long-run competitive supply curve LS is also the long-run marginal cost curve of the monopolist. The assumption that the industry operates under constant costs means that the long-run marginal costs curve and the long-run average cost curve of the monopolist coincide, and both are equal to LS in Figure 15.3. At equilibrium the monopoly produces Qm at price Pm. When the industry was competitive, quantity Qc was produced and sold at price Pc. Under monopoly there is therefore a lower quantity of output and higher prices than in a competitive situation.

Figure 15.3 can also be used to illustrate the welfare costs of introducing a monopoly. The monopoly reduces output from Qc to Qm. The fall in output releases resources and these can be used to create other products. In competitive markets the resources released can be used to produce output worth rectangle QmQcEcEm. The increase in price under monopoly causes a fall in consumer surplus of PmCEcPc. Rectangle PcEmCPm showing the monopoly profit is simply a transfer from consumers to producers so does not represent a net welfare loss to society. The net welfare loss to society is indicated by triangle CEcEm.

As explained below, one of the main aims of EU competition policy is to avoid abuse of monopoly power by firms in a dominant position. The simplified analysis here shows that competition policy may be aimed at reducing or avoiding the net welfare loss to society as a whole that results from the reduction in output and the rise in price, and limiting or eliminating (generally on equity grounds) the transfer from consumers to the producer represented by monopoly profit.

Monopoly is an extreme case, and in practice firms generally face some form of competition. Though beyond the present scope, most texts on microeconomic theory deal with situations of duopoly, oligopoly and monopolistic competition[8] and consider how outcomes vary according to the different market structure and assumptions about the behaviour of the firm – in particular, attitudes towards competitors. Here the discussion is limited to a model of collusion or cartel. As explained below, cartels are forbidden in the USA, but subject to heavy regulation in the EU.

The aim of collusion or the formation of a cartel by firms in a competitive industry is to co-ordinate their activities in order to earn monopoly profits. Figure 15.4 shows the downward-sloping industry demand curve D for the product, and the marginal revenue curve MR. SS is the short-run supply curve of the industry, that is the sum of the short-run marginal cost curves of all the firms. Under conditions of perfect competition, industry equilibrium occurs at Ec, with price Pc and quantity of output Qc.

Assume that the firms then form a cartel and agree to restrict output in order to raise prices. The firms will behave like a monopolist and will maximize their combined profits at Em, where the SS

---

[8] A duopoly consists of an industry with two firms, while in an oligopoly a few firms produce all or most of the output of the industry. Monopolistic competition occurs where entry and exit to the industry are unrestricted but firms produce differentiated products.

curve intersects the marginal revenue curve MR, with a combined output of Qm and a monopoly price of Pm. This outcome is the same as if a single monopoly controlled all the firms making up the cartel (see, for analogy, Figure 15.2 above).

The increase in total profits for all the firms in the cartel is given by the area EcEmC. By reducing the quantity produced from Qc to Qm, the firms eliminate all output for which their combined marginal costs exceed marginal revenue, and in this way the firms in the cartel can increase their combined profit.

However, as explained in Chapter 4, there are inherent economic reasons that cartels are unstable and tend to break down. As Figure 15.3 shows, the cartel can restrict output to raise prices, but at the higher prices each firm has an incentive to cheat since the individual firm could increase its profits by expanding output. Members of the cartel may find it difficult to reach agreement over price, output and profit sharing. Moreover, the monopoly profits earnt by a cartel may encourage other firms to enter the industry.

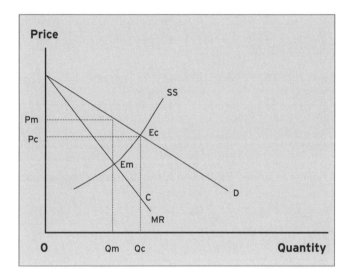

Figure 15.4 Profit maximization by a cartel

THE INSTITUTIONS RESPONSIBLE FOR EU COMPETITION POLICY

The Commission plays a central role in the implementation of EU competition policy. It may investigate rules at its own initiative, or upon the receipt of a complaint from an individual, company or member state. If a case of infringement is found, the Commission will generally attempt to convince the company or government in question to bring practices in line with EU competition law voluntarily. If this is not possible, the Commission can order enforcement or, in some cases, impose a fine.

The European Court of Justice was responsible for appeals, but subsequently this role was taken over by the Court of First Instance. The role of the Council of Ministers is limited to deciding on Regulations and Directives in the Community decision-making process. As explained below, with the reform of 2004 national courts and national competition authorities are to assume a more active role in competition policy in the EU.

One of the main criticisms of the procedures of EU competition policy was that the Commission acted as judge, jury and prosecutor and was subject to insufficient checks and balances. This was underlined by certain high-profile merger cases where the Commission blocked mergers, and the Court of First Instance subsequently reversed the decision (see below). In one case, Airtours/First Choice, the decision of the Court of First Instance came three years after the Commission had stopped the merger. Subsequently, to speed up the process it was decided that the court should use a 'fast track' for appeals.

In an attempt to meet the various criticisms, a series of internal reforms of the Competition Directorate-General were introduced before the EU enlargement of May 2004. The Commission staff involved in merger control and antitrust enforcement were integrated and reorganized on the basis of different sectors of the economy. The aim of the reform was to enhance sector-specific knowledge, facilitate the spread of the experience of best practices developed in the Merger Task Force to the whole of the DG and to ensure more effective and flexible use of limited staff resources.[9] In July 2003 a chief competition economist, Professor Lars-Hendrik Roller, was appointed to provide an independent economic viewpoint for policy analysis and offer guidance on individual cases throughout the investigation process. A system of peer review panels was established to reinforce internal scrutiny by the Commission. The aim of the panel system is to provide a second opinion on complex and high-profile merger and antitrust cases.

ANTITRUST ENFORCEMENT

Antitrust measures cover cartels and restrictive practices, and abuses of dominant position. Article 81 of the EC Treaty prohibits as 'incompatible with the Common Market' all agreements that affect trade between the member states and have the intention or effect of preventing, distorting or restricting competition. Collusive behaviour (or concerted action having the same effect as collusion) is considered contrary to consumer interests when it entails agreements to:[10]

- Raise prices;
- Restrict output, markets, technical development or investment;
- Share markets or sources of supply;
- Apply dissimilar conditions to equivalent transactions with other trading parties;
- Make the conclusion of contracts subject to supplementary obligations.

One of the major difficulties in implementing EU policy with respect to Article 81 is that in practice it may be difficult to establish that collusive behaviour has taken place. In the Franco-Japanese ball bearings case of 1972, representatives of firms and trade associations from the two countries met in Paris and wrote minutes recording their agreement to fix prices.[11] The minutes ended in the hands of the European Commission competition authorities, but rarely is such information readily available.

The onus is on the competition authorities to prove that collusive behaviour has taken place, and the task is further complicated by the fact that, for example, in a situation of oligopoly the outcome may appear collusive (with lower output and higher prices) without the firms actually having to collude in a legal sense.[12]

---

[9] Speech by Mario Monti on 'EU competition policy after 2004', Fordham Annual Conference on International Antitrust Law and Policy, New York, 24 October 2003.
[10] Article 81(1).
[11] Official Journal 343 of 21/12/74.
[12] This was evident in the wood pulp case of 1993 described in Martin (2001). The EU was supplied largely by firms in Northern Europe and North America, which tended to adjust prices by similar amounts at about the same time. Most of these firms met regularly at a trade association in Switzerland. The Commission maintained that there was collusion but was overruled by the Court of Justice on the basis of insufficient evidence. According to the court, the parallel pricing might be based on collusion, but it might simply be the consequence of transparent prices in an oligopoly market.

Horizontal co-operation involves firms at the same stage in the production process, and is generally found to violate EU competition policy when it can be established that there are agreements to set prices, impose entry barriers or reserve particular geographical areas for certain firms.

Vertical co-operation is between firms at different stages in the production process. The 1999 Regulation on vertical restraints forbids agreements on:[13]

- Exclusive purchasing;
- Resale price maintenance (the distributor agrees to sell at or above the price indicated by the manufacturer).

These types of vertical restraint typically infringe EU competition policy by fragmenting the Single Market and/or by introducing price discrimination. A frequently cited example is that of the car distribution system in the EU which for many years allowed car manufacturers to sell through designated dealers in specific territories.[14] The justification given was the repair and maintenance that cars require. Manufacturers were, however, obliged to allow dealers to sell cars to customers who were not resident in the designated sales area. On various occasions the Commission fined EU firms (VW in 1995 and 1999, and the Dutch General Motors in 2000) for attempting to block dealers from selling in other territories. In October 2002 a new regime came into operation which offers distributors greater freedom to operate multi-brand dealerships.[15]

Although collusion is forbidden, Article 81(3) of the EC Treaty permits other forms of co-operation between firms, which improve the production or distribution of goods, promote technical progress and allow consumers a fair share of the resulting benefit.

In 1999 a new Regulation established a block exemption and guidelines for vertical co-operation agreements. The exemption applies when the market share of the supplier (or buyer in the case of exclusive supply conditions) does not exceed 30 per cent and the turnover of each partner is less than €50 million.[16] In 2000 a new Regulation for horizontal co-operation was introduced to allow a block exemption when the market share of the firms involved was less than 20 per cent for specialization agreements and 25 per cent for co-operation in R&D.[17]

Even when the market share of the firms involved in horizontal co-operation exceeds these thresholds, further exemptions were envisaged provided the conditions of Article 81(3) were satisfied. Each case has to be examined individually, taking into account the impact of co-operation on market performance by examining such factors as:[18]

- The degree of seller concentration;
- The nature of entry conditions;
- Whether buyers and sellers are likely to exercise countervailing power;
- Other aspects of market structure.

The Commission also permitted agreements of minor importance under the *de minimus* principle. These were agreements useful for co-operation between small and medium-sized enterprises considered inherently incapable of affecting competition at the EU level and therefore not subject to authorization by the Commission. In 2001 the Commission fixed the market share of the firms concerned at less than 10 per cent for horizontal agreements and less than 15 per cent for vertical agreements.

---

[13] Official Journal 336 of 29 December 1999.
[14] See Martin (2001) for a more complete description.
[15] Regulation (EC) No.1400 of 31 July 2002.
[16] Commission Regulation No. 2790/1999 on the application of the Treaty to categories of vertical agreements and concerted practices, OJ L 336/21, 29 December 1999.
[17] Commission Regulation No.2658/2000 on the application of Art. 81(3) of the treaty to categories of specialization agreements, OJ L 304/3, 5 December 2000.
[18] European Commission (2000a).

In order to assess the market share of firms (and hence whether they could qualify for a block exemption) the problem of market definition arises. According to the Commission (1997):

> The main purpose of market definition is to identify...the competitive constraints that the undertakings involved face. The objective of defining a market in both its product and geographic dimension is to identify those actual competitors of the undertakings involved that are capable of constraining their behaviour and of preventing them from behaving independently of an effective competitive pressure.

In practice when deciding on market definition the Commission generally takes into account the availability of substitutes. Thus for example, in the 1978 dominant position case of United Brand Company (UBC) which controlled 40 per cent of the EC banana market, the Commission argued that the market was bananas, which have distinctive characteristics separating the demand for bananas from that of other fresh fruit. UBC tried unsuccessfully to argue that the market was fresh fruit, where the market share of UBC was too small to justify the claim that it had a dominant position. The Court of Justice upheld the Commission's definition.[19]

In the early years of competition policy, the Commission itself was responsible for granting exemptions, but the huge workload that this entailed meant that alternatives had to be developed. These include the block exemption system, 'comfort letters' from the Commission which indicated whether a firm was considered likely to qualify for an exemption or not (though, according to the Court of Justice, these letters were not legally binding) and a growing role for national competition authorities and courts. As explained below, with the 2004 reform, the block exemption system was developed into the idea of a 'safe harbour' for firms below a certain market share, and firms were no longer subject to the routine obligation to notify the Commission of agreements.

Article 82 of the EC Treaty prohibits abuse of dominant position by one or more firms. Types of behaviour that are found to constitute such abuse are:[20]

- Restriction of output;
- Price discrimination;
- Applying dissimilar conditions to equivalent transactions with other trading parties;
- Making the conclusion of contracts subject to supplementary obligations.

There are no exemptions to Article 82. Examples of decisions by the Commission against abuse of a dominant position were those against Microsoft (see Box 15.1) and Unilever and the ice-cream distribution market. Unilever provided freezer cabinets free to Irish distributors on condition they stocked only Unilever ice cream. This was found to limit the choice of Irish consumers.[21]

Box 15.1 The Microsoft decision

In 2003 the European Commission decided that Microsoft had abused its near-monopoly in the PC market (Windows is the operating system on more than 90 per cent of PCs) to extend its market power in two adjacent markets. According to the Commission, Microsoft had deliberately restricted interoperability between Windows PCs and non-Microsoft work group servers, and had tied sales of its Media Player to sales of the Windows operating system. As a result, the Commission claimed that Microsoft had used its PC market

---

[19] See Martin (2001) for a more detailed description of this case.
[20] EC Treaty Article 82.
[21] European Commission (2000b).

strength to acquire a dominant position in the work group server operating systems market and had significantly weakened competition in the Media Player market. The Commission decided to fine Microsoft €437 million and require Microsoft to take remedial action. The latter included disclosing information to competitors about interfaces allowing non-Microsoft work group servers to interoperate with Windows PCs and offering a version of Windows client PC operating system without Media Player in the EU. The Commission stated that the fine was calculated on the basis of EU sales and not on world-wide sales in deference to the USA.

The Commission turned down an offer of settlement by Microsoft. Microsoft decided to appeal against the Commission's decision, arguing that it had invested substantially in developing Windows and that its corporate strategy was to increase the sales of Windows. Microsoft stated that being forced to disclose interface information for servers runs against this strategy and would act as a disincentive to innovation. The company also maintained that Windows might not be able to function properly without Media Player. In 2003 a further complaint was filed against the Windows XP operating system, again with the claim that Microsoft was using its monopoly position to eliminate rivals.

From 1 May 2004 a new EU enforcement regime on restrictive practices and dominant position known as the 'modernization package' came into operation. Routine notification of agreements and practices to the Commission for clearance is no longer required. Instead, companies will make their own assessment. All agreements considered to have a net positive effect on the internal market are automatically valid. This will free the competition authorities to tackle serious violations, in particular the cases affecting cross-border trade. The fear was that with enlargement extension of the previous notification system to 25 member states would have led to a paralysis of enforcement activities.

The reform builds on the system of block exemptions and guidelines to introduce the notion of 'safe harbours' for firms. If a company is below a certain market share threshold, it can benefit from a 'safe harbour' and does not have to worry about the compatibility of agreements with EU competition law. At the same time guidelines will help to define 'hardcore restrictions' relating to practices that are prohibited because they have a negative impact on the common market (such as agreements to fix prices, limit output or share markets or consumers).

In order to ensure a more effective division of tasks, the Commission, national competition authorities and national courts are to share responsibility for enforcing EU antitrust rules. The Commission will focus on the infringements presenting the greatest risk of distortion at the EU level. To facilitate co-ordination between the various authorities a European Competition Network (ECN) has been set up. This is composed of the Commission and competition authorities of all the member states. The role of the ECN is to establish principles for the allocation of cases among the various authorities, exchange information, provide mutual assistance in investigations and co-ordinate the final decisions taken.

A number of flanking measures have been introduced to ensure consistent application of the new antitrust rules throughout the EU. These include guidance on key features of the new system, such as:

- When agreements and practices are considered to have an effect on trade between member states;
- What forms of co-operation between firms are permitted by Article 81(3);
- The treatment of complaints;

■ How co-operation among the Commission, national competition authorities and the courts is to operate.

Under the new framework consumers and companies that have been harmed by restrictive practices can bring the case to national courts and competition authorities. If necessary the courts can request an opinion or factual information from the Commission, while the Commission and national competition authorities can submit observations to the national courts on their own initiative.

MERGER CONTROL

While measures relating to restrictive practices and dominant position were already envisaged by the Treaty of Rome, the addition of merger control to EC competition policy came only in 1989. This was partly because the idea of promoting EC champions was popular in the 1970s and early 1980s, and, as explained below, there may be a tension between industrial policy and competition policy. However, it was also because the level of merger activity in the Community remained relatively low until the mid-1980s. During this period most mergers were between firms in the same country and were aimed chiefly at increasing market share on the domestic market.

The announcement of the Single Market Programme was accompanied by a spectacular increase in the number of mergers in the Community which rose from 200 in 1985 to 2000 in 1989 (Tsoukalis, 1997). Mergers were increasingly cross-frontier and also involved firms from outside the EU in an attempt to strengthen positions on world markets. The composition of mergers also altered, with a growing number of mergers in service sectors (such as banking, insurance and the retail trade).

The 1989 Merger Control Regulation (Reg. 4064/89) gave the European Commission the authority to control mergers that met a specified size and multi-nationality conditions, including mergers between non-EU businesses with substantial sales in the EU. The world-wide threshold based on the turnover of the companies involved amounted to €5 billion, and the Community-wide threshold to €250 million. Below these thresholds, the national authorities in the member states carried out merger control. Above the threshold the Commission had to be notified of the proposed merger. The number of notifications was growing by about 30 per cent annually, and reached about 300 each year in the late 1990s (European Commission, 2000b). The aim of the Regulation was to provide a 'one-stop shop' where firms could request clearance for the mergers and acquisitions in the whole EU, thereby reducing the costs, legal uncertainty and bureaucracy associated with multiple filings.

According to the 1989 Regulation, a merger should be blocked if it led to a potentially abusive dominant position and, therefore, was likely to result in higher prices, more limited choice for consumers and less innovation. The Commission and European courts interpreted this concept as applying also to joint dominance (Gencor/Lonrho) or collective dominance (Airtours/First Choice).[22] This is different from the US concept of 'avoiding a lessening of competition'. The Commission's use of the notion of 'collective dominance' was frequently challenged as offering a blank cheque to veto mergers.

During the 1989–95 period the Commission's approach to merger control was sometimes criticized as being too cautious and bland (Tsoukalis, 1997). Of 398 mergers considered during this period, only 4 were blocked. Over the 1990–2004 period the Commission examined more than 2400 mergers and 18 were stopped.[23] In 171 of these cases remedies were adopted to resolve

---

[22] European Commission (2004a).
[23] European Commission (2004a).

competition problems and allow the merger to proceed. However, in 2002 the Court of First Instance upheld three high profile cases of appeal against the Commission's merger decisions (Airtours/First Choice, Schneider/Legrand and Tetra Laval/Sidel), giving rise to heated debate about the powers and procedures of the Commission.

For instance, in the case of the British Airtours proposed takeover of First Choice, the Commission argued that the merger would reduce the number of tour operators in the UK to three, and that their UK collective dominance could impede competition. In June 2002 the Court of First Instance overruled the decision, arguing that it was not clear that there were significant barriers to other (foreign) operators entering the market or that smaller operators would not have access to favourably priced seats.

In October 2002 the merger between Tetra Laval and Sidel was blocked because the Commission argued that Tetra Laval was carrying out leverage, i.e. using its dominant position in the packaging sector to obtain a dominant position in another sector, that of machinery for making plastic (PET) bottles. While the court did not rule out the underlying theoretical argument, it maintained that so far there had been no evidence of this type of behaviour. Subsequently the Commission obtained new evidence about Tetra activities in developing a new stretch blow moulding (SBM) technology called Tetra Fast which gave rise to doubts about dominant position in the SBM market, and in January 2003 the Commission lodged an appeal against the decision by the Court of First Instance.

The new merger control regulation that came into operation from May 2004 attempted to meet the criticisms of EU competition policy by building on the experience of the past but adding some important innovations.[24] The main features of the new merger rules entailed:

- Reinforcing the one-stop shop concept;
- Extending the authority of the Commission to investigate all types of harmful scenarios resulting from a merger and not just cases of market dominance;
- Adding some flexibility to the investigation timeframes;
- Providing guidelines for the assessment of mergers between competing firms;
- Adopting a set of best practices on the conduct of merger investigations.

Despite the 1989 Regulation, the problem of multiple filings for authorization (i.e. notification of the same operation having to be made to several competition authorities in the EU) was still widespread. The new legislation aims at strengthening the concept of the 'one-stop shop' and maintains the same turnover thresholds for exclusive jurisdiction of the Commission. According to the new merger rules, companies can ask to benefit from the one-stop shop if they are required to notify in three or more member states. If none of the authorities in the competent member states object within 15 working days, the merger case is subject to examination by the Commission.

With the new merger rules the 'substantive test' of whether a merger should be challenged or not has been modified. Now any merger that will 'significantly impede effective competition in the common market or in a substantial part of it' is to be blocked. Dominance will remain a major concept, but the test will now extend to oligopolistic markets where the merged company may not be dominant. The central question becomes whether there is competition to provide consumers sufficient choice (European Commission, 2004a).

Under the 1989 Regulation after an initial scrutiny period of one month, the Commission would decide whether to authorize the merger (90 per cent of cases) or to continue with a four-month

---

[24] Council regulation EC9 No. 139/2004 of 20 January on the control of concentrations between undertakings. For further information see www.europa.eu.int/comm/competition/mergers/legislation.

investigation. At the end of this period the Commission could authorize the merger conditionally or unconditionally, or prohibit it.

According to the Commission, the new legislation should maintain the predictability of this timeframe but introduce more flexibility. The initial scrutiny period is fixed at 25 working days with the possibility of extension to 35 working days. The investigation period is 90 workings days extendible by 15 working days if companies offer remedies, or 20 working days if the Commission or notifying parties so request. Under the new legislation it will be possible to notify a transaction prior to conclusion of a binding agreement provided there is evidence of good faith to enter into that agreement.

The Commission has issued a set of guidelines to assess mergers between competing or potentially competing firms (horizontal mergers).[25] The Guidelines aim at providing indications to companies and the legal community about which mergers are likely to be challenged. As part of the assessment the Commission will also take into account possible increases in efficiency arising from a merger. For instance, mergers may allow firms to reorganize their activities or bring together complementary capabilities that allow them to compete better (European Commission, 2004a).

The Commission has also adopted a set of Best Practice Guidelines on the day-to-day aspects of merger investigations, covering issues ranging from economic indicators to assess mergers to the rights of the defence.

LIBERALIZATION AND STATE AIDS

Whereas Articles 81 and 82 and the 1989 Merger Control Regulation relate to the behaviour of firms, Articles 86–88 of the EC Treaty attempt to prevent competition being undermined by government intervention.

Article 86 covers the monopoly rights granted by member states to private or public undertakings to perform services in sectors such as the postal service, energy, telecommunications and transport. However, the Commission argues that these special rights should not go beyond what is necessary to provide the service, otherwise competition could be restricted. Many of these services require expensive infrastructure, and the Commission makes the distinction between infrastructure and services. While monopoly of the infrastructure is permitted, the monopolist must allow access to other competitors to provide the services.

EU competition rules aim at ensuring that impediments to effective liberalization are removed. This entails monitoring the liberalization process to prevent incumbents from raising new barriers or introducing restrictive practices to protect themselves against emerging competition (Commission, 2004a).

An example of an Article 86 ruling is that by the Commission against Spain in 1997 over the liberalization of the mobile phone market. A private company, Airtel Móvil, was charged €510 million to operate, while the state firm Telefonica could enter the market without payment (European Commission, 2000b). The Spanish government was required to introduce corrective measures.

Article 87 prohibits state aids to business if they distort competition, since this is incompatible with the common market. State aid may take various forms, including subsidies, capital investment, tax breaks and sales of assets at favourable prices.

Article 87 (2) and (3) indicate that exceptions are allowed for state aid:

■ With a social character;
■ For natural disasters or exceptional occurrences;

---

[25] Guidelines on the assessment of horizontal mergers under the Council Regulation on the control of concentrations between undertakings, No. C 31, 5 February 2004.

■ For regional development;
■ To promote an important project of common EU interest;
■ To develop certain economic activities of certain areas; and
■ To promote culture and heritage conservation.

According to the 1999 Regulation on state aid procedures, member states had to notify the Commission before introducing state aid and could not implement the measure until Commission consent had been given. Aid not notified could not benefit from the 87(3) exemptions. However, in practice even after the 1999 Regulation, many cases of state aid were still not notified, and the requirement that firms return aid that is judged incompatible with the common market was frequently not met.

At the Stockholm European Council of 2001 member states committed themselves to continue reducing the level of aid as a percentage of GDP by 2003. At the Barcelona European Council the member states called for 'less and better state aid', and fixed the target of 3 per cent of EU GDP for research and development spending. 'Better aid' is interpreted to mean measures to correct market failures by, for instance, promoting research and development, training, or increasing the level of risk capital. Rather than being aimed at a specific sector, these forms of aid address 'horizontal' objectives such as the development of small and medium enterprises, employment and regional development. Such measures can increase competitiveness, but the Commission argues that care must be taken to ensure that they target the market failure and avoid distortions to competition.

The Commission's state aid scoreboards suggest that member states are respecting the commitments set out at Stockholm and Barcelona. The overall volume of state aid fell from €67 billion in 1997 to €52 billion in 1999, and €49 billion in 2002.[26] Aid as a share of GDP fell from 0.64 per cent in 1999 to 0.56 in 2002 in the EU(15) (excluding aid to agriculture, fisheries and transport).

Member states also succeeded in redirecting their aid to horizontal objectives, and between 1998 and 2002 the share of horizontal objectives in total state aid increased by 7 per cent. In 2002 73 per cent of aid was on horizontal objectives, while the remaining 27 per cent was aid for specific sectors such as manufacturing, coal and financial services.

State aid has proved a particularly sensitive issue in the new member states of Central and Eastern Europe, which need to restructure their economies and had to prepare for EU membership. It is estimated that enlargement would increase the state aid workload by about 40 per cent.[27] An interim framework was adopted to assess state aids in operation before accession. National monitoring authorities had to decide whether state aid measures were compatible with the *acquis* and then provide the Commission with a list of such measures. The Commission then had to assess whether the notified measures were compatible with the common market.

In 2005–06 a large number of state aid rules came up for renewal including all the state aid exemptions, the regional aid guidelines, the framework for research and development and the risk capital guidelines. The environmental aid guidelines expire at the end of 2007. With enlargement and the need to take decisions on the 2007–13 financial perspective, the Commission decided that the moment was right to introduce fundamental changes in its approach to state aid. The review of state aids was to take into account the wider framework of realizing the Lisbon objectives and introducing a new policy to ensure economic and social cohesion over the 2007–13 period.

One of the aims of the reform is to ensure a more economic approach to state aid. Member states will be encouraged to use more economic analysis to assess whether an intervention in the form of state aid is the best way to address a particular market failure and to carry out *ex ante* and *ex post*

---

[26] The data in this paragraph are taken from European Commission (2004b).
[27] Mario Monti, 'State aid enforcement in context: Competitiveness, economic reforms and enlargement', Speech to the Mentor Group Forum for EU/US Legal–Economic Affairs, Brussels, 24 April 2004.

evaluations of individual state aid schemes to monitor the effectiveness of aid and its impact on competition.[28] Increased dialogue and exchange of information with and between member states is to be encouraged. Higher priority is to be given to ensuring that state aid policy is compatible with other EU objectives.

The state aid reform also aims at simplification and acceleration of procedures, increased transparency and legal certainty. In the case of aid for small and medium enterprises, training and employment, the old frameworks have been replaced by block exemption regulations that eliminate the need for notification by member states of individual aid schemes. In some cases (for example, capital for high-risk company start-ups), rules are to be rendered more flexible. The Commission is to draw up a 'practitioner's guide' providing guidance on measures in support of innovation that are consistent with state aid rules. Agreement has been reached on measures for specific sectors, such as the new framework on state aid to shipbuilding, and guidelines for the maritime transport sector.[29]

In 2003 a Green Paper was published on state aids to services of general economic interest. The Judgement of the Court of Justice of 24 July 2003 on Altmark (see Box 15.2) helped to clarify the conditions under which compensation for the provision of public services does not constitute state aid. However, most systems of public service compensation fail to meet the conditions set out in the Altmark case, and the aim of the Commission is to specify the conditions under which compensation that constitutes a state aid is compatible with the Treaty.

Box 15.2 The Altmark case

The Altmark case concerns the arrangements for granting licences for passenger transport on buses in the rural Stendal district in Germany and the public financing of those services. Altmark Trans had been given licences in 1990, 1994 and 1996 but in return was subject to certain obligations set by the authorities with regard to fares and timetables. A competing company whose application for the licence had been rejected brought an action to the German courts claiming that Altmark was not financially sound since it was incapable of surviving unaided. According to the Commission, under conditions where the company is simply compensated for an obligation imposed by the state this compensation does not constitute a form of state aid incompatible with the Common Market. The European Court of Justice confirmed this compensation approach but argued that there should be strict limits on the conditions under which the compensation does not qualify as aid.

Difficulties often arise in recovery of aid that should not have been permitted. Member states generally attach a low priority to recovering illegal aid, in particular if the beneficiary has financial difficulties. The proposed reform entails setting up a new unit in the Commission responsible for rescue and recovery measures. The Commission maintains that large enterprises should make a substantial contribution to the financing of restructuring (see also Box 15.3).

The Commission is also to carry out a review of regional aid in the enlarged EU. The Lisbon Strategy attaches high priority to the least developed regions, and the aim of the reform is to reconcile cuts in state aid with increased economic and social cohesion. This entails identifying the most appropriate strategies to reduce regional disparities (see Chapter 14) and stimulate growth, rather than subsidizing inefficient firms and distorting competition.

---

[28] Mario Monti, 'New challenges for state aid policy', Speech to the European State Aid Forum, June 2003.
[29] See European Commission (2004b) for a more detailed discussion of these measures.

Box 15.3 The Alstrom case

In August 2003 France informed the European Commission about a package of measures in favour of the Alstrom engineering group, which (among other things) produces high-speed trains. The package included a commitment by the French state to subscribe irrevocably half of a capital increase worth €600 million. The package was to be put immediately into effect without waiting for clearance from the Commission and so, according to the Commission, violated the obligation of prior notification of aid.*

In September 2003 the Commission began its investigation and considered introducing an injunction to suspend the participation in the capital increase because of its irreversible structural effects. In the event the Commission gave France five days to renounce the measure, and France agreed to introduce debt instruments instead, which will not have irreversible structural effects on the market. France also agreed to subject the envisaged entry into Alstrom's equity to prior authorization by the Commission.

The Commission then began its analysis of whether the package is in line with the rescue and restructuring guidelines and, in particular, whether the restructuring plan will restore Alstrom's viability and if compensatory measures are necessary to counterbalance the distortions of competition.

In 2004 the Commission agreed to a package of €3.2 billion government aid to Alstrom including an €800 million debt-for-equity swap on condition that Alstrom disposed of businesses accounting for 10 per cent of revenues worth about €1.5 billion. The Commission argued that industrial partnerships were necessary to ensure the viability of Alstrom and compensate for the distortions in competition caused by state aid.

*Speech by Mario Monti, 'Intervening against government restraints on competition: Reflections from the EU expertise', Lewis Bernstein Memorial Lecture, Department of Justice, Washington DC, October 2003.

EVALUATION OF EU COMPETITION POLCY

According to a survey carried out in June 2003 by the Global Competition Review, EU competition authorities are generally considered relatively efficient.[30] The survey was based on over 500 questionnaires sent to business groups, legal departments and competition authorities. However, some respondents claimed that there were insufficient checks and balances on the Commission's powers, that some decisions could be grounded in more economic analysis and that legal certainty could be increased.

In 2002 the Court of First Instance overruled the Commission on three high-profile merger cases, leading to calls for reform of rules and procedures. Enlargement also threatened to swamp the Commission competition authorities with an overload of work. The response of the Commission was to introduce the changes in organization and legislation described above, but a question mark hangs over how effective these reforms may prove in practice.

One of the initial aims of vesting so much power in the Commission was to limit the opportunities for political pressure and lobbying over decisions (in particular on state aid). Now responsibility is to be decentralized with a greater role for national authorities, many of which (such as those in Finland, Portugal, Austria and most of the new member states) have limited experience in applying competition law. Decentralization could lead to many merger decisions being referred

---

[30] See www.globalcompetitionreview.com.

back to member states, increasing uncertainty as rules and substantive tests still differ among member states.

The once-powerful Merger Task Force (sometimes referred to as the 'ayatollahs' of Brussels!) is to be disbanded and spread around the Competition DG. In theory this should add to flexibility and the diffusion of experience, but in practice it could simply lead to the weakening of an effective unit. A further question mark concerns how far EU competition policy will change after Commissioner Mario Monti leaves in November 2004, since he has taken an active hand in shaping the evolution of policy.

In recent years there have been increased efforts to co-operate on competition policy and investigations with major trading partners such as the USA, Japan and Canada. However, relations with the USA were strained by the Commission rulings over General Electric's proposed takeover of Honeywell in 2001 and the Microsoft case (see Box 15.1 above). US authorities had approved the General Electric–Honeywell merger, and though the Commission attempted to co-operate with US antitrust authorities over the Microsoft case, the USA maintained that its own settlement with Microsoft was the appropriate framework for dealing with the case. US politicians also criticized the Commission's ruling on Microsoft, arguing that it would lead to loss of jobs.

The Commission participates in attempts to encourage international convergence of enforcement standards and practices in the International Competition Network,[31] and was also in favour of negotiating a framework agreement on competition in the WTO context (see Chapter 17). However, competition was one of the issues that had to be dropped in the negotiations at Cancún in 2003 in the face of opposition, mainly from developing countries.

THE THEORETICAL BASIS OF INDUSTRIAL POLICY

One of the difficulties in discussing industrial policy is that of separating industrial policy from all the other measures having an impact on industry. The European Commission defines industrial policy as relating to manufacturing industry, but in the literature a wider concept is sometimes used which includes agriculture and certain services. Most industrial policy is carried out by the member states rather than at the EU level.

In general the aim of industrial policy is to increase competitiveness. The Commission defines competitiveness as the ability of an economy to provide its population with high and rising standards of living, and high rates of employment on a sustainable basis.[32] There are very different views of how this is best achieved, depending on differing opinions about the effectiveness of the market mechanism. At the risk of oversimplification, it is useful to distinguish certain main tendencies.

According to the market-orientated approach to industrial policy, the most effective way of promoting competition and efficiency is by allowing the market mechanism to operate as fully as possible. The removal of trade barriers and the creation of a common market will intensify international competition. The role of policy is to allow the market to operate by preventing abuse of monopoly power and ensuring that state aids do not distort competition. The role of industrial policy is therefore 'negative' in the sense that it is mainly concerned with eliminating distortions to competition.

At the other end of the scale, a selective, interventionist industrial policy may be used to favour certain firms or industries. An active industrial policy is sometimes advocated in order to support

---

[31] See www.internationalcompetitionnetwork.org.
[32] European Commission (2002b).

declining industries and avoid loss of jobs. For instance, if a declining industry is important in a particular region, allowing it to fail could lead to a high level of long-term unemployment in that region, with a heavy social cost. However, in many cases it seems likely that a subsidy to the declining industry will simply postpone unemployment.

An active industrial policy may also be seen as a means of promoting key or strategic industries, such as the aerospace industry, telecommunications and the audiovisual industry, in an effort to create national or EU champions. This is very similar to the strategic trade theory and infant industry arguments described in Chapter 4. According to this approach, public intervention may be used to create a competitive advantage for firms. However, there are numerous objections to these arguments on theoretical grounds. These include the negative implications of protection, insufficient information and the difficulty of picking winners, and the risk of retaliation by other countries.

Measures to encourage R&D and innovation are generally a central component of industrial policy. The traditional economic justification for such measures is in terms of externality. The social return on R&D and innovation is higher than the private return, so public intervention is justified to favour such activities.

An alternative justification for measures to promote R&D and innovation can be found on the basis of evolutionary economics. As described in Chapter 13, evolutionary economics makes the distinction between codified and tacit knowledge. Codified knowledge is formalized and can be stored and transmitted easily, while tacit knowledge is obtained through experience, so requires a process of learning-by-doing in order to be transferred. According to evolutionary economics a large part of knowledge needed for innovation is tacit, so contacts between people are important. As innovation depends on interaction between people, public intervention can be used to encourage that interaction. Measures may be introduced to encourage networking and co-operation on research and technological development between public authorities, firms, research institutions and universities. There may also be a case for favouring the creation of economic clusters, or networks of production of strongly interdependent firms. Highly skilled labour is often relatively mobile and may help to transmit tacit knowledge, so there may be a role for public intervention in attempts to attract highly qualified people to an area.

The instruments of industrial policy are various and include: financial assistance, tax breaks, aid for R&D, public contracts, trade barriers, export assistance and measures to encourage technology diffusion.

THE EVOLUTION OF EU INDUSTRIAL POLICY

Two of the original Communities, the European Steel and Coal Community and Euratom, covered key industrial sectors, and the approach used was essentially *dirigiste*, with an active role envisaged for public intervention. At the time, this type of approach was also deemed appropriate for sectors such as agriculture and transport, which were subject to intensive state intervention. It was considered easier to introduce a common policy for these sectors rather than attempt to harmonize the diverse national approaches.

The Treaty of Rome failed to make any mention of industrial policy, though a legal basis for industrial policy can be found in various articles. With the exception of the sectors mentioned above, the Treaty seems to be based on a market-orientated approach. The removal of trade barriers was seen as the means of promoting competition and efficiency, and the role of public intervention was to eliminate obstacles to the functioning of the market. Many of the articles in the Treaty of Rome considered most relevant for industrial policy were therefore those setting out competition policy. As discussed above, these articles dealt with cartels and restrictive practices, abuse of dominant position and state aids. Other articles were also intrinsically linked to industrial policy, such as those on the movement of capital and labour, the right of establishment and the creation of the common market. Industrial policy measures could also be justified on the basis of general treaty objectives set out in Article 235 (now Article 308 of the EC Treaty).[33]

In the 1960s the market-orientated view of the role of the Community continued to prevail, and industrial policy consisted mainly in removing barriers to operation of the common market. In 1967 the Directorate-General for Industry (DG III) was set up to promote cross-border co-operation. However, the industry of the member states seemed to encounter difficulty in adapting to the enlarged market and was less active than US and Japanese firms in setting up FDI in the Community (Hitiris, 2003).

At the time there were considerable differences in prevailing ideologies with regard to industrial policy in the member states, with Germany favouring a neo-liberal approach, while France and Italy were traditionally more in favour of intervention. Under the *laissez-faire* approach of the Commission, national industrial policies of the member states failed to converge.

As the market-orientated approach to Community industrial policy was not realizing the expected results, in 1970 the Commission published a Memorandum on Industrial Policy, also known as the Colonna Report. This called for a Community industrial policy aimed at economic expansion and technological development. However, the differing ideologies in the member states meant that there was little consensus on what Community industrial policy should be, and a change in approach failed to materialize.

In 1972, with the prospect of enlargement, the Paris Summit called for the establishment of 'a single industrial base for the Community as a whole'. In December 1973 the Commission published the Spinelli Memorandum proposing a competition-orientated Community policy based on harmonization of national regulations, company law and capital markets, the opening of public procurement and measures to encourage the creation of EC-wide firms. Again the consensus necessary to implement the measures was not forthcoming.

As described in Chapter 6, the 1973 oil crisis was followed by the years of Europessimism, with stagflation and growing fragmentation of the Community market as member states attempted to assist their own industries. Many of the interventionist policies were taken over, at times reluctantly, by the Community in order to co-ordinate assistance and render it more transparent. Community industrial policy during these years was mainly characterized by crisis management for specific sectors such as steel, shipbuilding and textiles. These are 'problem' industries with excess supply at a world level, and/or competition from lower-cost producers abroad.

Etienne Davignon, Commission vice-president with responsibility for industry from 1981 to 1985, attempted to 'build Europe' by increasing the competitiveness of Community firms and gained the support of industrialists for cross-border collaboration on technology. At the Copenhagen European Council of 1982 agreement was reached on strengthening the Single Market, increasing research related to industry and providing more funding for investment in industry, technology and energy. While interventionist measures for declining industries continued,[34] from about 1985 there was a shift in emphasis in Community policy away from saving declining industries towards promoting high-technology industries.

Despite the obvious advantages of pooling R&D, the Treaty of Rome made no mention of a common Community R&D effort. During the early 1980s the first Community research and development programmes were launched. ESPRIT (European Strategic Programme for Research

---

[33] See note 12 of Chapter 1.
[34] Davignon sponsored 'crisis cartels' for problem industries such as steel. In order to avoid chaotic price-cutting, there were common scrapping programmes that entailed common and binding floor prices, or public intervention to fix prices.

and Development in Information Technology) came into operation from 1984 in response to lobbying by prominent firms active in the information technology sector. ESPRIT was a joint Community and private sector programme to promote co-operation in research with potential industrial applications. The emphasis was on 'pre-competitive' or basic research in order to ensure compatibility with Community competition law. The private sector was required to make a substantial contribution to the financing of projects to ensure their commitment and avoid accusations, in particular on the part of the USA, that the Community was subsidising industry.

Firms in other sectors soon became aware of Community financial support for information technology and began lobbying the Commission for similar measures in their favour. The Community responded by introducing the First Framework Programme covering the 1984–87 period. This aimed at proving coherence and continuity by incorporating all Community aid for R&D into a single instrument and by extending the programme over a number of years.

Programmes for other industries were also introduced including JET (Joint European Torus) on thermonuclear fusion, BRITE/EURAM (Basic Research in Industrial Technology for Europe/Advanced Materials for Europe) and RACE (Research and Development in Advanced Communications Technology in Europe). RACE was subsequently replaced by ACTS (Advanced Communications Technology and Services), whose aims include the development of broadband technology.

In 1985 Eureka (European Research Co-ordination Agency) was set up partly as a response to Reagan's Star Wars initiative. It was established as a French initiative to reduce the fragmentation of European industry. Eureka is pan-European, including members such as Turkey, and involves public support for firms to launch new high-technology products and increase competitiveness in key areas for the future.

The early R&D programmes of the Community probably had a fairly limited impact on competitiveness, but they established the tradition of firms working with the Commission, and laid the basis for the Single Market. If the Commission were encouraging co-operation between firms and financing R&D to overcome the fragmentation of EC industry, why not tackle the causes of fragmentation directly?

This was the aim of the Single European Act, which also called for measures to promote research and technological development, to assist small and medium enterprises and to encourage co-operation between firms from different regions of the Community.

Not only did the prospect of the Single Market provoke the spate of cross-border mergers and acquisitions described in Chapter 6, but these changes in European industry in turn led to a reassessment of Community industrial policy. An intense debate ensued, with lobbying from industries in difficulty, such as electronics firms, and some member states (notably France) for Community support in favour of certain industries.

In contrast, the Commission view was that effective competition was the best means of ensuring the success of industry, and this position was set out in the Bangemann Memorandum of 1990,[35] named after the then commissioner responsible for industry. The report established the broad principles on which EU industrial policy has been based ever since. According to the Memorandum, the main role of the Community was not to provide selective intervention for individual firms or industries but rather to adopt a 'horizontal' approach aimed at:

■ Maintaining a competitive environment;
■ Providing catalysts for structural adjustment, including completion of the Single Market; and
■ Developing instruments to accelerate structural adjustment.

---

[35] European Commission (1990).

According to the Memorandum, a competitive position could be best be ensured by measures to control state aids, avoid abuse of dominant position and eliminate barriers to international trade. The main responsibility for structural adjustment was said to lie with economic operators, but the Community could help to provide the necessary prerequisites for adjustment, including a high level of educational attainment, social cohesion and environmental protection. Community assistance was therefore to be aimed at ensuring a 'level playing field' through an appropriate combination of the Single Market and trade, competition, regional, social and environmental policies. In order to accelerate the process of structural adjustment, measures could be introduced to promote research and technology, encourage a better use of human resources, ensure the conditions for the development of business services and favour small and medium enterprises (SMEs).

This view of the role of the Community also permeates the Maastricht Treaty, where the Community received explicit responsibility for industrial policy for the first time. Article 130 of the Maastricht Treaty called on the EU and its member states 'to ensure that the conditions needed to make the Community competitive are met in a system of open and competitive markets'. However, unanimity voting was required in the Council, limiting the possibilities for the Community to extend its role.

In the years following the 1990 Bangemann Memorandum, the 'horizontal' approach continued to characterize Community industrial policy, even though certain modifications and refinements were introduced.[36] For instance, two Commission documents of 2002 called for more effort in:[37]

■ Knowledge;
■ Innovation; and
■ Developing entrepreneurial capacity better able to take bigger risks and set up new businesses and expand existing ones.

Small and medium enterprises are considered central to the realization of this third objective. In line with the European Charter for Small Enterprises adopted at the Fiera European Council of 2000, the Commission therefore called for a business environment conducive to SMEs, improved education and training, measures to encourage co-operation between firms, and improved access to R&D programmes.

The aim was to build on previous measures for SMEs, including the reorganization of the Commission in 2000, with the creation of a new DG for Enterprise Policy. The Action Programme for the DG over the 2000–05 period entailed:

■ Action plans to promote entrepreneurship, competitiveness and enterprise policy in a knowledge-based economy;
■ Multi-annual programmes for enterprises, in particular SMEs;
■ An Action Plan for Innovation;
■ Improved industrial competitiveness of European industry;
■ Technical harmonization;
■ A strategy for integrating the environment into industrial policy.

Following the Bangemann Memorandum the EU moved away from selective industrial policy, but the EU still continued to take measures aimed at the specific requirements of several sectors including: steel (see Box 15.4), textiles and clothing, shipbuilding, the automobile industry and advanced technology industries such as aerospace, communications biotechnology, and

---

[36] See European Commission (1993, 1994 and 1998).
[37] European Commission (2002a and b).

Box 15.4 Measures to assist the EU steel industry

Concern with the steel industry was one of the reasons for creating the ECSC in 1951. During the 1950s and 1960s the problem was adjusting to meet growing demand, but during the 1970s the steel industry became characterized by overcapacity at a world level. Since 1974 output and employment in the Community's steel industry have been falling. The situation was worsened by falling demand for steel products with the development of substitutes and the emergence of new competitors on world markets such as Japan, South Korea and Brazil. The Community implemented a series of restructuring plans in the 1970s (such as the Simonet Plan and the Davignon Plan) aimed at modernization and reductions in capacity, but state aids and resistance to capacity cuts at a national level continued. Following the second oil price increase in 1979, the Community was forced to declare the steel industry in 'manifest crisis'. The Commission responded with mandatory production quotas on firms and restrictions on imports. The effort to restructure the industry and cut excess capacity continued, but one of the effects was to reinforce the oligopolistic structure of the sector.

Difficulties continued into the 1990s with falling employment in the sector and rising EU trade deficits, in particular, after the 1992–93 recession. The Community responded with financial incentives to cover some of the costs of restructuring, and foreign trade measures aimed at stabilizing the EU steel market. As these measures initially proved insufficient, the Commission tightened the application of state aids and controls on cartels in the steel sector. State aids were only to be tolerated if accompanied by capacity reductions. Social measures were introduced to assist workers who lose or change jobs, support was given to R&D and to measures to reduce regional disparities, improve the environment, modernize economic and social infrastructure, and develop alternative economic activities.

After a long and costly adjustment, according to the Commission the EU emerged with a modern and competitive steel sector. Over a 20-year period the EU closed down 50 million tonnes of excess capacity and reduced manpower from 900 000 to 250 000. However, the need for restructuring continues in some of the new member states.
* European Commission (2002b).

---

information technologies and so on.[38] The EU attempted to avoid direct intervention, instead relying on measures to:

- ■ Reduce capacity;
- ■ Limit the use of state aids;
- ■ Avoid cartels;
- ■ Promote technology;
- ■ Assist regional and social adjustment;
- ■ Promote environmental objectives;
- ■ Control competing imports.

EU funding of research continued to be covered by Framework Agreements, and the Sixth Framework Programme was introduced for the 2003–06 period. The budget amounted to €17.5 billion, an increase of 17 per cent compared with the Fifth Framework, and accounted for 3.9 per cent of the Community Budget. Seven priority areas for research were chosen: genomics and

---

[38] See, for example, European Commission (2002b); or the factsheets of the European Parliament for descriptions of these measures (www.europarl.eu.int/factsheets).

biotechnology for health; information science technologies; nanotechnologies and nanosciences; aeronautics and space; food safety; sustainable development and economic and social sciences. The Barcelona European Council also agreed to launch a European Research Area in a further effort to overcome the fragmentation of research efforts in the EU.

Article 157 of the Nice Treaty replaced Article 130 of the Maastricht Treaty, and states that the Community and its member states should 'ensure that the conditions necessary for the competitiveness of the Community's industry exist'. To achieve this objective, action is to be aimed at:

- 'Speeding up the adjustment of industry to structural changes;
- Encouraging an environment favourable to initiative and to the development of undertakings throughout the Community, particularly small and medium-sized undertakings;
- Encouraging an environment favourable to co-operation between undertakings;
- Fostering better exploitation of the industrial potential of policies of innovation, research and technological development.'

Enlargement poses challenges for the application of EU industrial policy in the new member states where various industries are still undergoing restructuring (see Chapter 20). The experience of the EU in supporting earlier adjustments suggests that it is necessary to find an appropriate combination of competition, R&D, training, environmental and regional policies.

THE OUTLOOK AND EVALUATION OF EU INDUSTRIAL POLICY

As described in Chapter 6, the EU is experiencing considerable difficulty in moving towards the Lisbon goal of making the EU 'the most competitive and dynamic knowledge-based economy in the world, capable of sustainable growth with more and better jobs and greater social cohesion'. Productivity, in particular in high-technology sectors, has been slowing down and was lower than in the USA. The EU seems unlikely to meet the Barcelona Council objective of R&D spending at 3 per cent of GDP by 2010, with shortfalls in private sector spending well below the levels to realize the target. Slow growth and the increasing strength of emerging competitors at a world level, such as China and India, led to questioning of the 'horizontal' approach to industrial policy adopted by the EU since 1990.

In this context the old debate about promoting national and European champions re-emerged, in what the commissioner responsible for the Internal Market, Frits Bolkenstein, called a 'time warp' reverting to the 1970s.[39] In May 2004 French President Jacques Chirac and German Chancellor Gerhard Schroeder called a meeting to discuss encouraging 'the creation of the industrial champions of the Europe of tomorrow, of which France and Germany could build a certain number'.[40] Steps in this direction had already been taken at a national level, with public support in France for firms such as Alcatel, Alstrom (see Box 15.3 above), Bull and Crédit Lyonnais. In Germany Schroeder had favoured the creation of a German 'superbank' based on Deutsche Bank taking control of Postbank.

Revival of this old debate also found echo at the EU level. Concern that the EU was undergoing a process of deindustrialization led the 2003 Brussels European Council, and France, Germany and Britain in particular, to request a Commission inquiry into the question in order to identify appropriate remedies if necessary. The underlying argument was that EU industry was having

---

[39] *Financial Times*, 14 June 2004.
[40] *Financial Times*, 19 May 2004.

increasing difficulties in the face of competition, which it perceived as 'unbeatable and sometimes unfair'.

The Commission failed to find evidence for a generalized process of deindustrialization, though it pointed to some negative developments such as slow productivity growth and insufficient R&D.[41] Deindustrialization was said to pose problems for the EU as growth in the productivity of manufacturing industry was higher than in services, but the declining share of industry in GDP is a characteristic of most developed economies, and the dividing line between industry and services has become less distinct. Many industrial firms make use of outsourcing for services such as transport, information technology and so on previously performed in house.

The solution proposed by the Commission was threefold:

- Creating a regulatory framework favourable to industry.
- Increasing synergy between the different Community policies having an impact on competitiveness. This should entail a higher priority for innovation, research, training and competition. The functioning of markets should be improved, and policies to ensure cohesion and sustainable development should be strengthened. The international aspect of industrial policy should be reinforced, and, in particular, Community access to third markets should be improved.
- Ensuring that the EU 'continues to develop the sectoral dimension on industrial policy'.

The first two prescriptions echo many previous Commission documents. Introduction of the Single Market and EMU have rendered the regulatory framework more favourable to industry, but there is space for further progress in areas such as financial services (see also Chapter 6). The main criticism of the second proposed solution is that so far words have generally failed to be matched by actions for many of the objectives (and notably the higher priority for R&D and innovation), and there seems little reason to suppose that this time will be different.

The most surprising aspect of the 2004 Commission document is the call for development of a sectoral policy. The Commission argues that 'this does not indicate a return to the interventionist policies of the past' but consists in adapting the horizontal approach to the specific needs of certain sectors. However, this change in orientation has to be read against recent developments in some of the member states where there does seem to be a revival of interventionist policies. Such policies tend to breed rent-seeking activities and politicization of decisions and, as explained above, are difficult to justify on the grounds of economic theory. The 'synergy' between EU competition and industrial policies could prove crucial in this context. After three high profile merger cases were overruled by the Court of First Instance in 2002, the Commission seemed a little more cautious in decisions such as those involving Alstrom and Microsoft. Mario Monti will leave the Commission in 2004, and it remains to be seen how far his successor, Neelie Kroes, is able to take an active stand on state aids. As Commissioner Bolkestein reminds us, supporting national or EU national champions has rarely proved successful in the past and is not a very promising path for policy either at the member state or EU level.

Summary of Key Concepts

- Competition policy is aimed at preventing distortions in competition caused either by private firms or by government actions.
- Article 81 of the EC Treaty prohibits as 'incompatible with the Common Market' all agreements that affect trade between the member states and have the intention or effect of preventing, distorting or restricting competition. Although collusion is forbidden, the EC Treaty permits other forms of co-operation between firms that are not considered to threaten consumers.

---

[41] European Commission (2004b).

- Article 82 of the EC Treaty prohibits abuse of dominant position by one or more firms.
- The announcement of the Single Market Programme was accompanied by a spectacular increase in the number of mergers in the Community. The 1989 Merger Control Regulation (Reg. 4064/89) gives the European Commission the authority to control mergers that meet a specified size and multi-nationality conditions.
- Article 86 covers the monopoly rights granted by member states to private or public undertakings to perform public services, but these rights should not go beyond what is necessary to provide the service, otherwise competition could be restricted.
- Article 87 prohibits state aids to business that have the effect of distorting competition. Exceptions are allowed for certain types of aid.
- A reform of competition policy was introduced in May 2004. Companies will no longer be subject to the obligation of routine notification to the Commission for antitrust clearance. National competition authorities and national courts are to share responsibility for enforcing EU antitrust rules. New merger rules alter procedures and extend the authority of the Commission to investigate all types of harmful scenarios resulting from a merger and not just market dominance. The state aid reform aims at simplification and acceleration of procedures, and encouraging member states to use a more economic approach in assessing state aids.
- A market-orientated industrial policy aims at removing the barriers to the operation of competition.
- Selective, interventionist industrial policy involves support for declining industries to avoid loss of jobs and the promotion of industries considered 'key' or strategic.
- During the 1960s Community industrial policy was based on a market-orientated approach, but in the 1970s and 1980s more selective intervention was used in favour of specific sectors.
- Following the 1990 Bangemann Memorandum, the Community adopted a 'horizontal' approach to industrial policy.
- In recent years the debate about supporting national and EU champions has revived.

Questions for Study and Review

■ Explain how the integration process may be undermined by distortions in competition.

■ Describe the role of the various EU institutions with regard to competition policy. What criticisms can be made, and what reforms could be introduced?

■ Explain the difficulties in establishing whether collusive behaviour between firms has taken place.

■ Describe what kinds of behaviour by firms are considered evidence of abuse of dominant position. Explain why market definition may pose difficulties in this context.

■ How has EU merger control changed over the years?

■ How successful do you think that EU policy with regard to state aids has been?

■ Describe the different forms industrial policy may take.

■ How successful has Community industrial policy proved?

■ What difficulties arise in the promotion of national and EU champions? Give some examples.

References

Begg, D., Fischer, S. and Dornbusch, R. (2000) *Economics*, 6th edn, McGraw-Hill Education, Maidenhead, UK.

Browning, E.K. and Browning, J.M. (1992) *Microeconomic Theory and Applications*, 4th edn, Harper Collins Publishers Inc., New York.

European Commission (1990) 'Industrial policy in an open and competitive environment: Guidelines for a Community Approach', COM(90)556.

European Commission (1993) 'Growth, competitiveness, employment – The challenges and ways forward into the 21st century', COM(93) 700.

European Commission (1994) 'An industrial competitiveness policy for the European Union', COM(94) 319 final.

European Commission (1997) 'Notice on the definition of the relevant market for the purposes of Community competition law', Official Journal C 372, 9 December.

European Commission (1998) 'The competitiveness of European enterprises in the face of globalization – How it can be encouraged', COM(1998) 718 final.

European Commission (2000a) 'Draft Guidelines on the applicability of Article 81 to horizontal co-operation'.

European Commission (2000b) 'Competition policy in Europe and the citizen'.

European Commission (2002a) 'Productivity: The key to competitiveness of European economies and enterprises', COM(2002) 262 final.

European Commission (2002b) 'Industrial policy in an enlarged Europe', COM(2002) 714 final.

European Commission (2004a) 'A pro-active competition policy for a competitive Europe: Communication from the Commission', COM(2004) 293 final, 20 April 2004.

European Commission (2004b) 'XXXIII Report on competition policy – 2003', SEC(2004) 658 final, 4 April 2004.

European Commission (2004c) 'Fostering structural change: An industrial policy for an enlarged Europe', COM(2004) 274 final.

Hitiris, T. (2003) *European Union Economics*, 5th edn, Prentice Hall, Harlow, UK.

Laudati, L.L. (1998) 'The impact of Community competition law on member state competition law', in Martin, S. ed. (1998) *Competition Policies in Europe*, Elsevier, Amsterdam.

Martin, S. (2001) 'Competition policy' in Artis, M. and Nixson, F. (eds), *The Economics of the European Union: Policy and Analysis*, 3rd edn, Oxford University Press, Oxford.

Navarro, L. (2003) 'Industrial policy in the economic literature: Recent theoretical developments and implications for EU policy', Enterprise papers No. 12, www.europa.eu.int/comm/enterprise.

Tsoukalis, L. (1997) *The New European Economy Revisited*, 3rd edn, Oxford University Press, Oxford.

Varian, H.R. (1999) *Intermediate Microeconomics: A Modern Approach*, 5th edn, W.W. Norton & Co., London and New York.

Useful websites

The website on competition is one of the best organized of the European Commission's websites, with explanations of policy and transcripts of speeches explaining recent reforms and cases:
www.europa.eu.int/comm/competition
The European Parliament factsheets provide descriptions of EU competition and industrial policies:
www.europarl.eu.int/factsheets
Information on industrial policy issues is available under Enterprise, and under Research, Development, Technology and Information on the European Commission website:
www.europa.eu.int/comm
For a description of issues in competition policy at a wider international level see:
Global Competition Review www.globalcompetitionreview.com
International Competition Network
www.internationalcompetitionnetwork.org

List of abbreviations

AC	average cost
AR	average revenue
ACTS	Advanced Communications Technology and Services
BRITE/ EURAM	Basic Research in Industrial technology for Europe/Advanced Materials for Europe
DG	Directorate-General
ECN	European Competition Network
ECSC	European Coal and Steel Community
EMU	economic and monetary union
ESPRIT	European Strategic Programme for Research and Development in Information Technology
Eureka	European Research Co-ordination Agency
FDI	foreign direct investment
GDP	gross domestic product
JET	Joint European Torus on thermonuclear fusion
LAC	long-run average cost
LMC	long-run marginal cost
MC	marginal cost
MR	marginal revenue
RACE	Research and Development in Advanced Communications Technology in Europe
R&D	research and development
SAC	short-run average cost
SMC	short-run marginal cost
SBM	stretch blow moulding
SME	small and medium enterprise
UBC	United Brand Company
WTO	World Trade Organization

16

Transport Policy

LEARNING OBJECTIVES

By the end of this chapter you should be able to understand:

▶ The reasons for public intervention in transport;

▶ The forms of public intervention in transport;

▶ Why the Treaty of Rome envisaged the creation of a common transport policy;

▶ The difficulties encountered in introducing a common transport policy;

▶ How and why the pace of introducing common transport measures increased from the mid-1980s;

▶ The proposals for the development of EU transport until 2010;

▶ What measures the EU has taken with regard to trans-European networks, road, rail and air transport, and shipping.

INTRODUCTION

Transport plays an essential role in the EU economy, accounting for over 10 per cent of GDP and employing about 7 million people in 2001.[1] Private households in the EU spend about €695 billion per year, or 14 per cent of their total consumption on transport. Transport is also important for its links to other sectors and absorbs about 40 per cent of public investment. In 2000 transport accounted for 32.4 per cent of total final energy demand in the EU and caused about 29 per cent of all carbon dioxide emissions, of which 24 per cent was due to road transport and 5 per cent to other modes.[2]

Transport costs may act as a barrier to trade, and from the beginning the need to develop a common transport policy was considered an essential element of the integration process. Together

[1] European Commission (2003a).
[2] European Commission (2003b).

with agriculture and trade, transport was one of the three common policies envisaged by the Treaty of Rome, but unlike the other two, a common transport policy was slow to develop.

PUBLIC INTERVENTION IN TRANSPORT

Transport has traditionally always been a heavily regulated sector. As in other sectors, such as agriculture, many of the justifications for public intervention in transport are based on the concept of market failure. Market failure occurs where it is either impossible to establish a market, or markets operate inefficiently.[3] A further justification sometimes given for public intervention in transport is the danger of 'excessive' competition, so the reasons for public intervention in transport become:

1. **Economies of scale and natural monopoly.** Increasing returns to scale are a common reason for markets not being competitive, since economic efficiency requires a limited number of firms. At the extreme, increasing returns will be so significant that only one firm should operate in the market, and this is referred to as 'a situation of natural monopoly'. The expensive infrastructure required in many forms of transport creates barriers to entry. In order to realize the benefits of economies of scale, and prevent duplication of expensive infrastructure, it may be necessary to permit just one or a few firms to operate. The state may either regulate this monopoly or run the monopoly itself.

2. **Externalities** can be defined as the difference between private (to the individual) and public (to the community) costs and benefits. In other words, externalities are the positive or negative effects of the production or consumption by one individual on others, which are not reflected in prices. Externalities may arise, for example, from the implications of transport for regional development, social policy and the environment.

3. A third form of market failure may arise from **costly and/or scarce information**. For instance, in the case of transport public intervention may be required to ensure adequate safety standards.

4. **Excessive competition** could destroy all but one or two firms, which would then set higher prices by, for example, forming a cartel. Capacity is geared to peak demand and fixed costs are high, so in times of low demand there may be intense price competition, leading to bankruptcies.[4]

Government intervention in transport may also be justified on the grounds of ensuring an appropriate mix of the different modes of transport (see Tables 16.1 and 16.2), in particular, to avoid congestion and bottlenecks (forms of negative externality).

Between 1990 and 2000 the increase in overall passenger transport in the EU was 19.7 per cent, but the relative proportion of rail, bus and even passenger car transport declined in favour of air transport. The share of air transport in total passenger transport rose from 3.7 percent in 1990 to 5.8 per cent in 2001. The number of cars in the EU is increasing by 3 million per year, and car numbers have trebled in the last 30 years.[5] Car numbers are also predicted to rise rapidly in the new CEEC member states.

---

[3] Public goods are not included in the list of forms of market failure used to justify intervention in transport here. Although this argument may apply to transport, it does not appear to be a major reason for intervention. Pure public goods are defined as having the characteristics of non-rivalry (i.e. the consumption by one individual does not imply less for others) and non-excludability (nobody can be kept from consuming the good). Mixed public goods have just one of these characteristics. There is no extra cost to producing a pure public good for an additional consumer, so consumers will tend not to reveal their preferences for the good and instead will attempt to free ride. This means that the public good is likely to be supplied insufficiently, or not at all. An example of a public good in transport could be a road system from which exclusion is costly.

[4] In other words, the price elasticity of demand is low, and supply remains inelastic at times of low demand. See Hitiris (2003) for a discussion of this point.

[5] European Commission (2003c).

	Goods		Passengers	
Road	43.8%	Road		78.3%
Sea	41.3%	Buses and coach		8.5%
Rail	8.1%	Tram and metro		1.1%
Inland waterways	4.1%	Rail		6.3%
Pipeline	2.8%	Air		5.8%

Table 16.1 The share of different modes in EU transport, 2001

Source: European Commission (2003a and c), www.europa.eu.int/comm/dgs/energy_transport.

With regard to freight transport, road transport grew by 40.3 per cent between 1990 and 2001, followed by inland waterways (an increase of 15.2 per cent) and rail (6.1 per cent).[6] There are large differences in the modal split of different member states, with the share of road transport ranging from 40 per cent in Austria to 98 per cent in Ireland. Inland waterways only accounted for a significant share of freight transport in six member states, but reached 45 per cent in the Netherlands. The ongoing process of relocation of some industries in the Single Market has increased heavy goods traffic, which is predicted to grow by a further 50 per cent by 2010 compared to its 1998 level if nothing is done.[7] According to the European Commission,[8] rail freight in the EU travels at only 18 km/h on average and is 'facing marginalization', in marked contrast to the USA where 40 per cent of goods are carried by rail.

	1980-90	1991-2001	2000-01
GDP (real growth)	2.3	2.1	1.6
Industrial production	1.8	1.0	0
Passenger transport pkm	3.0	1.7	1.1
Freight transport	1.6	2.7	-0.2

Table 16.2 Annual growth rates of transport (per cent)

Source: European Commission(2003a).

TRANSPORT COSTS AS A FORM OF TRADE BARRIER

Figure 16.1 can be used to show how transport costs can operate as a barrier to trade, and so should be reduced as part of the integration process. A homogenous good will only be traded between two countries if the difference in the prices for the good in the two countries exceeds the transport costs. The approach used here is that of partial equilibrium. The vertical axis indicates the price Px of good X in country 1 and country 2. The quantity of X is shown along the horizontal axes, with increasing quantities of X indicated by movements to the right from the origin for country 2 (as is usually the case). In contrast, increases in the quantity of X are shown by movements from the origin to the left for country 1. As a result the demand curve for product x slopes down to the left, while the supply curve slopes up to the left.

Without trade, the equilibrium for country 1 is at E where country 1 will produce and consume 50x at price €5. The equilibrium for country 2 is E′ where 50 X are produced and consumed at €11. With the opening of trade, country 1 will export to country 2, and the price of X will rise in country 1 and fall in country 2. Assuming transport costs of €2 per unit of X, the price of X in country 2 will be €2 higher than in country 1. The price of X becomes €7 in country 1, and country

---

[6] European Commission (2003b).
[7] European Commission (2003c).
[8] European Commission (2003c).

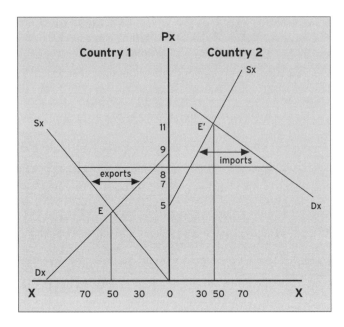

Figure 16.1 Transport costs as a trade barrier

Source: From *International Economics* by Dominick Salvatore, Copyright © 2001, John Wiley & Sons, Inc. This material is used by permission of John Wiley & Sons, Inc.

1 exports 40 X. The price of X in country 2 becomes €9 and country 2 imports €40. Without transport costs, with trade the price in both countries would be €8, and 60 X would be traded. The transport costs therefore act as a barrier to trade.

FORMS OF PUBLIC INTERVENTION IN TRANSPORT

Government intervention in transport may take various forms:

■ Responsibility for the infrastructure;
■ Providing the services that run on the infrastructure, or subsidising those that do and/or controlling the number of operators;
■ Introducing legislation to regulate the sector.

Traditionally transport technology has tended to require large, relatively indivisible infrastructure and this has created problems for investment appraisal. In principle all costs and benefits (including externalities) of a scheme should be taken into account in deciding on an investment, but in practice this often proves difficult. Problems may arise in finding reliable monetary measures of the various costs and benefits, in particular of externalities, and choice of the project may be influenced by equity considerations.

Difficulties also arise with regard to the pricing of transport services. A pricing principle frequently proposed to ensure efficiency in the allocation of resources is to set prices equal to the marginal social cost of the service. In other words the price should reflect the social opportunity cost of the services used, and in this way externalities would also be taken into consideration. The externalities include the costs of adding to congestion, pollution, the number of accidents and so on. Again in practice it may be difficult to calculate these social costs. The pricing of transport services is also likely to take into account equity considerations.

Control over the number of operators offering services entails limiting entry to the market. This may be carried out through quotas or licences. There may be restrictions on cabotage or the right of non-resident carriers to operate in another member country, in particular by obtaining business for the return journey.

TRANSPORT IN THE TREATY OF ROME

Articles 3 and 74–84 of the Treaty of Rome (now Articles 70–80 of the EC Treaty) envisaged the creation of a common transport policy. Article 71 (Formerly Article 75) sets out the main features of the common transport policy which include common rules applicable to the internal transport of member states, the conditions for operating in other member states, and measures to improve safety. According to Article 80, the common transport policy applies to rail, road and inland waterways, but the Treaty envisages the Council extending its provisions to sea and air transport, and an amendment to this effect was included in the Single European Act.

The common transport policy was therefore to be based on non-discrimination, different regimes for different modes and the right of establishment but not freedom of services (access to other EC markets was dependent on EC provisions). This rather contradictory list already showed the difficulty in reaching common positions. The Treaty of Rome lacks details about how the common transport policy was to operate, and the actual design of the common policy was left to the Council.

According to Swann (1995), three main factors account for the inclusion of a common transport policy among the objectives of the Treaty of Rome:

■ Transport costs could act as a trade barrier (see Figure 16.1 above), and measures to promote a cheap, efficient transport system in the Community could help to stimulate trade.
■ Transport has traditionally always been a heavily regulated sector and failure to harmonize policies could lead to distortions (as the experience of the ECSC showed).
■ The Treaty of Rome was a compromise, balancing the national interests of the founding countries, and the Netherlands in particular was anxious to include transport policy as part of the deal. Transport, especially through Rotterdam and along the Rhine, makes an important contribution to Dutch GDP.

THE DIFFICULTIES IN IMPLEMENTING A COMMON TRANSPORT POLICY

Progress in introducing common transport measures proved slow and controversial for three main reasons (Hitiris, 2003):

■ Differences in interpreting the Treaty;
■ Different attitudes about the form that intervention in transport should take; and
■ Conflicts of interest among the member states.

In 1961 the Commission presented its proposals for the general principles of the common transport policy in a document known as the 'Schaus Memorandum' after the first commissioner responsible for transport, Lambert Schaus. The purpose of the Schaus Memorandum was to begin discussion of the basic principles underlying the common policy. According to the Commission, this would involve an attempt to 'create healthy competition of the widest scope'. National transport policies were to be replaced by a common policy based on competition. Measures would be introduced to eliminate discrimination, to liberalize the provision of services and to harmonize measures such as the weights and dimensions of vehicles, the conditions of work in road transport and the taxation of vehicles. The emphasis of the Commission's proposals was therefore on deregulation. The proposals were bound to create controversy given the highly regulated nature of transport policy in the member states at that time.

Though Ecosoc and the European Parliament accepted the principles of the Commission's recommendations, the Council took little action to implement the proposals. In 1962 the Commission presented an Action Programme setting out the measures that the Commission thought necessary to implement the common transport policy. The emphasis was still on competition and liberalization, and the Commission also proposed extending these principles to national transport systems. Again the Commission's proposals met with opposition from the member states. It was argued that 'excessive' competition would cause safety standards to be undermined, lead to bankruptcies and render railways incapable of competing with road haulage (Swann, 1995).

Following the first enlargement of the Community in 1973, the Commission attempted a change in strategy and called for harmonization of national policies as a first step in introducing a common policy. A revised version of the Action Plan was presented in 1973. After a substantial delay, the Council called on the Commission to define its priorities. Over the next few years the Commission presented various proposals, but the Council failed to agree on the necessary steps for their implementation. Eventually, in 1982 the European Parliament decided to take the Council to the Court of Justice for failing to respect its obligation to introduce the common transport policy set out in the Treaty of Rome.

DEVELOPMENTS IN TRANSPORT POLICY SINCE 1985

Since 1985 progress in introducing common transport measures has been rapid for a number of reasons:

- Transport was an integral part of the 1993 Programme.
- In 1985 the European Court ruled that the Council should adopt measures to liberalize transport 'within a reasonable time'.
- There was an international trend towards the liberalization of transport that was particularly evident in the United States during the Reagan years.
- In 1986 in the Nouvelles Frontières case the European Court of Justice ruled in favour of a French firm which had been charging prices below those fixed by the French authorities. This ruling gave leeway to the EC Commission to overrule national agreements.

In 1992 the EC Commission published a White Paper, 'The future development of the common transport policy', which set out three main aims:

- To remove distortions and implement the Single Market;
- To ensure the proper functioning of the EC transport system, in particular by reducing modal and geographic imbalances and by improving safety and social aspects;
- To further environmental aims by raising standards to safeguard against pollution and by encouraging 'sustainable' mobility.

Measures to achieve these aims included the liberalizing of transport markets, harmonizing of technical standards, improving interconnections between networks, correcting the modal balance and combining different transport modes, increasing links with remote regions and neighbouring countries, researching new technologies and improving the quality of services. Considerable progress was made in realizing the basic aim of the White Paper to open up the transport market, with the exception of the rail sector (see below).[9] In 1993 a further White Paper of the Commission,

---

[9] European Commission (2003c).

'Growth, competitiveness and employment', called for substantial investment in infrastructure also to reduce bottlenecks and congestion in the EU, which were said to be causing a loss of competitiveness.

The Maastricht Treaty reinforced the legal, decision-making and financial bases of the common transport policy. In principle unanimity was replaced by qualified majority voting even though Council decisions still tend to be by unanimity. The Treaty also laid the basis for TENs, or trans-European networks, to improve transport, energy and telecommunications infrastructure with the help of Community financing (see below).

The Cardiff European Council of 1998 requested various sectoral Councils, including that on transport, to develop strategies with regard to sustainable development. In 1999 the Transport Council indicated five sectors where measures should be taken to correct negative trends:

- Growth in carbon dioxide emissions as a result of transport;
- Pollutant emissions and their effect on health;
- Anticipated growth in transport, in particular, after enlargement;
- Modal distribution;
- Noise in transport.

The Amsterdam Treaty and the Gothenburg European Council also stressed the importance of a sustainable development strategy (see Chapter 12), maintaining that the balance between different modes of transport was central to maintaining this strategy.

In 2001 the European Commission published the White Paper, 'European transport policy for 2010: Time to decide'.[10] The White Paper set out 60 measures to be introduced, and includes an Action programme extending until 2010, a monitoring process and a mid-term review in 2005. The proposals are aimed at:

- **Reinforcing passengers' rights**, for example by ensuring compensation for delays, denied boarding due to overbooking and accidents, not only in air travel but also for other modes.
- **Improving road safety**. In 2001 39 849 people were killed on EU roads and 70 were killed in rail accidents. The aim is to cut the number of victims by 50 per cent by 2010 by encouraging better technologies, improved signposting and information exchange on good practice. Road safety in towns could be improved by developing cycling. Though the member states are reluctant to transfer authority for such matters to the EU level, if progress is too slow the Commission will start making regulatory proposals from 2005. The Commission also proposed two measures for the trans-European networks. These entailed harmonization of signs at particularly dangerous black spots and harmonization of the checks and penalties for international commercial transport with regard to speeding and drink-driving.
- **Encouraging sustainable mobility.** In a Green Paper of 2000 on security of supply, the Commission argued that if nothing were done, carbon dioxide emissions from transport could increase by 50 per cent by 2010. The main cause of the increase was predicted to be road transport, which accounts for 84 per cent of the carbon dioxide emissions caused by transport.[11]

  The objective is to reduce dependence on oil from the 2000 level of 98 per cent by encouraging the use of alternative fuels and by improving efficiency in using energy. Tax reductions for bio fuels would also help increase their share in consumption to the target of 6 per cent by 2010. Research into clean, efficient transport is to be encouraged.

---

[10] European Commission (2001).
[11] European Commission (2003c).

The Commission called for alignment of the principles of charging for infrastructure use, with integration of external costs. The revenue raised in this way could be used to reduce or offset external costs.

■ **Preventing congestion**. According to the European Commission (2003c), 10 per cent of the EU road network is affected daily by traffic jams, 20 per cent of the rail network is classed as bottlenecks and 16 major EU airports recorded delays on more than 30 per cent of their flights. The cost of road traffic congestion alone was estimated at 0.5 per cent of EU GDP and predicted to rise to 1 per cent of GDP by 2010 if nothing were done.

The Commission aims at correcting the imbalance between different modes of transport by promoting rail, maritime and inland waterway transport in order to allow their shares in total transport to return to 1998 levels. Measures would also be taken to encourage links between the different modes of transport. This would require technical harmonization and interoperability between systems, in particular for containers. The programme Marco Polo with an annual budget of about €103 million for the 2003–2006 period was to be set up to encourage interconnections between different modes of transport.[12]

■ **Developing high-quality urban transport,** which would involve exchanges of good practice aimed at better use of public transport and infrastructure, and a more rational use of the car.

■ **Harmonizing taxes on fuel for professional road transport.**

■ **Major infrastructural** work is to be carried out in the context of trans-European networks (see below).

■ **Gallileo, Europe's satellite radionavigation system,** is to become operational by 2008. At present only the USA (GPS) and Russia (GLONASS) have radio navigation technology. Gallileo would offer services such as: measurement of car speeds, tracking of goods carried by rail, positioning of ships carrying dangerous cargoes and remote monitoring of medical patients.

■ **'Managing globalization'** is necessary because regulation of transport is becoming an increasingly international matter, but international rules sometimes take insufficient account of environmental protection or safety considerations. The aim is to raise the profile of the EU in international organizations such as the IMO (International Maritime Organization), the ICAO (International Civil Aviation Organization), the Central Commission for Navigation on the Rhine and the Danube Commission.

TRANS-EUROPEAN NETWORKS (TENS)

The Maastricht Treaty (Article 129b–d, replaced by Articles 154–56 of the EU Treaty) called for the creation of trans-European networks (TENs) in transport (see Box 16.1), energy, telecommunications and environmental infrastructure. The aim of these programmes is to assist completion of the Single Market, reinforce economic and social cohesion, increase competitiveness and promote sustainable development. The programmes were intended to ensure the interconnection and interoperability of national networks and improve access to them.

The Commission's White Paper, 'Growth, competitiveness and employment', of 1993 stressed the importance of TENs in helping to improve infrastructure and eliminate bottlenecks. The Essen European Council of 1994 selected 14 priority transport projects. In 1996 (Decision 1692/96) the

---

[12] This replaced the PACT Programme (Pilot Actions for Combined Transport), which had been active from 1997 to 2001.

Community developed the guidelines for implementation of the network and identification of projects of common interest and fixed the time horizon of 2010 to complete the network. The estimated cost was about €400 billion at the time, but only about 10 per cent of financing was to come from the TENs budget of the EU. The bulk of financing was expected to come from national governments and the private sector, though additional funds were available from the European Investment Bank, the Cohesion Fund and the European Regional Development Fund.

Box 16.1 Priority TEN-T projects

Railway axis Berlin-Verona/Milan-Bologna-Naples-Messina-Palermo

High-speed railway axis Paris-Brussels/Brussels-Cologne-Amsterdam-London

High-speed railway axis of south-west Europe

High-speed railway axis east

Betuwe axis

Railway axis Lyon-Trieste/Koper-Ljubiana-Budapest-Ukrainian border

Motorway axis Igoumenitsa/Patras-Athens-Sofia-Budapest

Multimode link Portugal/Spain-rest of Europe

Conventional rail link Cork-Dublin-Belfast-Larne-Stranraer (completed in 2001)

Malpensa airport (completed in 2001)

Nordic triangle railway/road axis

UK/Ireland/Benelux road link

West coast main axis

Freight railway axis Sines-Madrid-Paris

Railway axis Paris-Strasbourg-Stuttgart-Vienna-Bratislava

Rhine/Meuse-Main-Danube Inland waterway axis

High-speed axis interoperability on the Iberian Peninsula

Fehmarn Belt railway axis

Railway axis Athens-Sofia-Budapest-Vienna-Prague-Nürnberg-Dresden

Railway axis Gdansk-Warsaw-Brno/Bratislava-Vienna

Railway axis Lyon/Genova-Basel-Duisburg-Rotterdam/Antwerp

Motorway axis Gdansk-Brno/Bratislava-Vienna

Railway/road axis Ireland/UK/continental Europe

'Rail Baltica' axis Warsaw-Kaunas-Riga-Tallinn

'Eurocaprail' on the Brussels-Luxembourg-Strasbourg railway axis

Railway axis of the Ionian/Adriatic intermodal corridor

Source: European Commission (2003d).

However, progress in implementing the TENs was slow. According to the European Commission (2001), by 2001 only about one-fifth of the infrastructure projects had been carried out. Large projects that had been completed included the Brussels–Marseilles high-speed train, the Øresund bridge-tunnel linking Sweden and Denmark, and Spata airport. Public and private funding was not always forthcoming and private investors were often not convinced of the commercial viability of the projects. There were bureaucratic delays and uncertainties associated with the choice of routes and planning process. Governments were often only interested in the national dimension of projects and the co-ordination of cross-border projects was complex.

The Commission's White Paper of 2001 called for a revision of the TENs guidelines, with more concentration on removing the bottlenecks in the railway network, completing the routes identified as priorities for absorbing traffic flows generated by enlargement and improving access to outlying areas.[13]

In 2003 a high-level group was set up under Van Miert to examine ways of improving the functioning of the TEN-T (trans-European network transport) programme. The tasks of the group were to identify priority programmes up until 2020, propose a methodology for subsequent updating of the list of priority projects and develop the concept of 'motorways of the sea'. The group presented its recommendations in June 2003, which included:

■ Finishing 8 of the 14 priority projects by 2010;
■ Starting 22 new TEN-T projects with a time horizon of 2020;
■ Increasing the share of Community funding to 20 per cent for all cross-border transport projects (subsequently agreed by the Council);
■ Introducing new financial engineering techniques and strengthening the private-public partnership.

The Brussels European Council of December 2003 endorsed the European Action for Growth, which included steps to encourage private financing and set up a Quick-start programme for projects with a strong cross-border impact. The Quick-start programme would include the TEN-T priority list, three broadband projects, the Gallileo satellite navigation system and projects under the TEN-Energy (TEN-E) programme to improve cross-border gas and energy links. Among the proposals by the Italian Presidency for improving the TEN-T infrastructure was a bridge to Sicily, but the proposal was not accepted since other member states were sceptical about the contribution of the project to EU competitiveness.

ROAD HAULAGE

EC road haulage has always been characterized by a large number of operators, many of whom are very small. The sector is tightly regulated partly to avoid the negative aspects of excess competition, such as inadequate respect for safety conditions, bankruptcies and excessive cutting of costs but also to reduce competition with the railways.

Before the Single Market Programme there were restrictions on the number of operators (with quotas both at the national and EC levels), on tariffs and on cabotage, i.e. the right to pick up a load on the return journey.

The Single Market Programme entailed agreement on common minimum rates of excise on petrol and on minimum duties on licences (though agreement on minimum levels still leaves ample scope for divergence). A Directive of 1985 called for harmonization of maximum weights and dimensions and was to take full effect from 1999. Quantitative restrictions on road haulage were to be phased out, with surveillance and EC intervention if cases of oversupply resulted. The limits on cabotage were to be gradually reduced, with liberalization from 1998. Various measures were also introduced on mutual recognition of licences, safety belts, driving hours, traffic safety, environmental considerations (such as the emission of exhaust fumes and energy consumption) and the transport of dangerous goods and so on.

The 2001 White Paper[14] again refers to the problems of excessive competition of road haulage with fragmentation and pressure exerted on prices by consignors and industry. As a result there may be a risk of some road haulage companies resorting to dumping and failing to respect social

[13] European Commission (2001).
[14] European Commission (2003c).

and safety legislation. The White Paper called for an improvement in inspection procedures to ensure legislation is respected and the harmonization of contracts to protect road haulage firms from consignors and enable them to revise tariffs in the event of a sharp rise in fuel prices.

RAIL TRANSPORT

The share of railways in total freight transport in the 15 EU countries fell from 21 per cent in 1970 to 8.1 per cent in 2000, with the share of road freight transport increasing from 30.8 per cent to 43.8 per cent over the same period (see also Table 16.1 above).[15] The share of railways in total passenger transport also fell from 10.2 per cent in 1970 to 6.3 per cent in 2000. A major reason for this decline was that rail transport is less reliable than road haulage with regard to delivery times. One of the aims of EU policy is to revitalize the railways as a safe, relatively clean mode of transport, and as a means of reducing road and air congestion.

Traditionally rail services were considered a natural monopoly because of the costly infrastructure required. Railways were also considered a strategic asset for the economic development of countries. National governments maintained close links with railway authorities and regulated them tightly, generally also providing subsidies. Rail transport has always been characterized by the difficulty of reconciling the objective of efficiency with the need to operate as a public service, taking into account regional, social and environmental considerations.

A major aim of Community policy was to increase the transparency of state financing of the railroads and to reduce distortions. In addition there was a need to overcome technical barriers by ensuring compatibility of networks and rolling stock. In 1991 as part of the Internal Market Programme, a Community Directive (91/440/EEC) made the distinction between infrastructure and the management of rail services operating on that infrastructure, stipulating that:

- Operating services should be carried out according to commercial criteria, based on competitiveness and sound financial management;
- There was to be free access to all rail systems in the EC for international groupings operating rail services between EC member states;
- The infrastructure was to remain the responsibility of the member state.[16]

In 1995 a further Directive (95/18/EC) set out the common criteria that railway undertakings operating in the EU had to respect. The criteria relate to good repute, financial standing, professional competence and civil liability and were updated in 2001 (see below).

In 1996 a Commission White Paper proposed to create 'rail freight freeways' or major routes on which the carriage of freight would be market-driven and paths would be shared fairly among operators. However, these freeways were not as successful as expected as little use was made of this open access.[17]

In 2001 a 'Rail Infrastructure Package' was agreed which called for member states to allow access of international freight services to the national sections of the Trans European Rail Freight Network (TERFN) by 2008.[18] Different organizational entities are to be set up for transport operations and infrastructure management. The package defines the financial, economic and safety conditions for railway operators to obtain a licence and deals with the levying of charges for the use of infrastructure and safety certification.[19]

---

[15] The data here are taken from www.europa.eu.int/comm/transport/rail.
[16] This also involved the development of a pricing mechanism for infrastructure use that would cover social costs.
[17] See www.europa.eu.int/comm/transport/rail.
[18] Directive 2001/12 (which modified Directive 91/44).
[19] Directive 2001/13 and Directive 2001/14.

The White Paper of 2001 calls for the modal share of railways in total transport to return to the same level as 1998 by 2010. The Commission called for the gradual evolution of a network dedicated exclusively to goods transport and further measures to increase rail safety and interoperability, including the establishment of a European Safety and Interoperability Agency.

The White Paper also called for improved access to the railway network for freight transport, but in October 2003 the Commission referred nine member states to the Court of Justice for failure to notify the Commission of transposition of the necessary legislation for the Rail Infrastructure Package of 2001.[20] In 2004 the Commission again called for measures to open freight services in the railway sector.[21]

AIR TRANSPORT

Throughout the world air transport remained highly regulated until the mid-1980s. The basis for regulation was the 1944 Chicago Conference, which recognized:

- Flag-carrying airlines with non-commercial objectives;
- Bilateral agreements about flight routes and landing rights (typically services were divided 50:50 between the two national airlines involved);
- Fares negotiated in the IATA (International Air Transport Association) and then subject to the approval of national governments.

As a result, air transport operated on the basis of a system of bilateral agreements in which designated carriers provided services whose cost, capacity and conditions were directly or indirectly regulated. While the aim was to guarantee a safe, reliable and not too expensive service, by the mid-1980s the system came increasingly under attack. Prices tended to be high, services inadequate, and it was argued that deregulation would increase social welfare.

The Commission attempted to introduce limited deregulation by extending Community competition rules to air transport, but after many years of failing to induce the Council of Transport Ministers to implement measures, the Commission referred the case to the Court of Justice. In 1986 the Court ruled that competition rules also apply to air transport, and that the member states should not approve fares if they knew that they resulted from a cartel or concerted actions among airlines. However, progress on liberalization in the Council continued to be slow, leading some member states (Belgium, Germany, Italy, Ireland, the Netherlands and the UK) to introduce unilateral measures to free market entry and pricing on certain routes (Hitiris, 2003).

In order to force liberalization, the Commission proceeded by presenting cases of infringement of competition law by bilateral agreements on fares, capacity-sharing and other restrictive practices. Eventually in 1987 the Council of Transport Ministers agreed a package liberalizing fares, capacity, market access and the application of Community competition law to air transport. Other packages on air deregulation followed in 1989 and 1992.

Since 1993 any airline has the right to set its own fares without government approval. The Council also agreed that any EU carrier satisfying certain basic conditions with regard to safety, financial fitness etc. could obtain an operating licence, permitting it to fly anywhere in the EU, with full access to international routes. Virtually all routes were gradually opened to European operators, and airlines were free to determine fares subject to certain safeguards designed to protect the interests of consumers and the industry. Strict controls on state aids were maintained. Safety

---

[20] The nine countries were: Austria, Germany, Greece, Ireland, Luxembourg, Portugal, Spain, Sweden and the UK.
[21] European Commission (2004).

measures were to be harmonized through the work of national authorities co-operating in the Joint Aviation Authorities, even though considerable differences in national practices remain.

As a result of liberalization the number of routes and carriers has increased, while it is estimated that promotional fares fell by 41 per cent between 1992 and 2000.[22] Air traffic increased by an average of 7.4 per cent a year between 1980 and 2001, while the traffic in airports of the EU(15) grew fivefold since 1970.[23]

However, growth in aircraft traffic has also added to greenhouse gas emissions. It is estimated that carbon dioxide emissions because of aviation will rise by 3 per cent per year on average between 1990 and 2010, lower than the rate of traffic growth, thanks largely to improved technology.[24]

In order to reduce noise pollution, in 1992 a Directive was introduced to ban the noisiest aircraft from EU airports. In 1998 the Commission proposed further legislation to limit the operation in the EU of aircraft fitted with 'hushkits', or muffler devices aimed at rendering engines less noisy. The limited success of this measure, and objections by the USA led in 2002 to its replacement by Directive 2002/30/EC, introducing a more 'balanced approach' to noise around airports. Noise management is to be based on reduction of aircraft noise at source, land-use planning and management measures, noise-abatement operational procedures and operating restrictions.

The more competitive environment of air traffic has also contributed to a radical process of restructuring of EU airlines in recent years. This has been characterized by a series of new entrants (such as Easy-Jet or Ryanair, see Box 16.2) and the creation of global alliances (which sometimes prove unstable), typically involving an EU airline, a US airline and a few others.

> ### Box 16.2 Ryanair subsidies
> Ryanair became the EU's leading low-cost airline by cutting out the frills, using one type of aircraft, flying its aircraft more frequently and concentrating on smaller regional airports to cut costs and shorten turnaround times. In February 2004 the European Commission ruled against airport subsidies granted by Charleroi (the airport used for Brussels) to Ryanair. The owner of Charleroi, the Walloon regional government, had given a 50 per cent reduction in landing fees to Ryanair, and contributed in money or kind to Ryanair's local hotel, office, training and marketing costs. According to the EU Commission such assistance was discriminatory and ran counter to EU legislation on state aids.

One of the aims of the 2001 White Paper was to tackle the delays in air traffic by improving air traffic control capacity. In 2001 one flight in four was delayed due to air traffic problems, wasting fuel and undermining the competitiveness of EU airlines. The Commission proposed introducing effective Community legislation on air traffic by 2004 with the aim of creating a 'single European sky'. This would be based on co-operation with military authorities and Eurocontrol. EU airport capacity would be expanded (also in view of enlargement) but subject to tighter regulation of pollution and noise. However, the Commission's proposals ran into difficulties as member states wanted to maintain responsibility for air traffic control centres and were reluctant to force military authorities to co-operate.

The Commission also aimed to create an open aviation area between the EU and the USA by removing restrictions and allowing airlines to merge. It was estimated that this would benefit consumers by €5billion a year and increase passengers by over 17 million.[25] However, the USA seemed

---

[22] European Commission (2001).
[23] See www.europa.eu.int/comm/transport/air.
[24] See ww.europa.eu.int/comm/transport/air.
[25] *Financial Times*, 30 June, 2003

more in favour of building on existing deals with EU member states and extending them to the whole EU.[26]

SHIPPING

Over 90 per cent of extra-EU trade and some 43 per cent of intra-EU trade is carried by sea, and EU ports deal with over 1 billion tonnes of freight a year.[27] Maritime companies belonging to EU nationals control one-third of the world's fleet, and about 40 per cent of EU maritime trade is carried on ships controlled by EU interests.

EU policy has been based on the principles of liberalization and opening up of national markets, together with a concern for safety and environmental protection. With a few exceptions (passenger services between the Greek islands will not be liberalized until 2004), since 1999 there has been almost total freedom to provide maritime services in the EU.[28]

However, the EU maritime transport fleet has been shrinking both in terms of absolute tonnage and world market share. In part this reflects the drift to flags and ports 'of convenience' and the widespread recourse to off-shore registration (in countries such as Panama or Liberia) where taxation is lower and social, safety and environmental requirements tend to be less stringent.

The EU aims to meet these difficulties through measures to render EU fleets competitive and to ensure strict enforcement of international safety and environmental standards in the EU. Accidents such as those of the *Erika* and the *Prestige* have led to higher priority for these objectives. In the 2001 White Paper[29] the Commission proposed collaboration with international organizations such as the International Maritime Organization and the International Labour Office to establish minimum social rules to be observed in ship inspections. The White Paper also proposed creation of a European maritime traffic management system. In an attempt to improve EU maritime competitiveness and relieve road and air congestion, 'sea highways' were to be established through better links between ports, railways and inland waterways, and improvements in EU ports.

According to the 2001 White Paper, inland waterways in the EU were underexploited, offering a cheap, reliable and environmentally friendly means of transport and a way of reducing the congestion of the road network. In 1999 the inland waterways accounted for about a third of intra-EU commercial transport. Since 2000 the internal waterway market has been fully deregulated (Directive 96/75/EC). The 2001 White Paper called for the creation of 'waterway branches' with improved connections with other modes of transport and harmonization of the technical conditions for vessels and the social conditions for crews.

EVALUATION

The common transport policy has met with mixed results. Although envisaged as one of the first three common policies by the Treaty of Rome, embedded national interests meant that progress in introducing common measures was slow until the late 1980s. The modal split between different forms of transport has been increasingly biased towards road and air transport, inducing additional problems of congestion and pollution. Infrastructure (for example, for rail freight transport) remains inadequate, and attempts to improve the situation through programmes such as the TENs

---

[26] *The Economist*, 4 October 2003.
[27] See www.europa.eu.int/comm/transport/maritime.
[28] In accordance with Regulation EEC/3577/92.
[29] European Commission (2003c).

suffer from inadequate financing, bureaucratic delays and complexities of co-ordination. The new and different traffic patterns expected with EU enlargement, and the need to ensure sustainable development represent important challenges for the EU. The 2001 White Paper of the Commission is an ambitious attempt to meet these challenges, but it remains to be seen how successful its practical implementation will prove.

Summary of Key Concepts

- Transport plays a key role in the EU economy, accounting for a high percentage of energy consumption, public investment and relatively large shares of GDP and employment.
- Market failures, such as situations of natural monopoly, externalities and costly or scarce information, help to explain why there is so much public intervention in transport. A further reason is the possible negative consequences of 'excessive competition'.
- High transport costs act as a barrier to trade, so common measures for transport are an essential part of the integration process.
- Government intervention may take the form of responsibility for the infrastructure, controlling the prices and/or the number of operators providing services on the infrastructure, and regulating the sector through legislation.
- The Treaty of Rome envisaged a common transport policy as one of the first common policies.
- Difficulties in interpreting the Treaty of Rome, and different interests of the member states, meant that progress in introducing a common transport policy was slow.
- The Single Market Programme, and the deregulation prevalent from the mid-1980s, lent a new emphasis to introducing common transport measures.
- The White Paper published by the Commission in 2001 set out the main objectives of EU transport policy until 2010. These include: reinforcing passengers' rights, improving road safety, encouraging sustainable mobility, preventing congestion, improving infrastructure and managing globalization.
- The TENs are trans-European networks in transport, energy, telecommunications and environmental infrastructure. The EU identifies priority networks and part-finances them.
- The EU aims at rebalancing the modal split of transport by measures such as revitalization of the railways.
- The objective of the EU is to create a 'single European sky' with improved air traffic control to reduce delays and congestion.
- The EU wants to create 'shipping highways' and improved international maritime regulation.

Questions for Study and Review

- ■ What are the reasons for public intervention in transport?
- ■ What forms does public intervention in transport take?
- ■ How can transport costs act as a barrier to trade?
- ■ Why was the introduction of a common transport policy considered so important for the integration process?
- ■ Why was it so difficult to introduce a common transport policy?
- ■ What developments from the mid-1980s led to acceleration in introducing common transport measures?
- ■ What measures do you consider necessary for the improvement of the EU transport system, and how far is the EU introducing such measures?

References

European Commission (2001) 'Updating and Development of Economic and Fares Data Regarding the European Air Travel Industry, 2000 Annual Report', Commissioned by DG Transport and Energy.

European Commission (2003a) 'Energy and transport in figures 2003', www.europa.eu.int/comm/dgs/energy_transport.

European Commission (2003b) 'Energy and transport outlook to 2030', www.europa.eu.int/comm/ dgs/energy_transport.

European Commission (2003c) 'European transport policy for 2010: Time to decide', www.europa.eu.int/comm/dgs/energy_transport.

European Commission (2003d) 'A European initiative for growth', www.europa.eu.int/comm/dgs/energy_transport.

European Commission (2004) 'Implementation report on the internal market strategy', COM 2004/22, January, www:europa.eu.int/comm/internal_market.

Hitiris, T. (2003) *European Community Economics*, 5th edn, Harvester Wheatsheaf, Hemel Hempstead.

Salvatore, D. (2001) *International Economics*, 7th edn, John Wiley & Sons, New York.

Swann, D. (1995) *The Economics of the Common Market*, 8th edn, Penguin, London.

Useful websites

Directorate-General for Energy and Transport of the European Commission provides explanations of EU transport policy, statistics and key documents: www.europa.eu.int/comm/dgs/energy_transport

List of abbreviations

CEEC	Central and Eastern European country
Ecosoc	Economic and Social Committee
ECSC	European Coal and Steel Community
Gallileo	European satellite radionavigation system
GDP	gross domestic product
IATA	International Air Transport Association
ICAO	International Civil Aviation Organization
IMO	International Maritime Organization
km/h	kilometres per hour
Marco Polo	EU Programme to encourage interconnections between different modes of transport
PACT	Pilot Actions for Combined Transport
TEN	Trans-European Network
TEN-E	Trans-European Network – Energy
TEN-T	Trans-European Network – Transport
TERFN	Trans-European Rail Freight Network

17

The EU and the GATT/WTO

LEARNING OBJECTIVES

By the end of this chapter you should be able to understand:

▶ The main functions of the GATT/WTO;

▶ The most important results of the GATT Uruguay Round;

▶ The difficulties encountered in launching a new round of multilateral trade negotiations;

▶ Why agriculture is always at the centre of the GATT/WTO negotiations;

▶ The links between trade negotiations and environmental, health and safety issues.

THE GATT/WTO

The GATT (General Agreement on Tariffs and Trade) came into operation in 1948 with the aim of providing a framework for international trade negotiations, and attempts to regulate world trade. The original intention after the Second World War was to create an International Trade Organization, but difficulties in ratification (in particular, by the US Congress) led to the ITO Convention being abandoned. In its place the 'temporary' GATT arrangement was adopted. The World Trade Organization replaced the GATT from 1995, and its framework was reinforced.

The functions of the GATT/WTO can be divided into three main categories:

■ Setting out regulations governing the conduct of international trade;

■ Making provisions for the settlements of disputes and retaliatory actions;

■ Providing the framework for multilateral negotiations to liberalize world trade.

The GATT system has traditionally been based on three principles: tariff reductions, reciprocity and non-discrimination. Tariffs were preferred to other barriers on trade since they were considered the most transparent form of protection. Reciprocity implies that the concessions made by the parties should be more or less balanced. This generally involves matching tariff concession with tariff concession. When a country joined the GATT, it received the benefit of trade concessions already negotiated within that framework on the basis of the MFN (most favoured nation) principle.[1] The MFN principle was conceived as a means of ensuring non-discrimination. Since 1971 the rule of non-discrimination does not apply to trading privileges granted to developing countries.

Among the GATT principles with particular implications for the European Community was Article XXIV dealing with regional groupings. By its nature a customs union is regional and the trade preferences involved are not extended to all GATT members, and this seems to run counter to the principle of non-discrimination.[2] To meet this difficulty Article XXIV sets out certain conditions for the creation of regional groupings that aim at ensuring that customs unions are trade creating.[3] The underlying assumption of the GATT therefore seemed to be that regional integration arrangements were a building block rather than a stumbling block to global liberalization of trade.[4]

Typically the liberalization of world trade proceeds in series of successive 'rounds' of negotiations. To date eight such rounds have been completed (see Box 17.1). Following the failed attempt to launch a new Round at Seattle in 1999, in November 2001 the Doha Round began, but encountered a further setback at the Cancún meeting of September 2003. In July 2004 agreement was reached on the parameters for continuing negotiations in five areas: agriculture, industrial products, development issues, trade facilitation and services.

Box 17.1 GATT/WTO Rounds

Name of the Round	Year	Topic of negotiation
Geneva	1947	Tariffs
Annecy	1949	Tariffs
Torquay	1951	Tariffs
Geneva	1956	Tariffs
Dillon Round	1960–62	Tariffs
Kennedy Round	1964–67	Tariffs and anti-dumping
Tokyo Round	1973–79	Tariffs, non-tariff barriers, multilateral agreements
Uruguay Round	1986–94	Tariffs, creation of the WTO, agriculture, textiles, services, TRIMs, TRIPs and VERs*
Doha Round	2001–?	

*See text and Annex 17 for a more detailed explanation.

---

[1] In return the principle of reciprocity meant that the country had to offer 'equivalent' concessions.

[2] Further controversy arose concerning the trade preferences granted by the Community under the Association System. The preferences given by France, Italy, Belgium and the Netherlands to former dependencies were acceptable to the GATT because they had been granted before 1947. However, the GATT opposed the extension of these preferences so that all EC members could grant them. The question was examined in a working party with GATT and EC representatives, and it was decided that the EC should take mitigating action if damage to third parties were proved.

[3] Article XXIV requires that the move to implementation must take place within a reasonable time and that such arrangements should cover 'substantially all' trade. The common external tariff must also be no higher than the average of previous tariffs. However, even in this case some countries could still experience trade diversion.

[4] These expressions are used in the debate about whether regional blocs permit a quicker, more efficient move to multilateral trade liberalization, or whether they are inward-looking, competing blocs with different views of the world scene (see Chapter 5).

THE WORLD TRADE ORGANIZATION

Created in 1995, the WTO differs from the GATT in having full institutional status and legal personality, and in providing a permanent forum for the discussion of trade issues. By 2003 146 countries were members of the WTO, and at the Cancún meeting it was agreed to extend membership to Cambodia and Nepal.

The decision to transform the GATT into the WTO was based on a belief that interdependence was reducing the effectiveness of unilateral action on the part of countries, and on a growing awareness of the failings of the GATT. In particular, there was a tendency to disregard GATT rules with the widespread use of 'grey-area' measures or non-tariff barriers, and the GATT dispute settlement procedure was weak.

At the time it was considered that much of the future reputation of the WTO would depend on the performance of the new Disputes Settlement Mechanism (DSM). This established procedures for consultations, the setting up of panels, the presentation of panel reports and the possibility of appellate review, with precise deadlines for each. The consensus was now to be *against* the establishment of panels, or the adoption of panel reports for decisions not to be made, and so represented a reversal of the GATT condition. Moreover, the possibility of appeal against a decision was now introduced. The WTO may also sanction levies on imports as a form of cross-retaliation if a member fails to implement a panel recommendation.

THE URUGUAY ROUND

The Uruguay Round launched in 1986 at Punta del Este was far more ambitious than earlier GATT trade negotiations, which had been almost exclusively concerned with tariff reductions. The aim of the Uruguay Round was to further the process of tariff reduction, but also to extend fair trade disciplines to areas that hitherto had been largely exempt from GATT rules and regulations, including agriculture, textiles, services (through the GATS or General Agreement on Trade in Services), trade-related investment measures (TRIMs) and trade-related intellectual property rights (TRIPs). Despite initial US reluctance, it was also agreed to replace the GATT with the WTO.

The Uruguay Round was protracted well beyond all initial deadlines, and during the seven tortuous years of negotiations the Round seemed near to breaking down on various occasions, usually over the question of agriculture. Though falling short of many expectations, the results were substantial and are presented in the Appendix.

LAUNCHING A NEW TRADE ROUND

A new 'Millennium Round' of multilateral trade negotiations was to be launched at Seattle in December 1999 with the aim of furthering the achievements of the Uruguay Round, both in terms of trade liberalization and extension of the coverage of the WTO. The proposed aims of the new Round were extremely ambitious, and the backlash of criticism and the violence of the demonstrations outside were unexpected. The failure to launch the round at Seattle was partly due to poor organization but was also due to heated differences between:

- Developed countries, in particular between the USA, EU and Japan;
- Developed and less developed countries (LDCs); and

■ Non-governmental organizations (or NGOs) including environmentalists, consumer groups, trade unions, etc. who criticized both the WTO and official government positions.

Differences among developed countries arose even over the agenda for the negotiations. The USA was in favour of a relatively narrow, 'manageable' agenda based on a core of Uruguay Round 'leftovers', with a few additional issues such as the further liberalization of e-commerce and the linking of trade concerns to environmental questions and labour rights.

The EU (backed by Japan) favoured a wider agenda that would include subjects like investment and competition (antitrust) policy, but the USA accused the EU of attempting to widen the agenda in order to talk about 'anything but agriculture'. The US was reluctant to include trade-related investment measures (TRIMs) in the discussions as earlier attempts to tackle this issue had achieved so little. In particular, in 1998 OECD negotiations to draw up a Multilateral Agreement on Investment (MAI) broke down, partly because of differences between industrialized countries and protests by NGOs but also because of criticisms from less developed countries at their exclusion from the discussions. A central concept with regard to TRIMs is that of 'equal treatment' for nationals and foreigners. In its strongest form this implies strong commitments with regard to opening markets, providing adequate guarantees with regard to repatriation of assets and profits and a multilateral surveillance system. In practice regulations relating to foreign direct investment raise sensitive issues relating to ownership and national sovereignty, helping to explain why agreement is so difficult to reach.

The argument for linking competition policy to trade issues is that otherwise the effects of trade liberalization may be undermined by restrictive practices by firms that, for example, may collude to divide markets. Differences in national antitrust policies may also distort international competition and influence the decisions of firms on where to locate. However, the USA preferred to leave competition policy off the agenda since countries such as Japan, South Korea and others tended to use this as a pretext for introducing criticisms of US anti-dumping measures (in particular on steel) into the discussion. On agriculture the USA pushed for larger reductions in export subsidies and tariffs, and tighter obligations to cut domestic support than the EU or Japan were prepared to concede (see below).

While there was general agreement that WTO procedures should be subject to 'review, reform and repair', and that developing countries should be given more say in procedures, there was no common view of how this should take place. The less developed countries argued that the Uruguay Round Agreement was biased against them, and that multilateral discussions failed to take adequate account of their needs on a number of grounds:

■ They had difficulty in meeting the Uruguay Round commitments on TRIPs, TRIMs, subsidies and anti-dumping, and wanted their obligations reduced in these areas.

■ They argued that the benefits of the Uruguay Round in sectors of interest to them were less than expected. The EU was criticized for continuing high levels of agricultural protection, while the USA was said to have backloaded its liberalization of textile imports, so that most of the increased access would occur towards 2005.[5]

■ The LDCs interpreted the proposals to liberalize e-commerce and services such as telecommunications as an attempt by developed countries to further extend the markets of their multinationals and hinder the creation of indigenous LDC industries.

■ Finally the US proposal to include environmental issues on the agenda, and to link core

---

[5] For example, in 2003 an Oxfam report, *Running into the Sands* (www.oxfam.org.uk), showed how US and EU tariffs on imports from developing countries were often far higher that those on imports from other developed countries. The discrepancies arise because developed countries apply heavy tariffs on products such as textiles, clothing and agricultural goods that figure strongly in the exports of developing countries.

labour standards[6] to trade, was regarded as a pretext for higher protectionism on the part of industrialized countries.

Before the event the scale of participation of NGOs and individual protesters at the Seattle negotiations was hugely underestimated.[7] In 1998 about 1200 NGOs signed a statement calling for reform of the WTO, and many of them sent activists to Seattle.[8] NGOs differ considerably in size and vary from huge agencies such as Greenpeace to tiny fringe groups. Their interests are also extremely diverse, ranging from issues such as the environment, labour standards, to protests against multinational enterprises (MNEs) since these are said to be those gaining most from freeing trade. Farm groups were strongly represented at Seattle, as were labour unions expressing fears that trade liberalization could lead to widening wage disparities or higher unemployment.

Agreement was finally reached on launching the Doha Development Agenda in November 2001 in Qatar. Rather optimistically, a deadline of January 2005 was given for completing these negotiations. The phrasing of the mandate was often vague, trying to accommodate very different positions (in particular on agriculture). The Agenda included:

- Strengthening of WTO rules, and 'improvements and clarifications' to the dispute settlement procedure;
- Increasing the role of developing countries in the global trading system and stronger provisions for special and differential treatment of poorer members;
- Agreeing a declaration on international drugs patents and access to medicines (which was one of the TRIP reforms requested by developing nations);
- Liberalization of trade in industrial goods and services;
- Liberalization of agricultural trade (see below for a more detailed discussion);
- Negotiations on investment and competition rules following two years of preparatory work;
- Negotiations on trade facilitation (customs procedures etc.) and transparency in government procurement;
- Negotiations on 'clarifying and improving disciplines' on anti-dumping and anti-subsidy rules;
- Further work on e-commerce;
- Further work on environmental matters, but no commitment to negotiations;
- On labour issues note was taken of the work on the social dimensions of globalization by the International Labour Organization.

FAST TRACK

One of the question marks hanging over the Doha Round of trade negotiations was whether President Bush would be able to obtain Trade Promotion Authority (TPA), or 'fast track'. Fast track binds Congress to vote on trade agreements without amendment and was introduced to limit the influence of lobbies in Washington.

In December 2001 President Bush succeeded in obtaining fast-track authority, but in a deal that entailed huge concessions to US producer interests, thereby seemingly undermining the basic aim of fast track. In order to gain the support of the steel lobby Bush accepted a recommendation from

---

[6] The effectiveness of insisting on trade measures to push for core labour standards in developing countries has been the subject of much debate. If, for example, children are forced out of work in LDCs, there may be a risk that they become simply poorer. It is argued that child labour is a development, not a trade issue, and should be treated as such.
[7] Clinton initially called on such groups to come and express their opinions in Seattle, undoubtedly not anticipating the havoc this would create.
[8] *The Economist*, 10 November 1999.

the International Trade Commission for tariffs of up to 40 per cent on steel. On textiles the fast-track bill called for withdrawal of trade benefits granted in 2000 to textile exporters in sub-Saharan Africa and the Caribbean. The Bush administration also stated that US tariffs on textiles and clothing would not be reduced unless developing countries agreed to reciprocate.[9] Agriculture is another sector of vital importance to developing countries, and also here the Congress insisted on being consulted on tariff cuts, enabling US producer interests for products such as sugar and citrus fruits to maintain protectionist measures.[10]

THE DÉBÂCLE AT CANCÚN

In September 2003 negotiations at Cancún in Mexico on the Doha Round were suspended and, according to the EU trade commissioner, Pascal Lamy, the Doha Round, if not dead after Cancún, was in need of 'intensive care'. Hopes that progress would be made had been raised by an EU reform of the CAP in June 2003, followed in August by an EU–US framework agreement on farm trade negotiations. After years of negotiations a deal was also reached in August 2003 to allow poor countries to import cheaper genetic drugs to fight illnesses such as AIDS and malaria.

Some developing countries seemed to consider the lack of agreement a success, but as the arguments presented in Chapter 4 suggest, these countries could be the main losers if the process of trade liberalization stalls, or if the multilateral system is replaced by bilateralism. According to the WTO, tariffs levied between developing countries tend to be higher than those of developed countries.[11] A study by the World Bank suggested that a successful outcome to the Doha Round would generate up to $520 billion in additional income in 2015, of which $300 billion could flow to developing countries, lifting some 140 million people out of poverty.[12]

One of the main aims of the Doha Round was to ensure greater participation of the developing countries. At Cancún the G-20 group of countries including Brazil, India, China and South Africa (though its membership kept changing) emerged as an important force (see Box 17.2). The ACP countries joined together in expressing their fears that agricultural trade liberalization would erode their preferential access to EU markets. African cotton-producing countries, in particular Benin, Burkina Faso, Chad and Mali, were allied in their criticism of the US and EU subsidies.

Box 17.2 The G-20 plus 2 countries

At the December 2002 ministerial meeting Colombia, Costa Rica, Ecuador, El Salvador, Guatemala and Peru were not present, while Indonesia, Tanzania and Zimbabwe were.

Argentina	Ecuador	Paraguay
Bolivia	Egypt	Peru
Brazil	El Salvador	Philippines
Chile	Guatemala	South Africa
China	India	Thailand
Colombia	Mexico	Venezuela
Costa Rica	Nigeria	
Cuba	Pakistan	

---

[9] *Financial Times*, 17 December 2001.

[10] According to Brazil, if the agricultural provisions of the fast-track bill stand, they could place at risk the initiative on the Free Trade Area of the Americas (FTAA).

[11] According to www.wto.org the average tariff applied on industrial products by the USA was 4 per cent, compared with 14 per cent by Brazil and 30 per cent by India.

[12] See www.worldbank.org, 'Global economic prospects 2004'.

The talks at Cancún broke down on the so-called Singapore issues, or proposals for:

- Investment rules;
- Competition;
- Trade facilitation (including easier customs procedures);
- Transparency in government procurement.

The EU supported Singapore issues though they were a fairly low priority for EU business and member states. The EU argued, for example on investment, that the issue was not opening markets – since international investment was driven by globalization – but rather the need to provide rules. The EU was accused of a Machiavellian attempt to broaden the agenda, and so reduce the pressure for agricultural trade liberalization.[13] Asian and African countries refused to negotiate on all four Singapore issues, maintaining that they neither had the resources to negotiate nor to implement them. The EU offered to drop the two most controversial issues (competition and investment) at the last moment, but Japan and Korea were unprepared for the change in position by the EU and stood their ground. The Mexican chairman, Derbez, concluded the debate, arguing that 'despite considerable movement in consultations, members remained entrenched, particularly on the Singapore issues'.

Difficulties also arose on the question of geographical indications. The EU wanted world-wide protection for geographical indications, not only on wines and spirits (such as champagne, or Scotch whisky) but also on a wide range of products such as Parma ham, Roquefort cheese, Darjeeling tea and so on. The EU argued that quality guarantees were necessary to compensate for the liberalization of agricultural markets. The proposal was opposed by countries such as the USA, Australia, Canada and South Africa who maintain that well-known geographical indications have either become generic terms or have been registered by a trademark in their country.

Various explanations have been put forward for the Cancún débâcle, many of which echo the criticisms of Seattle:

- By September 2003 WTO membership had reached an unwieldy 146 (with two further members, Cambodia and Nepal, being accepted at Cancún), rendering consensus difficult to reach. Pascal Lamy referred to the WTO as a 'medieval organization' whose rules (i.e. the fact that decisions had to be agreed by consensus) could not support the weight of its tasks.
- Some participants were surprised when Derbez closed the debate and maintained that had discussions been switched to other topics, such as agriculture where some progress had been made, the negotiations could have continued.[14] According to the Director General, Panichpadki, 'We seemed to be making real progress. We were very, very close to a final agreement.'
- The EU change in position on the Singapore issues came late and was unexpected by other participants. Agreement on reform of the CAP was only reached in June 2003, leaving little time for bargaining before Cancún.
- Many countries, and in particular the G-20 and the Cairns group, considered the concessions offered by Japan, the EU, and the USA on agriculture (see below) inadequate.
- The USA failed to offer adequate concessions to the poorest African countries to meet their claim that US cotton subsidies were depressing world prices and forcing African cotton growers out of the market (see Box 17.3).

---

[13] See *Financial Times*, 19 September 2003, 22 September 2003 and 24 September 2003.
[14] *Financial Times*, 16 September 2003.

■ LDC countries were vehement in criticizing the developed countries but slower in presenting viable initiatives, common positions or concessions. The US trade representative, Zoellick, complained of the transformation of the WTO into a 'forum for the politics of protest'.[15] Whether the tougher negotiating stance adopted by LDCs leads to an improvement in their situation remains to be seen, but it certainly renders attempts to reach consensus in the WTO more difficult.

■ Various parties accused certain NGOs of inflammatory behaviour and attempting to radicalize the issues.[16]

Box 17.3 The African cotton-producing countries

The issue of African cotton farmers became emblematic at Cancún. Benin, Burkina Faso, Chad and Mali had been encouraged by the World Bank to produce their high-quality cotton, but argued that they encountered difficulties due to falling prices and the expansion of exports from developed countries, from the USA in particular. For 10 million people in Central and West Africa cotton is the main cash crop. In 1999/2000 the share of cotton in exports was 79 per cent for Mali, 65 per cent for Benin and 56 per cent for Chad.

US subsidies to its 25 000 cotton farmers amount to $3–4 billion a year, which is more than the GDP of Burkina Faso, and three times the US aid budget for Africa (*Financial Times*, 16 September 2003). The USA agreed to help build up Africa's textile industry, diversify from cotton production and address market distortions but was only prepared to discuss cotton subsidies in the general context of agricultural negotiations. The African countries did not consider such proposals adequate.

In 2004 the EU introduced a reform of its cotton regime that decoupled 65 per cent of support from production (see Chapter 10) and introduced limits on the areas that could produce cotton in Spain, Greece and Portugal. The EU also announced that it was prepared to eliminate exports subsidies on cotton to the least developed countries and allow duty- and quota-free access for cotton from these countries. The African cotton-producing countries expressed disappointment since they had hoped that the EU would completely decouple its support for cotton.

As a consequence of Cancún the USA announced that it would pursue bilateral and regional trade talks with more vigour. The EU has refused to open any new bilateral talks since 1999, arguing that priority should be given to multilateralism and the WTO negotiations, and that bilateral relations were complex and time-consuming.

Agreeing a framework for continuing negotiations in July 2004 was an important step in preventing collapse of the Doha Development Round. The main issues agreed were:

■ On agriculture there are to be substantial cuts in trade-distorting support, the elimination of all trade-distorting export competition measures and a significant opening of agricultural markets.

■ The importance of cotton for certain developing countries is recognized.

■ For industrial products there are to be tariff reductions with larger cuts for higher tariffs, though the least developed countries will be exempt. Guidelines for reducing non-tariff barriers to trade will also be agreed.

---

[15] *Financial Times*, 22 September 2003.
[16] See, for instance, the interview with EU commissioner for agriculture, Fischler, in the *Financial Times*, 20 September 2003.

- Negotiation of the liberalization of trade in services is to continue, with a new round fixed for May 2005.
- Negotiations are to be launched on trade facilitation, or cutting down the red tape at borders. There was agreement to drop the other three Singapore issues.
- The special and differential treatment for developing countries was to be reinforced.

AGRICULTURE IN GATT/WTO NEGOTIATIONS

Ever since agricultural issues have been included in GATT/WTO negotiations they have been the main source of contention, threatening to spill over and block progress in other areas. It is therefore useful to describe this central role of farm trade negotiations in more detail. The position of the various participants on agriculture in the Doha Round was heavily influenced by their experience in implementing the 1994 GATT agreement, so a brief review of the main features of that agreement is necessary.

Before the 1986–94 Uruguay Round, agriculture had never been included in GATT negotiations in more than a marginal way.[17] The declaration at Punta del Este in 1986, which marked the launching of the Uruguay Round, referred to: 'an urgent need to bring more discipline and predictability to world agriculture by correcting and preventing restrictions and distortions including those related to structural surpluses so as to reduce the uncertainty, imbalances and instability in world agricultural markets'.

The US opening position in the negotiations was the so-called zero option which involved the elimination in 10 years of all policies directly affecting international agricultural trade. The US Department of Agriculture (USDA) was convinced of the comparative advantage of American agriculture and believed that mutual elimination of the huge EU and US subsidies to agriculture would be to US benefit.

The Cairns Group of agricultural exporting countries[18] (see also Table 17.1) was also in favour of substantial, but more moderate, liberalization of world agricultural trade. In contrast, the initial EC and Japanese positions seemed to be aimed at introducing as little change as possible.

Table 17.1 World agricultural trade, 2001

Exporters	Value $bn	% in world	Importers	Value $bn	% in world
EU (including intra-EU trade)	213.5	39.0	EU (including intra-EU trade)	235.51	39.7
EU to rest of world	57.81	10.6	EU from rest of world	79.8	13.5
USA	70.0	12.8	US	68.4	11.5
Canada	33.6	6.1	Japan	56.9	9.6
Brazil	18.43	3.4	China	20.12	3.4
China	16.6	3.0	Canada	15.6	2.6
Australia	16.6	3.0	Mexico	12.8	2.2
Argentina	12.2	2.2	Rep. of Korea	12.5	2.1
Thailand	12.1	2.2	Russian Fed.	12.5	1.9

Source: www.wto/org.

[17] For instance, the treatment of agriculture in the Tokyo Round was limited to tariff reductions on some tropical products. The USA was largely responsible for the exclusion of agriculture for the most part from earlier GATT Rounds and for insisting on its inclusion in the Uruguay Round.
[18] Named after the town in Australia where they first met, during the Uruguay Round the Group numbered 14. By 2002 its membership had increased to 17 countries: Argentina, Australia, Bolivia, Brazil, Canada, Chile, Colombia, Costa Rica, Guatemala, Indonesia, Malaysia, New Zealand, Paraguay, Philippines, South Africa, Thailand and Uruguay.

Given such diverse starting points, it was not surprising that negotiations dragged on long past initial deadlines, and risked collapsing on numerous occasions over EU–US differences on agriculture (see also Table 17.2).

	USA	EU
Production (farm gate value) OECD data for 2000	$190 billion	$197 billion
Number of farms (holding in 1996	2 058 000	7 370 000
Farmland (utilizable agricultural area 1997)	425 million ha	134 million ha
Average size of holding	207 ha	18 ha
Producer support estimate (PSE) in 2000 (OECD data)*	$49.0 billion	$90.2 billion
PSE/full-time farmer equivalent (OECD data)	$20 000/farmer	$14 000/farmer

Table 17.2 US-EU farming structure

*The Producer Support Estimate (PSE) is an internationally accepted measure of the support to farmers. It can be defined as the subsidy necessary to leave farmers' revenues unchanged if all policies having an impact on agricultural revenues were removed. Each year the OECD provides estimates of PSEs in total money value for various countries and in percentage terms as a percentage of the value of total agricultural production at farm gate in that country. Source: www.wto.org.

Conflict was exacerbated by the ongoing row over oilseeds (see Chapter 10).[19] The interest of the industrial lobby and certain member states (notably the UK, Germany and the Netherlands) in obtaining a successful outcome to the negotiations meant that there was pressure to reach an agreement on agriculture. The director general of GATT, Arthur Dunkel, was also instrumental in presenting a series of proposals that ultimately became the basis of the final agreement. The main aspects of the Uruguay Round Agreement on Agriculture, signed at Marrakech in 1994, are set out in Box 17.4.

Box 17.4 The Uruguay Round Agricultural Agreement (URAA)

The Uruguay Round Agricultural Agreement (URAA) introduced a series of commitments with regard to agricultural policies (with slower liberalization envisaged for developing countries) to be implemented over a six-year period (1995-2000):

■ **The domestic support provisions**

Domestic agricultural support was to be reduced by 20 per cent from a base period of 1986-88 in terms of an Aggregate Measure of Support (AMS).

■ **The export competition provisions**

Export subsidies were to be reduced by 21 per cent in terms of volume, and 36 per cent in terms of expenditure from a base period of 1986-90. No new export subsidies were to be introduced.

■ **The market access commitments**

Non-tariff barriers were to be converted into tariffs (tariffication) from July 1995, and the resulting tariffs were to be reduced by 36 per cent compared to a base period of 1986-88. All the resulting tariffs were to be cut by a minimum of 15 per cent.

---

[19] The USA complained to the GATT that the EC introduction of tariffs and subsidies to domestic crushers ran contrary to a 1962 EU–US agreement. EC changes to the regime following a GATT ruling were considered insufficient, and in 1992 the USA threatened to introduce 200 per cent punitive tariffs on imports worth $300 million from the EU.

Minimum market access was to rise from 3 per cent of domestic consumption to 5 per cent in 1999. Special Safeguard (SSG) Provisions could be invoked if a country experiences an import surge, or, on a consignment basis, if prices fell below the 1986–88 level.
■ The **peace clause** protects policies (such as decoupled domestic subsidies or export subsidies) conforming to the URAA from certain kinds of challenge under the WTO until December 2003.
■ The **Sanitary and Phytosanitary (SPS) Agreement** was technically separate from the URAA but has close connections (see below).

The GATT Uruguay Round contained a 'built-in agenda' with a commitment to begin a new round of negotiations on agriculture within 1999. After the initial fiasco at Seattle in 1999, the mandate of the Doha Development Agenda on agriculture called for: [20]

■ 'Comprehensive negotiations aimed at substantial improvements in market access';
■ 'Reductions, with a view to phasing out, all forms of export subsidies';
■ 'Substantial reductions in trade-distorting domestic support';
■ 'Special and differential treatment for developing countries'; and
■ Note to be taken of 'non-trade concerns reflected in the negotiating proposals of some Members'.

The EU (together with countries such as Japan and Korea) has been pushing for recognition of 'non-trade concerns'. According to this view, agricultural negotiations should take account of the 'multifunctional' role played by farmers in protecting the environment and countryside, and in promoting food quality and safety, rural development and animal welfare. The EU position was interpreted by the USA as a means of maintaining farm subsidies.

The 'peace clause' sheltering EU and US agricultural regimes from legal challenge expired on 31 December 2003 (see Box 17.4). This may lead to the opening of numerous new disputes, which could provide an incentive for reaching agreement in the agricultural negotiations.

In order to overcome the substantial differences between participants on various agricultural issues, in February 2003 Stuart Harbison, the WTO chairman of agricultural negotiations, presented a draft proposal on farm trade reform. This was to provide the basis for a framework agreement on agricultural negotiations accepted by the USA and EU in August 2003. The framework agreement covered the so-called three main pillars of agricultural negotiations: market access, export subsidies and domestic support. There was also mention, but no agreement, on other issues such as non-trade concerns, the peace clause, the implementation period and geographical indications. Developing countries argued that the framework failed to go far enough in the direction of liberalization.

The deadline for agreeing on the mandate for negotiating the liberalization of agricultural trade was the Ministerial Conference in Cancún of September 2003, but in the event negotiations on agriculture did not even begin there.

It is useful to set out the positions of the EU, the USA, and some of the other main parties on the principal issues in the agricultural negotiations to see where the differences lie and how far they could have been resolved.

---

[20] WTO (2002).

MARKET ACCESS

On market access, as a result of the Uruguay Round Agreement the EU was required to convert variable levies for most products into tariffs.[21] However, 'tariffication' involved very generous calculation of the tariff equivalent for many products because:

■ World prices in the base period 1986-88 were very low.
■ The calculation of domestic prices tended to be rather generous, for example 10 per cent was added to the intervention price for milk.
■ Subsequent reform poured more 'water' into the tariffs. For example, Agenda 2000 did not cut import tariffs, though it entailed cuts in minimum guaranteed prices for milk, cereals and beef.

The tariff rate quotas (TRQs) used to meet the Uruguay Round requirements with regard to minimum access and continuation of current access ran into a series of operational problems:

■ Lack of transparency;
■ Because they entail economic rent they may encourage rent-seeking, fraud or corruption;
■ Many quotas were not used in full.

Although the Uruguay Round achieved little reduction in protection, the tariffs that emerged from tariffication are more transparent for negotiating subsequent reductions in successive rounds.

In the WTO framework agreement of July 2004 it was accepted that market access should be substantially increased. Tariffs would be reduced on the basis of a single tiered approach, by which the higher the tariff, the larger the cut, and the functioning of tariff rate quotas would be improved. The agreement also addressed the EU concern to protect sensitive products.

EXPORT SUBSIDIES

On export subsidies the EU and some of the new CEEC member states have encountered difficulties in meeting their GATT commitments for certain products.[22] An earlier fear was that enlargement would lead to increased production for a number of products, requiring additional export subsidies for the disposal of surpluses, but as explained in Chapter 20, the impact of enlargement on the level of EU agricultural production is expected to be less than initially predicted.

The USA noted that in 2000 the EU spent $2 billion in export subsidies, compared with US export subsidies of $20 million in that year.

The EU position at the start of the Doha Round was to propose a reduction of export subsidies by 45 per cent on average and to argue that all such support should be treated 'on an equal basis.' In particular, the Community wanted to discipline less transparent forms of export subsidy such as state trading enterprises (the Canadian and Australian Wheat Boards) or the use of export credits or food aid to boost domestic markets (the USA).

In May 2004 the commissioners for trade, Lamy, and agriculture, Fischler, signed a letter expressing their willingness to consider the elimination of export subsidies on agricultural products.[23] This was taken up in the July 2004 WTO agreement on parameters to continue

---

[21] However, some NTBs prevail, such as the entry price for fruit and vegetables or the maximum import duty for cereals.
[22] WTO, 24 November 1999. This is the case for dairy products for the EU, Slovakia and the Czech Republic, for sugar for Slovakia and Poland, and for various products for Hungary (Tangermann 2000; Buckwell and Tangermann, 1999).
[23] As reported in the *Financial Times*, 10 May 2004.

negotiations when it was also agreed that other trade-distorting measures such as export credits, food aid or state-trading enterprises should be eliminated.

DOMESTIC SUPPORT

The obligation to reduce domestic support by 20 per cent agreed in the Uruguay Round brought about changes in the policy mechanisms used by various countries but in most cases did not constitute a binding constraint. In part this was because the commitment applied to the farm sector in aggregate and did not require a reduction in support product-by-product. Moreover, reforms introduced after the base period of 1986–88 could also be taken into account. The commitment also excludes certain categories of policy and, in particular, those falling into the green and blue boxes.

The WTO classification of policies follows a traffic-light analogy: red measures must be stopped, amber box policies should slow down (by means of reduction), while green measures can go ahead. The distinction between boxes is based on the presumed impact of policies on trade:

- Green box measures can be freely adopted and are generally not negotiated at the international level. They are said to be 'decoupled' from production, as they have a minimal effect on production and trade, and include training, research, environmental measures, payment for natural calamities and so on.
- Red box policies (such as import quotas) are forbidden, but no agricultural measures are included in this category.
- The amber box covers policies permitted within the limits agreed in international negotiations (such as export subsidies).
- Blue box measures refer only to agriculture and are those temporarily allowed as a result of an EU-US deal. They include support under 'production-limiting schemes' on the basis of acreage or animal numbers and were initially designed to cover the 1992 EU direct payments and the US deficiency payments.

The Community initially hoped that the 1992 MacSharry direct payments (see Chapter 10) would fall into the green box, but this was not accepted by the USA. Instead the EC and USA agreed on the blue box that was specifically designed to cover the US deficiency payments and MacSharry compensatory payments. These are excluded from the obligation to reduce domestic support, but after 2003 when the peace clause no longer applied (see Box 17.4), their exemption could be subject to challenge.

The EU was only able to meet its Uruguay Round commitment to reduce domestic support because its direct payments were classified in the blue box.[24] Initially in the Doha Round the EU called for an average reduction in domestic support provided the blue and green boxes remained. However, the June 2003 reform of the CAP involved a decoupling of EU agricultural support from production, aimed also at reducing its trade distorting effect (see Chapter 10). The EU objective was to enable the 'single farm payments' to be introduced from 2005 to be included in the green box and so exempt from WTO obligations to reduce domestic support.

At Seattle the Clinton administration joined the Cairns Group of agricultural exporting countries in calling for the abolition of the blue box and tighter definition of the green box. It was argued that with the 1996 US FAIR Act (Federal Agricultural Improvement and Reform Act), which averaged agricultural assistance over a seven-year period), the USA no longer required the

---

[24] See Buckwell and Tangermann (1999) for a more complete discussion of this issue.

blue box. However, this position was somewhat undermined by the additional emergency aid to US farmers in most of the following years and the 2002 Farm Bill which increased support to US farmers by an estimated 70 per cent over 10 years.[25] In the 2003 EU–US framework agreement the USA insisted on maintaining the blue box.

The starting position of the USA in the Doha Round was to call for a cut in all trade-distorting support to 5 per cent of the value of agricultural production. This would entail no reductions for the USA, but a cut in domestic support from $47 billion to $12 billion for the EU and from $33 billion to $4 billion for Japan.

The G-20 proposed eliminating the blue box and reducing all domestic support having a distorting effect on trade on a product-by-product basis and revaluing or eliminating all support in the green box. The EU would have no difficulty in eliminating the blue box but would have problems in accepting cuts in support on a product-by-product basis. The EU would also challenge the G-20 proposal to call into question green box policies, i.e. those having minimal or no implications for international trade. By its nature the WTO deals with international trade, so, according to the EU, should not have responsibility over measures with almost exclusively domestic implications.

In the WTO framework agreement of July 2004 it was agreed that overall levels of the most trade-distorting domestic support would have to be cut, with the biggest subsidisers making the largest cuts. The green box would remain and the blue box would be limited to 5 per cent of agricultural production. As a result of the agreement the recent reforms of the CAP would be locked in, and the USA would have to reform its Farm Bill. EU concern for the most sensitive products would be recognized.

THE GATT/WTO AND ENVIRONMENTAL, HEALTH AND SAFETY ISSUES

One of the most controversial areas in international trade negotiations is the link between trade liberalization and environmental protection. Conflicts may arise from trade-offs between different policy objectives and the different priorities of countries. Countries with higher standards are concerned that the liberalization of international trade, or more specifically, WTO rulings, may lead to a 'race to the bottom' with legislation on environmental, safety or health issues being relaxed or undermined. It has also been argued that there may be a tendency towards the concentration of the most polluting industries in developing countries where environmental regulations are less strict.

GATT/WTO rules have always allowed countries to impose restrictions for environmental or health or safety motives, and, according to Article XX of the WTO, these are defined as measures necessary 'to protect human, animal or plant life or health'. Under WTO agreements subsidies are also permitted for environmental protection, and environmental objectives are recognized in agreements dealing with product standards, food safety and intellectual property protection. Otherwise 'like products' have to be treated identically, and this has led to some extremely controversial rulings.

For instance, in 1991 Mexico brought a case against a US embargo of imports of tuna from Mexico under the Marine Mammals Protection Act because the Mexican fishing techniques resulted in a higher level of accidental deaths of dolphins than the Act permitted. The embargo was also extended to other countries that could not prove that the tuna had not come from Mexico.

---

[25] See www.europa.eu.int/comm/agriculture/external/wto/usfarmbill, 'The US farm bill – Questions and answers'.

Mexico won since it was argued that in this case other GATT rules should not override the basic prohibition of import restrictions. In the event, the controversy was resolved by Mexico and the USA agreeing to improve fishing methods.

In a similar case the WTO Appellate Body upheld a complaint by five Asian countries (India, Malaysia, Pakistan, Thailand and the Philippines) over restrictions on imports imposed by the USA because their shrimps were caught by methods that incidentally caught sea turtles, an endangered species. According to the WTO, members could take measures relating to the conservation of exhaustible natural resources, including turtles, but these measures should not be applied in a way that is arbitrary or unjustifiable, or which constitutes a disguised restriction on international trade. The justification given for the ruling against the USA was that it had treated some WTO members less favourably than others, failed to recognize that the sea-turtle protection programmes of other countries were equivalent to that of the USA, and who banned imports of shrimps, even if the country complied with US regulations but if the country of origin had not been certified under the US regulation. Moreover the USA had given only four months' notice to these countries to adopt US-type legislation on turtle-excluding devices.

Two aspects of the 1994 GATT Uruguay Round Agreement deal specifically with health and safety matters.[26] The Agreement on Sanitary and Phytosanitary measures (SPS) sets out certain basic rules concerning the setting of standards for food safety and animal and plant health. The Agreement on Technical Barriers to Trade deals with other standards, such as those establishing safety requirements for cars and electrical equipment, and labelling requirements.

The reference standard of the SPS Agreement is based on the food standards established by the Codex Alimentaris, which is a joint body of two international organizations, the World Health Organization (WHO) and the Food and Agriculture Organization (FAO). SPS measures also have to be based on an appropriate assessment of risks, taking into account available scientific evidence and other relevant factors such as testing and inspection methods, or potential damage from spread of disease.

In discussions of such issues, certain countries, and the EU in particular, have placed increasing emphasis on the 'precautionary principle,' also known as being 'better safe than sorry'. Faced with incomplete knowledge, and uncertainty regarding the possible consequences of some actions, the principle allows regulators to intervene, though the measures taken should only be proportionate to suspected risks. A justification sometimes given for the precautionary principle is that in such uncharted territory if disaster occurs it may be irreversible.

According to the SPS agreement, in the absence of sufficient scientific evidence, a country is permitted to take a take a provisional measure on the basis of information available. If a country takes such a measure, it is obliged to seek further information and review the measure in this light.

In practice trying to evolve policy guidelines on the basis of the precautionary principle proves extremely complex. How, for example, are the 'suspected risks' to be assessed, and what measures are deemed 'proportionate'? Again in this context cultural differences may play an important role, and a negative experience (such as the BSE or 'mad cow' crisis, see Chapter 10) may render countries far more sensitive to such issues.

EVALUATION

The Uruguay Round took seven long years of negotiations, with talks threatening to collapse over the question of agriculture on numerous occasions. After the false start in Seattle in 1999, the Doha

---

[26] See http:/heva:wto-ministerial.org, 'Seattle: What's at stake? Concerns...and responses (2)' for a summary of these issues.

Round was launched in November 2001, and looks like being equally protracted. Though agriculture remains a bone of contention, the June 2003 reform of the CAP leaves the EU (generally considered the main culprit) considerable room for manoeuvre, even allowing space for concessions such as the elimination of export subsidies.

The main difficulty now seems to lie in the weak organizational capacity of the WTO and the difficulty of reaching consensus with so many members, in particular, as developing countries seem destined to play a more active role. The aim of certain developed countries to include issues such as investment, competition and the environment in negotiations encountered the opposition of many developing countries and was to prove excessively ambitious. The July 2004 agreement on the parameters for continuing negotiations accepted a more limited agenda. However, the details of the agreement still have to be filled in, and agreement still has to be reached on reform of the WTO. Though the July 2004 agreement was an important step, many hurdles still have to be overcome before the Doha Development Round can be completed.

Summary of Key Concepts

● The GATT came into operation in 1948. The GATT was replaced by the WTO in 1995.

● The functions of the GATT and subsequently the WTO are: to set out regulations governing the conduct of international trade; to make provisions for the settlements of disputes and retaliatory actions and to provide the framework for multilateral negotiations to liberalize world trade.

● The GATT/WTO system has traditionally been based on three principles: tariff reductions, reciprocity and non-discrimination.

● The liberalization of world trade proceeds by 'rounds' of negotiations, the last of which to be completed was the Uruguay Round (1986–94).

● The aim of the Uruguay Round was to further the process of tariff reduction but also to extend fair trade disciplines to areas that hitherto had been largely exempt from GATT rules and regulations, including agriculture, textiles, services (through the General Agreement on Trade in Services), trade-related investment measures and trade-related intellectual property rights. It was also agreed to replace the GATT with the WTO.

● Following the failure to launch a trade round at Seattle, the Doha Development Agenda eventually began in November 2001.

● At Cancún in September 2003 negotiations broke down on the Singapore issues (competition, investment, trade facilitation and transparency in government procurement).

● For the first time in the 1986–94 Uruguay Round agriculture was included in GATT negotiations in more than a marginal way. The Uruguay Round Agricultural Agreement signed in 1994 introduced a series of commitments with regard to agricultural policies (with slower liberalization envisaged for developing countries) to be implemented over a six-year period (1995–2000). The commitments relate to domestic support, export subsidies and market access for agricultural products.

● Differences soon emerged between the EU and USA over agricultural questions in the Doha Round and, in particular, over further reductions in domestic support and export subsidies and improvements in market access.

● In July 2004 agreement was reached in the WTO on the parameters for continuing negotiations in the Doha Round.

● GATT/ WTO rules have always allowed countries to impose restrictions for environmental or health or safety motives, but otherwise 'like products' have to be treated identically, and this has led to some extremely controversial rulings.

Questions for Study and Review

■ What were the main functions of the GATT, and how effective was it in meeting its objectives?

■ How is the WTO different from the GATT?

■ Why have attempts to launch a new trade round encountered so many difficulties?

■ What are the tensions between trade liberalization and environmental considerations?

■ How has the GATT/WTO attempted to reconcile these objectives?

Appendix

The main results of the Uruguay Round Agreement

■ A detailed timetable was agreed for tariff cuts of about 40 per cent on average, which is well beyond the initial objective of 30 per cent.

■ Despite initial US reluctance, it was agreed to replace the GATT with the WTO.

■ Agriculture was incorporated in the GATT framework, and some agricultural trade liberalization was achieved, with commitments to improve market access, cut domestic support and reduce export subsidies (see the discussion above).

■ Textiles had remained largely outside the GATT framework and were covered by the Multifibre Agreement (MFA) of 1974, subsequently renewed in 1977, 1981 and 1986.[27] The Uruguay Round Agreement entailed progressive liberalization of international trade in clothing and textiles over the 10 years to 2005.[28] During the 10 transitional years bilateral quotas would remain, but measures were introduced to ensure more rapid growth of the ceilings fixed by quantitative restrictions. However, even after the Uruguay Round, tariff rates on clothing and textile imports remain high.

■ For the first time in the GATT framework the Uruguay Round included a General Agreement on Trade in Services (GATS). It is estimated that services account for about two-thirds of world GDP, while the share of manufacturing is only about a third. In developed countries the share of manufacturing is even lower, accounting for only about a fifth of the US GDP or a quarter of that of the EU.

The term 'services' covers a wide range of activities, and the GATT classification covers seven categories: distribution, education, communication, health, transport, tourism and professional activities (such as architecture, engineering, legal services, accounting etc.). Moreover the international 'trade' in services can take various forms: cross-border supply, moving the customers to the supplier (as in the case of tourism) and vice versa. One of the main reasons that services remained largely outside the GATT is that it is difficult to provide rules for such diverse phenomena, and in the event the Uruguay Agreement on GATS was extremely limited.

The Agreement on GATS comprised three main elements:

(a) That GATT members open up service industries listed in a schedule of commitments. However, countries were left discretion in drawing up these schedules, so the outcome depends heavily on what each country wished to include in its schedule and the number of exemptions to the MFN clause invoked.

---

[27] The MFA permitted industrial countries or groups of countries to impose restrictions on imports from over 30 countries, but it also imposed obligations on the industrial countries. However, if a country pleaded threat of market disruption, bilateral agreements were allowed with the exporting country and these may contain departures from the obligations. In practice market disruption was so widely invoked that the MFA became far less important than the bilateral agreements introduced under its aegis.

[28] From January 1995 each country would liberalize a quota of its trade equal to 16 per cent of its imports in 1990. Further quotas of 17 per cent from 1998 and 18 per cent from 2002 would be liberalized and from 2005 no barriers would remain.

(b) Signatories to the Uruguay Round have to subscribe to certain general principles, including the agreement to prohibit practices such as limitations on the number of suppliers, the volume of output or transactions and on the percentage of foreign capital.
(c) GATS negotiations were to resume in 2000.

■ Though much energy was devoted to discussing trade-related investment measures (TRIMs) during the Uruguay Round, in the final act it is one of the shortest texts. The main element of the Uruguay Round Agreement on TRIMs is a list of measures inconsistent with GATT requirements (such as local content obligations, limits on imported inputs, trade balancing requirements or limits on the percentage of production which may be exported).

■ The Uruguay Round also included an agreement on trade-related intellectual property rights (TRIPs). Growing difficulties in enforcing respect for copyright, patents and trademarks, in particular in newly developed countries, led to increasing demands (also on the part of business) for multilateral rules. The Uruguay Round Agreement on TRIPs was rather limited, calling simply for increased transparency, inclusion of TRIPs under the Dispute Settlement Procedure and a general commitment to reducing disparities in national legislation in this area.

■ The phasing out of VERs over 10 years (see Chapter 4).

References

Buckwell, A. and Tangermann, S. (1999) 'The future of direct payments in the context of Eastern Enlargement', *MOCT/MOST, Economic Policy in Transition Economies*, Vol. 9, pp. 229–52.
Burrell A. (2000) 'The World Trade Organization and EU agricultural policy', in Burrell A. and Oskam, A. (eds), *Agricultural Policy and Enlargement of the European Union,* Wageningen University Press, Wageningen, NL.
OECD (2000) *Agricultural Policies in Emerging and Transitional Economies, Monitoring and Evaluation,* OECD, Paris.
Tangermann, S. (2000) 'Widening the EU to Central and Eastern European countries: WTO and perspectives of the new member countries,' in Burrell, A. and Oskam, A. (eds), *Agricultural Policy and Enlargement of the European Union,* Wageningen University Press, Wageningen, NL.
WTO(2002) 'WTO agricultural negotiations. The issues and where we are now', http://www.wto.org.

Useful websites

The European Commission explains the EU position and provides statistics and key reports:
www.europa.eu.int/comm/trade
The Institute for International Economics in the USA publishes various studies of trade and international monetary economics:
www.iie.com
The Organization for Economic Co-operation and Development publishes reports and statistics on international trade:
www.oecd.org
Oxfam provides a critical view of international economic relations:
www.oxfam.org.uk
The United Nations publishes international trade statistics, though with a certain delay:
www.un.org
The US position is presented by:
The US Department of Commerce, International Trade Administration:
www.ita.doc.gov

The US Trade Representative:

www.ustr.gov

The US International Trade Commission:

www.usitc.gov

The World Bank provides statistics and analysis, in particular of the developing countries' prospective:

www.worldbank.org

The World Trade Organization provides statistics, explanations and key documents on the Doha Round:

www.wto.org

List of abbreviations

ACP	African, Caribbean and Pacific countries covered by the Lomé Conventions and the Cotonou Agreement
AMS	aggregate measure of support
BSE	bovine spongiform encephalopathy
CAP	Common Agricultural Policy
CEEC	Central and Eastern European country
DSM	Disputes Settlement Mechanism
FAIR Act	Federal Agricultural Improvement and Reform Act introduced in the USA in 1996
FAO	Food and Agriculture Organization
FTAA	Free Trade Area of the Americas
GATS	General Agreement on Trade in Services
GATT	General Agreement on Tariffs and Trade
ITO	International Trade Organization
LDC	less developed country
MAI	Multilateral Agreement on Investment
MFN	most favoured nation
MNE	multinational enterprise
NGO	non-governmental organization
OECD	Organization for Economic Co-operation and Development
PSE	producer support estimate (previously producer subsidy equivalent)
SPS	Sanitary and Phytosanitary Agreement
SSG	Special Safeguard Clause
TPA	Trade Promotion Authority
TRIM	trade-related investment measure
TRIP	trade-related intellectual property rights
URAA	Uruguay Round Agricultural Agreement
USDA	United States Department of Agriculture
TRQ	tariff rate quota
VER	voluntary export restraint
WHO	World Health Organization
WTO	World Trade Organization

18

EU Trade and Aid Policies

LEARNING OBJECTIVES

By the end of this chapter you should be able to understand:

▶ What we mean by the 'hierarchy' of trade preferences of the EU;

▶ What we mean by the General System of Preferences;

▶ How the foreign aid policy of the EU works;

▶ The trade and investment relations between the EU and the USA;

▶ What the institutional framework for the transatlantic dialogue involves;

▶ Some possible explanations of the conflictual co-operation between the EU and the USA;

▶ What are the main features of EU relations with neighbouring countries, the Mediterranean area, the former Soviet Republics, Asia and Latin America.

EU TRADE POLICY

Although the EU has primarily been concerned with promoting integration internally, it has also had to develop a trade policy towards the rest of the world. The Common Commercial Policy (CCP) of the EU was based on Article 113 of the Treaty of Rome which required a common Community tariff regime and common trade agreements with third countries. EU trade policy is intrinsically linked to other policy areas, and notably the Common Agricultural Policy, the Single Market and the CFSP. The European Commission represents the Community in multilateral trade negotiations. Table 18.1 indicates the main trading partners of the EU.

Rank	Partner	Imports to EU (billion euros)	Exports to EU	Percentage of total trade (exports + imports)
	EU global trade	985	990	100
1	USA	174	239	20.9
2	The ten new member states	107	125	11.7
3	Switzerland	59	71	6.5
4	China	81	34	5.8
5	Japan	68	42	5.6
6	The 77 African Caribbean and Pacific countries (ACP)	46	40	4.4
7	Russia	48	30	3.9
8	Norway	45	26	3.6

Table 18.1 Main destination of extra-EU exports and main origin of extra-EU imports, 2002

Source: Eurostat.

At times the gradual extension of EU responsibility into questions of external relations not strictly related to trade has been hotly contested by the member states. The external aid policy of the EU has been influenced by historic and strategic considerations, with former French and British colonies receiving particularly favourable treatment, and continuation of this historical bias in policies has at times been challenged.

Over time the EU has developed a patchwork of preferential agreements with other countries or groups of countries. Reference is frequently made to the 'hierarchy of EU preferences' or the 'pyramid of privileges'. In practice it is no longer possible (if it ever was) to discern a clear hierarchical pattern since the system is complex, in flux, the concessions are generally riddled with exceptions and the agreements rarely refer exclusively to trade issues.

The trade arrangements of the EU include:

- The European Economic Area (see Chapter 2);
- Customs unions with Turkey, Andorra and San Marino (and, before enlargement these were proposed, but overtaken by the accession process, with Cyprus and Malta);
- The pan-European trading bloc that came into operation from 2002 and covers 31 countries[1] – the agreement entails the elimination of tariff barriers between members and the harmonization of rules of origin, so the parts and components produced in any country belonging to the European trading bloc are treated as domestic components;
- Wider Europe or the European Neighbourhood Policy;
- The Euro-Mediterranean Partnership which involves introducing a free trade area for the Mediterranean by 2010;
- Trade and Co-operation Agreements, and Co-operation and Partnership Agreements with Russia and other former Soviet Republics;
- Before enlargement Europe Agreements established free trade areas with the Central and East European countries (see Chapter 20);
- Stabilization and Association Agreements with South-Eastern European countries (see Chapter 20);
- Bilateral free trade areas with the African Caribbean and Pacific (ACP) countries;

---

[1] The pan-European cumulation system was established at the request of the 1993 Copenhagen Council and includes the EU(25), Romania, Bulgaria, Turkey, Iceland, Norway and Switzerland.

■ Agreements with regional groupings such as those in Latin America and Asia;
■ The Generalized System of Preferences or GSP (see below);
■ Free trade agreements with countries such as Mexico;
■ MFN treatment for countries such as the USA, Japan and Australia.

The aim of this chapter is to discuss certain of these arrangements and, in particular, those with developing countries, the USA, neighbouring countries, the Mediterranean area, Russia and the CIS, Asia and Latin America.

THE GENERALIZED SYSTEM OF PREFERENCES

As trade is generally considered one of the most effective tools in fostering development, in 1968 the UNCTAD (United Nations Committee on Trade and Development) called for a Generalized System of Preferences under which industrialized countries would grant autonomous preferences to all developing countries. In 1971 the Community established a Generalized System of Preferences (GSP) which entails the elimination or reduction of tariffs on a non-reciprocal basis and is now applied to 178 developing countries.[2] In 2002 EU imports under the GSP amounted to €53 billion.

The GSP is applied in the framework of 10-year programmes, and the current cycle covers the 1995–2005 period. The scope and availability of preferences depend on which of five GSP arrangements is applied to the country:

■ General arrangements;
■ Special arrangements for the least developed countries, also known as 'anything but arms';
■ Special arrangements to combat drugs production and trafficking;
■ Special incentive arrangements to protect labour rights, on request from the country in question;
■ Special incentive arrangements for the protection of the environment on request from the country in question.

The general arrangements cover about 7000 products, with products classed as 'non-sensitive' entering the EU duty-free, while 'sensitive' products are subject to tariff reductions, generally in the order of 3.5 per cent. The classification of products by sensitivity depends on the market situation of the product in the EU.

The special incentive arrangements for the protection of labour rights and the environment entail additional tariff reductions (generally of a further 5 per cent) on sensitive goods for countries respecting core labour standards and international environmental standards (in particular, those relating to tropical forests) respectively.

The UN identifies the 49 'least developed countries' on the basis of their low GDP per capita, weak human assets and economic vulnerability (see Figure 18.1). In 2001 the EU launched its 'everything but arms' (EBA) initiative for these countries. This implies that apart from arms and ammunition all imports (with a few exceptions) from these countries enter the EU duty free. Import duties on bananas, sugar and rice are being removed in stages between 2002 and 2009. The special arrangements to combat drug production and trafficking are aimed at providing beneficiary countries with export opportunities for substitute crops, and encouraging economic and social development.

---

[2] The description of the GSP here is based on European Commission (2004a).

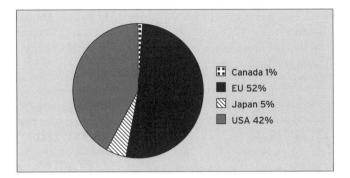

The EU defends the GSP system as being transparent and relatively easy to administrate, but in practice the system is complex (Nixson, 2001) and has given rise to lobbying over the inclusion of goods and the way in which their sensitivity should be categorized.

EU FOREIGN AID AND EXTERNAL ASSISTANCE

The EU and its member states provided about half of the total €57 billion in Overseas Development Assistance (ODA) given to developing countries in 2002 (European Commission, 2004b). EU development policy is implemented through instruments such as trade preferences, development finance and humanitarian aid.

EU development policy is centred on the 77 ACP, or African, Caribbean and Pacific countries, many of which are former colonies of EU member states. However, aid is also given to other countries, such as those in the Mediterranean area, the former Eastern bloc, Latin America, Asia and Africa. In the European Commission the responsibility for policy and programming of aid is divided among the ACP countries (DG Development), the non-ACP countries (DG External Relations) and the candidate countries (DG Enlargement). Since 2001 EuropeAid has carried out the implementation of measures, while humanitarian aid is managed by a separate agency, ECHO.

The results of attempts to encourage development are far from satisfactory. According to the World Bank, in 1999 1.2 billion people in the world, or 23 per cent of the population in the developing countries, earned less than $1 a day.[3] The difficulties in sub-Saharan Africa and Southern Asia remain particularly acute. It is estimated that 800 million people in the world (200 million of them children) suffer chronic malnutrition (European Commission, 2004b). The relentless spread of HIV/AIDS continues, and other illnesses such as malaria and tuberculosis are rife in developing countries. In 2002 and 2003 there were new conflicts and famine in sub-Saharan Africa.

The share of ACP countries in trade has been falling. According to Eurostat data, the share of ACP countries in world exports fell from 3.4 per cent in 1976 to 1.9 per cent in 2000, and their share in EU imports fell from 6.7 per cent in 1976 to 3.1 per cent in 2002. For most ACPs (and all African ACPs) the EU is the main trading partner. LDCs attract less than 1 per cent of foreign direct investment in the world.[4] In some countries (the HIPCs or highly indebted poor countries) the high level of indebtedness remains a problem.

LDC exports tend to be concentrated in a few commodities, with nine products accounting for 57 per cent of ACP exports in 1999 (see also Figure 18.2). Millions of people in developing countries are dependent on commodities for their employment and income, but prices for a wide

---

[3] See www.worldbank.org.
[4] See www.europa.eu.int/comm/development/body/cotonou/overview_en.htm.

range of commodities are very volatile and have been experiencing a long-term declining trend. For instance in terms of constant dollars, between 1970 and 2000 prices for some key agricultural commodity exports of developing countries such as sugar, cotton, cocoa and coffee fell by 30 to 60 per cent (European Commission, 2004c).

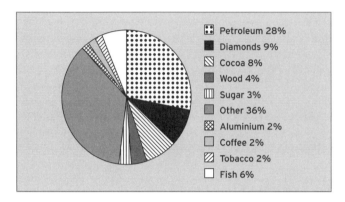

Figure 18.2 Main products imported by the EU from the ACP, 2002

Source: European Commission: www.europa.eu.int/comm/trade.

Petroleum 28%
Diamonds 9%
Cocoa 8%
Wood 4%
Sugar 3%
Other 36%
Aluminium 2%
Coffee 2%
Tobacco 2%
Fish 6%

The evolution of EU development policy has been influenced by changes within the EU itself but also by the political, strategic and economic changes on the international scene, decolonialization, changing views of economic and social development, the ending of the Cold War and globalization.

Community development policy dates from the Treaty of Rome when France wanted to maintain its links with its colonial territories but share some of the financial costs with other Community members (see Box 18.1). For this purpose in 1958 the European Development Fund (EDF) was set up, and financed social and economic infrastructure projects mainly in French-speaking Overseas Countries and Territories (OCTs). Subsequently the EDF financed aid to the ACP countries.

Box 18.1 The evolution of EU development Policy

Articles 131 and 136 of the Treaty of Rome provide for the association of non-European countries and territories with which the EEC states had particular relations.

1958: The European Development Fund (EDF) was established.

1963 Yaoundé I: trade concessions and financial aid to African ex-colonies.

1969 Yaoundé II.

1975 Lomé I: non-reciprocal trade preferences to ACP countries, equality of partners and introduction of Stabex.

1980 Lomé II: no major changes apart from the introduction of Sysmin.

1985 Lomé III: attention was shifted from the promotion of industrial development to self-reliant development on the basis of self-sufficiency and food security.

1990 Lomé IV (revised in 1995): covered a 10-year period and gave more emphasis to the promotion of human rights, democracy, good governance, the situation of women, protection of the environment (including forests), decentralization of co-operation and increased regional co-operation.

2000 Cotonou: covers a 20-year period and uses an approach based on politics, trade and development to tackle poverty.

The EDF is not funded from the general Community budget but from direct contributions from the member states. The funding from a member state is partly based on GDP and partly on their historic links with the ACP country concerned. The Commission proposes to include the EDF in the EU budget for the 2007–13 period. Most aid to non-ACP countries is financed through the EU Budget.

During the 1960s many of the overseas territories gained independence, and a new framework of assistance was provided with the Yaoundé agreement of 1963 (renewed in 1969) covering trade and aid arrangements between the EC and former French colonies in Africa.

The entry of the UK into the Community in 1973 led to a reappraisal of development policy, resulting in the first Lomé Convention of 1975. Subsequent Conventions followed in 1980, 1985 and 1990 (which covered a 10-year period) and the Cotonou Agreement of 2000.

In line with the then widely discussed objective of creating a New International Economic Order (NIEO), the initial ambitious aim of the Lomé conventions was to create a 'partnership of equals'. The main instruments adopted were non-reciprocal and included:

- Tariff preferences;[5]
- Preferences for agricultural products;
- Financial aid; and
- Stabex arrangements (subsequently also Sysmin for mining sectors), which are funds to stabilize export earnings.[6]

However, the global economic instability following the oil shocks of 1973 and 1979 hit Sub-Saharan economies particularly hard and the ACP countries were disappointed with the Lomé Conventions. The Conventions were criticized for poor use of aid since projects were often badly designed and hindered by a hostile policy environment, and for weak management on the part of donors, with slow and cumbersome disbursement procedures and accusations of 'meddling'.[7]

The need to tackle poverty, instability and political conflict led to a renewed debate on EU development policy in the late 1990s. To facilitate discussion the Commission published a Green Paper in 1996 and a discussion paper in 1997 setting out its proposals for a post-Lomé agreement.[8] Negotiations began in 1998, and in 2000 the Cotonou Agreement was signed between the EU and 77 ACP countries.[9] This was to cover a period of 20 years, with a five-year review clause. It is based on a perspective that combines politics, trade and development. The central objective of the agreement was the reduction and eventual eradication of poverty, and for that purpose five interdependent pillars were indicated:

- A comprehensive political dimension;
- Participatory approaches;
- Strengthening the focus on poverty reduction;
- A new framework for trade and co-operation; and
- A reform of financial co-operation.

An innovation of the agreement is the added emphasis on the political dimension, and the need to promote respect for human rights, democratic institutions and the rule of law. Increased dialogue

---

[5] Ninety-nine per cent of ACP products enter the EU free of duty (Weidenfield and Wessels, 1997, p. 69). The EU tariffs are generally non-reciprocal (there are certain exceptions, such as South Africa), and the ACP countries are required to grant imports from the EU the same favourable treatment as that given to the most favoured developing country.

[6] Stabex applied on over 40 agricultural raw materials and guaranteed compensation for a fall in income from sales subject to maximum rates, and provided certain conditions were met.

[7] See Stevens (1990) for an early criticism of these agreements.

[8] European Commission (1996 and 1997).

[9] Cuba was admitted as a new member of the ACP in December 2000, but was not a signatory of the Cotonou Agreement.

and co-operation strategies are to be aimed at peace-keeping strategies and conflict prevention and resolution. There is also an explicit attempt to address corruption.

The EU stress on the link between economic development and democratic institutions is shared by other international organizations such as the World Bank and European Bank for Reconstruction and Development (EBRD).[10] Democratic elections and freedom of the media render politicians more answerable for their choices. Effective rule of law ensures that contracts are enforceable and, if necessary, redress is possible through the courts. Corruption and criminal activity may impede the establishment of new firms, and disrupt the activities of existing ones. Protection of property rights is necessary to ensure the efficient allocation of resources, and to encourage innovation and investment. Participation is aimed at encouraging ownership of policies and implies the involvement of civil society, and a wide range of economic and social actors in development co-operation.

Poverty is not defined simply as lack of income or financial resources, but encompasses the notion of vulnerability and factors such as lack of access to adequate food supplies, education, healthy drinking water, employment, and political involvement (European Commission, 2004b). The focus on poverty reduction entails emphasis on three main areas for support:

- Economic development, including private sector development and investment, macroeconomic and structural policies and reforms, and sectoral policies (including transport, food security and rural development);
- Social and human development, including social sector policies, youth issues and cultural development;
- Regional co-operation and integration.

At the same time three horizontal themes are to be taken into account in all areas of co-operation (in accordance with the principle of 'mainstreaming'):

- Gender equality;
- Environmental sustainability; and
- Institutional development and capacity building.

The Cotonou Agreement envisaged the introduction of Economic Partnership Agreements (EPAs) to create a new framework for trade and economic co-operation. In the past ACP–EU trade relations had been exclusively concerned with promoting bilateral trade, ignoring the potential offered by national, regional and international markets. Moreover, trade measures were often limited to tariff reductions at a time when non-tariff barriers such as standards and technical restrictions were playing an increasingly important role. Too often trade promotion was regarded as an end in itself, rather than as a means of promoting development.

Negotiations on the Economic Partnership Agreements began in 2002, and they are expected to come into operation from 2008. They take the form of agreements between the EU and groups of neighbouring ACP countries. The objective is to strengthen regional economic integration within different ACP regions. The EPAs would aim at building free trade areas between the parties by progressively eliminating all barriers to trade and simplifying procedures.

The Cotonou Agreement earmarks about €25 billion for the 2000–07 period. In order to simplify and speed up disbursement each recipient country will receive an indication of the lump sum of resources for a five-year period, rather than numerous allocations from different instruments.

The aim is also to ensure 'the three Cs': coherence, co-ordination and complementarity in development policy. Coherence and co-ordination are necessary to render aid more effective, while

---

[10] See, for example, EBRD *Transition Report*, 2003.

coherence requires an integrated approach to external relations, security, economic and development policies. Programming of EU development policy was also strengthened with the introduction of Country Strategy Papers for 140 countries, established in consultation with national governments, other donors and civil society.

In 2000 the international community agreed on the Millennium Development Goals (MDGs) up to the year 2015. These entail:

- Halving the number of people in extreme poverty;
- Achieving universal primary education; and
- Reducing child mortality by two-thirds.

In 2002 the EU worked with member states and other international organizations such as the OECD, the World Bank and the UNDP (United Nations Development Programme) to develop a core set of indicators to assess progress in meeting the MDGs. *Inter alia* these indicators relate to the health and education of children and women, and access to water (European Commission, 2003b). To reach the Millennium Development Goals, the World Bank estimates that total overseas development aid (ODA) needs to be increased from its 2002 level of €57 billion to €100 billion.

In 2002 the EU agreed to the Monterrey Consensus adopted by the International Conference on Financing for Development (FfD) in Mexico. The 2002 Barcelona European Council defined the EU contribution to the FfD process. The commitments include enabling each EU member state to meet the UN target of ODA equal to 0.7 per cent of gross national income, with an intermediate target of 0.33 per cent by 2006. Other measures include increased co-ordination between donors, debt relief, and untying aid (so that aid is no longer dependent on the recipient buying the goods or services of the donor) (see Table 18.2).

	% gross national income		% Gross national income
Austria	0.26	Portugal	0.27
Belgium	0.43	Spain	0.26
Denmark	0.96	Sweden	0.83
Finland	0.35	UK	0.31
France	0.38	EU total	0.35
Germany	0.27	USA	0.13
Greece	0.21	Japan	0.23
Ireland	0.40	Canada	0.28
Italy	0.20	Norway	0.89
Lux.	0.77	Switzerland	0.32
Netherlands	0.81	New Zealand	0.22

Table 18.2 Overseas development aid as a percentage of gross national income, 2002

Source: OECD.

EVALUATION OF EU DEVELOPMENT POLICY

There has already been much debate about how effective this new approach to EU development assistance will be. In 2002 the EU member states increased their overseas development aid by 5.7 per cent, reaching 0.35 per cent of their collective gross national income. ODA rose significantly in Sweden, France, Greece and Italy (European Commission, 2004f). The large portfolio of old EU commitments that were never likely to be spent were reallocated, but some observers argue that the financial provisions are inadequate to meet the ambitious aims of the Cotonou Agreement.

Difficulties have been encountered in introducing common, simplified procedures and ensuring co-ordination and the complementarity of different aid measures and the activities of donors. Insufficient progress has also been made in realizing the third 'C', namely coherence with other EU policies. Enlargement and the CFSP may focus attention on 'near neighbours', but poverty reduction requires more priority being given to the poorest countries (House of Lords, 2004). Ongoing attention is necessary to ensure that decisions in areas such as trade and agriculture are compatible with development co-operation.

The organizational structure of EU policy is complex, and there would seem a case for bringing all measures under one Directorate-General. Continuation of the historical distinction between ACP and other countries seems difficult to defend, but its abolition is likely to encounter the opposition of the ACP Group. There also seems a case for including the EDF under the EU budget.

Economic development is a complex process depending on a whole series of factors including the internal situation of the recipient countries, the international economic environment, globalization, the evolution of EU policies (such as the CAP or CFSP) and the outcome of the Doha Round. As the quantity of ODA seems likely to remain limited, it is essential to ensure its quality (House of Lords, 2004). Candidates for ensuring the quality of aid include:

- Emphasis on promoting economic growth;
- Focusing on essential priorities such as poverty reduction and fighting disease;
- Building democratic institutions that can ensure the rule of law and respect for minorities, the reduction of corruption and guarantees of property rights;
- Applying conditionality so that building democratic institutions, rule of law and respect for human rights are consistently applied as conditions for receiving aid;
- Promoting sustainable development;
- Simplifying the procedures and ensuring better co-ordination of aid programmes.

EU-US TRADE AND INVESTMENT

In recent years trade relations between the EU and the USA have at times been tense, degenerating into surprisingly acrimonious disputes over issues as varied as bananas, beef, trade legislation and subsidies to aircraft. At the same time there have been various initiatives to construct an institutional framework for transatlantic co-operation. The aim here is to describe and attempt to provide explanations of this conflictual co-operation.

In terms of economic dimension, the EU and the USA are roughly compatible. In 2003 the EU(25) had a population of 455 million, while that of the USA was 278 million.[11] The land area of the USA was considerably greater at 9.4 million square kilometres, compared with the 4.3 million of the EU(25). The 2003 GDP of the EU(25) amounted to €11.1 billion in purchasing power parity terms, while that of the US was €10.9 billion.

The EU and the USA are the world's most important traders. The EU(15) share of total world trade (exports plus imports excluding intra-EU trade) was 19.4 per cent for goods in 2002, and the new member states accounted for a further 3.4 per cent. The EU(15) accounted 24.3 per cent of world trade in services in 2001, while the share of the new member states was 3 per cent. The equivalent US shares were 19.1 per cent for goods in 2002 and 20.2 per cent for services in 2001.

The EU and the USA are each other's single largest trading partner in goods and services. The USA accounted for 17.7 per cent of total EU(15) imports of goods and 24.2 per cent of total EU

---

[11] Unless otherwise stated, all the statistics in this chapter are taken from Eurostat. See, in particular, www.europa.eu.int/comm/external_relations/us.

exports of goods in 2002. The EU accounted for 21 per cent of total trade (exports and imports) in goods of the US in 2002. In 2001 transatlantic trade represented 39 per cent of EU(15) and 35 per cent of US total cross-border trade in services.

They are also each other's most important source and destination of FDI (foreign direct investment).[12] Over the 1998–2001 period the USA accounted for 61.6 per cent of all FDI in the EU(15) (see Figures 18.3 and 18.4), while the USA received 52.4 per cent of EU(15) investment abroad. About a quarter of EU–US trade consisted of transactions within firms based on their investments on either side of the Atlantic.

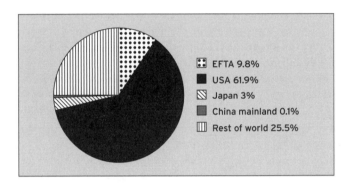

Figure 18.3 Share in EU(15) FDI inflows, 1998-2001

Source: Own elaborations based on Eurostat data.

EFTA 9.8%
USA 61.9%
Japan 3%
China mainland 0.1%
Rest of world 25.5%

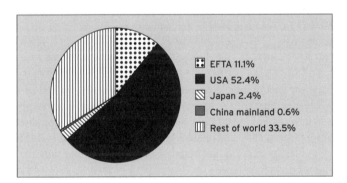

Figure 18.4 Share in EU(15) outflows of FDI, 1998-2001

Source: Own elaborations on the basis of Eurostat data.

EFTA 11.1%
USA 52.4%
Japan 2.4%
China mainland 0.6%
Rest of world 33.5%

FDI by the EU(25) in the USA, was estimated at €49 billion in 2003 compared with a disinvestment of €3 billion in 2002. US investment in the EU(25) fell by two-thirds from €51 billion in 2002 to €18 billion in 2003. The United States was the main FDI partner of the EU(25), receiving 42 per cent of extra-EU(25) investment in 2003 and supplying 23 per cent of investment into the EU(25) from the rest of the world.

THE INSTITUTIONAL FRAMEWORK FOR TRANSATLANTIC CO-OPERATION

During the post-Second World War period, the USA demonstrated unequivocal support for the integration process in Europe. Marshall Aid was conditional on regional co-operation of the recipient

---

[12] This was despite US popular fears of a Japanese takeover in the 1980s, though this was probably largely fuelled by some high profile deals such as the Sony purchase of Colombia Pictures or the New York Rockerfeller Centre by Mitsubishi.

countries and led to the creation of the OEEC.[13] The early European federalists hoped this would become a supranational institution, but in the event the OEEC and its successor, the OECD, were firmly based on intergovernmental co-operation (thanks largely to Britain and the Scandinavian countries, see Chapter 2). The USA also expressed strong support for the creation of the European Community and was disappointed when the West European integration split into two blocs with the establishment of EFTA in 1960.

An ongoing feature is the rhetorical character of statements made about EU–US relations (even when they are conflictual).[14] This, for instance, is typified in Kennedy's 'Declaration of Interdependence', or 'Grand Design', announced at Independence Hall, Philadelphia, on 4 July 1962. The aim was to create a concrete Atlantic partnership based on a declaration of inter-dependence with a united Europe.[15] The EC was viewed as an ally that could be induced to assist in the fight against communism (both at an international level and internally in countries such as Greece and Italy) and to bear part of the bill for international security.

Recent years have been characterized by several concrete attempts to promote EU–US co-operation, as summarized in Box 18.2.

Box 18.2 Recent landmarks in EU-US relations*

1990 the Transatlantic Declaration

1995 the New Transatlantic Agenda (NTA)

1998 the Transatlantic Economic Partnership (TEP)

1999 Bonn Declaration

2002 Positive Economic Agenda (PEA)

*See text for a description of these initiatives.

In 1990 the **Transatlantic Declaration** institutionalized a framework for consultation and co-operation on all matters, including foreign policy, the economy, education, science and culture and transnational changes. Within this framework President Clinton and EU leaders met in December 1995 to reaffirm their 'strong historic relationship' and their vision of a post-Cold War world 'united around values of democracy and free markets'. This led to the 1995 **the New Transatlantic Agenda (NTA)**, which entailed joint action in four areas:

■ Promoting peace, stability, democracy and development around the world;

■ Responding to global challenges;

■ Contributing to the expansion of world trade and closer economic relations;

■ Building bridges across the Atlantic (which implies promoting contacts at the level of individual citizens).

The institutional structure of the NTA entails twice-yearly meetings between the US president and the presidents of the EU Council and Commission. The NTA also involved an Action Plan to implement the above objectives. The Action Plan sets out 150 specific actions to further the objectives of the NTA through co-operation in fields such as trade and economic issues, fighting international crime and drug trafficking, promoting civil society, supporting democracy, the environment, migration, health, and establishing links between colleges, research institutes and universities.

---

[13] For a description of US attitudes towards European integration in the 1950s, see Chapter 2 of Guay (1999).

[14] On the negative side, in 2000 at the beginning of his term of office the EU commissioner for trade, Pascal Lamy, referred to the need to replace megaphone with telephone diplomacy.

[15] For a more detailed description see Guay (1999), p. 32.

The NTA led to a number of bilateral agreements, covering, for example, co-operation and mutual assistance on customs matters (1997), science and technology (1997), competition laws (1998) and veterinary equivalence (1999).

In 1997 the Mutual Recognition Agreement was signed to meet complaints about customs formalities that often involve requests for additional documentation and information, and lengthy sampling and inspection procedures. Regulatory barriers are now the main obstacles to trans-atlantic business,[16] and the agreement is a move towards reciprocal recognition of standards and technical regulations. It covers telecommunications equipment, pharmaceuticals, medical devices, computers, electronic devices, electromagnetic compatibility, electrical safety and recreational craft.

The EU maintained that the agreement was undermined by the refusal of the US authorities to recognize European product safety standards and testing as equivalent to those in the USA. While US companies in sectors such as computers and telecommunications can sell in the EU simply by declaring that their products meet local standards, EU companies were encountering costly delays for product certification. It was estimated that mutual recognition of regulations could lead to savings of more than $1 billion annually.[17] The Mutual Recognition Agreement has encountered strong opposition from consumer interest groups in the USA who fear that it will undermine the stringency of the US regulatory system.

The NTA also established the Transatlantic Business Dialogue (TABD) that came into operation from 1995. The TABD involves top businessmen in a forum to discuss ways of reducing barriers to trade and investment. Annual meetings take place alternately in the EU and the USA, and businessmen have been called on to make recommendations relating to the evolution of common standards, the reduction of tariffs and the implementation of anti-corruption measures. Governments have subsequently endorsed many of the recommendations. Topics discussed at the 2003 meeting of the TABD included the Doha Round, security issues, regulatory convergence and capital market convergence.

The commitment of the New Transatlantic Agreement to expand trade led in 1998 to the proposal to create a New Transatlantic Marketplace. This aimed at eliminating barriers to the flow of goods, services and investment between the EU and USA by 2010. Although the European Commission approved the New Transatlantic Marketplace, it was subsequently blocked by France, who was not convinced that audio-visual services (which had sensitive cultural implications) and agriculture would receive special treatment.

Following this failure, in 1998 a **Transatlantic Economic Partnership (TEP)** was agreed. The TEP aimed at creating an open and more accessible world trading system, and improving economic relations between the EU and the USA. This involves tackling trade issues, and, in particular, regulatory barriers. The aim of the TEP is also to integrate labour, business, and environmental and consumer interests into the process. An Action Plan was also agreed, which entails a rolling work programme with specific target dates for implementation of the TEP.

In 1999 an EU–US summit resulted in the **Bonn Declaration** which aimed at developing an effective early warning system to identify problems at an early stage and avoid the risk of conflicts undermining EU–US relations.

In 2002 the **Positive Economic Agenda (PEA)** was set up to enhance bilateral co-operation between the EU and the USA. It provides a framework for setting up new objectives, starting negotiations or increasing the momentum of existing dialogues. The PEA entails bilateral projects, with reports each year to the EU/US Summit in order to take stock of progress.

---

[16] For descriptions of the ways in which standards and technical restrictions act as barriers in EU–US trade, see, for example, the annual publication of the European Commission, *US Barriers to Trade and Investment*, or the annual *US Trade Review*.
[17] *Financial Times*, 9 November 2000.

TRADE DISPUTES BETWEEN THE EU AND THE USA

In addition to the difficulties in reaching agreement in the 1987–94 Uruguay Round, and differences in the Doha Round (see Chapter 17), there have been numerous trade disputes between the EU and the USA. However, despite their high profile, in general most disputes only touched a minimal percentage of trade.

Between 1960 and 1985 the USA initiated 17 legal cases against the EC in the GATT, 13 of which (or 76 per cent) concerned agriculture and fisheries (Hudec, 1993).[18] The USA objected to the system of variable levies used by the EC on its imports of agricultural products from the rest of the world; the level of EC domestic support to agriculture and the use of export subsidies on agricultural products.

In March 2004 the EU was active in 29 WTO disputes, of which 14 were with the USA. In 11 of these cases the EU was the complaining party, and in 3 cases (genetically modified organisms (GMOs), beef hormones and trademarks/geographical indications) the EU was the defendant.[19]

Direct disputes between the EC and USA cover a wide variety of issues such as:[20]

- The EU banana regime, which discriminated in favour of ACP countries;
- The UN ban on imports of beef from the USA and Canada containing growth-promoting hormones;
- The US use of foreign sales corporations to reduce the taxes of US firms exporting abroad;
- The EU failure to authorize additional genetically modified organisms;
- US public procurement (the Massachusetts–Burma case raised by the EC in 1997);[21]
- US use of trade defence instruments (such as anti-dumping and safeguards);
- EU protection of trademarks and geographical indications for agricultural products and foodstuffs; and
- Preferential loans for the development of a flight management system by the French government to Airbus, and the 2004 Airbus–Boeing case.[22]

POSSIBLE EXPLANATIONS FOR EU-US TRADE CONFLICTS

The increasing number of disputes may simply reflect the interdependence and the higher level of international trade and FDI between the EU and the USA. It may also be an indication that countries are more willing to refer their conflicts to a multilateral forum, since the WTO is considered to be more effective in settling disputes than its predecessor, the GATT.

The increase in EU–US trade disputes may also reflect the changed international environment since 1989 with the end of the Cold War. Earlier reliance of West European countries on the US nuclear umbrella constrained the extent to which they could provoke the USA with bitter trade wars.

---

[18] The first dispute, the 1962 US/EU 'Chicken War', was the direct result of the 1962 EC agreement creating the CAP. See Chapter 10 for a more detailed discussion of these questions.
[19] See www.europa.eu.int/comm/trade.
[20] Some of these disputes (such as those over the EU banana regime, beef hormones, foreign sales corporations, subsidies to Airbus and Boeing, and GMOs) are taken up as case studies and discussed in more detail on the OLC website for this book.
[21] The Commonwealth of Massachusetts forbade business with anyone having official relations with Burma (Myanmar). The EU maintained that sub-national action violated international trade agreements signed by national governments. See www.wto.org:wto/dispute/bulletin.htm for a description of these disputes.
[22] France granted, and the EU accepted, preferential loans to a French company, Sextant, over three years to develop a new flight management system adapted to the Airbus. The USA considers this to be a specific subsidy that could impede or displace US exports and could permit a price advantage to the subsidized product.

According to international relations theory, the increased strength and changing role of the EU could imply a decline in the hegemonic stability of the USA.[23] The basic hypothesis of this type of approach is that the existence of a single hegemonic nation will lend stability to the international economic and political system, but if rival countries emerge to challenge the hegemony, the system may become unstable. The picture that emerges varies considerably according to the policy area considered. Few would contest the continued hegemonic role of the USA with regard to international security. In the international monetary sphere there has been much speculation as to whether the euro would challenge the dollar, both as a reserve currency, and in the invoicing of international trade (see Chapter 8). However, it is in the area of international trade that the real discussion about possible decline of US hegemony emerges.

Domestic pressures, and, in particular interest groups, and big business have generally played a role in the disputes. The USA challenged the EU banana regime, though bananas are not produced in the USA. However, the US government appeared subject to pressure from large multinationals, Chiquita and Dole, while in the EU the firms controlling banana licences had a vested interest in not reforming the regime. The banana lobby was also strong in some of the ACP countries. In 1998 the prime minister of Dominica, Edison James, was a former general manager of the Dominica Banana Growers Association. He was elected on a platform to 're-energise the banana industry', with bananas accounting for half the export earnings of the island. The GMO market is controlled by large multinationals, and in most cases producer lobbies (such as the National Cattlemen's Beef Association in the beef-hormone case) were active in claiming compensation for their losses.

In certain cases sanctions were applied (as in the banana and beef hormone cases), and these took the form of tariffs on a certain value of imports. These sanctions hit consumers, but the general public may have been unaware of these effects. Alternatively, in the beef hormone case, EU authorities may have considered sanctions a worthwhile price to pay in view of the strong preferences of consumers with regard to possible health risks. It seems likely that other lobbies quite unconnected to the case in question influenced the choice of products on which to apply sanctions.

Disputes may arise from different regulatory approaches that reflect economic, social, historical and cultural diversity, or different sensitivities and societal values with regard to health, consumer and environmental protection. Both the USA and EU have numerous technical regulations relating to health, safety and the environment, and the existence of these regulatory systems frequently constitutes a structural impediment to access. The increasing complexity of the issues renders it difficult to draw up clear and unambiguous rules, in particular when there may be conflicts between policy objectives, such as between free trade and the environment (see also Chapter 17).

The EU has frequently complained about US attempts to apply extra-territoriality and unilateralism in trade policy. The EU objects to extra-territorial application of US domestic legislation when it requires individuals or companies in the EU to comply with US laws or policies. This was said to be the case for the 1996 Cuban Liberty and Solidarity Act (formerly the Helms–Burton Act) applying sanctions against Cuba, and the 1996 Iran and Libya Sanctions Act (otherwise known as the D'Amato Act). The EU criticized the use (or threat of use) by the USA of unilateral sanctions or retaliatory actions based on Sections 301–10 of US trade legislation, as in the banana dispute. Such actions are said to undermine the authority for multilateral settlement of disputes, which the WTO was supposed to provide.

The EU and the USA have different views about the effectiveness of linking strategic and commercial objectives. While the USA sees trade as a useful diplomatic weapon in dealing

---

[23] See the OLC website of this book.

with rogue countries (as in the D'Amato Act or Cuban Liberty and Solidarity Act cited above), the EU is more sceptical about the effectiveness of sanctions and tends to favour a policy of engagement.

Point scoring and the personal objectives of national politicians and bureaucrats may also lead to a process of reciprocal retaliation that can gather its own momentum. Between 1999 and 2004 the personal friendship of the two leading trade negotiators, Pascal Lamy for the European Commission, and Robert Zoellick, the US trade representative, often appeared to counterbalance this difficulty. However, at least Lamy is to be replaced in 2004, and the outlook for improved trade relations in the near future does not appear very promising.

WIDER EUROPE: THE EUROPEAN NEIGHBOURHOOD POLICY

In March 2003 the European Commission published the Communication on Wider Europe, setting out the European Neighbourhood Policy (ENP) to deal with relations between an enlarged EU and its eastern and southern neighbours.[24] The aim is to prevent new dividing lines emerging between the EU and its neighbours and to enhance security and narrow the prosperity gap on the new external borders of the EU.

The European Neighbourhood Policy is for countries with no immediate prospect of EU membership, covering countries such as Russia, the western NIS (newly independent states) and Southern Mediterranean countries (see Table 18.3), but not South East Europe. The Commission has held preliminary talks with countries with Partnership and Co-operation or Association Agreements in force[25] and intends to extend the process to countries that have ratified these agreements such as Egypt and Lebanon. The Commission has also recommended the inclusion of Armenia, Azerbaijan and Georgia in the ENP.

	Population millions	GDP per capita % of EU(15) average	Trade with EU(15) as % of total	FDI millions of euros
Israel	6.4	79.7	26.7	3397
Algeria	30.7	7.8	66.4	1335
Egypt	65.3	7.3	31.5	569
Libya	5.4	n.a.	82.3	-112
Morocco	29.2	5.6	70.0	2966
Tunisia	9.7	9.9	79.8	534
Jordan	5.2	8.3	3.8	189*
Lebanon	3.6	19.1	26.6	278*
Occupied Palestinian Territory	3.0	6.4	0.0	57*
Syria	17.1	4.8	61.2	229*
Belarus	10.0	5.7	11.1	189
Moldova	4.3	1.8	21.4	167
Russian Fed.	114.8	8.3	38.9	2835
Ukraine	49.1	3.4	20.5	862

Table 18.3 Basic data on the countries covered by the European Neighbourhood Policy, 2001

Source: European Commission (2003b).

---

[24] European Commission (2003b).
[25] Israel, Jordan, Moldova, Morocco, Palestinian Authority, Tunisia and Ukraine.

The approach is based on mutual commitment to common values such as the rule of law, good governance, respect for human rights, including minority rights, the promotion of a market economy, sustainable development and certain foreign policy goals. The Neighbourhood Policy aims at establishing a pan-European integrated market, functioning on the basis of rules that are similar or harmonized with those of the EU. A European Neighbourhood Instrument would also be introduced to focus on cross-border co-operation along the new external border of the EU.

If the partner country agrees, it would define a set of jointly agreed priorities in an Action Plan aimed at bringing the partner country as close as possible to the EU. The Action Plans would be differentiated, and the pace at which the EU develops links with each partner will be based on benchmarks reflecting the extent to which common values are effectively shared.

The Action Plans will cover areas such as:

- Political dialogue, including measures against terrorism and to prevent the spread of weapons of mass destruction and the encouragement of regional co-operation;
- Economic and social development policy, offering partner countries a stake in the EU Internal Market based on regulatory and legislative convergence, participation in certain EU programmes (such as education, training, research and innovation) and improved interconnections and physical links with the EU (in transport, energy, the environment and telecommunications);
- The promotion of trade, including convergence with EU standards;
- Justice and Home Affairs, including co-operation on issues such as border management, migration, the fight against terrorism, organized crime, trafficking in human beings, the drugs trade and so on.

The Action Plans could pave the way to a new generation of European Neighbourhood Agreements to replace existing bilateral agreements.

While it seems a positive move to avoid new divisions with neighbouring countries, it is difficult to see how a single policy can be applied to countries with such different characteristics and needs, even with a differentiated approach. Moreover, most of the countries included in the ENP are already covered by EU geographical co-operation programmes (see below). The use of benchmarks in applying the Action Plans seems to imply that the EU is attempting to introduce some form of conditionality, but as the experience of the former Yugoslav Republics of South-East Europe and other countries (including those of the Mediterranean Area) has shown, conditionality is a very blunt weapon without the prospect of EU membership (see Chapter 20). The idea that European Neighbourhood Policy is extended to countries with no immediate prospect of EU membership might also be interpreted as a 'cold shoulder' by some of them.

THE MEDITERRANEAN REGION

In 1995 what is known as the Mediterranean Partnership, or Barcelona Process, began. This provides a framework for co-operation between the 15 EU members and 10 Mediterranean countries: Algeria, Egypt, Israel, Jordan, Lebanon, Morocco, the Palestinian Authority, Syria, Tunisia and Turkey. Turkey is a candidate country for EU membership, but (as was the case for Cyprus and Malta) can participate in Euro-Mediterranean regional co-operation until accession. Libya currently has observer status.

The Euro-Mediterranean Partnership is composed of bilateral and regional relations. At a bilateral level the EU has concluded Euro-Mediterranean Association Agreements with nine

Mediterranean countries, and negotiations are at an advanced stage with Syria. The Euro-Mediterranean Agreements differ between countries, but their main features include:

- ■ Respect for human rights and democratic principles. To further this aim common political dialogue is to occur at regular intervals and at various levels.
- ■ Free trade is to be established, with dismantling of tariffs by the Mediterranean countries over a transitional period of up to 12 years (EU tariffs on industrial goods have already been eliminated). Trade in agriculture and services is to be 'gradually liberalized'.
- ■ Provisions relating to intellectual property rights, public procurement, competition rules, state aids and monopolies.
- ■ Financial assistance from the Community (except to Israel).
- ■ Co-operation on economic and cultural matters.
- ■ CFSP themes.
- ■ Co-operation on workers' rights and social policy, and the possibility of re-admission of illegal immigrants (though the terms vary between countries).

At regional level the aim is to promote activities in all three domains of the Barcelona Declaration:

- ■ The political and security dimension;
- ■ The economic and financial dimension;
- ■ The social, cultural and human dimension.

Within the political and security dimension emphasis is placed on creating a zone of peace and stability. The aim is also to encourage 'horizontal' or 'South–South' integration through the creation of free trade areas among the Mediterranean Partners themselves. In 2001 the Agadir Initiative entailed agreement to set up a free trade area between Egypt, Jordan, Morocco and Tunisia.

The MEDA Programme is the main financial instrument of the EU for the implementation of the Euro-Mediterranean Programme, and was allocated €5,350 million for the 2000–06 period. Examples of projects financed by MEDA at the bilateral level are the structural adjustment programmes in Morocco, Tunisia and Jordan, the social fund for employment creation in Egypt, rehabilitation of the public administration in Lebanon and rural development in Morocco.[26]

In July 2003 the Palermo Action Plan was launched to facilitate the free movement of industrial goods. This involved trade facilitation and the simplifying of customs procedures, and the incorporation of provisions into the Association Agreements of provisions for the creation of a common pan-Euro-Mediterranean origin protocol.

From 1980 to 2002 EU imports from the nine Mediterranean countries (MED9) grew by 5.6 per cent on average each year, while EU exports to MED9 grew by 4.84 per cent.[27] Trade with these countries represented 4.35 per cent of EU imports from the rest of the world in 2002 and 5.03 per cent of EU exports. The MED9 accounted for 11.3 per cent of EU energy imports, 9.7 per cent of textile imports, 3.2 of imports of chemical products and 3.7 per cent of agricultural imports in 2002. The MED9 countries accounted for 11.4 per cent of EU textile exports and 7.12 of EU agricultural exports in 2002.

The main weakness of the Euro-Mediterranean Partnership is that the aspiration of creating an area of peace, prosperity and progress around the Mediterranean is constantly threatened by the ongoing unsettled international situation, in particular in the Middle East. To try to meet this problem, at the March 2004 European Council an Interim Report on 'An EU Strategic Partnership

---

[26] European Commission (2001).
[27] The MED9 are Morocco, Algeria, Tunisia, Israel, Egypt, Jordan, Lebanon, Syria, Gaza and Jericho.

with the Mediterranean and the Middle East' was presented. The aim is to work towards a common agreed view towards the area, but, as explained in Chapter 19, the difficulties in reaching common positions should not be underestimated.

Despite the Mediterranean Partnership, the income gap between the Northern and Southern Mediterranean was been widening (see also Table 18.3). The Mediterranean partners criticize the EU for limited concessions in the sectors that interest them most, namely agriculture and textiles and clothing. Co-operation over immigration is inadequate, and attempts to insist on improvements in human rights are hampered by limited EU leverage when there is no prospect of EU membership.

Shortcomings were also encountered in the implementation of the Mediterranean Partnership, and in 2003 it was agreed to improve working methods, which included measures such as setting up *ad hoc* groups to prepare discussions and increasing the sense of co-ownership of programmes by enhancing the role of Mediterranean partners.

THE RUSSIAN FEDERATION

The legal basis for EU relations with Russia is the Partnership and Co-operation Agreement (PCA) which was signed in 1994 and came into operation in 1997.[28] The Agreement covers a 10-year period and entails:

■ Trade and economic co-operation. Trade liberalization is to entail MFN treatment, the elimination of quantitative restrictions and legal harmonization. There are also provisions on the establishment of companies, capital movement and competition and intellectual property rights. Both sides are committed to creating a free trade area as soon as circumstances permit.

■ Co-operation in sectors including science and technology, energy, the environment transport, space and so on.

■ Political dialogue, which also includes democratization and respect for human rights.

■ Justice and Home Affairs, which entails co-operation to combat illegal activities, drug trafficking, money laundering and organized crime.

Bilateral trade agreements between the EU and Russia cover sectors such as steel, and entail the progressive removal of restrictions on EU imports. The PCA also envisages an agreement on trade in nuclear materials.

Since 1991 the EU has provided technical assistance to Russia through the TACIS Programme (Technical Assistance for the Commonwealth of Independent States). By 2001 a total of €2.4 billion had been given through TACIS, and the EU was the main provider of economic and technical aid to Russia.

Faced with the prospect of EU enlargement, Russia submitted to the European Commission a list of 14 points for urgent negotiation, threatening to block extension of the PCA to the new member states if these questions were not addressed. Russia remains an important economic partner of the CEEC new member states. In 2002 14.2 per cent of Russian exports worth €13.8 billion went to the CEEC(8), with energy products accounting for 82 per cent of these exports. Of Russian imports 5.9 per cent came from these countries.[29] Russia believed that enlargement would

---

[28] Unless otherwise stated, the data in this section are taken from www.europa.eu.int/comm/external_relations and www.europa.eu.int/comm/trade/issues/russia.

[29] *Revue Elargissement*, No. 61, 8 March 2004.

lead to a loss of its trade in this area, and Russian economists estimated that the cost to Russia could amount to between €150 and 400 million.

Russian iron and steel exports would be subject to quotas, while agricultural products would have difficulty meeting EU standards and would also be subject to quotas. Russia was also concerned that EU anti-dumping measures would be applied on certain chemicals and steel products. There were also non-economic issues on the list, such as transit to Kaliningrad (see below) and the treatment of Russian minorities in the Baltics.

Had Russia been a WTO member, these issues could have been raised there. However, although the EU supports the acceleration of negotiations for Russia to join the WTO, in return it has requested adjustment of the very low energy prices that Russian firms pay.

A compromise on Russian steel imports, EU anti-dumping measures and veterinary standards was reached, and in April 2004 a protocol was added to the Partnership and Co-operation Agreement so that its provisions could be extended to relations between Russia and an enlarged EU. The tariffs on imports of goods of Russian origin to the new member states will decrease on average from 9 per cent to 4 per cent as a result of application of the Common External Tariff. Russia also stands to benefit from dealing with an enlarged Single Market that applies common standards.

In 1999 the EU presented its 'common strategy' for Russia, which covers a four-year period and sets out four priority areas:

■ Consolidation of democracy, rule of law and public institutions;
■ Integration of Russia into a common European economic and social space;
■ Stability and security in Europe and beyond;
■ Common challenges on the European Continent (including the environment, crime and illegal immigration).

At the EU–Russian summit of 2001 the Common European Economic Space (CEES) was launched. This covers mainly trade and economic issues and aims at the elimination of trade barriers mainly through regulatory convergence. So far the CEES does not foresee the creation of shared institutions with rule-making capacity or the replacement of the PCA.

In 2003 the Final Declaration of the EU–Russian Summit in St Petersburg defined four 'common spaces' or areas for co-operation:

■ The economy;
■ Liberty, security and justice;
■ Research, education and culture;
■ External security.

However, despite such intentions, a leaked European Commission paper criticized the EU strategy towards Russia as being 'ineffective, flawed and lacking in an overall strategy'.[30] In particular, different positions emerged between the Commission and the member states in the Council. An extreme example arose in the November 2003 European Council when the then president, Berlusconi, refused to criticize Russia over human rights violations in Chechnya and for not ratifying the Kyoto Protocol.

Since enlargement part of the Russian Federation, Kaliningrad, is surrounded by EU member states. This raised the sensitive question of how to guarantee transit between Kaliningrad and the

---

[30] As reported in the *Financial Times*, 23 February 2004.

rest of Russia. In 2002 at the Brussels Summit, agreement was reached on a package of measures addressing this problem, which included:

- A facilitated transit document;
- Assessing the feasibility of a non-stop, high-speed train;
- Discussions on the long-term goal of visa-free travel between the EU and Russia; and
- Full use of existing international conventions to simplify transit of goods, including energy.

The commitment to implement this package was confirmed in a joint EU–Russian statement following enlargement in 2004.

The EU is Russia's main trading partner, accounting for about 50 per cent of trade in 2003, and this percentage is expected to rise after enlargement. Total EU trade with Russia amounted to €85 billion in 2003, and the main EU imports from Russia in that year were energy (57 per cent), agricultural products (4 per cent) and chemicals (4 per cent). The principle EU exports to Russia in 2003 were machinery (34 per cent), chemicals (13 per cent), agricultural products (11 per cent), transport materials (11 per cent) and textiles (6 per cent). A large share of EU imports from Russia is granted GSP treatment.

To date Russia has not succeeded in attracting sufficient FDI to meet its huge investment requirements, and European FDI amounted to only €2.2 billion in 2002. Capital outflows remain a problem, even though capital flight declined in 2002/2003.

OTHER FORMER SOVIET REPUBLICS

The EU signed Partnership and Co-operation Agreements with Ukraine and Moldova in 1994 that entered into force in 1998. These cover a wide range of areas including political dialogue, trade and investment, legislative co-operation, culture, science, the promotion of peace and security and of respect for democratic principles and human rights. Since enlargement there seems a strong case for developing tighter EU links with Ukraine in particular, given its size (see Table 18.3 above) and borders with three new EU member states and one candidate country. The EU has held discussions with both countries over inclusion in the European Neighbourhood Programme, but Moldova has expressed a preference for joining the Stabilization and Association Process of South-East Europe (which offers the prospect of eventual EU membership).

A PCA was completed with Belarus in 1995, but failed to enter into force because of objections by the EU to violations of human rights and the controversial constitutional changes introduced in 1996, with replacement of a democratically elected parliament by a national assembly nominated by President Lukashenko. Since that time EU relations with Belarus have been effectively frozen.

In 2002 the European Commission adopted a Strategy Paper for Central Asia. This reviews co-operation with five countries of Central Asia (Kazakhstan, Kyrgyzstan, Tajikistan, Turkmenistan and Uzbekistan) and sets out the strategy for providing an annual €50 million in aid to the region for the 2002–06 period. The core objective of the strategy is to promote stability and security, economic development and reduced poverty in these countries.

Partnership and Co-operation Agreements are in force between the EU and Kazakhstan, Kyrgyzstan, and Uzbekistan, and a similar agreement has been signed with Turkmenistan. The EU has a Trade and Co-operation Agreement with Tajikistan. These five countries receive various forms of aid from the EU, including technical assistance through TACIS, GSP treatment, humanitarian aid and macro-financial loans and grants. TACIS assistance is also granted to Armenia, Azerbaijan, Belarus, Georgia, Moldova, Mongolia and the Ukraine.

EU RELATIONS WITH ASIA

In 1994 the European Commission published the document 'Towards a New Asia strategy' which was the first attempt to take an overall view of relations with Asian countries.[31] The higher priority attached to relations with Asia reflected an awareness of the growing economic weight of these countries in the world. The strategy has evolved over time, and in 2001 the Commission published a communication setting out its main points:

- Recognition of the diversity of Asia;
- A strengthened EU political and economic presence in Asia;
- A better balance between the economic, social and political aspects of the relationship; and
- A partnership of equality.

The strategy has six main objectives:

- Political dialogue, both at a bilateral level and in the ASEM, or Asia-Europe Meeting (see below);
- Strengthening trade and investment flows;
- Development of the less prosperous countries;
- Encouraging democratization and the protection of human rights;
- Building global alliances;
- Heightening the awareness of Europe in Asia.

The ASEM (Asia–Europe Meeting) was set up in 1996 to encourage dialogue and co-operation between the EU and 10 Asian countries.[32] It involves summits (which have taken place every two years), ministerial meetings and conferences and seminars at expert levels to discuss political, economic and cultural issues. Action Plans have been drawn up to facilitate trade and investment. There are also meetings on a regular basis of civil society and of the private and public sectors in the Asia–Europe Business Forum. The Asia–Europe Foundation was set up in 1997 in Singapore in order to promote cultural and intellectual meetings between the two regions. The dialogue encouraged by the ASEM process has recently concentrated more on political issues such as the fight against terrorism and transnational crime, and the management of international migration.

For the EU ASEM was seen as a balance to the APEC forum that links 21 Asian-Pacific countries, including the USA. During the early 1990s APEC seemed to be moving towards a free trade area, and the Community feared that it would lose its market share in the Asian-Pacific market (Yeo Lay Hwee, 2004). For the Asian partners, ASEM was seen as a means of diversifying and reducing dependence on the USA. In 2003 ASEM accounted for 24.7 of EU imports and 13.8 per cent of EU exports to the rest of the world.

The ASEM framework has provided numerous opportunities for dialogue and exchange of information, and on the economic front the meetings are considered to have helped in promoting

---

[31] The strategy covers relations with 26 Asian countries. The Commission documents setting out the strategy are available at www.europa.eu.int/comm/external_relations/asia.
[32] Brunei, China, Indonesia, Japan, S. Korea, Malaysia, the Philippines, Singapore, Thailand and Vietnam.

networking and co-operation.[33] However, Yeo Lay Hwee (2004) criticizes ASEM as being little more than a talking shop and of not providing institutions and mechanisms for problem solving and rule setting. He argues that an ASEM contribution to global governance would require tighter integration among the Asian partners and a greater willingness of the EU to become a global rather than simply a regional actor.

The EU also has relations with sub-regional Asian groupings such as ASEAN (the Association of South-East Asian countries), and SAARC (the South Asian Association for Regional Co-operation), as described in Table 18.4.

The EU also has bilateral relations with individual Asian countries, such as Japan. EU relations with Japan are covered by the 1991 Political Declaration which set out common principles and shared objectives in the political, economic, co-operation and cultural areas, and established a consultation framework for annual summits between the EU and Japan. In 2000 an Action Plan was established to move EU–Japanese relations from consultation to joint action.[34] The Action Plan extends EU–Japanese political co-operation to cover the promotion of peace and security through measures such as arms control, non-proliferation, conflict prevention and the promotion of human rights and democracy. The EU and Japan have also attempted to co-ordinate their positions with regard to the WTO.

In the past EU relations with Japan tended to be dominated by trade disputes, and the EU continues to complain of difficulties in market access. In recent years there has been increased Japanese willingness to meet EU requests for structural reforms and deregulation. Since 1994 the Regulatory Reform Dialogue has provided a forum for reciprocal requests for reducing the number of unnecessary regulations that may obstruct trade. In 2002 an EU–Japan Mutual Recognition Agreement entered into force, and in 2003 an Agreement on Co-operation on Anti-Competitive Activities was adopted.

Between 1980 and 2002 EU imports from Japan grew by 7 per cent on average a year, and EU exports by 10 per cent. Historically Japan has had a large trade surplus with the EU, but in recent years trade with Japan has become more balanced. In 2003 EU merchandise exports to Japan amounted to €40.0 billion, while imports amounted to €66.6 billion.[35] In 2002 EU exports of services to Japan amounted to €17.4 billion, while imports amounted to €8.9 billion. At the end of 2002 4.48 per cent of the stock of EU inward FDI came from Japan, and 1.26 per cent of EU outward investment was in Japan. EU firms complain of structural obstacles to FDI in Japan, and the sectors that have attracted most FDI (telecoms, financial services and a few areas in distribution) are those that have benefited from regulatory reform.

In recent years trade between the EU and China has been growing rapidly, and in 2003 China became the second trading partner of the EU (overtaking Switzerland) after the USA.[36] According to official Chinese statistics, the EU was also China's second trade partner, behind Japan and roughly on a par with the USA.

Whereas the EU(15) had a surplus with China at the beginning of the 1980s, its deficit has been growing and reached €55 for the EU(15) and €64 billion for the EU(25) in 2003 (the largest bilateral deficit of the EU). China is the main supplier of textiles and clothing to the EU, and in 2003 amounted to 14.3 per cent of total textile and clothing imports to what is now the EU(25). EU textile and clothing imports from China are expected to expand rapidly with the abolition of quotas from 2005 in line with WTO commitments.

The EU grants China GSP treatment. The EU supported China's WTO membership and is

---

[33] See www.europa.eu.int/comm/external_relations/asem.
[34] The data in this section are taken from www.europa.eu.int/comm/trade/issues/bilateral/countries/japan.
[35] European Commission, www.europa.eu.int/comm/trade Greek data are missing for December 2003.
[36] The data in this section are taken from www.europa.eu.int/comm/trade/issues/bilateral/countries/china.

Table 18.4 EU relations with certain integration blocs

Integration bloc	Current membership	Characteristics/ weaknesses of bloc	Links with EU
ASEAN (Association of South-East Asian countries) created in 1967.	10 countries: Indonesia, Malaysia, Philippines, Singapore, Thailand, Brunei, Vietnam, Laos, Myanmar and Cambodia	Differences between the countries meant that for many years it was difficult to move beyond co-operation to integration. The six more developed countries agreed to create the Asian Free Trade Area, cutting tariffs to between 0 and 5 per cent on all but a few goods from January 2003. The four less developed members (Cambodia, Laos, Myanmar and Vietnam) are to reduce tariffs in the next decade. However, there have been derogations and delays. The consensus-based approach to decision-making has helped to resolve political differences but has meant slow progress in integration.	The EU has regular ministerial meetings with ASEAN. In 2002 ASEAN accounted for 6.3 per cent of EU imports and 3.9 per cent of EU exports to the rest of the world.
SAARC (the South Asian Association for Regional Co-operation) set up in 1985.	Bangladesh, Bhutan, India, the Maldives, Nepal, Pakistan and Sri Lanka	There is an asymmetry between India (with 76 per cent of the population and 77 per cent of regional GDP) and the other members. Slow and cumbersome procedures, and tensions between members have limited the effectiveness of this bloc.	The EU maintains this bloc could play a useful role in encouraging regional co-operation. In 2001 SAARC accounted for 2 per cent of EU imports and 1.7 per cent of EU exports to the rest of the world.
Mercosur ('EL Mercado del Sur') set up in 1991.	Argentina, Brazil, Paraguay and Uruguay, with Chile, Bolivia and Peru as associate members	After some success in promoting trade liberalization and export growth during the 1990s, economic crises first in Brazil and then in Argentina acted as a setback to further attempts at integration. With a gradual improvement in the economic situation, the governments of Kirchner in Argentina and Lula in Brazil expressed a new determination to revive Mercosur. This was also considered a way of strengthening their bargaining position in negotiations to create the Free Trade Area of the Americas, and in developing tighter links with the EU.	In 2003 Mercosur accounted for 3 per cent of EU(25) imports and 1.8 of EU(25) exports to the rest of the world. The main Mercosur export to the EU(25) was agricultural products, amounting to €14 billion in 2003. In 1995 the Madrid Treaty marked the beginning of negotiations to set up a free trade area between the Mercosur and the European Union, but the treaty was too generic in its means and goals. Actual negotiations began in 1999 but stalled as fallout from the economic crisis undermined the internal cohesion of Mercosur. In 2004 negotiations for a Framework Agreement

Table 18.4 (continued)

Integration bloc	Current membership	Characteristics/ weaknesses of bloc	Links with EU
			between the two blocs began, eased by the reform of the CAP of June 2003 and the willingness of the EU to grant more generous agricultural trade concessions to Mercosur. In return the EU requested Mercosur to lower industrial trade barriers, liberalize investment and open services and government procurement to EU firms.
In 1969 the Carthegena Agreement established the Andean Pact, which in 1996 became the Andean Community.	Bolivia, Colombia, Ecuador, Peru and Venezuela	It is considered that regional integration could increase regulatory stability and create a market of sufficient size to attract trade and development. The EU maintains that tighter regional integration is a pre-condition for signing a free trade agreement with the bloc.	EU trade with the Andean Community increased from €9 billion in 1980 to €15.5 in 2002. With the exception of Venezuela (oil and oil-related products), food, agriculture and mining products accounted for 90 per cent of EU imports from the area. In 1993 a Framework Co-operation Agreement was signed between the EU and Andean Community. One of the highest priorities is the fight against drugs. A new Political Dialogue and Co-operation Agreement was signed in 2004 and aims at reinforcing the political and economic stability of the Andean countries, encouraging regional integration and fostering sustainable development.
Caricom (the Caribbean Community and Common Market) was formed in 1973.	Caricom consists of Antigua and Barbuda, The Bahamas, Barbados, Belize, Dominica, Grenada, Guyana, Haiti, Jamaica, St Kitts and Nevis, St Lucia, St Vincent and the Grenadines, Antilles and Turks and Caicos Islands	Cariforum is the forum of the EU and ACP Caribbean states, which includes the Caribbean Community and Common Market (Caricom) and Haiti, Surinam and the Dominican Republic. Cariforum aims at better co-ordination of support from the EU and improved regional co-operation and integration.	In 1984 the EU and Central American countries set up the San José dialogue to promote democratization, peace and closer economic ties. A co-operation programme was established to address the socio-economic causes of unrest in Central America, and reduction of vulnerability to natural disasters. The EU will not begin negotiations for a free trade area with Central American countries until an adequate level of regional integration has been reached, with dismantling of trade barriers and harmonization of regulations and customs procedures.

now concerned to ensure implementation of China's WTO commitments, in particular with regard to market access and intellectual property rights. In 2004 an EU–China Co-operation Programme was launched to support the integration of China into the world trading system.

EU-LATIN AMERICAN RELATIONS

With the entry of Spain and Portugal into the Community, relations with Latin America acquired a higher priority. Trade between the EU and Latin America more than doubled between 1990 and 2002. The EU is Latin America's second trading partner, with EU imports from the area of €53.7 billion and exports worth €57.6 billion in 2002. The EU is also Latin America's largest source of FDI (though inflows have declined since 2000), and the total EU FDI stock in Latin America reached €206 billion in 2002. Machinery, equipment and chemicals are the main EU exports to Latin America, while agricultural products are the main EU import. The EU has granted GSP treatment to Andean and Central American countries, also with the aim of combating the international drugs trade.

However, the EU share of Latin American trade fell from 20 per cent in 1980 to 15 per cent in 2000, while the US share rose from 35 per cent to 47 per cent over the same period. The EU is concerned that Latin America should maintain a balanced relationship between its two principal partners, also in view of the US proposal to create a Free Trade Area of the Americas (FTAA) by 2005.[37] The EU has developed a parallel set of ties with Latin America and the Caribbean, and relations are carried out simultaneously at regional, sub-regional and bilateral levels.

At a regional (sub-continent) level, in 1986 six Latin American countries set up the Rio Group in order to discuss matters of common interest. Membership of this group has gradually expanded, and it now includes all the Latin American countries and representatives of Caribbean countries. Since 1987 annual meetings have been held between the EU and Rio Group.

In 1999 at the Rio Summit it was decided to develop a strategic partnership between the EU and Latin America and the Caribbean (EU–LAC) in order to develop political, economic and cultural understanding between the partners. A second EU–LAC summit was held in Madrid in 2002. Emphasis was traditionally placed on developing democracy, the rule of law, human rights, pluralism, peace and security and political stability. Over time, however, more priority has been given to international challenges affecting the region such as the environment, new technologies and WTO negotiations. The most recent meeting was at Guadalajara in Mexico in 2004 and concentrated on social cohesion, regional integration, and bi-regional co-operation in international forums. In order to support social cohesion, in 2004 EUROsociAL was set up with a budget of €30 million for a five-year period.

At a sub-regional level, as shown in Table 18.4, the EU has relationships with the three main integration blocs in Latin America: Mercosur, the Andean Community, and Central America. The EU also has bilateral links with individual countries and, in particular, Mexico and Chile, which are not members of Latin American integration blocs. In 2002 the EU signed an Association Agreement with Chile that envisages trade liberalization and political co-operation. An Economic Partnership, Political Co-operation and Co-operation Agreement (Global Agreement) was signed between the EU and Mexico in 1997. This envisages a free trade area with Mexico, that aimed at full liberalization of trade in industrial products by 2003 on the part of the EU, and 2007 for Mexico. There should also be substantial liberalization of trade in agriculture and fish products.

---

[37] It was hoped that this would build on the success of NAFTA (the North American Free Trade Association which came into operation between the USA, Mexico and Canada in 1994).

EVALUATIONS

The EU seems to have become more willing to take a more active role in promoting initiatives to tighten links with its main trading partners and encourage the efforts of other regional integration blocs. This probably reflects an awareness of the weight of an enlarged EU in the world and of the need to present a counterweight to the USA. None the less it seems likely that much time will elapse before the EU can evolve common positions and extend its perspective beyond the predominantly regional viewpoint.

Summary of Key Concepts

- The Common Commercial Policy of the EU is based on Article 113 of the Treaty of Rome and entails a common Community tariff regime and common trade agreements with third countries. Over time the EU has developed a patchwork of preferential agreements with other countries or groups of countries.
- In 1971 the Community established a Generalized System of Preferences. This entails a list of products negotiated each year on which tariffs are reduced by an amount that depends on the 'sensitivity' of the product and degree of development of the exporting countries.
- EU development policy is centred on the now 77 ACP countries, most of which are former colonies of EU member states. However, policies to reduce world poverty have met with limited success.
- Following the four Lomé Conventions, the 2000 Cotonou Agreement between the EU and ACP countries aims at poverty reduction and covers a 20-year period. It places a new emphasis on the political dimension (respect for human rights, democracy and rule of law) and on improved implementation.
- In terms of economic dimension, the EU and the USA are roughly compatible. The USA and the EU are each other's largest trading partner and most important source and destination of FDI.
- During the post-Second World War period, the USA demonstrated unequivocal support for the integration process in Europe. Marshall Aid was conditional on regional co-operation of the recipient countries and led to the creation of the OEEC.
- Recent years have been characterized by several concrete attempts to promote EU–US co-operation, such as the Transatlantic Declaration of 1990, the New Transatlantic Agenda (NTA) of 1995, the Transatlantic Economic Partnership (TEP) of 1998, the Bonn Declaration of 1999 and the Positive Economic Agenda (PEA) of 2002.
- There have been numerous trade disputes between the EU and the USA on issues such as bananas, meat containing growth-promoting hormones, foreign sales corporations and genetically modified food.
- Various explanations for these disputes have been advanced: the interdependence and the growing level of international trade and FDI between the EU and the USA; the increased willingness to refer conflicts to a multilateral forum; the changed international environment since 1989; a possible decline in the hegemonic stability of the USA in the trade context; the role of domestic pressures and interest groups; differences in regulatory approaches; the increasing complexity of the issues which renders it difficult to draw up clear and unambiguous rules; EU complaints about US attempts to apply extra-territoriality and unilateralism in trade policy; different views about the effectiveness of linking strategic and commercial objectives, and point-scoring and the personal objectives of national politicians and bureaucrats.
- In March 2003 the European Commission published the Communication on Wider Europe setting out the European Neighbourhood Policy to deal with relations between an enlarged EU and its eastern and southern neighbours.

- What is known as the Mediterranean Partnership, or Barcelona Process, began in 1995. This provides a framework for co-operation between the 15 EU members and 10 Mediterranean countries. The MEDA Programme is the main financial instrument of the EU for the Euro-Mediterranean Programme.
- The Partnership and Co-operation Agreement is the legal basis for EU–Russian relations. In 1999 the European Commission set out a 'common strategy' towards Russia. Certain other members of the CIS also have Partnership and Co-operation Agreements with the EU and, like Russia, receive technical assistance through TACIS.
- The document, 'Towards a new Asia strategy' sets out the framework of policy towards all Asian countries. The Asia–Europe Meeting was set up in 1996 to encourage dialogue and co-operation between the EU and 10 Asian countries. The EU also has bilateral links with ASEAN and SAARC, and individual countries such as Japan and China.
- EU relations with Latin America are carried out simultaneously at regional, sub-regional and bilateral levels. The EU is concerned that Latin American countries maintain a balance in their links with major partners when the Free Trade Area of the Americas is set up.

Questions for Study and Review

■ What are the main features of EU trade policy?

■ What are the main criticisms of EU development policy? How successful do you think that the Cotonou Agreement will be in overcoming these shortcomings?

■ What is the link between economic development and democracy?

■ What strategies should be used to ensure the effectiveness of development policies?

■ Indicate the main features of EU-US economic relations.

■ Describe the main attempts at EU-US co-operation. How successful do you consider these initiatives?

■ Describe some of the main trade disputes between the USA and the EU (see the OLC website for this book and the WTO website).

■ How can we account for the increase in trade disputes between the EU and the USA in recent years?

■ How successful do you consider the WTO in resolving these disputes?

■ How do you envisage the future of EU-US relations?

■ Do you think that the European Neighbourhood Policy will prove successful?

■ What criticisms can be made of the Euro-Mediterranean Partnership?

■ How could the EU develop a more coherent policy towards Russia?

■ How could Europe-Asia relations be strengthened?

■ Describe EU and US rivalry in Latin and Central America.

■ Do you think that the EU is right to insist on regional integration in its dealings with Latin and Central America?

References

European Bank for Reconstruction and Development, various years, *Transition Report and Transition Update,* London.

European Commission (1996) 'Green Paper on the relations between the European Union and the ACP countries on the eve of the 21st century - Challenges and options for a new partnership', COM(96)570, 20 November 1996.

European Commission (1997) 'Guidelines for the negotiation of new co-operation agreements with the African, Caribbean and Pacific countries', COM(97)537, 29 October 1997.

European Commission (2001) 'Euro-Mediterranean Partnership. Euromed information notes', www.europa.eu.int/comm/external_relations/euromed.

European Commission (2003a) 'Annual Report 2003 from the Commission to the Council and the European Parliament on the EC development policy and the implementation of external assistance in 2002', Brussels, COM (2003)527, 3 September 2003.

European Commission (2003b) 'Wider Europe – Neighbourhood: A new framework for our relations with our eastern and southern neighbours', COM(2003)104final.

European Commission (2004a) 'The EU's Generalized System of Preferences – GSP', www.europa.eu.int/comm/trade.

European Commission (2004b) 'The European Community's Development Policy' – Statement by the Council and Commission.

European Commission (2004c) 'Agricultural commodity chains, dependence and poverty – A proposal for an EU action plan'. Communication from the Commission to the Council and the European Parliament, COM(2004)89, 12 February 2004.

European Commission (2004d) 'Making globalization work for everyone. The EU and world trade', www.europa.eu.int/comm/trade.

European Commission (2004e) 'Economic Partnership Agreements', www.europa.eu.int/comm/trade.

European Commission (2004f) 'Translating the Monterrey Consensus into practice: The contribution of the European Union', Communication from the Commission to the Council and the European Parliament, COM(2004)150, 5 March 2004.

Guay, T.R. (1999) *The United States and the European Union: The Political Economy of a Relationship*, Sheffield Academic Press, Sheffield.

Hitiris, T. (1998) *European Community Economics*, 4th edn, Prentice Hall, Hemel Hempstead.

House of Lords (2004) 'EU development aid in transition', www.parliament.uk/parliamentary_committees/lords_s_comm_c/lords_s_comm_c_reports_and_publications.cfm.

Hudec, R.E. (1993) *Enforcing International Trade Law: The Evolution of the Modern GATT Legal System*, Butterworth Legal Publishers, Salem, NY.

Nixson, F. (2001) 'Foreign and external assistance', in Artis, M. and Nixson, F. (eds), *The Economics of the European Union. Policy and Analysis*, 3rd edn, Oxford University Press, Oxford.

Stevens, C. (1990) 'The Lomé Convention', in Kiljunen, K. (ed.), *Region-to-Region Co-operation between the Developed and Developing Countries: The Potential for Mini NIEO*, Avebury, Aldershot.

Weidenfeld, W. and Wessels, W. (1997) *Europe from A to Z. Guide to European Integration*, European Documentation, Luxembourg: Office for Official Publications of the European Community.

Yeo Lay Hwee (2004) 'Dimensions of Asia–Europe co-operation', *Asia Europe Journal*, Vol. 2, No. 1, pp. 19–32.

Useful websites

The European Commission for information on EU development policy and external relations: www.europa.eu.int/comm

The Food and Agricultural Organization for data and analysis on world food and agricultural issues: www.fao.org

The Organization for Economic Co-operation and Development for statistics and country reviews: www.oecd.org

Oxfam for a less orthodox view on trade and development questions:
www.oxfam.org.uk
For data and analysis of development issues see:
United Nations Development Programme (UNDP):
www.undp.org
United Nations Educational, Scientific and Cultural Organization (UNESCO):
www.unesco.org
UNICEF:
www.unicef.org
The World Bank:
www.worldbank.org
For the US position, see US Trade Representative:
www.ustr.gov
The World Trade Organization is useful for statistics and reports on international economic relations and accounts of trade disputes:
http://www.wto.org

List of abbreviations

ACP	African, Caribbean and Pacific countries covered by the Lomé Conventions and the Cotonou Agreement
APEC	Asia-Pacific Economic Co-operation
ASEAN	Association of South-East Asian Nations
ASEM	Asia–Europe Meeting
CAP	Common Agricultural Policy
Caricom	the Caribbean Community and Common Market
Cariforum	the forum of the EU and Caricom together with Haiti, Surinam and the Dominican Republic
CCP	Common Commercial Policy
CEEC	Central and Eastern European country
CEES	Common European Economic Space
CIS	Commonwealth of Independent States
CFSP	Common Foreign and Security Policy
DG	Directorate-General
EBA	everything but arms
EBRD	European Bank for Reconstruction and Development
ECHO	European Community Humanitarian Office
EDF	European Development Fund
EFTA	European Free Trade Association
ENP	European Neighbourhood Policy
EPA	Economic Partnership Agreement
EU–LAC	partnership between the European Union and Latin American and Caribbean countries
EuropAid	Office of the European Commission responsible for foreign aid and co-operation
EUROsociAL	EU support for social cohesion in Latin America
FDI	foreign direct investment
FfD	Financing for Development
FSC	foreign sales corporation

FTAA	Free Trade Area of the Americas
GATT	General Agreement on Tariffs and Trade
GMO	genetically modified organism
GDP	gross domestic product
GSP	General System of Preferences
HIPC	highly indebted poor countries
MDGs	Millennium Development Goals
MEDA	principal financial instrument for the implementation of the Euro-Mediterranean Partnership
Mercosur	'El Mercado del Sur'
MFN	most favoured nation
NAFTA	North American Free trade Association
NIEO	New International Economic Order
NTA	New Transatlantic Agenda
OCTs	Overseas Countries and Territories
ODA	overseas development assistance
OECD	Organization for Economic Co-operation and Development
OEEC	Organization for European Economic Co-operation
PCA	Partnership and Co-operation Agreement
PEA	Positive Economic Agenda
SAARC	South-Asian Association for Regional Co-operation
Stabex	System for the stabilization of ACP and OCTs' export earnings
Sysmin	Special financing facility for ACP and OCTs' mining products
TABD	Transatlantic Business Dialogue
TACIS	Technical Assistance for the Commonwealth of Independent States
TEP	Transatlantic Economic Partnership
UNCTAD	United Nations Conference on Trade and Development
UNDP	United Nations Development Programme
WTO	World Trade Organization

19

The Common Foreign and Security Policy

LEARNING OBJECTIVES

By the end of this chapter you should be able to understand:

▶ What the Common Foreign and Security Policy is;

▶ The difficulties of the EU countries in reaching common positions on foreign policy;

▶ What we mean by the capability-expectations gap;

▶ The role of Mr CFSP (or Monsieur PESC);

▶ The changes that occurred in the international security environment after 1989;

▶ What the Petersberg tasks are;

▶ What the St Malo Declaration involved;

▶ The difficulties encountered in establishing a Rapid Reaction Force;

▶ The debate on the future of an EU defence.

THE COMMON FOREIGN AND SECURITY POLICY

The Common Foreign and Security Policy forms the second pillar of the European Union and covers the various means by which the EU attempts to influence foreign affairs. Its aim is to present the identity of the EU at the international level. This entails exchange of information and opinions on international political issues in order to align national approaches and forge common positions, which can be put into practice through joint actions. In practice, however, over time very different opinions have emerged from the member states as to how active the EU should be in such matters (see Box 19.1).

Box 19.1 Important steps in the evolution of the Common Foreign and Security Policy

1970 European Political Co-operation is set up.

1993 The Maastricht Treaty creates the CFSP.

1999 The Amsterdam Treaty creates the post of High Representative for the CFSP.

2003 The Constitutional Treaty proposes creating a Union Minister for Foreign Affairs combining the role of Mr CFSP and the Commissioner for External Relations.

In terms of economic power the EU is already a heavyweight actor at the international level. The Common Commercial Policy was one of the first Community policies to be implemented, and the EU represents a major trading bloc and generally (but not always) presents a united front towards the rest of the world on economic issues.[1]

However, the frequent criticism is that in practice the EU is essentially a civil power, and while it acts as an economic giant, the EU remains a political pygmy. The EU member states have extreme difficulty in evolving common positions on foreign policy and defence issues, let alone imposing them. Differences between the member states on such matters frequently erupt, and countries often act unilaterally with little or no consultation. Despite some common initiatives (such as administration in Bosnia and missions to Macedonia and the Congo), the EU has proved largely ineffectual in halting the horrors on its doorstep that accompanied the disintegration of Yugoslavia and reaching a common position with regard to Iraq and the ongoing tensions in the Middle East.

The evolution of the EU on the international stage therefore appears lop-sided. Even Margaret Thatcher in her famous 1988 Bruges speech argued that 'On many great issues Europe should try to speak with a single voice. Europe is stronger when we do so whether it be in trade, in defence, or in our relationship with the world.'

Part of the co-ordination difficulty arises because the various member states arrived at the integration process with very different historical baggage in terms of traditional alliances, geographical situation, perceived cultural interests and so on. Some member states (Austria, Denmark, Finland, Ireland and Sweden) have a tradition of neutrality. Britain emphasizes its 'special relationship' with the USA and until the late 1990s was reluctant to see the Community develop as a forum for foreign policy and defence issues. For many years French attitudes were shaped by the decision to leave the military structure of NATO in 1966. Until recently Germany was hesitant to participate in military initiatives.

Foreign policy and security matters are areas in which governments are reluctant to sacrifice sovereignty, and not all are convinced that the EU is the appropriate framework for such issues. In addition, as Hill (1993) argues, there also appears to be a capability-expectations gap: not only does the EU often lack a common front on foreign policy questions but it also frequently seems unwilling or unable to supply the necessary means to deliver what is expected.[2]

Despite the decision of the founding fathers of the Community not to pursue a co-ordinated

---

[1] In late 1992, for example, France challenged the negotiating stance of the Commission in the GATT Round.
[2] Not surprisingly the head of the US Senate's Foreign Relations Committee, Jesse Helms, was reputed to have said that the EU could not fight itself out of a wet paper bag.

foreign policy, from the 1960s it was becoming increasingly evident that there was scope for co-operation and concerted action on the part of the member states (Bainbridge, 1998).

At the Hague Summit of 1969 the foreign ministers of the Community were requested to consider methods to increase co-operation between the member states in foreign policy. This led to European Political Co-operation (EPC) that was based on intergovernmental co-operation, or consensus between the governments of the member states, and operated outside the framework of the Community institutions. There was no voting, decisions were not binding and military aspects of security were excluded from EPC (Jones, 2001). The first recognition of EPC in the treaties was in the Single European Act of 1987, which stated that the member states would jointly attempt to formulate and implement a common foreign policy, though still on the basis of intergovernmental co-operation.

The CFSP was formally established by the Maastricht Treaty (see Box 19.2). The member states are required to co-ordinate their actions in international organizations, uphold common positions in international forums and support the common external and security policy. The instruments of the CFSP are common positions, joint actions, decisions and the conclusion of international agreements.

In dealing with the CFSP the EU Treaty was mainly concerned with institutional procedures for arriving at 'concerted and convergent action'[3] rather than setting out the substance of policy. Like EPC, the CFSP was still to be based on intergovernmental co-operation. Unlike EPC, there was an increased obligation for the member states to develop joint action, and the CFSP was also extended to cover defence issues. The Maastricht Treaty refers to 'the eventual framing of a common defence policy which could lead to a common defence'. However, the Treaty stated that no agreement would be binding on a member state (such as Ireland), which calls into question the requirements of its own constitution.

Given the weak formulation of the CFSP in the Maastricht Treaty, and its evident ineffectiveness, Germany (with some backing from Belgium) was in favour bringing the CFSP into the Community pillar in the Amsterdam Treaty. However, this was opposed by France, the UK and most of the other member states. In the event the Amsterdam Treaty simply allowed for an increased role of the Commission in drafting CFSP proposals, and the possibility of taking decisions under certain circumstances in the Council.[4] The Treaty also stated that the CFSP includes the progressive framing of a common defence policy 'which might lead to a common defence should the European Council so decide'.

The Amsterdam Treaty also established a High Representative, or individual responsible for the Common Foreign and Security Policy for a five-year period, soon to become known as 'Mr CFSP', or in the French version, 'Monsieur PESC'. This was an attempt (at least in this policy area) to meet the famous problem raised by Kissinger: 'Who shall I phone if I phone Europe?' The High Representative assists the Council by helping to formulate and implement decisions and, where necessary, acting on behalf of the Council at the request of the Presidency. The first Mr CFSP who was appointed in 1999 was the Spaniard, Javier Solana, the former secretary general of NATO.

Although the budget and staff of the High Representative are smaller than those of the Commissioner for External Relations (Chris Patten in the 1999–2004 Commission), the representative role of Mr CFSP confers certain degree of authority. This was increased by the personal prestige of Solana (also because of his former role in NATO) who soon achieved a high profile. The Constitutional Treaty proposed replacing the High Representative with a Union Minister for Foreign Affairs (see Chapter 3). The minister would be responsible to both the Commission and Council, though in practice this dual role could be difficult to balance.

---

[3] Article J of the Maastricht Treaty.
[4] See Jones (2001) for a more detailed account of this issue.

The Nice Treaty contained new CFSP provisions relating, in particular, to an increase in the areas that fall under the qualified majority vote and an enhanced role for the EU in crisis management.

THE EVOLUTION OF A EUROPEAN SECURITY AND DEFENCE POLICY (ESDP)

A substantial change in European attitudes towards international security came with the collapse of communism in 1989 and the subsequent disintegration of the Soviet Union. Even then common positions were slow to emerge. Fundamental questions had to be addressed concerning the future role of NATO, the possibility of the EU developing its own defence capacity and the relation of the latter to NATO structures.

Box 19.2 Main events in the creation of the European Security and Defence Policy

1955 Creation of the WEU.

1992 Definition of the Petersberg tasks.

1998 Anglo-French declaration at St Malo.

1999 Helsinki European Council creates the European Security and Defence Policy and calls for an EU Rapid Reaction Force to be set up.

2002 Berlin-plus agreement allowing EU missions possible use of NATO assets.

2003 Iraq War reveals wide differences in the positions of EU countries.

2003 Britain, France and Germany agree to create a common military planning cell.

In the changed international environment a tacit agreement seemed to emerge between the USA and the Community that NATO should remain responsible for territorial defence (in this case the defence of Europe against external aggression) but that the EC should play an increasing role in crisis management. Crisis management was interpreted to mean ethnic and regional conflicts in the vicinity of the EU and also problems relating to nuclear safeguards, organized crime (including drugs and international terrorism), mass migration, and environmental disasters. In 1992 at a meeting in Petersberg near Bonn this new role was defined in what became known as the Petersberg tasks, namely:

- Crisis management, including combat-force tasks;
- Peace-keeping;
- Humanitarian and rescue missions.

These tasks were incorporated into the Treaty of Amsterdam.

After 1989 there was also debate about whether it was better to create new institutions to cope with the changed international environment or adjust existing arrangements *ad hoc*. At least initially the choice seemed to fall on the latter solution, even though this entailed a certain amount of overlap and duplication of tasks between institutions such as NATO and the WEU.

As explained in Chapter 2, the framework for European co-operation on defence issues for many years was the Western European Union (WEU). This was created by the original EC(6) plus Britain in 1955 but remained relatively inactive for a long time. Following Reagan's decision to launch the Strategic Defence Initiative (SDI or 'Star Wars') in 1983 without consulting the Europeans, a meeting of the WEU in Rome in 1984 decided to revive the organization as a forum for the discussion of European security questions. At the Hague in 1987 a Platform on European Security Interests was adopted with the aim of developing a 'more cohesive European defence identity'.[5] In 1990 the WEU was responsible for the co-ordination of the military response of the Western European countries to the Gulf crisis.

The Maastricht Treaty assumed that the WEU would develop into the EU defence arm, and refers to the WEU as 'an integral part of the development of the European Union'. It was also described as the executive arm of the CFSP, which was to elaborate and implement all decisions taken under the CFSP. The Amsterdam Treaty still envisaged WEU as the framework for common EU defence initiatives and stated that the EU should foster closer institutional links with the WEU with a view to the possible integration of the WEU into the Union should the Council so decide.

One of the main limitations of the WEU is that its membership coincides neither with that of the EU, nor with that of NATO (see Figure 19.1). This creates difficulties both in defining the responsibilities of the WEU and in establishing the division of powers among the three organizations. Five EU members (Austria, Denmark, Finland, Ireland and Sweden) are only observers at the WEU.[6] Ten EU members (Benelux, France, Germany, Greece, Italy, Portugal, Spain and the UK) are also full members of the WEU. Iceland, Norway, Turkey, the Czech republic, Hungary and Poland are associate members of the WEU.[7] Seven CEEC countries (Bulgaria, Estonia, Latvia, Lithuania, Romania, Slovakia and Slovenia) are also associate partners of the WEU.

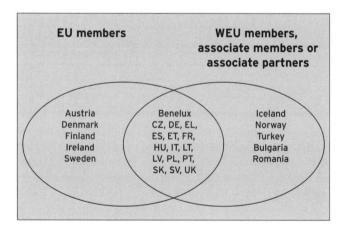

Figure 19.1 WEU members

In view of the shortcomings of the WEU and, in particular, the problem of its membership, at the Cologne and Helsinki Summits of 1999 it was decided to transfer most of the WEU's role and operational resources to the EU, though (at least for the time being) the WEU will continue to exist.

Rather surprisingly for Britain, which is not generally known for its propulsive role in the integration process, the next step in the evolution of a common defence policy came from an Anglo-French initiative. The evident ineffectiveness of the EU in the Balkans convinced Tony Blair and

---

[5] See Bainbridge (1998).
[6] Observers may attend WEU Council meetings and working groups where they may also speak on request (Jones, 2001).
[7] Associate members of the WEU may take full part in Council meetings and working groups, and can take part in WEU operations.

Jacques Chirac of the need to strengthen EU defence structures. This led to the St Malo Declaration of December 1998 which called for the development of a stronger European defence capacity to enable the EU to act without the USA, providing this did not jeopardize the transatlantic alliance.

The European Council of Helsinki in December 1999 decided on the creation of a European Security and Defence Policy (ESDP). The ESDP was to form part of the CFSP but with responsibilities for:

- The development of a temporary bureaucratic framework for the ESDP;
- The creation of an EU capacity to respond independently to crises and prevent conflicts, and eventually to run military operations;
- The establishment of a Rapid Reaction Force (see below).

At the Helsinki and Nice European Councils decisions were taken regarding the new political and military bodies for the day-to-day running of the ESDP, namely:

- A Political and Security Committee (PSC) that, in the event of crisis, is responsible for the political and strategic control of the operation, though subject to control by the Council. This is composed of national representatives at senior ambassadorial level.[8]
- The EU Military Committee composed of Chiefs of Staff that is responsible for giving military advice and recommendations to the PSC.
- The EU Military Staff that provides military expertise and support.

The EU Rapid Reaction Force (RRF) requires the member states to deploy a force of up to 60 000 troops within 60 days for up to a year to deal with the Petersberg peacekeeping tasks. It has been repeatedly stressed that this force does not represent a European army and that the commitment and deployment of troops was to be based on sovereign decisions by member states. The Laeken European Council of December 2001 rather optimistically declared the Rapid Reaction Force 'operational' and able to conduct some crisis management operations. A European Capability Action Plan (ECAP) was launched to boost the development of EU crisis-management capability.

After 11 September 2001, the task of building a European defence capability was felt to have become more urgent, but EU member states were slow to increase defence spending in line with the needs of the Rapid Reaction Force. Rendering the RRF operational required additional capabilities with regard to intelligence, logistics, communications and air transport systems.[9] There were arguments concerning the proposed division of the cost, and though it was agreed that multinational co-production and acquisition would increase effectiveness, there was little progress in this direction. Denmark decided against contributing troops to the Rapid Reaction Force on the basis of its opt-out from EU decisions and actions with defence implications.

In the 'Berlin plus' agreement of December 2002 EU countries were granted access to NATO assets and capabilities if the EU carried out missions independently from NATO. The agreement placed EU–NATO relations on a formal basis for the first time and pledged both sides to transparency.[10] Consultation and co-operation between the EU and NATO were to be tightened. It was also decided that non-EU–NATO countries and other interested states could also contribute to EU crisis management.

The 'Berlin plus' agreement was only reached when tensions over the Rapid Reaction Force with

---

[8] The Nice Treaty adds that the PSC will be able to take certain decisions to implement crisis management.

[9] Solana argued that the Airbus A44M transport aircraft could play an important role in building up capability, but Italy decided against its purchase, and the German proposal to buy 73 aircraft was controversial domestically. See for instance, the *Financial Times*, 20 November 2001 and 19 December 2001.

[10] *Financial Times*, 20 October 2003.

Turkey were overcome. As a long-standing NATO member in a strategic geographical position, Turkey was displeased at being excluded from the project and initially opposed the guaranteed access of EU initiatives to NATO military assets and capabilities.

Although the USA supported the EU bearing more of the defence burden, it was concerned about the duplication and overlap of efforts, and the lack of co-ordination and transparency which might result from EU 'go it alone' initiatives.

The Iraq War underlined the difficulties in developing the CFSP by bringing out differences among the EU member states. Britain was strongly in favour of the US decision to intervene militarily even without a second UN resolution. President Bush's policy was also supported by Spain, Portugal and Italy, but France and Germany preferred a multilateral solution. In January 2003 eight European countries signed a joint letter calling for Europe to stand behind the policy of Bush, and the following month 10 Central and East European countries went even further in expressing support for US policy.[11] President Chirac of France expressed the view that the future new EU member states had missed a good opportunity to remain silent. In a much-publicized comment US Secretary of Defence Donald Rumsfeld contrasted the 'new Europe' that supported US policy with the 'old Europe'.

After the official 'end' of hostilities, in April 2003, there was an initiative by Belgium, Luxembourg, France and Germany to launch a common defence effort with the notable exclusion of Britain. The proposal deepened the divisions caused by the Iraq War and led to US fears that France and Germany were attempting to undermine NATO.

At the European Council in Thessaloniki in June 2003 there was an attempt to resolve differences among the member states, and it was agreed that the EU could exert influence to prevent conflicts or to take 'pre-emptive engagement' through 'effective' multilateral institutions. Subsequently in what became known as the 'Solana doctrine' presented in 2003, the reference to pre-emption was watered down at French and German request to read 'preventive engagement'.[12]

In December 2003 Britain, France and Germany agreed to create a common military planning cell in Brussels, that could eventually develop into a headquarters for military planning if everyone agreed. This would only be able to operate a military operation in narrowly defined circumstances as a last resort, but it would be independent from NATO's operational planners at SHAPE (Supreme Headquarters Allied Powers Europe).[13]

The proposed articles on defence in the Constitutional Treaty were also the subject of much controversy. France, Germany and the UK pushed for an article permitting enhanced or structured co-operation so a core group of countries could take the lead developing defence policy. However, the UK wanted to ensure that any such initiative was as inclusive of as many member states as possible.

The proposed Constitutional Treaty includes an article on mutual defence whereby if any country were 'the victim of armed aggression on its territory, the other member states shall have towards it 'an obligation of aid and assistance'.[14] This commitment is subject to compatibility with NATO commitments, though the UK expressed concern about duplication. Austria, Finland, Ireland and Sweden feared that inclusion of the article in the Constitutional Treaty would threaten their neutrality.[15] The commitment cannot therefore 'prejudice the specific character of the security and defence policy of certain member states'.

---

[11] The eight countries signing the letter in February 2003 were: Spain, Britain, Italy, Portugal, the Czech Republic, Hungary and Poland. The 'Vilnius' Group a month later were: Estonia, Latvia, Lithuania, Slovakia, Slovenia, Croatia, Macedonia, Bulgaria, Romania and Albania.

[12] European Commission (2003).

[13] The EU headquarters would be used only with approval of all EU states and only when NATO was not involved and NATO or national headquarters of EU states were not used.

[14] Article 41.7.

[15] Denmark already has an opt-out of defence matters in the treaties.

EVALUATION

It is difficult not to conclude that there is still a long way to go in reaching common EU positions on defence and foreign policy issues, and in overcoming the capabilities-expectation gap. Despite Tony Blair's attempts to placate the Bush administration, the USA continues to worry about the duplication or competition with NATO posed by an EU military structure and the problems of co-ordination and transparency involved. Although the USA is in favour of the EU sharing more of the burden for collective security, at times it seems wary of challenges to US primacy. In the absence of unconditional EU support for US policies, the Bush administration seemed to prefer a fractured Europe from which it could select a 'coalition of the willing'. What was perhaps surprising was the scale of the differences between the EU member states revealed by the Iraq War and the bitterness of the debate. The aim of relegating this débâcle to the past may yet provide a strong incentive to renewed efforts to develop a more effective EU defence and foreign policy capacity.

Summary of Key Concepts
- The Common Foreign and Security Policy forms the second pillar of the European Union, and covers the various means by which the EU attempts to influence foreign affairs.
- In practice the EU remains essentially a civil power, and while it acts as an economic giant, the EU remains a political pygmy. Part of the difficulty arises because the various member states arrived at the integration process with very different historical baggage in terms of traditional alliances, geographical situation, perceived cultural interests and so on.
- There also appears to be a capability-expectations gap since the EU frequently seems unwilling or unable to supply the necessary means to deliver what is expected.
- The CFSP evolved out of European Political Co-operation.
- 'Mr CFSP' is the High Representative responsible for the Common Foreign and Security policy. The first Mr CSPC, Javier Solana, was appointed in 1999.
- In the changed international environment after 1989 there seemed agreement that NATO should remain responsible for territorial defence but that the EC should play an increasing role in crisis management.
- The Petersberg tasks agreed in 1992 are: crisis management, peacekeeping and humanitarian missions.
- Until 1999 the WEU was generally regarded as providing the framework for developing a common EU policy on security and defence issues, but its membership does not coincide with that of the EU.
- An Anglo-French initiative led to the St Malo Declaration of December 1998 calling for the development of a stronger European defence capacity.
- The Helsinki European Council of 1999 called for creation of an EU Rapid Reaction Force. Member states were reluctant to make the necessary increases in defence spending to finance the RRF.
- Although the USA supported the EU Rapid Reaction Force, it was concerned about possible duplication and lack of co-ordination. Tensions over the Rapid Reaction Force also arose with Turkey.
- After the Iraq War there have been various proposals for common defence initiatives, but the differences in view between member states remain substantial.

Questions for Study and Review
■ **Why do you consider it so difficult for the EU member states to reach common positions on foreign policy questions?**

■ How do you explain the capabilities-expectation gap?
■ How did the international security environment alter after 1989?
■ Describe the various attempts of the EU to evolve a common defence policy.

References

Bainbridge, T. (1998) *The Penguin Companion to European Union,* 2nd edn, Penguin Books, London.

European Commission (2003) 'A secure Europe in a better world: European security strategy', www.europa.eu.int.

Hill, C. (1993) 'The capability-expectations gap, or conceptualising Europe's international role', *Journal of Common Market Studies*, Vol. 31, no. 3, pp. 305-28.

Jones, R.A. (2001) *The Politics and Economics of the European Union. An Introductory Text,* 2nd edn, Edward Elgar, Cheltenham, UK.

Useful websites

Information about the CFSP is available on:

www.ue.eu.int/PESC

More general statistics and analysis of security and defence issues are presented by the ISS-EU, the EU Institute for Security Studies:

www.iss.eu.org

NATO

www.nato.int

The WEU

www.weu.int

List of abbreviations

CEEC	Central and Eastern European countries
CFSP	Common Foreign and Security Policy
ECAP	European Capability Action Plan
EPC	European Political Co-operation
ESDP	European Security and Defence Policy
NATO	North Atlantic Treaty Organization
PESC	Politique européenne de sécurité commune, the French acronym for the CFSP
PSC	Political and Security Committee
RRF	Rapid Reaction Force
SDI	Strategic Defence Initiative
SHAPE	Supreme Headquarters Allied Powers Europe
WEU	Western European Union

20

EU Enlargement

LEARNING OBJECTIVES

By the end of this chapter you should be able to understand:

▶ What measures were introduced by Western countries to assist the transition process and with what success;

▶ The differences between aid for transition and the Marshall Plan;

▶ The changing pattern of trade and investment in the Central and East European countries (CEECs);

▶ EU policy towards South-Eastern Europe;

▶ The difficulties encountered in trying to apply the Copenhagen criteria;

▶ The main steps involved in the pre-accession strategy;

▶ The difficulties of extending the CAP and the Structural Funds to the new member states;

▶ The links between Economic and Monetary Union and Enlargement;

▶ The issue of labour movement in an enlarged EU;

▶ How public opinion may react to the enlargement issue.

INTRODUCTION

In May 2004 10 new countries joined the EU, and Bulgaria and Romania could join in 2007. In April 2004 the European Commission published an Opinion favourable to opening negotiations for membership with Croatia. Turkey has also been declared a candidate, and a decision on whether to open negotiations with Turkey will be taken in December 2004. Table 20.1 presents some of the basic characteristics of these countries.

EU enlargement raises fundamental questions about the future of the Union. Will, for instance, an expansion in membership from 15 to 25 or more lead to a change in identity of the EU? Is widening on this scale compatible with deepening? Will the EU be condemned to endless arguing about the relative size of contributions to and receipts from the Community budget? Will some equitable solution be found to the problem of extending the CAP and Structural Funds to the new member states, or is the EU to be involved in a protracted debate about reform of these policies? Will the EU be able to develop an institutional framework that enables it to avoid deadlock in decision-making and at the same time increase its transparency and democratic accountability? The EU is committed to further enlargements, but where should its borders end?

Table 20.1 **Basic data on the new member states and candidate countries**

	Population in 2002 (millions)	GDP €billions PPP 2001	GDP per capita €/PPP 2002	GDP per capita as % of EU average (PPP) 2002	GDP growth in 2002 (%)
Bulgaria	7.9	51.5	5900	25	4 8
Cyprus	0.8	14.1	17 400	72	2.2
Czech Republic	10.2	136.1	14 400	60	2.0
Estonia	1. 4	3.4	10 000	42	6.0
Hungary	10.2	121.3	13 600	57	3.3
Latvia	2.4	18.1	8500	35	6.1
Lithuania	3.5	30.3	9400	39	6.7
Malta	0.4	4.6 #	11 700 #	55 #	1.2
Poland	38.6	355.5	9500	39	1.6
Romania	21.8	132.2	5900	25	4.9
Slovakia	5.4	59.7	11 400	47	4.4
Slovenia	2.0	31.9	17 700	74	3.2
Turkey	68.6	356.8	5500	23	7.8
Croatia	4.4	23.8	$(US) 8267	36	5.2

#1999
Source: European Commission: www.europa.eu.int/comm/enlargement.

A BRIEF CHRONOLOGY OF THE ENLARGEMENT PROCESS

Before dealing with the main aspects of enlargement in more detail, it is useful to provide a brief chronology of the main steps in the process.

As soon as the central planning system collapsed in 1989, many of the smaller Central and East European countries (CEECs) were anxious for tighter links with or membership of the European Community. The Community responded with a series of trade and aid measures, but a strategy with regard to enlargement emerged only gradually.

It was as late as 1993 that the Copenhagen European Council set out the conditions that applicant countries have to fulfil in order to join the EU. The 1994 Essen Summit established a 'pre-accession strategy' to help prepare the candidate countries for eventual membership.[1] As described below, this entailed the PHARE Programme of assistance, the Europe or Association Agreements and a 'structured dialogue', bringing together the EU and candidate countries to discuss questions of common interest.

---

[1] See Annex 20.1 for an outline of the main steps in the pre-accession process.

On the basis of the accession criteria, in July 1997 the EC Commission published 'Opinions' on the readiness of the applicant countries to join the EU. These Opinions were included in the document, Agenda 2000, which represents a milestone in the enlargement process. Agenda 2000 analysed the necessary steps to prepare both the EU and accession countries for enlargement and set out the Commission's proposals for the 2000–06 financial perspective.

Following the decision of the Luxembourg European Council in December 1999, accession negotiations started with Cyprus and with five of the 10 Central and East European countries in March 1998.[2] Each year the European Commission published Regular Reports on the progress made by applicant countries in preparing for EU membership.

At the 1999 Helsinki European Summit it was decided to extend negotiations to a further six countries.[3] Malta's application lapsed in 1993 but was subsequently resumed in 1998, and Malta was included in the Helsinki group. The Commission stressed that each country would be judged individually on the basis of its preparations for accession and that this could lead to some countries of the second 'Helsinki wave' overtaking those of the Luxembourg group.

Turkey applied for EU membership in 1987. In December 1997 it was decided to establish the European Conference that would entail an annual meeting of the EU member States and the 'European States aspiring to accede to it and sharing its values and internal and external objectives'.[4] The aim was to reassure those countries not included in the first wave of negotiations and, in particular, Turkey. However, Turkey was offended by the fact that it had been overtaken by so many countries in the accession queue, and refused to attend the first two meetings of the European Conference. At the Helsinki Summit Turkey was declared a candidate, and Turkey began to participate in a reinforced pre-accession strategy similar to that of the other candidate countries.[5]

At the Berlin European Council of March 1999 agreement was reached on the Agenda 2000 package, including the financial perspective for the 2000–06 period and reform of the Common Agricultural Policy and Structural Funds.[6] The financial package for the new member states was subsequently amended at the 2002 Copenhagen European Council. Following the rather disappointing results of the Amsterdam and Nice treaties, the Constitutional Treaty set out further proposals for reform of EU decision-making, also with a view to enlargement.

The 2001 Gothenburg Summit confirmed the 'road map' for enlargement set out at Nice and fixed the objective of completion of negotiations with the first applicant countries by the end of 2002 so that they could participate in the elections to the European Parliament of 2004. At the Copenhagen European Council of December 2002 the deadline of May 2004 was confirmed for 10 of the applicant countries, with 2007 being indicated as a possible date for the accession of Bulgaria and Romania. In a referendum on 24 April the Greek Cypriots voted against a UN proposal for settlement and, as a result, in May 2004 only the Greek Cypriot part of the island joined the EU.[7]

TRADE AND AID ARRANGEMENTS BETWEEN THE EU AND CEECS: THE 'FIRST GENERATION' TRADE AND CO-OPERATION AGREEMENTS

After a long history of stormy relations between the European Community and the Eastern integration bloc, the CMEA (Council for Mutual Economic Assistance), in June 1988 a Joint

---

[2] The Czech Republic, Estonia, Hungary, Poland and Slovenia.
[3] Bulgaria, Latvia, Lithuania, Romania, Slovakia and Malta.
[4] Conclusions of the European Council, Luxembourg, December 1997, where the decision to establish the European Conference was taken.
[5] See Annex 20.2 for a summary of the main events in EU–Turkish relations.
[6] The Berlin Agreement is discussed in Chapter 9 on the EU budget, though some aspects are taken up in the sections on the CAP and Structural Funds here.
[7] See Senior Nello (2004) and Annex 20.3 for a summary of the main events in EU–Cypriot relations.

Declaration of Mutual Recognition was signed.[8] This opened the way for tighter links between the EC and individual Central-East European countries.

In September 1988 Hungary signed a trade and co-operation agreement with the Community, and similar 'first generation agreements' with the other CEECs and the USSR soon followed. The agreements related to trade and to commercial and economic co-operation. The first generation agreements were soon overtaken by events, but remain important as a milestone in EC–CEEC relations.

WESTERN AID MEASURES TO ASSIST TRANSITION

The question of whether to aid transition was decided in July 1989 when, encouraged by President Bush, the EC Commission chaired a meeting of the then 24 OECD countries (the G–24) to seek ways of facilitating the process of moving towards democracy and market-orientated economies. Also involved in the programme were the EIB (European Investment Bank), the World Bank, the IMF and the OECD.

The main argument advanced in favour of giving aid to the CEECs and former Soviet Republics was Western self-interest. Despite the low levels of East–West trade at the end of the 1980s, and the difficulties of transition, the CMEA countries represented a potential market of some 450 million consumers. For generations the objective of ensuring Western security *vis-à-vis* the Eastern bloc had entailed huge defence budgets, and now a different type of effort was needed to further peace and prosperity. If transition failed, the West could risk experiencing external costs in the form of migratory pressures and/or spillover of ethnic and nationalistic tensions.

The term 'PHARE' (Economic Reconstruction Aid for Poland and Hungary) was adopted for the Community's programme, though this soon became something of a misnomer as aid was soon extended to the other CEECs. After a heated debate on possible political and economic consequences, assistance was also extended to the Soviet Union and, subsequently, to former Soviet Republics through the TACIS Programme (Technical Assistance for the Commonwealth of Independent States).

The PHARE Programme came into operation from 1990 and was initially demand-driven and based on the requests of the recipient countries (see Tables 20.2 and 20.3, and Figure 20.1). The measures included:

- Food aid to Poland, Romania, Bulgaria and the USSR;
- Agricultural assistance;
- Training and human resources;
- Energy and the environment;
- Improved market access;
- Assistance for privatization and restructuring (for small and medium enterprises, the financial system, technical assistance, investment guarantees etc.);
- Medical aid.

In addition loans were granted for stabilization and to cover balance-of-payments difficulties, and debt relief was extended to countries such as Poland and Bulgaria.

The European Bank for Reconstruction and Development (EBRD) was established in 1991 to

---

[8] Also known as the Comecon, the CMEA was founded in 1949 and formally dissolved in 1991. It was composed of the USSR, Bulgaria, Czechoslovakia, East Germany, Hungary, Poland, Romania, Cuba, Mongolia and Vietnam. Angola, Ethiopia, Laos and North Korea had observer status, while Yugoslavia only participated with regard to certain sectors. For a more detailed account of EC–CMEA relations up until 1988 and a description of the CMEA and its activities, see Senior Nello (1991).

1990	475.3
1991	769.7
1992	979.6
1993	966.1
1994	946.1
1995	1114.0
1996	1207.8
1997	1135.1
1998	1153.9
1999	1481.7
2000	1651.5
2001	1635.4
2001	1695.1

Table 20.2 Expenditure on PHARE 1990-2002 (million euros)

Source: European Commission (2003a).

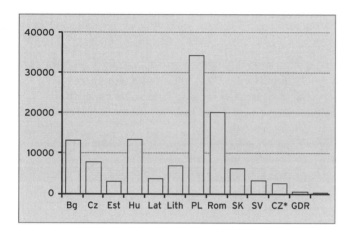

Figure 20.1 PHARE assistance to selected economies in transition, 1990-2002 (euros, millions)

*Czechoslovakia
Source: European Commission (2003a).

encourage investment in transition countries and reduce financial risks. From 1993 PHARE became more concerned with preparing CEECs for accession (with priority given to institution building, infrastructure, and promoting economic and social cohesion). Increasingly PHARE used the procedures of the Structural Funds in order to familiarize the CEECs so they could use the Structural Funds more efficiently upon accession.

One of the main mechanisms used in the task of institution building was 'twinning'. Twinning brings administrations and semi-public organizations in the EU and candidate countries together to work on common projects related to the *acquis*. Typically twinning involves secondment of civil servants from the EU member states working on Community policies to a candidate country for a certain period of time.

The 1999 Berlin Council established PHARE as one of the three pre-accession instruments for the 2000–06 period to help prepare the candidate countries for membership (see also Chapter 9). The three pre-accession instruments are:

■ PHARE, which has an allocation of €1.56 billion per year, 30 per cent of which is earmarked for institution building, 35 per cent is for the regulatory infrastructure required for implementation of the *acquis*, and 35 per cent for economic and social cohesion. The new CEEC member states will continue to receive PHARE for three years after 2004, and the programme might continue longer for Bulgaria and Romania.

■ ISPA (Instrument for Structural Policies Pre-Accession) is to receive €1.04 billion per year for assistance for the environment and transport infrastructure (see Table 20.3).

	PHARE	SAPARD	ISPA	Total
Bulgaria	185.3	54.1	106.8	346.2
Czech Rep.	86.6	22.9	66.9	176.4
Estonia	29.3	22.9	66.9	176.4
Hungary	109.9	39.5	90.8	240.2
Latvia	36.2	22.7	48.1	107.0
Lithuania	106.2	30.9	50.5	187.6
Poland	468.5	175.1	406.6	1050.2
Romania	289.1	156.3	245.6	691.0
Slovakia	80.5	19.0	48.1	147.6
Slovenia	28.5	6.6	16.0	51.1
Others *	221.1			
Total	1641.0	539.6	1109.3	3289.9

Table 20.3 PHARE, ISPA and SAPARD assistance to selected economies in transition, 2001 (euros, millions)

* Horizontal, regional and nuclear safety programmes
Source: European Commission (2003a), 'General Report on the pre-accession instruments (PHARE, ISPA, SAPARD) in 2001'.

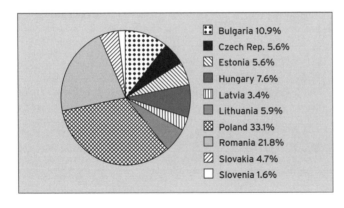

- Bulgaria 10.9%
- Czech Rep. 5.6%
- Estonia 5.6%
- Hungary 7.6%
- Latvia 3.4%
- Lithuania 5.9%
- Poland 33.1%
- Romania 21.8%
- Slovakia 4.7%
- Slovenia 1.6%

Figure 20.2 PHARE, ISPA and SAPARD assistance, 2001

Source: European Commission (2003a), 'General Report on the pre-accession instruments (PHARE, ISPA, SAPARD) in 2001'.

■ SAPARD, or the Special Accession Programme for Agriculture and Regional Development, has been allocated €0.52 billion per year. Measures include improving quality, applying veterinary and plant controls, setting up producer groups and creating land registers.

There was much debate about whether Western assistance to the transition countries could be construed as a new Marshall Plan. However, there were substantial differences from the Marshall Plan:[9]

■ Post-war reconstruction is very different from transition;
■ Most of Marshall Aid came from one donor, so the co-ordination problems were fewer;
■ The scale of financing, and the share of grants (80 per cent compared with 15 per cent, according to Mayhew, 1998) were higher under the Marshall Plan.

According to some observers,[10] the financial assistance under the Marshall Plan was probably less important than the conditionality imposed. In order to receive aid West European countries were encouraged to opt for market economies, liberalized trade and regional co-operation.

[9] As reported in Mayhew (1998).
[10] De Long and Eichengreen (1993).

Western measures to assist the transition process were also conditional. For instance PHARE aid to Romania was suspended on human rights grounds in 1990 and was not extended to Albania until 1991. However, as a growing literature demonstrates, it is the prospect of EU membership that ultimately renders the conditionality imposed on the CEECs effective.[11]

Regional co-operation was also a condition of EU assistance, and this was a major factor leading to the creation of arrangements such as the CEFTA (Central European Free Trade Area) in 1992[12] and the South East Co-operation Initiative of 1996.[13] However, a major shortcoming of these initiatives among transition countries was that they were generally more interested in co-operation with the EU than with each other.

Given the size and number of post-communist economies and the cost of transition, it was inevitable that the role played by external financial assistance would be relatively modest.[14] Much aid was in the form of loans, and much consisted of export credits, which also benefit Western firms. However, at times aid may arrive at a crucial, vulnerable time. The policy advice and training given was often criticized as being contradictory, inconsistent and not always tailored to the needs of the recipient country. Another complaint was that the main beneficiaries were often Western consultants. There was also criticism of the insufficient co-ordination and excessive bureaucracy in giving aid. With the benefit of hindsight, trade liberalization, FDI and the prospect of EU membership were probably more important catalysts in encouraging transition.

THE 'SECOND GENERATION' EUROPE AGREEMENTS

Between 1991 and 1996 the EU signed second generation 'Europe Agreements' with 10 CEECs deemed to have made sufficient progress in economic and political transition (these were the same 10 that were subsequently the first to start accession negotiations).[15] The Europe Agreements were the basic legal instruments covering the relationship between the EU and the CEEC(10).[16] The Agreements covered trade-related issues, political dialogue, legal approximation, 'phased introduction' of the four freedoms (though the EC failed to grant any access to workers beyond what was guaranteed by its member state) and co-operation in other areas, including industry, environment, transport and customs (Mayhew, 1998).

The Europe Agreements created a free trade area between the EU and associated CEECs. Because the CEEC partners needed more time to become competitive, the tariff cuts were asymmetric, with the Community proceeding more rapidly. The removal of tariffs on certain sensitive sectors such as steel and textiles and clothing was to be phased over several years, but by 1998 most restrictions on industrial products had been removed.[17] The concessions granted on agricultural trade were less favourable than in other sectors, and it was only in 2003 that agricultural trade with the new member states was liberalized for products meeting EU standards.[18]

As a result of the provisions of the Europe Agreements, a free trade area in manufactured products was in place before enlargement. For the CEECs, joining the EU means moving from a

---

[11] Grabbe (2002), Smith (2001), Vachudova (2001), and Smith (2003).
[12] CEFTA is composed of the Czech Republic, Hungary Poland and Slovakia; Bulgaria, Romania and Slovenia subsequently joined.
[13] This was composed of Albania, Bosnia & Herzegovina, Bulgaria, FYR of Macedonia, Hungary, Romania, Moldova and Turkey, with Croatia as an observer.
[14] However, the EU and IFIs have played an important role in attracting additional financing from official sources, including debt relief through the Paris Club. They have been rather less successful in attracting complementary private financing or private (London Club) debt relief.
[15] From 1992 negotiation began leading to the signing of less far-reaching 'trade and partnership' agreements with various former Soviet Republics, including Russia, Belarus, Ukraine, Kazakhstan, Georgia and Kyrgyzstan (see Chapter 18).
[16] See Senior Nello (1991) for a more detailed description of these agreements.
[17] See Mayhew (1998) or Senior Nello (2002a) for descriptions of the timing of trade liberalization for various groups of products.
[18] See Senior Nello (2002b) for a description of the agricultural concessions.

free trade area to a customs union (by adopting the Common Commercial Policy with its 'hierarchy' of trade preferences) and the Single Market.[19]

TRADE AND INVESTMENT IN THE CEECS

What is significant about the level of trade between the EU and CEECs is the speed of its reorientation from Eastern to Western markets, as shown in Table 20.4. The redirection of Czech and Slovak trade towards the EU was less than in other CEECs such as Hungary or Poland because when the two countries split, what had been internal trade became trade between two transition economies. The redirection of trade to the EU was also relatively low for Lithuania,[20] but this is largely due to the continuing importance of transit trade from Russia, in particular of mineral fuels and oils.

Table 20.4 The increase EU(15)–CEEC(10) trade over the 1989-2002 period

	Exports to EU as % all exports, 1989	Exports to EU as % all exports, 2002	Imports to EU as % all imports	Imports to EU as % all imports, 2002	Trade balance with EU (million euros) 2002
Bulgaria	5.5% (EC) 1.5% (EFTA)	55.6 (EFTA)	10.8% (EC) 3.9%	50.2	-606
Czech Republic and Slovakia	Czechoslovakia 18.2 (EC)# 4.6 (Austria) 6.6 (GDR)	68.4 (Czech Rep.) 60.5 (Slovakia)	Czechoslovakia 17.8 (EC)# 5.5 (Austria) 7.8 (GDR)	60.2 (Czech Rep.) 50.3 (Slovakia)	-1673 (Czech Rep.) +982 (Slovakia)
Estonia	n.a.	68.0	n.a.	57.9	847
Hungary	24.8 (EC)# 6.4% Austria 5.4% GDR	75.1	29 (EC)# 8.6% (Austria) 6.2% (GDR)	56.3	+68
Latvia	n.a.	60.4	N/a	53.0	620
Lithuania	n.a.	48.4	N/a	44.5	-1290
Poland	31.8 (EC)# 1.5 (EFTA)	68.7	34.2 (EC)# 3.9 (EFTA)	61.7	-9156
Romania	28.5 (EC) 3.2 (EFTA)	67.1	13.8 (EC) 1.3 (EFTA)	58.4	-1003
Slovenia	n.a.	59.4	n.a.	68.0	-1806

Source: Own elaboration based on Eurostat data. n.a. = not available

The rapid switch in trade patterns was reinforced by the difficulties experienced in most former Soviet Republics following the dismantling of the USSR. Over time the pattern of trade growth with the EU also appears to have reflected the evolution of real exchange rates[21] and cyclical changes in Western import demand, but it seems likely that EU trade concessions played an important role.

---

[19] In contrast, many empirical studies of integration effects are based on the assumption of a move from free trade to a customs union (see Chapter 5).
[20] The other main Lithuanian trade partners were Russia, the Ukraine, Belarus and Latvia.
[21] Halpern and Wyplosz (1995).

The incomplete liberalization of agricultural trade until 2003 was subject to particularly severe criticism, especially with the transformation of an EU agricultural trade deficit into a surplus from 1993.[22] The EU had a deficit in trade in agricultural products with the CEEC(10) of €1 billion in 1988, but a surplus of €1.5 billion in 2000 (see Figure 20.3).[23]

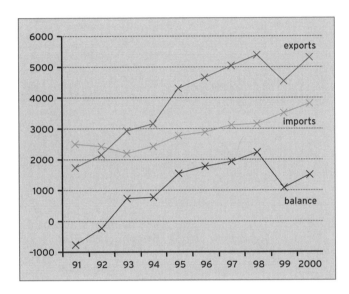

Figure 20.3 EU-CEEC agricultural trade

Source: Elaboration based on Eurostat data.

Early studies found that the composition of CEEC trade was changing relatively slowly.[24] Subsequently, the countries most advanced in transition, and, in particular Hungary and the Czech Republic, succeeded in gradually moving to a larger share of higher-skilled, higher-technology products in exports.[25] The turn-around for these countries came in 1993/4 with the end of transitional recession and the beginning of positive economic growth. The exports were generally produced in firms that were either newly established or restructured, and firms that had not modernized often had problems in maintaining their share in foreign markets. Outsourcing[26] and foreign direct investment (see Table 20.5 and Figures 20.4 and 20.5) played an important role in helping the CEECs to adjust the structure of their exports. In 1999 the EU(15) accounted for 73 per cent of all foreign direct investment in the CEEC (10).[27]

However, despite the rapid increase in exports of more skilled human-capital-intensive, technology-intensive products, even in countries such as Hungary and the Czech Republic the largest share of exports remained in 'traditional' so-called sensitive sectors. The sensitive sectors are generally defined as: agriculture, textiles, clothing, coal, footwear, steel and chemicals.[28] Eichengreen and Kohl (1998) found that if agriculture is excluded,[29] the share of sensitive sectors in the exports of

---

[22] See Tarditi, et al. (1995) for a criticism of the agricultural provisions of the Europe Agreements.

[23] Eurostat statistics.

[24] Such as Drábek and Smith (1995); EC Commission (1994) and Faini and Portes (1995).

[25] See for example, World Bank (1999a and b), or Kaminski (2000).

[26] Outsourcing, or outward processing trade (OPT), is the international fragmentation of production. It entails previously integrated production activities being segmented and spread over an international network of production sites. OPT is a kind of subcontracting whereby exports of semi-finished products or components flow from the main contractor's country and, after some processing, imports of more elaborate intermediate or final products return to the main contractor's country.

[27] European Commission (2003b).

[28] The large share of EU anti-dumping measures in this sector justifies the inclusion of chemicals among the sensitive sectors, but not all authors accept it. For instance in CEPR (1992) chemicals are not included in the list of sensitive sectors.

[29] The exception of agriculture is largely to be explained by continuing EU protectionism, the disruption associated with transition (and, in particular, privatization), but difficulties in meeting the requirements of the EU market with regard to standards and quality requirements also played a role.

	a) Flows 2003 $ million	b) Total Stock 2003 $ million	Inward stocks % GDP (2003)
Bulgaria	1419	5082	29.1
Czech Rep.	2583	41033	48.0
Estonia	891	6511	77.6
Hungary	2470	42915	51.8
Latvia	360	3320	35.1
Lithuania	179	4960	27.2
Poland	4225	52125	24.9
Romania	1566	12693	23.4
Slovakia	571	10248	31.5
Slovenia	181	4290	15.6

Table 20.5 Foreign direct investment in 2003

Source: World Investment Report 2004 www.UNCTAD.org

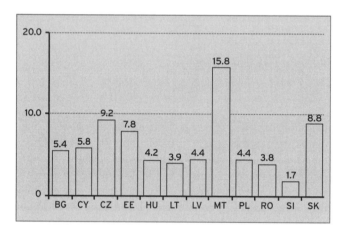

Figure 20.4 FDI in the new member states as a percentage of GDP (average 1999-2001)

Source: European Commission (2004a).

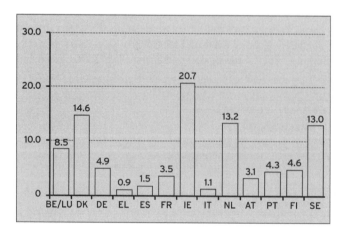

Figure 20.5 FDI in the EU(15) as a percentage of GDP (average 1999-2001)

Source: European Commission (2004a).

the CEEC(6) actually increased over the 1988–96 period.[30] According to Eichengreen and Kohl (1998), the duality in export composition (with the presence of both traditional, sensitive sectors and fast-growing new products) was even more pronounced in Poland, Slovakia and Romania.[31] These findings were confirmed by a more recent study by De Benedictis and Tajoli (2004), as can be seen from Table 20.6.

Despite the increase in machinery exports, the exports of the Baltic States are still dominated by wood and wood products, textiles and clothing, chemicals and base metals, and transit trade of mineral fuels and oils.[32]

	Increased share in exports	Reduced share in exports
Poland	furniture auto vehicles electrical machinery machinery iron articles paper	copper, iron apparel, glues fuels, seeds fruit, vegetables fish, meat, animals
Hungary	auto vehicles electrical machinery machinery	iron, footwear apparel organic chemicals fuels, vegetables plants, fish meat, animals
Romania	electrical machinery, machinery footwear apparel fuels	furniture aluminium
Bulgaria	copper iron footwear apparel	electrical machinery, machinery organic chemicals inorganic chemicals tobacco beverages seeds, dairy fish, meat animals

Table 20.6 Sectors whose share in CEEC exports increased over the 1989-2002 period

Source: De Benedictis and Tajoli (2004).

EU POLICY TOWARDS SOUTH-EASTERN EUROPE

South-Eastern Europe (SEE) is generally taken to refer to the five Western Balkan countries: Albania, Bosnia/Herzegovina, Croatia, FYR Macedonia and Serbia-Montenegro, though Bulgaria and Romania are also included in certain initiatives.

The poor long-term economic performance of SEE has been compounded by the series of wars that resulted from the disintegration of Yugoslavia. The instability in SEE also imposes costs on the EU in terms of military intervention, migration, trade disruption, ecological damage and the need for humanitarian and other aid. Between 1991 and 1999 EU assistance (including EBRD

---

[30] The study covers: Bulgaria, the Czech Republic, Hungary, Poland, Romania and Slovakia.
[31] According to Eichengreen and Kohl (1998) Bulgarian exports continued to fall mainly into this latter category.
[32] See Pautola (1999) and Kaitila and Widgrén (2001) for detailed analyses of trade between the EU and Baltic States.

measures) to the five Western Balkan countries amounted to €8.2 billion, of which roughly half was humanitarian aid (Uvalic, 2002).

Initially the EU underestimated the political problems arising from the collapse of Yugoslavia and failed to develop a long-term strategy towards the area, relying instead on *ad hoc* measures and 'day after' actions. It was only after the Dayton Peace Agreement of 1995 that the EU began to evolve a regional approach to SEE. In 1995 the EU launched the Royaumont Process aimed at promoting stability and good neighbourly relations in SEE. In 1996 the Regional Approach of the EU was introduced, but it was not well defined, had limited financial resources, arrived late, and failed to offer the SEE counties any incentive for compliance.

In 1999 the EU attempted to bring an end to its crisis-by-crisis approach by introducing the Stability Pact, which aimed at fostering peace, democracy, human rights and economic prosperity as a means of bringing stability to the region. Importantly, the EU attempted to reinforce its leverage in SEE by offering the prospect of eventual EU membership. The EU insisted that its approach would be differentiated according with the compliance of a country to the relevant conditions, including increased emphasis on regional co-operation. Central to the approach was the Stabilization and Association process that offered eligible West Balkan countries the possibility of signing Stabilization and Association Agreements. By 2004 Agreements had been signed with Croatia and Macedonia, and Albania was negotiating an Agreement. In April 2004 the European Commission published an Opinion favourable to opening negotiations for membership with Croatia. Macedonia also applied for membership.

The Thessaloniki European Council and the Summit between the EU and Balkan countries of 2003 set out the 'Thessaloniki Approach', which entailed extending some of the more successful instruments of the pre-accession process to the SEE countries. In particular, European Partnerships were introduced to set out the short- and medium-term priorities these countries need to address. As progress was achieved, these Partnerships would be increasingly geared to the task of taking on the *acquis*. Over the 2000–06 period EU assistance for SEE was to be provided mainly through the CARDS (Community Assistance for Reconstruction, Development and Stabilization), and about €5 billion was earmarked for this purpose.

THE COPENHAGEN CRITERIA

In 1993 the Copenhagen European Council agreed that 'accession will take place as soon as the applicant country is able to assume the obligations of membership by satisfying the economic and political conditions required'. The conditions for accession are:

- The applicant state must have a functioning market economy with the capacity to cope with competitive pressures and market forces within the Community;
- The applicant state must have achieved stability of institutions, guaranteeing democracy, the rule of law, human rights and respect for and protection of minorities;
- The applicant state must be able to take on the obligations of membership, including adherence to the aims of political and economic and monetary union.

At the Copenhagen Summit it was also stipulated that enlargement is subject to the condition that the EU is able to absorb new members and maintain the momentum of integration.

The criteria are generally divided into political criteria, economic criteria, and ability to take on the *acquis communautaire* and to establish the administrative and judicial capacity to ensure its effective implementation.

There are three political criteria:

■ Stability of institutions guaranteeing democracy, the rule of law, human rights and respect for and protection of minorities;

■ Adherence to the objective of political union; and

■ Maintaining the momentum of integration.

The economic criteria are similarly divided into three:

■ The existence of a functioning market economy;

■ Capacity to cope with competitive pressures and market forces within the Community; and

■ Adherence to the aim of economic and monetary union.

The accession criteria are presumably intended to provide some kind of objective basis for selecting those CEECs ready to join the EU, as well as indicating to the applicant countries the tasks they are expected to perform. The introduction of the Copenhagen criteria would therefore seem aimed at replicating the experience of the Maastricht criteria but in a different field, that of enlargement.

However, although there is a certain flexibility and political leeway in deciding whether the Maastricht criteria have been met, this is far more the case for the accession criteria. This arises from the number of criteria and, in some cases, from the vague and imprecise nature of the concepts involved. This is the case, for instance, in deciding whether a country has a 'a functioning market economy' or the 'capacity to cope with competitive pressures'. There are different models of market economies, and no indication is given as to which model is appropriate, or how to assess when the CEEC has 'arrived'.

In deciding whether the CEECs are ready to cope with competitive pressures in an enlarged EU, a detailed analysis of their economies is necessary, together with predictions about which sectors will be able to cope in the internal EU market. The International Institute for Management Development in Switzerland (IMD) carries out annual studies of competitiveness in 59 countries (see Table 20.7). Just how complicated the task is can be seen from the fact that the IMD takes into account more than 300 variables. These reflect current economic performance, business surveys and factors such as infrastructure and innovation.

For other criteria, such as the obligation to take on the objective of political union, or the requirement that the momentum of integration can be maintained (which presumably requires some form of enhanced co-operation or flexibility, see Chapter 3) the objective in question has yet to be defined fully.

Overall ranking		EU rankings		EU rankings	
country	rank	country	rank	country	rank
USA	1	Denmark	7	France	30
Singapore	2	Finland	8	Spain	31
Canada	3	Luxembourg	9	Portugal	39
Australia	4	Ireland	10	Slovak Republic	40
Iceland	5	Sweden	11	Hungary	42
Hong Kong	6	Austria	13	Czech Republic	43
Denmark	7	Netherlands	15	Greece	44
Finland	8	Germany	21	Slovenia	45
Luxembourg	9	UK	22	Italy	51
Ireland	10	Belgium	25	Romania	54
		Estonia	28	Poland	57

Table 20.7 World competitiveness in 2004: overall scoreboards

Source: International Institute for Management Development (IMD).

The simple rule 'when a CEEC meets the accession criteria, it can join the EU' is misleading given the degree of discretion in deciding whether the accession criteria have been met. In the end choice of who joins when becomes a political issue. Poland could not be left out of a first wave without undermining the image of 'reunifiying Europe', and the ratification process and institutional changes in EU decision-making suggested that there would be less disruption admitting a larger group simultaneously.

Though at the time of the Copenhagen European Council no indication was given with regard to the weights of the different criteria, subsequently the European Commission indicated that predominance was to be given to the political criteria, so a country must fulfil these before joining and must be making substantial progress towards meeting the economic criteria. Agenda 2000 stresses that 'the effective functioning of democracy is a primordial question in assessing the application of a country for membership of the Union'.[33]

Political criteria were also introduced into the Amsterdam Treaty and Article 6 states: 'the Union is founded on the principles of liberty, democracy, respect for human rights and fundamental freedoms, and the rule of law, principles which are common to the member states'. According to Article 49, any country that respects these principles may apply to become a member of the Union. The 1999 Helsinki European Council again stressed that democracy is the requisite for beginning negotiations on EU membership.

At the 1997 Luxembourg European Council Slovakia was not considered to meet the accession criteria on political grounds. Following the electoral defeat of Meciar in September 1998, this decision was reversed, and the Helsinki European Council decided that Slovakia was sufficiently advanced in both economic and political transition for accession negotiations to begin. It is mainly on the basis of the political criteria that the European Commission expresses misgivings about Turkey (see Appendix 2).

Treatment of minorities has also been a sensitive question in accession negotiations. There are large Hungarian minorities in Romania and Slovakia, a Slovak minority in Hungary, substantial Russian minorities in Estonia and Latvia, a Turk minority in Bulgaria and a large Roma population in countries such as Romania, Bulgaria, Slovakia, the Czech Republic and Hungary (see Box 20.1).

Box 20.1 Ethnic minorities in Central and Eastern Europe

Hungarians in Romania
Estimated 1.6–2 million (about 8% of the population).
Hungarians in Slovakia
Estimated 600 000 (about 11% of the population).
Slovakians in Hungary
Estimated 100 000

Russians in Latvia
Estimated roughly 43% of the population
Russians in Estonia
Estimated 28% of the population

---

[33] Agenda 2000, p. 40. The experience of sanctions on Austria following the inclusion of Haider in the governing coalition in early 2000 suggests that in the future political issues will become predominant.

> Roma
> Estimated 1–1.5 million in Romania
> 400 000–600 000 in Hungary
> Officially 1.6% of the population in Slovakia (unofficially 4–10% of the population;
> 5% in Bulgaria
>
> **Turkish Minority in Bulgaria (10% of the population or 800 000).**
> Sources: Vachudova (2000); European Commission, www.europa.eu/comm.

Also in this context the European Commission has emphasized the need for regional co-operation and good neighbourly relations before accession,[34] and the applicant countries have generally taken this condition seriously. Agenda 2000 maintained that outstanding border disputes between applicant countries should be referred to the International Court of Justice. In 1992, for example, the Czech Republic and Slovakia were careful to ensure their break-up was peaceful. In 1993 Hungary and Slovakia agreed to refer a dispute over the Gabcikovo dam on the Danube to the International Court of Justice.

In the context of the 1994–95 Pact for Stability (which was one of the first joint CFSP actions) the EU co-ordinated a multilateral framework in which the CEECs were encouraged to conclude agreements with each other on borders and treatment of minorities, as well as to use regional round tables to agree cross-border co-operation projects (with EU financial support). Agreements followed between Hungary and Slovakia (1995), and Hungary and Romania (1996) regardless of opposition in all three countries.

Despite the Commission's insistence on being good neighbours, tensions among the accession countries have at times run high, as, for instance, over the call by Austria and Hungary for repeal of the Czechoslovak Benes decrees under which some 2.5 million Germans and 30 000 Hungarians were deported at the end of the Second World War.[35]

THE PRE-ACCESSION STRATEGY

The Essen European Council of 1994 set out a pre-accession strategy to help the candidate countries prepare for EU membership. An enhanced pre-accession strategy was launched at the 1997 Luxembourg European Council and was set in motion in 1998. In addition to the Europe Agreements and pre-accession assistance (through PHARE, ISPA and SAPARD), the enhanced strategy includes Accession Partnerships and National Programmes for the Adoption of the *Acquis* (NPAA), the opening of Community programmes and agencies, and a review procedure.

The Accession Partnerships set out the main priorities for each of the candidate countries in preparing for EU membership and provide a single framework for coordinating the various forms of EU assistance. Each of the candidate countries drew up a NPAA that indicated in detail how the country aimed to meet the priorities of the Accession Partnership. In 2002 the Commission also prepared Action Plans with the 12 countries with whom negotiations were underway to reinforce their administrative and judicial capacity.

The opening of Community programmes and agencies was aimed at promoting co-operation between the member states and applicant countries in areas such as public health, the environment,

---

[34] See Smith (2003) for a more detailed discussion of this point.
[35] See, for example, the *Financial Times*, 3 April 2002.

energy, research, small and medium enterprises, culture, vocational training and support for student and youth exchanges (such as Socrates). In this way it was hoped that the new member states could be familiarized with the way in which EU policies and instruments are put into practice.

Following the Opinions of the applications of the candidate countries for accession, each year in order to assess progress in preparing for membership the Commission submitted Regular Reports to the Council. The Regular Reports on each applicant country were generally published in October/November, together with a Composite or Strategy Paper. While useful as a source of information, often the style of these publications was not far removed from school reports, though the comments 'could try harder', or 'could do better' were usually expressed in slightly more diplomatic terms.

THE ACCESSION NEGOTIATIONS

A first step in preparing for the accession negotiations was the 'screening' of the *acquis*. It began in March 1998 with all the accession countries, whether negotiations had been opened or not. The purpose of the exercise was to identify issues likely to arise in the negotiations. It consists of a detailed presentation by Commission experts on the application of the 31 chapters of the *acquis* (see Table 20.8) to the applicant countries. The first chapters of the *acquis* opened in the screening process were the least controversial and included Chapters 15–19 (see Table 20.8), Consumers and Health Protection (Chapter 23) and Statistics (Chapter 12).

Though the Commission stressed that political criteria remained primordial, the 'screening' of the applicant countries to assess their progress in taking on the 'obligations of membership' encouraged a shift of emphasis away from the other Copenhagen criteria. The speed and progress of accession negotiations appeared to depend heavily on the ability of a country to adopt and implement the *acquis*. According to the Commission, the administrative and judicial capacity of a country were also key factors in implementing the *acquis*.

Following the screening process, negotiations were opened with the candidate countries, chapter by chapter. A chapter was considered 'provisionally closed' with a candidate country when the EU considered that further negotiation was not required on the chapter, and the candidate concerned

Table 20.8 Chapters of the *acquis*

1. Free movement of goods	19. Telecommunications and information technologies
2. Freedom of movement for persons	20. Culture and audio-visual policy
3. Freedom to provide services	21. Regional policy and co-ordination of structural instruments
4. Free movement of capital	
5. Company law	
6. Competition policy	22. Environment
7. Agriculture	23. Consumers and health protection
8. Fisheries	
9. Transport policy	24. Co-operation in the fields of justice and home affairs
10. Taxation	
11. Economic and monetary union	25. Customs union
	26. External relations
12. Statistics	27. Common foreign and security policy
13. Social policy and employment	
14. Energy	28. Financial control
15. Industrial policy	29. Financial and budgetary provisions
16. Small and medium-sized enterprises	
17. Science and research	30. Institutions
18. Education and training	31. Other

accepted the EU common position. The EU reserved the right to return to the chapter at a later stage during the negotiation if new *acquis* were adopted, or if the candidate country concerned failed to implement the commitments it had taken on the chapter. As a result, though chapters could be 'provisionally closed', the Commission's negotiating stance was based on the principle that 'nothing is agreed until everything is agreed' and that a final overall compromise deal was necessary to conclude negotiations.

For the areas linked to the functioning of the Single Market, according to the Commission, any transition periods were to be few and short (though there were exceptions to this general rule as, for instance, the derogation on movement of people requested by existing member states). For areas where considerable adaptations were necessary, and which required substantial effort (including large monetary outlays) such as the environment, energy and infrastructure, transition periods involving 'temporary derogations' were to be granted, but in some areas (nuclear safety, the fight against crime) the new members were expected to go 'beyond the *acquis*'.

The new member states criticized the Commission's attitude to the adoption of the *acquis* on a number of counts:

- The asymmetry of treatment compared with present EU members (e.g. the Nice Treaty does not require respect for minorities, while the Copenhagen criteria do);
- The CEECs were given little opportunity to voice objections to the conditions, and their preferences seemed to be marginalized at times (while the EU(15) have on occasion challenged the overriding nature of the *acquis*);
- Taking on the *acquis* does not always further transition;
- The *acquis* is constantly evolving;
- The insistence on taking on all the *acquis* might divert attention from the need for a hierarchy of priorities.

EXTENDING THE CAP TO THE NEW MEMBERS

Agriculture frequently threatened to prove a stumbling block in the enlargement process. As shown in Table 20.9, agriculture continues to play an important role in many of the CEECs. The numbers employed in agriculture in the EU will increase from about 7 to 11 million, raising the share in employment from 4 per cent to 5.5 per cent, which would become 7.5 per cent with Bulgaria and Romania. At the same time, the CAP continues to absorb just under half of the Community budget, while food and agricultural measures account for roughly half the *acquis communautaire*. The applicant countries have the complex task of adapting to EU policies and standards, while the EU wanted to ensure that enlargement does not result in excessive transfers from the Community budget.

As described in Chapter 10, the 1992 MacSharry Reform, the 1999 Berlin Agreement and the June 2003 reform entailed cuts in support prices for some of the main Community products. The impact of these price cuts for farmers in the EU(15) was (more or less, see Chapter 10) offset by direct income payments. By 2002 direct aids accounted for roughly 60 per cent of the CAP budget.

There was considerable debate about extending direct income payments to farmers in countries joining the EU. At least initially, such payments were introduced as compensation for the reductions in price support. At first the Commission argued that farmers in applicant countries would not generally experience price cuts and so should not benefit from direct payments.[36]

---

[36] See, for example, the Agricultural Strategy Paper (Commission of the European Communities, 1995), and Agenda 2000 (Commission of the European Communities, 1997).

Table 20.9 Basic data on agriculture in the new member states and selected candidate countries

	Land area (m. ha) 2001	Gross value added in ag. € billion 2000	Agriculture as % gross value added 2002	Agriculture employment (1000s) 2000	Ag. as % total employment 2002	Food expenditures % income 1999
Bulgaria	5.5	1.6	12.5	342[b]	10.7	54[a]
Czech Rep.	4.3	1.9	3.7	193	4.9	32
Slovakia	2.4	0.8	4.5	119	6.6	32
Hungary	5.9	1.8	4.3[d]	227	6.0	42[a]
Poland	18.4	5.0	3.1	2698	19.6	30
Romania	14.8	4.6	13.0	4861[b]	37.7	58
Slovenia	0.5	0.6	3.3[d]	81	9.7	24
Estonia	1.0	0.3	5.4	32	6.5	36
Latvia	2.5	0.3	4.7	118	15.3	39
Lithuania	3.5	0.8	7.1	262	18.6	40
CEEC(10)	58.8	17.8	5.1[c]	8933	21.4[c]	37
Cyprus	.1[c]	0.3[b]	4.3	14[b]	5.3	19
Malta	.01	0.08	2.8	3	2.3	
EU(15)	130.0	167.5	2.0[c]	7129	4.3[c]	17

[a]= 1998, [b]=1999, [c]= 2000, [d]=2001
Source: European Commission www.europa.eu.int/comm/enlargement.

According to the European Commission, prices for most agricultural products were below EU levels,[37] and it was argued that farmers in the CEECs would receive the benefit of higher prices when they joined the EU, so compensation in the form of direct payments was superfluous. However, this argument was somewhat undermined by rapid price increases for agricultural products in the CEECs.[38] The proposed differential treatment between 'rich' Western farmers and their poorer counterparts in the CEECs was subject to fierce criticism in those countries.

In March 2002 the Commission published an extensive study of the impact of enlargement on agricultural markets and incomes,[39] confirming the view that immediate payment of 100 per cent direct payments on accession of the CEECs would lead to social distortions and inequalities. Moreover there would be non-rural beneficiaries who had generally become landowners as a result of the privatization process that included restitution in most CEECs. The report took into account four different policy scenarios:

- No enlargement;
- Application of the 1999 CAP without direct payments;
- Introduction of the CAP with full, immediate direct payments; and
- Acceptance of the candidate countries' negotiating positions.

The working assumption of the analysis was accession of eight CEEC candidates from 2007.[40] According to the Commission report, even without direct payments the CEEC farmers would benefit on average from a 30 per cent increase in income as a result of EU market support. With the scenario of full application of direct payments in the new member states, the average expected income gain tripled, reaching a level of 89 per cent, while assuming that the applicant countries'

[37] The European Commission (1995) maintained that, depending on the product, CEEC prices were between 40 and 80 per cent of EU levels.
[38] According to *Euro-East*, No. 90, July 2000, p.6, grain prices in Slovenia were 70–80 per cent higher than in the EU, and Polish beef prices were well above EU averages.
[39] EC Commission (2002).
[40] It was assumed Bulgaria and Romania would join later.

negotiating positions were accepted, the predicted gain quadrupled to reach an estimated 123 per cent.

At the Copenhagen European Council of December 2002 it was agreed that direct aids for the new member states would be phased out gradually in over 10 years. These countries would receive direct payments equivalent to 25 per cent of the present system in 2004, 30 per cent in 2005 and 35 per cent in 2006, rising to 100 per cent only in 2013. The new member states were offered the possibility of topping up direct payments through national funds and their rural development funds to 55 per cent in 2004, 60 per cent in 2005 and 65 per cent in 2006.

In order to meet problems of administrative costs and fraud, the new member states could opt for simplified system of direct payments for three years, renewable for up to two more years.[41] This would entail area payments per hectare on the whole of the agricultural area of the applicant countries. There would be no obligation for farmers to produce in order to receive these payments, and so the direct aids would be 'decoupled' from the level of production.[42]

Difficulties also arose in deciding on production quotas for milk and sugar (see Chapter 10) for the new member states. The EC Commission proposed taking 1995–99 as the reference period, but this was contested by some of the CEECs as not being representative. For instance, since milk production fell during these years due to the process of restructuring, countries such as Poland and the Czech Republic argued in favour of a quota based on production in the 1980s or some estimate of 'productive potential'. The Copenhagen European Council agreed on production quotas on the basis of 'the most recent historical reference periods for which data is available', though in fact some concessions were granted.

A further sensitive issue was whether the CEECs would be allowed a derogation on land ownership. Land prices are much lower in the CEECs, and though a general derogation of seven years, with the option of extending the derogation for a further three years, was eventually agreed (12 years for Poland), the initial requests were higher (18 years in the case of Poland).[43]

THE STRUCTURAL FUNDS

As Table 20.10 illustrates, in earlier enlargements the addition to the population and GDP of the EU were roughly in line. Although they have been growing faster than the EU(15) since the mid-1990s, Table 20.11 shows that in all the CEECs the per capita income in terms of purchasing power parity (PPP) is well below the EU average.[44] With enlargement the gap between the most and the least prosperous member states will widen.

The Third Report on Economic and Social Cohesion (European Commission, 2004a) divides the countries in an enlarged EU into three groups according to GDP per head in PPP terms. For the first group, consisting of 12 of the present 15 member states, GDP per head is well above the EU(25) average (10 per cent or more). In the second group of seven countries (Spain, Portugal, Greece, Cyprus, the Czech Republic, Slovenia and Malta) GDP per capita is between 68 per cent and 94 per cent of the EU(25) average. In the third group, which comprises the other new member states and Bulgaria and Romania, GDP per capita is less than 60 per cent of the EU(25) average.

Despite the rapid growth of the CEECs, it appears likely that it will take some years to eliminate the income disparity compared with existing EU member states. Baldwin (1994) estimated that

---

[41] The need for a simplified system arose because the EU applies 30 types of direct payment, and six for beef alone. The various types of direct payments are listed in an Annex to Council Regulation No. 1259/1999.

[42] As explained in Chapter 17, this has important implications for GATT/WTO commitments.

[43] The general derogation applies to the three Baltic states, the Czech Republic, Hungary and Slovakia.

[44] It is essential to bear in mind the limitations of comparisons of this type. All the CEECs have rapidly growing private sectors, part of which fails to show up in official statistics, though it must be recalled that most EU economies also have substantial 'informal' sectors.

with 5 per cent growth, the catch-up period ranges from eight years for Slovenia to 22 years for Poland and 26 years for Slovakia. A later study by the European Integration Consortium suggested an average period of 30 years to catch up, with Slovenia possibly requiring only 10 years.[45]

The EU(15) stand to gain from the catching-up process of the CEECs, given their high dependency on imports (over half of GDP). About 60 per cent of these imports come from the EU, of which about 25 per cent from Germany and 10 per cent from Italy.[46]

Year	New entrants	Increase in population	Increase in GDP
1973	From 6 to 9 Denmark, Ireland, UK	+33.4%	+32.4%
1981	From 9 to 10 Greece	+3.7%	+2.8%
1986	From 10 to 12 Spain and Portugal	+17.7%	+11.6%
1995	From 12 to 15 Austria, Finland, Sweden	+6.2%	+6.3%
2004	Accession of 10 new member states May 2004	+20%	+5%
2007?	Romania and Bulgaria	+8%	+1%

Table 20.10 The impact of successive enlargements of the EU

Source: *Le Cacheux* (1996) for enlargements until 1995; European Commission (2004a) for subsequent enlargements.

Table 20.11 Extending the Structural Funds to the CEECs

	Population 2002	GDP € billions PPP 2002	GDP per capita at PPP (% EU average, 2002)	Average GDP growth 1995–2000	Growth in 2002	Unemployment % labour force 2002
Bulgaria	7.9	47.4	25	-1.7	4.8	18.1
Cyprus	0.8	14.0	72			3.8
Czech Rep.	10.2	146.9	60	0.6	2.0	7.3
Estonia	1.4	13.5	42	4.3	6.0	9.1
Hungary	10.2	138.2	57	4.0	3.3	5.6
Latvia	2.4	19.9	35	3.7	6.1	12.8
Lithuania	3.5	34.3	39	2.7	6.7	13.1
Malta	0.4	4.6	55		1.2	7.4
Poland	38.6	363.0	39	5.4	1.6	19.9
Romania	21.8	128.9	25	-2.2	4.9	7.0
Slovakia	5.4	61.3	47	4.2	4.4	18.6
Slovenia	2.0	35.3	74	4.0	3.2	6.0
Acceding 10	74.3	831.0				
EU(15) total/ average	378.7	9166.5	100	4.0		

Source: EC Commission: www.europa.eu.int/comm/enlargement.

[45] Boeri and Brücker (2000).
[46] European Commission (2004a).

Enlargement will also increase income disparities between regions in an enlarged EU. Between 1999 and 2001 some 19 per cent of the population of the the EU(15), or 73 million, live in Objective 1 regions, where income per capita is less than 75 per cent of the EU average. It is estimated that some 69 million of the 74.5 million in the 10 new member states, or 92 per cent of the total, live in regions where the GDP per capita is less that 75 per cent of the average in EU(25).[47]

The average GDP per capita will be reduced with the increase in the number of member states from 15 to 25 (see Table 20.12). As a result, if the criterion for Objective 1 remains unchanged, some regions that now qualify for Objective 1 status will no longer do so in an enlarged EU. This is the case for four regions in Eastern Germany, four in the UK, four in Spain, one in Greece and one in Portugal.[48] It is estimated that some 19 million people in the EU(15) live in such regions.

Table 20.12 The statistical effect in Objective 1 regions (based on GDP per capita in PPP, average 1999-2001)

	For EU(15) in EU(15)	For EU(15) in EU(25)	In 10 new member states in EU(25)	In EU(25) in EU(25)
Number of regions falling below 75% of average GDP/head	50	33	36	69
Population in those regions (millions)	73	54	69	123
Population as % of EU(15) for 10 new states	19.2	14.2	92.4	
Population as % of EU(25)		11.9	15.2	27.1
Average GDP/head PPP of those regions as % of EU(15)/EU(25) average	65.1	69.3	46.0	56.2

Source: European Commission (2004a).

In 2004 Michel Barnier, the commissioner responsible for regional affairs, suggested splitting the 2007–13 expenditure on the Structural Funds so that half goes to the new member states and half remains for the poorer existing member states. Barnier proposed transitional assistance to poorer regions in existing member states who would otherwise lose their rights to assistance.

With enlargement employment disparities between regions in the EU will also increase. Unemployment is generally higher in the CEECs than the existing member states (see Table 20.11). In the new member states only Cyprus and three regions in the Czech Republic exceed the Lisbon target of 67 per cent employment of the active population for 2005.[49] In an EU of 25 members there will be 14 regions where the employment rate is less than 50 per cent: six in Southern Italy, one in Spain (Ceuta e Melilla), one in France (Corse), five in Poland and one in Hungary (E'szak Alfold). A further three regions in Bulgaria fall into this category.

In general areas with low employment are associated with low GDP per capita. However, there are many rural areas, in particular in Poland, Romania and Lithuania, where semi-subsistence farming provides employment, but GDP per capita remains low.

The financial package agreed for the new member states at the December 2002 Copenhagen European Council allocated €14 156 million for the Structural Funds, and €7591 million for the Cohesion Fund for the 2004–06 period (see Chapter 9). Total support including that from the

---

[47] European Commission (2004a).
[48] European Commission (2004a).
[49] European Commission (2004a).

Cohesion Fund amounts to just over €7.3 billion a year in 1999 prices. The requirement of national co-financing seems likely to place a strain on the budgets of the new member states during these years.

To limit the scale of transfers and 'resolve the absorption problem', the Berlin Agreement also set a limit on the size of transfers, which could not exceed 4 per cent of the GDP of the recipient country. This ceiling entails a kind of inverse logic whereby the lower the GDP, the lower the transfer from the Structural Funds. It is estimated that over the 2004–06 period Poland will receive €67 per capita annually, and Hungary €49 compared with Greece receiving €437 per head and Ireland receiving €418 per capita in 2000.[50]

In order to simplify implementation, during the 2004–06 period support is to be concentrated on a few priority areas (see Table 20.13). The activities programmed reflect the transitional nature of the period, and appear largely as a means of preparing the ground for the strategies and procedures to be followed subsequently (European Commission, 2004a). In particular, there seems a need for better analytic tools and information sources, and increased selectivity to ensure the quality of programmes. Administrative capacity to implement measures also needs to be improved.

Table 20.13 Indicative breakdown of commitment appropriations for Structural Funds in new member states, 2004-06

	CY	CZ	EE	HU	LT	LV	MT	PL	SI	SK
Basic infrastructure		16.9	37.2	16.4	39.4	32.6		14.1		40.5
Competitiveness industry/enterprise		17.9	19.7	21.5	25.3	25.0	60.0	15.2	57.5	14.5
Human resource development		21.9	20.5	28.2	18.3	21.2	17.0	17.8	31.9	27.2
Agriculture, rural development and fisheries	67.5	12.0	18.7	15.9	15.3	18.5	11.0	16.7	9.9	17.7
Regional development		31.2		18.0			10.0	35.9		
Urban regeneration	30.0									
Other*	2.5		3.9		1.7	2.7	2.0	0.3	0.8	
Total	100	100	100	100	100	100	100	100	100	100

*including technical assistance
Source: European Commission (2004a).

ECONOMIC AND MONETARY UNION

One of the main challenges for the EU in the coming years is to reconcile the twin programmes of deepening and widening. This also creates tensions between enlargement and EMU.

As described in Chapter 8, enlargement will further complicate the already cumbersome decision-making institutions of the European Central Bank (ECB) and add to the complexity of the division of responsibility between the ECB, Ecofin, the Eurogroup and national governments.

Full participation of the new member states in EMU is unlikely to occur for some time. The Maastricht criterion on exchange rates entails that a country should remain within the 'normal' band of the exchange rate mechanism (ERM 2) without tension and without initiating depreciation for two years. For the new member states, this means that full participation in the third stage of EMU has to wait for two years after joining the EU since they were not allowed to join the

---

[50] *Financial Times*, 22 April 2004.

ERM 2 before they become EU members.[51] In the meantime the CEECs have a free choice of exchange rate regime, though 'this does not mean the EU would treat these choices with indifference'.[52]

Even without participating fully in the third stage of EMU, with enlargement the new member states will have to accept the EMU *acquis*, which involves:

- Adherence to the objective of EMU;
- Respect of the Stability and Growth Pact including regular submission of convergence programmes in the context of EU surveillance (Art. 99 § 2-5);[53]
- The prohibition of direct public sector financing by the Central Bank and the ending of privileged access to that bank (Art. 101);
- Treatment of the exchange rate and of other economic policies as a matter of 'common concern' (Art. 99 and Art. 124) to be co-ordinated within the Council (Art. 99 §1);
- The orderly liberalization of capital movements not only *vis-à-vis* other EU members but also third countries (Art. 56);
- Independence of the central bank (Art. 108) and its adherence to price stability as the primary objective (Art. 105).

The European Commission has repeatedly warned the CEECs against premature attempts to meet the Maastricht criteria in order to join the euro early.[54] The new member states could encounter difficulties in meeting the fiscal deficit criterion on a sustainable basis (see Table 20.14). Although external discipline can play a useful role where fiscal deficits are too high, excessive concern for budgetary constraint may hinder transition. The CEECs face pressure for additional government spending from a number of sources. Most of these countries are engaged in

	Inflation rate (%) annual average	Government debt % GDP	Fiscal deficit % GDP
Bulgaria	5.8	53.0p	-0.6
Cyprus	2.8	59.0	-3.5
Czech Republic	1.4	20.0	-3.9
Estonia	3.6	5.2	1.3
Hungary	5.2	54.3	-9.2
Latvia	2.0	14.6	-3.0
Lithuania	0.4	29.5	-2.0
Malta	2.2	60.6 (2000)	-6.2
Poland	1.9	46.0	-4.1
Romania	22.5	22.7p	-2.2
Slovakia	3.3	42.7	-7.2
Slovenia	7.5	26.9	-2.6
Turkey	45.0	95.0	-10.0

Table 20.14 **The Maastricht criteria and 2002 data for the new member states and candidate countries**

p = provisional
Source: European Commission; European Bank for Reconstruction and Development for government debt for the eight CEECs that joined the EU in 2004.

[51] In the past the Council has demonstrated a certain flexibility in interpreting this criterion: for example, both Finland and Italy were accepted even though they had been in the ERM less than two years.
[52] Ecofin meeting, 7 November 2000.
[53] The references are to the relevant articles in the Nice Treaty.
[54] As discussed elsewhere (see Krenzler and Senior Nello, 1999), problems of definition or specification may also arise in applying the Maastricht criteria in transition economies. For example, assessing public deficit may run into difficulties since many CEECs do not present consolidated accounts, while some are only now in the process of setting up regional governments (whose accounts should also be included). Many CEECs do not issue 10-year government bonds, which are the basis for the interest rate criterion.

fundamental reform of their pension and social security systems, health care and education. Improvements in infrastructure are urgently required, and the bad debts of state enterprises remain a problem in some CEECs. The task of taking on the *acquis* also calls for budgetary expenditure, in particular in areas such as the environment, increasing nuclear safety and improvement in administrative and judicial capacity.

Further difficulties could arise with inflation (see Table 20.14). Price liberalization in some CEECs is incomplete, in particular in the housing and energy sectors. When the formerly closed and inefficient centrally planned economies were opened up to market forces, a process of catching up, with rapid gains in productivity, occurred. If the productivity gains are faster in the traded than in the non-traded sector, this can generate inflation.[55] If the CEECs attempt to peg their exchange rate when inflation is higher than in their main trading partners, this can lead to loss of competitiveness and may result in currency crises.[56]

It is important to stress that although the applicant countries have to adhere to the aim of EMU, they are not obliged to meet the Maastricht criteria at the time of their accession. The Commission has repeatedly stated that the Maastricht criteria should not be regarded as a short-run objective but a goal for the medium to long term.

FREEDOM OF LABOUR MOVEMENT

As discussed in Chapter 7, most studies suggest that if ethnic upheaval and major civil strife are avoided (and this is one of the main reasons for applying the Copenhagen criteria), migration in an enlarged EU will be on a manageable scale.[57] None the less, a general transition period of five years before requiring the extension of freedom of labour movement to the new member states has been agreed, with the possibility of being extended for a further two years by individual member states. During that time member states can decide on what national measures to implement, and individual countries are free to proceed more rapidly with liberalization of labour movement if they so decide. Cyprus and Malta, which have labour shortages, will be excluded from these transition periods. An automatic review will take place after the first two years, when member states can decide to shorten or lift the transition period.

ENLARGEMENT AND PUBLIC OPINION

Any enlargement has to be ratified by all the EU member states, the European Parliament and the accession country in question. With the exception of Cyprus, for constitutional reasons all the new member states decided on ratification by referendum (see Table 20.15). The process proceeded surprisingly smoothly, though in some countries the majority in favour of accession was rather small (notably Malta), while in others (Hungary in particular) the turnout was low.

Enlargement has largely been a process carried forward by élites, so the annual opinion surveys also carried out by Eurobarometer in the new member states provide a useful indication of the attitudes of the general public to the EU. The results presented in Table 20.16 suggest that support for the EU was higher on average in the then 13 candidate countries (62 per cent on average

---

[55] This phenomenon is called the 'Balassa–Samuelson–Harrod effect'. When a small economy opens to international trade, its export prices are set at the world level. If the country is on its production possibility frontier, increased productivity in traded goods leads to increased wages in the traded-goods sector. However, if wages are equalized between the traded and non-traded goods sectors, and the non-traded goods sector has lower productivity, inflation will increase.

[56] As, for instance, occurred in the Czech Republic in 1997 and Slovakia in 1998.

[57] See, for instance, Alvarez-Plata et al. (2003); Boeri and Brücker (2000); CEPR (1992) or Layard et al. (1992).

Country	Date of referendum or ratification	Referendum outcome
Cyprus	Ratification notified 6 August 2003	
Czech Republic	13-14 June 2003	Yes 77.33%, No 22.67% Turnout 55.21%
Estonia	14 September 2003	Yes 66.92%, No 30.98% Turnout 63.9%
Hungary	12 April 2003	Yes 83.76, No 16.24% Turnout 45.62%
Latvia	20 September 2003	Yes 66.69%, No 32.2% Turnout 72.53%
Lithuania	10-11 May 2003	Yes 91.04%, No 8.96% Turnout 63.3%
Malta	8 March 2003	Yes 53.65%, No 46.35% Turnout 91%
Poland	7-8 June 2003	Yes 77.45%, No 22.55% Turnout 58.85%
Slovakia	16-17 may 2003	Yes 92.46%, No 6.20% Turnout 52.15%
Slovenia	23 March 2003	Yes 89.61%, No 10.39% Turnout 60.29%

Table 20.15 Referenda and ratification of the Accession Treaty

	A good thing	Neither good nor bad	A bad thing
Romania	81%	10%	2%
Bulgaria	73%	17%	3%
Turkey	67%	18%	10%
Cyprus	59%	26%	11%
Slovakia	58%	31%	8%
Hungary	56%	24%	10%
Lithuania	55%	29%	9%
Malta	55%	22%	17%
Poland	52%	28%	13%
Slovenia	50%	37%	8%
Latvia	46%	37%	16%
Czech Republic	44%	34%	15%
Estonia	39%	37%	16%
	A good thing	**Neither good nor bad***	**A bad thing**
Austria	35%	45%	20%
Belgium	56%	32%	12%
Denmark	57%	21%	22%
Finland	39%	39%	22%
France	44%	39%	17%
Germany	46%	44%	10%
Greece	62%	31%	7%
Ireland	73%	21%	6%
Italy	58%	32%	10%
Luxembourg	77%	17%	6%
Netherlands	62%	26%	12%
Portugal	55%	34%	11%
Spain	62%	31%	7%
Sweden	40%	28%	32%
UK	28%	43%	29%

Table 20.16 Support for EU membership

* includes 'don't know' percentage.
Source: European Commission (2004b and 2004c).

thought that membership was a 'good thing') than in the 15 member states (48 per cent on average). Among the candidate countries, support for the EU seemed highest in the three countries not joining in 2004. In the EU(15) support has fallen since the early 1990s when 72 per cent considered the EU a 'good thing', but support remains high in the Cohesion countries, in countries hosting a large share of EU institutions (Luxembourg and Belgium) and in the Netherlands and Denmark.

EVALUATION AND OUTLOOK FOR AN EU OF 25 OR MORE

Though the EU was slow to respond to the requests of the CEECs for membership, there were few illusions that transition and preparing for accession could prove other than lengthy and complex. Many aspects of transition (such as those relating to infrastructure, energy, the environment, human capital, and social capital and institution building) will have to continue long after enlargement.

Though an enlargement on the scale of that of 2004 has never been attempted, it seems set to become simply one in an ongoing process. In addition to Bulgaria, Romania, Turkey (see Appendix 2), Croatia and Macedonia have presented requests for membership. As part of the Stability and Association Process, the possibility of eventual membership has been offered to other countries in South-Eastern Europe. The Wider Europe policy foresees tighter links with CIS countries, and even if the prospect of enlargement has not yet been voiced, it cannot be indefinitely excluded for at least some of these countries.

With previous enlargements (and those of 1973 and with the Mediterranean countries, in particular) there were fears that larger membership would profoundly change the nature of the Community. Inevitably, this is even more the case for a move from 15 to 25 members or more. What kind of changes can be expected?

To date decisions in the EU have generally been taken on the basis of consensus. Even on issues where qualified majority voting is foreseen in the Council, votes are rarely taken and efforts are made to find a compromise. In a larger EU confrontational politics will probably be more difficult to avoid, and efforts to find compromise could lead to a slowing of the integration process. There may be a shift to more application of the QMV rule, but even after Nice or with the Constitutional Treaty, many areas remain subject to unanimity. Confrontational tactics could lead to a return to situations like the Empty Chair Crisis of 1965 or the eurosclerosis of the 1970s.

However, eurosclerosis 30 years later would be a different animal. The *acquis* has grown, and achievements like the Single Market and the euro seem irreversible, though less stringent application of, for example, competition or industrial policy could erode some of the advantages.

Member states will continue to benefit from the advantages of a larger market with more price transparency, but the aim of the Lisbon Strategy is to move beyond this and create a knowledge-based economy of world quality reference by 2010. The date 2010 is drawing closer, and we do not seem much nearer this aim. Part of the difficulty is that the Lisbon goals are disparate and also rely on the efforts of national governments and private business for their realization. Insufficient resources are still devoted to education and research, and to reaching the goals of the European Employment Strategy, which include increasing employment, the quality of work and social cohesion.

One of the main aims of the 2007–13 financial perspective is to give these goals a higher priority. However, the member states that are net contributors to the EU budget oppose any increase in spending (and, indeed, favour its reduction as a share of gross national income). The October 2002 European Council precluded the possibility of releasing substantial resources from the CAP for other spending. There have been calls for radical cuts, if not the elimination of the CAP, from some quarters. However, as argued in Chapter 10, there are well-founded reasons for public intervention in agriculture. The public has repeatedly expressed a strong preference for safe food and a healthy environment. Though there is still space for improvement in gearing policy to these objectives, the CAP has been radically transformed by the 1992, 1999 and 2003 reforms. Goals such as food safety and protection of the environment are not achieved cheaply, but there may be an argument for shifting more of the burden to national governments, with a partial renationalization of the CAP.

Since the scope for increased spending on the Structural Funds is therefore limited, the emphasis will have to be on increasing the effectiveness of measures.[58] Many of the new member states would like to repeat the Irish experience, which, as argued in Chapter 14, was partly due to the Structural Funds. However, when Ireland joined it was the only poor member state, and now there are many.

In December 2004 a decision will be taken on Turkey.[59] It is difficult to pretend that accession will not pose difficulties for the EU, given the size of the Turkish population, the level of GDP per capita and the share of agriculture in the economy. Against this, the urgent need to provide security in such an unstable corner of the globe could prove overriding. The prospect of EU membership has encouraged the Turkish government to undertake an active policy of democratization, and there are strong reasons for continuing this process. Similar arguments apply for many of the countries in South-Eastern Europe, but here their relatively small size poses fewer problems for the EU.

One of the main challenges for the EU remains establishing its democratic legitimacy. When consulted in referenda or opinion polls the people of Europe have frequently expressed negative opinions of the integration process (as, for instance, the Danish and Swedish votes against the euro, or the Irish vote on the Nice Treaty). Even if the Constitutional Treaty is ratified, as anyone who has attempted to consult it on the Internet can verify, the Constitutional Treaty has severe limits as an attempt to 'sell Europe' to its citizens. As Siedentop (2000, p. 1) argues, ongoing debate on the constitutional form of the EU is the only way to convince Europeans that 'what is happening in Europe today is not merely the result of inexorable market forces or the machinations of élites, which have escaped from democratic control'.

Clearly prescriptions to resolve this situation are beyond the present scope, but further forms of flexibility, or enhanced co-operation, will have to emerge. They will probably do so in the time-honoured, piecemeal EU method of reaching compromises and allowing exceptions. Grand designs for Europe invariably have to be whittled down and adjusted so that one size is stretched into shape to fit all.

Summary of Key Concepts

- In May 2004 10 countries joined the EU: Cyprus, the Czech Republic, Estonia, Hungary, Latvia, Lithuania, Malta, Poland, Slovakia and Slovenia. Bulgaria and Romania could join in 2007, and a decision on Turkey will be taken in December 2004. In April 2004 the European Commission published an Opinion favourable to opening negotiations for membership with Croatia.
- The PHARE Programme that came into operation from 1990 was initially demand-driven, and based on the requests of the recipient countries. From 1993 PHARE became increasing concerned with preparing CEECs for accession.
- PHARE is one of the three pre-accession instruments for the 2000–06 period. The other two instruments are ISPA and SAPARD.

---

[58] For suggestions of how this might be achieved see, for example, the Sapir Report of 2004.
[59] See the OLC website of this book for an updating of this issue.

- Western assistance to the transition countries was different from the Marshall Plan. Post-war reconstruction is very different from transition, while the co-ordination problems were fewer, the scale of financing was higher and the conditionality was tighter under the Marshall Plan.
- As a result of the provisions of the Europe Agreements, a free trade area in manufactured products was in place before enlargement.
- The CEECs succeeded in redirecting their trade rapidly towards the EU(15) and, in some cases, in attracting substantial foreign direct investment.
- South-Eastern Europe is generally taken to refer to the five Western Balkan countries: Albania, Bosnia/Herzegovina, Croatia, FYR Macedonia and Serbia-Montenegro, though Bulgaria and Romania are also included in certain initiatives. In 1999 the EU introduced the Stabilization and Association process, which offered eligible West Balkan countries the possibility of signing Stabilization and Association Agreements and eventual EU membership.
- The conditions for accession set out at the 1993 Copenhagen European Summit are: a functioning market economy with the capacity to cope with competitive pressures and market forces within the Community; stability of institutions guaranteeing democracy, the rule of law, human rights and respect for and protection of minorities and ability to take on the obligations of membership, including adherence to the aims of political and economic and monetary union. It was also stipulated that enlargement is subject to the condition that the EU is able to absorb new members and maintain the momentum of integration.
- Difficulties arise in applying the Copenhagen criteria because of the number of criteria and, in some cases, the vague and imprecise nature of the concepts involved.
- The Essen European Council of 1994 set out a pre-accession strategy to help the candidate countries in preparing for EU membership.
- Agenda 2000 of July 1997 set out the Commission's proposals for the 2000–06 financial perspective and for reform of the Common Agricultural Policy and Structural Funds.
- Agriculture continues to play an important role in many of the CEECs and to account for a high share of EU spending and the *acquis*. The applicant countries have to adapt to EU policies and standards, while the EU(15) wanted to ensure that enlargement does not result in excessive transfers from the Community budget.
- The proposals for extending the Structural Funds to the new member states appear to discriminate in the treatment of the existing member states, new members and so-called pre-ins. The new member states are likely to challenge this discrepancy in treatment.
- Enlargement will further complicate the already cumbersome decision-making institutions of EMU, but the new member states will only be able to adopt the euro two years after accession.
- Most studies suggest that migration in an enlarged EU will be on a manageable scale, but a transition period has been agreed before applying full movement of labour in an enlarged EU.
- Opinion polls suggest that support for the EU was generally higher in the new member states than in the EU(15).

Questions for Study and Review

■ What criticisms can be made of Western measures to assist transition?
■ How far can Western measures to facilitate transition be considered a new Marshall Plan?
■ Discuss the conditionality applied by the EU in its dealings with the CEECs.
■ Describe the main features of the Europe agreements.
■ When the CEECs joined the EU, they passed from a free trade area to membership of the Single Market. What does this imply?

■ Describe the main features and limitations of the policy of the EU towards SEE.

■ Why did the accession of Cyprus to the EU create difficulties (see Appendix 3)?

■ What criticisms can be made of the Copenhagen criteria?

■ With enlargement, what are the main obstacles facing agriculture?

■ What difficulties arise in extending the Structural Funds to the new member states?

■ What difficulties are likely to arise in reconciling EMU and enlargement?

■ How far is migration likely to pose a problem in an enlarged EU?

■ Discuss public perceptions of the EU and enlargement.

Appendix 1 Steps in pre-accession

1988 the Joint Declaration of Mutual Recognition between the EC and CMEA

From 1989 the PHARE Programme

From 1991 the TACIS Programme

1988–90 First Generation Trade and Co-operation Agreements

1992–95 Second Generation Europe Agreements

1994–1997 Trade and Co-operation Agreements with the former Soviet Republics

June 1993 Copenhagen European Council

■ The accession criteria;

■ The structured relationship;

■ Accelerated market access;

■ Additional financial assistance (an additional 15 per cent of PHARE annual commitments for infrastructure);

■ Assistance for the harmonization of laws.

December 1994 Essen European Council

■ Development of the structured relationship;

■ Call for White Paper to prepare CEECs for inclusion in Single European Market;

■ Call for a study of appropriate means to develop relations in agriculture (leading to the Agricultural Strategy Paper of 1995);

■ Encouragement of regional co-operation among accession countries.

1995 Cannes European Council

■ Approval of the White Paper on the Single Market;

■ Agreement that technical assistance under PHARE should be concentrated on implementation of the White Paper, and that more resources should be devoted to improving infrastructure (including TENs).

1995 Madrid European Council

■ The necessary decision should be taken to begin accession negotiations within six months of the conclusion of the Intergovernmental Conference (IGC) to be launched in Turin in March 1996;

■ Studies of countries to prepare Opinions as soon as possible after the conclusion of the IGC;

■ Decision to prepare a composite paper on enlargement;

■ Further strengthening of structured dialogue.

June 1997 Amsterdam Treaty

Aimed at creating more efficient operating procedures and facilitating decision-making in an enlarged EU, as well as increasing the legitimacy of EU institutions and meeting the problem of the democratic deficit.

July 1997 Agenda 2000 and Opinions on the applications for EU membership

December 1997 Luxembourg European Council

- Decision to open accession negotiations with five CEECs (Poland, Hungary, Czech Republic, Slovenia and Estonia) and Cyprus;
- Accession partnership extended to all 10 CEEC applicants;
- European Conference to include CEEC(10) and Cyprus (Turkey refused to participate).

March 1998 opening of negotiations with CEEC(5) and Cyprus

- 'Screening' of CEEC progress in implementation of *acquis*;
- Infringement procedures where progress in implementing the *acquis* is inadequate;
- Feedback into Regular Reports.

March 1999 Berlin Agreement on Agenda 2000

- The financial perspective for 2000–06;
- Reform of the CAP;
- Reform of the Structural Funds.

1999 December Helsinki European Council

Decision to extend negotiations to Bulgaria, Latvia, Lithuania, Malta, Romania, and Slovakia and to declare Turkey a candidate.

February 2000 opening of negotiations with these six further candidates

December 2000 Nice European Summit

- Limited extension of the qualified majority vote, and reweighting of votes in the Council of Ministers;
- Ceilings on the number of commissioners and members of the European Parliament;
- An increased possibility to use flexibility or enhanced co-operation;
- A new IGC to be called in 2004 to decide on the future architecture of the EU.

June 2001 Gothenburg Summit

- Confirmed the 'road map' set out at Nice with the objective of completing negotiations with the first applicant countries in 2002 so that they could participate in the European Parliament elections of 2004.

December 2002 Copenhagen Summit

- Confirmed 1 May 2004 as the objective for the date of entry of 10 of the applicant countries;
- Indicated 2007 as the possible date of accession for Bulgaria and Romania;
- Decision on whether to open negotiations with Turkey to be taken December 2004.

February 2003 Nice Treaty comes into effect

December 2003 failure to agree on the Constitutional Treaty at the Brussels European Council

May 2004 10 new member states join the EU

June 2004 the European Council agrees on the Constitutional Treaty, but ratification still has to take place

Appendix 2 EU–Turkish Relations

Turkey became a member of the OECD in 1948, the Council of Europe in 1949 and NATO in 1952. It applied for Associate Membership of the EEC in 1959 (a few days after Greece), but following the coup in 1960, talks were suspended for two years.

In 1963 Turkey signed an Association Agreement, the Ankara Treaty, with the Community. Since being European is one of the conditions of Community membership, in 1963 the president of the European Commission, Hallstein, ruled in favour of Turkey, announcing that it was 'part of Europe'. However, debate about the dual European and Muslim identities of Turkey and the implications for EU membership continues.

In 1970 the Association Agreement was modified by an Additional Protocol that called for the creation of a customs union by 1995. However, during the 1970s tensions arose over the 1974 Cyprus crisis and the Greek application of 1975 for full membership. In 1978 Turkey requested participation in EPC (European Political Co-operation) in order to prevent Greece using its position to hinder the development of tighter Turkish–EC relations. This request was rejected, and in 1978 Turkey issued a unilateral declaration freezing its relations with the EC. The military took over in Turkey in 1980, and relations with the EU remained suspended. Relations were resumed in 1986, leading to a reactivation of the Association Agreement from 1988.

Turkey presented a request for EU membership in 1987, and received a negative reply two years later. The official reason given by the Commission was the need to complete the Single Market Programme. In 1990 the EC implemented a package to improve relations with Turkey, that included financial and technical assistance and the creation of a customs union by 1995.

At the Luxembourg European Council of December 1997 Turkey was not even included among the slow-track countries being considered for EU accession. The Council decided to establish the European Conference, but Turkey refused to attend its first two meetings. In 1999 meetings were suspended, but were resumed with Turkish participation after the 1999 Helsinki European Council. At the 1999 Helsinki European Council Turkey was declared a candidate. The 2002 Copenhagen Summit agreed that a decision on whether Turkey was ready to join the EU would be taken in December 2004, and if so that negotiations would begin 'without delay'.

Despite substantial reforms in Turkey, the 2003 Regular Report still concluded that further efforts were needed with regard to:

> the strengthening of the independence and the functioning of the judiciary, the overall frame-work for the exercise of fundamental freedoms (association, expression and religion), the further alignment of civil-military relations with European practice, the situation in the South-east and cultural rights. Turkey should ensure full and effective implementation of reforms to ensure that Turkish citizens can enjoy human rights and fundamental freedoms in line with European standards.

Membership would also pose economic problems because of: Turkey's size, population (69.6 million in 2002), level of development (GDP per capita was only 23 per cent of the EU average in 2002), the importance of the agricultural sector (33.2 per cent of employment and 11.2 per cent of GDP in 2002), the dominant role of the state in the economy, the weakness of the financial sector, corruption and inflation (45 per cent in 2002).

In 2002 the EU accounted for 51.5 per cent of Turkish exports and 45.5 per cent of Turkish imports.[60] The main exports to the EU were textiles (41.4 per cent), transport material (13.4) and agricultural products (9.5 per cent). The main EU exports to Turkey were machinery (29.7 per cent), chemical products (19.1 per cent) and transport material (14.2 per cent).

---

[60] The data here are taken from the European Commission: www.europa.eu.int/comm/trade. See the OLC website of this book for an updating of this issue.

Appendix 3 The EU and Cyprus

Since 1974 the island of Cyprus has been divided into the Greek Republic of Cyprus (population 689,000 in 2002), and what in 1983 was declared the Turkish Republic of Northern Cyprus (TRNC). The TRNC (population 211,000 in 2002) is recognized only by Turkey.

Cyprus obtained its independence from Great Britain in 1960, and the Treaty of Guarantee placed the independence, territorial integrity and security of the island under the joint guarantee of Greece, Turkey and the UK. The Treaty envisaged a complex power-sharing arrangement and a bi-communal structure. The Turkish Cypriots claimed that representation in municipal authorities and the army failed to conform to planned ethnic proportions and began to exercise their veto rights. In 1963 President Makarios proposed constitutional amendments to reduce the opportunities for the Turkish Cypriots to block legislation, and there was a political crisis. Intercommunal violence broke out, Turkish Cypriots moved into enclaves and withdrew from the common institutions.

In 1964 the UNFICYP (United Nations Peacekeeping Force in Cyprus) was established to prevent a recurrence of fighting and to contribute to the maintenance of law and order.

In 1974 the Greek junta staged a coup against President Archbishop Makarios and claimed annexation of Cyprus to Greece. Also committed to the protection of Cypriot independence, Turkey intervened on 20 July 1974. Two conferences were held in Geneva between Greece, Turkey and the UK, with the second also attended by Greek and Turkish Cypriots. The talks were inconclusive, and on 14 August the Turkish army launched a second offensive. According to the Greek Cypriots, this second invasion was not justified by the Treaty of Guarantee since the constitutional order had already been restored.

In 1974 Cyprus was divided by a 'Green Line', with the Turkish Cypriots holding almost 37 per cent of the island. In 1974 some 140 000–160 000 Greek Cypriots moved to the South, while an estimated 30 000–40 000 Turkish Cypriots fled to the North (Brewen, 2000). It is estimated that some 50 000 Turkish Cypriots left the island, while between 85 000 and 115 000 settlers (in particular from Anatolia) came over from the Turkish mainland, though the statistics are controversial.[61] A large Turkish force (estimated at 35 000 in 2003) remained in Northern Cyprus.

In 1990 the Republic of Cyprus applied for EC membership. In 1993 the EC Commission published its Opinion on application for EC membership, that appeared to make accession conditional on internal political settlement.

In 1994 Greece threatened to veto negotiations for a customs union between the EU and Turkey if Cyprus were not included in the next EU enlargement process, and at the 1997 Luxembourg European Council it was agreed to include Cyprus among the first-wave countries.

The EU continued to push for a settlement, but the Presidency Conclusions of the 1999 Helsinki European Council announced that 'if no settlement has been reached by the completion of accession negotiations, the Council's decision will be made without the above being a pre-condition'.

In 2002 the UN presented a proposal to set up a Swiss-type confederation between the two parts of the island, that would also permit Northern Cyprus to join the EU. The European Commission made it clear that if agreement were reached, Northern Cyprus could join the EU in May 2004 with no further negotiation of the Accession Treaty. A referendum on the UN proposal, or Annan Plan, was held in both parts of the island on 24 April 2004, and while 65 per cent of Turkish Cypriots voted in favour of settlement, 76 per cent of Greek Cypriots voted against. As a result only the Greek Cypriot part of the island joined the EU. The EU introduced a series of measures to compensate the Turkish Cypriots for their favourable vote, but were still not prepared to recognize the Turkish Republic of Northern Cyprus.

---

[61] The data here are taken from www.un.int/cyprus/cyissue.htm.

References

Alvarez-Plata, P., Brücker, H., and Siliverstovs, B. (2003) 'Potential migration from Central and Eastern Europe into the EU-15 – An Update', Report for the European Commission DG Employment and Social Affairs, http://europa.eu.int/comm/employment_social

Baldwin, R. (1994) *Towards an Integrated Europe*, Centre for Economic Policy Research, London.

Boeri, T. and Brücker, H. (2000) 'The impact of Eastern enlargement on employment and labour markets in the member states', http://europa.eu.int/comm/dgs/employment social/news_en.htm

Brenton, P. and Gros, D. (1993) 'The budgetary implications of EC enlargement', CEPS Working Document no. 78, Centre for European Policy Studies, Brussels.

Brewen, C. (2000) *The European Union and Cyprus*, Eothen Press, Huntingdon, Cambridgeshire.

Buckwell et al. (1997) 'Towards a common agricultural and rural policy for Europe', *European Economy Reports and Studies*, No. 5, pp. 1–97.

Buckwell, A. and Tangermann, S. (1999) 'The future of direct payments in the context of Eastern Enlargement', *MOCT/MOST, Economic Policy in Transition Economies*, No. 9, pp. 229–52.

CEPR (1992) *Is Bigger Better? The Economics of EC Enlargement,* Monitoring European Integration 3, Centre for Economic Policy Research, London.

Courchene, T. et al. (1993) 'Stable money – sound finances', *European Economy*, No. 53.

Cremona, M. (ed.) (2003) *The Enlargement of the European Union*, Oxford University Press, Oxford.

De Benedictis, L. and Tajoli, L. (2004) 'Economic integration, similarity and convergence in the EU and CEECs trade structures', paper presented at the XIVth conference of the AISSEC, Naples, 27–28 February 2004.

De Long, B. and Eichengreen, B. (1993) 'The Marshall Plan: History's most successful structural adjustment programme', in Dornbusch, R., Nölling, W. and Layard, R. (eds) *Postwar Economic Reconstruction and Lessons for the East Today*, MIT Press, Cambridge, Massachusetts.

Drábek, Z. and Smith, A. (1995) 'Trade performance and trade policy in Central and Eastern Europe', CEPR Discussion Paper no. 1182, Centre for Economic Policy Research, London.

Eichengreen, B. and Kohl, R. (1998) 'The external sector, the state and development in Eastern Europe', in Zysman, J. and Schwartz, A. (eds) *Enlarging Europe: The Industrial Foundations of a New Political Reality,* Research Series no. 99, University of California, Berkeley, pp. 169–201.

EC Commission (1994) 'The economic interpenetration between the European Community and Eastern Europe', *European Economy Reports and Studies,* no. 6.

European Commission (1995) *The Agricultural Strategy Paper*, CSE(95)607.

European Commission (1997) *Agenda 2000, COM (97) 2000 final,* 15 July 1997, Supplement to the *Bulletin of the European Union*, May.

European Commission (2002) SEC(2002)95 'Enlargement and agriculture: Successfully integrating the new member states into the CAP', Issues Paper, Brussels, January.

European Commission (2003a) 'Relation on PHARE and the pre-accession instruments for Cyprus, Malta and Turkey'.

European Commission (2003b) 'Enlargement of the European Union. An historic opportunity'.

European Commission (2004a) 'Third report on economic and social cohesion'.

European Commission (2004b) 'Candidate Countries Eurobarometer 2003–4'.

European Commission (2004c) 'Eurobarometer 60, Public Opinion in the European Union'.

Faini, R. and Portes, R. (eds) (1995) *European Union Trade with Eastern Europe: Adjustment and Opportunities*, Centre for Economic Policy Research, London.

Grabbe, H. (2002) 'EU conditionality and the *acquis communautaire*', *International Political Science Review*, Vol. 23, No. 3, July.

Halpern, L. and Wyplosz, C. (1995) 'The role of exchange rates in the process of economic transformation', CEPR Discussion Paper no. 1145, Centre for Economic Policy Research, London.

Kaitila, V. and Widgrén, M. (2001) 'Revealed comparative advantage in trade between the European Union and the Baltic countries', European University Institute, Robert Schuman Centre for Advanced Studies, Working Paper 2001/02.

Kaminski, B. (2000) 'Industrial restructuring as revealed in Hungary's pattern of integration into European Union Markets', *Europe–Asia Studies*, Vol. 52, pp. 457-87.

Krenzler, H.G. and Senior Nello, S.M. (1999) 'The implications of the euro for enlargement', Robert Schuman Centre Policy Paper, European University Institute, Florence.

Layard, R., Blanchard, O., Dornbusch, R., and Krugman, P. (1992) *East-West Migration: The Alternatives*, MIT Press, Cambridge, MA.

Le Cacheux, J. (1996) *Europe, la nouvelle vague: perspectives économiques de l'élargissement*, Presses de la Fondation des Sciences Politiques, Paris.

Mayhew, A. (1998) *Recreating Europe. The European Union's Policy towards Central and Eastern Europe*, Cambridge University Press, Cambridge.

Pautola, N. (1999) 'Preferential trading areas: The specific aspects of the integration of the Baltic states into the EU', European University Institute, Robert Schuman Centre for Advanced Studies, Working Paper 2000/64.

Sapir, A. et al. (2004*) An Agenda for a Growing Europe. The Sapir Report*, Oxford University Press, Oxford.

Senior Nello, S.M. (1991) *The New Europe: Changing Economic Relations between East and West*, Harvester Wheatsheaf, Hemel Hempstead.

Senior Nello, S.M. and Smith, K.E. (1998) *The Consequences of Eastern Enlargement of the European Union in Stages*, Ashgate Publishers Ltd, Aldershot, UK.

Senior Nello, S.M. (2002a) 'Preparing for enlargement in the European Union: The tensions between economic and political integration', *International Political Science Review*, Vol. 23, No. 3, July.

Senior Nello, S.M. (2002b) 'Food and agriculture in an enlarged EU', EUI Working Paper RSC No. 2002/58, Robert Schuman Centre for Advanced Studies, European University Institute, Florence.

Senior Nello, S.M. (2004) 'Cyprus and EU accession' in Landuyt, A. (ed.), *Lo spazio politico nell'intergrazione europea. Gli allargamenti della CEE/UE dal 1961 al 2002*, Il Mulino, Bologna.

Siedentop, L. (2000) *Democracy in Europe*, Penguin Books, London.

Smith, K.E. (2001) 'Western actors and the promotion of democracy', in Zielonka, J. and Pravda, A. (eds), *Democratic Consolidation in Eastern Europe*, vol. 2, International and Transnational Factors, Oxford University Press, Oxford, pp. 31-57.

Smith, K.E. (2003) 'The evolution and application of EU membership conditionality', in Cremona, M. (ed.), *The Enlargement of the European Union*, Oxford University Press, Oxford.

Swinnen, J.F.M. (2002) 'Transition and integration in Europe: Implications for agricultural and food markets, policy and trade agreements', *The World Economy*, vol. 25, pp. 481-501.

Tangermann, S. (2000) 'Widening the EU to Central and Eastern European Countries: WTO and perspectives of the new member countries', in Burrell, A. and Oskam, A. (eds), *Agricultural Policy and Enlargement of the European Union*, Wageningen University Press, Wageningen, NL.

Tarditi, S., Marsh, J. and Senior Nello, S.M. (1995) 'Agricultural strategies for the enlargement of the European Union to Central and Eastern Europe', Study prepared for DG-1 of the Commission, Faculty of Economics, University of Siena.

Uvalic, M. (2002) 'The economies of South-Eastern Europe - From international assistance to self-sustainable growth', Bertlesmann Foundation Risk Reporting 2001/2002 South-Eastern Europe Economics and Reform Assistance Strategy Report, Gütersloh, Germany, www.stiftung.bertlesmann.de.

Vachudova, M.A. (2000) 'Eastern Europe as gatekeeper: The immigration and asylum policies of an enlarging European Union', in Andreas, P. and Snyder, T. (eds), *The Wall around the West: State Borders and Immigration Control in North America and Europe*, Rowman & Littlefield, Lanham, MD.

Vachudova, M.A. (2001) 'The leverage of international institutions on democratizing states: Eastern Europe and the European Union', EUI Working Paper RSC No. 2001/33, Florence, Italy.

World Bank (1999a) *Czech Republic: Toward EU Accession*. Main Report, The World Bank, Washington DC.

World Bank (1999b) *Hungary. On the Road to the European Union*, The World Bank, Washington DC.

Useful Websites

European Commission provides data, description of policies and key documents:

www.europa.eu.int/comm/enlargement

www.europa.eu.int/comm/external_relations

The Countdown site of the Wiener Institut für Internationale Wirtschaftvergleiche provides an extensive bibliography, abstracts of publications and debate on key issues in transition:

http://wiiwsv.wsr.ac.at/Countdown/f_liter.htlm

European Bank for Reconstruction and Development presents statistics, country reports and analyses of key issues in transition countries:

www.ebrd.org

The Council of Europe provides analyses of democratic consolidation and human rights in transition countries:

www.coe.int

Reports on the international competitiveness of countries are available from the Institute of Management Development, Lausanne:

www.imd.ch

World Economic Forum:

www.weforum.org

Data on FDI is available from UNCTAD:

www.unctad.org

List of abbreviations

CAP	The Common Agricultural Policy
CARDS	Community Assistance for Reconstruction, Development and Stabilization
CEEC	Central and Eastern European country
CEFTA	Central European Free Trade Area
CFSP	Common Foreign and Security Policy
CIS	Commonwealth of Independent States
CMEA	Council for Mutual Economic Assistance
EBRD	European Bank for Reconstruction and Development
ECB	European Central Bank
Ecofin	Council of Economic and Finance Ministers
EMU	economic and monetary union
EPC	European Political Co-operation
ERM	Exchange Rate Mechanism
Europgroup	Group of Economic and Finance Ministers of the euro area
IFI	international financial institution
IGC	Intergovernmantal Conference
IMF	International Monetary Fund
ISPA	Pre-Accession Structural Instrument
NATO	North Atlantic Treaty Organization
NPAA	National Programme for the Adoption of the *Acquis*

OECD	Organization for Economic Co-operation and Development
OPT	outward processing trade
PHARE	Poland, Hungary Aid for Economic Reconstruction
PPP	purchasing power parity
SAPARD	Special Accession Programme for Agriculture and Rural Development
SEE	South-Eastern Europe
Socrates	EU programme for the mobility of students
TACIS	Technical Assistance for the Commonwealth of Independent States
TEN	Trans-European Network
UNFICYP	United Nations Peacekeeping Force in Cyprus
UNCTAD	United Nations Conference on Trade and Development
WTO	World Trade Organization

Index